KU-681-551

AA

KEYGUIDE

THAILAND

240

CONTENTS

194

71

150

120

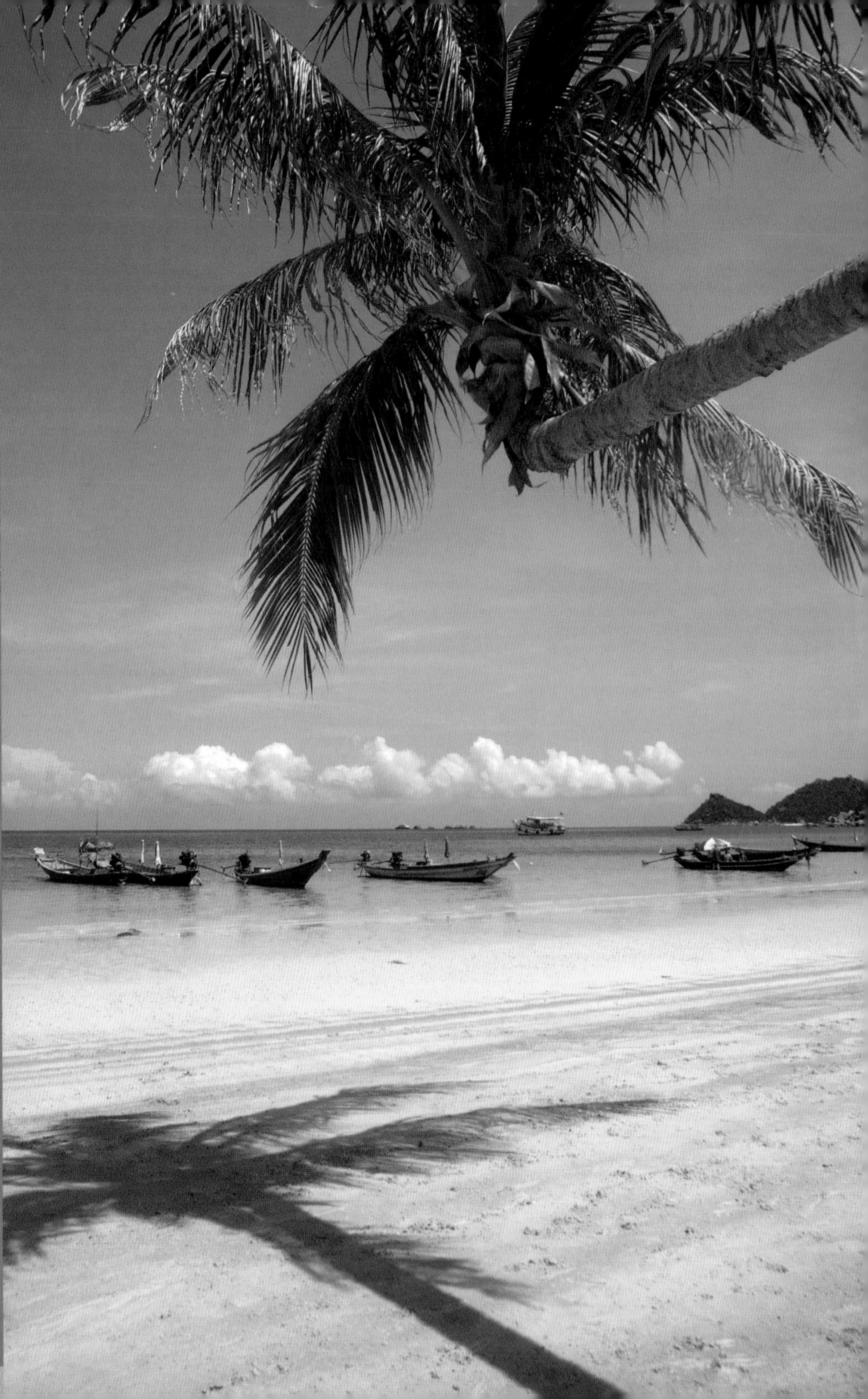

UNDERSTANDING THAILAND

Understanding Thailand is an introduction to the country, its geography,
economy, history and its people, giving a real insight into the nation. Living
Thailand gets under the skin of Thailand today, while The Story of Thailand
takes you through the country's past.

Thailand is popularly known as the "land of smiles," while the country's tourist board lures visitors with the slogan "Amazing Thailand." Visitors to this Southeast Asian country are struck by the friendliness of its people and by the great variety of its attractions: its islands and beaches, mountains and jungles, exotic culture and temples, and celebrated cuisine. Thailand is a very easy country to explore, with an excellent transportation network that's the envy of its neighbors, and even the most remote villages of the north and east are accessible by local bus. The range of its hotels, guesthouses, restaurants and nightspots is unrivaled in Asia, and Bangkok is among one of the most exhilarating of Asia's capitals.

LANDSCAPE

Thailand is one of Southeast Asia's largest countries, stretching nearly 1,240 miles (2,000km) from north to south, from a mountainous border with Myanmar (Burma) to the Malaysian peninsula. Its terrain conveniently divides the country into four regions: the mountainous north, the undulating central plains, the vast northeastern plateau and the coastal south, with its islands and archipelagos. Bangkok sits like a bulky megalith at its center, at the head of the great bay called the Bight of Bangkok.

POLITICS

Thailand's formal political system resembles that of any other democracy with distinct executive, legislative and judicial branches. However, dynamic Thai-style politics often do not.

Since Thailand adopted a constitutional monarchy in 1932—itself the result of a coup—the country has been embroiled in political intrigue, including at least 18 further coups d'état. The latest, in 2006, removed Prime Minister Thaksin Shinawatra and his Thai Rak Thai party from office.

Thaksin came to power in 2001 promising to tackle the poverty. A universal healthcare package, a debt moratorium for farmers, and a locally managed development fund for villages all proved successful and, importantly, established a strong support base among the rural sector of society.

It was this elecoral support that saw Thaksin reelected by an overwhelming majority in 2005 (with Thai Rak Thai sweeping 374 of the 500 seats in Parliament) and gave him the distinction of being the first elected prime minister in Thai history to complete his term in office.

However, increasing criticism at home and abroad was leveled at other policies, including the "War on Drugs" and Thaksin's response to the resurgence of separatist violence in the southernmost provinces of Thailand. To add to Thaksin's woes were allegations of corruption, which he denied. In September 2006, the Thai Army staged a coup against the government, suspended the Constitution and dissolved Parliament. The Council for Democratic Reform (CDR), as they called themselves, appointed General Surayud Chulanont as prime minister under an interim charter and promised to restore democratic government within one year.

In August 2007, voting took place in Thailand's first-ever referendum on a new constitution. Successfully passed, this paved the way for the nation's 18th constitution. In elections in December 2007, the People Power Party (PPP), made up largely of politicians from the now illegal Thai Rak Thai party, claimed victory in what had become a poll on Thaksin's policies. Samak Sundaravej, leader of the PPP, was elected prime minister on January 28, 2008.

The country was anything but stable and protests continued in 2008 and 2009. A year later, political unrest surfaced again in Bangkok when anti-government demonstrations by Red Shirts (supporters of former Prime Minister Thaksin Sinawatra) turned into bloody riots as they stood their ground against the Thai military. The battle lasted nine weeks and resulted in many protestors' deaths as well as much damage to the city. An apparent calm has been restored to the capital—the clean up was swift—but, as the nation prepares to go to the polls in the winter of 2010, more incidents are likely.

ECONOMICS

From the ashes of the 1997–98 Asian economic crisis, Thailand emerged with one of Southeast Asia's most robust and vibrant economies. This economy has proven its durability in the years since, remaining relatively unchecked in growth from those dark days despite a number of subsequent blows from factors both internal and external. The SARS epidemic of 2003, bird flu, the devastation of the 2004 tsunami, and a climate of uncertainty for investors following the 2006 coup, continued protests and rebellion in 2010, and occasional terrorist incidents in the far south and north have all seemingly been taken in their stride. Even the Thai baht, which experienced its biggest loss in almost three years following news of the coup, rebounded in the following days and has remained steady since.

There have, however, been problems for the economy. In 2009, revenue from tourism was 2 percent lower than in 2008. The reduction has been attributed to a variety of factors, including the 2008–2009 political crisis, H1N1, and the 2008 economic crisis. Export-oriented manufacturing and farm output are also important to the Thai economy and account for almost 60 percent of GDP. Under the Thaksin government, policies aimed at developing open markets and foreign investment were successful. After the coup, however, some of this stalled.

A number of further issues must now be tackled to encourage continued growth of Thailand's economy: reform of the financial sector, increasing exports, and attracting foreign investment by restoring confidence in the midst of political instability. Other issues have painted Thailand in an unfavorable light to investors and tourists, including its poor treatment of refugees from Myanmar and Laos, as well as conflicts with its own Muslim community in the far south.

SOCIETY

The social structure of Thailand has the form of three concentric circles. At its heart are the king and the royal family. They are surrounded by the community of Buddhist abbots and monks. The outer ring is made up of the Thai populace. This structure is supported by a foundation of special forms of behavior and language. The king and his immediate family are so remote from the general public that special terms of language have to be used in talking of them; they command total loyalty and respect, and any form of criticism or ridicule is not only taboo but also a punishable offence. Yet the king is referred to by the simplest peasant as "father"; he is benefactor and protector—not only of the nation but also of the individual. The popular love felt for King Bhumibol, the world's longest-reigning monarch, is palpable and genuine, and Thais talk with true dread of the day when he no longer rules over them. The second circle of Thailand's social structure is populated by representatives of the Buddhist faith, which dominates popular thought and action. Abbots and monks are held in great esteem, but at the same time they lead hard lives of frugal simplicity, supported materially by their congregations. Housewives rise before dawn to fill the begging bowls of monks on their daily rounds. Outside these two formal circles of society is grouped the general populace, which is developing its own rules of social order as the country's increasing prosperity produces a growing middle class.

Opposite *Guarding the gate of Wat Pho, Bangkok*
Below *Buddhist monks in Chinatown, Bangkok*

THAILAND AT A GLANCE

Thailand divides neatly into four distinct regions, each of which developed over the centuries its own separate history and economic structure. The huge metropolitan area of Bangkok is also often regarded as a separate region because of its size. Subdivided into 76 provinces, Thailand occupies a landmass about the size of France, enclosed by mountains in the north and two seas in the south. The distance from the Myanmar border in the north to the southern frontier with Malaysia is nearly as great as the distance between the Baltic and the Mediterranean. It takes at least two days to travel the length of the country by train or bus, and even flying takes up most of the day by the time Bangkok connections are taken into account. Visitors planning to tour Thailand in less than two weeks often underestimate the distances they have to cover, and many holiday itineraries are rapidly rewritten within a few hours of arrival in Bangkok.

Bangkok Thailand's capital is classed as a region simply because of its sheer size: 594sq miles (1,538sq km), home to one-tenth of Thailand's 66 million people. Its center is inland from the great Gulf of Thailand, and Bangkok dominates the urban landscape, industry and economy.

The Northeast The country's largest region is known as Isan. It stretches from the eastern upland reaches of the north to the frontiers of Laos and Cambodia, bordered for much of its eastern length by the Mekong River. Much of the region is a hot, largely arid plateau, where farmers eke out a difficult existence. Yet the food of the Isan is prized highly, and the hospitality of its people is legendary. The towns and villages along the Mekong see few visitors and are true explorer territory. Even more interesting is Isan's southern border with Cambodia, where a string of ruined Khmer temples gives a fascinating insight into a civilization that shaped this part of Thailand.

The North At the northern end of the country lie the mountains of the north, including Thailand's highest mountain, Doi Inthanon. From the northern capital, Chiang Mai, the mountains rise in thickly forested ranges to form natural frontiers with Myanmar to the north and west and with Laos to the east. The north was a separate kingdom, the realm of Lanna, for nearly 800 years and gave up the last vestiges of its independence to Bangkok only in the 20th century. It still retains a proud sense of nationhood, reflected in the numerous Lanna festivals held. The region's seasons are more pronounced than elsewhere in Thailand, and temperatures can drop to near freezing in the mountains in the cool months from November to March.

Central Thailand Anchored by Bangkok, the Central Plains form Thailand's rice bowl and the country's most densely populated region. The rivers flowing from the mountainous north, tributaries of Thailand's main waterway, the Chao Phraya, feed the vast patchwork of rice paddies that distinguishes the landscape of this largely flat region. Riverside farming communities are grouped around market towns and local administrative centers.

The South To the south of Bangkok lie the coastal areas. The eastern seaboard is becoming rapidly industrialized, with vehicle-manufacturing plants shooting up around the port of Bang Lamung. But between the industrial zones and the Cambodian border to the south lie such holiday playgrounds as Pattaya and Ko Chang island. The true south is the long peninsula running from Bangkok to the Malaysian border, a tropical region of rain forests, palm-fringed beaches and tourist resorts.

On the western side are the Andaman coast and a chain of islands of which Phuket is the biggest. On the east is the gulf coast, with resorts like Hua Hin and Chumphon and the islands of Ko Samui and Ko Pha Ngan. The far south is predominantly Muslim, and endures political and social instability.

Left The landscape is dominated by a picturesque patchwork of rice paddies near the upland town of Mae Hong Son

CHIANG RAI

PHAYAO

NAN

MAE HONG SON

CHIANG MAI

LAMPANG

LAMPHUN

PHRAE

UTTARADIT

LA

VN

NONG KHAI

SUKHOTHAI

LOEI

NONG BUA LAMPHU

UDON THANI

SAKHON NAKHON

NAKHON PHANOM

TAK

PHITSANULOK

KHON KAEN

KALASIN

MUKDAHAN

KAMPHAENG PHET

PHICHIT

PHETCHABUN

CHAIYAPHUM

MAHA SARAKHAM

YASOTHON

AMNAT CHAROEN

MM

NAKHONSAWAN

ROI ET

UTHAITHANI

CHAINAT

SINGURI

LOPBURI

NAKHONRATCHASIMA

SURIN

UBON RATCHATHANI

SI SAKET

SUPHANBURI

KANCHANABURI

1

SARABURI

BURIRAM

2

NAKHONNAYOK

3

PRACHINBURI

4

BANGKOK

SAKAEO

RATCHABURI

5

6

CHACHOENGSAO

7

CHON BURI

CHANTHABURI

PHETCHABURI

RAYONG

KH

TRAT

PRACHUAP KHIRI KHAN

Ko Chang

1   ANGTHONG
2   AYUTTHAYA
3   PRATHUMTHANI
4   PHRAE
5   UBON RATCHATHANI
6   SAMUTPRAKAN
7   UDON THANI

CHUMPHON

RANONG

Ko Pha Ngan

Ko Samui

VN

SURAT THANI

PHANG-NGA

KRABI

NAKHON SI THAMMARAT

Ko Phuket

TRANG

PHATTHALUNG

Ko Lanta

SATUN

SONGKHLA

PATTANI

YALA

NARATHIWAT

MY

BANGKOK

Baan Jim Thompson's House (▷ 69) This traditional house has been gorgeously furnished and decorated by an expatriate connoisseur of Thai art.

Bed Supper Club (▷ 99–100) Bangkok's chic symposium, with white linen sheets, food, drink and an air of stylish decadence.

Chao Phraya River (▷ 70) Beat the road traffic and get around by boat.

Chatuchak Market (▷ 70) On a Saturday or Sunday, shop at the world's benchmark for street markets.

Chinatown (▷ 71) Take a noisy, sweaty, exhausting and insightful walk through the capital.

Grand Palace (▷ 87–90) If you visit only one temple in Thailand, make it this one—and bring a camera.

May Kaidee's (▷ 107) Feast on delicious Thai vegetarian food at this wonderful restaurant tucked away off the Khao San Road.

National Museum (▷ 77–79) See art and beautiful objects from across the country, and the Buddha in all his sublime poses.

The Peninsula (▷ 112) Stay at the best hotel in the capital for views of the Chao Phraya River.

Siam Square (▷ 82) A huge range of shopping, eating, and entertainment opportunities under one roof.

The Sky Bar (▷ 102) Sip cocktails on top of the world.

Wat Pho (▷ 86) See the longest reclining Buddha in the world and an authentic massage center.

THE NORTHEAST

Ban Khwao (▷ 118) Be amazed by the home-based production process that results in quality silk and, perhaps, buy some silk to take home.

Chiang Khan (▷ 119) Wander through this laid-back little town on the banks of the Mekong.

Khao Phra Viharn (▷ 119) Visit this remote Khmer temple complex just over the border in Cambodia, off-limits for nearly a century, but visitable in a day without a visa.

Khao Yai National Park (▷ 122) See wild elephants and hornbills and take night safaris and treks through the rain forest with knowledgeable nature guides.

Khon Kaen (▷ 120–121) Explore this sophisticated city offering good food and some of the best-quality shopping in the northeast of Thailand.

Lamai Homestay (▷ 146–147) Stay a night or two in a quiet rice village, where you will experience Thai rural life as it is really lived.

Nakhon Ratchasima (▷ 125) Enjoy Thai curries at their most authentic and shopping without the hassle.

Nong Khai (▷ 124, 141–142) Sit back and relax with a drink, as you take in the scenery, on a river cruise along the Mekong River.

Above *Wat Suthat, Bangkok, built in early-Bangkok style and surrounded by Chinese pagodas*
Opposite T*he crystal clear waters of Erawan Waterfall, Kanchanaburi*

THE NORTH

Chiang Mai (▷ 188–189) Reserve a table at one of Chiang Mai's several *kantoke* restaurants, where a performance of traditional music and dance accompanies the Thai food.

Chiang Mai Get up before dawn and hike up Chiang Mai's mountain, Doi Suthep (▷ 164), reaching the top before the sun gets too hot and the crowds at the Phra That Doi Suthep temple too dense.

Chiang Mai (▷ 155, 158) Join in the daily "monk chat" in the park-like grounds of Wat Chedi Luang in central Chiang Mai.

Chiang Mai (▷ 155) Get up early browse for bargains and eat breakfast from one of the many food and drink vendors at the Sunday Walking Street market.

Chiang Mai and Chiang Rai (▷ 155, 160) Browse the night markets of Chiang Mai and Chiang Rai, where you're certain to find just the souvenir or keepsake you've been looking for.

Chiang Rai (▷ 160) Instead of motoring to Chiang Rai, arrive there by boat—there's a daily service down the Kok River from Thaton.

Lampang (▷ 166–167) Switch off for a day's meditation at a Lampang temple.

Lamphun (▷ 168–169) Shop for locally made textiles on Lamphun's covered bridge and then stroll in the twilight through the nearby Wat Haripunchai.

Mae Hong Son (▷ 170) Rent a car and drive the Mae Hong Son loop road (▷ 176–177), making sure to find time for stops in Pai and Mae Sariang.

Spa towns Soak the day away in the hot springs of one of Northern Thailand's many spas—Chiang Mai (▷ 154–159), Lampang (▷ 166–167), Mae Hong Son (▷ 170) and Pai (▷ 172)—and enjoy a traditional Thai massage.

Tak (▷ 175) Join a houseboat party on any of Northern Thailand's big lakes (the Bhumiphol Dam, for instance) and cruise its waters, stopping for lunch at a floating restaurant.

CENTRAL THAILAND

Ayutthaya (▷ 196–199) Cruise the canals of Ayutthaya by boat, or amble around the ruins of the old city on the back of an elephant.

Chanthaburi (▷ 201) Tour the jewelry shops of Chanthaburi, Thailand's gem-trade center.

Damnoen Saduak (▷ 202) Take an early bus from Bangkok to the Damnoen Saduak floating market, one of Thailand's top visitor attractions.

Kanchanaburi (▷ 203–204) Ride the "Death Railway" from Kanchanaburi to the end of the line, Nam Tok—but also find time to cruise the famous Kwai River in a longtail boat.

Lop Buri (▷ 205) Throw a few bananas to the monkeys at Lop Buri's Wat Phra Gan, but don't go too close.

Pattaya (▷ 208–209) Overnight in Pattaya, sample its hedonistic, anything-goes nightlife and vow to return—or to stay away forever.

Si Satchanalai (▷ 210–211) Seek out the ruined royal city of Si Satchanalai, near Sukhothai, and tour the site on elephant back.

THE SOUTH

Hua Hin (▷ 238) Visit this seaside resort with a sparkling white beach, a historic hotel, good food and easy access from Bangkok.

Ko Lanta (▷ 240) Chill out on a beach, read a long novel and explore the island's east coast.

Ko Samui (▷ 242–243) The palm-fringed beaches make this a hugely popular island, but it is large enough for those seeking a quiet retreat.

Ko Similan (▷ 241) Explore the islands that offer the best underwater experience in Thailand.

Krabi (▷ 246–247) This small and well-provided town is a great base for island trips and water-based activities such as kayaking in mangrove swamps, snorkeling or diving.

Phetchaburi (▷ 249) Take a walking tour through a town renowned for its historic temples, including the photogenic Wat Mahathat.

Phuket (▷ 250–252) Base yourself at one of the most sophisticated beach resorts in the country and enjoy some welcome relaxation—or make the most of the water sport and nightlife opportunities.

Railay Beach (Krabi ▷ 247) Climb towering karsts or lounge on the white beach amid Thailand's stunning coastal scenery.

TOP EXPERIENCES

Deepen your knowledge of Thai history by touring the magnificent Khmer ruins along the country's border with Cambodia (▷ 29).

Get sporty Experience Chiang Mai's more rugged scenery by mountain bike, raft or canoe, with an experienced adventure tour company (▷ 182, Active Thailand).

Join a trekking tour in Chiang Rai (▷ 160) to remote hill-tribe villages.

Learn to ride elephants as the mahouts do at the National Elephant Institute and Conservation Center near Lampang (▷ 165).

Pamper yourself with a day's spa treatment in Bangkok or Chiang Mai (▷ 103–104, 183–184).

Rent a longtail boat at Chiang Saen on the Mekong River and tell the skipper to take you to the true Golden Triangle, where the borders of Thailand, Myanmar and Laos meet (▷ 161).

Sip wine at Thailand's leading vineyard, Chateau de Loei, in Loei province (▷ 123).

Spend the night in a timber-built cabin at one of Thailand's national parks and rent a guide the next morning to lead you on a trek through virgin rain forest (▷ 122, 123).

Stay overnight in a floating cabin on the Kwai River in Kanchanaburi province (▷ 203–204).

Surprise friends at your next dinner party by serving a complete Thai menu after taking a cooking course at one of Bangkok's many cookery schools (▷ 102–103).

Tackle the rapids of the Pai River in Northern Thailand in a canoe or, more safely, on a raft (▷ 186).

Try a new water sport at Pattaya (▷ 208–209) or Patong (▷ 251), where instructors in sailing, windsurfing, waterskiing and paragliding operate at the beaches.

Watch Thai boxing, or *Muay Thai*, at Lumphini Stadium in Bangkok (▷ 100–101).

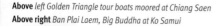

Above *left Golden Triangle tour boats moored at Chiang Saen*
Above right *Ban Plai Laem, Big Buddha at Ko Samui*

LIVING THAILAND

Thailand's social fabric dictates all the country's actions and the daily routine of its people, from government procedures to the way the humblest farmer conducts his life. At the center stands the monarch, whose picture hangs not only in schools, offices, workplaces and everywhere the public congregates, but also in most homes. The present king, Bhumibol Adulyadej, Rama IX, is genuinely and universally loved by the Thai people, a true father figure. Great reverence is also paid to the community of monks, the Sangha, which is held at a respectful distance by a population that is more than 90 percent Buddhist. Society's third level is taken up by the commoners, increasingly divided into a burgeoning middle class and a peasant majority. Despite past demonstrations of student political engagement and fervor, Thailand's youth is quiescent and more concerned with carving out careers than with addressing the political, economic and social problems that beset the country. Thailand even has "yuppies"—a class of young professionals sometimes called "tuppies." Their rapid acquisition of wealth and influence is having a polarizing effect on Thai society, which is in danger of becoming a two-class state, divided between those who control the wealth and the millions of rural peasants.

Clockwise from above *Members of the Hmong (or Meo) tribe sitting in front of their wooden dwellings in a hill village in the Phu Hin Rong Kla National Park; doorman at the Royal Orchid Sheraton Hotel in Bangkok; Akha tribeswoman at the Doi Mae Salong morning market in Chiang Mai*

WOMEN FARE BEST IN THAILAND?

Recent years have seen a significant and positive change to the status and role of women in Thai society, according to a 2004 World Bank report. This view is supported by findings of the MasterIndex of Women's Advancement (a composite index measuring the socio-economic level of women in 13 Asia-Pacific markets). In 2005, Thailand topped the index. While the country's rating has dropped since, Thailand has improved in all rated categories.

While women in Thailand are making steps toward equality in the workplace, traditional values still hold their ground. Only on rare occasions will a woman relinquish taking care of her family in order to continue her career.

LANGUAGE-TEACHING PROBLEMS

English-language skills are seen as a vital tool with which to succeed in the "global community." Thailand has long been well served thanks to its desirability as a location for ESL (English as a Second Language) teachers—foreign professionals or backpackers looking to make money to fund their travel.

Recently, however, political unrest and changing immigration procedures have had a detrimental effect. In a 2007 study by the Office of Basic Education Commission, a test of native Thai English-language teachers revealed that of the 14,189 participants, a massive 75 percent scored less than 41 marks out of 100.

LADYBOYS

Thailand is famous for its refreshingly open and populous gay and transsexual community. While public displays of affection are generally frowned upon, Thailand is otherwise tolerant of outward expressions of sexual preference.

Thailand's flamboyant transsexuals ("ladyboys") draw a lot of attention in tourist areas, where many also work as prostitutes. However, the vast majority of transsexuals in Thailand work conventional jobs, but choose to go about their daily business wearing full drag. Transsexuals are seen in all stages of transition, from cross-dressers to others almost indistinguishable from the female sex.

THAILAND'S REMOTE HILL TRIBES

Wherever you travel in northern Thailand you'll encounter hill-tribe people and have the opportunity to visit or stay in their picturesque villages. There are nine hill tribes, numbering about half a million people, in Thailand, most originating in the remote regions of northeastern Myanmar (Burma) and northwestern China. One, the gentle Akha people, trace their origins to Tibet. The Karen are the most numerous, with more than 200,000 people inhabiting most of Thailand's western border with Myanmar. Although the Karen are by tradition animists, many of them are Christians, converted by missionaries. A large number of hill-tribe villages existed for years on the opium trade, growing poppies on mountainside plots difficult for the police to access. But a government program introducing alternative cash crops is weaning them away from their illegal business.

THE PRACTICAL SIDE OF THAI CUSTOMS

Some of the obscure Thai customs, originating in the ancient northern kingdom of Lanna, actually serve a practical purpose. Each year, Buddhists—particularly in rural communities—bring sand to their local temple and seem to the outsider to busy themselves building sandcastles in the monastery compounds. In fact, they are symbolically but also practically replacing the soil, sand and gravel carried away from the temple compound by the feet of monks and visitors. Buddhist belief considers it inappropriate to take anything from a temple, including the soil, sand or gravel. So once a year, at the Songkran New Year festival, people make merit, easing their way to Nirvana, by taking bags of sand to the local temple.

In the north, the sand is built into elegant *chedis*, rather like building a sandcastle on the beach, and decorated with flowers, paper flags and money.

Visitors to Thailand's historic cities often ask why virtually the only surviving buildings are temple structures. The answer is that secular homes were usually constructed of wood, and have not withstood the ravages of time. Stone and masonry were reserved for palaces and temples, as if early rulers knew they would be building for posterity. No wooden building in today's Thailand is more than a century or so old, making it difficult for historians to trace a precise line of architectural development. The ruins of temples and royal buildings, however, follow a 1,500-year course that embraces Indian, Sri Lankan, Mon, Khmer, Chinese and Burmese influences within a recognizably Siamese context. Sandstone was the earliest construction material, to be replaced in the 12th century by brick. By the 16th century, stucco was being used more and more. Increasing contact with the outside world in the 19th century brought Western architectural styles and building methods to Siam, and neo-Gothic, Victorian and even classical Greek structures arose in Bangkok and royal country retreats. During the late 20th century, renowned architects were employed to give Bangkok a Manhattan look and skyline, and soaring glass and steel skyscrapers now share space with century-old wooden pavilions and shophouses.

LANNA REVIVAL

A new style has entered Thailand's architectural vocabulary—the Lanna Revival. It's not without controversy, however. A conference attended by Buddhist academics and abbots in Chiang Mai complained that the Lanna Revival style increasingly seen in hotel construction was exploiting temple architecture and icons for commercial purposes.

They pointed to the example of a new luxury hotel that had built on its grounds a replica of a famous Lampang temple. Furthermore, the same hotel had built its entrance in imitation of another Lampang temple. Worse still, hotels were displaying Buddha images and statues as decorative items in bedrooms. Stripped of its Buddhist decorations, the Lanna Revival style is actually very ascetic, combining dark teak flooring and paneling with stark white stucco.

Clockwise from above Beautiful gardens surround the five raised traditional Thai houses, built for Princess Chumbhot, in the grounds of the Suan Pakkad Palace, Bangkok; Le Royal Meridien Hotel in downtown Bangkok; an ancient temple and modern skyscraper jostle together in Bangkok

SPECTACULAR SKYLINE

Bangkok is not known as a city of architectural beauty, yet the boom years of the early 1990s left the city with a collection of spectacular skyscrapers that wouldn't look out of place in Manhattan. More than 700 high-rise buildings, 35 of them taller than 330ft (100m), pierce the skyline of Thailand's sprawling capital, many designed by leading architects. The highest is the Baiyoke Tower II, in Ratchatewi district, which tops 984ft (300m). The 85 floors include a 673-room hotel. When it was built in 1996 it was the tallest building in Southeast Asia and the world's third-highest hotel. Among the most spectacular is the Thai Wah Tower II, a thin wafer that reaches 636ft (194m), with the topmost of its 60 floors framing a graceful arch.

SPIRIT HOUSES

The building industry in Thailand has a very lucrative offshoot—the construction of spirit houses. Office blocks, condominium buildings, hotels and even petrol stations all have a spirit house for the *pi* (or spirits) who previously lived on the site.

The spirits are given food and offerings to ensure that they don't cause problems for the new occupants of their territory and encourage good luck. In more rural areas, when a new house is built, ceremonies are regularly held to appease and thank the spirits who lived in the forest that supplied the timber used in the construction. If a property is enlarged, the spirit house also has to be made bigger to accommodate an increased number of spirits.

BANKING ON ARCHITECTURAL AWARD

Thailand's innovative and popular architect Sathaporn Srikaranonda won the country's 1993 award for best work of architectural conservation by brilliantly converting a temple sermon hall into a boat museum. He found his inspiration in the depiction of the wooden pavilion structure on the back of a rare one-baht banknote from the reign of King Rama VIII. The superb sermon hall, its high ceiling supported by massive beams and pillars, was built in 1927 and renovated in 1988.

BANGKOK'S HIGH-RISE TEMPLE

Thailand has some of Southeast Asia's most distinctive temple architecture, but not all of it is in traditional style. The capital's tallest temple structure, built in 1985, is a modern pyramid-shape high-rise of 10 floors, topped by a traditional stupa or *chedi*, containing relics said to be strands of the Buddha's hair. The temple building, Wat Dhammamongkol (Soi 1, Thanon Sukhumvit), is 312ft (95m) tall and contains the world's largest jade Buddha image.

Although Thailand's King is now a constitutional monarch and no longer an absolute ruler, he and his family are held in the highest reverence, and any form of disrespect or lese majesty is a punishable offense. At royal audiences, government officials approach the monarch on their knees and keep their heads below his at all times. The occasional television interviews with the royal family are staged so that the prince or princess sits on a raised dais, and pictures of the King, or earlier monarchs, are hung above head height. These elaborate displays of reverence are accepted without question by the majority of Thais, who regard the King as the true father of the nation. There have been occasions—notably during confrontations between students and the government in 1992—when he has used this paternal influence to end a crisis. The King is also the guardian of Thailand's customs and traditions, and he is present at all important Buddhist rituals within the palace compound and often attends other temple events. In 1960, he resurrected the ancient Brahman custom of plowing a section of the park adjacent to the palace, the Sanam Luang. The token plowing, held in May, is accompanied by a prediction of how the next rice harvest will turn out. In December, the King and Queen review the royal guard in a Trooping the Color ceremony very similar to the British one.

Above *Constitution Day Parade through Bangkok is held annually in December*

THE NATIONAL ANTHEM

First-time visitors to Thailand are often startled to see Thais stop what they are doing and stand stiffly to attention in public places while loudspeakers blare out a stirring melody.

Twice a day, at 8am and 6pm, the national anthem is played in open spaces, such as railway station concourses and markets. No Thai would ever dare ignore the call to stand in honor of their nation while the anthem is played; foreigners aren't required to follow the practice, but they get approving looks if they do.

Theater and cinema performances are preceded by the royal anthem, and there it's highly disrespectful to sit and munch popcorn while it's played.

60TH ANNIVERSARY CELEBRATIONS

The reverence felt for King Bhumibol, the world's longest-reigning monarch, was no more apparent than during celebrations of the 60th anniversary of his accession to the throne, in 2006. The celebrations began on June 8 with The Meritorious Royal Ceremony on the Merit Offering to the Royal Ancestors and continued to June 12, during which time kings, queens and dignitaries from around the world came to pay their respects. Even after the official celebrations ended, unofficial events continued throughout 2006 and 2007. Wristbands inscribed with "We love the King" are still a common sight.

"RENAISSANCE MAN"

King Bhumibol plays saxophone and clarinet, loves jazz and has written 35 registered compositions. His love of jazz developed during the years of his youth that he spent in the United States and Switzerland; he once played saxophone with the great Benny Goodman. Among his jazz compositions are such numbers as "HM Blues" and "Friday Night Rag," but he has also written love songs with titles like "Lovelight in My Heart." He also dabbles successfully in science and technology. His keen interest in agriculture and the environment doesn't stop at theory—he has patented a rain-making idea involving "seeding" clouds over drought areas.

Above *Girls wearing formal Thai dress*
Below *Portrait of Queen Sirikit*

HOW TO *WAI*

The *wai* is Thailand's universal form of greeting, and every visitor should get to know the subtle rules governing its use. The height of your palms when brought together before the face or upper body is critical—too low and you may be mildly offending somebody, too high and surprised amusement may be the reaction. Basically, wait for a Thai to *wai* you before returning the gesture. Some Thais welcome foreigners by shaking hands, and in that case a *wai* is not only unnecessary but impossible. Monks and venerable people older than yourself receive the highest *wai*, with the fingertips reaching forehead level. Other adults and young people are the easiest to *wai*—just keep the palms of your hands above chest level. There is no need to return the *wai* of hotel or restaurant staff, or any service personnel.

QUEEN OF SILKS

Thailand's Queen Sirikit is responsible for putting mudmee silk on the international fashion map. She financed a program to encourage women in rural areas to take up traditional handicrafts as a way of supplementing family incomes and keeping alive age-old skills. In Thailand's northeastern provinces, silk-weaving is a means of livelihood in many villages, and Queen Sirikit launched a project to promote one particularly fine silk, mudmee. She wore mudmee silk on state occasions, at home and abroad, attracting the attention of textile companies and designers. The high point of her campaign came when the French designer Pierre Balmain featured mudmee creations in one of his collections. Now mudmee, once a peasant cloth, is one of Thailand's most fashionable fabrics.

Nearly 67 percent of Thailand's population of almost 66 million people live in the rural areas, and one of the problems faced by successive governments in Bangkok has been to maintain their living standards in a booming industrial economy. The latest United Nations report on world poverty levels classes nearly 10 million Thais as "poor"—that is, existing on less than the equivalent of US $1 per day—and most of these are living on the land. A further 5.8 million people are said, in the report, to be existing on less than 80 cents a day and therefore "ultra poor," while 19 million are listed as being on the poverty line. A parallel report by the UN Development Programme used other factors to measure Thailand's poverty: access to healthcare, housing, education, employment, transportation and environmental considerations. When these factors were considered, the report said, just 5 percent of Thailand's population could be classified as really poor. Nevertheless, most of Thailand's farmers, who form the backbone of the rural economy, exist on little more than $1 per day. City incomes average more than 10 times that, a growing disparity that Bangkok governments have difficulty in combating. Nobody starves in Thailand; subsidized medical services and education and a basic "survival" pension of B600 per month for needy elderly stave off total penury. But many rural dwellers watch in disbelief the antics of Thailand's high-living nouveau riche on TV soap operas.

PROTECTIVE CLOTHING OF THE FOREST

Although illegal logging remains a serious threat to Thailand's vanishing forests, villagers are aware of the problem and have their own way of dealing with it.

To protect the teak forests that provide an income to rural communities, most village temples have a festival known as *Wat Pa*—the Holy Forest. Animist beliefs and Buddhist ritual are blended in a ceremony in which the trees are "clothed" in saffron-colored monks' robes to deter thieves from entering the forest and disturbing the spirits that dwell there.

Above *Once common, tigers are now a rare sight in Thailand*

THE ROYAL PROJECTS

In an effort to wean hill-tribe farmers away from cultivating poppies for the production of opium, Thailand's King Bhumibol launched a program of "royal projects" in 1969 to offer them alternative sources of income. Since then, the number of projects has grown to more than 4,000, transforming Thailand's agriculture, particularly in the far north. The projects have introduced new varieties of crops once unknown in Thailand—temperate-zone fruits such as apples, pears, plums, strawberries and raspberries, potatoes, artichokes and asparagus. The King called on experts from all over the world to assist in the enterprise: dispossessed white farmers from Zimbabwe helped nurture Thailand's embryonic tobacco industry, French vintners taught Thais to make wine, and German experts discovered the perfect soil conditions for growing asparagus.

OTOP

A new road sign has appeared at the entrance to most Thai towns and villages: OTOP. It stands for One Tambol One Product and indicates that the local community is specializing in the production of traditional handicrafts. Tambol (pronounced and sometimes written as "Tambon") is the administrative term for a small town or village. The idea of encouraging people in rural areas to supplement their income by starting "cottage industries" was borrowed from Japan, which is now closely involved with Thailand in the OTOP program. Thai communities are actively encouraged to revive traditional skills, from simple basket-weaving to the production of fine teak, bamboo and unusual water hyacinth furniture. There are major OTOP retail outlets throughout Bangkok and in some provincial centers, notably Chiang Mai, and a visit to one of them should definitely be on any foreign shopper's schedule.

THAILAND'S VANISHING TIGERS

Once a frequent sight, tigers are now so rare in Thailand that when two were sighted northwest of Chiang Mai in July 2005, a general warning not to shoot them was issued.

The World Wildlife Fund (WWF) estimates that there are a maximum of 500 wild tigers remaining in Thailand. Tigers are a strictly protected species, and severe penalties await any hunter who kills one. Trading in tiger skins or body parts is also a serious offense, but that doesn't prevent some villagers in remote areas from offering visitors tiger teeth, claws and even penises. Such wares should not, of course, be bought.

Above *Tower block and town houses in Bangkok*
Left *A Thai farmer*

UNHEALTHY BANGKOK

Latest statistics confirm what everybody knew anyway: Bangkok is a dangerously unhealthy city. A report by the National Economic and Social Development Board shows that nearly half of the capital's 10 million inhabitants suffer from respiratory ailments. Air pollution regularly exceeds World Health Organization danger levels—on the main shopping street, Silom Road, dust levels are often nearly 10 times the WHO limits. Road accidents account for a huge number of casualties—more than 2,000 people die every year on Bangkok's roads. These statistics contributed to Bangkok's decline in the Mercer Human Resource Consulting list of "liveable cities" in the 12 months to 2007: Bangkok dropped from 107th place to 109th.

First-time visitors to Bangkok find a vibrant city that not only never sleeps, but also never stops eating. Noodle stands line the streets, serving hot food around the clock, while restaurants are rarely more than a few paces apart. One reason given for this preoccupation with food is that Thais prefer to eat little and often rather than indulge in large Western-style meals twice a day. Rice and noodles are the staple diet, introduced from China more than 1,000 years ago. There are two kinds of rice: the popular "sticky" variety and boiled *kao suay*, which is sometimes jasmine flavored. Sticky rice is eaten with curries and sauces, while *kao suay* is normally served as a side dish or stir-fried with meat or vegetables. Sticky rice is also a component of a delicious dessert: sliced mango and sticky rice soaked in coconut milk. The coconut milk used to thicken curries and sauces is not the sweet juice of a ripe coconut (that's served complete with the coconut, like an exotic cocktail), but is obtained from the crushed white flesh of the fruit. It was first developed by French chefs at the 17th-century court of Ayutthaya, where they shunned the watery sauces and curries prepared by local cooks. The ample supply of wood in Thailand resulted in an early development of grilling techniques, while a flourishing ceramics tradition provided pots for preparing the curries and soups. Herbs gathered from the forest, chilies and other spices grown domestically added the distinctly Thai character and flavor.

Clockwise from above *The markets in Thailand are packed with superb fresh produce; outdoor food vendors are a common sight all over Thailand: here a woman is grilling fish at Sirikit Reservoir; a traditional Kaeng matsaman curry dish*

LEARNING THAI CUISINE
Cookery schools have shot up all over Thailand in response to the profound international popularity of Thai cuisine. Most are concentrated in Bangkok, Chiang Mai and holiday islands such as Phuket and Ko Samui, but they are also to be found in any city and town on the visitor route. The largest concentration of cookery schools is in Chiang Mai, which has more than 20. Among the more established ones are Gaps House (3 Thanon Ratchadamnoen, Soi 4, tel 053 27 81 40; www.gaps-house.com) and the Chiang Mai Cookery School (47/2 Thanon Moon Muang, tel 053 20 63 88; www.thaicookeryschool.com), which has a restaurant outlet, The Wok (44 Thanon Ratchamanka, tel 053 20 82 87). Courses at all schools last from one day to one week and cost around B990 per day.

HERBS AND SPICES

Around 30 fragrant herbs and spices are used in Thai cuisine. Three of them are varieties of basil: *horapa* (similar to the kind in Italian pesto), a sweeter version called *gaprao*, and *mangluk*, which has a slight peppery taste. The most important addition to traditional Thai cuisine is lemongrass *(takrai)*, which gives soups such as *tom yam gong* (spicy shrimp soup) a distinctive flavor. Medicinal powers are ascribed to most of Thailand's herbs and spices. Three varieties of ginger are especially valued: *khing* (young green ginger used as a condiment with meat), *galangal* or *khaa* (Siamese ginger used to make curry paste) and *grashai* (added to fish and curries).

THAI TABLEWARE

When you eat at a typical Thai restaurant you'll be presented with a spoon and fork, but no knife. Chopsticks are usually kept in a metal container on the table. All are relatively new additions to the table in a country where people traditionally eat with their fingers.

If you're invited to join a family at their meal in a country village, don't be surprised if you're expected to sit on the floor and eat with your fingers from common bowls. Sticky rice was once the staple food of the Thais and is still eaten in country areas in preference to the more refined kao *suay* (or "fine rice"). The only practical way to eat sticky rice is with the fingers, using it to soak up the soup.

TABLE HABITS

When dining with friends or business colleagues, etiquette in a Thai restaurant requires that you share your ordered dish with others at the table. The usual practice is for each diner to order one or two items from the menu, which should be different from those requested by the others. Each dish should have its own serving spoon, but don't be shocked if your neighbor dips directly into your curry! Rice is usually served from a common bowl. Don't expect dishes to come to the table in the order common in the West—soups and salads are served at the same time as other savory dishes. Only desserts come at the end of the meal. Water is usually drunk, but you will often see Thai businessmen lacing it with whisky.

"ROYAL" THAI CUISINE

The best Thai restaurants serve dishes that date back to the 17th-century reign of King Narai the Great, who introduced many Western influences to his magnificent court. Portuguese missionaries and traders brought luxury items, such as eggs to the kitchen and syrups for desserts and cakes *(kanom)*. French visitors showed the Thais how to make bread, which is still called *kanom pang* (*pang* being a transliteration of the French *pain*). The first Western ambassador welcomed to Ayutthaya was a French diplomat. The nobleman brought with him a retinue of cooks, who transformed the court kitchens. The dishes they prepared became known as "royal Thai", and can still be found on restaurant menus.

After many years in the wilderness, Thailand is beginning to make a significant contribution to the international arts and entertainment scene. The award of a Cannes Film Festival Jury Prize to the Thai avant-garde film *Tropical Malady* (2004) gave a big boost, and martial arts films starring Tony Jaa (Jaa Panom)—*Ong-Bak* (2003), *Tom-Yum-Goong* (2005) and *Ong-Bak 2* (2008)—have put Thai action films on the international map. The burgeoning film production infrastructure now attracts numerous big-budget international productions to Thailand. Thai theater and serious music, meanwhile, seem still rooted in tradition and the few brave attempts at experimenting with new styles and themes have found little popular resonance. The pop music scene, though dominated by artless Korean boy-bands, has a few bright and shining local stars.

Above *A Thai man performing a traditional dance during the Longan Fair, which takes place every August in Lamphun*

THAILAND'S STRUGGLING THEATER

The curtain has never risen on a truly contemporary theater scene in Thailand, where the stage is still associated in the public's mind with displays of traditional music and dancing and epic drama. There are only three major annual performing arts festivals, and the chief of these, the Bangkok International Festival of Music and Dance, is dominated by foreign productions. The other two, the Bangkok Theater Festival and the Fringe Festival, attract only small audiences.

Government or corporate grants are rare, and the country's 10 professional theater companies have difficulty financing more than one or two productions a month between them. Even Bangkok has no theater devoted solely to drama.

ASIAN POP SENSATION

Daughter of an American father and a Thai mother, Tata Young has put Thai pop music on the international map. Tata's music shot her to success and she has cut nearly a dozen albums for 10 different studios, the fifth of which, "I Believe," launched her onto the world's stage.

Born in December 1980, she made her first album, singing in both Thai and English, at the age of 15. It sold one million copies within five months of its release and her career was launched.

Tata is also a movie star and won a best actress award in her debut role in the Thai film *Red Bike Story*, which beat box office records when it was released in 1997.

Her third English album, "Ready for Love," was released in 2009.

THE STORY OF THAILAND

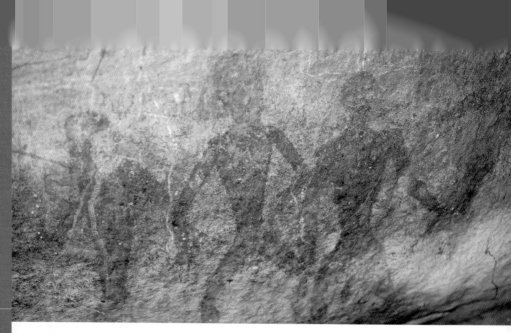

Scholars still disagree over the true origins of the inhabitants of present-day Thailand, their theories often confounded by new archeological discoveries. It was long thought that Thai civilization arrived from China, until a Bronze Age settlement was discovered that predated any found to date in China. Yet all agree that migratory patterns and linguistic evidence show that large areas of northern Thailand were settled thousands of years ago by people from Chinese Yunnan. These newcomers, grouped under the generic term "Tai," either absorbed or displaced an aboriginal population who appear to be the ancestors of the hill tribes that inhabit remote areas of northern Thailand. The newcomers introduced agriculture, rearing livestock and cultivating rice that has since formed the basis of Thailand's rural economy and the country's national product. The few records that exist show that these communities formed into ever larger units—called (then as now) *Muang*—at first for trade but also for mutual defense. Village chiefs rose to become *Muang* leaders, who formed regional ruling dynasties, assigning sons to take over neighboring *Muang*. Dynastic realms grew in size and importance, worrying even the emperors of China, who demanded tribute. In central and northeastern regions, the Mon and Khmer empires were penetrating deeper into Tai territory, bringing with them Hinduism and Buddhism. The Tai absorbed the religions but resisted domination by the Khmer and Mon, and a struggle for supremacy grew from the sixth century onward.

POWS' DISCOVERY
One of Thailand's most interesting neolithic sites was uncovered by chance by Dutch prisoners working on the "Death Railway" near Kanchanaburi in 1943. Japanese troops overseeing work on the railway ignored pleas to protect the site, but after the war Dutch survivors alerted archeologists to the existence of the riverside site, near the village of Ban Kao, 22 miles (35km) northwest of Kanchanaburi. Among the objects displayed at a small museum (Wed–Sun 9–4.30) adjoining the site is decorative jewelry carved from bone more than 3,000 years ago. Stone axes and clay pots are also among the exhibits.

Clockwise from above *Rock paintings by Brahmin and early Buddhists have been discovered near Ban Phu in the Phu Phra Bat Historical Park; sandbanks on the Mekong River near Sangkhon; original pottery from the early Bronze Age settlement excavated during archeological digs at Ban Chiang*

BRONZE AGE BEGINNINGS

For many years it was thought that the Bronze Age had virtually bypassed Southeast Asia. But then in the late 1960s archeologists uncovered evidence in a small Thai village that a thriving Bronze Age civilization existed here for up to 4,000 years, until around AD200. The discovery made the village of Ban Chiang world famous and injected money from tourism and scientific research funds into this poor region of northeastern Thailand. The community that settled here some 4,000 years ago on the 20-acre (8ha) site not only mastered the craft of creating implements and ornaments from iron and bronze but also developed a very artistic pottery style, known as the "Ban Chiang Ceramic Tradition." Fine examples of the work are on show at a museum on the excavation site in Ban Chiang.

BONES OF CONTENTION

When archeologists discovered the remains of prehistoric ancestors of the elephant and crocodile in Thailand's Korat Basin in 2005, their discoveries proved that 10 million years ago this arid region of eastern Thailand was richly forested and teeming with wildlife. The archeologists ran into trouble when they sought to move their finds to Bangkok—local people regarded the fossils as sacred and imbued with magic powers. One large piece of petrified wood was venerated as a female deity. Among the animal bones were the skulls of two large fish-eating crocodiles, now extinct in Thailand, and of a hyena that has long disappeared from Asia. An incomplete skeleton of a Stegadon, an ancestor of both the mammoth and the elephant, was also recovered—and was thought by locals to have superhuman powers.

WHERE DINOSAURS ROAMED

Thailand has some of the world's most spectacular prehistoric fossil sites. Most are in the eastern Isan region, where eight previously unknown species of dinosaurs have been discovered. They include the world's oldest sauropod, *Isanosaurus attavipachi*, which roamed the area 210 million years ago. Remains of the world's oldest tyrannosaur were also discovered in Isan. Two dinosaurs unique to Thailand are the huge plant-eating sauropod *Phuwiangosaurus sirindhornae* and a fish-eating theropod, *Siamosaurus suteethorni*, which lived on the Isan plateau more than 100 million years ago. More than 800 bones of six different dinosaur species and an almost complete skeleton have been discovered in the Phu Khum Kao National Park, in Kalasin province, where a research center is being set up. There is a small museum at the site, and another in the village of Phu Wiang in Khon Kaen province.

HOW THE WORLD BEGAN

A catastrophic flood features in a legend still told in northeastern Thailand to explain the origins of this part of Southeast Asia. The king of the gods, angered by the ingratitude of mortals, inundated the earth with a huge flood. Only three local chiefs survived and lived with the gods until the flood subsided. They returned to earth with a buffalo, which helped them restore the devastated fields before dying. From its nostrils then grew a plant that produced a crop of gourds, which in turn produced two races of people—dark-skinned Aboriginals and lighter-skinned Lao. The three chiefs taught the Lao to till the land and raise crops and domesticate animals (presumably leaving the Aboriginals to their own devices) and the king of the gods sent his son to help them. The son produced seven of his own, whom he appointed to rule over a territory stretching all the way from Yunnan to Myanmar (Burma) and from Laos to northern Thailand.

The story of how the Siam region emerged from prehistoric times has been pieced together from the art and architecture of the period. This era is called Dvaravati, from the one decipherable word on a coin discovered from those times. The word Dvaravati is Sanskrit for "doors." Scholars have long mused over the significance of the name, with the most credible explanation being that the "doors" are actually "portals" to a country or territory. Perhaps the name was imprinted on coins used by traders and recognized as legal tender by one region. The portals, according to the theory, must have been the trading centers established along the frontiers of this region. These towns were the one unifying element of the region. The traders were mostly from India and Sri Lanka, Hindu holy men and Buddhist monks among them. These spiritual men spread not only their beliefs but also their art and architecture. The rise of the Dvaravati "empire" coincided with expansionist moves by the Khmer. They established outposts in today's central and eastern Thailand and inevitably came into conflict with local Dvaravati rulers. The end of the Dvaravati era and the retreat of the Khmer followed the formation of regional alliances that were strong enough to challenge both.

Clockwise from above *A door guardian* (kala) *of the Khmer sanctuary of Ku Phra Ko Na; Wheel of the Law, a symbol of Buddhist wisdom; entrance to Khao Phra Viharn, in Cambodia, built by the Khmer kings*

THE UNLUCKY SUITOR
In the absence of a written Dvaravati history, myths inevitably surround Queen Chamthewi, many of them focusing on her apparent celibacy. Was she akin to England's Virgin Queen? Like Elizabeth I, she appears to have had her share of suitors, but none managed to conquer her heart. According to a fable, one smitten chieftain was told that if he could throw a spear from his hilltop home south of Chiang Mai to her palace in Haripunchai she would marry him. His first two attempts fell short and the third throw went totally amiss, the spear rising vertically and then falling into the unfortunate man's heart.

KHMER RUINS STILL CAUSE CONFLICT

The ancient Khmer ruins of Cambodia are still the subject of dispute with Thailand. The latter nearly broke off diplomatic relations with Phnom Penh in 2003, when its embassy was attacked: Cambodian protesters feared that Bangkok was resurrecting claims on the ancient city of Angkor. Siamese forces in previous centuries had overrun Angkor three times, and many Cambodians believe present-day Thailand still harbors a territorial claim. Their fears erupted into anti-Thai rioting at the start of 2003, when a Thai actress seemed to remark that Angkor belonged to Thailand. The Thai embassy and other Thai property were badly damaged in the rioting, and Thailand hurriedly evacuated its citizens from Phnom Penh. One ancient Khmer compound on Cambodia's thickly forested northern border, Prasat Khao Phra Vihanalong (Preah Vihear), is more accessible from Thailand, which continued to be a source of military dispute as late as 2009.

QUEEN CHAMTHEWI

The Dvaravati era produced the most glamorous and favored monarch in Thailand's history—Queen Chamthewi of Haripunchai, now the little town of Lamphun. Chamthewi is pictured in history books as a young woman of great beauty and courage, adored by her subjects and feared by her enemies: a female ruler who added grace and glamor to the Haripunchai court but who regularly donned armor and fearlessly rode into battle on an elephant. Chamthewi was sent to rule Haripunchai by her father, the king of Lop Buri. She ruled wisely for nearly 40 years, abdicating at the age of 60. Chamthewi chose to spend most of her remaining years meditating in a beautiful temple she had built on the edge of Haripunchai. When she died, at the grand old age of 92, she was cremated within the temple compound and her ashes were sealed in a *chedi* that still stands—one of Lamphun's most revered monuments. A *chedi* on the other side of town marks the place where her favorite battle elephant was buried.

DVARAVATI ART

Dvaravati sculptures found at sites in central Thailand offer proof that this ancient culture had a highly sophisticated and talented community of craftspeople, judging by the fine works discovered there. Among them was a circular stone representing the "Wheel of the Law," the symbol of Buddhist wisdom. The limestone wheel, 3ft (95cm) in diameter, and dating from the seventh or eighth century, incorporates a statue of a deer as a reminder that the Buddha attained enlightenment in a deer park. The wheel is a central exhibit at the National Museum in Bangkok, where other examples of Dvaravati art include an exquisite Buddha bust, 8 inches (20cm) high but as detailed as the greatest Buddha statues.

DVARAVATI PALACES

Dvaravati palaces were probably constructed entirely of wood, so virtually no traces remain of them. A bas-relief found at Muang Fa Daet Sung Yang in Kalasin province gives a good idea, however, of how splendid they must have been. The carved picture shows a scene from a Jataka legend, with prominence given to the palace home of the Buddha's former wife, Yasodhara. The palace compound is entered through an imposing three-tiered gateway, and the princess's home is a handsome mansion with elaborate roof ornamentation. The house was built with each of its four facades facing a cardinal point of the compass, a Dvaravati architectural feature copied by later Siamese rulers.

Although the Sukhothai dynasty lasted less than 150 years, it is regarded as the cradle of modern Thailand. Until the early 13th century, most of Thailand was ruled by weak vassal states and communities controlled by the Khmer from their stronghold in Angkor. It was a vast area to govern from so far away, and disintegration and political unrest was inevitable. In 1238, two local princes, Phi Khun Pha Muang and Pho Khun Bang Klang Thao, joined forces and marched on Sukhothai, routing the Khmer. Pho Khun Bang Klang Thao, the victor, was proclaimed king and took the royal title Pho Khun Si Indradit, starting a dynasty that was to last until the mid-14th century. He was succeeded by his eldest son, Pho Khun Ban Muang, who died young, vacating the throne for his brother, Pho Khun Ramkhamhaeng. Under Ramkhamhaeng's rule, Sukhothai flourished as no other Southeast Asian realm, and his reign is known as the "golden period" of Thai history. Ramkhamhaeng abolished slavery and most taxes, and he built up a thriving economy. He also extended his realm into today's Myanmar (Burma) and Laos, and into the Malay peninsula, and forged productive diplomatic relations with China. Sukhothai's decline began with Ramkhamhaeng's death and the subsequent rise of the Ayutthaya court. It was annexed by Ayutthaya in 1350 and became a northern outpost of Siam's new center of power.

Clockwise from above *There are superb ceramics all over Thailand (this one is for sale in a ceramics shop in Sawankhalok); the Kilns Museum in Sawankhalok charts the history of ceramics in Thailand; Buddhas for sale at one of the many craft shops in Sukhothai*

BIRTH OF THE THAI ALPHABET

Sukhothai gave birth not only to the first Siamese empire but also to the Thai alphabet in use today. The introduction of a truly Siamese alphabet was part of King Ramkhamhaeng's plan to create an autonomous state free from the traces of the Khmer and Mon rulers he had defeated. In the dying years of his rule he developed a script incorporating the original Khmer and the ancient Brahmi script, brought by Buddhist monks and scholars from southern India and Sri Lanka. The new alphabet became known as the "Sukhothai Script," and a famous late 13th-century inscription by King Ramkhamhaeng (now in the National Museum, Bangkok) is the earliest example of its use. The Sukhothai Script was modified over the years, and King Ramkhamhaeng's grandson Li Thai gave his name to one of the embellishments.

A GREEN AND FRUITFUL CITY

A stone inscription by King Ramkhamhaeng, now in Thailand's National Museum in Bangkok, gives a vivid picture of the Sukhothai he ruled, indicating that the city really was a haven of peace and plenty. It was a very green city, full of fruit and nut trees—"betel nut and betel-vine woods are all over this city," says the inscription. Groves and orchards of coconut, mango, areca nut and tamarind are listed in a kind of inventory. The trees belonged to whomever planted them. The city was surrounded by orchards, plantations and rice paddies, punctuated by farmhouses ("large and small"), a palace, "residences" and temples. The landscape was so beautiful, says the inscription, that it appeared to be "faked." Fish were abundant, and the water in the city's reservoir was as clean "as the Mekong river in the dry season."

THE DIPLOMAT KING

King Ramkhamhaeng was not only a great monarch but also a skilled diplomat, who recognized the necessity of sealing good relations with his mighty neighbor to the north, China. He undertook two journeys to China, meeting the Mongol emperor Kublai Khan in 1282. On his second visit, in 1300, he persuaded Kublai Khan's successor to allow him to return to Sukhothai with Chinese artisans, who taught the Siamese to make pottery. In no time at all, the kilns of Sukhothai, Si Satchanalai and Sawankhalok were turning out ceramics fine enough to be exported to China and beyond. Examples of Sukhothai ceramics have been found as far away as Japan and the Philippines. The courts of Sukhothai were so proud of the skills their craftspeople had learned from China that they weren't too shy to send examples back to Chinese emperors as tribute.

RING-THE-BELL JUSTICE

Outside one of the gates in the walls of Sukhothai, King Ramkhamhaeng hung a bell, which any citizen could ring and seek royal redress. Historians have argued over this example of the democracy. But the bell's original inscription, now in the National Museum, states: "King Ramkhamhaeng, the ruler of the kingdom, hears the call; he goes and questions the man, examines the case and decides it justly for him. So the people ... praise him."

SUKHOTHAI ART AND ARCHITECTURE

Sukhothai produced a style of art and architecture that left its stamp on succeeding centuries and still wields a tangible influence on Thai design. Its greatest contribution was in sculpture, producing Buddha statues of unmatched grace and beauty, with serene, reflective and often gently smiling faces and aristocratic features. Sukhothai craftspeople developed the art of casting in bronze, and they took the then daring step of removing the ancient image of the walking Buddha from its conventional two-dimensional form, in bas-relief, and giving it three-dimensional realism. The "walking Buddha" created in Sukhothai strides confidently, one arm swinging and one raised in the "teaching" pose.

Several Sukhothai architectural features— notably the concave flow of roofs and gables and the cloistered galleries and pillars—persist today. And much of the jewelry you'll find in boutiques and markets has an art nouveau look that dates back to 14th-century Sukhothai.

In the mid-13th century, migrating tribes from present-day Laos crossed the Mekong River and established a citadel where the northern Thai river port town of Chiang Saen now stands. Their leader, Mengrai, was proclaimed ruler of a new realm, Annachak Lanna Thai, in 1259. As Mengrai's influence grew, his expanding empire came to be known as Lanna—the land of a "million rice fields." He founded his first true capital south of Chiang Saen, at Chiang Rai, an easily fortified site sitting on a bend of the Kok River. Over the next 30 years he and his followers pushed steadily farther south and built an even larger capital at Chiang Mai, meaning "new city," after overrunning the nearby northern Dvaravati stronghold, Lamphun. Over the following two centuries, Chiang Mai grew into an important religious and cultural center, developing its own distinctive style of art and architecture, which still influences the appearance of this northern Thai capital. In the mid-16th century, Burmese forces, advancing steadily from the south and west, lay siege to Chiang Mai and finally broke its defenses, sacking the city and carrying most of the population off as slaves. For almost 200 years, Chiang Mai was a ghost city, until the Burmese were finally driven out of Thailand in 1774. By then Ayutthaya had laid claim to suzerainty over the north, and the rebuilt Chiang Mai became a provincial outpost, ruled by a prince answerable to the kings of the far-off capital.

Above *Mural of the Burmese Army who ruled Chiang Mai for almost 200 years*

CHIANG MAI'S CALAMITY CORNER

The first Lanna monarch, King Mengrai, was killed by a lightning bolt in the exact center of Chiang Mai in 1311. A shrine marks the spot, and terra-cotta friezes depict his death and achievements. Mengrai's death was the first of three calamities in this corner of the city, earning the area an ominous reputation. An earthquake in the 18th century felled the top of the city's highest *chedi*, in the grounds of Wat Chedi Luang, and in early 2005 a violent storm broke a particularly sacred tree in half. The 150ft (46m) yang tree was planted by a successor of Mengrai, Chao Kawila, and local lore said that if it ever died Chiang Mai would also fall. Religious ceremonies were held in the Wat Chedi Luang grounds to pray for deliverance from any further calamity after the top half of the tree fell.

LANNA "STYLE"

Although nearly 1,000 years old, the Lanna style of architecture and design is enjoying a renaissance in contemporary Thai hotel and home construction, particularly in Chiang Mai, but also in Bangkok. Boutique hotels are shooting up in both cities that employ the traditional Lanna look, which emphasizes simplicity. Dark teak woods and white exteriors are combined in a two-color synthesis where line and form are more important than decoration. Cool cloisters enclose hidden gardens and courtyards, where fountains play amid lily ponds and winding walkways. Low multi-eaved roofs of red clay tiles keep out the sun, and high, ceilingless living areas keep interiors cool. The only concession to color is found in the richness of the silk soft furnishings, whose patterns echo the graceful sarongs worn on special occasions by Thai women.

A ROYAL "AFFAIR"

The alliance between the three monarchs is said to have nearly foundered on an affair between Sukhothai's celebrated King Ramkhamhaeng and the wife of Phayao's King Ngam Muang.

King Mengrai was called on to sit in judgment on Ngam Muang's serious complaint that the younger Ramkhamhaeng had seduced his wife. The Lanna king had to employ all his legendary diplomacy to reconcile the cuckolded ruler and Ramkhamhaeng, who stood in danger of execution for his adultery. It's said that Mengrai ruled in favor of sparing Ramkhamhaeng's life in the interests of maintaining the alliance between Sukhothai, Lanna and Phayao. The fortunate Ramkhamhaeng got away with an apology and the payment of large damages to Ngam Muang.

MENGRAI'S "TROJAN HORSE"

Lanna King Mengrai was a wily ruler, who is said to have conquered the Dvaravati city Nakhon Haripunchai (now Lamphun) by a cunning trick.

The Dvaravati realm's northern outpost was too heavily garrisoned and defended for Mengrai to take by sheer force of arms. So he sent one of his cleverest scholars, Ai Fa, to seek employment in the court of the Nakhon Haripunchai ruler, King Yi Ba. Over the following 10 years, Ai Fa consolidated his position in Yi Ba's court, securing the king's favor while at the same time secretly stoking up public opposition to his rule. The ruse worked. At Ai Fa's signal, Mengrai and his army marched on Nakhon Haripunchai and were able to take a demoralized and divided city.

THE THREE KINGS OF CHIANG MAI

A remarkable alliance of three provincial rulers is said to have brought about the founding of the city of Chiang Mai in 1296.

History records state that when King Mengrai began work on his new capital, two neighboring rulers came to his assistance. Instead of resisting the Lanna advance into their sphere of influence, the ruler of Phayao, Phya Ngum Muang, and the king of Sukhothai, Phra Ruang, offered their support and protection to King Mengrai.

The three kings are said to have sealed their alliance by opening their veins and mingling their blood in a fraternal bond. Today their statues stand side by side in the "Three Kings Monument" outside the former home of Chiang Mai's last provincial ruler, now the city museum.

Below *Temple wall painting of the Thai Burmese conflict, which was fought on the backs of war elephants*

The rise of Ayutthaya coincided with the decline not only of Sukhothai but of the Angkor-based Khmer empire, the Lanna kingdom in the north and the Lao nation on the Mekong. There had long been a settlement on this fruitful tract of territory at the confluence of three rivers: the Chao Phraya, the Pasak and the Lopburi. Regular flooding enabled the cultivation of wet rice and provided moats for its defense. As the 14th century progressed, another great advantage of Ayutthaya's location emerged; trade between China and India was growing at a staggering rate, and Ayutthaya found itself at the crossroads of the trade routes. Later, explorers and traders from the West arrived, looking for routes that would save them the journey around the Malay peninsula. Another major factor boosting the growth of Ayutthaya was the arrival of Buddhist monks from India and Sri Lanka. Theravada Buddhism made its base in Ayutthaya and spread from there. The date of Ayutthaya's founding is officially given as 1350, when a Chinese merchant's son, U Thong, was proclaimed its first king, Ramathibodi I. During his 18-year reign he laid the administrative and legal foundations not only of Ayutthaya but of the future kingdom of Siam. In 1431 Ayutthaya conquered Angkor, and in 1438 it annexed the Sukhothai state. But Myanmar (Burma) remained an intractable foe, and after many wars Ayutthaya was overrun by the Burmese in 1767. The city was destroyed, its inhabitants either killed or carried off into slavery.

Clockwise from above *Buddhas surround the Wat Yai Chai Mongkhon, built in 1384 in Ayutthaya; Khmer-style prang at Wat Ratburana, Ayutthaya; King Taksin the Great Memorial in Chanthaburi*

ELEPHANT DUELS

In Ayutthaya's days, kingdoms were won and lost and battles for succession decided in deadly elephant-back duels. King Naresuan the Great earned his grand title—one of only five Siamese rulers to win the addition of "Great" to their names—after (among other courageous feats) killing the crown prince of Burma in a duel fought on the backs of their battle elephants. Naresuan's army engaged a massive Burmese invasion force west of Ayutthaya in 1592.

According to contemporary records, he spotted the Burmese crown prince in the middle of the fray and challenged him: "Let us fight an elephant duel for the honor of our kingdoms." Naresuan cut the Burmese leader down with his sword, and the entire Burmese army fled. Burma left Ayutthaya alone for the next 25 years.

BUREAUCRATIC BEGINNINGS

Thailand's modern bureaucracy derives directly from the administrative structures created by the early Ayutthaya kings. As the Ayutthaya empire grew and took on ever more important responsibilities, successive rulers built up a compartmentalized structure to deal with policy areas. Departments corresponding to today's government ministries were set up to handle such administrative areas as foreign affairs, trade and taxation. Officials, most of them close to the throne, were given "honor marks" according to their duties, and in time a hierarchical system of government took shape. The officials occupied a middle rank, known as *Khunnang* (or "nobles"), in a three-tiered system headed by the king and his family. Below the officials was a bottom class of commoners and slaves. The large and powerful community of monks, the *sangha*, remained outside the class system but held great influence over state affairs.

WOMEN WARRIORS

Women warriors played a key role in protecting the 18th- to 19th-century Ayutthaya realm from outside invasion. When King Anuwong of Vientiane led a large army against northeastern Siam in 1771, the town of Nakhon Ratchasima (Korat) called on the wife of the deputy governor to organize the local defense forces. Madam Mo not only succeeded in breaking a siege of Korat by King Anuwong, but pursued the invader and his army back to the banks of the Mekong River. Taksin the Great rewarded her with the royal title Lady Suranari.

Farther south, on the island now known as Phuket, two famous sisters rallied the islanders in a successful defense against an invading Burmese naval force in 1785. The two, Lady Thepsatri and Lady Srisunthorn, were daughters of the governor of Phuket, then known as Thalang. They are commemorated today by an impressive monument located at a highway crossroads in the center of Phuket island.

BLOODY INTRIGUES

The courts of Ayutthaya were hotbeds of intrigue, often fueled by foreign interests plotting to win influence and trading advantages. Thrones were won and lost in schemes hatched behind palace walls and even in the confines of the royal concubines' quarters. One king, Ekathotsarot, ordered the execution of his young son, Prince Suthat, in 1610, on the flimsiest of evidence. Suthat was accused of plotting a coup, denounced by a court official in the pay of a powerful group of Japanese merchants. Ekathotsarot outlived his executed son by only a few months. A century previously, an Ayutthaya queen-regent, Lady Si Sudachan, had her 11-year-old son poisoned and put her lover, a court official, on the throne in his place. The usurper was assassinated after only six weeks of rule.

AYUTTHAYA'S GREEK INTRUDER

For a critical period of its 17th-century history, Ayutthaya was effectively ruled by a powerful Greek opportunist and adventurer, Constantine Phaulkon. Son of a hotelier, he came to Asia in 1678 as an official of the East India Company. In Ayutthaya he cleverly insinuated himself into the court of King Narai. Phaulkon's influence grew to the point where he was the equivalent of King Narai's prime minister, running the affairs of state. Phaulkon was also responsible for introducing Jesuit missionary priests into the court and was apparently close to converting Narai when the monarch died, in 1688.

While Narai lay on his deathbed, a struggle for succession broke out, and the dying monarch's regent arrested Phaulkon and had him beheaded.

With Ayutthaya in ruins and its population either in flight or in Burmese captivity, Siamese unity seemed finally at an end. But a remarkable military leader, Phraya Taksin, took control and within 15 years had founded a new capital, Thonburi, and rid Siam of the Burmese. Despite his remarkable feat, the general took on increasingly fanatical traits, and in 1782 he was deposed and executed. He was succeeded by a fellow general, Chao Phraya Chakri. At his coronation he took the title Rama I, and one of his first acts was to move the capital to a small village called Bangkok, across the river and safe from further Burmese incursions. Rama I laid the administrative and legal foundations of today's Thailand. At his death in 1809 he was succeeded by his son, a highly cultured man who patronized the arts and literature. He and his successor, Rama III, built up Siam's international trade routes, and established their country's first links with Western colonial powers. The two monarchs who came after him—Mongkut (Rama IV) and Chulalongkorn (Rama V)—performed the delicate balancing act that kept their country free of colonial occupation while ushering their people into the modern world. Road and rail communications were laid, schools and universities founded, civil rights legislation promulgated and, in 1892, Siam's first ministerial government was appointed.

VELVET SACK MYSTERY

Under Ayutthaya law, a king or queen found guilty of serious wrongdoing or who was just unwanted on the throne was executed in a very bizarre manner. He or she was placed in a velvet sack and beaten to death. This painful fate, according to contemporary accounts, awaited Taksin, the ruler whose death opened the palace doors to the Chakri dynasty.

But rumors persist to this day that an innocent commoner was put in the sack instead of Taksin, who was allegedly smuggled into hiding in the mountains near Myanmar (Burma). He is supposed to have died there in 1825, in his late 60s. Many years later his remains—or those of his unfortunate "stand-in"— were given a royal burial, and the once-reviled ruler was given the title Taksin the Great.

Clockwise from above French warships at Bangkok after the Pak Nam incident; King Mongkut (Rama IV) and Queen Rampuy; portrait of King Chulalongkorn (Rama V)

KING RAMA I, THE POET AND TRANSLATOR

King Rama I not only oversaw the first blossoming of a vibrant Siamese literature, but also actively contributed to it as an author and translator. He and a select circle of scribes and academics translated and reworked the Indian epic *Ramayana* and published it in 1797 as the *Ramakien*. The lengthy, colorful story, originally more than 3,000 pages long, is the subject of countless temple frescoes and still features in artistic representations. Works from China, Sri Lanka and Persia were also translated at the behest of King Rama I, and a distinct Siamese literary style arose, in which formal verse gave way to prose. Appointed the first "Supreme Patriarch of Thai Buddhism," King Rama I was particularly concerned with preserving ancient religious texts. He translated original Pali texts from India and salvaged many Buddhist texts that were lost during the sacking of Ayutthaya in 1767.

ANNA AND THE KING

King Mongkut hired a governess to educate his children and some of his wives and concubines, but by all accounts Anna Leonowens was nothing like the character portrayed in the movie *The King and I*. Nor did Mongkut at all resemble the autocratic, bare-chested monarch played by Yul Brynner. Welsh-born Anna grew up a lonely child in India, where her soldier father had been stationed. In 1851, the year Mongkut took the throne, Anna married a British officer, Major Thomas Leonowens. He died young, and Anna took up teaching to support herself and her two small children. In 1862 she was hired by the royal court in Bangkok. Anna herself wrote two books on her experiences there, but skepticism has arisen over the truth of her reminiscences. Three movies have been made—the third and latest movie, *Anna and the King*, was released in 1999. Like the books, it has been banned in Thailand.

PALACE INTRIGUES

Although the reign of the first Chakri monarch was just and civilized, it was still not entirely free of the palace intrigues and bloody retributions that marked the Ayutthaya period. Tensions frequently surfaced between the king and his younger brother, reaching a head in 1796, when the king ordered his guard to surround his brother's palace after rumors of a coup plot. Only the intervention of the royal princesses prevented a bloody confrontation. The king's brother died in 1803, but the palace intrigues continued, and two of the ruler's nephews were shortly afterward accused with a group of courtiers of plotting against the monarch and were summarily beheaded. Rama I subsequently held fast to the throne, and ruled until his death in 1809.

MONGKUT—MONK AND MONARCH

King Mongkut is one of the most interesting figures in Thailand's rich history. Before taking the throne in 1851, he spent 27 years as a monk, spending most of the time in meditation. He learned English, French, Latin, Sanskrit and the language of Buddhist monks, Pali. He also gained knowledge of the natural sciences and astronomy and successfully predicted a solar eclipse. After his coronation, the 47-year-old monarch abandoned monastic precepts and took 39 wives, fathering 82 children. The youngest of these, Chulalongkorn, succeeded him, although he nearly died from malaria during a trip with his father to southern Siam. Mongkut also fell ill and died from the disease in 1868.

The death of King Chulalongkorn (Rama V) in 1910 ushered in a century of profound social and political change. Chulalongkorn was succeeded by one of his many sons, Vajiravudh, a fun-loving monarch who introduced many Western-influenced reforms and customs. Vajiravudh steered Siam through World War I without conceding any of the country's sovereignty, and he left a successful, viable state to his brother, Prajadhipok. The 10-year reign of Rama VII was a much less happy one, and in 1932 Siam's last absolute ruler was forced by a group of reformers to agree to the introduction of a constitutional monarchy. The leaders of the coup, Phibun Songkhram and Pridi Phanamyang, dominated the political scene for nearly 20 of the following 25 years. Prajadhipok abdicated in 1935, and a council of regents chose Ananda, then a schoolboy in Switzerland, to succeed him. Phibun became prime minister in 1938 and took a pro-Japanese line during World War II. His former fellow student, Pridi, organized an anti-Japanese resistance and took power from the disgraced Phibun at the war's end in 1945. Ananda returned from Switzerland in 1946 to assume the Siamese throne, but died in mysterious circumstances. His younger brother, Bhumibol Adulyadej, succeeded him, as Rama IX, and is now the world's longest-reigning monarch. Phibun returned from the shadows and overthrew Pridi in 1947, establishing a military dictatorship. He in turn was ousted in 1957. Student demonstrations in 1992 led to an intervention by the King.

Clockwise from above *Golden hand sculpture outside the museum, Mae Salong; Akha people buying and selling produce in the market at Doi Mae Salong*

THE *MANHATTAN* COUP
The most unusual of the several coup attempts that marked Thailand's recent history involved the seizure of an American ship, the *Manhattan*, in the waters off Bangkok in June 1951. Navy rebels took over the ship as Prime Minister Phibun Songkhram, a veteran army officer, was officially accepting it as a gift from the United States. Phibun was taken prisoner and held on the Thai navy flagship *Sri Ayudhya* while negotiations proceeded between the two sides. The talks broke down and the Thai air force bombarded the ship. Phibun jumped overboard and swam to safety—soaked, shaken but still in control of the government.

More than a 1,000 men died in the coup attempt, which was followed by a inevitable wave of arrests and drastic cuts in the strength of the navy.

A TRAGIC MONARCH

King Rama VIII, Ananda Mahidol, was Thailand's most tragic monarch. He was a schoolboy in Switzerland when he succeeded Rama VII, King Prajadhipok, who abdicated in 1935 after confrontations with the military. A council of regents guarded the throne until Ananda's return to Thailand in December, 1945. Six months later, Ananda was dead—found with a bullet wound in the head in his palace quarters in Bangkok. The government at first said he had died accidentally, but a commission of inquiry, which included British and American doctors, concluded he had probably been murdered. But by whom? Suspicion fell on three of the palace staff, and they were put on trial, convicted and executed. Prime Minister Pridi also came under pressure and went abroad, precipitating a government crisis. Ananda was succeeded by his younger brother, Bhumibol Adulyadej, the present King Rama IX.

THE RAILWAY AGE

When King Chulalongkorn visited London in 1898, Queen Victoria presented him with a clockwork train set, instilling in the monarch an enthusiasm that laid the foundations of one of Asia's most efficient railway networks. Chulalongkorn returned home determined to give his country the best railway system money could buy. He engaged British and German engineers, who laid track in record time through impenetrable jungle and through mountain ranges. Locomotives and rolling stock were imported from Europe, and by 1920 Bangkok was linked with Malaya and with cities that had previously been remote outposts of the realm, accessible only by unpaved roads or rivers. Chulalongkorn and his successors ordained that railway stations should become architectural features of the landscape, and today even the smallest railway stop in Thailand is a picture-postcard attraction.

CHIANG KAI-SHEK SOLDIERS REWARDED

The Thai government suppressed a communist insurgency in the 1970s with the help of Chinese nationalist soldiers who had fled the advancing Red Army of Mao Tse Tung. The refugees, remnants of General Chiang Kai-shek's Kuomintang, were rewarded with Thai nationality and permanent residence in northern Thailand, where they established several communities. The most famous of these is Santikhiri ("Mountain of Peace") in the Mae Salong mountain range near the Burmese border. Visit Santikhiri and you'd be excused for thinking yourself in China—the small town of 20,000, most of them descendants of the original soldiers, has Chinese temples, schools, shops and noodle stands. There's even a home for disabled veteran soldiers, and a museum where the story of Santikhiri is recounted with a display of interesting contemporary pictures and documents.

WHEN SIAM BECAME THAILAND

Three name changes occurred before Siam finally became called Thailand. The nationalist military leader Phibun Songkhram discarded the historic name of Siam in favor of Thailand on June 23, 1939, in a controversial move interpreted as an attempt to free the country from its negative associations with ancient monarchies. Phibun's post-war successor, Pridi Phanamyang, changed the country's name back again to Siam in 1945 in a package of measures intended to repudiate all policy decisions by the now-discredited Phibun. Two years later, Phibun overthrew Pridi—and one of his first acts as leader was to change the country's name back to Thailand. The name Thailand is derived from the dominant ethnic group of the country (Thai). Due to Thailand's large ethnic diversity, a movement persists to revert back to the old name of Siam.

21ST-CENTURY THAILAND 2000–TODAY

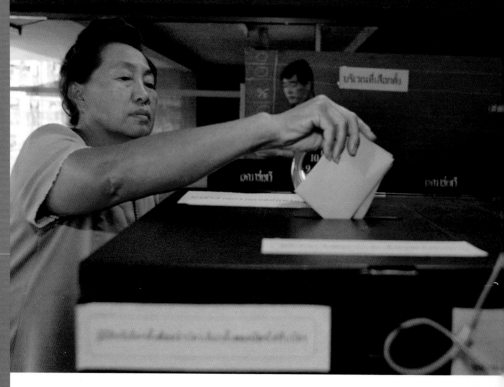

The new century began in style for Thailand. January 2001 general elections (the first held under the 1997 "People's Constitution") were considered to be the most corruption-free in Thai history. Thaksin Shinawatra became prime minister and his Thai Rak Thai party made further history by completing the first ever four-year term in Thai government. Following his reelection in 2005, early 2006 saw a marked change in fortune for Thaksin's government, which found itself facing increasing criticism. In September 2006, a military coup removed the government from power. Elections took place in December 2007 (▷ 6). Globally, the devastating 2004 tsunami, Muslim insurgency, political demonstrations in 2008 and 2009, skirmishes with Cambodia at Khao Phra Viharn (Preah Vihear), arguments with Cambodia over their support of Thaksin, mistreatment of refugees from Myanmar, and violent riots on the streets of Bangkok in 2010 have all kept Thailand in the global spotlight, but tourism and industry continue to thrive.

THAILAND'S RESTIVE SOUTH

Unrest and violence broke out in Thailand's southernmost provinces (ethnically Malaysian Muslim) in 2004, and the government has been struggling ever since to bring it to an end. Thaksin at first used strong-arm methods to quell the violence, but after clashes that resulted in the deaths of a number of protesters, he tried a more conciliatory approach. Discontent and violence continue, but it has been overshadowed by clashes between "red-shirts" (supporters of the overthrown Thaksin) and "yellow-shirts" (supporters of the current government).

Above *Elections in Thailand now take place amid strict new laws enacted to prevent electoral fraud*

ON THE MOVE

On the Move gives you detailed advice and information about the various options for traveling to Thailand before explaining the best ways to get around the country once you are there. Handy tips help you with everything from buying tickets to renting a car.

BY AIR

There are currently eight international airports in Thailand: Suvarnabhumi (Bangkok), Phuket, Chiang Mai, Chiang Rai, Ko Samui, Krabi, Hat Yai and Sukhothai. You are most likely to arrive in Bangkok, even if your final destination is Phuket, Ko Samui or one of the other regional airports, though there are direct flights to Phuket from Europe. Asian airlines, especially from Malaysia, Singapore and Laos, have direct flights to the other international airports. In 2006, Suvarnabhumi airport replaced Don Muang as Thailand's principal point of entry into the kingdom, though Don Muang continues to operate somewhat as a domestic airport.

Suvarnabhumi Airport (BKK)

Despite the controversy, delays and technical problems that have dogged Thailand's new international airport since the beginning, Suvarnabhumi opened to business in September 2006 with much fanfare and relatively minor teething problems. While various problems continued in the wake of the opening, the airport has become one of the finest in the world, and thus plays an essential role in making Bangkok the tourist hub of Southeast Asia. The airport consists of one huge main terminal, housing the check-in counters for both international and domestic flights, branching off into seven concourses (A to G) with a total of 120 gates, eight of which are capable of accommodating the Airbus A380.

The Tourism Authority of Thailand (TAT) has an office on the second floor of the main terminal, right next to the Thai Hotels Association (THA) counter, where you can make hotel reservations. For general information about the airport and flight times tel 02 132 1888 or visit www.bangkokairportonline.com.

Phuket Airport (HKT) is on the
northwest coast of Phuket island, 20 miles (32km) from Phuket town. There is a tourist office, car rental and hotel accommodations counters, post office, banks, ATMs and exchange booths, left-luggage office, internet access, and places to eat and drink. For general information about the airport tel 076 327 230-7.

Chiang Mai Airport (CNX),
2 miles (3km) southwest of town, is now an international terminal. There are booths for currency exchange, ATMs, car rental and hotel accommodations counters, left-luggage facilities, a restaurant and post office. For general information about the airport tel 053 270 233 (www.airportthai.co.th).

Ko Samui Airport (USM) is in the
northeast of the island, 3 miles (5km) from Chaweng, and has booths for currency exchange, ATMs, car rental and hotel accommodations counters, restaurant and bar, and post office. For general information about the airport tel 077 425 011.

GETTING TO THE CITY FROM BANGKOK'S SUVARNABHUMI AIRPORT

By taxi: Metered taxis are available 24 hours a day, departing from the taxi stand at Level 1. A B50 surcharge is payable to the counter before entering the taxi. Officially the trip should be metered and the passenger pays for the expressway tolls along the way, although some drivers will seek to bargain a flat fare, usually to their advantage. If you arrive at rush hour, expect to pay up to B500 for a trip into the city.
By airport bus: An airport express bus service operates from 5am

---

Suvarnabhumi Airport The airport was originally to be called Nong Ngu Hao Airport (Cobra Swamp Airport), after the local name of the swampy area which was reclaimed for the project. However, not long before its opening, the King bestowed the more glamorous title of Suvarnabhumi (more correctly pronounced "Suwanapoom"), meaning "Golden Land."

to midnight. There are four routes covering most of the major hotels in the city, with termination points at Silom, Banglamphu, Sukhumvit and the Hua Lamphong railway station. The fare is B150 for all stops. For more information, head to the Airport Bus Express counter near Entrance 8 on level 1.

GETTING TO DON MUANG AIRPORT FROM SUVARNABHUMI AIRPORT

Take the shuttle bus from the main terminal to the Suvarnabhumi bus station (a five-minute ride), then board the 554 or 555 air-conditioned bus directly to Don Muang airport. Buses leave every 30 minutes, and the journey usually takes 45 to 90 minutes, depending on the time of day. The fare is B35. If you are hurrying to catch an internal flight, a metered taxi should get you there for no more than B400, including the tollway fares, which you will be asked to pay at each gate.

GETTING TO DON MUANG AIRPORT FROM THE CITY

Taxis are the best way to get to the airport as there is no longer an airport bus service for Don Muang. A metered taxi from the heart of Bangkok costs around B350, excluding tolls. If your hotel is convenient to the Skytrain, you might consider taking the train to Mo Chit, then continuing from there by taxi. Trains also run from Hua Lamphong station to Don Muang station (B5; allow one hour). This is the cheapest way to go and puts you within five minutes' walk of the terminal, although longer in the rush hour.

GETTING TO THE BEACH AREAS OR PHUKET TOWN FROM PHUKET AIRPORT

By taxi: Fares to the beaches and Phuket town are B500 to B600.
By airport bus: Minivans and buses, booked at counters in the airport, travel to all the hotels: B100 to

Opposite *Thai Airways plane*
Right *View of Mae Hong Son airport*

MAJOR AIRLINES	
AIRLINE	**WEBSITE**
AirAsia	www.airasia.com
Air France	www.airfrance.com
Bangkok Airways	www.bangkokair.com
British Airways	www.ba.com
Cathay Pacific	www.cathaypacific.com
Emirates	www.emirates.com
Lao Airlines	www.laoairlines.com
Lufthansa	www.lufthansa.com
Jetstar	www.jetstar.com
Malaysia Airlines	www.malaysiaairlines.com
Qantas	www.qantas.com
Royal Jordanian	www.rj.com
Singapore Airlines	www.singaporeair.com
Thai Airways	www.thaiair.com
Tiger Airways	www.tigerairways.com
United Airlines	www.united.com
Valuair	www.valuair.com

Phuket town; B170 to Ao Patong; and B200 to Ao Kata or Ao Karon. The journey takes 25 to 35 minutes.

GETTING TO TOWN FROM CHIANG MAI AIRPORT

By taxi: A reservations system operates at the airport; the fare to the middle of town is a fixed rate of B120 to anywhere in the city. There is a taxi counter outside the airport exit.

GETTING TO THE BEACH AREAS FROM KO SAMUI AIRPORT

By taxi: The fare to the beaches is around B300 to B400; taxis are not metered so agree on the fare.
By airport bus: Minivans meet incoming flights for transport to the beach areas. Fares are fixed, depending on the number of passengers, and cost around B150 to Chaweng and B200 to Lamai.

BY TRAIN

The train service connecting Thailand with Malaysia and Singapore is well established. As it is possible to obtain short visas on arrival for each of the three countries, it is easy and relatively inexpensive to enter or leave Thailand by train. See page 47 for information on Bangkok's Hua lamphong station, for trains from Malaysia. Afternoon departures from Penang (Butterworth) in Malaysia arrive in Bangkok around mid-morning the next day (B1,600 for a first-class sleeper with air-conditioning).

The State Railway of Thailand (SRT; www.railway.co.th), KTMB (Keretapi Tanah Melayu Berhad; www.ktmb.com.my) of Malaysia and Singapore Railways coordinate the train route between Singapore and Bangkok, via Kuala Lumpur and Penang (Butterworth) in Malaysia. Through travel to Thailand can be reserved in Singapore or Malaysia. However, in Thailand it is only possible to reserve train travel through to either Penang (Butterworth) or Kuala Lumpur, from where a train ticket on to Singapore can be reserved. When crossing the border between Thailand and Malaysia, you will need to get off the train with your luggage and clear immigration and customs before reboarding the train. Coming from Singapore or Kuala Lumpur, you change at Penang (Butterworth) for onward travel to Bangkok, and vice versa.

The international trains to and from Bangkok travel down the east coast of southern Thailand, stopping at Hua Hin, Chumphon and Hat Yai; you can reserve your journey to arrive at or depart from any of these stations.

It is also possible to travel by train between the east coast of peninsular Malaysia and Thailand, although the trains do not actually cross the border. Coming from Malaysia, trains stop at Kota Bahru, from where buses and taxis run to Rantau Panjang, only 1 mile (1.6km) from the international border. Taxis wait to take passengers to the border crossing, as they also do on the other side of the border to take you to Sungai Kolok station on the Thailand side. From here, trains travel to Hat Yai, where you connect with the main train line north to Bangkok. Train schedules work around this arrangement so it is possible to cross the border and pick up a train on the other side without the need for an overnight stay at the Thailand–Malaysia border.

The level of service on trains is high, and on long-distance journeys there is always a dining carriage, with the option of table service. The most stylish and expensive way to travel by train in Thailand is on the Eastern & Oriental Express (www.orient-express.com). There are trips (three days/two nights) from Singapore to Bangkok, costing B2,355 with all meals and tours included, and onward from Bangkok via Chiang Mai via Ayutthaya for B1,253 for a first-class sleeper with air-conditioning.

BY BUS

Buses are comfortable and usually safe; those from Malaysia and Singapore have a better safety record than long-distance, overnight buses within Thailand.

Hat Yai in southern Thailand is the transportation hub for buses between Malaysia and Thailand. There are buses all the way to Hat Yai from Singapore, but they involve sleeping on board for the 18-hour journey. Buses from Kuala Lumpur in Malaysia take about 12 hours, while the most manageable bus connection is the 6-hour journey from Penang in Malaysia. From Penang, Kuala Lumpur and Singapore, there are also buses to Phuket, Krabi and Surat Thani (for Ko Samui). All these bus routes work both ways should you want to visit Malaysia and/or Singapore from Thailand. With the price of budget air travel so low, though, you may choose to fly instead. Buses are also available via Koh Kong and Siam Reep, Cambodia.

BY BOAT

From the Malaysian resort island of Langkawi, there are daily boats to Thammalang in Thailand, 6 miles (9km) south of the Thai town of Satun; the journey to Thammalang, where immigration formalities are conducted, takes just under one hour. From Satun, there are buses to Hat Yai, and to Trang (for Krabi and Phuket). Boats also travel to Thammalang from Kuala Perlis in the far northwest of Malaysia; the journey time is 45 minutes. Note that there are no banks or ATMs at Thammalang, and the opening times of the money exchange facility are sporadic, so make sure you have some Thai currency to hand to pay for a taxi to Satun.

FROM LAOS

Crossing the Friendship Bridge that spans the Mekong River is both an adventurous and easy-to-organize way to arrive in Thailand. Vientiane, the capital of Laos, is only 15 miles (24km) away from the Friendship Bridge, and taxis and buses make the journey on a regular basis. Minibuses cross the bridge from early in the morning until 9pm, and a 14-day Thai visa will be issued to you at the bridge crossing. From the Thai side of the river, a five-minute *tuk-tuk* ride will take you into the middle of Nong Khai. From here, there are trains to Bangkok, taking about 12 hours; buses to Bangkok take 10 hours. It takes one hour by bus to Udon Thani, from where there are one-hour flights to Bangkok. Another crossing point to the northeast of Thailand is from Khammouan/Tha Khaek to Nakhon Phanom, where there are flights to Bangkok. It is also possible to enter Thailand from Houayaxi, a two-day boat ride on the Mekong River from Louang Prabang to Chiang Khong. If traveling from Thailand to Laos, a visa to enter Laos can be purchased at some crossing points for US$30 to $44, in cash, plus two passport-size photos. Alternatively, you can organize a visa in advance at the Laos embassy in Bangkok.

Getting around Thailand is made easy by an extensive range of transportation options: planes, boats, cars, taxis, buses, coaches, minivans, *songthaews*, motorcycle taxis, *tuk-tuks* and *samlors*. Travel is relatively inexpensive, reliable and efficient, but long-distance journeys can be time-consuming unless you're flying.

BY AIR

Journeys across Thailand that easily take the best part of a day or more by bus or train can be reduced to an hour or so by an internal flight. For example, from Chiang Mai to Phuket takes about two hours by plane as opposed to two days by bus; the journey covered in a one-hour flight from Bangkok to Ubon Ratchathani takes 10 hours by train. Internal flights are available through the national airline and a number of smaller airlines, and an internet reservation is the most efficient way to purchase a ticket. See page 50 for further information.

BY TRAIN

The rail network is run by the State Railway of Thailand (SRT), and there are four main lines covering the northern, southern, northeastern and eastern parts of the country. Tickets can be reserved in advance, which is advisable for popular routes like Bangkok to Chiang Mai or Bangkok to Surat Thani (for Ko Samui). Within Thailand, train tickets can be reserved in advance in Bangkok or through mainline stations; outside of Thailand, tickets can be reserved online. It is not possible to purchase tickets on the train itself without paying an excess charge. There are no super-fast trains, but for long journeys the best option is to take one of the night trains, which are comfortable and fitted with sleepers.

Above *Arriving by boat in Chumphon, southern Thailand*

BY BUS

Buses belonging to the government-run Baw Khaw Saw go mostly everywhere in Thailand, covering short inter-town routes as well as the more obvious long-distance routes. There is also a variety of private companies running buses and minivans on all the popular long-distance routes. On the whole, bus travel, whether government-run or private, is reliable, with the exception of some budget-price private buses between Bangkok and Chiang Mai, Phuket and Surat Thani. There is often a choice of classes of bus travel, air-conditioning being the most important distinction. Long, overnight bus journeys are not as safe or as comfortable as overnight train travel.

BY BOAT

There are scheduled boat services to all the main islands using a variety of vessels. Popular routes to islands such as Ko Samui and Ko Lanta use large, ocean-going craft with interior seating and air-conditioning, and hovercraft and jetfoils are also in use on some routes. Tickets are either bought on board or, increasingly

common, through agents or your island accommodation in advance. Apart from boats to Ko Samui, services are usually reduced during the wet months of May to October.

DRIVING

Outside Bangkok, getting around using a rented vehicle is a feasible option. This is especially so in the northeast and southern regions of Thailand, where roads are pleasantly uncongested. Distances in Thailand are measured in kilometers and, apart from in some rural areas off the main network, road directions are in English. Road signs follow easy-to-understand, international conventions.

LOCAL TRANSPORTATION

Within towns—because walking is an option only for short distances due to the heat—there is always some form of transportation available. Buses and *songthaews* follow set routes with fixed fares, while taxis and *tuk-tuks* have negotiable rates. Apart from in Bangkok, where metered taxis are the rule, it is essential to agree on the fare beforehand.

TRAINS

Trains are not the speediest way to travel across Thailand but they are safe and quite comfortable, and can provide an insight into Thai lifestyle and culture that you might not see otherwise, as people seem more willing to strike up a conversation on a train. While trains will generally depart and arrive on time, delays in the course of a journey are still quite common. Trains designated as Ordinary are the slowest and are best avoided unless there is no choice. Rapid trains are not rapid at all and only a little faster than Ordinary ones. Express and Special Express are the ones to use whenever possible.

ROUTES

The northern line runs between Bangkok and Chiang Mai, via Ayutthaya, Lop Buri and Phitsanulok. The southern line runs between Bangkok and Hat Yai, via Hua Hin, Chumphon and Surat Thani. At Hat Yai the line branches into two, one heading down to Malaysia's west coast and the other to Malaysia's east coast. The southern line also has a branch that connects Kanchanaburi with Bangkok. The northeastern line splits into two north of Bangkok, with one line terminating at Ubon Ratchathani, via Nakhon Ratchasima (Korat) and Surin, and the other one heading up to Nong Khai via Khon Kaen and Udon Thani. The eastern line branches to connect Bangkok with Pattaya.

CLASSES

Travel in first class provides cabins for two passengers, with air-conditioning, a washbasin, a small table and seats that convert into beds. Travel in second class provides comfortable padded seats in cabins, some with air-conditioning and some with fans, with toilet facilities for each carriage. Travel in third class can mean hard seats that are uncomfortable for long journeys but fine for short trips. Trains to Kanchanaburi from Bangkok take about three hours, and only third-class seats are available. Carriages are clean, though, and with open windows looking out across rural scenes, the journey is very enjoyable.

OVERNIGHT TRAVEL

On overnight journeys the seats convert into lower sleeping berths, and the upper berths fold out from the side of the carriage above the windows. Fresh linen is provided and there is a curtain for each berth that

Below *Bangkok Railway Station; trains are safe and comfortable but slow, so use Express and Special Express trains when possible*

gives a reasonable degree of privacy. Luggage is stored in racks nearby, but keep valuables with you in your berth. In first class you have a two-bed cabin with a door that locks.

FARES

The basic fare for any journey is subject to supplements determined by the class of seat, type of train and whether air-conditioning is available. Even when these are added, you will find fares to be relatively inexpensive, though first-class fares are notably higher. From Bangkok to Surat Thani, for example, the journey of 400 miles (650km) costs approximately B850 for an overnight berth in second class (air-conditioned). The fare for an upper berth is a little less than that for a lower berth—a difference of less than B100 on the Bangkok–Surat Thani route. Children aged under three and less than 39 inches (100cm) tall travel free; those aged 4 to 11 and under 59 inches (150cm) pay half the adult fare.

Rail passes for unlimited travel over 20 days are available for B3,000 for adults and B1,000 for children. However, unless you intend to tour the country, the rail pass is not an especially economical offer.

BUYING TICKETS

Seats on some short journeys with third-class seating, like the Bangkok–Kanchanaburi route, cannot be reserved in advance. For all other journeys it is advisable to reserve at least a day or two in advance, longer for trains to Chiang Mai and Surat Thani (for Ko Samui), and especially for overnight and weekend journeys. For travel during mid-April, covering the Thai New Year, and over the Chinese New Year period (which changes each year), reserve as far ahead as possible. Tickets are checked on board.

In Thailand tickets can be reserved up to one month in advance from any mainline station: a computerized system issues you with a ticket stating train departure time and seat number. Bangkok's

JOURNEY TIMES AND FARES FROM BANGKOK		
TO	**JOURNEY TIME**	**FARE**
Chiang Mai	13 hours	B1,253 (first-class air-conditioned sleeper)
Hua Hin	3 hours 30 min	B382 (second-class air-conditioned train)
Kanchanaburi	3 hours	B30 (third-class train)
Ubon Ratchathani	11 hours	B1,180 (first-class air-conditioned sleeper)

USEFUL WEBSITES
For reserving tickets online:
Asia-Discovery: www.asia-discovery.com/train.htm
Thaifocus: www.thaifocus.com/travel/train
Traveller2000: www.traveller2000.com/train
Other useful websites:
Seat Sixty-One: www.seat61.com/Thailand.htm
Good information, including pictures of the different classes of travel, timetables and fares.
State Railway of Thailand (SRT): www.railway.co.th
Timetables, seat availability and sample fares, but online reservations are not possible. In Thailand, SRT can be contacted on a 24-hour information line (tel 1690) or at Bangkok's Hua Lamphong station (tel 022 250 300).
Tales of Asia: www.talesofasia.com
Information on train transport scams in Thailand.

Hua Lamphong station has a special advance reservations office.

From outside Thailand there are a number of agencies that will reserve train tickets for you through their websites (see above); a reservation charge will apply.

BANGKOK'S HUA LAMPHONG STATION

In the middle of Bangkok and with its own subway station, Hua Lamphong station is used as the arrival and departure point for nearly all Bangkok trains. Entering the station from the subway, walk directly ahead, keeping the platforms on your left, for the information booth on the other side of the concourse. To the left of this, parallel with the platforms, is the advance reservations office (open daily 8.30–4), where payment can be made with Visa/MasterCard. Take a numbered ticket from the machine just inside the entrance. The ticket windows by the platforms and under the departures display board are for same-day travel, but when the advance reservations office is closed you can use windows 2 to 11. The station has a food court, as well as small shops, a post office, ATMs

and exchange facilities, internet access and a left-luggage office (4am–10.30pm).

TIPS

>> Trains from Malaysia to Thailand can be reserved online.

>> Reserve train travel as far in advance as possible: Seats with sleepers are the first to go.

>> Bangkok's Don Muang Airport has a station on the northern line, between Bangkok and Chiang Mai via Ayutthaya, and on the northeastern line to Nong Khai. If arriving at the airport, these trains can be boarded there without traveling to Bangkok's Hua Lamphong station.

>> It pays to check timetables carefully because the difference between a slow and fast train can be anything from one hour to four or more.

>> In Bangkok, nearly all trains depart from Hua Lamphong station, but if traveling to Kanchanaburi you need to go to Bangkok Noi station in Thonburi, close to the Thonburi Railway/Bangkok Noi pier, via a Chao Phraya River Express boat.

>> At Hua Lamphong station, beware of anyone proffering help and bearing official-looking insignia suggesting they work for the Tourist Authority of Thailand (TAT)—they are touts for private travel agents.

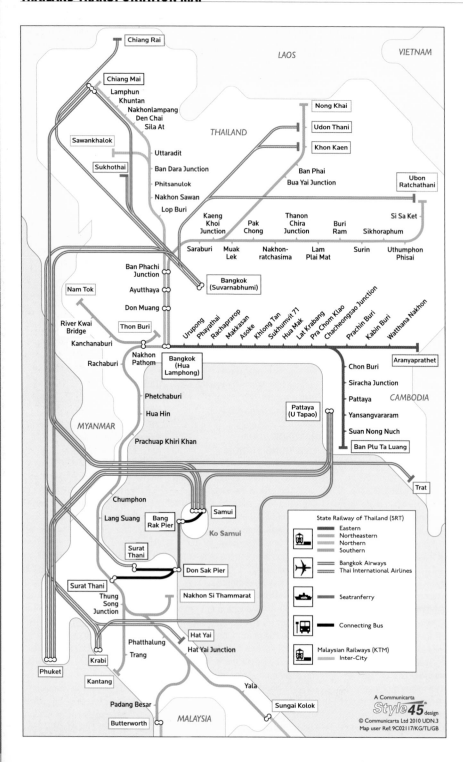

Chiang Rai

LAOS

VIETNAM

Chiang Mai
Lamphun
Khuntan
Nakhonlampang
Den Chai
Sila At

THAILAND

Nong Khai

Udon Thani

Khon Kaen

Sawankhalok

Uttaradit

Sukhothai

Ban Dara Junction

Ban Phai
Bua Yai Junction

Ubon
Ratchathani

Phitsanulok

Nakhon Sawan

Lop Buri

Kaeng
Khoi
Junction

Pak
Chong

Thanon
Chira
Junction

Buri
Ram

Si Sa Ket

Sikhoraphum

Ban Phachi
Junction

Saraburi

Muak
Lek

Nakhon-
ratchasima

Lam
Plai Mat

Surin

Uthumphon
Phisai

Nam Tok

Ayutthaya

Bangkok
(Suvarnabhumi)

Don Muang

River Kwai
Bridge

Thon Buri

Urupong
Phayathai
Rachaprarop
Makkasan
Asoke
Khlong Tan
Sukhumvit 71
Hua Mak
Lat Krabang
Pra Chom Klao
Chacheongsao Junction
Prachin Buri
Kabin Buri
Watthana Nakhon

Kanchanaburi

Rachaburi

Nakhon
Pathom

Bangkok
(Hua
Lamphong)

Chon Buri

Aranyaprathet

Siracha Junction

Phetchaburi

Pattaya

CAMBODIA

Hua Hin

Pattaya
(U Tapao)

Yansangvararam

MYANMAR

Suan Nong Nuch

Prachuap Khiri Khan

Ban Plu Ta Luang

Trat

Chumphon

Lang Suang

Bang
Rak Pier

Samui

State Railway of Thailand (SRT)

Ko Samui

Eastern
Northeastern
Northern
Southern

Surat
Thani

Bangkok Airways
Thai International Airlines

Surat Thani

Don Sak Pier

Thung
Song
Junction

Nakhon Si Thammarat

Seatranferry

Connecting Bus

Hat Yai

Phatthalung

Hat Yai Junction

Malaysian Railways (KTM)
Inter-City

Phuket

Krabi

Trang

Kantang

Yala

Padang Besar

Sungai Kolok

Butterworth

MALAYSIA

BUSES

With the exception of the smaller islands in Thailand, the chances are that anywhere you want to get to will be served by a public or private bus service. Every town has a bus station of some description with a ticket office, and they are often used by both government-run and private buses.

GOVERNMENT-RUN BUSES

For short journeys between towns, up to a distance of under 100 miles (around 150km), there are government-run buses that depart whenever there is a sufficient number of passengers. These buses do not usually have air-conditioning if the journey is a short one, and they can get crowded, but you are usually not stuck on one long enough for this to be a hardship. These buses run throughout the day, with the frequency of services always highest in the morning and tending to fizzle out during late afternoon.

For longer routes, the buses are larger, air-conditioned and with a good level of service. For popular routes there is usually the option of a VIP bus that costs more but provides more leg room and a shorter journey time. Complimentary water, soft drinks and snacks are usually served on longer routes.

PRIVATE BUSES

On longer routes you often won't know whether the bus you have a reserved seat on is a private or government-run one, and most of the time it makes little or no difference. Large towns and cities will have companies competing for business through travel agents: Rival ticket offices are alongside each other at bus stations, but usually there is little variation in their prices. The differences in fares between private and government-run buses running the same route is often negligible, though private buses may be more frequent and offer a slightly higher standard of service. There will be a reason that fares on private buses are noticeably less expensive than rival ones plying

Above Bus in Thailand

the same route, and it is not always prudent to go for the cheapest fare. As well as buses, private minivans are often available for mid-length journeys such as, for example, the Bangkok–Hua Hin route.

BUYING TICKETS

For short journeys on ordinary government-run buses, fares are paid on the bus to a conductor, not the driver, and passengers are picked up and dropped off along the route. For longer journeys, on government-run and private buses, tickets are usually purchased before boarding from a ticket office at the bus station, and a seat number is specified. Sometimes your stored luggage will also be ticketed.

In large towns, timetables and fares are displayed for long-distance routes, and you can see the choices between VIP and regular services.

TIPS

>> Some VIP buses have toilets, but do not rely on this. Bus stations have toilet facilities and on long routes there is usually a rest and meal break at a restaurant with toilet facilities.

>> Tickets for long-distance routes can be reserved in advance and to be sure of a seat on a popular route it is best to reserve the day before departure; it is advisable to at least confirm timetable details the day before traveling.

>> Tourist offices have local bus information and larger ones dispense leaflets listing timetables and fares.

JOURNEY TIMES AND FARES

Fares are based on air-conditioned, first-class or VIP bus services

FROM	TO	JOURNEY TIME	FARE
Bangkok	Ayutthaya	2 hours	B65
	Chiang Mai	10–11 hours	B695
	Hua Hin	3 hours	B165
	Khon Kaen	7 hours	B585
	Korat	3 hours 30 min	B180
	Loei	11 hours	B480
	Pattaya	2 hours 30 min	B140
	Phuket	13 hours	B970
	Surat Thani	10 hours	B600
	Ubon Ratchathani	9 hours	B470
Chiang Mai	Chiang Rai	3 hours	B295
	Mae Hong Son	7 hours 30 min	B250
	Sukhothai	5 hours	B320
	Udon Thani	12 hours	B800
Krabi	Hat Yai	4 hours	B210
	Phang Nga	2 hours	B90
	Phuket	3 hours	B250
	Surat Thani	3 hours	B280
Phuket	Chumphon	7 hours	B320
	Hat Yai	7 hours	B420
	Phang Nga	2 hours 30 min	B70
	Surat Thani	5 hours	B500

FLIGHTS WITHIN THAILAND

Internal flights reach most corners of the country and are not especially expensive. In recent years a number of budget airlines have entered the domestic market—during off-peak periods the price of a ticket on some routes approaches that of a VIP bus or sleeping berth on the train.

Thai Airways has an extensive set of domestic routes, and its timetables are reliable. Hot on its heels comes AirAsia, winners of the Best Low-Cost Airline Asia title (2007, Skytrax research) and Nok Air. Bangkok Airways has been around for longer and all but monopolizes the Bangkok–Ko Samui route.

A one-way Bangkok–Phuket flight (85 minutes; about 25 flights daily) costs from B3,500 (including surcharges and taxes) during off-peak seasons; expect to pay up to another thousand baht during the high season and on public holidays. A slightly cheaper-rate scale applies for flights between Bangkok and Chiang Mai (60 minutes; about 20 flights daily) or Bangkok and Krabi (80 minutes; about 10 flights daily). Prices are usually displayed at a basic rate, so be prepared to pay an extra B500–B700 for additional surcharges and taxes.

RESERVING TICKETS

All the airlines have websites for online reservations. After paying by credit card you will receive a reference number; turn up at the airport with this number and your passport. Flights with Thai Airways can also be reserved through Thai Airways travel agent, and AirAsia has a call center for telephone reservations (025159 999). Check the websites for timetables and fares, and note the luggage limits.

Most hotels allow guests to store baggage in their locked storage area and pick it up days or weeks later.

REGIONAL AIRPORTS

After the grand opening of the Suvarnabhumi International Airport in September 2006, Bangkok's Don Muang Airport reopened in March 2007 as a domestic airport used by Thai Airways, Nok Air and One-Two-Go. There are shuttle buses running between the two airports (▷ 43). The airport express-bus service or a taxi is the best way of getting from Suvarnabhumi airport to the city center, while a taxi is the best option from Don Muang. A rail service linking Suvarnabhumi to central

DOMESTIC AIRLINE WEBSITES

AIRLINE	WEBSITE
AirAsia	www.airasia.com
Bangkok Airways	www.bangkokair.com
Nok Air	www.nokair.com
One-Two-Go	www.fly12go.com
PB Air	www.pbair.com
Thai Airways (THAI)	www.thaiairways.com

FLIGHTS WITHIN THAILAND

FROM	TO	AIRLINE
Bangkok	Chiang Mai	Thai Airways, Bangkok Airways, Nok Air, One-Two-Go, AirAsia
	Chiang Rai	Thai Airways, One-Two-Go, AirAsia
	Hat Yai	Thai Airways, Nok Air, One-Two-Go, AirAsia
	Khon Kaen	Thai Airways, AirAsia
	Ko Samui	Bangkok Airways, Thai Airways
	Krabi	Thai Airways, Bangkok Airways, One-Two-Go
	Mae Hong Son	Thai Airways
	Nakhon Phanom	PB Air
	Nakhon Si Thammarat	Thai Airways, PB Air, One-Two-Go
	Nan	PB Air
	Phitsanulok	Thai Airways, Nok Air
	Phuket	Thai Airways, Bangkok Airways, Nok Air, One-Two-Go, AirAsia
	Roi Et	PB Air
	Sukhothai	Bangkok Airways
	Surat Thani	Thai Airways, One-Two-Go
	Ubon Ratchathani	Thai Airways, AirAsia
	Udon Thani	Thai Airways, Nok Air, AirAsia
Ko Samui	Bangkok	Bangkok Airways, Thai Airways
	Chiang Mai	Bangkok Airways
	Krabi	Bangkok Airways
	Pattaya	Bangkok Airways
	Phuket	Bangkok Airways
	Sukhothai	Bangkok Airways

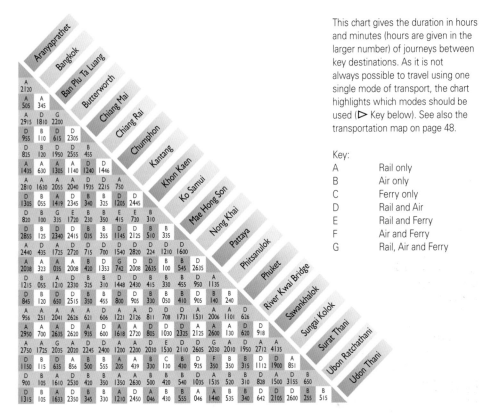

This chart gives the duration in hours and minutes (hours are given in the larger number) of journeys between key destinations. As it is not always possible to travel using one single mode of transport, the chart highlights which modes should be used (▷ Key below). See also the transportation map on page 48.

Key:
A	Rail only
B	Air only
C	Ferry only
D	Rail and Air
E	Rail and Ferry
F	Air and Ferry
G	Rail, Air and Ferry

ON THE MOVE | GETTING AROUND

Bangkok via the Skytrain and subway systems is due for completion soon.

Thailand's regional airports are usually not far from the city center or the main beach resorts. Chiang Mai's airport is only 2 miles (3km) from the center, though Phuket's airport is 12–19 miles (20–30km) from the main west-coast beach resort area.

All Thailand's regional airports have a taxi or minibus service into the local town and for busy destinations this is a well-organized system with fixed rates that are clearly displayed at counters in the arrivals hall. Many resort hotels and the better city-center hotels have their own minivans bringing guests to and from the airport. If your hotel is reserved in advance, it is worth checking and confirming the transfer arrangements.

AIR PASSES

There are only two types of air passes available. Thai Airways sells a Thailand Air pass that covers three internal routes for just US $149 and up to three additional flights can be purchased at US $45 each. All flights must be specified upon purchase, but dates can be changed. The Bangkok Airways air pass operates on a coupon system; a minimum of three coupons are purchased for US $55 each, which you use to pay for your flights when you book. Air passes for Thai Airways and Bangkok Airways must be purchased outside of Thailand, through registered agents.

Right *Check-in area of Phuket International Airport for domestic departures*

Taxis are available throughout Thailand and take different forms, but, with the exception of those in Bangkok, they do not use meters. This means that the fare must be established beforehand. *Songthaews* are a cross between a bus and a shared taxi, but fares for regular routes are fixed.

TAXI FARES

Establishing a taxi fare is more of an art than a science, though it is always easier to handle if you have some idea beforehand of the likely fare for a particular journey. Ask the staff where you are staying, talk to other visitors or check the asking rate with more than one taxi. Sometimes, especially when arriving somewhere for the first time, you simply have to ask the taxi driver what the fare is and use your own judgment. Some degree of bargaining is usually taken for granted, but try to bear in mind,

especially with *samlor* drivers, that most of them earn very little and you may be disagreeing over a very small amount in terms of your currency.

TUK-TUKS

Tuk-tuks are small, three-wheeled vehicles driven by two-stroke engines. They look attractive, but the name, *tuk tuk*, comes from the distinctive noise they make and after a while the charm may wear off. Apart from the noise and exhaust fumes, some drivers resemble kamikaze pilots as they dart in and out of traffic and take right-angle turns with reckless abandon. On a good day, though, they can be fun to ride in and will take you wherever you want to go with alacrity and little expense.

Samlors are also three-wheeled vehicles; their unmotorized form is the bicycle rickshaw. The ones with motors make as much noise as *tuk-tuks*.

MOTORCYCLE TAXIS

Motorcycle taxis are found in urban and rural areas and are usually identified by the drivers' conspicuous vests, sometimes bearing numerals, and the tendency for them to gather in small clusters at junctions, outside stations or shopping malls. Thais use them for short journeys. While the driver may or may not wear a helmet, they do not usually carry one for passengers, despite the fact that they are a legal requirement. They are not suitable or safe if you are carrying luggage, but in out-of-town locations they are sometimes the only readily available alternative to a long walk. For short hops, their fares are usually between B10–B30.

SONGTHAEWS

In small towns, rural areas and large islands, public transportation takes the form of open-ended pick-up trucks with two rows of seats facing one another. These are *songthaews* (Thai for "two rows") and passengers can flag them down or be dropped off anywhere along their route. The conventional time for paying the driver varies, either at the start or end of your journey. in Phuket, one *songthaew* runs between the beaches and Phuket town, and the driver stops halfway and collects all the fares. Many *songthaews* are equipped with bells for passengers to press when they wish to alight, but in others you may need to give a shout or tap the railings with a coin to alert the driver. Observe the practice of other passengers.

TIP

>> Carry coins and small notes for paying taxi drivers.

Left *A couple riding on a trishaw, or three-wheeled bicycle taxi, through the streets of Chiang Mai*
Opposite left *Colorful signs advertising bike rentals on Ko Lanta Yai*
Opposite right *Bicycling is a great way to get between places of interest*

BICYCLING AND WALKING

Despite the heat, bicycling leisurely around a small town or rural area is one of the most pleasant ways of getting around. The larger and more congested the urban area, the less attractive bicycling becomes, and as a bicyclist you cannot assume that the hard shoulder of a road will not be used by motorists and truck drivers. In Bangkok, of course, bicycling is just not an option, but outside the capital, bicycles and tricycles are used regularly by Thais, and motorists are well aware of bicyclists sharing the roadways with them.

BICYCLE RENTAL

Bicycle rental shops and bicycling tours are now becoming quite common in the major tourist areas, where entrepreneurs have realized there is a steady demand from visitors. In Chiang Mai, Kanchanaburi and Nong Khai it is not difficult to find places renting out bicycles, usually by the day for around B50 and often with a discount for a longer rental period. They open up the local countryside in a way not possible with other means of transportation. In these places, bicycle rental is often also available through guesthouses, and it is not always necessary to be a guest to rent one of their bicycles. In Ayutthaya, where bicycle shops dot the road between the station and the ferry jetty, a bicycle is the ideal way to get around the *wats* (temples) that are too spaced out to reach on foot.

WALKING

Traveling on foot for more than half an hour can be an exhausting and dehydrating experience in the hotter hours of the day. Having said that, longer periods spent walking are quite feasible if you carry or stop for drinks, maintain a moderate-to-slow pace and use shaded areas as much as possible. The suggested walks in this guide will take well over an hour but are very manageable. Depending on the temperature and time of day, far longer walks are possible. It is a good idea to always carry a supply of water and a hat.

TIPS

›› Road and street signs are usually translated into English, but you will find minor differences in the spellings used for maps and brochures.
›› *Thanon* means road, so Thanon Sukhumvit is Sukhumvit Road.
›› *Soi* means a smaller road branching off a main road. Soi 20 Thanon Sukhumvit, for example, means *soi* number 20 off Sukhumvit Road.

DRIVING IN THAILAND

If Bangkok provides your first experience of Thailand's roads, you are likely to shun the idea of renting a car, but outside the capital driving is a manageable proposition. Rental through a reputable company is as uncomplicated as in your home country, and in many areas of Thailand the roads are uncongested and drivers generally show consideration and drive responsibly. At the same time, expect to encounter some reckless drivers, often behind the wheel of a bus or truck, with little consideration for cars. This is especially so after dark, and long-distance driving at night is not recommended for this reason. Bear in mind, also, that a vehicle flashing its lights is not giving way—he is indicating that he is coming through, regardless of who has right-of-way.

Apart from rural areas off the main road network, road signs are clearly posted in English and Thai, with distances to main destinations indicated in kilometers. On main roads there will be signs warning of sharp bends and/or the need to reduce speed.

In Bangkok the density of traffic and the bewildering mix of traffic directions and lanes—which are subject to constant changes and not signposted in English—make driving around the city challenging for most foreign drivers; it is not recommended. Car rental at Bangkok's Don Muang or Suvarnabhumi airports is feasible if you are not heading into the city, and expressways, signposted in English, connect the airports with routes to other parts of the country. There is very little vehicle crime, and parking is rarely a problem outside Bangkok.

RULES OF THE ROAD

›› Drive on the left.
›› All directions and speed limits are in kilometers. In towns and built-up areas the limit is 37mph (60kph), and on other roads the limit varies

Above *Cattle heading home at dusk*

between 55mph (90kph) and 74mph (120kph).
›› You must wear seat belts in the front seats.
›› Large vehicles assume they have priority on roads and drive accordingly.
›› Hard shoulders are often used by slower vehicles or by cars yielding to a larger vehicle.
›› If the vehicle in front of you is indicating left, the driver may be signaling that it is safe to pass; indicating right may mean it is not.
›› Until recently, it was common and accepted practice to hand over some cash to a traffic officer to avoid paying a fine for not wearing a seat belt or helmet, or failing to present a valid license. This is no longer the case—getting caught usually involves the inconvenience of not only a B200–B500 fine, but also an hour or two being "processed" at the local police station. For speeding or drunk-driving the punishment is more serious.

CAR RENTAL

Cars and jeeps can be rented at airports or through many hotels and travel agents, as well as reserved and paid for in advance through a company's website. Expect to pay comparable prices to rentals in the West. Company websites will provide quotes.

In popular destinations, especially Phuket, Ko Samui and Chiang Mai, there are countless places offering car rental at less expensive rates than the better-known, franchised companies. If you use these you need to check the insurance cover very carefully to be sure that the vehicle is actually insured.

It is not advisable to use companies that ask for your passport and expect to retain it until you return the vehicle. The local TAT office should be able to recommend reliable companies, and car rental desks in good hotels will be from reputable and trustworthy companies.

The general rule, and one that is enforced by the larger and more reputable car rental companies, is that the driver is over the age of 21 and able to pay by credit card.

It is normal to ask for pre-authorization for a security deposit from your credit card of B20,000.

A non-Thai driver is supposed to show an international driver's license when renting a vehicle, but in practice it is often sufficient to show your national license.

CAR RENTAL COMPANIES	
COMPANY	**WEBSITE**
Avis	www.avis.com
Budget	www.budget.co.th
Hertz	www.hertz.com
National	www.nationalcar.com

Cars are usually supplied with a full tank of fuel and should be returned with a full tank. There should be no charge for mileage.

Loss damage waiver, subject usually to a B5,000 charge in the event of a nonrecoverable loss or damage to the vehicle, should be included in the car rental price, and you should check this is the case before you rent the car. A drink-related driving offense will invalidate your insurance-covered liability on the vehicle.

Also available is an optional Personal Accident and Effect insurance, which costs around B100 per day. Check your general travel insurance to see if you are covered for accidents while driving a rented vehicle.

Good car rental companies use cars in good condition, but they should have a clear policy in the event of a breakdown. Make sure you know how to contact your rental company if you break down or have an accident. Before you drive off, check the condition of the car and ensure that any defects are marked on the rental form.

MOTORCYCLE RENTAL

In Phuket, Ko Samui and Ko Lanta, as well as smaller islands and in the north, visitors commonly rent a motorcycle. This can often be arranged where you are staying. Expect to pay around B200 for one day's rental. Insurance is not usually available.

Some of the visitors you see driving rented motorcycles have never driven one before, and as you may yourself be in this category, careful riding is essential.

On some islands, roads can be uneven and in poor condition, with unexpected potholes.

Always wear a helmet while riding and check the condition of the motorcycle before leaving the shop, as rental bikes tend to suffer a lot of damage and some can become quite unsafe to ride.

FUEL

Newer cars usually use unleaded 95 (B28 per liter) or Gasohol 95 (B25), a gasoline/ethanol mix that is becoming widely available and is set to replace unleaded 95 eventually. Vans mostly use diesel (B25). But always check before you fill up. Larger fuel stations will accept payment by recognized international credit cards, but in rural areas cash may be required by the fuel garage attendant.

ROAD DISTANCES

This chart shows the distances in kilometers of a car journey between key destinations.

	Ayutthaya	Bangkok	Chanthaburi	Chiang Mai	Chiang Rai	Chumphon	Khon Kaen	Lampang	Lamphun	Lop Buri	Mae Hong Son	Mukdahan	Nakhon Phanom	Nakhon Ratchasima (Korat)	Pattaya	Phetchaburi	Phuket	Sukhothai	Surat Thani	Ubon Ratchathani
Bangkok	75																			
Chanthaburi	320	245																		
Chiang Mai	625	695	1000																	
Chiang Rai	715	785	1200	180																
Chumphon	535	465	720	1160	1250															
Khon Kaen	405	450	695	650	730	910														
Lampang	530	600	850	90	225	1062	565													
Lamphun	600	670	915	20	200	890	630	65												
Lop Buri	100	155	360	580	670	610	390	490	560											
Mae Hong Son	855	925	1170	350	440	1390	955	410	370	815										
Mukdahan	640	640	700	900	975	1100	245	805	875	680	1200									
Nakhon Phanom	695	740	810	950	1030	1105	300	860	920	680	1250	105								
Nakhon Ratchasima (Korat)	215	260	505	775	1015	720	190	685	755	200	1010	385	480							
Pattaya	225	145	170	845	930	610	595	745	815	300	1070	720	820	335						
Phetchaburi	200	125	365	820	910	340	570	720	790	275	1050	765	860	380	270					
Phuket	940	860	1110	1560	1630	412	1310	1460	1530	1015	1785	1500	1600	1120	1005	740				
Sukhothai	360	425	690	300	400	890	380	205	275	330	580	620	675	515	570	550	1290			
Surat Thani	720	645	870	1340	1430	190	1095	1240	1310	800	1568	1285	1385	905	790	520	290	1070		
Ubon Ratchathani	580	630	875	935	1015	1090	280	845	915	570	1240	165	270	370	775	750	1490	660	1275	
Udon Thani	520	565	810	400	845	1025	115	680	745	505	1070	280	250	305	620	685	1425	495	1210	400

Bangkok is a large, sprawling city and getting around depends on establishing, before setting out, the most convenient means of transport for where you want to go. The Skytrain, the subway system and the Chao Phraya River Express boats are most commonly used by visitors to get about, but taxis, plentiful and inexpensive, are sometimes necessary. The bus network reaches every part of the city.

SKYTRAIN

The BTS Skytrain (www.bts.co.th) system offers comfortable, efficient, non-smoking, air-conditioned transportation on two lines between 6am and midnight. Trains run every few minutes. Drinking or eating is not allowed on the trains (although refreshment booths are located inside the terminals), and stations have no toilets. The name of each station is announced in English as the train approaches the platform.

Lines

The Sukhumvit Line runs from Mo Chit in the north (station N8), close to the Northern Bus Terminal and Chatuchak Market, to On Nut (E9) on Thanon Sukhumvit; the entire journey takes half an hour. All trains stop at every station, including the interchange at Siam for connecting trains on the Silom Line.

The Silom Line runs from National Stadium (W1), one stop west of Siam, to Saphan Taksin (S6), which is two minutes away on foot from a Chao Phraya River Express boat pier.

Tickets

Tickets are issued by touch-sensitive machines in all stations, with clear instructions in English. Only B5 and B10 coins are accepted. After inserting your ticket into one of the turnstiles to enter the platform area, the ticket is returned to you. Upon exiting through a turnstile, the ticket is retained. Non-turnstile access is available for large luggage and staff will assist. Men, in particular, should use caution when passing through the turnstiles, as they slam shut just below the waist without warning.

Fares

Tickets cost between B15 and B40 depending on the distance. There is a useful three-day/four-night Tourist Pass—if purchased in the morning it serves for four days—for B280. The one-day pass for B100 would need a lot of journeys to make it economical. There are also 30-day passes that cover any 10 trips for B250, 15 trips for B300 and 30 trips for B540 (B160, B210 and B360 respectively for those aged under 23). Children under 35.5 inches (90cm) travel free.

SUBWAY

Bangkok's MRT subway system (www.mrta.co.th) operates from 5am to midnight, with trains running

every 10 minutes on average. Air-conditioned and non-smoking, the subway has one line, running between Hua Lamphong railway station in the middle of the city and Bang Sue in the north, two stations beyond Chatuchak, where it connects with the Mo Chit Skytrain station. Subway station Silom also connects with the Skytrain station of Sala Daeng, and subway station Sukhumvit connects with Asok Skytrain station, though the latter connection entails leaving the subway and walking to another station nearby.

Drinking or eating is not allowed on trains; stations have toilets but no other amenities.

The name of each station is announced in English as the train approaches the platform.

Tickets and fares

Tickets, in the form of a small black, plastic disc, are issued by machines along the same lines as the Skytrain. The disc is used to activate entry through a turnstile and should be

inserted into the turnstile, which retains it, when exiting a station. Fares are approximately the same as for the Skytrain.

CHAO PHRAYA RIVER EXPRESS BOATS

The Chao Phraya River Express Boat Company runs boats up and down Bangkok's river every day from 5.50am–7.40pm.

Tha Sathorn pier, next to Saphan Taksin Skytrain station and close to the Shangri-La hotel, has been designated Central Pier. The piers north of this are numbered N1, N2 and so on.

You are most likely to use boats between Central Pier and Tha Phra Athit (N13) for reaching places like the Royal Palace, National Museum and Banglamphu. Some of the piers are on the west side of the river, useful for Wat Arun and Thonburi station (for trains to Kanchanaburi).

Types of boats

Boats not flying any flag will stop at piers where people are waiting to board or passengers are waiting to disembark. Boats flying a yellow or orange flag are express boats that

do not stop at every pier. A dark blue flag shows that this is the last one of the day.

Special Tourist Boats run between Central Pier and Banglamphu (▷ 70), and the ticket lasts all day and allows you to hop on and off any of these boats at your convenience.

Tickets and fares

Tickets cost from B9 to B32, depending on the distance, and whether the boat is an express type or not, and are bought on board.

The boats get busy and you need to be ready to disembark by making your way toward the back of the boat, which is where you boarded.

Cross-river boats

These boats ply back and forth across the Chao Phraya River and have their own access and exit points alongside the piers that service the Chao Phraya River Express boats. The fare is B3, which you pay at a booth at the pier; no tickets are issued.

CANAL BOATS

On the *khlongs* (canals), longtail boats operate like the Chao Phraya

River Express boats, stopping at piers along their routes. On the Bangkok side of the river, you are most likely to use the route that runs between Tha Phanfa (for Wat Rachanada, Wak Saket and Banglamphu) and Asok (for Thanon Sukhumvit), a useful way of moving between the east and west parts of the city.

The piers are not conspicuous, but *The Official Map of Bangkok* (free from Bangkok airport and tourist offices) clearly shows the course of the canal and the different piers and is useful for monitoring your journey and anticipating arrival at the pier you want. Tickets are purchased from a conductor on board; follow everyone else when they change boats at Tha Pratunam (due to bridge height restrictions).

Fares are between B9 and B32 depending on distance. Have a B20 note ready and state your destination to the conductor. Sitting near the end of each seat row makes it easier to get off; the disadvantage is an occasional light splash from the water.

TAXIS
Metered taxis
Comfortable, air-conditioned taxis with meters, displaying "TAXI" on the roof, are plentiful, and those available display a red light in the windscreen on the passenger's side.

Fares start at B35. Expect to pay from B80 to B120 for a typical journey across town—from the vicinity of Thanon Sukhumvit around the Asok (E4) Skytrain station, for example, to Central Pier near the Shangri-La hotel. The meter increases according to distance and time, so try to avoid the busiest parts of the day, from 8 to 9.30am and 5.30 to 7pm: traffic jams can be horrendous, the fare will increase and your patience will be tested by sitting for what feels like interminable lengths of time.

A tip is not obligatory but rounding up a fare is customary. There is no charge for pieces of luggage and, apart from journeys

to and from the airport, there are no other supplements to pay.

Many taxi drivers speak a little English, but this cannot be taken for granted: do not assume they can read English on a map. Most will know common destinations, and hotel staff will often help by hailing a taxi for you and stating the destination to the driver.

Tuk-tuks
You will find these everywhere in Bangkok and they are useful for short trips when you are in a rush. A ride in a *tuk-tuk*, even the rare one driven in a calm manner, will expose you to traffic fumes and noise to an alarming degree. Two people, three at the very most, can sit comfortably. Having coins helps when paying the fare, which should always be agreed beforehand. Expect to be cheated. Haggle vigorously and be wary of discounts that include obligatory stops at tailor shops.

Motorcycle taxis
Motorcycle taxis are used by Bangkok residents but they are not recommended for visitors, except perhaps for short trips from one end of a long *soi* to your hotel at the other end. A short trip costs about B15. It is against the law not to wear a helmet, which should be made available to you by the taxi driver.

BUSES
Buses go everywhere in Bangkok, albeit slowly most of the time, but the difficulty is knowing when to get off for a destination with which you're not familiar—buses are often crowded and you cannot expect the driver to help or assume another passenger will speak English. Once you have some familiar landmarks and a map, buses can be useful, but to begin with it is best to use a metered taxi or the Skytrain and/ or subway. Bus fares for different classes start at B5, B8 and B12, and are paid to either the conductor or dropped in a box by the entrance.

Right *Motorcycle taxi in Bangkok*

LEAVING BANGKOK
By air
Thai Airways, AirAsia and Nok Air operate their domestic flights from Don Muang airport. Bangkok Airways, PB Air and SGA Airlines use Suvarnabhumi.

By bus
There are three terminals for long-distance buses. For buses to northern and northeastern Thailand use the Northern Bus Terminal on Kamphaeng Phet 2 Road, a short taxi ride or 15-minute walk from Mo Chit Skytrain station or Chatuchak subway station. For southern Thailand use the Southern Bus Terminal on Borommarat Chonnani Road in Thonburi, on the west side of the Chao Phraya River. For eastern Thailand, use the Eastern Bus Terminal on Sukhumvit Road at Soi 40, which is next to Ekkamai Skytrain station.

TIPS
>> *The Official Map of Bangkok*, a fold-out map freely available at the airport, tourist offices and some hotels, shows clearly all the Skytrain and subway stations and river and canal piers. Free Skytrain maps are available at all Skytrain stations.
>> Keep a supply of coins to avoid waiting in line for change at Skytrain and subway stations and for purchasing boat tickets.
>> For returning to your hotel by taxi, it helps to carry a hotel card with the address in Thai.

GETTING AROUND IN OTHER MAJOR CITIES AND ISLANDS

Getting around in cities, towns and on islands is inexpensive. While not always fast, transportation is usually efficient and reliable.

GETTING TO YOUR HOTEL
From airports

Every regional airport has taxis waiting, and airport staff should be able to give you an idea of an acceptable fare to bear in mind when negotiating a price with the driver. Some airports will have desks for taxis and/or airport buses with fixed prices to your hotel.

If your hotel has been reserved in advance, and especially if it is a resort hotel, there may be a minivan waiting for guests at the airport; check this in advance with your hotel.

From bus and railway stations

Bus and railway stations are not usually within walking distance of hotels, but there will always be *tuk-tuks* and *samlors* waiting, as well as taxis, and some stations will have a *songthaew* service into town.

From island piers

Your hotel may well have its own transportation waiting at the pier for guests and this should be checked in advance. On disembarking, you are likely to be approached by a variety of touts and/or staff offering accommodations, and at busy times of the year, especially between November and February in southern Thailand, these may be worth considering as they will have transportation waiting. Usually there will be no shortage of taxis—whether cars, motorcycles or *samlors*—available to take you to wherever you are staying.

GETTING AROUND PHUKET

Airport buses to beach hotels or into town cost from B120 and B180. *Songthaews* run between the beaches and town, a well-organized service with destinations and fares marked in English. The fare between Phuket town and Karon beach, for

example, is B40, while a *tuk-tuk* from Karon beach to Phuket Town is B300. The bus station is on Thanon Phang Nga, a 10-minute walk from where the *songthaews* congregate. An air-conditioned VIP sleeper bus from town to Bangkok costs B970; a minibus to Surat Thani costs B180–B200. For more details of Phuket transportation, ▷ 251 or visit www.phuket-guide.net.

GETTING AROUND KRABI

A taxi from the airport into town costs around B300. Thai Airways also runs a minibus service, meeting their flights, for B60. Budget (tel 075 637 913) has a desk at Arrivals. *Songthaews* run from Thanon Maharat to Ao Nang for B40–B80 and to the bus terminal, 3 miles (5km) north of town. A VIP sleeper from Krabi to Bangkok costs B1,100, while first-class air-conditioned buses to Phuket are B250 and to Surat Thani B280. Reservations for boats include transportation from your hotel to the departure pier. For more details on Krabi transportation visit www.yourkrabi.com.

GETTING AROUND KO SAMUI

At the airport, where Budget has a car rental desk (tel 077 427 188), minibuses meet flights and charge around B100 to B200 to the beach

hotels. *Songthaews* run between the beaches and the pier at Na Thon, with destinations marked in English, while at night they become taxis available for individual rental. For more details on Ko Samui transportation, ▷ 242 or visit www.faraway.co.th.

GETTING AROUND CHIANG MAI

A taxi system with fixed prices operates at the airport. *Songthaews* and *tuk-tuks* run between the train and bus stations into town and will take you directly to your accommodation; rates are negotiable, but expect to pay up to B100. Bicycles are a good way of getting around town; there are several rental outlets. For more details on Chiang Mai transportation visit www.chiangmai-thai.com.

TIP
➤ Tourist offices and most hotels, guesthouses and restaurants have maps and English-language magazines freely available showing bus stations and other transportation locations, as well as transportation timetables and local fares.

Above *Ferry waiting at Phi Phi Don on Ko Phi Phi; regular ferry services operate in Southern Thailand making it easy to get around and see the many beautiful resorts and islands*

Above *Access to beaches for wheelchair users is improving in Thailand*

Visitors with a disability should not be deterred from visiting Thailand, even though the country has not made great strides to create wheelchair access at places of interest and on public transportation. On the plus side, Thai people are usually as accommodating as possible, and it is not too costly to make generous use of taxis and to ask tour guides to arrange access to temples and museums.

PREPARATION AND PLANNING

There are a number of excellent organizations worldwide that offer useful advice and information and some companies that specialize in adventure holidays to Thailand for visitors with disabilities, including for travelers in wheelchair, for the hearing impaired and slow walkers. **http://members.chello.nl/ danblokker** lists accommodations close to the hub of Chiang Mai that are equipped to accommodate travelers with disabilities.

www.disabilitytravelers.com/ airlines.htm gives relevant information about the airlines for passengers with disabilities. **www.disabilitytravel.com** offers a range of accessible journeys and exciting lifestyle vacations for travelers with disabilities. **www.sath.org** (Society for Accessible Travel and Hospitality) and **www.miusa.org** (Mobility International USA) are both reputable organizations devoted to assisting disabled travelers have successful holidays abroad.

www.disabledtravelers.com has a list of travel agents that are experienced in assisting travelers with disabilities.

www.apparelyzed.com includes a useful list of travel agents, travel tips, hotel and resort reviews and a traveler's forum.

ARRIVING BY AIR

Check with your airline about the arrangements they can offer and the facilities at Don Muang and Suvarnabhumi airports. Both airports have elevators and wheelchairs. A taxi will take you to your hotel; check with your hotel beforehand about their facilities. Better hotels, especially in Bangkok, Phuket, Ko Samui and Chiang Mai, have excellent, up-to-date facilities for travelers with disabilities.

GETTING AROUND IN BANGKOK

Bangkok presents difficulties because of the lack of provision for people with disabilities or walking difficulties and the density of human and vehicular traffic. Sidewalks are often high, uneven at the best of times, and curbs are rarely sloped for wheelchair use. Underpasses with ramps are even more rare, and bridges for pedestrians are accessible only by stairs. The Chao Phraya River Express boats have no wheelchair access, but all the subway stations and many of the Skytrain ones have elevators.

REGIONS

This chapter is divided into five regions of Thailand (▷ 8–9). Region names are for the purposes of this book only and places of interest are listed alphabetically in each region.

Thailand's Regions

BANGKOK

Bangkok was founded in 1782 by Rama I in a gradual transition after the former capital of Ayutthaya was burned by the Burmese in 1767. Bangkok's official name is the longest place-name in the world: "Krung Thep Mahanakhon Amon Rattanakosin Mahinthara Yuthaya Mahadilok Phop Noppharat Ratchathani Burirom Udomratchaniwet Mahasathan Amon Phiman Awatan Sathit Sakkathattiya Witsanukam Prasit," which translates as: "The city of angels, the great city, the eternal jewel city, the impregnable city of God Indra, the grand capital of the world endowed with nine precious gems, the happy city, abounding in an enormous Royal Palace that resembles the heavenly abode where reigns the reincarnated god, a city given by Indra and built by Vishnukarm". Most Thais simply refer to is as Krung Thep or "City of Angels."

Thailand's capital city is the center of all things Thai, from traditional to pop culture, cuisine, commerce, art and entertainment, and, of course, politics. Bangkok's influence extends far outside Thailand's borders, and is a major metropolitan hub for all of Southeast Asia. For the metropolitan traveler, Bangkok is a utopia of vast shopping malls, world-class restaurants and endless food markets stocked with some of the best food Asia has to offer. Urbanites can spend the day wandering Royal Palaces, atmospheric temples and bustling neighborhoods in the old city, then party all night in Asia's hottest clubs.

Bangkok is not a city to see in a hurry—the heat and the traffic will defeat you—its rich culture and long history are worth spending some time exploring. But for some travelers not so enamored with the high-octane city life, the pollution, noise, traffic and endless crowds can be overwhelming. The flourishing red-light districts with marauding prostitutes and infamous sex shows, con artists and obnoxious *tuk-tuk* drivers may convince some travelers that a few days in "The Big Mango" is plenty of time. Whether angel or devil, most travelers will at least pass through Bangkok, and some may spend their entire trip in this one city—there's certainly plenty to keep you busy.

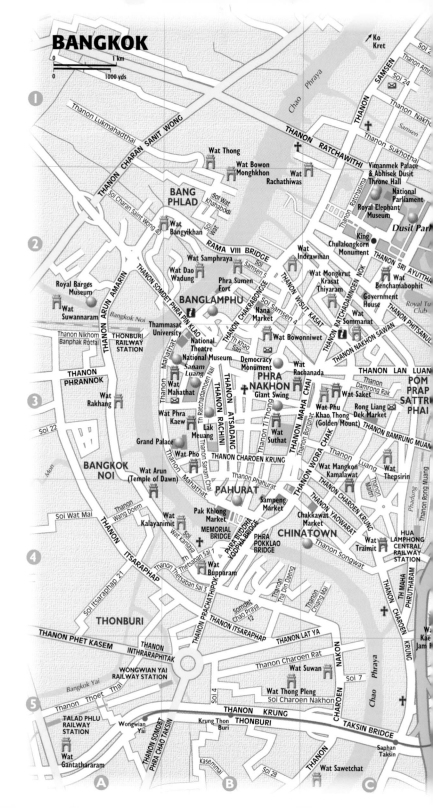

BANGKOK

0 — 1 km
0 — 1000 yds

→ Ko Kret

Chao Phraya

THANON RATCHAWITHI

Thanon Lukmahadthal

THANON CHARAN SANIT WONG

THANON SAMSEN

Soi 24

Thanon Nak

Samsen

Thanon Sukhothal

Thanon Samsen

Vimanmek Palace & Abhisek Dusit Throne Hall

Wat Thong

Wat Bowon Monghkhon

Wat Rachathiwas

National Parliament

Royal Elephant Museum

Dusit Par

BANG PHLAD

Soi Wat Khahabodi

Thanon Ratchasima

King Chulalongkorn Monument

THANON SRI AYUTTHA

Wat Bangyikhan

RAMA VIII BRIDGE

Wat Indrawihan

Wat Mongkrut Krasat Thiyaram

Wat Benchamabophit

Wat Samphraya

Samsen 5

THANON RATCHADAMNOEN NOK

Government House

THANON PHITSANUL

Wat Dao Wadung

Phra Sumen Fort

Soi Samsen 4

THANON WISUT KASAT

Wat Sommanat

Royal Tu Club

Royal Barges Museum

Wat Suwannaram

BANGLAMPHU

Nana Market

THANON CHAKRABONGSE

THANON RATCHADAMNOEN KLANG

THANON NAKHON SAWAN

Bangkok Noi

Thammasat University

Th Khao San

Wat Bowonniwet

THANON ARUN AMARIN

THANON SOMDET PHRA PIN KLAO

THANON LAN LUAN

Thanon Nikhom Banphak Rotfai

THONBURI RAILWAY STATION

National Theatre

Democracy Monument

Wat Rachanada

POM PRAP SATTRU PHAI

National Museum

Sanam Luang

PHRA NAKHON

Wat Saket

THANON PHRANNOK

Wat Mahathat

Giant Swing

THANON MAHA CHAI

Wat Phu Khao Thong (Golden Mount)

Rong Liang Dek Market

Wat Rakhang

THANON ATSADANG

THANON RACHINI

Thanon Damrong Rak

Thanon Boriphat

Wat Phra Kaew

Lak Meuang

Wat Ti Thong

Wat Suthat

THANON BAMRUNG MUAN

BANGKOK NOI

Grand Palace

Wat Pho

Thanon Sanam Chal

THANON CHAROEN KRUNG

Thanon Luang

Thanon Maitri

Wat Thepsirin

Soi 22

Men

Thanon Phahurat

Wat Mangkon Kamalawat

THANON CHAROEN KRUNG

Phadung

Thanon Rong Muang

Wat Arun (Temple of Dawn)

PAHURAT

Sampeng Market

THANON WORA CHAK

THANON YAOWARAT

Soi Wat Mai

Pak Khlong Market

Chakkawat Market

CHINATOWN

Wat Traimit

HUA LAMPHONG CENTRAL RAILWAY STATION

Wat Kalayanimit

MEMORIAL BRIDGE

PHRA BUDDHA YODPHA BRIDGE

PHRA POKKLAO BRIDGE

Thanon Songwat

Wat Kaniaja

THANON ITSARAPHAP

THANON PRACHATHIPOK

Th Thetsaban Sal 1

Th Thetsaban Sal 3

Wat Bupparam

Somdet Chao Praya 12

Tha Din Daeng

Thanon Chiang Mai

TH MAHA PHRUTHARAM

THANON CHAROEN

Soi Itsaraphap 21

THONBURI

THANON ITSARAPHAP

THANON INTHRAPHITAK

THANON LAT YA

NAKON

Kae Jam

THANON PHET KASEM

THANON

Thanon Charoen Rat

Wat Suwan

Chao Phraya

Bangkok Yai

WONGWIAN YAI RAILWAY STATION

Soi 4

Wat Thong Pleng

Soi 7

THANON

Thanon Thoet Thai

Soi Charoen Nakhon

THANON KRUNG THONBURI

TAKSIN BRIDGE

TALAD PHLU RAILWAY STATION

Wongwian Yai

THANON SOMDET PHRA CHAO TAKSIN

Krung Thon Buri

Saphan Taksin

Wat Gantahararam

Kasemmal

Soi 28

Wat Sawetchat

A   B   C

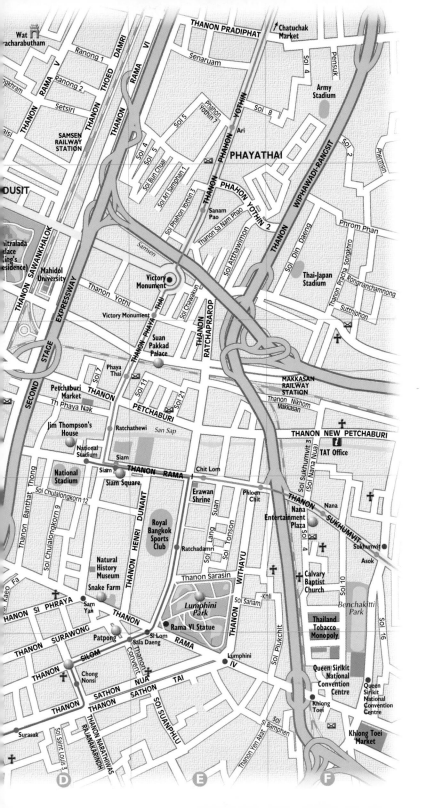

Wat racharabutham
ngkhram
aisi
RANONG V
Ranong 1
Ranong 2
Setsiri
THANON RAMA V
THANON THOED DAMRI
THANON RAMA VI
THANON PRADIPHAT
Senaruam
Chatuchak Market
Pensuk
Soi 4
Army Stadium
SOI 5
Phahon Yothin 7
SOI 8
SAMSEN RAILWAY STATION
SOI 4
SOI 5
Soi Bun Chuai
Soi Ari Samphan 1
THANON PHAHON YOTHIN
Ari
SOI 2
Phetmin
DUSIT
Soi Phahon Yothin 3
THANON PHAHON YOTHIN
PHAYATHAI
THANON PHAHON YOTHIN 2
WIPHAWADI-RANGSIT
nitralada alace ing's esidence)
THANON SAWANKHALOK
Mahidol University
EXPRESSWAY
Samsen
Thanon Yothi
Sanam Pao
Thanon Sa Nam Phao
THANON
Thanon Soi Din Daeng
Soi Pracha Songkhro
Phrom Phan
Thanon Pracha Rongrianchamnong
Thai-Japan Stadium
Suttiphon
Victory Monument
Victory Monument
STAGE
SECOND
THANON PHAYA THAI
Soi Chanakun
THANON RATCHAPRAROP
THANON RATCHAPRAROP
Soi Atthawimon
Phaya Thai
Suan Pakkad Palace
MAKKASAN RAILWAY STATION
Petchaburi Market
Soi 7
THANON
SOI 11
SOI 21
PETCHABURI
Thanon Nikhom Makkasan
Th Phaya Nak
THANON NEW PETCHABURI
Jim Thompson's House
Ratchathewi
San Sap
TAT Office
Soi Sukhumvit 3
(Soi Nana Nua)
National Stadium
Siam
THANON RAMA I
Chit Lom
THANON SUKHUMVIT
Nana
National Stadium
Siam
Siam Square
Soi Chulalongkorn 12
THANON HENRI DUNANT
Erawan Shrine
Phloen Chit
Nana Entertainment Plaza
SOI 4
Sukhumvit
Thanon Banthat Thong
Soi Chulalongkorn 9
Royal Bangkok Sports Club
Soi Lang
Soi Tonson
Soi Suan
WITHAYU
Asok
Ratchadamri
SOI 10
Natural History Museum
THANON RAMA
Thanon Sarasin
Calvary Baptist Church
Benchakitti Park
aeo Fa
Snake Farm
Sam Yan
Soi Sanam
-Khli
Thailand Tobacco Monopoly
SOI 16
THANON SI PHRAYA
THANON
Lumphini Park
THANON SARASIN
THANON SURAWONG
Patpong
Rama VI Statue
RAMA IV
Lumphini
Soi Piukchit
Queen Sirikit National Convention Centre
Chong Nonsi
Sala Daeng
Si Lom
Convent
TAI
SILOM
THANON
THANON
NUA
SATHON
SATHON
SOI SUANPHLU
Queen Sirikit National Convention Centre
Khlong Toei
Surasak
THANON NARATHIWAS RAJANAKARINDHA
Soi Saint Louis 3
Thanon Yen Akat
Soi Bamphen
Khlong Toei Market

D   E   F

65

BANGKOK TRANSPORTATION MAP

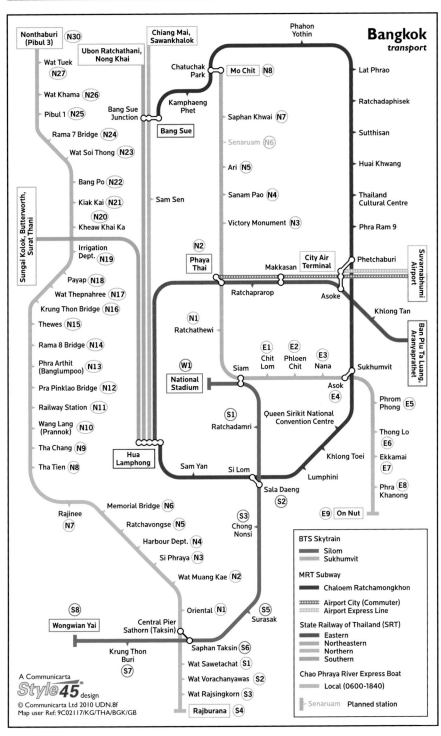

Bangkok
transport

BTS Skytrain
- Silom
- Sukhumvit

MRT Subway
- Chaloem Ratchamongkhon

- Airport City (Commuter)
- Airport Express Line

State Railway of Thailand (SRT)
- Eastern
- Northeastern
- Northern
- Southern

Chao Phraya River Express Boat
- Local (0600-1840)

Senaruam Planned station

A Communicarta
Style45 design
© Communicarta Ltd 2010 UDN.8f
Map user Ref: 9C02117/KG/THA/BGK/GB

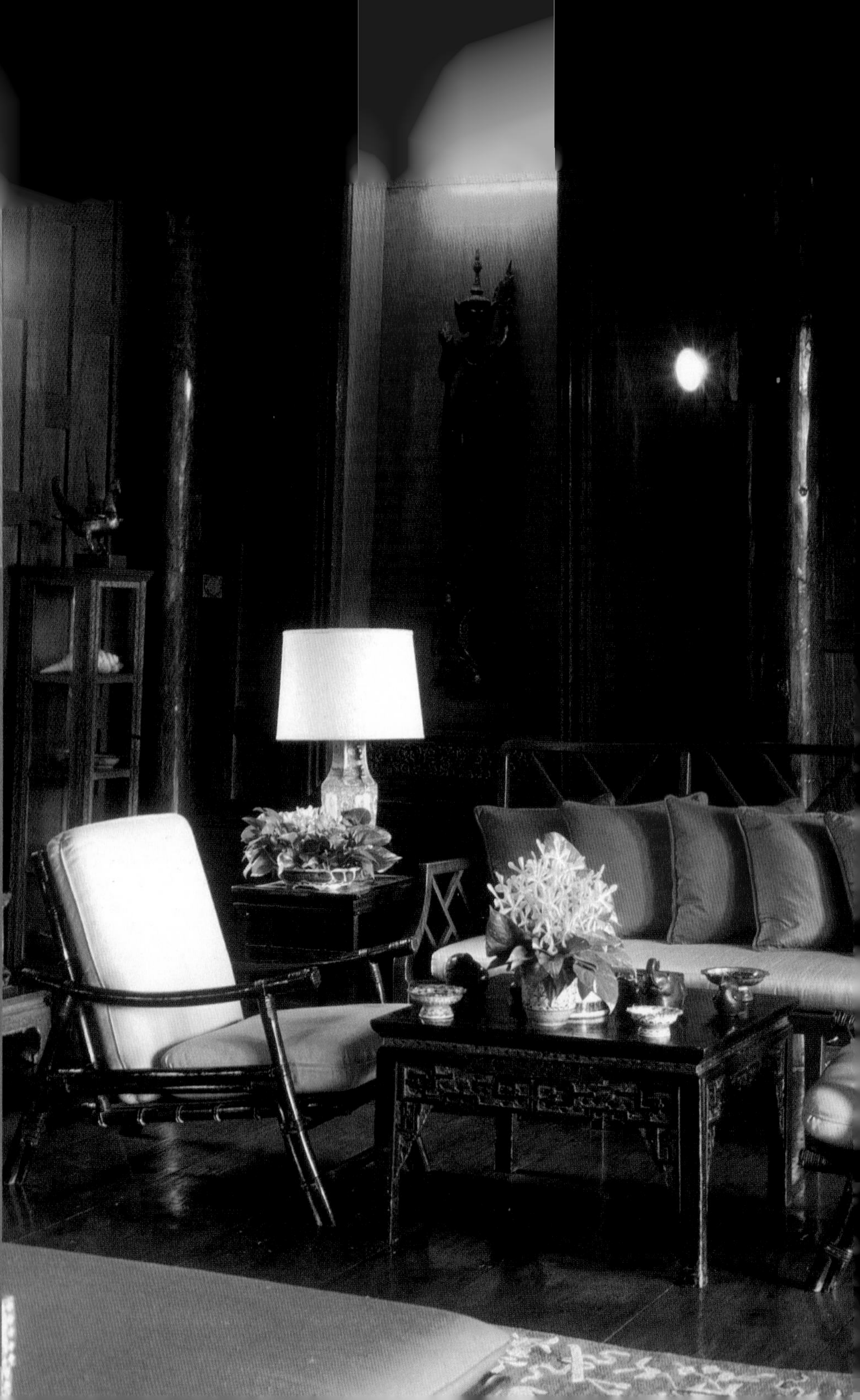

BAAN JIM THOMPSON'S HOUSE

Here you'll find traditional Thai domestic architecture, a collection of fine Thai arts and antiques, a legacy of silk and an extraordinary man responsible for it all. Jim Thompson was an American, born in Delaware in 1906, who first came to Bangkok as an intelligence officer in World War II and returned to live in Thailand after the war. He built his home close to where silk weavers lived, by transporting and reassembling traditional teak houses from the outskirts of the city and filling them with his personal collection of Thai art. In 1947, together with Thai investors, he founded the Thai Silk Company and was largely responsible for introducing Thailand's silk industry to the West and reviving its importance within the country itself. The Jim Thompson brand is now known internationally, with shops throughout Thailand, Malaysia and Singapore and outlets in Germany and the USA.

ELEGANT THAI LIVING

Thompson lived in Thailand for 22 years, although he only spent 8 years in this elegant home. Tucked away at the back of an alley, and in stark contrast to the surrounding modern hotels and residences, inside the entrance, visitors can see an exhibition on Thai textiles above the shop that sells Thai silk. Tours of the house begin in a rice storage barn, brought from Ayutthaya and filled by Thompson with superb Thai paintings, and continue past a precious headless Buddha statue from the seventh century. In the main house, where Thompson lived in the 1960s, the floors are laid in beautiful marble imported from Italy, but nearly everything else you see in the house—exquisite porcelain, 17th- to 19th-century cotton paintings, a 13th-century sandstone Buddha, and furniture—was bought or acquired by Thompson in Thailand. Look out for the rare eighth-century limestone statue of Buddha in his study.

Jim Thompson disappeared in mysterious circumstances in 1967 after setting off for a walk while on holiday in Malaysia. His body was never found, and various conspiracy theories have emerged as a result.

INFORMATION

www.jimthompson.com
⊞ 65 D3 ⊠ Soi Kasem San 2, Thanon Rama I ☎ 022 167 368 ⊕ Daily 9–5 ✋ Adult B100, under 25 B50
◪ National Stadium (Exit 1)
⛴ Hua Chang canal boat pier
◪ 30-min tours (up to 13 people) every 20–30 min ⭤ Cafe, bar and restaurant
⊞ 64 C5 (tourist boats departure point)
⛴ Chao Phraya Tourist Boats depart every 30 min 9.30–3 ☎ 022 253 002
✋ B75 (including guidebook)

TIPS

>> Be aware that touts linger outside and occasionally dupe people by claiming that the house is shut and offering to take you on a shopping tour instead.
>> Photography is not allowed inside the house, but is permitted outside, around the tropical gardens, silk shop, restaurant and fishponds.

Opposite and above *Jim Thompson's beautiful house is a gracious museum to Thai textiles*

BANGLAMPHU
(KHAO SAN ROAD)
www.khaosanroad.com

Backpackers have traditionally headed for Khao San Road in the Banglamphu District, because it has the highest concentration of budget accommodations in the city. This remains the case, although the area's evolving identity is reflected in the development of mid-range hotels in the heart of what was once solely a backpackers' ghetto. The area deserves a visit, and the idea of staying here for a couple of nights should not be dismissed, because of its self-conscious image as the gathering place for voyagers in search of the Asian experience. There is a multitude of travel shops, internet access points, stands shifting bootleg CDs and DVDs and stores selling hip clothing. The easiest way to experience the neighborhood is by the Chao Phraya River Express boat to Tha Phra Athit, and then walking to Khao San Road. This is the nucleus of Banglamphu, and at night it has a high-pulse atmosphere fueled by bars and restaurants. Tha Phra Athit, the road outside the boat pier, is more genial because it is close to Thammasat University and attracts students to its funky bars and restaurants.

🕂 64 B2 🔝 Bangkok Information Office, Thanon Phra Athit, under Pinklao Bridge (turn right on Thanon Phra Athit after exiting from boat pier); daily 9–7 🚤 Tha Phra Athit pier G3, on the boat pier side of Thanon Phra Athit (for the Northern Bus Terminal); 53, on the south side of Thanon Phra Athit (for the Grand Palace); 15, 30, 47, 79, on Thanon Ratchadamnoen Klang (for Siam Square)

CHAO PHRAYA RIVERFRONT
Sometimes it is easy to forget that Bangkok was built around a river and that the Chao Phraya River is still a main artery that bisects the metropolis. The amphibious origins of the city are best appreciated by taking a boat trip on a Chao Phraya River Express boat. You will see how shops and houses were built on the banks of the river and you will still spot people's homes with boats

moored alongside or hooked up by what are now their rear entrances. The famous Oriental (▷ 112), the only hotel with a boat pier named after it, was built to receive its guests from the river, and every day thousands of Bangkok residents use cross-river ferries to make their way to and from Thonburi on the west side. Beyond Banglamphu, the riverfront has its own commercial life, and barges carrying produce are constantly on the move.

Chao Phraya Tourist Boats depart from Sathorn pier, next to the Skytrain Saphan Taksin station, for a tour up the river as far as Banglamphu, stopping at 10 of the piers. There is on-board commentary. The ticket allows unlimited trips for the day so you can hop on and off and also use their regular boats (▷ 94–95) for an extended tour of the river.

🕂 64 C5 (tourist boats departure point) 🚤 Chao Phraya Tourist Boats depart every 30 min 9.30–4 ☎ 022 253 002 ✋ One-day pass B150 (including guidebook)

CHATUCHAK MARKET
Situated next to the Northern Bus Terminal, Chatuchak is the weekend home to Bangkok's largest market and a visitor attraction in its own right because of the sheer size of the place and the exuberant diversity of its many thousands of stands. It is spread out over 30 acres (12ha). Maps of the market are posted up at various points throughout the area, and they can also be picked up at the market's information office. There is a systematic and thematic arrangement of the market stands, but if you are arriving here with other people, be sure to identify a meeting point at an early stage and keep your bearings in mind as you head off into the market. There is plenty to consider buying—facilitated by ATM machines near the information office—especially in the way of art and craft items from every corner of Thailand, plus other souvenirs, and clothing and textiles. Some of the best buys include antique lacquerware, traditional

musical instruments, silver jewelry and ceramics. Money-conscious Bangkok residents come here for household goods, clothes, plants and pets (including illegal trade in protected species). Fatigue can kick in prematurely at Chatuchak, but there are quite a few places to rest and have a meal, many of which are aimed at visitors rather than Thais.

🕂 Off map 65 F1 🖂 Corner of Thanon Kamphaeng Phet and Thanon Phahon Yothin 🕐 Sat–Sun 9–6 (crowds build up from around 11am onward) 🔝 Thanon Kamphaeng Phet 2, inside Gate 1 (closer to the metro station than the Skytrain one) ☎ 022 724 440 🕐 Sat–Sun 8.30–4.30 🚇 Mo Chit 🚇 Chatuchak Park

CHINATOWN
▷ 71.

DEMOCRACY MONUMENT
This monument was constructed in 1939–40 to commemorate the establishment of the constitutional monarchy, its ideological foundations being the 1932 revolution. This is signified by the 75 cannons buried around it, referring to the Buddhist year 2475 (which is AD1932). The political symbolism of the monument helped make it a gathering point on October 14, 1973, when hundreds of thousands protested against the undemocratic government then ruling the country. Many hundreds were killed by the police and army on that day, and in 1992 there were further killings when protests against another set of military rulers were suppressed. Democracy Monument is a 10-minute walk from Thanon Khao San in Banglamphu (▷ above), 5 minutes from Wat Saket (▷ 91) or 15 minutes from the National Museum (▷ 77–79). It is also close to a canal pier (▷ Khlongs, 74), Tha Phanfa, from where boats plow their way to and from the Tha Asoke pier at the top of Soi 21 off Thanon Sukhumvit.

🕂 64 B3 🖂 Thanon Ratchadamnoen Klang 🚤 Tha Phra Athit pier, then walk, via Banglamphu (▷ above) 🚌 15, 30, 47, 79 on Thanon Ratchadamnoen Klang travel to/from Siam Square and the Skytrain station

CHINATOWN

Chinatown is congested, noisy and smelly but a sensory and cultural experience. A guided walk (▷ 92) minimizes the chances of losing your bearings amid the warren of small streets and narrow, mostly pedestrianized alleyways. Bangkok's Chinese community used to live in Ratanakosin, but in the late 18th century, when King Rama I decided to move his capital to the eastern side of the river and build his palace in Ratanakosin to escape Burmese incursions, the people who were already living there were forced to move downriver. They settled down anew and created their Chinatown situated between Thanon Charoen Krung and the river and bordered by what is now Hua Lamphong railway station to the east and the Indian neighborhood of Pahurat (▷ 75) to the west.

SHOPPING FOR THE AFTERLIFE

First impressions of Chinatown suggest a consumer's nightmare, a chaotic and confusing jumble of shops and stands thrown together in a crazy fit, but despite this there is method to the madness. Merchandise is concentrated in different areas according to type. Thanon Yaowarat is full of gold dealers selling jewelry items strictly by weight and with the day's fixed price on show; Thanon Ractchawong is the place to go if you want to purchase household goods; while Sampeng Lane has fabric stalls at its eastern end, followed by hair and beauty items, and then clothes. The near-claustrophobic Soi 16 is crammed full of stalls displaying strange-looking seafood and vegetables, dried fish and freshly butchered chickens and ducks.

Chinatown is very much about buying and selling, and the materialistic considerations extend to the afterlife. In the vicinity of Wat Mangkon Kamalawat (▷ 85) there is a multitude of shops selling incense sticks and votive offerings for the temple. The paper replicas of consumer goods, cars, planes, mobile phones and banknotes that you see on sale here are purchased for burning at Chinese funerals as a way of ensuring that the dead have everything they might need in the next world. There is also a landmark Buddhist temple in Chinatown: Wat Traimit.

INFORMATION

✚ 64 C4 ✉ Streets and lanes around Thanon Ractchawong, Thanon Yaowarat and Thanon Charoen Krung ⊗ Best time to visit is 8–5; Sat pm is especially hectic 🚊 Hua Lamphong

Below *You can buy everything from dried fish to funeral offerings at the busy market in Chinatown*

REGIONS • BANGKOK • SIGHTS

INFORMATION

64 C2 ✉ Thanon Sri Ayutthaya, Thanon Ratchasima and Thanon Ratchawithi 🍴 Food center 🛥 Tha Thewet pier 🚇 Phaya Thai, then take a taxi 🚌 10, 12, 18, 28, 56, 70, 72, 108, 510, 515

TIP

>> A useful free map of Dusit, dispensed by the information office, will guide you around the complex of buildings and exhibition halls that make up Dusit. Vimanmek Palace and the Abhisek Dusit Throne Hall are the major sights, but there are other exhibitions and places of interest.

Above *Suan Bua Residential Hall built by King Chulalongkorn (Rama V) for Princess Saisavali Bhiromya*

INTRODUCTION

Dusit Park, in the northeast of the city, has royal associations that give the area's grand buildings an air of studied elegance. A statue of Rama V, the king whose interest in European culture shaped Dusit, and its distinctive identity, stands in the Royal Plaza on Thanon Sri Ayutthaya, across from Dusit Park. The statue is worshiped and presented with offerings, particularly on Chulalongkorn Day (October 23). Across the street, royal guards march around Suan Amporn on December 2 for the magnificent annual Trooping the Color ceremony. It is possible to enter Dusit from Thanon Sri Ayutthaya, but there are also entrances on Thanon Ratchasima and on Thanon Ratchawithi. Whichever way you enter Dusit, follow the signs for Vimanmek Palace and the nearby information office.

WHAT TO SEE

VIMANMEK PALACE

Graceful and airy, this well-crafted house was designed on a grand scale, amid landscaped gardens, and conveys a calm and cultured feel that would have pleased its royal patron. Vimanmek Palace lies in the Dusit Park area of the city, away to the north of the Grand Palace quarter of Ratanakosin, and the European tone of the district seems quite in fitting with the character of this teakwood mansion. It was erected here in 1901 by Rama V, who visited Europe on two occasions and employed a large retinue of foreign advisers to further his ambitious plans to modernize the country and add some sophistication to Siam's image in the world. Vimanmek Palace was first built on Ko Si Chang as part of a royal resort, but was dismantled and rebuilt in Dusit, where it blends in very nicely with the manicured lawns and lotus ponds. It became a favorite getaway for Rama V, who lived here for extended periods of time with a large entourage of officials, concubines and officials until 1906, and royals continued to use the palace until 1935. It was restored and opened as a museum in 1982 as part of Bangkok's bicentennial celebrations.

Despite aspects of the exterior and interior that are reminiscent of Victorian architecture, tried and tested Thai methods were used in its construction. The three stories are built of teak, naturally resistant to tropical heat, and the task of rebuilding was made easier by the fact that nails weren't used in its original construction. The Vimanmek Palace is now considered to be the largest teak building in the world. There are more than 80 rooms and the guided tour takes you through 30 of them. Ironically, while the American Jim Thompson (▷ 69) wanted to furnish his Bangkok house with Thai arts and crafts, Rama V, king of Thailand, was keen to add items of European provenance to his collection. The private apartments have been carefully restored to show some of the modern inventions brought to the country by the King. There are also a number of early Ratanakosin antiques on display.

ABHISEK DUSIT THRONE HALL

The building of a throne hall for King Rama V was completed in 1904, on a site that is now part of the grounds of Vimanmek Palace, in an architecturally playful style that continues to please the eye. Its interior has been converted into a small exhibition of arts and crafts produced in rural communities under the patronage of the Queen Sirikit's Promotion of Supplementary Occupations & Related Techniques (SUPPORT) Foundation. Displays include fine examples of neilloware (an ancient type of metalwork with silver or gold patterns on a black background), handmade gold- and silverware, silk textiles from different regions, bamboo and lipao fern basketry, soapstone carvings of animals and people, and unusual wood carvings.

THE ROYAL CARRIAGE EXHIBITION

Close to the Thanon Ratchawithi entrance, the Royal Carriage Exhibition displays more than 20 carriages used by royalty over the last century. The earliest ones date from the time of Rama V and include the state coach used for the opening of parliamentary sessions. Many of the carriages are English in origin and the landaus and phaetons you see here look like scenery props from a Jane Austen film set. Quite different in character are the golden palanquins, with their ornate roofs. The other exhibition halls are of less interest. The Royal Paraphernalia Building houses an exhibition of portraits of various royals and items used by them, including a three-tiered umbrella, sedan chairs and a portable throne.

➕ 64 C2 🕐 Daily 9–5 ✋ Free

DUSIT ZOO

www.zoothailand.org

The entrance to Dusit Zoo is on Thanon Ratchawithi, and children in particular will enjoy seeing the wide range of animals that live here, which includes more than 300 mammals, 800 birds and 200 reptiles. As well as elephants, orangutans, rhinoceros, gaur and other large mammals, there are other rare species endemic to Thailand and those not usually seen in zoos. The area is well shaded and there is a lake with pedalos for rent, as well as numerous places to eat and drink. The night zoo, open on Friday and Sunday evenings, provides a rare opportunity to observe the habits of nocturnal animals not usually seen by the public. On weekends the zoo can be busy and noisy with Thai families, who come here for a stroll and a meal at the food stands.

➕ 64 C2 ☎ 022 819 027/8 🕐 Mon–Thu, Sat 8–6; Fri, Sun 8am–9pm ✋ Adult B100, child B50

MORE TO SEE

AROUND THE PARK

Several other sites of interest are located within the park. The royal cloth collection is displayed at the Ancient Cloth Museum. The Royal Elephant Museum is held in two stables near the U-Thong Nai entrance that once housed three white elephants. One stable contains a photographic exhibition illustrating the importance of white elephants in Thai history, while the other contains a shrine to the remaining white elephant, which lives in the private residence of the King. These elephants owe their lack of pigment to naturally occurring albinism, and are considered property of the Crown.

INFORMATION

www.vimanmek.com

➕ 64 C2 ✉ Thanon Ratchawithi

☎ 026 286 300 ext. 5120–5121

🕐 Daily 9.30–4 ✋ Adult B100, child B50, or free with Grand Palace ticket (valid for one month) ℹ Free guided tours are obligatory and take place every half-hour (first tour at 9.45, last at 3.15)

❓ Grand Palace dress code applies (▷ 87)

TIPS

➤➤ Time your visit to take in the traditional Thai dance show that takes place at 10.30am and 2pm each day.

➤➤ Don't miss Wat Benchamabophit, also known as "The Marble Temple," close to the U-Thong Nai gate. The temple is a typical synthesis of Rama V's European tastes and Thai upbringing. King Rama V's ashes are watched over by a revered Phra Buddha Chinnarat image of Phitsanulok in a small room inside. Between 6 and 7.30am, the monks of the temple line up on Thanon Nakhon Pathom to receive rice and a variety of other offerings from merit makers.

KHLONGS

When Rama I planned the Grand Palace in his new capital, Bangkok, he chose a site by the river for defensive reasons and constructed a series of canals that would further protect his residence. As the city grew, the river and an increasing number of canals were the main means of travel and transporting goods and it was only over many years that roads and streets were laid out. For many Bangkok residents, canals (khlongs) are still an important means of getting around the city—some mail deliveries are still made using canal networks and for the visitor they provide eye-opening views. Instead of the facades presented by shops, businesses and hotels, you will see the homes of ordinary citizens, and gain some insight into what lies behind the glitzy exterior that Bangkok presents.

Tours of the canals of Thonburi on the west side of the river are organized by a number of tour companies, but for many of them the canals are only part of the trip: you may find yourself spending time at a less-than-arresting snake farm and a visitor-oriented floating market.

Other canal tours include trips to Wat Arun (▷ 84) and the Royal Barges Museum (▷ 80). Alternatively, a longtail boat with a driver can be rented from many of the piers on the Bangkok side of the river for about B500 (after some bargaining). You can cruise the canals for an hour and get a better idea of why Bangkok, its houses built on rafts and moored on the water, was once called the Venice of the East.

On the Bangkok side of the river, longboats ply their way along a lengthy canal that helpfully connects the west and east sides of the city, from Tha Phanfa near Democracy Monument to a series of piers at the top ends of different sois that connect with Thanon Sukhumvit. Useful stops along the way include Hua Chang for Bann Jim Thompson's House (▷ 69) and a Skytrain station. The canal piers are not always clearly marked, especially if you are on board and plonked in the middle of the seat row, so bring a map with you and some loose change for the fare. You will feel like an intrepid explorer and, if you find yourself sitting at the end of a row, be prepared for a slight splashing when the boat gathers speed, even if the plastic wraps are unfolded to shield passengers from getting wet.

🚤 Canal tours; contact Real Asia (www.realasia.net) or Bangkok.com (www.bangkok.com/tours)

KO KRET

A visit to Ko Kret (also called Koh Kred) can make a welcome change from central Bangkok. With an area of only 4sq miles (10sq km), this island provides a haven for an more laidback and peaceful way of life. One of its main attractions is the opportunity to see Mon potters at work. Mon people, whose origins are Burmese, have been here for centuries, and pottery is their specialty. Allow yourself two hours for a walk around the island, observing the potters at work and looking at the completed pots and jars exhibited in the Ancient Mon Pottery Center. There are no cars on the island, and although motorcycle taxis are available, it is much more relaxing just to wander along the tracks at your own pace. The least troublesome way of reaching Ko Kret is by joining the Chao Phraya River Express cruise on a 40-seat boat from Sathorn Pier in downtown Bangkok on Sundays. This tour includes a visit to a Mon temple, Wat Poramaiyikawas to see the superb murals, a lunch break near Baan Kanom, where sweet-making is observed, and a short canal ride, which takes you to a small floating market. The alternative to the Sunday cruise is to take any Chao Phraya River Express boat to Nonthaburi and then charter a longtail boat to the island, but this will be expensive unless you can make up a group to share the cost.

✚ Off map at 64 C1 🚤 90-min cruise from Sathorn Pier at 10am Sun with English-

Above A busy longtail boat on the canal
Opposite Lumphini Park looking toward modern Bangkok

speaking tour guide, returning from Ko Kret at noon ☎ 026 236 143 💵 Adult B300, child (under 39 inches/100cm) B250

LAK MEUANG

Every Thai city has a foundation stone, and Bangkok's was laid down in the form of a pillar by Rama I in 1782 at the precise time of 6.54 on the morning of April 21, pinpointed by the court astrologers as the most auspicious moment for such an important event. The associated shrine is believed to facilitate people's wishes, and this brings worshipers to the spot every day; as with Erawan Shrine (▷ 82), a troupe of dancers is at hand to perform for those who want to express their gratitude for a wish granted. A visit to Lak Meuang could be taken in before or after seeing the nearby Grand Palace (▷ 87–90) or as part of a walkabout in Sanam Luang (▷ 81).

✚ 64 B3 ✉ Corner of Thanon Ratchadamnoen Nai and Thanon Lak Meuang 🕐 Daily 24 hours
🚢 Tha Chang pier

LUMPHINI PARK

A small town in southern Nepal where the Buddha was born gives its name to this large and attractive park in downtown Bangkok. It is a vast expanse of green where the sound of traffic is rarely intrusive, encircled by concrete paths—a tranquil place to seek some respite from urban blues and enjoy some moments of peace and quiet. Rowing boats and pedalos are available for rent on both of the park's two lakes, and youngsters will enjoy feeding breadcrumbs to the resident carp. There is also a children's playground. Lumphini is a relaxing place, dotted with picnic tables, pavilions and shaded areas so that even in the heat of the day you will see Bangkok residents whiling away some time here. As the sun begins to go down, and very early in the morning also, small battalions of both sexes take up their positions for sessions of t'ai chi. Joggers of all ages pound their way around a running track and there is an open-air gym and a public swimming pool.

Between early February and the end of April, kite-flying is a popular activity in the park. The statue in the southwest corner of the park near the main entrance is of Rama VI, the king who owned the parkland before he donated it to the city in 1925.
➕ 65 E4 ✉ Thanon Rama IV ☎ 022 527 006 🕐 Daily 5am–8pm 🎟 Free 🚇 Sala Daeng 🚇 Si Lom or Lumphini 🚌 2, 4, 5, 7, 13, 15, 47, 505 🍴 A food court within the park opens in the evening ❓ Boat and pedalo rental B30 per half-hour

NANA ENTERTAINMENT PLAZA

Along with Patpong (▷ 76) and a small area known as Soi Cowboy on Thanon Sukhumvit, between *sois* 21 and 23, the Nana Entertainment Plaza completes an unholy trio of street locations dedicated to the darker side of Bangkok nightlife. Patpong can at least offer a bustling night market, but Nana Entertainment Plaza and Soi Cowboy have no such redeeming feature. Nana Entertainment Plaza is an open-air, neon-lit amphitheater off Soi 4 with three levels of sleazy bars fronted by bored-looking young women whose job is to cajole passing males to step inside, buy an expensive beer and stare at girls dancing perfunctorily. Soi Cowboy consists of one street packed with about 40 bars, indistinguishable from those in Soi 4. It is named after an American, T. G. Edwards, who ran the first bar here in the early 1970s after he left the army. The women working in the bars in Soi Cowboy and the Nana Entertainment Plaza are mostly prostitutes who come mainly from the poverty-stricken northeast of Thailand.
➕ 65 F4 ✉ Soi 4, Thanon Sukhumvit 🚇 Phloen Chit or Nana

PAHURAT

The west side of Chinatown comes to an end at Khlong Ong Ang, and on the other side of the canal lies the fascinating Indian quarter of Pahurat, separating the old city of Ratanakosin from Chinatown. An urban ramble in Pahurat is not as rewarding as a stroll through the streets of Chinatown, but it does have a distinct ethnic identity and a visit here could be enjoyably combined with a meal at one of the Indian restaurants. There are many shops retailing fabrics and clothes, an above-average number of shops selling guns, and along Thanon Pahurat the Old Siam Plaza department store is worth browsing.
➕ 64 B4 ✉ Thanon Chakrawat and Thanon Pahurat ⛴ Tha Saphan Phut pier 🚌 25, 40 (to/from Thanon Sukhumvit and Siam Square) ❓ Grand Palace dress code applies (▷ 87)

PATPONG

Patpong 1 and 2, two small streets that run off Thanon Silom, gave their name to a notorious red-light area of Bangkok that began attracting such a multitude of visitors, many of them curious peeping toms, that clever street traders moved in and turned Patpong 1 into a thriving night market (▷ 98) for fake designer watches, branded clothes, designer bags and similar sought-after items.

By day, Patpong is a rather desultory place of no interest, but every night it bustles with human traffic. The go-go bars are still there, a legacy of the Vietnam War, when off-duty American servicemen used Bangkok as a recreation center, and some very sleazy joints operate in the vicinity. Nowadays, many people come to Patpong to shop, but as street markets go the place is overrated as there are no bargains to be had and time-consuming bargaining is necessary before reasonable prices come into play.

Having said that, Patpong is unlikely to lose its popularity and you may well find yourself coming here just to experience its atmosphere and see what all the hype is about.
✚ 65 D4 ✉ Patpong 1 and Patpong 2 🚇 Sala Daeng 🚇 Si Lom

PIPITAPHAN

▷ 77–79.

QUEEN SAOVABHA MEMORIAL INSTITUTE (SNAKE FARM)

Though popularly known as the Snake Farm, its official title is a reminder that this is a professional herpetological institute. It was founded in the 1920s as the Pasteur Institute, and the Thai Red Cross now runs the place. It came up with the idea of attracting public interest in snakes by organizing shows around the milking of snakes. The sessions begin with a slide show presenting practical information about how to deal with snake bites, followed by a live demonstration involving some highly venomous creatures. The venom that is milked from the snakes is used in the production of serum. Children love the Snake Farm, but arrive early to be at the front of the audience.
✚ 65 D4 ✉ Corner of Thanon Rama IV and Thanon Henri Dunant ☎ 022 520 161 🕐 Mon–Fri 9.30–3.30, Sat–Sun 9.30–1; milking: daily 11; snake-handling: Mon–Fri 2.30 👆 Adult B200, child B50 🚇 Sala Daeng 🚇 Sam Yan

ROYAL BARGES MUSEUM

▷ 80.

ROYAL ELEPHANT MUSEUM

Alongside Vimanmek Palace, the two stables that once provided a home for the royal white elephants now make up a museum devoted to the role of elephants in Thailand's history and society. There are displays of elephant equipment and information on the contribution elephants have made to the country's economy and folklore. The importance of white elephants is explained: the animals are albinos (more brown than white) whose rarity made them sacred and, de facto, the personal property of the king. When a white elephant was spotted in the wild, and its authenticity accredited by a team of experts, an elaborate ceremony accompanied its presentation to the king prior to it being received into the royal stables. Photographs of the elephants are on display, but the one white elephant, still housed in Dusit, is not shown to the public.
✚ 64 C2 ✉ Thanon Ratchawithi ☎ 022 823 336 🕐 Daily 9–4 👆 Price included in the entry to Vimanmek Palace (▷ 72–73) 🚤 Tha Thewet pier 🚇 Phaya Thai, then a taxi 🚌 10, 56, 70, 72, 510 ❓ Grand Palace dress code applies (▷ 87)

Below *The busy market in Patpong*

PIPITAPHAN

INTRODUCTION

The National Museum (Pipitaphan) is the country's foremost museum and is full of treasures from prehistoric times onward. Rock art, funeral chariots and rare Buddha images are only some of the museum's many rich and fascinating exhibits. Wang Na, now the central palace buildings, was built in 1792 as a palace for the person officially designated as the heir to the throne. King Rama V abolished this position of the "Second King" in 1887 and used the palace to house the collection of antiquities his father, Rama IV, had built up and left to him. Rama V had already established a museum of sorts here in 1874 when he first made these antiquities open to the public, keeping them in a pavilion inside the Grand Palace.

An easy way to reach the museum from the boat pier is by walking straight ahead after disembarking, crossing the first intersection and turning left at the next intersection on to the signposted Thanon Na Phrathat. The museum is along this road on your left. A map of the galleries is issued with your ticket and, although it is not cross-referenced with the room numbers, it is not difficult to find your way about the various exhibitions. Just by the ticket office, the Gallery of Thai History provides an overview of the historical periods that are represented by the exhibits; this makes a useful start point.

WHAT TO SEE

THE NORTHERN WING

The first room at the entrance side of the museum houses ornate funeral chariots that make the average European royal funeral carriage seem tame by comparison. The most resplendent one was built in 1799, first used for the funeral of a princess in 1923 and last wheeled out in 1985 for the queen

INFORMATION

www.thailandmuseum.com
✚ 64 B3 ✉ Thanon Na Phrathat
☎ 022 241 333 ◷ Wed–Sun 9–3.30
🖐 B200 ⛴ Tha Chang pier 🚍 3, 6, 9, 15, 19, 30, 32, 33, 43, 53, 59, 64, 65, 70, 80, 84 ☛ English, German, Japanese, French, Wed and Thu 9.30 🍽 Café, and an ice-cream parlor by the ticket office
📖 Good selection of books on sale, covering most aspects of Thai art

Above *The beautiful and ornate exterior of Pipitaphan, the National Museum*

of King Rama VII. On the upper floor of the next gallery, in rooms 8 to 10, Sukhothai (13th to 15th centuries) and Ayutthaya (14th to 18th centuries) art is displayed. The walking Buddha, an innovation of Sukhothai art with no known precedent, is represented by an unusual example in room 8; it looks fine from the front but viewed from the side lacks the graceful curves of Sukhothai art.

The museum's cafe is next door and serves simple but adequate lunchtime meals and drinks, but is often a more relaxing option than trying to find something to eat in the hectic food scene between the pier and the museum.

THE SOUTHERN WING

The Asian Art gallery goes beyond Thailand's borders for gems of Asian art with absorbing examples from early Indian culture, including a Buddha that reveals the influence of Alexander the Great and his Greek army in the northwest of India. Here too is an exquisite standing Buddha, with the thumb and first finger of the right hand touching in the Vitarkamudra manner to represent the spinning of the Wheel of Law.

Upstairs, the Dvaravati Art gallery covers the Thai Mons kingdom of the sixth to 11th centuries, influenced in its sensuality by Indian art, with some very ancient Buddha images. The centerpiece here is a Wheel of Law. The adjoining Gallery of Prehistory has a terrific example of prehistoric rock art.

BUDDHAISAWAN CHAPEL

Housed between the northern and southern wings, the central galleries begin at the museum's entrance and end with the Buddhaisawan Chapel, home to the revered Phra Sihing Buddha. There is a legend about its magical arrival from Ceylon, but experts regard it as a Ceylonese-influenced example of early Sukhothai art. There are also two other images in Thailand that claim to be the original miraculous one. What cannot be disputed is the outstanding quality of the 200-year-old murals that surround the chapel, depicting moments in the life of the Buddha.

CENTRAL PALACE BUILDINGS

The maze of galleries in the central palace buildings has a large collection of artistic and ethnographic items where visitors will discover their own favorites. The Transportation Gallery is enlivened by a selection of elephant seats and an impressive royal palanquin that took 56 men to carry one passenger. Room 11, Old Weapons, contains an awesome model of an elephant equipped for war.

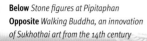
Below *Stone figures at Pipitaphan*
Opposite *Walking Buddha, an innovation of Sukhothai art from the 14th century*

INFORMATION

64 A2 Khlong Bangkok Noi
024 240 004 Daily 9–5 B100
Tha Phra Pinklao pier, or a cross-ferry
boat from Tha Phra Athit pier to Tha
Phra Pinkalo; either way, walk up the
road from the boat pier and take the first
left, signposted Soi Wat Duistaram, and
follow the signs to the museum
3, 7, 9, 11, 503, 507, 509, 511
B100 charge for taking photos and
B200 for using video cameras

ROYAL BARGES MUSEUM

Take a trip across the Chao Phraya River to view a visually stunning collection
of barges. Elaborately carved and exquisitely decorated, these are the Rolls
Royces of the marine world and unbelievably beautiful. When Thai kings made
a journey along the Chao Phraya River, they impressed and dazzled their
subjects by traveling in these specially crafted and brightly decorated barges.
They plowed through the water in as stately a manner as the rhythmic rowing
of up to 50 oarsmen could make possible.

Royal processions occurred annually until the late 1960s, when they became
reserved for special occasions only, such as the 60th anniversary of the King's
coronation in 2006. Just seeing them in their dignified boatyard will give you a
good idea of how spectacular a show these gilded vessels must make when
decked out with uniformed crews and carrying a band of choral singers.

The design of the barges is based on representations of those used when
Ayutthaya was the capital of Thailand; they were first built for Rama I (1782–
1809), and then restored and partly rebuilt by Rama VI in the early part
of the 20th century.

THE *SUPHANNAHONGSA*

The signature barge, extravagantly and elegantly decorated, is the
Suphannahongsa, first winched out in 1911 after being carved from one piece
of teakwood. It is nearly 164ft (50m) in length and the golden canopy makes
it obvious where the king and queen had their seats. The gleaming prow
is ornately decorated and ends in the shape of a mythical bird-like creature
associated with Brahma, the Hindu god. The prow on the *Anantainagaraj*, the
barge that comes closest in size and magnificence to the *Suphannahongsa*, is
equally distinctive, with its traditional multi-headed serpent, the *naga*. A new
royal barge was built for the king's golden jubilee celebrations in 1996 and is
also in the museum.

SEEING THE ROYAL BARGES MUSEUM

Many of the city's canal tours (▷ 70) include a visit to the Royal Barges
Museum, but it is easy to get there by yourself from the Bangkok side of the
river by boat. Taking a bus is also straightforward because you hop off at the
first stop over the Pinklao Bridge.

Above *The magnificent Royal Barge
Suphannahongsa would have been
rowed by up to 50 oarsmen*

SANAM LUANG

A large green area was created close to the Grand Palace for the purpose of conducting royal cremation ceremonies. This is still the case—the last such occasion was in 1996 for the mother of the present king—and the green is also used for the annual Plowing Ceremony in May. The actual day of the Plowing Ceremony, determined by astrologers for its auspiciousness for farmers to set about a new rice season, attracts large crowds that come to watch the symbolic plowing by a team of oxen and the sprinkling of blessed rice.

From late-February through to the end of April, kite-flying is popular here, and kites can be bought locally from vendors. The rest of the year Sanam Luang is a rather unattractive lot used mainly by locals for parking and selling street food. Unfortunately, it is also popular with con artists who untruthfully warn passing tourists that the surrounding sites are closed for the Buddhist holidays, and then try to divert them to visit gem and tailor shops. It is a good idea to ignore anyone who approaches you here and attempts to offer advice or tour services.

✚ 64 B3 ✉ Thanon Ratchadamoen Nai 🕐 Daily 7am–8pm 🚢 Tha Phra pier 🚆 Phaya Thai, then a taxi 🚌 3, 6, 7, 8, 9, 12, 25, 30, 32, 47, 53

SIAM SQUARE

▷ 82.

SUAN PAKKAD PALACE

▷ 83.

THANON SILOM

Running from near the Chao Phraya River to its junction with Thanon Rama IV and Lumphini Park (▷ 75), Silom Road (Thanon Silom), along with the *sois* running off it, is a hive of activity day and night. The lower end has a number of airline offices, mid-range places to stay, shops and restaurants, including the Silom Village Trade Center (▷ 99), and the area between the river and the Skytrain at Chong Nonsi makes for a nice place for a stroll.

At a midway point along this pleasant stretch of the road, on your left, if walking down from Chong Nonsi, is the Sri Mariamman Hindu temple. The exterior, with its vibrant display of Hindu deities, makes it hard to miss. There is also usually a stall outside selling garlands for devotees who come here to worship, especially around midday.

The *sois* at the other end of Silom Road are home to Patpong (▷ 76) and a busy commercial and entertainment district where a number of top-notch hotels boast their own shopping arcades. Here, too, is the Silom Complex department store, as well as others in the immediate vicinity (Central Department Store, Robinson Department Store and Thaniya Plaza). The *sois* numbered 2 to 8 connect this end of Silom Road with Thanon Surawong; they are packed with nightspots that range from the seedy to the salubrious and offer plenty of choice for those in search of a night out on the town.

✚ 65 D5 ✉ Thanon Silom 🚢 Tha Sathon pier 🚆 Saphan Taksin (for the Chao Phraya River Express); Chong Nonsi (the middle of Silom Road); Sala Daeng (top end of Silom Road) 🚇 Si Lom (top end of Silom Road)

Below *Kite-flying in Sanam Luang Park*

INFORMATION

www.siam-square.com

🕂 65 D3 ✉ Thanon Rama I 🚇 Siam
🚌 15, 47, 79 (for Banglamphu); 25 (for
Eastern Bus Terminal and Chinatown);
29 (Victory Monument); 8, 508 (for Grand
Palace, Sukhumvit)

SIAM SQUARE

Siam Square itself is an unremarkable *sois* lined with shops and haunted by touts waiting to divert tourists to disreputable gem shops, out-of-the-way travel agents and over-priced tailors. The surrounding mega-malls, however, form one of Southeast Asia's most renowned shopping districts. The shopping centers straddle Thanon Rama I, beginning with the MBK (▷ 98) on the southwest corner of Rama I and Phayathai, then continues to the opposite corner with Siam Discover, Siam Center, Siam Paragon and Central World Plaza (▷ 97).

The MBK (daily 10–10) is the most well-known shopping center in Bangkok, and a good place to find deals on clothes and electronic equipment. There is a large cinema on the top floor. Siam Discovery and Siam Center (daily 10–9) are the smallest in the group. Discovery is topped with a cinema and free Asian pop concerts are held on either side of Siam Center nearly every week. Siam Paragon (daily 10am–2am) is the best place for families with a large bowling alley, opera house, convention center and several IMAX screens, as well as Asia's most exclusive Cineplex all on the top floor. In the basement is Siam Ocean World, an aquarium with penguins and walk-through shark tank.

Siam Square was at the center of the 2010 riots in Bangkok and Central World Plaza, in particular, suffered a lot of damage. At the time of writing (mid-2010) rebuilding the area was well underway and Central World Plaza should be back in business by the end of 2011.

ERAWAN SHRINE

The Erawan Shrine, on the corner of Thanon Rama I and Thanon Ratchadamri, can be seen from the window of a Skytrain passing overhead, but if you are walking you might miss it altogether. Bangkok citizens regularly drop by to make offerings of garlands in the hope that their wishes will be granted. A dance troupe is usually standing by to perform at the paid behest of worshipers. This happens frequently, so you may see them in action. It is a surreal and incongruous sight: a Thai dance to a Hindu god in the shadow of glass edifices and the constant traffic at one of the city's busiest junctions. The shrine was created when a series of accidents accompanying the construction of a nearby hotel was attributed to resident spirits put out by the building work. To placate the spirits, this shrine was built and there were no further mishaps.

Below *People shopping in Siam Square*

SUAN PAKKAD PALACE

The name Suan Pakkad, which translates as "cabbage farm," serves as a reminder of the homely origins of the superb landscaped garden around this royal palace. Today, the traditional Thai houses are filled with fine art and set in a restful garden with an exquisite Lacquer Pavilion. Their Royal Highnesses Prince and Princess Chumbhot of Nagara Svarga, now deceased, had a number of old houses moved here from northern Thailand to serve as their residence in the early 1950s, and they guided the transformation of the original cabbage patch into the garden you see today. They also built up a collection of art and objects, largely dating from the era of H.R.H. Prince Paribatra Sukhumbandhu, son of His Majesty King Chulalongkorn, Rama V and Her Majesty Queen Sukhumala Marasri, and these now make up the content of the houses.

SPEARHEADS, BETEL NUT BOXES AND MURALS

In the modern Chumbhot–Pantip Center of Arts building there are exhibits of pottery, spearheads, axes and other finds from the Bronze Age site of Ban Chiang (▷ 117). Some artifacts date back to neolithic cultures from 3600BC. There are also first-rate examples of Khmer art from the seventh century onward and figures of the Buddha dating from the 14th century. A garden footbridge leads across to two houses where the exhibits include a howdah (a seat that is placed on the back of an elephant or camel), betel nut boxes, musical instruments, and European drawings from the Renaissance period.

THE LACQUER PAVILION

This beautiful pavilion, posed on stilts, dates to the mid-17th century and was originally part of a temple in Ayutthaya. It was reassembled here in 1959 and, more recently, renovated. Inside, the walls are filled with delicate murals of gold and black lacquer narrating the life of the Buddha and depicting scenes from the *Ramayana*. The paneled pictures are worth examining because of the wealth of detail they contain and, in the case of some of the *Ramayana* panels, the glimpses of social life of the period they portray. Look for the depiction of European gentlemen riding horses, reflecting the presence of Western traders and suggesting the work was completed before the fall of Ayutthaya in 1767.

INFORMATION

www.suanpakkad.com
🕂 65 E3 ✉ 352–354 Thanon Sri Ayutthaya ☎ 022 454 934 🕒 Daily 9–4 ✋ B100 🚇 Phaya Thai 🚌 14, 18, 38, 72, 74, 77, 204 🎧 Optional guided tours in English

TIPS

›› Don't miss the remarkable and rare bronze jewelry and ceramics from Ban Chiang.
›› Take a look at the Kao Kung Bayam royal barge, made of teak and white thingan wood, in the grounds of the palace. It was once used in spectacular royal river processions by King Rama V.

Above *The traditional Thai houses in the grounds of Suan Pakkad Palace are filled with beautiful objects and art*

INFORMATION

✚ 64 A4 ✉ Thanon Arun Amarin
☎ 028 911 149 🕐 Daily 9–5
✋ B20 🚢 Tha Thien pier, then a cross-river ferry ❓ River tours (▷ 70) invariably include a visit to Wat Arun

TIP

» Boat tours restrict your time at Wat Arun but the cross-river ferries are frequent and give you more freedom.

WAT ARUN

This towering temple on the cityscape offers views across the river and images from Khmer mythology. It is an architectural marvel and should not to be missed while you are in Bangkok. Wat Arun is in Thonburi, on the west side of the Chao Phraya River, where King Taksin first set up his new capital in 1768. It is also called the Temple of Dawn because this was the time of day when King Taksin selected the spot for a new palace. There was already a temple on the site that dated back to the 17th century, and it was here that Taksin housed the Emerald Buddha until his successor Rama I moved it across to Wat Phra Kaew. Rama II and Rama III rebuilt and enlarged Wat Arun, creating the monumental structure you see today.

PILES OF PORCELAIN

When you first see Wat Arun from the river it is the elongated *prang* (tower) that first strikes you. Rising higher than any other *prang* in the city, its soaring shape has helped make it a familiar logo for Bangkok's Thai identity. The chief *prang* is bordered by four smaller ones and they all glitter and gleam in the sunshine. It is only when you get closer that you realize that the sparkling effect is caused by the light catching countless thousands of pieces of porcelain that have been embedded into the stucco and painstakingly patterned to represent a floral display. The porcelain was provided by local people, pleased to contribute to the building of a shrine, and came in bulk form from merchant ships from China that used discarded porcelain as ballast.

KINARI, YAKSAS AND MONDOPS

The temple design as a whole is a representation of Mount Meru, and includes individual figures of various mythical life forms from Khmer legends. It is not difficult to identify the half-human and half-bird creatures called *kinari* and the devilish-looking *yaksas* (titans).

The four square-shaped structures on the first terrace are *mondops*; they house statues of the Buddha in different postures. On the second terrace are four images of the Hindu god Indra and, in the niches of the smaller *prangs*, statues of Phra Pai, the god of the wind.

Below *The rooftops of Wat Arun*

Left Making offerings at the temple of Wat Mangkon Kamalawat in Chinatown

✚ 64 B3 ✉ Thanon Mahathat ☎ 035 248 000 🕐 Daily 7–8 ⛴ Tha Chang pier 🚌 3, 6, 8, 12, 39, 508, 512

WAT MANGKON KAMALAWAT

This busy temple can be taken in while exploring Chinatown on foot (▷ 92–93), but it justifies a journey on its own merit. Also known as Wat Leng Nee Yee, this is the most popular temple for Bangkok's Chinese, and the place is never empty. Arrive here on a Saturday afternoon and the atmosphere is like a busy beehive, with some devotees departing after making their offerings of incense and flowers and others just arriving to do the same. Although this is a Buddhist temple, some of the deities represented in statues vividly painted in shades of red and yellow are more evocative of a Chinese Taoist temple. So too is the behavior of those devotees, whom you may see kneeling to rattle hollow tubes of bamboo. When chance rolls out a piece of paper, it is studied for what it portends.

As you enter the temple there are four gigantic statues of sagacious-looking bearded men, two on each side of the passageway, looking down on you. Each is holding a different object—a pagoda, the head of a snake, a mandolin and a parasol. Beyond them lies the main chapel, a large, airy space filled with images of large and small Buddhas and, hanging from the ceiling, attractive lanterns that subdue the amount of light and help create a hushed and devotional atmosphere. Again, the mixture of gold and deep reds is redolent of a Chinese place of worship. Sometimes, the main chamber is filled with the sound of group chanting as a choir of Buddhists dressed all in white read from their hymn sheets.

✚ 64 C4 ✉ Thanon Charoen Krung 🕐 Daily 9–6 ⛴ Ratchawongse pier, then walk 🚇 Hua lamphong, then a taxi ride or 25-min walk ❓ Photography is not allowed inside the temple

WAT BENCHAMABOPHIT

Rama V commissioned a close relation, the architect Prince Naris, for the building of this temple, completed in 1911. It is a distinctive structure because of the way it blends innovative design ideas, borrowing elements of European architecture with traditional Thai concepts. The building material is white Carrara marble, hence the "White Marble" epithet it has acquired, and you will also discover stained-glass windows that would not be out of place in an English country church were it not for the Asian mythological scenes they depict. The ashes of Rama V are inside the temple, as is a well-executed copy of the very holy Phra Buddha Chinnarat image in Phitsanulok (▷ 206). In a courtyard at the back of the temple is a large collection of Buddha images from different parts of the country showing the various ways in which the Buddha has been depicted over the ages. For a real-life display of Buddhism in action arrive at Wat Benchamabophit early in the morning, between 6.30 and 7, when monks from the temple line up on Nakorn Pathom (which runs parallel with Thanon Rama V) to receive alms from citizens of the city. It is a sight that not many visitors have ever experienced.

✚ 64 C2 ✉ Thanon Sri Ayutthaya and Thanon Rama V 🕐 Daily 7–5 💷 B20 ⛴ Tha Thewet pier, then walk; or walk from the zoo (▷ 73) or from Vimanmek Palace (▷ 72–73) 🚇 Phaya Thai, then take a taxi 🚌 10, 56, 70, 72, 510

WAT MAHATHAT

www.mcu.ac.th

In an area where the Grand Palace acts like a magnet for purposeful visitors and pilgrims, Wat Mahathat goes about its own business. The temple itself, occupying a cramped space, is fairly undistinguished, but the monastery here dates back to the early 18th century and is older than the city around it. The monks you see around the place belong to a Buddhist university that is attached to Wat Mahathat. Also established here is a respected meditation center that conducts courses in English. Across the road from the main entrance on Thanon Mahathat there is a religious amulet market that is always busy.

INFORMATION

www.watpho.com

✚ 64 B3 ✉ Entrances on Thanon Thai Wang and Soi Chetuphon ☎ 022 219 911 🕐 Daily 8–5 💷 B50; foot massages B220 per hour 🚤 Tha Tien pier, then turn right onto Thanon Maharat and then left for Soi Chetuphon; Thanon Thai Wang is straight on from the pier 🚌 1, 6, 7, 8, 12, 44, 508, 512 🎧 Guides can be hired inside the temple for B200 for two people

TIP

>> If you use the Soi Chetuphon entrance you will avoid the tour groups congregating around the main entrance on Thanon Thai Wang.

WAT PHO

The gilded reclining Buddha in shining gold, with feet decorated with mother-of-pearl is what everyone comes to see in Wat Pho, known also as Wat Phra Chetuphon since Rama I gave it this name at the beginning of the 19th century. The working temple that houses this magnificent statue is far older than this, dating back to well before Bangkok became the capital, and it also functions as a center for the study and teaching of traditional medicine.

Thai massage training courses are conducted and day visitors to the temple can experience for themselves an invigorating massage. There are *chedis* all around the temple grounds but the ones that will catch your eye are the four largest ones, clad in garish ceramic tiles. Two of them contain the remains of Rama III and Rama IV.

THE RECLINING BUDDHA

There are various buildings and *chedis* (monuments housing a Buddhist relic) inside the temple compound, and the chapel with the reclining Buddha is only one of them: Follow the crowds and you cannot miss it. The Buddha is 148ft (45m) in length—behind the gold leaf are plain old bricks and plaster—and because of the size of the chapel it is impossible to stand far enough back to take in the figure as a whole. So what you experience, instead, as you file past, is an intense close-up of a sublimely happy Buddha with inordinately long earlobes about to enter the state of nirvana. The soles of the feet are intricately inlaid with mother-of-pearl depicting the 108 *lakshanas*, the auspicious signs of the Buddha.

THE *BOT*

The *bot*, or *ubosot* (main temple chapel), is on the eastern side and accessed from the outside by the Soi Chetuphon entrance, although you can also get there from the Reclining Buddha inside the temple. It is reached via galleries of nearly 400 assorted Buddha images and entered by teak doors superbly decorated with scenes from the *Ramayana*. The interior, lavishly adorned with pillars and an ebulliently decorated ceiling, holds the remains of Rama I.

Below *The stunning reclining Buddha*

WAT PHRA KAEW AND THE GRAND PALACE

INTRODUCTION

After the fall of Ayutthaya, Rama I decided to move across the Chao Phraya River from the site of the first palace on the west side. He wanted a base that would be more able to withstand an attack, and work began in Ratanakosin constructing the Grand Palace with its own temple. An open field, Sanam Luang, was created in front of the palace as a royal cremation site. The palace is still an official residence for the royals and although their day-to-day home has moved to Dusit, a number of buildings inside the palace remain in use and are closed to the public. On certain occasions, like the ordination or death of a royal, important ceremonial events take place here. The royal temple of Phra Kaew, Thailand's major Buddhist site, and the Grand Palace should not be missed. Highly theatrical in appearance, these buildings are frequented by Thai pilgrims as well as sightseers. The dress code for all visitors signifies the respect and reverence accorded this sacred site.

WHAT TO SEE

ENTERING WAT PHRA KAEW

You will never be alone on your visit: tour groups mill around the entrance and ticket office. There is only one gated entrance to the palace and the driveway leads to the ticket office. The psychedelic tones and the sheer variety of shimmering shapes will overwhelm you at first, but the map that comes with the ticket can help guide your walk. There are separate entrances for Wat Phra Kaew, Dusit Maha Prasat and the museum, but most of your time is likely to be spent looking around the temple. The guided tours are a useful way to glean information about what you see because it can be difficult to make sense of it all amid the bewildering array of stupas, mosaics, glittering roof tiles, fabulous images, statues, pillars and pediments that make up the palace and Wat Phra

INFORMATION

✚ 64 B3 ✉ Thanon Na Phra Lan
☎ 026 235 500 ⏰ Daily 8.30–3.30
💲 B350 for Grand Palace and the buildings open to the public inside, including Wat Phra Kaew 🚌 4 from Siam Square 🚢 Tha Chang pier 🎫 Free English-language tours 10, 10.30, 1.30 and 2.30; 1-hour personal audioguide B200 ❓ Dress code: no T-shirts, sleeveless vests, shorts, short skirts, tight-fitting or see-through clothing; no bare feet. Nearby booth can loan suitable clothing to visitors but a credit card or passport must be left as a security deposit.

Above *The 18th-century Ramayana mural at Wat Phra Kaew tells the epic adventure of Rama and his wife Sita*

Kaew. The temple, Thailand's major Buddhist site, is home to the venerated Emerald Buddha. The *bot* (chapel) that houses the Buddha image is therefore suitably guarded by a series of garishly painted demons. You will be confronted by these devilish-looking figures immediately after entering the temple. There are more statues and structures to contemplate outside the *bot* itself, including a lotus-topped pillar which was a gift to the king by the city's Chinese.

THE EMERALD BUDDHA
The size of the tiny image of the Buddha bears no relation to the enormous reverence in which it is held. Credited with miraculous powers, it was discovered by accident inside a *chedi* (monument housing a Buddhist relic) in the 15th century and then carried off to Laos where it was kept for 200 years. The prince who would become Rama I expropriated it in 1779 and constituted it as the symbolic and religious heart of his new capital and the nation.

UPPER TERRACE
On the upper terrace there stands the glamorous Prasat Phra Thep Bidorn. It is known as the Royal Panetheon because inside, which is rarely open to the public, there are life-size statues of all the kings since Rama I established Bangkok as the capital. The outside is a blaze of different hues, with floral patterns enlivening the gables, a green *prang* (tower) and tiles of shining blue and red. A row of eight *prangs* makes up the east side of the temple. The other buildings visible from the terrace are not open to the public: the royal mausoleum, a library and a *mondop* (a square-shaped building housing a sacred object), as well as a scale model of Angkor Wat, a renowned temple in Cambodia that was under Thai rule in the mid-19th century. The building of the model was commissioned at that time, when Rama IV was king.

THE *RAMAYANA* MURALS
Shaded in arcades along the walls, the paneled murals date back to the late 18th century, but all of them have been repainted at various times over the

TIP
▶▶ Ignore anyone around the Grand Palace who, telling you that it is closed for the day, offers what will turn out to be a shopping tour of the city.

Opposite *A bejewelled temple guard stands before Wat Phra Kaeo*
Below left *The elegant Grand Palace*
Below right *Yak Temple guardian*

Below *The striking tiered roof of Dusit Maha Prasat*

years. They tell the story of Rama and his wife Sita, an epic adventure story that originated in India and spread into other parts of Asia under the influence of Hinduism. The narrative begins on the side where the palace entrance is situated, with a panel depicting the baby Sita floating down a stream, Moses-like, and being discovered by a stranger. Without a guide it is impossible to follow the whole story (which ends happily), but the intricacy and fine detail of the panels can be appreciated in isolation.

DUSIT MAHA PRASAT

This building, outside Wat Phra Kaew and one of the oldest of all in the Grand Palace, was built as an audience hall and is now used to hold the corpse of a royal before the cremation ceremony. The tiered roof is eye-catching, with its gold, green and red tiles. It's crowned by a golden spire and each part of the stepped roof is decorated with stylized birds *(chofas)*.

CHAKRI MAHA PRASAT

Another part of the Grand Palace, recognizable by the portrait of Rama V over the entrance, is a large hall, the Chakri Maha Prasat, that is not open to the public except for a small and less-than-arresting weapons museum occupying part of the ground floor. The unusual exterior is what catches the eye. It was designed by an English architect in 1882, which explains the neoclassical features that reach as far as the roof. The story goes that members of the monarch's family persuaded him to have traditional Thai spires added so as to redeem the structure's foreignness; hence the epithet "the *farang* (foreigner) with a Thai crown" that has been given to the building.

MORE TO SEE

WAT PHRA KAEW MUSEUM

Close to the Dusit Maha Prasat, the museum collection consists of objects relating to the Emerald Buddha and the restoration of the palace in 1982. The scale models of the Grand Palace show it has developed over the years.
✉ Thanon Na Phra Lan 🕒 Daily 8.30–3.30

WAT RACHANADA

From Democracy Monument, walk along Thanon Ratchadamnoen Klang to the junction where The Queen's Gallery stands and cross where pictures of the king decorate the roadway. The grouping of edifices across the road is Wat Rachanada (variant spellings are common).

To reach the entrance to the most peculiar of these religious buildings walk down Thanon Mala Chai for 110 yards (100m) (the sign on the corner points to Wat Ratchanatdaran). You enter a courtyard/parking area; the pink-tone structure in front with the black spires is Loh Prasat (the "Iron Monastery"). There are 37 spires, representing the number of stages on the journey to enlightenment. Having deposited your footwear, you enter a strange interior—a cross between a scene from a Kafka novel and something from *Gormenghast*—where narrow passageways criss-cross in every direction and tiny meditation cells remain eerily empty. A tiring climb up a spiral staircase eventually brings you to the top level (save your legs if you're going on to see nearby Wat Saket—the views from there are far better). When leaving through the courtyard, it is worth heading over to your right for an indoor amulet market, the sign overhead identifying it as the temple's Buddha Center. It is packed with stalls and shops selling religious paraphernalia, with the tiniest Buddha image alongside large statuettes of assorted Hindu deities. ✚ 64 B3 ✉ Corner of Thanon Maha Chai and Thanon Ratchadamnoen Klang ⊙ Daily 9–5 ⛴ Tha Phra Athit pier, then walk through Banglamphu (▷ 70) to Democracy Monument; Tha Phanfa canal boat pier (▷ right) ⊟ 15, 30, 47, 56, 79, 505 on Thanon Ratchadamnoen Klang travel to/from Siam Square and the Skytrain station

WAT SAKET

From Wat Rachanada walk back to the junction of Thanon Maha Chai and Thanon Ratchadamnoen Klang and turn right for Wat Saket and the Golden Mount. The route is signposted. At the Tha Phanfa

canal boat pier you turn right and the entrance is on your left. Wat Saket was built outside the city walls by Rama I, and it served as a crematorium before Rama III decided to build a *chedi* (monument housing a Buddhist relic) here. This collapsed before completion and it was left to Rama V to finish the project with the monument you see today. It is a short but steep climb to the top of the 262ft-high (80m) hill, passing evidence of the collapse, the retaining walls of concrete and an information panel about the *chedi*. From the spacious summit you are rewarded with fine views over the city. You can enter the *chedi* at the top of the hill. The relics are said to be some of the Buddha's teeth discovered in an urn in 1899, and the interior murals are of some interest, though you may spend longer on the open terrace identifying landmark buildings on the skyline. If you have just come from Wat Rachanada, or are going there next, the aerial view from here helps make sense of its layout. ✚ 64 C3 ✉ Thanon Boriphat ☎ 022 234 561 ⊙ Daily 8–5 ⊟ B50 ⛴ Tha Phanfa canal boat pier ⊟ 508, 511

WAT SUTHAT AND THE GIANT SWING

Within walking distance of Democracy Monument (▷ 70) and Wat Saket (▷ left), the building of Wat Suthat, an archetypal Thai temple, was started in the late 18th century under Rama I but not completed until Rama III was on the throne. The lavish endowments that three monarchs could afford show themselves in the grand style of the main chapel, the *viharn*, which is exceptionally tall in order to accommodate its 26ft-high (8m) Buddha figure. This 14th-century Buddha was brought to Wat Suthat by river from Sukhothai, a journey of over 248 miles (400km), signifying its importance as an object of reverence. It sits on a gleaming dais in the aisled interior, and all around it are impressive paintings depicting innumerable incarnations of the

Buddha. The courtyard area outside the *viharn* is filled with a variety of statues of Chinese sages and not-so-sagacious Western sailors.

Lofty teak posts, painted red, are all that remain of Sao Ching Cha, the Giant Swing. In an annual Brahman ceremony, teams of men would stand on the now-missing seat, which was nothing more than an open board, and swing dangerously high in order to try to catch between their teeth bags of silver coins that hung from a post nearly 82ft (25m) in height. Accidents were common, sometimes fatal, and the event was banned in 1932. ✚ 64 B3 ✉ Corner of Thanon Ti Thong and Thanon Bamrung Muang ☎ 022 249 846 ⊙ Daily 9–8 ⛴ B20 ⊟ 15, 30, 47, 79, 508

WAT TRAIMIT

With a Buddha figure over 10ft (3m) high and made of solid gold, this temple is bound to attract visitors in large numbers—hence the signs warning of the danger of pickpockets. The Buddha is an example of Sukhothai art and was probably cast in the 13th century, though it was not until 1955, when a Buddha in stucco was being moved, that it saw the light of day. The stucco figure was accidentally damaged, something shining was detected below the surface and then all was revealed. It seems likely that the plaster cover was a ruse to deceive robbers or the invading Burmese during the Ayutthaya period. The security in its present location seems remarkably lax for an object of such huge value, and it is open to view in a very ordinary building. Although the Buddha's face is not especially serene, there is a viscous quality about the gold surface that makes it special.

Try to time your visit to coincide with the fair at Wat Saket in the first week of November. ✚ 64 C4 ✉ Thanon Traimit, at junction of Thanon Yaowarat and Thanon Charoen Krung ☎ 022 259 775 ⊙ Daily 9–5 ⛴ B20 🚉 Hua Lamphong ⊟ 25, 53

CHINATOWN

This walk introduces you to Bangkok's Chinatown, its hustle and bustle, shops and stands and everyday life. You may not end up purchasing anything, but more than one of your senses will be stimulated by this walk.

THE WALK

Distance: 2 miles (3.5km)
Allow: 2–3 hours
Start/end at: Tha Ratchawongse pier
➕ 64 B4

HOW TO GET THERE

Take any Chao Phraya River Express boat to the Ratchawongse pier.

★ The Ratchawongse boat pier is at the end of Thanon Ratchawong; food and drink stands are on hand.

Walk along Thanon Ratchawong to a pedestrian crossing (if you reach traffic lights you have gone too far). Turn left down a congested lane.

❶ You have entered Sampeng Lane. This section of the lane was once home to opium addicts and brothels but is now filled with fabric shops.

Continue along Sampeng Lane to reach a crossroads with a pedestrian crossing and vehicular traffic. Turn right here, for Thanon Wora Chak.

❷ The first shop on your right is Eain Nee Kok, a Chinese medicine store, selling traditional ingredients.

Walk along to the traffic lights and turn right onto Thanon Yaowarat.

❸ Thanon Yaowarat is a busy thoroughfare. You will pass pre-World War II Chinese buildings with rickety balconies and enter the hub of Thailand's retail gold trade. Gold shops become a common sight.

Cross the main intersection with traffic lights, staying on the left-hand side where the Grand

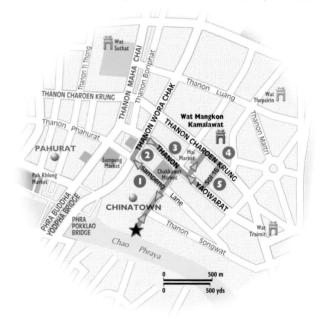

China Princess Hotel stands, but stay on Thanon Yaowarat. Look for the signed Thanon Mangkan on your left and turn down here, past fruit vendors, and right at the first crossroad intersection onto Thanon Charoen Krung. Stay on the left-hand side for 27 yards (25m) and look for the Wat Mangkon Kamalawat temple entrance.

❹ Wat Mangkon Kamalawat (▷ 85) is one of Chinatown's busiest temples, with lots to look at.

Return to Thanon Charoen Krung, turn left and cross the road at the pedestrian crossing. Go down the lane, signposted Soi 16.

❺ Along Soi 16 you will pass a smaller temple on your left, amid the many food stands.

Opposite *The Chinese-Buddhist temple of Wat Mangkon Kamalawat, known in Chinese as Wat Leng Nee*

Soi 16 brings you to an intersection with Thanon Yaowarat. Turn right, passing Thanon Mangkan again, until you arrive at the intersection with Thanon Ratchawong on your left, just after the Shangarila restaurant. Turn down here to return to the Chao Phraya River Express boat pier.

WHERE TO EAT
GRAND CHINA PRINCESS HOTEL
▷ 111.
✉ 215 Thanon Yaowarat ☎ 022 249 977; www.grandchina.com 🕒 Daily 11.30–2.30

TOURIST INFORMATION
BANGKOK INFORMATION CENTER
✉ Pinklao Bridge, Thanon Phra Athit, Banglamphu ☎ 022 257 612

BANGKOK RIVER TOUR

This tour takes you up the Chao Phraya River to Nonthaburi, a town beyond Bangkok's northern boundary, taking in some sights along the way. At Nonthaburi you can take a short walk through the town's market area and cross the river to a little-visited temple on the west side before returning to Bangkok.

THE RIVER TOUR

Distance: 20 miles (32km)
Allow: 4–6 hours
Start/end at: Central Pier
✚ 64 C5

HOW TO GET THERE

Take the Skytrain to Saphan Taksin.

★ Central Pier, next to the Saphan Taksin Skytrain station, is designated as N1 on the route traveled by the Chao Phraya River Express boats. Boats travel throughout the day, from early morning until 5.30pm, and tickets are purchased on board.

Chao Phraya River Express boats with no flag stop at every pier. Boats displaying an orange flag stop at 15 piers and take an hour to reach Nonthaburi. Boats with a yellow flag only make seven stops. The fare to Nonthaburi is B13 to B28.

❶ The first stretch of the river, up until the N13 pier, is the busiest, with river traffic and plenty to observe. After the N7 pier, look to the left for views of Wat Arun (▷ 84). Disembark at the N10 pier, Wang Lang (Siriaj). From the pier go along Thanon Phrannok to enter the

hospital from its side entrance and walk through the hospital grounds for about 330 yards (300m). Turn left just before the sign for the History of Thai Medicine Museum. The Anatomical Museum is on your left.

❷ Visit the Anatomical Museum and see its ghoulish abnormalities.

Return to the N10 pier and board a Chao Phraya River Express boat.

❸ After the N13 pier, you approach the asymmetric but graceful Rama VIII suspension bridge, completed in 2002. The B20 banknote depicts King Rama VIII standing before the bridge that commemorates his life.

Pier N15, brings you to Vimanmek and Dusit Park (▷ 72–73).

❹ After the N22 pier and before the railway bridge over the river, you will see glistening temples on your right. After the N25 pier, there is a mosque on the right and houses built on stilts.

Disembark at Nonthaburi, the terminal pier for Chao Phraya River Express boats.

❺ Outside the pier, the old City Hall by the clock tower is a reminder that you are now in the provincial capital of Nonthaburi province.

Outside the pier station, head for the market on the right-hand side of the road and walking along the covered sidewalk (pavement).

❻ Nonthaburi is a market town, well known for its orchards, and the produce grown in the vicinity is on sale every day of the year in the street market. Among the pyramids of fruit on offer, look for the mangosteen—unattractive but a delicacy—and the foul-smelling durian. As well as fruit, the market is teeming with inexpensive clothing, watches, wallets and all sorts of useful household items.

Continue through the market until you reach some traffic lights. Turn right here and continue walking until you reach a pedestrian bridge over the road. Cross the bridge to the other side of the street.

Above *The River Express boats on the Chao Phraya River are a convenient way to get around and see the sights in Bangkok*

7 The view from the bridge may resemble a typical Bangkok street, but you will also see *samlors*, a form of unmotorized transportation. The River Plaza mall is Nonthaburi's concession to modernity.

Walk back to the traffic lights, turn left and return to the pier on the other side of the street to the covered market. At the pier look for the smaller boats—most of them displaying 120AV on their side—that continuously ply their way across the river. Step aboard and have B10 ready to pay on the other side.

Exiting the pier on the west side of the river, take a *tuk-tuk* to Wat Chalerm Phra Kiat. It's a five-minute drive away, and you should haggle hard for a cheap fare. Ask the *tuk-tuk* driver to wait for you at the temple.

8 Wat Chalerm Phra Kiat was built by Rama III, on the site of a 17th-century fortress, in memory of his mother. It is now a restful spot among trees, one that lends the temple a quiet dignity. The roofs and shapely gables are decorated with ceramic tiles, revealing a Chinese character in this shrine to Thai Buddhism. The doors and windows, rich in stuccowork, are equally impressive, and the peaceful interior has been carefully restored.

Return to the pier and cross back to the east side of the Chao Phraya River to catch a boat back to Bangkok. Unless you want a long journey, wait for a boat with a yellow or orange flag. The Rim Fang Floating Restaurant, on the promenade downriver from the pier, is a few minutes away on foot and a good place to stop for a drink. The last boat to Bangkok departs at around 5.30pm.

WHERE TO EAT
RIVER PLAZA
Fast-food restaurants, ice-cream and sorbet parlors by the pedestrian bridge in Nonthaburi.
⏰ Daily 9.30–7

PLACE TO VISIT
ANATOMICAL MUSEUM
✉ Siriraj Hospital, Thanon Prannok
☎ 024 197 000 ⏰ Mon–Sat 8.30–3
✋ B40

TOURIST INFORMATION
BANGKOK INFORMATION CENTER
✉ Pinklao Bridge, Thanon Phra Athit, Banglamphu ☎ 022 257 612

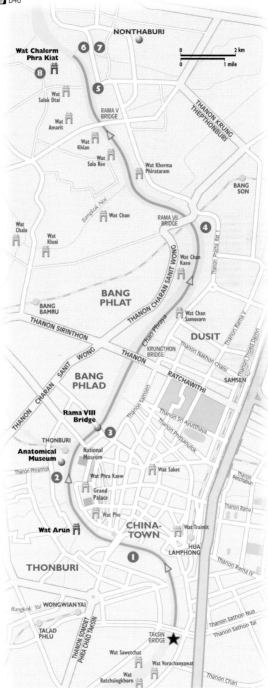

SHOPPING

ANITA THAI SILK
www.anitasilk.com
Established in 1959, Anita Thai silk
sells a wide range of gorgeous
silk and cotton fabrics, along with
a variety of desirable high-quality
silk goods, including photo frames,
cushion covers and many types of
purses and shoulder bags. Tailor-
made shirts and dresses can be
made to measure and are usually
ready within three days, though
allow time to return to the store for
a fitting in between.
✉ Anita Thai Silk, 298/2–5 Silom Road
☎ 022 342 481 ⏲ Daily 8.30–6
🚇 Surasak

ASIA BOOKS
The largest chain of English-
language bookstores in Bangkok
stocks a good range of maps,
guides, coffee-table books, fiction
and non-fiction. You can find
Asia Books outlets at:

Central World Plaza
✉ 6th Floor, Central World Plaza,
Skydome Zone C, Thanon Ratchadamri
☎ 022 556 209 ⏲ Daily 10.30–8

Siam Discovery Centre
✉ 4th Floor, Siam Discovery Centre,
Thanon Rama I ☎ 026 580 418
⏲ Daily 10–9

Sukhumvit
✉ 221 (near Robinson's Department
Store), Thanon Sukhumvit, between Soi 15
and 17 ☎ 022 527 277 ⏲ Daily 10–7

✉ 1st Floor, Landmark Hotel, Thanon
Sukhumvit, between Soi 4 and 6
☎ 022 525 839 ⏲ Daily 10.30–7.30

✉ 2nd Floor, Times Square Building,
Thanon Sukhumvit, between Soi 12 and 14
☎ 022 500 162 ⏲ Daily 10.30–7.30

✉ 3rd Floor, Emporium Shopping Complex,
Thanon Sukhumvit, between Soi 22 and 24
☎ 026 648 545 ⏲ Daily 10.30–9.30

BATH & BLOOM
www.earthfactory.com
A small store packed with bath
products, especially handmade,
fragrant soaps scented with unusual
ingredients like mango, rice and
charcoal. A range of detoxifying
products uses exotic blends of kaffir
lime, mint and lemon grass.
✉ 25/11 Ekachai, Soi 25 ☎ 028 948
860/1 ⏲ Mon–Sat 8–5 🚌 43, 120
🚇 Siam

CENTRAL CHIDLOM
This is the flagship store of
Bangkok's largest chain of
department stores. There are seven
floors dedicated to quality shopping,
including clothes, electronics and
a supermarket, all at fixed prices.

Opposite *An antique shop in the River City Shopping Complex in Bangkok*

A trip here can be an exhausting experience, but body fatigue can be relieved on the top floor's Food Loft (▷ 107), where there is also a free internet facility.

✉ 1027 Thanon Phloenchit ☎ 026 557 777 🕙 Daily 9am–10pm 🚇 Chit Lom

CENTRAL WORLD PLAZA
www.centralworld.co.th
Visible from passing Skytrains, it was once hard to miss this monumental edifice on the corner of Thanon Rama IV and Thanon Ratchadamri, one of the largest shopping malls in the country. The mall suffered significant damage in the 2010 riots in Bangkok but, at the time of writing in 2010, the mall was under construction and should be rebuilt by the end of 2011.

✉ Thanon Rama IV ☎ 026 351 111 🕙 Daily 10–10 (currently closed) 🚇 Chit Lom

CHATUCHAK MARKET
▷ 70.

CHINATOWN
▷ 71.

EMPORIUM
An upmarket center with a reasonable spread of quality shops and the flagship Emporium department stores. As well as big-name boutiques like Christian Dior and Armani, there are two bookshops, a Jim Thompson silk outlet, a Boots pharmacy, a gourmet supermarket and some craft shops on the fourth level. Places to eat are on the fifth level; above that is a cinema.

✉ Thanon Sukhumvit between Soi 22 and 24 ☎ 022 691 000 🕙 Daily 10–8 🚇 Phrom Phong

GAYSORN
Gaysorn has securely positioned itself at the luxury end of consumer shopping: Louis Vuitton, Fendi, Dior, Celine, Gucci, Prada, Loewe and La Perla are all here, plus many lesser-known but equally pricey stores. The atmosphere inside Gaysorn, in tune with the overall minimalist style, is more sedate and less busy than your average Bangkok shopping mall.

✉ Corner of Thanon Ratchadamri and Thanon Ploenchiton ☎ 026 561 149 🕙 Daily 9–10 🚇 Chit Lom (with direct access from Skybridge)

JADE THONGTAVEE
Jade jewelry and objects carved from jade are the specialty of this shop in River City. Best of all, everything you see is small enough to fit in your luggage. Prices are displayed but expect a discount of around 10 percent.

✉ Rm. 202, 2nd Floor, River City ☎ 022 370 077 🕙 Daily 12–7 🚢 Sri Praya pier

JIM THOMPSON'S THAI SILK
www.jimthompson.com
This shop at Jim Thompson's House (▷ 69) is a good introduction to the range of high-quality Thai fabrics available in the city. Silk is sold by the yard, and there are ready-to-wear dresses as well as cushions and other home furnishings. Jim Thompson shops are also located in the Peninsula, Sheraton Grande, Amari Watergate and Oriental hotels, the Emporium, Central Chidlom department store and Terminal 1 at the airport.

✉ Soi Kasem San 2, Thanon Rama I ☎ 026 123 603 🕙 Daily 9–5 🚇 National Stadium (Exit 1) 🚢 Hua Chang canal boat pier

KHAO SAN ROAD
In the heart of Banglamphu (▷ 70), Khao San Road was once known only as a place where backpackers came to find dirt-cheap lodging, but it has since evolved into a lively street market. It's lined with stands selling inexpensive but iconic items of Thai clothing, CDs and DVDs, jewelry and handicrafts small enough to squeeze into a rucksack. If you wander down the adjoining backstreets, where a pleasant Thai atmosphere prevails, you'll find some more individual and characterful shops.

✉ Thanon Khao San 🕙 Daily 9am–11pm 🚢 Tha Phra Athit pier

LA LANTA FINE ART
www.lalanta.com
Regular exhibitions are hosted here to give emerging Thai and Asian artists a platform to promote their paintings, sculpture and photography. This stylish and spacious art gallery also houses an extensive selection of local and international art prints, as well as art-related products such as notebooks and picture frames. Even if you don't intend to make a purchase, this place gives a good insight into the contemporary fine arts scene in Asia.

✉ 657 Baan Silom (corner of Silom 19), Silom Road ☎ 022 040 582 🕙 Tue–Fri 10–9, Sat–Sun 12–7 🚇 Surasak

L'OCCITANE
www.loccitane.com
Similar to The Body Shop in its concept—environmentally friendly products with recyclable packaging and no animal testing—but with an Asian accent. A wide selection of soaps, candles and beautifully scented incense for meditation, fragrances and skin creams.

✉ Central Chidlom, Thanon Ploenchit ☎ 022 545 032 🕙 Daily 10–8 🚇 Chit Lom

LOFTY BAMBOO
www.loftybamboo.com
This "fair trade" shop with two locations sells high quality, handmade crafts including Lisu fabrics and Karen Silver, and their Saori Project supports tsunami survivors in Phang Nga.

✉ Floor 2, MBK Center, Siam Square ☎ 026 294 716 🕙 Daily 10–10 🚇 National Stadium

MARCO TAYLOR
This trusted, but pricey, men's tailor has two locations in Bangkok and makes beautifully cut suits from wool, cotton and silk in less than three weeks.

✉ 430/33 Soi 7, Siam Square ☎ 022 520 689 🕙 Mon–Fri 10–5 🚢 Siam

MBK
www.mbk-center.com

For general shopping and especially if you're looking for clothes, shoes, leather goods, handbags and luggage, it is hard to beat the seven-floor MBK (Mah Boon Krong (▷ 82 Siam Square). Some of the shops have fixed prices, while others allow for some flexibility and you can usually cut quickly to the chase and get their bottom price. MBK is just west of the National Stadium Skytrain station, and a covered walkway takes you directly inside the mall. Try to avoid weekends, when the place is busy; the best time is mid-morning on a weekday, when most of the shutters are down and your energy levels are up. There are places to eat and drink on the ground floor and throughout MBK.
✉ Corner of Thanon Phayathai and Thanon Rama I ☎ 026 209 000 ⏰ Daily 10–10 🚆 National Stadium

NARAI PHAND
www.naraiphand.com

Large, government-run craft center, which is entered next to Gaysorn

just across the road from the Erawan Shrine (▷ 82), not to be confused with the private enterprises of the nearby Thai Craft Village. Fabrics and cloth by the meter on the first floor, crafts on the second, and furniture and wood-carved elephants on the third. There are fixed prices, shipping can be arranged and there's internet access on the second level by the cafe.
✉ 127 Ratchadamri Avenue, off Thanon Ratchadamri ☎ 022 524 670 ⏰ Daily 10–8 🚆 Chit Lom

OLD MAPS & PRINTS
www.classicmaps.com

A wide selection of beautiful maps, engravings and prints of Southeast Asia from before 1900 can be found here. The shop is run by two German expatriates who know a great deal about their subject and can offer advice, or there is a search facility on their website, useful if you are looking for a particular item.
✉ Shop 432, River City, Trok Rongnamkhaeng, off Thanon Charoen Krung (New Road) ☎ 022 370 077 ⏰ Daily 11–7 🚢 Tha Si Phraya

PANPURI
www.panpuri.com

A philosophy of holistic well-being underpins Panpuri's gorgeous bath and beauty products, found in many of the luxury spas across Asia. All the products are hypoallergenic, of course, and contain only natural ingredients and plant oils to create the relaxing and rejuvenating scents.
✉ 2/F Gaysorn Plaza, Thanon Ploenchit ☎ 026 561 362 ⏰ Daily 10–9 🚆 Chit Lom

PATPONG NIGHT BAZAAR
Bangkok's red-light area (▷ 76) is also the site for a very popular night market. The sidewalks of Patpong 1 and nearby Thanon Silom fill with stands displaying clothes with counterfeit designer labels, counterfeit Rolex watches, bootleg music and movies, leather items, trinkets and assorted other merchandise. There are no bargains to be had here, but it can be a fun shopping experience.
✉ Patpong 1 ⏰ 7–11 🚆 Si Lom 🚆 Sala Daeng

PRATUNAM CLOTHING MARKET
This vast maze is the place to find clothes at rock-bottom prices. Lanes bisect each other at random, with tiny stalls and shops displaying every category of clothing: casual and formal evening wear, beachwear, winter jackets, children's clothes, shoes, socks and watches. This is a good time to practice your bargaining skills and stock up on cheap clothes to take home. Be aware that "designer brands" on sale here are likely to be fakes.
✉ Intersection of Thanon Phetburi and Thanon Ratchprarop ⏰ Daily 9–6 🚆 Ratchathewi, Chit Lom

RIVER CITY SHOPPING COMPLEX
www.rivercity.co.th

More than a hundred art and antiques shops line the first, third and fourth floors of this complex, a haven for antiques collectors. A wide

Left *Interior view of the Jim Thompson's Thai Silk shop in Bangkok*

range of rare and genuine artifacts from China, Thailand, Myanmar, Laos, Cambodia, Vietnam and even Europe are to be found here. An auction is held on the fourth floor on the first Saturday of every month.
✉ 23 Trok Rongnamkhaeng, Thanon Charoen Krung ☎ 022 370 077 🕐 10am–8pm 🚇 Saphan Taksin 🚢 River City

SIAM SQUARE
www.siam-square.com
A series of interlocking *sois* rather than a square, packed with tiny shops and boutiques catering to Bangkok's fashion-conscious youth. Clothes and accessories are reasonable value and often have fixed prices. The nearby Novotel hotel is a useful landmark and rendezvous point.
🕐 Daily 10–10 🚇 Siam

SILOM VILLAGE TRADE CENTER
www.silomvillage.co.th
The most conspicuous visitor-oriented attraction on Thanon Silom is a series of shopping arcades, a hotel, spa, the Ruen Thep Thai dance center and restaurants. The outlets mostly sell handicrafts and jewelry, and there is also a clothes boutique, two luggage shops and a tailor's shop that sells Thai silk. It is a convenient cluster of shops, but prices are a bit steep and you need to bargain hard.
✉ 286 Thanon Silom ☎ 026 235 8760 🕐 Daily 10–10 🚇 Surasak 🚢 Central Pier

SUAN LUM NIGHT BAZAAR
This night market is easy to reach in the southeast corner of Lumphini Park and a short walk from a Skytrain and metro station. In many respects, it is the ideal place to shop for arts and crafts in Bangkok. The atmosphere is a lot less frenetic than Chatuchak Market, and there is far less chance of getting lost in a maze of shop stands. Nor do you have to walk past endless stands selling products you are not interested in. Suan Lum is devoted entirely to Thai arts and crafts, with

an emphasis on quality rather than tourist kitsch. Bargaining will secure a discount of around 10 percent or more. You'll find interesting ceramics, flatpacked lampshades, and a nice line of wooden Buddhas and spa products.
✉ Thanon Rama IV 🕐 Daily 3pm–midnight 🚌 Suan Si Lom 🚇 Lumphini

TAEKEE TAEKON
Turn left after exiting from the Tha Phra Athit pier, cross the road, and this shop is about 220 yards (200m) farther down on a corner. Prices are more or less fixed—expect around a 10 percent discount—and there is a choice of quality textiles, silk items, axe cushions, jewelry, baskets, stationery and bags. The store is easy to find if you're visiting Banglamphu.
✉ 118 Thanon Phra Athit ☎ 026 291 473 🕐 Mon–Sat 9–6 🚢 Tha Phra Athit pier

THANIYA PLAZA DEPARTMENT STORE
This four-floor complex is dedicated to selling golf merchandise. Here you will find independent retailers selling a wide array of products, as well as franchised dealers selling top brands such as Ping, Nike and Callaway, and plenty of facilities for testing clubs.
✉ Thaniya Plaza Building (next to Soi Patpong 2), Silom Road ☎ 022 231 2244 🕐 10–10 🚇 Sala Daeng

THANON SUKHUMVIT
The western end of Thanon Sukhumvit, between Soi 1 and 33, has numerous shops catering to the needs of overseas visitors, but they are not especially good value when compared to MBK (▷ 98). Up to Soi 11 the sidewalks are busy with stands retailing fake designer items and the like, but bargaining is essential in order to obtain a fair price. There is a branch of Robinson's department store, one notch below Central Chidlom (▷ 96–97) in terms of quality, between Soi 17 and 19, and across the road there is the swish Times Square shopping mall. Near Soi 24 you will find the

Emporium (▷ 97) while around Soi 71 the less touristy shops are usually good value for general merchandise.
🕐 Daily 9–11 🚇 Nana for Soi 1–13, Asoke for Soi 13–18, Phrom Phong for Soi 18–26, Thong Lo for Soi 26–33

ENTERTAINMENT AND NIGHTLIFE
AUTHOR'S LOUNGE
www.mandarinoriental.com
The full tea set, with a choice of Traditional, Spa for the health-conscious, or the Oriental Thai, comes with a three-tiered platter bearing delicacies like vegetable caponata on olive focaccia bread (Spa), cucumber and cream cheese on wheat bread (Traditional) or banana scones on pandanus leaf (Oriental). Sit back in what was the original hotel's lobby on white rattan chairs under palm fronds, surrounded by old photographs of famous guests over the years, or explore the Reading Room.
✉ The Oriental, 48 Oriental Avenue ☎ 026 599 000 🕐 Daily 12–6 💵 B300 for tea/coffee with a choice of cakes and pastries; B1,000 for the Traditional tea set 🚇 Saphan Taksin 🚢 The Oriental

BAMBOO BAR
This bar, next to the lobby of the Oriental Hotel, is considered by most jazz fanatics to be the best live jazz spot in town. It often features internationally acclaimed singers and has been legendary for its live jazz since 1946. The jungle theme creates a very laid-back ambience, yet with all the class, sophistication and style to be expected of a five-star hotel bar. The live music gets into full swing around 10pm every night.
✉ Oriental Hotel, 48 Oriental Avenue ☎ 022 360 400 🕐 Daily 11am–1am 💵 Free entry; cocktails B300 🚇 Saphan Taksin 🚢 The Oriental

BED SUPPER CLUB
www.bedsupperclub.com
With an innovative interior design and concept that has attracted

international attention, this is one of Bangkok's most chic nighttime destinations. Lines form for the bar and reservations are essential for the dining section, where you can stretch out and relax on the white linen of sofa beds, eat from bowls, drink and watch a fashion show or whatever event has been planned for the night. Photo ID is required at the door.

✉ 26 Sukhumvit Soi 11 ☎ 026 513 537 🕐 Daily 7.30pm–1am ✋ Sun–Mon B500, including 2 drinks from 10pm, Wed B500, including 2 drinks from 7.30pm, Thu B800, all you can drink from 10pm, Fri–Sat B600, including 2 drinks from 10pm

BROWN SUGAR
Located just to the north of Lumphini Park, Brown Sugar is one of the top live-jazz venues in the city and a popular social hub for locals and tourists. Lounge in style while listening to visiting artists, or the nine-piece house band, Zao-za-dung. Recommended for an enjoyable evening in the city.

✉ 231/19–20 Soi Sarasin ☎ 022 501 825/6 🕐 Daily till late 🚇 Ratchadamri

BULLY'S BAR
Bully's Bar attracts a regular local clientele and plenty of visitors. Stop here to eat lunch or dinner, to taste some great pub food, perhaps shoot a few games of pool (four tables away from the main bar area), play darts or listen to some live music. Featuring five beers on tap, including Guinness and Kilkenny's.

✉ Between Soi 2 and 4, Sukhumvit Road, (next to the J.W. Marriott) ☎ 026 564 609 🕐 11am–1am 🚇 Ploenchit

CINEMAS
www.movieseer.com
Cinemas are not conspicuous because they are usually on the top floor of shopping malls, but there are plenty to choose from. Programs are listed in the *Bangkok Post* and *The Nation* newspapers and at www.movieseer.com. First-run releases with original soundtracks and Thai subtitles are

the norm. Patrons stand for the national anthem, which is played before each performance. Tickets cost between B60 and B180.

CHAO PHRAYA RIVER EXPRESS BOAT
www.chaophrayaboat.co.th
The River Express Boat also runs a Sunday cruise to Bang-Pa-In and passes Wat Arun and the Grand Palace. This boat cruise is convenient if Central Pier is easy to reach from your accommodation.

✉ Central Pier ☎ 026 236 143 🕐 Sun: departs at 7am, returns 6.30pm ✋ Adult B1,400, child B1,200 ⛴ Sathon pier

CLUB CULTURE
www.club-culture-bkk.com
This trend-setting dance club is housed in old Thai ballroom, built in the early 1970s. International DJs play trance, dance, techno and house till the early hours for crowds of expats, locals and visitors.

✉ 346/29 Thanon Sri Ayutthaya ☎ 089 497 8422 🕐 Tue–Sun 9pm–2am ✋ B400 includes 2 drinks 🚇 Phayathai

CONCEPT CM2
www.cm2bkk.com
A well-established nightspot where international bands usually play live pop, funk or R&B on Friday to Wednesday nights in the main stage area. There is also the Boom Room, where DJs play house and techno, a karaoke area and an informal eatery serving pizza and pasta.

✉ Basement Novotel Hotel, Siam Square, Soi 6 ☎ 022 098 888 🕐 Daily 5pm–2am; ladies night Mon (free admission) ✋ Sun–Thu B250, Fri–Sat B450–650; price includes B170 discount on first drink 🚇 Siam

EGV CINEMA
www.egv.com
There are cinemas and then there is Gold Class at the EGV cinema, the equivalent of traveling first class. Your reclining seat is electrically adjustable and comes with a footrest, a pillow, blanket and socks. arrive in time to enjoy the private lounge and complimentary drink. The

Gold Class Suite is a double-seat complete with massage. Economy class is on the seventh floor.

✉ 6/F Siam Discovery Centre, Thanon Rama I ☎ 026 580 458 ✋ B120; B1,000 for Gold Class Suite 🚇 Siam

ERAWAN SHRINE
▷ 82.

JAZZIT NIGHTCLUB (THE RCA CLUB)
This popular party house and nightclub hosts parties, contests and mini concerts. Local bands play everything from mainstream to indie. Some nights international and Thai DJs play soul, funk and techno.

✉ 21/39–40 Royal City Avenue (RCA), Block C, Huay Kwang ☎ 022 031 053 🕐 6pm–2am 🚇 Asoke

JOE LOUIS PUPPET THEATER
www.thaipuppet.com
Puppet theater dates back to the middle of the 19th century. The art was resuscitated by Sakorn Yangkeowsod, who was nicknamed Joe Louis. The shows are fascinating for people of all ages, and as the puppets act out episodes from the *Ramakien*, a voice-over in English recounts the narrative. Arrive early to stroll through the night bazaar, and enjoy dinner on the terrace in front of the theater.

✉ Suan Lum Night Bazaar, Thanon Rama IV ☎ 022 529 683 🕐 Sat–Sun 7.30pm ✋ Adult B900, child B300 🚇 Ratchadamri 🚇 Lumphini

LOY NAVA
www.loynava.com
Enjoy five-star dining and traditional culture as you sail past historic places such as Wat Arun and the Grand Palace on the only antique rice barge on the river in Bangkok. The set menu includes Royal Thai Cuisine, seafood and vegetarian dishes. Drinks on board are extra.

✉ Oriental Hotel Pier ☎ 024 374 932 🕐 6–8pm, 8–10pm ✋ Set menu B1,620

LUMPHINI STADIUM
Thai boxing, *Muay Thai*, is fast and furious and the frenzied atmosphere

has more to do with the serious gambling that accompanies the bouts than appreciation of the finer skills of the contestants. There is no need to reserve seats but turn up half an hour before the first fights to get the seat you want. If you want instruction in *Muay Thai*, check out www.muaythai-institute.net

✉ Thanon Rama IV ☎ 022 514 303
🕐 Tue, Fri 6.30–10.30pm, Sat 5pm, 8pm
🖐 B1,000–B2,000 🚇 Lumphini

MAJOR CINEPLEX
www.majorcineplex.com
Eight-screen cinema, downtown in the city's largest shopping mall.
✉ 7/F, Central World Plaza ☎ 025 155 555 🕐 Currently closed; reopening 2011
🚇 Chit Lom

THE MALL, BANG KAPI
www.themalldepartmentstore.com
A modern and spacious mall, for shopping, leisure and entertainment. The top floor holds an amusement park and a water park where you can cool off, while the SF Cinemacity on the fourth floor has almost a dozen movie theaters to give you a wide range of movies in English.
✉ 3522 Lat Phao, Bang Kapi ☎ 021 731 000 🕐 Daily 10–10 🚍 Sri Nakharin

MOJOS
The top-notch live bands playing blues and jazz can be watched from the floor of the club or from above on the mezzanine. Mojos takes its food seriously too, with popular dishes like smoked ribs and burgers and fries as well as well-prepared Thai dishes. The interior is decked out in 1950s style, and Mojos is deservedly popular.
✉ 10/20 Sukhumvit Soi 33 ☎ 022 608 430 🕐 4pm–2am 🚇 Asok 🚇 Sukhumvit

MOLLY MALLONE'S
This old stand-by remains one of the most popular Irish pubs in the country, and is trimmed and furnished in leather, dark wood, and traditional decor from the Emerald Isle. All the Irish standards are on tap, including Guinness and Kilkenny Bitter. Come every night for live

Above *Watch a performance of classical Thai dancing at The Oriental*

music, except Sunday nights when sports are shown on the large-screen TV.
✉ 1/5–6 Thanon Convent ☎ 022 667 160 🕐 Daily 11am–1am, Happy Hour 4–7
🚇 Sala Daeng

MOON BAR AT VERTIGO
Located high up in the sky and open to the night air, the Moon Bar is a cool place to spend the evening, literally and metaphorically. Soft jazz plays in the background, and there is a telescope to view the city landscape. The 61st level is a good place to enjoy a pre-dinner drink and watch the sun set over the metropolis. If you like the Moon Bar, you might also like to try the open-air Sky Bar (▷ 102).
✉ 61/F Banyan Tree Hotel, 21/100 Thanon Sathorn Tai ☎ 026 791 200
🕐 Daily 5pm–1am (weather permitting)
🚇 Lumphini

PARAGON CINEPLEX
www.paragoncineplex.com
This is one of the best and most comfortable cinemas in the city. All the latest movie releases are shown here on the IMAX screens and there is a VIP service.
✉ 991 Rama 1 Road, Pathumwan
☎ 026 901 000 🚇 Siam

PATRAVADI THEATRE
www.patravaditheatre.com
Over the weekend, visitors are welcome to come along and join the excellent classes in Thai dance and drums or the meditation and yoga sessions. A busy program ensures there are often evening performances.
✉ Soi Wat Rakhang, Thonburi
☎ 024 127 287 🕐 Evening performances at around 7pm; meditation and yoga Sun 2pm; Thai dance and drum classes Fri, Sat 5pm 🖐 Thai dance class B500; meditation and yoga classes take donations; evening shows vary in price 🚤 Wat Rakhang or Wang Lang pier

Q BAR
www.qbarbangkok.com
This is one of the most popular clubs in the city, and the big draw is the likelihood of there being a celebrity DJ, usually from the US or UK, in residence. There's a mix of cocktails, and a lively and gregarious atmosphere prevails throughout, guaranteeing a good night. The music is usually house, acid jazz, hip-hop or pure chill-out. Photo ID is often required at the door. Food is served until 11.30pm.
✉ 34 Sukhumvit, Soi 11 ☎ 022 523 274
🕐 Daily 8pm–2am 🖐 Cover charge

Mon–Thu B500, Fri–Sun B700, includes 3 free drinks 🚇 Nana

RATCHADAMNOEN BOXING STADIUM

This is the other venue for Thai boxing in the city and the quality of the fights is no different than at the Lumphini Stadium. The best seats are always those nearer the ringside but these are also most expensive; the cheapest seats are for the Sunday bouts.

✉ 1 Ratchadamnoen Nok ☎ 022 814 205 🕐 Mon, Wed, Thu 6–11pm, Sun 5pm–midnight ✋ B1,000–2,000

RIVER KING CRUISE

A tour bus departs from your hotel in Bangkok (free pickup service within selected areas) to take you around the historical palace and temple sites of Ayuttaya and Bang-Pa-In. You'll return to Bangkok via boat. Once you're on board, an international buffet lunch is served, and the tour continues downriver. You'll pass more places of interest, Ko Kret island and the Nonthaburi provincial offices, housed within the largest teak wood structure in Thailand. As the tour draws to a close, you pass under the Rama 5 Bridge, with picturesque views of the Grand Palace and Wat Arun. The journey ends at the River City pier, where transportation is waiting to take you back to your hotel. Bus fares, admission to sights, lunch and afternoon snacks are included in the price.

☎ 081 199 2784 🕐 Daily 7am–4.30pm ✋ Adult B1,700, child B900

RUEN THEP

www.silomvillage.co.th
Thai classical dance, with or without a set dinner, takes place every evening in the popular Silom Village complex. Shoes are deposited at the entrance, and you enter a low-ceilinged chamber, where everything has a red hue, to watch Thai dancers in elaborate and glittering costumes perform a series of classical dances.

✉ Silom Village Level 2, 286 Thanon Silom ☎ 026 635 6313 🕐 Show 8.20–9.10;

dinner 7.30–9.10 🍽 B600–B900 🚇 Surasak ⛴ Central Pier

SALA RIM NAAM

www.mandarinoriental.com
Classical Thai dancing, performed by beautifully costumed dancers, at The Oriental (▷ 112) takes place nightly in a teak pavilion on the western side of the Chao Phraya River. The hotel's shuttle boat will bring you over from the hotel's terrace, and the evening's entertainment includes a Thai dinner, served at long, low tables (footwear deposited outside) shared with other guests, making this a sociable rather than an intimate experience. The dancers are glamorous and photographs can be taken. The food can be rather bland and drinks are extra.

✉ The Oriental, 48 Oriental Avenue ☎ 024 372 918, ext. 3344 🕐 Dinner from 7pm, dance from 8.30pm 🍽 B1,850 🚇 Saphan Taksin ⛴ The Oriental

SAXOPHONE PUB & RESTAURANT

A well-established venue for good music and food. The atmosphere is easygoing, and live jazz is played every night of the week.

✉ 3/8 Victory Monument, Thanon Phayathai ☎ 022 465 472 🕐 Daily 6pm–1am 🚇 Victory Monument

SF CINEMA CITY EMPORIUM

Multiplex comfortable movie theater in an upscale mall.

✉ 6/F, Emporium Shopping Centre, Sukhumvit, Soi 24 ☎ 022 609 333 🚇 Phrom Phong

SF CINEMA CITY MBK

http://booking.sfcinemacity.com
A modern and comfortable movie theater, which screens all the latest Asian and Hollywood releases.

✉ 7/F, MBK Centre, corner of Thanon Phayathai and Thanon Rama I ☎ 026 116 444 🚇 National Stadium

SKY BAR

www.thedomebkk.com
Open-air bar some 820ft (250m) above the ground of the State Tower, close to the Chao Phraya River, at

the bottom end of Thanon Silom where it meets Thanon Charoen Krung. A strict if idiosyncratic dress code means that if you are wearing shorts—however well pressed and whatever the designer label—or even sandals, you will not be allowed in (but scruffy old jeans are permissible). The Sky Bar vies with the Moon Bar (▷ 101) as the coolest place to go for a drink before or after a meal. There is live music, with a band and singer, every night except Monday (band only), and the Sirocco restaurant (▷ 109).

✉ 63rd level, State Tower, 1055 Thanon Silom ☎ 026 249 555 🕐 Daily 6.30pm–1am 🚇 Saphan Taksin

SUNSET STREET

Sunset Street is a square on the busy and bustling Khao San Road (Thanon Khao San, ▷ 70) where there are three bars. Sabai is the most relaxing of them, and the music encourages you to linger and lounge around. Sanook Bar is a more hip-hop joint in comparison, while the Sunset Bar is always lively when a live band gets going.

✉ 199 Thanon Khao San ☎ 022 822 565 🕐 Sabai Bar 8am–5pm, Sunset Bar 11pm–2am 🚇 Tha Phra Athit pier

SPORTS AND ACTIVITIES

AMAZING BANGKOK CYCLIST

www.realasia.net
The price of a four-hour bicycle trip includes bicycle, drinks and lunch, and you are taken through backstreets, across main roads and over the river to Thonburi for a fascinating excursion on two wheels with a guide. This gives you an eye-opening perspective on Bangkok life. Trips start from 10/5–7 Soi 26, Thanon Sukhumvit.

☎ 081 812 9641 🕐 Daily 1pm ✋ B1000; special weekend tours (10am–4pm) B2000

BLUE ELEPHANT COOKING SCHOOL

www.blueelephant.com/bangkok
Located in a century-old mansion, the Blue Elephant Cooking School has fully equipped facilities and highly experienced chefs offering

you the chance to put your hand to cooking Royal Thai Cuisine. The course begins with a visit to the morning market for instruction on ingredient selection, then back to the school's classroom for cooking theory, before the hands-on training begins. Call at least three days in advance to make a reservation.

✉ 233 South Sathorn Road, Sathorn ☎ 026 739 353-8 ✋ B2,800 (half day) 🚇 Surasak

HASH HOUSE HARRIERS
www.bangkokhhh.com
Visitors are welcome to join the Hash House Harriers for one of their weekly runs, and you don't need to be a speed runner as there's not a competitive spirit; everyone runs, or walks, at their own pace. Each run lasts about 90 minutes and there is always a social drink at the end. Check the website or the sports section of Saturday's The Bangkok Post for details of the week's meeting place and contact numbers.

☎ 086 174 6806 ⏰ Sat 5pm ✋ B350

THE LANDMARK
Using the Nipa Thai restaurant and kitchen (▷ 108), the Thai chefs teach the art of cooking famous dishes like tom yam goong (spicy soup with prawns and lemongrass), and green curries with chicken or beef. The course fee includes a cooking apron to keep as a souvenir, a gift box of Thai spices and herbs and a lunch or dinner (not the one you've cooked!).

✉ 138 Thanon Sukhumvit ☎ 022 540 404 ext. 4305 ⏰ Daily 10.30–12.30, 2–4 ✋ 1-day course B2,250, 5-day course B9,900 🚇 Nana

MAY KAIDEE'S VEGETARIAN COOKING CLASSES
www.maykaidee.com
Chefs-to-be meet at May Kaidee's (▷ 107) at 9am and begin the course with a visit to the local market to purchase ingredients. By 10am you are in the kitchen and by 1pm you have cooked some ten dishes. To find the restaurant, turn left at the bottom of Thanon Khao San, cross the road and take the first lane on

the right to find the back lane where May Kaidee is situated.

✉ 33 Thanon Samsen ☎ 089 137 3173 ⏰ Daily 9am–1pm ✋ B1,000 🚢 Tha Phra Athit (N13)

SOI KLANG RACQUET CLUB
www.rqclub.com
An expanding club with facilities for all, with special focus on the family. Facilities include tennis, squash and badminton courts, a fully equipped gym, saunas and steam rooms, and two swimming pools. Snooker tables are also available.

✉ 68 Soi 14/9 Thanon Sukhumvit ☎ 027 147 200 ⏰ Daily 6am–11pm ✋ B225–B550 🚇 Thonglor

HEALTH AND BEAUTY
ANNE SEMONIN SPA
www.eurasiacosmetics.com
From Chong Nonsi it is just a 10-minute walk to this spa; head to Thanon Silom from the station then turn left, and the hotel is a little further along the road. A specialty here is the jet-lag treatment that involves coating your face in a self-heating mud that promises to revitalize tired skin and reduce "economy-class fatigue". There are other treatments, including waxing and massages. A private consultation can be booked and slimming programs are available.

✉ 4/F Sofitel Silom, 188 Thanon Silom ☎ 022 381 991, ext 1244 ⏰ Daily 10–10 ✋ From B2,000 🚇 Sala Daeng

AUDY MASSAGE AND BEAUTY SALON
After an hour or two of Banglamphu, a visit to the Audy Massage and Beauty Salon is a relaxing way to spend some down time. It offers a full range of makeover services for the hair and body, from shampoo to highlights, manicures to waxing. Massages include Thai and Swedish, mineral and oil. Friendly, professional service in air-conditioned premises, and reasonably priced treatments.

✉ Inside the Viengtai Hotel, 42 Rambuttri Road (off Khao San Road), Banglamphu ☎ 022 827 825 ⏰ Daily 9am–10pm ✋ Thai massage B180 per hour; face massage B200; oil massage B300 🚢 Tha Phra Athit pier

BANYAN TREE SPA
www.banyantreespa.com
The whole gamut of treatments is available, from the feet, hands or face to a whole-body massage or, the ultimate in spa pampering, the seven-hour Banyan Day. Reduced prices are offered to couples taking the same treatment.

✉ Banyan Tree Hotel, 21/100 Thanon Sathorn ☎ 026 791 054 ⏰ Daily 9–10 ✋ 90-min Back Reviver US$80, 2-hour hand, feet and face treatment US$150, 3-hour Thai Ginger Healer US$205, Banyan Day US$380 🚇 Lumphini

GOODWILL
Goodwill, opposite the BNH hospital, is a neat little place where meals are

Below *Relax after sightseeing or shopping with a therapeutic massage at the Banjan Tree Spa*

served, including vegetarian choices like tofu salad, alongside a health and treatment set-up. Treatments include facials, waxing, haircuts and styling, manicures, pedicures, Thai and oil massages and a Thai herbal scrub. The rooftop garden is open for tea and cakes.

✉ 44/16 Thanon Convent ☎ 026 320 626 🕐 Mon–Sat 10–10 ✋ Massages B350–B850; facials B500–B2,200; haircuts and styling B100–B5,000 🚊 Sala Daeng

GRANDE NAIL
www.grandenail.com
Grande Nail's premises is housed in a converted town house with a garden, and successfully conjures up the look and feel of a high-quality resort so that the pampering factor is satisfyingly high. Acrylic and gel extensions to fingernails are a specialty. A range of hand and foot massages are also offered and nail products are available to buy.

✉ 63 Soi 63, Thanon Sukhumvit ☎ 027 141 015/6 🕐 Daily 9.30–7 ✋ B400–B1,900 🚊 Ekamai

LET'S RELAX
A homely setting for a spa that pampers a tired body and relieves muscular tension. Sessions begin with a cup of herbal tea. The foot massage room has floor-to-ceiling windows looking out on a garden scene, while the main massage room is upstairs on the third floor.

✉ 77 Sukhumvit, Soi 39 ☎ 026 626 935 🕐 Daily 11am–midnight ✋ 45-min foot reflexology and 90-min hot stone massage B2,200 🚊 Phrom Phong

NAILS UP
www.nails-up.com
The ultimate in nail care, with professional attention and high standards of cleanliness. There is a range of treatments, from basic polishes to nail extensions. Take the free shuttle, departing every 15 minutes, from Central Pier for the Marriott Resort & Spa and walk through to the plaza.

✉ Royal Garden Plaza, Bangkok Marriott Resort and Spa, Thanon Charoen ☎ 028 779 971 🕐 Daily 10–8 ✋ B180–B2,500

ORIENTAL SPA
www.mandarinoriental.com
The hotel's boat will shuttle you across the river to the spa and bring you back invigorated, refreshed and rosy. There is a wide choice of treatments, including manicures and pedicures. The two-hour Essence of Acqa session starts with a 30-minute scrub on a heated table followed by half an hour in the Vitality Pool, a whirl tub, and then the special Rhassoul Bath. Here, clay and herbs are applied to the body and you sit down in the bath and wait for the aromatized steam to trickle down your skin as the lighting changes to resemble a starry night sky.

✉ The Oriental, 48 Oriental Avenue ☎ 026 599 000 🕐 Daily 9am–10pm ✋ Packages start from B1,700 🚤 The Oriental

SPA CENVAREE
www.spacenvaree.com
Thailand's premier resort and spa empire has two spa locations in Bangkok, conveniently located in prime shopping and entertainment areas. Enjoy a range of massages, facials, wraps, aromatherapy treatments and nail care, with special packages designed for him or her. Prices are relatively the same at both locations but offer different treatments and massages; offerings are detailed on the website.

✉ Centara Grand at CentralWorld: 999/99 Rama I Road, Pathumwan; Sofitel Centara Grand Bangkok: 1695 Phaholyothin Road, Chatuchak ☎ 021 001 234 🕐 Centara Grand: 9am–12am; Sofitel Centara: 10am–10pm ✋ 1-hr Swedish massage B1,800; 90-min Thai herbal facial B2,500 🚊 Chit Lom

TAMMACHART
An excellent beauty center, managed by the hotel, providing natural therapies for men and women. The available massages include a body slimming one and a Thai–Swedish Sports Massage, as well as more traditional Thai versions. Other options include a body exfoliating scrub using

milk, coffee and herbs, feet/hand reflexology sessions and a choice of seven different facial treatments. You'll need at least one session here if you spend too much time out and about in frenetic Siam Square.

✉ Novotel Bangkok Hotel, Siam Square, Soi 6 ☎ 022 098 888 🕐 Daily 8–10 ✋ B500–B2,500 🚊 Siam

FOR CHILDREN
CENTRAL WORLD PLAZA
▷ 70.

CHERUBIN
A shrine for chocolate lovers as well as a delightful cafe where the decor, all soothing chocolate brown and white vanilla, blends with comfortable sofas, teddy bears and a display of English animal books to help create a childlike atmosphere. On the menu are cheesecake, brownies and a Chocolate Shot that delivers instant gratification.

✉ Soi 31 (Soi Sawasdee), Thanon Sukhumvit ☎ 022 609 800 🕐 Tue–Thu 10.30–7, Fri–Sun 10.30–8 🚊 Phrom Phong

CHILDREN'S DISCOVERY MUSEUM
www.bkkchildrenmusuem.com
This modern-looking building, in the grounds of the Queen Sirikit Park, is a 10-minute walk from Chatuchak's Skytrain station. It is a lively, hands-on type of museum with various experiments, games, computer screens and puppet shows designed to encourage an interest in learning. The Rhythm of the Universe room is especially good.

✉ Thanon Kamphaengphet 4, Chatuchak ☎ 022 724 500/1 🕐 Tue–Fri 9–5, Sat–Sun 10–6 ✋ Adult B70, child B50 🚊 Chatuchak

DREAM WORLD
www.dreamworld-th.com
A busy and well-laid-out theme park with lots of exciting attractions for children that the adults will also enjoy, including a Hollywood Action Show and an Animal Talent Show. Weekends are a good time to visit as the shows are more regular and the crowds add to the atmosphere.

✉ Thanon Rangsit–Ongharak, 5 miles (8km) north of Don Muang Airport ☎ 025 331 152 🕙 Show times: Hollywood Action Mon–Fri 2.30, Sat–Sun 12.30, 2.30, 4.30; Animal Talent Show Mon–Fri 12, 2, Sat–Sun 12, 2, 3.15 💷 B1,000, including shuttle transportation from your hotel, buffet lunch and rides 🚃 Shuttle service

DUSIT ZOO
▷ 73.

EGV CINEMA
▷ 100.

JOE LOUIS PUPPET THEATER
▷ 100.

KITE-FLYING
Kite-flying is a national pastime in Thailand and not one confined to children. Contests between rival teams can be quite serious affairs. In Lumphini Park and Sanam Luang, however, the emphasis is on fun. Vendors sell kites around both parks.
✉ Lumphini Park and Sanam Luang 🕙 Daily Feb–Apr, daytime 🚇 Si Lom or Lumphini (Lumphini Park) 🚇 Sala Daeng (Lumphini Park); Phayathai and then a taxi (Sanam Luang) 🚢 Tha Phra pier (Sanam Luang)

THE MALL, BANG KAPI
▷ 101.

QUEEN SAOVABHA MEMORIAL INSTITUTE (SNAKE FARM)
▷ 76.

SIAM OCEAN WORLD
www.siamoceanworld.co.th
Over 30,000 marine animals are on display here, encased in seven distinct environments: weird and wonderful, deep reef, living ocean, rainforest, open ocean, rocky shore and sea jellies. It is possible to get face-to-face with some of them by getting into one of the oceanariums.
✉ Siam Paragon Center (floors B1 and B2) 991 Rama I Road, Pathumwan ☎ 026 872 000 🕙 Daily 9am–10pm 💷 Adult B850, child B650

FESTIVALS AND EVENTS

MAY
ROYAL PLOWING CEREMONY, SANAM LUANG
A ceremony to commemorate the beginning of the rice-planting season, conducted by brahmins in Sanam Luang (▷ 81). It is a more formal occasion than usual, but it attracts large crowds in the capital.
🕙 Early May 🖐 Free

BANGKOK INTERNATIONAL FILM FESTIVAL
The month of this festival varies so check the website (www.bangkokfilm.org) for details, but it usually takes place around May. It lasts 10 days, with over 150 feature films, seminars, special events and the Golden Kinnaree Awards for excellence in international film.

Right *Bangkok International Film Festival*

PRICES AND SYMBOLS

The prices given are the average for a two-course lunch (L) and a three-course dinner (D) for one person, without drinks or wine.

For a key to the symbols, ▷ 2.

BISCOTTI

www.fourseasons.com

An open kitchen helps create the informal atmosphere where diners can linger and enjoy the good food; not the place for a quiet romantic meal. The menu is Italian with pizza and pasta, but also dishes of tender beef and lamb dishes and fish.
✉ Four Seasons Hotel, 155 Thanon Rajadamri ☎ 022 501 000 🕐 Daily 12–2.30, 6–10.30 🖐 L B660, D B800, Sunday Brunch Buffet B2,350 🚇 Rajadamri

LA BOULANGE

A cheerful place offering air-conditioned comfort and quiet dining after a hectic shopping session. Look for the house specials on the blackboard and expect to find mouthwatering dishes of roasted chicken, steak tartare and smoked ham. Choose a table indoors or out on the street if you want to people-watch. It gets busy at lunchtime.

✉ 2–2/1 Thanon Convent ☎ 026 310 355 🕐 Daily 7–2.30, 6.30–10 🖐 L B300, D B400 🚇 Sala Daeng

CELADON

www.sukhothaihotel.com

The restaurant at the Sukhothai Hotel (▷ 113) is surrounded by lotus ponds, and has a sleek interior. Appetizers include mussels steamed with herbs, and the spicy ones like shrimp cakes and pickled vegetables go well with a frozen margarita. There are varieties of salads and curries, excellent seafood choices, including grilled lobster, vegetables like *shitake* mushrooms and bean curd salad with roasted rice. The menu covers regional specialties from the north, such as spicy sausages with herbs, and pork with yellow curry from the south. There are set menus for B900 and B1,200, and a vegetarian one for B800.
✉ The Sukhothai, 13/3 Thanon South Sathorn ☎ 023 448 888 🕐 Daily 12–3, 6.30–11 🖐 L B650, D B1,000 🚇 Sala Daeng 🚇 Lumphini Park

COCA SUKI

Look for the conspicuous Central Investigation Unit building on Thanon Henry Dunant, and Coco Suki is facing it on the other side of the road. A restaurant for the culinary adventurer, it specializes in a form of "hot pot" style of cooking, originating from northern China. Choose a selection of meat, seafood and vegetables from the illustrated menu, then your ingredients are cooked in a chicken broth. Choose noodles or rice to accompany the meal; alcoholic drinks are beer and Chinese saki.
✉ 416/3-8 Thanon Henri Dunant ☎ 022 516 337 🕐 Daily 11–11 🖐 L B200, D B250 🚇 Siam, take exit 6 and walk along the elevated walkway to the first set of steps, leading down to Thanon Henry Dunant; the restaurant is up on the right

LE DANANG

Superb Vietnamese dishes created by an experienced Hanoi chef with specialties like snow fish in tamarind soup, and smoked duck and foie gras. Superb dishes include sautéed prawns in orange sauce, sea bass in lime juice and spring rolls filled with smoked salmon and herbs. A band plays old favorites and on Friday nights there is time for dancing.

Opposite Informal dining at Biscotti

✉ Sofitel Centara Plaza Hotel, 1695 Thanon Phaholyothyhin ☎ 025 411 234, ext. 4041 🕐 Daily 11.30–2.30, 6–10.30 🍴 L B900, D B900 🚇 Mo Chit 🚉 Chatuchak Park

DON GIOVANNI
www.centarahotelsresorts.com
Don Giovanni offers Italian cuisine prepared by an Italian chef. On the menu there is a mix of traditional and modern Italian dishes. There are also plenty of wines and spirits. A violin and piano playing quietly in the background, top-quality service, the decor and the marble flooring all add to the ambience of the place.
✉ Sofitel Centara Plaza Hotel, 1695 Thanon Phaholyothyhin ☎ 025 411 234, ext. 4169 🕐 Daily 11.30–2.30, 6–10.30 🍴 L B1,500, D B1,800 🚇 Mo Chit 🚉 Chatuchak Park

FISHERMAN'S SEAFOOD RESTAURANT
Sit outside for views of the Royal Palace, or inside for interesting decorations—just two of the reasons why this place is enjoyed by both Thais and Westerners alike. There are plenty of seafood dishes, mostly with a Thai twist.
✉ 1/12 Soi Mahathat, Thanon Maharaj ☎ 022 228 082 🕐 Daily 11–2.30, 5.30–11 🍴 L B250, D B450 🚇 Taksin 🚢 Maharaj pier

FOGO VIVO
The entrance to this carnivore's heaven, a Brazilian *churrascaria*, is next to the Holiday Inn, and it leads to a stylish drinks area where a cigar menu is made available. A glass stairway leads down to the dining area and a sumptuous, eat-all-you-want buffet of appetizers, salads and an array of meat and fish that is being continually grilled in the wonderful open kitchen.
✉ Ground Level, President Tower Arcade, 973 Thanon Ploenchit ☎ 026 560 384 🕐 Daily 11.30–11 🍴 L B500, D B1,000 🚇 Chit Lom

FOOD LOFT
For the top floor of a huge department store, this is positively elegant dining, with a cool lounge area to enjoy drinks. Collect a bar-coded card at the entrance and use it to choose dishes from a variety of outlets. Vegetarians can enjoy meals from the Indian outlet or try the *laksa* at the Old Malayan stand.
✉ 7th Level, Central Chidlom, Thanon Ploenchit ☎ 027 937 777 🕐 Daily 9–10 🍴 L B200, D B250 🚇 Chit Lom

GALLERY ELEVEN
An enchanting little eatery, Gallery Eleven is an oasis of calm that makes you feel like you're in rural Thailand. To find Gallery Eleven, keep on the left walking down Sukhumvit Soi 11 and turn left by the 7–11 store opposite the Ambassador Hotel. The menu has plenty of Thai appetizers and traditional dishes. Check out the mobile bar serving superb cocktails.
✉ Sukhumvit Soi 11 ☎ 026 512 672 🕐 Daily 9.30am–1am 🍴 L B300, D B500, Cocktails B120 🚇 Nana

GANJI
With comforting views of the hotel's placid and manicured gardens, this excellent Japanese restaurant has a sushi bar, two *tempanyaki* counters and a main dining area. The set meals provide a gratifying introduction to Japanese food—appetizers, sashimi or sushi, grilled meat, seafood or tempura, miso soup, *chawanmushi* (a custard) or salad, rice and dessert—and aficionados will not be disappointed either. The à la carte choices are expensive.
✉ Nai Lert Park Hotel, 2 Thanon Withayu ☎ 022 530 123 🕐 Daily 11.30–2, 6–10 🍴 L B400, D B1,000 🚇 Chit Lom

GIANNI RISTORANTE
The interior could do with an overhaul, but the food more than makes up for it. Reserve ahead, because the 90 tables are usually packed with regulars. There is a good set lunch and the dinner menu provides you with everything you would expect from a good Italian restaurant. There are also red and white wines, beer and whiskeys.
✉ 34/1 Piya Place Soi Tonson, Ploenchit ☎ 022 521 619 🕐 12–2.30, 6–10.30 🍴 L B350, D B450 🚇 Ploenchit

GLOW
The tone is set upon arrival when you receive a cup of refreshing mulberry tea with jasmine. The set lunch offers a choice of one dish and one juice from the menu. The food is organic, created by Chef Amanda Gale, and features raw tuna, spirulina noodles with a sea vegetable salad, or a salad of asparagus, fennel and avocado or tiger prawns grilled with a sesame and tamarind dressing. The same menu is the à la carte one at night. Organic wine, vodka and gin, and delicious desserts, such as whole wheat pumpkin cake with nutmeg and yogurt are available.
✉ The Metropolitan, 27 Thanon South Sathorn ☎ 026 253 366 🕐 Daily 11–9 🍴 L B400, D B1,000 🚇 Suan Lum

GREAT AMERICAN RIB
If the weather is not too hot, get an outside table so you can smell your food cooking and watch the chefs work the BBQ. The menu is as the name suggests: plenty of ribs, as well as steaks and burgers. If dining with friends, there are large platters to share.
✉ 33 Sukhumvit, Soi 36 ☎ 026 613 801 🕐 Daily 11.30–11.30 🍴 L B250, D B400 🚇 Thonglor

MAY KAIDEE'S VEGETARIAN RESTAURANT
www.maykaidee.com
A small but friendly place, easy to miss because it is tucked away down a lane, parallel to but located behind Thanon Tanao. It is worth seeking out for the inexpensive but well-cooked tasty green curry, carrot salad, fried water spinach and other vegetarian delights. One of the best desserts is the black sticky rice with coconut milk, banana and mango. There are two other May Kaidee's venues to try, one at 111 Rachadamnuen Road, and another at 33 Samsen Road (Soi 1).
✉ 59 Rachadamnoen Road, near Thanon Khao San ☎ 089 137 3173

Daily 9am–11pm L B100, D B150
N13 New World Lodge

NIPA THAI

www.landmarkbangkok.com
Dimly lit with low ceiling, teakwood, polished floor and live classical Thai music. Start with the *koy kung* (hot-and-sour shrimp salad) or the *tom yam* soup—either goes well with the frozen martini—the spiciness can be toned down on request. Vegetarians, seafood- or meat-eaters all have choices, and the signature dessert is lemongrass and ginger ice cream. Nightly music except Monday.
The Landmark, 138 Thanon Sukhumvit
022 540 404, ext. 4305 Daily 11.30–2.30, 6–10.30 L B250, D B390
Nana

LE NORMANDIE

www.mandarinoriental.com
Fine French dining at this very famous Bangkok restaurant, now benefiting from its consultant Guy Martin, chef of the Michelin three-star Le Grand Vefour in Paris. Reservations are essential to enjoy the chandelier-lit splendor. A jacket and tie are mandatory for men.
The Oriental Hotel, 48 Thanon Oriental (off Thanon Charoen Krung) 026 599 000 Mon–Sat 12–2.30, 7–10.30, Sun 7–10.30 L B1,000, D B4,200 Saphan Taksin Oriental

N.P. FOOD CENTER

On the other side of the road to Central World Plaza, and looking north toward the Amari Watergate, turn right at the corner where the Aroma Hotel is situated. The entrance to the N.P. Food Center is down this side street on the right after 110 yards (100m). Popular with local workers, this is ideal for an inexpensive meal in air-conditioned comfort, and there is a wide choice of food stands and fresh fruit drinks. Vegetarians will be happy here, too.
Off Thanon Ratchadamri Daily 10–8
L B150, D B200 Nana

LES NYMPHÉAS

Global inflections to modern French food at its best. The set lunch

menu has a choice of six appetizers and five main courses, and any two courses are B440 (B540 with dessert). The evening menu includes Australian steak and dishes like sea bass with potato salad and citrus-basil sauce or snow fish with saffron. There is one romantic table that can be reserved on a balcony. Check out the life-size copies of Monet paintings—everything can be copied in Bangkok.
4th Level, Imperial Queen's Park Hotel, 109 Thanon Sukhumvit, Soi 22 022 619 000 Daily 11.30–2, 6–10 L B500, D B1,500 Phrom Phong

LE PRE GRILL

A well-priced French restaurant with a pleasant atmosphere and friendly, efficient service. There are plenty of mouthwatering delicacies to select from the menu. There is

also a well-priced set menu for lunch or dinner, and an excellent choice of wines available by the glass or the bottle.
73/2 Langsuan Soi 4, Langsuan Road 022 535 919 Daily 11.30–2.30, 6.30–10.30 L B260, D B850, Wine B1,200 Chidlom

SIAM PARAGON FOOD CENTER

This luxurious shopping center is the new focus of Bangkok's downtown shopping district, and has one of the largest food courts in the city. There are numerous American fast-food joints, and Asian restaurants—including Japanese, Korean and Thai—to choose from. Alternatively, there are several bakeries and cafes, as well as one of the country's largest grocery stores if you want to buy provisions for a picnic.

✉ Siam Square ☎ 026 901 000
🕐 Daily 11.30–2.30, 6.30–10.30
🍴 Daily 10–10 🍴 L B150, D B200
🚇 Siam

SIROCCO

The tallest alfresco restaurant in the world is waiting for you when you press the button for the 63rd level in the elevator of State Tower. Watch your step when walking down into the balustraded dining area, as your attention will be distracted by the astonishing views of the city. The food, Mediterranean with Asian hints, is expensive, but the setting is tremendous. The Sky Bar (▷ 102), just a few steps away, beckons.
✉ 63rd Level, State Tower, 1055 Thanon Silom ☎ 026 249 555 🕐 Daily 6pm–1am 🍴 D B2,750 🚇 Saphan Taksin 🚢 Sathorn pier ❓ Dress code: no sandals or shorts

THAI ON 4

The jazzy decor distinguishes this swish restaurant, and the walls are decorated with non-figurative art rather than Buddha images and Thai objects. Staff are dressed smartly but anonymously, and the stylish approach is maintained with the artistic presentation of traditional Thai cuisine with modern flourishes.

✉ Amari Watergate Hotel, 847 Thanon Petchburi, Pratunam ☎ 026 539 000
🕐 Daily 11.30–2.30, 6.30–10.30
🍴 L B850, D B850 🚇 Phaya Thai

VEGETARIAN FOOD

The vegetarian counter in this food center is at the top of the escalator. Buy coupons at the counter and return unused ones for reimbursement. Popular with local office workers; little is in English.
✉ 3rd Level, United Centre, Thanon Silom ☎ 022 893 560 🕐 Daily 11–9 🍴 L B80, D B130 🚇 Sala Daeng

VERTIGO

www.banyantree.com
"The highest alfresco city hotel restaurant in the world" is Vertigo's claim to fame and, indeed, it may be a hotel restaurant but certainly not a typical one when you are seated 61 floors up, out in the open air gazing down on the twinkling city lights. A tempting menu of grills and Mediterranean flavors, an especially appealing choice of steaks, alcoholic sorbets, a special mini-serving of five different desserts and a very good wine list. There is live music throughout the night.
✉ 61st Level, Banyan Tree Hotel, 21/100 Thanon South Sathorn ☎ 026 791 200

🕐 Daily 6.30pm–12 (last orders at 10.30)
🍴 D B2,900 🚇 Sala Daeng 🚇 Lumphini

VIMARN THAI

On the 32nd floor of the hotel, there are spectacular views and dancers fluttering around the tables (nightly 7–9pm). Deep-fried breaded prawns on a taro nest for starters and stir-fried chicken with cashew nuts mixed with dried chili are some of the terrific dishes on the menu. The food and atmosphere create a great night out.
✉ Windsor Suites Hotel, Sukhumvit Soi 20 ☎ 022 621 234 🕐 Daily 6pm–10.30pm 🍴 D B600 🚇 Asoke

WHITE ELEPHANT

The buffet lunch is good value and offers a safe introduction to Thai cuisine if you're new to the country and not sure what to try. At night you can enjoy the Thai music and dance while you eat.
✉ J.W. Marriott Hotel, Soi 2, Thanon Sukhumvit ☎ 026 567 700 🕐 Daily 11.30–2.30, 6–10.30 🍴 L B465, D B1,100 🚇 Nana

Opposite *The uncluttered style and beautifully presented food at the Celadon* **Below** *Sirocco is the tallest alfresco restaurant in the world*

PRICES AND SYMBOLS

Prices are the lowest and highest for a double room for one night. Breakfast is included unless noted otherwise. All the hotels listed accept credit cards unless otherwise stated. Note that rates vary widely throughout the year.

For a key to the symbols, ▷ 2.

A-ONE INN

www.aoneinn.com

If shopping is on your agenda, A-One is in a perfect location across the street from the MBK. Rooms are simple and clean. Water pressure is a little low, and there aren't many English-speaking cable channels, but the rooms are large and cheerful. Nearby are plenty of cheap, tasty eating options, and A-One has cheap WiFi rates too.

✉ 25/13–15 Soi Kasamsunt 1, Ramal Road ☎ 022 215 302 ✋ B600–B700 ☯ ⊛ National Stadium

THE ATLANTA

The lobby is wonderfully old-fashioned, and there is an eccentric charm that makes a stay here quite an experience. Bedrooms with a fan are inexpensive, and the standard rooms with air-conditioning are very good value. There are two pools, a restaurant where above-average consideration is given to vegetarians and a travel desk. No credit cards.

✉ 78 Soi 2, Thanon Sukhumvit ☎ 022 526 069 ✋ B450–B1,500 ① 49 ☯ Some ⛵ Outdoor ⊛ Phloen Chit or Nana

BUDDY LODGE

www.buddylodge.com

This boutique-ish hotel is in the heart of Thanon Khao San. All the rooms have safe deposit boxes, there is a cafe, tours can be arranged through a travel agency and the small pool on the fifth floor has a sun deck and pleasant bar.

✉ 265 Thanon Khao San ☎ 026 294 477 ✋ B2,400–B2,800 ① 76 ☯ ⛵ Outdoor ⊟ ⊟ 3, 30, 32, 64

THE CHINATOWN HOTEL

www.chinatownhotel.co.th

The photograph in the lobby shows what this hotel looked like before it was completely renovated. All the rooms now have modern bathrooms, satellite TV, minibar and safe deposit boxes, and there is internet access in the lobby.

✉ 526 Thanon Yaowarat ☎ 022 250 204/6 ✋ B1,170–B1,220 ① 75 ☯ ⊟ ⊛ Hua Lamphong

CITY LODGE

www.amari.com

Both these boutique hotels are squarely aimed at visitors to the city who want comfortable and smart accommodations without paying for the frills. At Soi 9 there is a restaurant for casual dining, while Soi 19 has La Gritta, an Italian restaurant open all day. The rooms are well appointed and comfortably furnished. You can use the pool and gym at the nearby Amari Boulevard hotel for free. The hotel also has a car park.

✉ Soi 9 and Soi 19, Thanon Sukhumvit ☎ 022 537 705 (Soi 9), 022 537 710 (Soi 19) ✋ B1,700–B2,100 ① 28 (Soi 9), 34 (Soi 19) (7 and 14 non-smoking, respectively) ☯ ⊛ Hua Lamphong

Opposite *Luxury rooms at J.W. Marriott*
Below *The modern Imperial Queen's Park*

GRAND CHINA PRINCESS

www.grandchina.com

If you want to stay in Chinatown then this is the hotel to choose. Rooms have all the amenities, including tea- and coffee-making facilities and a fridge, and a choice of places to eat, including a revolving restaurant at the top. There's music in the lobby at night, a fitness center and a Thai massage service.

✉ 215 Thanon Yaowarat ☎ 022 249 977 ⬛ B2,700–B4,900 🛏 155 (55 non-smoking) 🛗 ☲ Outdoor 📶 🚇 Hua Lamphong

HOLIDAY INN SILOM HOTEL

www.holidayinn.com

In the heart of Bangkok shopping, jewelry and entertainment area, this hotel has comfortable rooms. There's a baby-sitting and day-care service on request for people traveling with young children. The health club has a pool, sauna and Jacuzzi. The hotel itself does not have a spa but there are plenty to choose from nearby.

✉ 981 Silom Road, Silom ☎ 022 384 300 ⬛ B2,600–B3,200 🛏 700 🛗 ☲ Outdoor 📶 🚇 Surasak

IMPERIAL QUEEN'S PARK HOTEL

www.imperialhotels.com

This hotel has two 37-floor towers and a stupendously large lobby with teak, gold-topped columns and an elaborate ceiling inlaid with teak panels, all of which are illuminated at night by glistening chandeliers. The extravagance continues with seven restaurants, a squash court, a spa and a range of rooms from deluxe to premier and suites.

✉ Soi 22, Thanon Sukhumvit ☎ 022 619 000 ⬛ B3,200–B3,700 🛏 125 🛗 ☲ Outdoor 📶 🚇 Phrom Phong, exit 2 and a five-minute walk across the park

J.W. MARRIOTT

www.marriott.com/bkkdt

This is one of the best hotels along Thanon Sukhumvit, with a choice of deluxe or executive rooms or a suite. The sports facilities include a spa and a 24-hour gym. There is a Chinese and a Thai restaurant and a New York Steakhouse, as well as a gregarious bar that is usually full of guests. Wireless internet connection and broadband are available in all the bedrooms.

✉ Soi 2, Thanon Sukhumvit ☎ 026 567 700 ⬛ From B4,960–£7,250 excluding breakfast 🛏 441 🛗 ☲ Outdoor 📶 🚇 Phloen Chit

THE LANDMARK

www.landmarkbangkok.com

This is an ultramodern, 31-floor hotel with a range of bars and Thai (Nipa Thai ▷ 108), Japanese, Italian, Chinese and international restaurants. There is a pub—English in its decor and with live music—and a 24-hour coffee shop. Two levels, dedicated "Lifestyle Floors," have a more contemporary, less business-like style to the bedrooms, with beautiful Jim Thompson fabrics, and with broadband internet access.

✉ 138 Thanon Sukhumvit ☎ 022 540 404 ⬛ B4,575–B9,945 excluding breakfast 🛏 414 🛗 ☲ Outdoor 📶 🚇 Nana

MAJESTIC GRANDE

www.majesticgrande.com

Opened in 2005, this modern hotel has all the comforts you would expect and with a reasonable discount off the official rates it could be good value. It is down a quiet *soi*, a short walk from the hustle and bustle of Sukhumvit. There are two restaurants, with live jazz music at night, a cafe by the pool and smartly furnished bedrooms.

✉ 12 Soi 2, Thanon Sukhumvit ☎ 022 622 999 ⬛ B3,860–B5,200 🛏 251 🛗 ☲ Outdoor 📶 🚇 Phloen Chit

THE METROPOLITAN

www.metropolitan.como.bz

Bangkok's most chic and image-conscious accommodations are to be enjoyed at The Metropolitan, dwarfed in size by the nearby Banyan Tree and Sukhothai hotels but etching out a stylish identity of its own. The design is minimalist,

pared down to straight lines, clean hues and an air of sophistication. For dining there is the formal Cy'an restaurant but also healthy, organic cuisine at the informal Glow restaurant, and Asian cuisine at the cool Met Bar. The health and fitness center, Shambhala, has a menu of massage therapies, body and facial treatments, and nail care. Guests receive a free 15-minute massage.

✉ 27 Thanon Sathorn Tai ☎ 026 253 333 ✋ B8,400–B10,300 🚻 171 (79 non-smoking) 🅱 ➿ Outdoor 🔶 🚇 Sala Daeng

NAI LERT PARK
www.swissotel.com
This low-rise, five-star hotel with parking, formerly the Hilton, has been transformed and given a sophisticated, contemporary identity. The landscaped garden, the most delightful of any Bangkok hotel, surrounds the pool and provides a relaxed atmosphere. There are three restaurants, including an excellent Japanese one (Ganji ▷ 107), and a lounge bar that could feature in a *Star Trek* movie.

✉ 2 Thanon Withayu ☎ 022 530 123 ✋ B4,300–B5,800 🚻 338 (88 non-smoking) 🅱 ➿ Outdoor 🚇 Phloen Chit

NOVOTEL BANGKOK
www.novotelbkk.com
In the noisy heart of the city, this is a busy hotel where the lobby is so often bustling with people that you should only stay here if you enjoy a constantly convivial scene. There is a Chinese and international restaurant, a health center and a popular nightclub (Concept Cm²). Children under 12 stay for free if sharing their parents' room.

✉ Soi 6, Siam Square ☎ 022 098 888 ✋ B4,000–5,800 🚻 429 🅱 ➿ Outdoor 🚇 Siam

THE ORIENTAL
www.mandarinoriental.com
The most famous hotel in Bangkok has spread to both sides of the river. The bedrooms, where luminaries like Joseph Conrad, Graham Greene and Gore Vidal have stayed, and

most restaurants are on the east side; the gym, spa and tennis courts are across the river, reached by shuttle boat. It's a very business-like hotel, and the pool is small.

✉ 48 Oriental Avenue ☎ 026 599 000 ✋ B13,100–B14,100 excluding breakfast 🚻 393 🅱 ➿ Outdoor 🛥 The Oriental

PATHUMWAN PRINCESS
www.pprincess.com
If you are planning some serious shopping time in the giant MBK center and the Paragon, then this is the hotel for you. It has direct access to MBK and a Skytrain station is just outside. The atmosphere is a busy one. Japanese and Korean restaurants are just two of many dining choices, and there's also a lobby bar with live music, a health club, spa, tennis and squash courts.

✉ 444 Thanon Phayathai ☎ 022 163 700 ✋ B3,500–B4,700 🚻 462 🅱 ➿ Outdoor 🔶 🚇 National Stadium

THE PENINSULA
www.peninsula.com
On the west bank of the Chao Phraya River and adding a distinctive architectural statement to the Bangkok skyline, The Peninsula excels as perhaps Bangkok's best overall hotel. All the bedrooms look out across the river, but you need to be higher than the first few levels, in a deluxe room, to benefit from a bird's-eye view of the city. There is a superb pool, first-class Chinese, Thai and Pacific-Rim cuisine in the restaurants, and exemplary levels of service. The hotel's shuttle boat takes you across the river from a small pier next to Central Pier until midnight, after which you can take a taxi across the bridge.

✉ 333 Thanon Charoennakorn, Klongsan ☎ 028 612 888 ✋ From BB10,800–13,800 🚻 370 (288 non-smoking) 🅱 ➿ Outdoor 🛥 Sa Pan Tak Sin pier

RENO HOTEL
www.renohotel.co.th
The Reno is a good-value, comfortable and friendly hotel. The standard rooms have their own bathrooms, the superior ones

come with a TV and safe box and the deluxe rooms have a fridge. The pool is just large enough to swim in, there is internet access in the lobby, and there's a laundry service and a cafe.

✉ 40 Soi Kasemson 1, off Thanon Rama I ☎ 022 150 026 ✋ B1,280–B1,420 🚻 58 🅱 ➿ Outdoor 🚇 National Stadium

SATHORN INN
www.sathorninn.com
This is a well-run establishment, conveniently reached from the airport by the airport bus route that stops at the top of the *soi*. Standard and deluxe rooms are available, with the latter having balconies, a TV and fridge. There is a coffee shop and internet access in the lobby.

✉ 37 Soi 9, Thanon Silom ☎ 022 381 655 ✋ B950–B1,200 🚻 80 🅱 🚇 Chong Nonsi

SHANGRI-LA HOTEL
www.shangri-la.com
Facing the Chao Phraya River, the Shangri-La features in several world lists of top-10 hotels, so you will find a spa, two pools, tennis and squash courts, day cruises to Ayutthaya and dinner river cruises. There are Chinese, Thai, Japanese and Western restaurants.

✉ 89 Soi Wat Suan Plu ☎ 022 367 777 ✋ B5,900–B6,900 🚻 799 🅱 ➿ Outdoor 🔶 🚇 Saphan Taksin 🛥 Sathorn Pier

SHERATON GRANDE SUKHUMVIT
www.sheratongrandesukhumvit.com
A 33-floor tower hotel, the best on Sukhumvit, fronted by a well-turned-out lobby with a marble floor and high ceiling. Rooms are generously sized and richly furnished. There are two good restaurants to choose from, a cafe and an outdoor eatery by the pool, plus at Riva's there are bands most nights, and a jazz bar. The spa is impressive.

✉ 250 Thanon Sukhumvit ☎ 026 498 888 ✋ B4,500–B8,000 🚻 429 🅱 ➿ Outdoor 🔶 🚇 Asok

SIAMATSIAM DESIGN HOTEL AND SPA BANGKOK

www.siamatsiam.com

This boutique hotel proclaims that "each of the 203 artistically appointed rooms is an individual exhibit within this extraordinary gallery of a Bangkok hotel." Art and accommodations definitely become one here, providing a unique experience. The staff are friendly and helpful. A rooftop restaurant gives views of the city and the location offers easy access to many of Bangkok's attractions. ✉ Rama I Road, Wang Mai, Patumwan ☎ 022 173 000 🍴 B3,400–B4,850 🛏 203 ⛔ ⛱ Outdoor 🚇 National Stadium

SIAM HERITAGE

www.thesiamheritage.com

This hotel tries hard to maintain an air of elegance and culture, with polished floors, teak furniture and part of the lobby displaying Thai art. There is a spa and fitness center, although the pool is not large enough to swim in. Coffee and tea is available in the rooms, there's cable TV and a Thai restaurant. This is an interesting hotel, conveniently located with easy access to the Skytrain and the metro making it easier to get around Bangkok.

✉ 115/1 Thanon Surawong ☎ 023 536 101 🍴 B2,500–B5,2000 🛏 73 ⛔ ⛱ Outdoor 🚻 🚇 Sala Daeng 🚇 Sam Yan

SOFITEL CENTARA GRAND BANGKOK

www.centarahotelsresorts.com

The ease of access by train and subway, a nearby huge shopping center, the weekend Chatuchak market, and the top-class facilities within the hotel—including Vietnamese (Le Danang ▷ 106–107), Thai, Chinese, Italian and Japanese restaurants—all add up to an attractive proposition. ✉ 1695 Thanon Phaholyothin, Chatuchak ☎ 025 411 234 🍴 From B4,500–B7,500 🛏 607 ⛔ ⛱ Outdoor 🚇 Mo Chit 🚇 Chatuchak Park

THE SUKHOTHAI

www.sukhothai.com

Winner of various awards, The Sukhothai is among the world's top hotels, and offers an exceptional standard of service and accommodations. There are two good restaurants and a bar, plus an infinity-edge pool. ✉ 13/3 Thanon South Sathorn ☎ 023 448 888 🍴 B11,500–B22,900 🛏 214 (78 non-smoking) ⛔ ⛱ Outdoor 🚻 🚇 Sala Daeng 🚇 Lumphini Park

THE SWISS LODGE

www.swisslodge.com

A gorgeous boutique hotel and a fantastic place to stay right in the heart of the city. There is a small pool and sun deck for relaxing, bedrooms with teak furniture, 24-hour room service, a business center and laundry. ✉ 3 Thanon Convent ☎ 022 335 345 🍴 B3,800–B5,500 🛏 46 ⛔ ⛱ Outdoor 🚇 Sala Daeng

THAI COZY HOUSE

www.thaicozyhouse.com

Clean and tidy rooms—the more expensive ones have a window and include breakfast. ✉ 113/1–3 Thanon Tanee ☎ 026 295 870 🍴 B750–B1,000 🛏 53 ⛔ ⛱ Tha Praya Athit

VIENGTAI HOTEL

www.viengtai.co.th

Rooms at the Viengtai are modern and well appointed and the Thai restaurant has a daily buffet for lunchtimes and Thai and international food at night. ✉ 42 Thanon Rambuttri, Banglamphu ☎ 022 805 434/45 🍴 B2,200–B2,700 🛏 200 (49 non-smoking) ⛔ ⛱ Outdoor ⛱ Tha Praya Athit

Above *Riverside dining at The Peninsula*

THE NORTHEAST

Thailand's best-kept secret is its northeast, known as Isan, and its least-visited region also has the most surprises for tourists to the region. There are no beaches or palm-fringed islands, and relatively little in the way of organized activities. Life is not rushed here—a slow cruise along the Mekong River is characteristic of the lazy pleasures on offer. Instead, Isan is an enticing mix of culture and countryside: wild elephants and gibbons in Khao Yai National Park; the mighty 4,000km (2,500-mile) Mekong River; Khmer temple ruins at Phimai, Khao Phra Viharn and Phanom Rung; and Isan arts and crafts—gorgeous silk, especially—at prices lower than anywhere else in the country. There are pleasant cafes and bars to while away the time and nearly 50 national parks and forests to explore, so there's also plenty to keep the whole family happy. Observing cultural life in Isan brings you closer to the ordinary lives of Thais and, although fewer people speak English, you will find the people wonderfully patient and helpful.

The northeast is also Thailand's most highly populated and poorest area. Most families subsist on farming, despite poor soils, inadequate irrigation and intense rainy seasons. As a means of survival, many families resort to sending their daughters to Bangkok and Pattaya to work in the sex industry. The area is heavily influenced by the politics of its neighbors. From the 1950s through the mid-60s, communist insurgents lead a movement here to align with Marxists in Laos. The border received countless Hmong refugees during the Vietnam War and then Khmer refugees during the Khmer Rouge era. The border has continued to be a point of territorial dispute with Cambodia at Khao Phra Viharn (Preah Vihear).

Vibrant festivals are one of the biggest draws for visitors to the region—particularly Surin's Elephant Round-up in November. The 10-day event ends with a procession of 300 festooned elephants performing battle reenactments. Other must-sees include the May Rocket Festival in Yasothon and the Rain-making Festival, held during mid-summer near Loei in Dan Sai.

BAN CHIANG

Archeological excavations, discovered by accident at the village of Ban Chiang in the 1960s, completely repositioned Southeast Asia in the history of human civilization. Ban Chiang, 31 miles (50km) east of Udon Thani, is the site of a human settlement that dates back to around 3600BC. The people lived in huts, made pottery and conducted funeral ceremonies. Their food came mostly from the wild, but some domesticated animals were kept and a primitive form of rice cultivation was in use. From these beginnings, the people began to make bronze tools and ornaments, and by 1700BC there is clear evidence of a Bronze Age culture emerging in Ban Chiang, challenging the long-held idea that the Bronze Age started in the Middle East around 3000BC and only reached Southeast Asia some 2,500 years later. The significance of Ban Chiang in overturning this view led to UNESCO declaring it a World Heritage Site in 1992.

THE STORY OF BAN CHIANG

The site was discovered in 1966 by a Harvard College student, named Steve Young, who was conducting interviews for his senior thesis. While walking down a path in the village, he tripped and landed face-first in an exposed stash of red-painted Ban Chiang pottery. He took samples of the pottery to Princess Phanthip Chumbote, some of which are now on display at the Suan Pakkad Palace in Bangkok (▷ 83).

The story of Ban Chiang, and the accidental way in which the excavations got under way, is told in the village's national museum. There are two floors to the museum. downstairs has a metallurgy room and a ceramics room, devoted to the early culture that began around 3600BC. The more interesting Ban Chiang Exhibition is upstairs, beginning with a skeleton, dated 1500BC, of a man who was buried with a bronze axe at his shoulder and wearing four bronze bracelets. Other exhibits include infant burial jars and red-painted pottery that was placed over corpses. Upstairs, there is also a Ban Chiang Today exhibition that consists of tools currently used by the villages.

INFORMATION

🞡 310 H5 ✉ Ban Chiang ☎ 042 208 340 🕐 Daily 8.30–4.30 💷 B150
🚌 From Udon Thani take a *songthaew* to Ban Chiang or take a bus heading to Sakon Nakhon, get off Route 2 at Ban Palu and take a *samlor* from there to the village. There are no afternoon *songthaews* back to Udon Thani, so take a *samlor* back to Route 2 and wait for a bus from Sakon Nakhon bound for Khon Kaen

TIPS

❯❯ The locally made cotton fabrics, heavy enough for winter wear, available in the village shops are good buys.
❯❯ Ban Chiang village has a number of craft and souvenir shops selling attractive reproductions of the pottery unearthed by archeologists. Unfortunately these can be quite difficult to pack in your luggage.

Opposite and below *There are a number of craft shops in Ben Chiang where you buy beautiful pottery*

BAN KHOK SA-NGA
Known as King Cobra Village, Ban Khok Sa-Nga is a farming village 31 miles (50km) northeast of Khon Kaen with a population of around 700 king cobra snakes and raises them as pets. This allows the snakes to be tamed and trained for the "boxing" performances that take place on demand. The shows begin with children performing their own "boxing" acts with non-poisonous snakes. The main acts get under way when adult king cobras are released from their boxes. You will be either fascinated or repulsed by the spectacle that follows, depending on the degree to which you think the snakes are being goaded simply for the sake of entertainment. It becomes clear that the snakes want to be left alone—they have no wish to attack, and will only adopt aggressive postures under duress. Whatever your feelings about this, there is no doubting the dangers involved—look carefully, some of the snake handlers have missing fingers.

Below *Weaving silk on a traditional loom*

The performances are dramatic and involve the handlers getting dangerously close to the king cobras, looking them straight in the eye and, even occasionally, putting a snake's head in the mouth.
✚ 310 G6 ✉ Ban Khok Sa-Nga ☎ 081 974 9499 🕐 Daily 9–5 💲 Donation to look around the village and see the snakes; the admission cost for a performance depends on the number of visitors. Ask the tourist office in Udon Thani to telephone the venue and establish the payment for a performance 🚗 From Khon Kaen take Route 2 to Udon Thani, turning right at kilometer stone 33 onto road 2039. At kilometer stone 14, signs point the way to a right-turn for the village

BAN KHWAO SILK-WEAVING VILLAGE
Around Chaiyaphum (▷ 119) there are a number of communities that specialize in silk-weaving, and Ban Khwao is one of the more accessible villages. Here you will see the whole process that begins with the breeding of silkworms using mulberry leaves and finishes with the distinctive, tie-dyed *mutmee* silk. The production process takes place under village houses, and you will see the silkworms being fed and covered under large saucer-shape trays of rattan. When the silkworm has created its silk cocoon from a fiber secreted from the mouth, and just before the moth will emerge from inside it, the cocoon is boiled to help release the silk fiber. The dead silkworms are not discarded, and you may be offered one of them as a quick snack. The silk fiber is then carefully unraveled and reeled onto threads. The silk is then dyed in preparation for weaving on the handmade looms.
Children and adults alike find it a fascinating and educational experience to observe, and village shops sell some of the fabrics that are made here.
✚ 312 F7 ✉ Ban Khwao 🕐 Daily 7–7 🚌 From Chaiyaphum, buses to Ban Khwao depart every half-hour between early morning and 6pm 🚗 From Chaiyaphum head west on Route 225 for 8 miles (13km) to Ban Khwao village

BAN NONG SAMRONG ORCHID NURSERY
Known also as Udon Sunshine Orchid Garden, this nursery grows and sells a new species of orchid that has been cultivated for its fragrance. The orchid is known as Miss Udon Sunshine and is unique because its scent is the first to be extracted from an orchid to make perfume. If you arrive at the nursery between early morning and early afternoon, the scent from the orchid is unmistakable. The orchids and the perfume can be purchased at the nursery. Also worth seeing here is a hybrid of *gyrants* that has become known as the "dancing plant" because of the way some of its leaves move in response to particular rhythmic sounds.
✚ 310 G5 ✉ Soi Kamon Watthana on Route 2024 at Ban Nong Samrong ☎ 042 242 475 🕐 Daily 8–6 🚗 From Udon Thani, a *tuk-tuk* to Ban Nong Samrong will cost about B150 each way 🚗 From Udon Thani, head northwest out of town on Route 2024 and look for signs to Udon Sunshine Orchid Garden

BAN PHU
The region around Ban Phu, best reached with your own transportation from either Nong Khai or Udon Thani, is characterized by a strange landscape of odd-shape rock formations and a number of caves and cliffs with traces of prehistoric paintings. The peculiar geology of Ban Phu is thought to have been caused by river erosion working on the rock of a glacier's terminal moraine. The area has been turned into the Phu Phra Bat Historical Park. It is worth arriving when the information center is open (daily 8–4.30) to study the displays relating to the prehistoric paintings and the legends associated with some of the outcrops of rock. An easy-to-follow set of footpaths connects many of the outcrops, and you should give yourself at least two hours to reach some of the more interesting rock formations. It is worth walking to the mushroom-shape Hor Nang Ussa, a bizarre pillar of rock topped by a flat

stone and chiseled by human hands to form a shrine or shelter. Legend has it that a princess named Ussa, imprisoned here by her father, was visited by the faithful Baros, who climbed to the top and eventually rescued her. It is thought that Hor Nang Ussa was sculpted into its present shape about 1,000 years ago. There are other examples of such grottos in the park, though none as photogenic as this one. There is also a natural viewpoint at Pha Sadej from where you can gaze northward to the mountains of Laos, 43 miles (70km) away.

✚ 310 G4 ✉ Phu Phra Bat Historical Park ☎ 042 222 909 🕐 Daily 8–6 🚌 From Nong Khai, take an early bus to Ban Phu and check the time of the last bus back, usually departing around 3pm; from Ban Phu a *songthaew* and then a motorcycle will take you to Phu Phra Bat Historical Park 🚗 From Udon Thani or Nong Khai, turn off Route 2 onto Route 2021 for 26 miles (42km) to Ban Phu. At Ban Phu, continue for another 7 miles (12km) on Route 2348 to Phu Phra Bat Historical Park

CHAIYAPHUM

A Laotian named Phraya Lae founded a town in the area around Chaiyaphum in 1819, seeking to escape from the court politics of Vientiane. Seven years later, when the Laotian king decided to go to war with Bangkok, Phraya Lae chose to ally himself with Siam and alerted officials in Korat about the invading army. He was rewarded by King Rama II but was captured in battle by Laotian soldiers and executed outside the town he had founded. A statue of Phraya Lae stands in the heart of town on Thanon Banakran. About 2 miles (3km) west of town, on the banks of the river on Route 225, a large tamarind tree marks the spot where he was executed. Each year, between January 12 and 20, a festival featuring an elephant parade to the tree commemorates his loyalty. Geographically, Chaiyaphum is located in the exact heart of Thailand, yet it remains one of the least-known and least-visited towns in the country.

Tad Ton National Park (▷ 129) makes a pleasant day's excursion. ✚ 312 F7 🚌 Daily from Mo Chit station in Bangkok, as well as regular local services to/from Khon Kaen and Nakhon Ratchasima (Korat) 🚗 From Nakhon Ratchasima (Korat) or Nong Khai, turn west off Route 2 onto Route 202

CHIANG KHAN

Chiang Khan has more character than most small Thai towns, due partly to its setting on the banks of the mighty Mekong River but also because of its charming old wooden houses along the two long narrow streets, which evoke an earlier age. The town is on the backpackers' trail and there are a number of budget guesthouses and places to enjoy a meal or coffee. Boat trips up and down the Mekong can be arranged through guesthouses, whether you are staying there or not.

Chiang Khan has temples that are not typically Thai in the way they incorporate colonnades, arches and shutters—stylistic features that suggest a French influence originating from across the Mekong in Laos. A good example can be found opposite *sois* 11 and 12 on the inland side of the main street, Thanon Chiang Khan, that is part of Route 211. Another temple like this can be seen by turning down Soi 20 at the eastern end of town.

✚ 310 F4 🚌 *Songthaews* and buses travel throughout the day between Loei and Chiang Khan; coming from Nong Khai, *songthaews* travel between Chiang Khan and Pak Chom 🚗 Chiang Khan is 31 miles (50km) north of Loei on Route 201; Route 211 connects Nong Khai with Chiang Khan

KHAO PHRA VIHARN

With your own transportation it is easy to reach this well-preserved Khmer temple from Ubon Ratchathani, and it makes a rewarding and adventurous journey; the temple complex is just inside Cambodia but can be visited without a visa. Khao Phra Viharn (or "Preah Vihear" in Cambodia) is dramatically perched on a clifftop and, after crossing the border into Cambodia,

you will soon find yourself at the bottom of a broad stone-built avenue that makes its way up the cliffside through a series of four *gopuras* (pavilions) decorated with scenes from Hindu mythology. One of the best examples, depicting Vishnu as a tortoise alongside *nagas* (magical serpents), can be found above the last door of the second *gopura*. In this Hindu version of the Big Bang, the universe is shown being created by stirring the cosmic sea with a large churning stick.

The building of Khao Phra Viharn, dedicated to Shiva, began in the ninth century and was completed by the twelfth. It would have been an arduous journey reaching the temple, a retreat for Hindu priests and a pilgrimage site for devotees. Today, the main sanctuary and its Buddha image are watched over by Cambodian monks on the clifftop, and there are stunning views of the Cambodian plain from the summit if you clamber through one of the stone windows. The complex was occupied by the Khmer Rouge during the Pol Pot years and mines laid around the site. It finally reopened in 2003 after international arbitration. Due to ongoing disputes with Cambodia, however, visitors should verify that the site is open before making travel plans. There have been periodic military skirmishes here since 2008. Do not stray into the areas where warning signs indicate there are still mines. Note that the Thai baht is accepted by all the Cambodian vendors at Khao Phra Viharn.

✚ 313 J8 🕐 Daily 8–5 ✋ Entry to the park B200; border crossing B5; entry to the temple (to the Cambodian authorities) B200 🚗 From Ubon Ratchathani, take Route 24 and turn onto Route 221 near Kantharalak. From Si Saket, take Route 221 through Kantharalak 🚗 A car and driver can be arranged through the tourist office in Si Saket (▷ 130) 🍴 Food and drink stands at the temple parking area, but bring a picnic or eat at Kantharalak

KHAO YAI NATIONAL PARK
▷ 122.

INFORMATION

✚ 310 G6 ℹ 15/5 Thanon Prachasamosorn, Khon Kaen ☎ 043 244 498 🕐 Daily 8.30–4.30 🚉 Khon Kaen Station (☎ 043 221 112) 🚌 From Bangkok's Northern Bus Terminal to Khon Kaen's bus station (☎ 043 237 300) ✈ 16 miles (10km) northwest of town (☎ 043 246 661/74); hotel buses meet arriving flights ❓ Budget (☎ 043 345 460) car rental at the airport

Above *A golden dragon guards the steps of the city's most stunning temple, Nongwan Muang Kao*

INTRODUCTION

A university town in the heart of Isan, Khon Kaen has a good choice of high-quality hotels and restaurants, excellent shopping for silk and cotton fabrics, and a fine museum. There is an easy-going, confident feel to Khon Kaen that makes it a refreshing place for a sojourn or a base for excursions into the beautiful surrounding countryside.

Khon Kaen began to emerge as a city of some importance only in the 1960s, when the Thai government injected some capital into its development and the US made it a base for their air force in the Vietnam War. Now the fourth-largest city in the country and home to Isan's most prestigious university, Khon Kaen is emerging as an attractive commercial and cultural center, as reflected in the development of sophisticated hotels and restaurants.

With daily flights and trains to and from Bangkok (280 miles/450km away) and with buses traveling up and down the northeast's major road, Route 2, as well as connecting with Phitsanulok in northern Thailand, Khon Kaen is well placed to receive visitors. The tourist office has a good range of literature on local attractions and dispenses a city map showing the transportation links, places of interest and the hotels and restaurants. *Songthaews* ply their way up and down the main streets, and *tuk-tuk* rides around town average B50. Cars can be rented at the airport, and Khon Kaen is an easy city to drive around and find your way. Unlike Korat and Udon Thani, the city's air does not feel polluted.

WHAT TO SEE

NATIONAL MUSEUM

Khon Kaen's branch of the National Museum has a notable collection of Bronze Age finds from Ban Chiang (▷ 117), pottery and jewelry, and is well worth seeing if you do not have time to visit Ban Chiang itself. The boundary stones exhibited are from the Dvaravati period (seventh to eleventh century) and one in particular is finely carved, with a picture of the Buddha's feet being cleaned

by Princess Bimba with her hair. Upstairs, there is an interesting gallery devoted to local crafts, with a specialist collection of the trays used by betel nut-chewers, and a small but choice collection of Buddha statues and ceramics.
✉ Thanon Lang Soon Ratchakan, 3 blocks north of the tourist office ☎ 043 246 170
🕐 Wed–Sun 9–4 ✋ B10

WAT NONGWAN MUANG KAO

While the museum is off the north end of Thanon Klang Muang, the city's most visually arresting temple is at the south end of the same long road. Its nine tiers, completed in 1997, are painted in vivid red and gold and shine gloriously in the sunlight. Walk inside the pagoda to admire the murals on the first level before climbing to the top for panoramic views of the city. The lake you see, Bung Kaen Nakhon, is a good 10-minute walk away, and the pathway around it is dotted with restaurants and food stands.
✉ Thanon Klang Muang 🕐 Daily 8–7 ✋ Free

SHOPPING

One of the best reasons to visit Khon Kaen is the number of quality shops selling superb local silk and cotton, as well as Isan arts and crafts. Prices are fixed at the huge Prathamakant Local Goods Center (▷ 141), and in the private shops expect a discount of around 15 percent.

A gratifying aspect of shopping here is the fact that you do not need to indulge in prolonged bargaining to get a decent price. As well as the shops, there are vendors on the street—many congregate opposite the Pullman Khon Kaen Raja Orchid—and every year a Silk Festival takes place at the end of November and early December. The focus of the festival takes place around the Provincial Hall on Thanon Na Suan Ratchakan.

MORE TO SEE

PHU WIANG NATIONAL PARK

www.thaiforestbooking.com/nationalpark-eng.htm

You need your own transportation from Khon Kaen to reach the Phu Wiang National Park, although the best way to see the park itself is on foot or mountain bike. Phu Wiang is the name of a mountain and there are beautiful views over the valley from its peak. There is plenty to do and see in the park including spectacular waterfall walks, birdwatching and mountain-bike riding, but the main draw here are the fossils of dinosaur footprints and skeletons, which were first found in 1981.

The prize exhibit is in site 9: the fossil remains of a new species of dinosaur regarded as the ancestor of *Tryrannosaurus rex*. Visit the park's Phu Wiang Musuem to learn more about the dinosaurs that once roamed free in the park, as well as see life-size models of the dinosaurs themselves. A brochure on Phu Wiang, available from the tourist office in Khon Kaen has useful information and a map of the various sites. You can also reserve bungalow accommodation or pitch a tent in one of the campsites around the national park.
✚ 310 F6 ☎ 043 358 073 🕐 Daily 8–4.30 ✋ B400 🚌 Route 12 from Khon Kaen for 30 miles (48km), as far as Nong Rua, then a right turn onto route 2038 for 24 miles (39km) to Phu Wiang

CHONNABOT

Like Ban Khwao (▷ 118), the town of Chonnabot specializes in the production of silk, and you can see women working on different stages of the process in their wooden homes. The silk they produce can be purchased from vendors along the street.
✚ 312 G6 🚌 Khon Kaen–Korat buses stop at Ban Phai, then take a *songthaew* for 6 miles (10km) to Chonnabot 🚌 Route 2 south from Khon Kaen to Ban Phai, then right turn on Route 229 to Chonnabot

TIP
➤ The silk shop next to the Pullman Khon Kaen Raja Orchid (▷ 146) is one of the very few places where you can buy unstuffed axe pillows.

Below *Detail of golden statue at Nongwan Muang Kao temple*

INFORMATION

www.thaiforestbooking.com/
nationalpark-eng.htm
⊕ 309 E8 ⊠ Park Headquarters:
Thanon Thanarat, Pak Chong ☎ 081 877
3127 ◷ Daily 8am–8pm (information
center closes at 4pm) ✋ Entrance to
national park: adult B400, child B200
🚆 From Bangkok to Pak Chong (2.5
hours) 🚌 From Bangkok's Northern
Bus Terminal to Pak Chong; *songthaews*
travel between the park entrance and
Pak Chong, but your accommodations
will pick you up at Pak Chong 🍴 At park
headquarters

TIP

>> It's possible to get lost in the park on
some of the longer walking trails so it is
safer to have a guide.

Above *Bats in flight at dusk over Khao Yai
National Park*

KHAO YAI NATIONAL PARK

Thailand's oldest and best national park is easily reached from Bangkok, and
the availability of decent accommodations and knowledgeable nature guides
makes Khao Yai one of the most enjoyable destinations in northeast Thailand.
About 74 miles (120km) from Bangkok, the park was established in 1962.
Covering an area of over 770sq miles (2,000sq km), its diverse habitats include
mountains and forest, and there are short- and long-distance walks that provide
an opportunity to experience wildlife at close quarters.

STAYING IN THE PARK

Accommodations are available at the park headquarters, but are geared toward
large groups. It makes more sense to stay at one of the private lodges that
are dotted along the 20km (12-mile) stretch of road that connects the town of
Pak Chong with the entrance to the park. As well as offering more salubrious
accommodations, the best of these lodges have their own experienced guides
who will accompany you on half- and full-day tours around the park.

The park headquarters has displays about the park's wildlife, including the
dwindling number of tigers. After dark, you can take a night safari, where you
sit in the back of an open truck and hope that the park ranger's spotlight will
pick out some interesting creatures. Civet cats and barking deer are usually
seen, and a herd of elephants is not an uncommon sight.

PARK TOURS

The full-day tours offered by the lodges, which include the night safari, begin
early in the morning with a view to catching sight of the white-handed gibbons.
Their whooping duets claiming territorial rights are an unforgettable sound,
and just as memorable is the sight of any of the four species of hornbills that
inhabit the park. The birdlife varies with the time of year, but dollar birds, white-
crested laughing thrushes, black-crested bulbuls and trogons are commonly
seen. Half-day tours include a visit to caves in the vicinity and, at evening time,
an opportunity to observe thousands of birds flying out in wave upon wave for
their nightly food trips. Come prepared with suitable footwear for forest walks,
long trousers and insect repellent; a pair of binoculars is useful, but your guide
will have some and will supply leech socks if necessary. Opportunities for
nature photographs abound.

LOEI

Forming a border area between northern and northeastern Thailand, and 31 miles (50km) south of the border with Laos, Loei's transportation links with Udon Thani and Phitsanulok make it your most likely arrival and departure point for visiting Phu Kradung and Phu Rua national parks. The town makes a pleasant base and, although it has a distinctly frontier feel, Loei has a friendly atmosphere. There are good accommodations in the town, and Loei's dusty streets, with its shops selling agricultural tools and products, are worth wandering around.

PHU KRADUNG NATIONAL PARK

The park, 50 miles (80km) south of Loei and closed in the rainy season (June to September), has a picturesque trail that leads for 5 miles (8km) from the first visitor center to a viewing area on the plateau of Phu Kradung, three hours away. Here there is another visitor center, places to eat and accommodations in park bungalows (reserve ahead; go to www.thaiforestbooking.com/nationalpark-eng.htm). There are shorter walking trails that begin from the plateau's visitor center.

PHU RUA NATIONAL PARK

Some 31 miles (50km) west of Loei, Phu Rua National Park is best visited with your own transportation. Having paid the entrance fee, a paved road leads to the summit of a picturesque mountain at 4,478ft (1,365m). Before reaching a second visitor center, there are a number of guesthouses that offer alternative accommodations to the bungalows for rent at the second visitor center. At the summit there are a number of fantastic walking trails that provide plenty of birdwatching opportunities.

PHI TA KHON FESTIVAL

If you are in the region around the end of June, travel to the town of Dan Sai, 50 miles (80km) southwest of Loei, for its three-day *Phi Ta Khon* Festival, where young people dress up in ghost masks and bright clothes. Rockets are set off and live bands perform in the evening. If you can't make it to Dan Sai, stop by the Loei Center (tel 042 835 224, daily 8.30–4, Rte 201) to see fine examples of the masks. The Chateau de Loei, Thailand's foremost wine producer, is 37 miles (60km) from Loei town on route 203. You can taste the wines at the vineyard restaurant (daily 8–5; www.chateaudeloei.com).

INFORMATION

www.thaiforestbooking.com/nationalpark-eng.htm
309 F5 Loei tourist office, Thanon Charoenrat 042 812 812 Daily 8.30–4.30

Phu Kradung National Park

310 F5 Phu Kradung National Park 042 871 333 Oct–end May; visitor center Oct–end May daily 7–2 Adult B400, child B200 Loei–Khon Kaen buses stop at Phu Kradung village; take a *songthaew* to the visitor center Take Route 201 south to Phu Kradung, then turn right onto Route 2019 for 5 miles (8km) Restaurant at the first visitor center

Phu Rua National Park

309 E5 Phu Rua National Park 042 801 716 Visitor center daily 7–4 B200 Loei–Phu Rua buses travel throughout the day, but there is little public transportation to the visitor center Take Route 203 to Phu Rua village, then right for 2.5 miles (4km)

TIP

» If you're not staying in Phu Kradung, you need to reach the first visitor center before 10am to have time to get to the plateau and back.

Below *There are some fine walking trails at Phu Kradung National Park*

MUKDAHAN

You will feel like an intrepid explorer when you reach Mukdahan, an out-of-the-way and attractive town set along the Mekong River, some 105 miles (170km) north of Ubon Ratchathani. Trade links with Savannakhet, the second-largest town in Laos and directly across the river from Mukdahan, fuel the lively Indochina Market by the pier (▷ 141). To appreciate the town's scenic location, climb to the top of Mukdahan Tower (tel 042 633 211; daily 8–6; B20) for panoramic views of the river and the patchwork of the rice paddies around Laos.

US$30 buys you a 15-day visa to visit Savannakhet and the rest of Laos. Staying in Thailand, Mukdahan National Park (also known as Phu Pha Thoep National Park) is 9 miles (15km) south of town, reached by taking Route 2034 and turning off between kilometer stones 14 and 15. The park is characterized by unusual rock formations and a viewpoint reached after a 2km (1.2-mile) walk from the park headquarters. There is the usual B200 entrance fee.

🕀 311 J6 🚌 To/from Ubon Ratchathani, That Phanom, Nakhon Phanom, Bangkok, Udon Thani

NAKHON PHANOM

Nakhon Phanom's claim to fame is its location, on the picturesque banks of the Mekong with the best views of the river and the jagged mountains of Laos in the northeast. It is worth wandering along the town's streets to admire the interesting old buildings: the old Vietnamese-style temple by the pier, the Clock Tower and Custom House, and the French-style National Library on Thanon Apiban Bancha. With your own transportation, there are plenty of places to visit nearby, and at That Phanom (▷ 132) there is the village of Renu Nakhon, where high-quality silk and cotton is woven and available to purchase at good prices.

🕀 311 J5 🛈 184/1 Thanon Suntorn Vichit ☎ 042 513 490 🕓 Daily 8.30–4.30 🚌 To/from Nong Khai, Mukdahan,

Bangkok, Udon Thani ✈ Nakhon Phanom Airport for flights to/from Bangkok with PB Air (www.pbair.com)

NAKHON RATCHASIMA (KORAT)

▷ 125.

NAM NAO NATIONAL PARK

www.thaiforestbooking.com/nationalpark-eng.htm (for reserving bungalow accommodations in the park)
Covering about 390sq miles (1,000sq km), this is one of the country's least visited national parks, although it offers walks and a variety of habitats. Circular trails that are easy to follow begin from the visitor center and vary in length from 0.5 to 4 miles (1km to 6km). There are also longer trails of up to 15.5 miles (25km), although for these it would be advisable to hire a guide from the visitor center. Mammals, including elephants, thrive in the park, and you are most likely to spot barking deer or hear gibbons in the morning. More than 200 species of bird have been identified in the park.

🕀 309 F5 ☎ 056 810 724 🕓 Daily 6am–11pm 🖐 B400 🚌 Buses from Phitsanulok, Khon Kaen and Loei will drop you off at the turn-off on Route 12 🚗 Signposted off Route 12 at kilometer stone 50, 90 miles (145km) west of Khon Kaen, 100 miles (160km) southwest of Loei

NONG KHAI

Of all the border towns in the northeast, Nong Khai has the most developed infrastructure for visitors and an appealing charm that warrants a stay of more than just one night. There is a fair choice of accommodations and places to eat, an evening boat cruise on the Mekong (▷ 142) and some good places to shop for clothes, arts and crafts and souvenirs. The absence of heavy traffic and a laid-back atmosphere make Nong Khai an enjoyable town to walk around (▷ 136–137) and relax in. Bicycles can be rented from some of the guesthouses by the riverfront.

The Friendship Bridge, 2 miles (3km) out of town, opened to Thai–Laos traffic in 1994. You can obtain a

visa for Laos at the bridge for US$30 and a photograph. From the other side it is only 15 miles (24km) to Vientiane, and taxis and *songthaews* are available at the border.

The Pantawee Hotel is a good source of local information and, in addition to internet access, there is a travel desk for arranging car rental and tours in the area. If you are here in June, ask about the dates for the Rocket Festival—it varies each year—and if it is on then arrange for transportation to take you there.

Take a *tuk-tuk* to Sala Kaeo Kou, a temple 3 miles (5km) east of town with an interesting sculpture garden.

🕀 310 G4 🛈 On the road leading to the Friendship Bridge ☎ 042 411 132 🕓 Daily 8.30–4.30 🚌 Buses from Udon Thani, Khon Kaen, Loei and most other towns in the northeast; long-distance buses to and from Bangkok 🚉 Nong Khai station is 2.5 miles (4km) outside of town, near the Friendship Bridge 🚢 Tours to Vientiane and day tours of Nong Khai through Holiday Puyfay at Pantawee Hotel (www.pantawee.com)

Below *Herds of elephants and more than 200 species of birds thrive in Nam Nao National Park*

NAKHON RATCHASIMA (KORAT)

Thailand's second-largest city, known as Korat, is a transportation hub for the northeast and a base for visits to major Khmer ruins at Phimai and Phanom Rung. Although at first sight Nakhon Ratchasima lacks charm, and its sprawling size makes it a difficult city to get to know in a short space of time, when the traffic dies down a little and you gain a sense of direction it becomes less daunting. The old part of the city is still encircled by a moat, and the city gates have been rebuilt and serve as reference points.

If arriving at the large, well-organized bus station, on the main Route 2, you need a *tuk-tuk* to get into town. The train station and the tourist office are at the eastern end of town, while the city center is represented by the landmark Thao Suranari Shrine. The commercial heart of the city is to be found in the streets around the shrine; here you will find a modern shopping complex and a shop selling quality Isan silk (▷ 141).

A MONUMENT, MUSEUM AND CERAMICS

The Thao Suranari ("Courageous Lady") Shrine by the west gate is a striking monument commemorating Khun Ying Mo, the wife of the provincial governor who saved the city when it faced an invading army from Laos in 1826. The story goes that she gathered together the town's womenfolk, and they offered alcohol and sensual inducements to the Laotian soldiers; once inebriated, the soldiers were slaughtered. The monument has become a shrine and is venerated as a source of good luck and marital harmony. Each year, at the end of March, a festival celebrates the memory of Khun Ying Mo, and there are pageants and parades though the streets, dancing at the shrine and fireworks.

The Maha Wirawong National Museum, on Thanon Ratchadamnoen in the grounds of Wat Sutchnida (tel 044 242 958; Wed–Sun 9–4; B50) has a modest collection of Khmer and Hindu woodcarvings and sandstone images, including an eighth-century statue of Ganesh.

If you have your own transportation it is worthwhile making an excursion to visit the pottery village of Dan Kwian, 9 miles (15km) south of Korat on Route 224, to see pottery being made.

INFORMATION

312 F8 Thanon Mittaphap
044 213 666 Daily 8.30–4.30
Nakhon Ratchasima Station (044 242 044; Thanon Mukkhamontri)
Served by buses (044 256 006) to/from Bangkok, Chiang Mai, Khon Kaen, Ubon Ratchathani and smaller towns like Pak Chong (for Khao Yai National Park) and Phimai Budget (044 341 654) car rental

Above *Korat is a sprawling, bustling city with some fine buildings to admire*

PAK THONG CHAI

Pak Thong Chai is a silk-weaving village with a commercial awareness that has resulted in a number of shops retailing the silk by the meter. It is worth taking a look if you have your own transportation and are traveling along this stretch of Route 304, but a special trip hardly justifies itself because prices are high and there are no bargains to be had.

➕ 312 F8 🚌 Buses from Nakhon Ratchasima (Korat) 🚌 18.5 miles (30km) south of Nakhon Ratchasima (Korat) on Route 304; the village is 1.2 miles (2km) off the road

PHA TAM

Inside Pha Tam National Park there is a section of cliff-face, protected from the elements by an overhanging ledge, with prehistoric rock paintings in red that date back at least 3,000 years. You can make out human shapes, huge catfish and fish traps, elephants and geometric symbols, the significance of which can only be guessed at. The park opens at 5am because it is the first place in Thailand to receive the rising sun. On weekends Thais arrive very early in the morning for this reason.

➕ 313 K7 ✉ Kong Chiam 🕐 Daily 5am–6pm 💵 B200 🚌 From Ubon Ratchathani take Route 217 and then Route 2222 to Kong Chiam, from where Pha Tam National Park is signposted

PHANOM RUNG

Phanom Rung, only reachable with your own transportation, was built between the 10th and 13th centuries using sandstone and laterite. Over a period of 17 years its majestic remains were restored to make it the most impressive and important Khmer temple in Thailand. The quality of the carvings is on a par with those at Angkor Wat in Cambodia.

Phanom Rung stands on the top of an inactive volcano—Phanom Rung means "big mountain"—and is approached by way of a grand stone avenue over 164 yards (150m) in length and bordered by small pillars topped with lotus-bud finials. This processional way was completed in the 12th century. At the end of the avenue you walk across a bridge, representing the journey into the world of the gods, with balustrades formed by five-headed *nagas* (snakes). A second bridge, with *naga* heads spouting water from the mouth of a monster, accesses the eastern *gorupa* (Khmer doorway), where you will find a pediment depicting Shiva and female consorts. The eastern *gorupa* was the formal entrance to the temple sanctuary.

In the sanctuary itself there is an even more remarkable pediment with a dancing Shiva and, on the lintel below it, a reclining Vishnu framed by two neatly carved parrots. The Vishnu lintel was stolen from the temple but turned up in the Art Institute of Chicago in 1973 and was finally returned to Thailand in 1988. Other pediments depict battle scenes, thought to refer to the 12th-century Khmer ruler Narendraditya, who retired to the temple.

The north side of the sanctuary is decorated with scenes from the *Ramayana* that have been beautifully restored; the level of detail is extraordinary. Over the west door, Sita is shown being abducted and driven away in a chariot.

A visit to the information center (daily 9–4) is highly recommended before exploring the site because the exemplary display panels provide useful historical context for understanding the significance of the temple's many elements.

Less than 5 miles (8km) southeast of Phanom Rung is another beautiful temple complex, Prasat Muang Tam, worth visiting.

➕ 312 G8 ✉ Prasat Phanom Rung ☎ 044 782 715 🕐 Daily 6–6 💵 B100 🚌 From Nakhon Ratchasima (Korat), Route 226 to Buriram, then Route 219 to Prakhon Chai and straight over, then right

PHIMAI

▷ 127.

Right *A lady silk weaver in Pak Thong Chai, where you can buy beautiful handmade silks*

ROI ET

▷ 128.

SAKHON NAKHON

The agricultural town of Sakhon Nakhon is known in Thailand as the town where eating dog meat is relatively popular. A better reason to visit is to view its very sacred and ancient temple, Wat Phra That Cheong Chum, beside the town lake. The white, Lao-style *chedi* (monument housing a Buddhist relic) is 79ft (24m) high, and monks will allow you access if you ask. Northwest of town, off Route 22 and 2 miles (3km) past the airport at the village of Ban That (turn left at kilometer stone 156), there is another noted temple, Wat Phra That Narai Jaeng Weng. It boasts some carvings depicting Hindu motifs like a dancing Shiva, a reclining Vishnu and a *naga* engaging two lions.

➕ 311 J5 🚌 On Route 22 from Udon Thani or Nakhon Phanom

PHIMAI

This major Khmer temple was built in Phimai in the late 11th and early 12th centuries to face Angkor and was connected to the Khmer capital by a direct road. Restored in the 1980s, Prasat Hin Phimai is the biggest and most complete Khmer temple in Thailand.

The town of Phimai developed on the banks of the Mun River, a tributary of the Mekong, and there is evidence of settlements dating back to neolithic times. The Angkor empire in the 12th century included large parts of Thailand as well as Cambodia, and Phimai was part of this empire, 149 miles (240km) away from the capital at Angkor. It is thought that the sanctuary at Phimai was built before work was completed on Angkor Wat. It remained an important sanctuary until Thai forces under an Ayutthaya king defeated the Khmer empire in the 14th century.

SANDSTONE SANCTUARY

The sanctuary has a 92ft-high (28m) *prang* (tower) but when you first enter through the main gate to the southeast your attention is taken by the stone staircase and the decorative *nagas* (snakes) on the raised terrace. Inside Prang Bhranmathat, made of laterite, was found an armless sandstone statue, the original of which can be seen in the museum. The statue of a cross-legged man is thought to be King Jayavarman VII, who ruled in the 12th century. Prang Hin Daeng, on the left (southwest) side, dates to the 12th century, when Hinduism began to give way to Buddhism.

The main five-tiered *prang*, is decorated with fine carvings on the pediments and lintels that depict scenes from the *Ramayana*, while those on the southern side show the dancing Shiva. The pediment on the eastern side depicts Hindu deities. The one on the western side was never finished, but you can make out the figure of a *garuda* (a half-man and half-bird creature) flying to the rescue of Rama and Lakshmana.

PHIMAI NATIONAL MUSEUM

The single rarest exhibit in the museum is the statue of King Jayavarman VII, but there is a lot more to see relating to Khmer culture. In addition to background information on the history and architecture of Phimai, there are displays relating to contemporary religious beliefs. Hindu-inspired art is well represented by statues of Shiva and Ganesha, and there are finds on show from excavations at Phanom Rung (▷ 126).

✉ Behind, to the northeast of, Prasat Hin Phimai and just before the bridge ☎ 044 471 167
🕐 Daily 9–4 ✋ B100

INFORMATION

www.phimai.ca
✚ 312 G7 ☎ 044 471 568 🕐 Daily 8–6 ✋ B100 🚌 From Nakhon Ratchasima (Korat) throughout the day; coming from Khon Kaen, get off any Korat-bound bus at the turnoff for Route 206 and wait for a Korat–Phimai bus for the remaining 6-mile (10km) journey to Phimai 🚌 From Nakhon Ratchasima (Korat), 33.5 miles (54km) on Route 2 then 6 miles (10km) on Route 206

TIPS

➤➤ Buses from Nakhon Ratchasima (Korat) stop close by the temple. As the last bus back to Korat departs at around 6.30pm, a day trip to Phimai is quite feasible.
➤➤ Be sure to collect the English-language brochure when you buy your ticket as it contains a map of the temple complex and without it you may find sorting out the different elements confusing.
➤➤ The open-air restaurants opposite the huge banyan tree in Sai Ngam, 1.2 miles (2km) to the northeast of the temple on Route 206, are ideal for lunch. *Samlors* will take you between the sanctuary and Sai Ngam. Alternatively, hire a bike from the Bai Teiy restaurant on Thanon Chomsudasadet

Above *Buddhist monks entering the remains of the Khmer sandstone sanctuary of Phimai*

INFORMATION

313 H6 The bus station (043 512 546) is outside the middle of town, served by *tuk-tuks*

ROI ET

This attractive small town is built around an artificial lake and an island with a large walking Buddha. An even larger walking Buddha, one of the tallest in Thailand, dominates one of the town's temples. The tourist office in Khon Kaen dispenses a brochure on Roi Et that includes a useful map showing the town's lake, Bung Phalan Chai, in the heart of town. On the lake's island, reached by footbridges, is a large walking Buddha. Rowboats can be rented on the lake. The best place for a meal is along one of the roads surrounding the lake.

The oldest temple in town is Wat Klang Ming Muang, off Thanon Padung Panit, a 10-minute walk northeast of the Buddha statue. It dates back to the Ayutthaya period, before the town was founded, and around the outside of the *bot* (main sanctuary) there are murals, some showing their age, depicting the story of the Buddha.

EXCURSIONS

Wat Buraphaphiram, located farther along the same road but to the east of Wat Klang Ming Muang, has an especially large walking Buddha. Its height is around 197ft (60m) and you can walk up one side of the statue for beautiful views of the town.

With your own transportation, a short excursion can be made to visit a late 11th-century Khmer sanctuary called Prang Ku. Take Route 23 east of town for 5 miles (8km), turning right at kilometer stone 8. The ruins of the three-tiered *prang* are less than a 0.6 miles (1km) down this unpaved road.

To appreciate a more substantial example of Khmer architecture, you need to travel 37 miles (60km) south of town on Route 214 and make a right turn between kilometer stones 6 and 7. This leads to Ku Phra Ko Na, which also dates from the 11th century but was partly restored in the 1920s. Lintels on the northern side carry depictions of Hindu deities, a reclining Vishnu, and Shiva on a *garuda*, a half-man and half-bird creature.

Above *Walk up the Buddha at Wat Buraphaphiram for beautiful views*
Opposite *One of the waterfalls in Tad Ton National Park*

SI CHIANG MAI

This small town by the Mekong River is renowned throughout Thailand for its production of spring-roll wrappers, using rice flour. You will see them drying in the sun below people's village houses. Route 211 passes through the town, with a quieter road running parallel to it but closer to the river. There are Lao and Vietnamese families living here as well as Thais, and the French influence from Laos shows itself clearly in the town's bakery, which churns out row upon row of fresh baguettes each morning. The bakery is at the Nong Khai end of town, while the backpackers' traditional port of call, Tim Guest House, overlooks the river and is reached by turning down Soi 17—on your left if you're coming into town from the western end. This is the best place to go for a coffee, have a meal or just get some information on the area. Bicycles can be rented and boat trips along the Mekong River can be arranged, though the price only becomes economical if you can make up a small group of people to share the cost between you.

To the west, halfway between Si Chiang Mai and Sang Khom and clearly signposted off Route 211, Wat Hin Mak Peng is a famous temple by the banks of the Mekong. On display here are effigies of Luang Phu Thet, the temple's founder, an ascetic who died in 1994; the figure you first see on entering the temple is an alarmingly lifelike reproduction. The number of visitors to the *wat* drove him to relocate to a quieter temple near Sakhon Nakhon.

🕇 310 G4 🚌 From Nong Khai throughout the day; connections to/from Chiang Khan, Loei, Udon Thani and Bangkok

SI SAKET
▷ 130.

SURIN
▷ 131.

TAD TON NATIONAL PARK
www.thaiforestbooking.com/nationalpark-eng.htm (bungalow reservations in the park)

One of Thailand's smallest and less well-known national parks—84sq miles (217sq km) in size—Tad Ton can nevertheless boast some superb scenery. The highland landscape is characterized by dipterocarp and evergreen forest. With your own transportation it is easily reached on a day trip from Chaiyaphum (▷ 119), and outside of weekends or public holidays you are likely to have the place to yourself.

At the entrance to the park there is a track that leads to Nam Tok Tad Ton, a robust waterfall that is seen at its best between June and November during the rainy season. The water pours down from a large platform of stone and it is possible to swim in the basin below the waterfall. The nearby shrine, Chao Pho Tad Ton, is named after a hermit who lived in the area before it became a national park.

There is another smaller waterfall in the park, Pha Phuong, which is also signposted. Walks through the forest with a pair of binoculars reveal a rich birdlife, and you may also spot some barking deer and wild pigs. If you are here during the rainy season, when leeches are plentiful, you should come prepared with insect repellent and wear long trousers and suitable footwear.

Accommodations are available in simple two-bedroom bungalows with a fan. There is a small grocery shop for campers but no restaurant or food stands.

🕇 312 F6 ☎ 044 853 333, 044 853 293 (reservations) 🖐 B200 🚌 13 miles (21km) north of Chaiyaphum on Route 2051

THAT PHANOM
▷ 132.

UBON RATCHATHANI
▷ 133–134.

UDON THANI
▷ 135.

YASOTHON

The principal sight in Yasothon is Wat Mahathat, situated off the main road, which dates back to the foundation of the town itself. The La-style reliquary is thought to be from the seventh century, making Yasothon an ancient settlement.

If you are in Isan around the middle of May it is worth going out of your way to witness Yasothon's rocket festival, which is intended to encourage the gods to produce rain. Called Bun Bang Fai, it is the most exuberant of the rocket festivals that punctuate the skyline at the end of the dry season, and you will be astonished at the size (up to 27ft/8m long) and power (more than 44lb/20kg of gunpowder) of the bamboo rockets. They are fired from launching pads, made of concrete and wood, with local villages competing to see whose can ascend the highest and make the most impressive display. A panel of judges is involved and bets are laid amid the festive atmosphere. When you see spectators moving back from the launch pad, retreat further back because the explosive charge is dangerous and fatalities do occur.

Just over 12 miles (20km) to the east of Yasothon, reached by turning off Route 202 to the right between kilometer stones 18 and 19, the village of Ban Si Than is worth an excursion. It is a center for axe pillows production and you can observe villagers making them. They can be bought at competitive prices.

If you miss Yasothon's rocket festival, try to catch Nong Khai's pyrotechnic display in June (▷ 143). 🕇 313 J7 🚌 Bus station is on Thanon Rattanakhet, with daily services to/from Ubon Ratchathani

INFORMATION
✚ 313 J8 🏠 Thanon Lak Muang
☎ 045 611 283 🕐 Mon–Fri 8.30–4.30
🚌 Bus station (☎ 045 612 500) is in
the town, with regular services to Ubon
Ratchathani, Surin and Bangkok
🚆 Si Saket Station (☎ 045 613 871)
in the heart of town; Bangkok—Ubon
Ratchathani trains stop here

TIP
>> There is nowhere to eat at Prasat Hin Wat Sra Kamphaeng Yai so plan your excursion to take this into account.

SI SAKET

Close to the Cambodian border, Si Saket is a typical Isan town where visitors are few and far between. Good transportation links make it a convenient base for an excursion to the remarkable Khao Phra Viharn (▷ 119) and to another less well-known Khmer ruin in the vicinity.

The capital of Si Saket province, with a population of around 135,000, is easy to reach by bus or train from Surin or Ubon Ratchathani, or direct from Bangkok (354 miles/570km away), and a night spent in town before or after visiting the Khmer sites lets you experience small-town life in Isan at an unhurried pace.

Each evening at around 6pm, food stands take up their positions close to the railway line and station, and as the place begins to fill with diners there is a buzz of activity that enlivens the scene, making it the town's social center. Little English is spoken here though: it's a matter of finding something that looks tasty and pointing at what you want. If you can't find anything here to whet your appetite, the town's main concentration of restaurants is along Thanon Kukhan, perpendicular to the rail line. There are also several handicraft shops along this road, selling locally produced silk.

PRASAT HIN WAT SRA KAMPHAENG YAI

To reach this Khmer ruin, take Route 226 west of Si Saket for 25 miles (40km), turn off at kilometer stone 81 and the temple is 0.6 miles (1km) down the unpaved road. The site is thought to date back to the late 10th or early 11th century, before the influence of Buddhism made itself felt in this region, and it is thought to have converted to a Buddhist temple some time in the 13th century. It is an impressive ruin, with the main stupa surrounded by a gallery— made from laterite and restored in places—a grand ceremonial gateway and brick structures adjoining the central stupa. The style of the gallery is architecturally similar to the gallery on the summit at Khao Phra Viharn (▷ 119). The detailed figures carved out of sandstone on the lintels and pediments are very well preserved, and you can clearly make out Shiva with his wife Uma seated in his lap, both sitting atop the bull Nandin. Look too for the lintel in the brick structure on the east side of the stupa that shows Vishnu reclining on a *naga* (serpent) in the company of his wives.

Below *The night market in Si Saket, serving freshly cooked food*

SURIN

A provincial capital town, with a rich Khmer inheritance, Surin is famous for its annual Elephant Roundup in November, and is a retail center for locally produced silk. More than 280 miles (450km) from Bangkok and 125 miles (200km) east of Nakhon Ratchasima (Korat), Surin is close to the border with Cambodia—visas are issued at the border crossing—and Angkor Wat is only 93 miles (150km) away. Prasat Ta Moan, an evocative Khmer sanctuary built on the ancient road that connected Angkor with Phimai (▷ 127), lies 43 miles (70km) to the south of Surin and makes the most obvious excursion from town. Many of the villages in Surin province weave silk, and you will find women vendors selling their produce around town as well as through shops.

ELEPHANT ROUNDUP FESTIVAL

Surin erupts into life over the third weekend of each November, when festooned elephants parade the streets and mock battles and soccer games using elephants amuse the large crowds that flock to the town. Tickets can be reserved though travel agents in Bangkok and Surin. The village of Ban Ta Klang, 37 miles (60km) north of Surin on Route 214, is the traditional home for the Say people, who used to make their living out of training elephants. There is an Elephant Museum (tel 044 513 358; daily 8.30–4.30; free), and occasional elephant shows take place in the village.

PRASAT TA MOAN

To reach this Khmer chapel and resting place, travel south on Route 214 and turn right at kilometer stone 35 for the final 7.5 miles (12km). Small but finely proportioned and typically Khmer in its design, Prasat Ta Moan (daily 7.30–6; B30) has doorways at the four cardinal points in the gallery that encircles the main *prang* (tower), with minor *prangs* adjoining at the sides. Part of the attractiveness of the site is attributable to the four ponds that are part of the overall design, the need for water being part of the cleansing ceremony for travelers in addition to its sacred quality for the priests.

Prasat Ta Moan was built in the early 12th century, when Jayavarman VII adopted Mahayana Buddhism as the official religion of the Khmer empire. The site has a small tourist center (daily 9–4; free) that provides background information on the construction of the chapel complex.

INFORMATION

✚ 313 H8 ✋ Elephant shows during the festival B200–B500 🚌 Bus station (☎ 044 511 756) in the middle of town, with daily services to/from all the big towns in Isan, as well as Bangkok and Chiang Mai 🚆 Surin Station (☎ 044 511 295); several of the daily Bangkok–Ubon Ratchathani trains stop in Surin ✉ Saran Travel (☎ 044 520 174; sarentour@yahoo.com), with a desk at the Thong Train Hotel on Thanon Suit near the bus station, for car rental and tickets for elephant shows. Local tours to silk-producing villages through Pirom's House (☎ 044 515 140)

TIP

>> Accommodations during the Elephant Roundup Festival should be reserved a month or more in advance.

Above *The impressive ruins of Prasat Ta Moan near Surin*

✚ 311 J5 🚌 Buses to/from Ubon Ratchathani, Udon Thani, Mukdahan, Sakhon Nakhon and Nakhon Phanom. *Songthaews* from Nakhon Phanom pass by Phra That Phanom

TIP

➤➤ Try to plan your visit so you are in That Phanom between 8am and noon on a Monday or Thursday, to coincide with the market.

THAT PHANOM

The small town of That Phanom, with a delightful setting by the Mekong River, is home to a shrine revered by the locals. Tucked away in the far northeast of Isan, 31 miles (50km) south of Nakhon Phanom, That Phanom has always enjoyed close links with the Laotian communities on the other side of the river. For centuries the villagers of both countries have worshiped as one at Wat Phra That Phanom. Every February, when the town celebrates a religious festival at the temple, Lao people arrive in large numbers to participate. Every Monday and Thursday morning, the Mekong River also serves to bring the nationalities together when Laotian farmers cross the river in boats laden with their fruit, vegetables, pigs, animal skins and exotic herbal remedies from the forest, all of which they hope to sell to Thais. You may not buy anything, but the markets are lively riverside affairs.

THE LEGEND OF PHRA THAT PHANOM

Phra That Phanom was a monk who came here in the eighth year after the death of the Buddha (535BC), and five local rulers shared in the establishment of a simple brick shrine to house the Buddha relics in the monk's possession. The temple you see today, shining white and covered with gold leaf, was the result of restoration and rebuilding work in the 17th century and then again in the 1940s. Too high for its own good, the stupa collapsed in 1975 during a rainstorm and was rebuilt to its present height—still over 177ft (54m)—four years later. It's based on the That Luang in Vientiane, Laos. Devotees make offerings to the temple throughout the year.

LAO ARCH

A roadway connects the temple with the pier and passes under a Lao arch of victory—a version of the large one in the centre of Vientiane. As is the custom, the temple faces both water and the rising sun. This old part of town has a number of old houses that combine characteristics of Laotian-French and Chinese architecture.

Below *Wat That Phanom is dominated by a white and gold Lao-style* chedi, *fronted by a seated Buddha*

INTRODUCTION

Built on the north bank of the Mun River, Ubon Ratchathani is the best base for exploring out-of-the-way attractions in this eastern corner of the country close to the Cambodian border. The Mun River, one of the major Mekong tributaries that cuts through Isan, meets the Mekong River just to the east of Ubon at Kong Chiam, and the prehistoric rock paintings there testify to the ancient origins of human development in this area. Dvaravati and Khmer cultures flourished around Ubon, followed by a strong Laotian influence that is still evident. The town became an important US base during the Vietnam War. Today, Ubon is a prosperous urban center and continues to develop.

The tourist office provides a useful town map that shows the location of the train and bus stations and the main hotels. It also shows the main bus routes within town, very useful for getting around because Ubon Ratchathani (usually called just Ubon) is spread out across a large area and some places are too far apart for walking. It makes sense to base yourself around the middle of town and the landmark Thung Si Muang Park. This keeps you close to the tourist office and the best places to eat.

WHAT TO SEE

NATIONAL MUSEUM

Ubon's branch of the National Museum uses the old city hall building, an attractive one-floor edifice built in 1918, with exhibits housed in the rooms around a central courtyard. The region's prehistory is introduced with displays of cave paintings, iron and bronze tools and bracelets. Dvaravati culture of the sixth to tenth centuries is represented by some rich finds from the Ubon province, ninth-century boundary stones in particular. Pre-Angkor and Angkor civilization, from around the eighth to the thirteenth centuries, account for the museum's most important exhibits, including an exquisite Khmer lintel depicting a series of nine Hindu deities and a tenth-century statue of Ganesh. Other rooms are devoted to displays of local crafts and folk music and worth admiring is the wooden sugarcane press with a finely crafted gear mechanism.

INFORMATION

http://isan.sawdee.com/ubonratchathani
🕇 315 K7 ℹ Thanon Khuenthani
☎ 045 243 770 🕐 Daily 8.30–4.30
🚉 Ubon Ratchathani Station (☎ 045 321 004), on the south side of the Mun River, is served by *tuk-tuks* and bus from the middle of town 🚌 The main bus station (☎ 045 312 773), too far to walk to and best reached by *tuk-tuk*, is on Thanon Chayangkun and serves Korat, Roi Et, Si Saket, Surin and other local towns. Long-distance private buses to Bangkok, Chiang Mai and Phitsanulok use a separate terminal south of the river ✈ Just north of the middle of town (☎ 045 245 612); flights to/from Bangkok ❓ Budget (☎ 045 240 507) car rental at the airport

Above *One of the impressive monuments dotted around the city*

TIP

>> The time to be in Ubon is early July, when the city celebrates the start of a Buddhist retreat with festive parades of giant decorated candles. In early October, at the end of the retreat, there are more parades, fireworks and boat processions on the river.

✉ Thanon Khuenthani, one block south of the park and three blocks west of the tourist office ☎ 045 255 071 🕐 Wed–Sun 9–4 💷 B100 🚌 City bus 11, 12

MONUMENT OF MERIT

What will catch your eye in the park is the elongated and brightly painted Candle Sculpture, completed in 2000 and dedicated to the King, which showcases Isan art styles. It is worth also seeking out a less conspicuous monument in the northeastern corner. Here you will find a simple, brick-built obelisk and an explanation of its purpose provided nearby. The notice explains how it was put there by a group of men who were prisoners of war, held in an Ubon camp by the Japanese in World War II. The men, who erected the obelisk after the war, wanted to express their thanks to those residents of Ubon who secretly provided them with provisions despite the risks involved.

✉ Thung Si Muang Park, in the middle of town 🕐 Daily 7am–9pm 🖐 Free

WAT NONG BUA

This *wat* (temple), built in the mid-1950s, is modeled closely on the *wat* at Bodh Gaya in northeast India, the place where the Buddha is said to have achieved enlightenment. The lower part of its white tower is decorated with gold leaf, as is the *chedi* (monument housing a Buddhist relic) at the top, and the base is carved with fine reliefs from the *Jataka* tales. The niches at ground level are home to four standing Buddhas.

✉ Off Thanon Chayangkul 🕐 Daily 7am–8pm 🖐 Free 🚌 City bus 2 or a *tuk-tuk* 🚌 2.5 miles (4km) north of town on Route 212

SHOPPING

Ubon vies with Khon Kaen as the best place in the northeast for quality shops selling local silk and cotton. Shops worth visiting are listed in the Shopping section (▷ 140–143).

Below *Sacred objects and stone relief work at the royal temple of Wat Supatanaram in Ubon Ratchathani on the bank of the Mun River.*

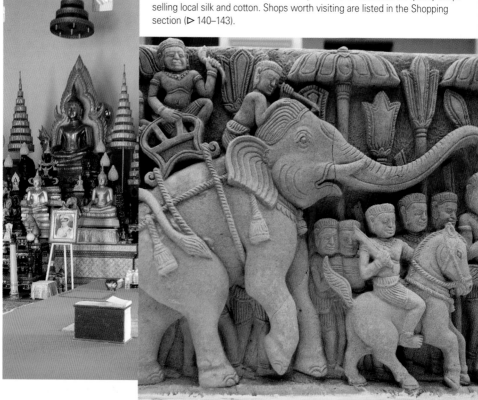

UDON THANI

Udon Thani is a busy commercial city, with good transportation links, and a likely resting stop while journeying through Isan or visiting Ban Chiang (▷ 117). It is a city with two centers; they're too far apart to comfortably walk between them but *tuk-tuks* are plentiful and a fare from one to the other is B50. The city is a manufacturing center for *tuk-tuks* and you will see some splendidly upmarket versions, far larger than normal ones and looking like giant motorcycles with posh seating attached.

The train station and the main bus station are both on the eastern side of town, and close to a modern shopping mall, the Charoensri Complex on Thanon Prachak (▷ 143), which has a Robinson's department store, a movie theater and a food center, plus banks and ATM machines. Next door is the Charoensri Grand Royal, the city's main hotel and one of the best places in town to eat. Internet access is available from the small shops opposite the Charoensri Complex.

PARKLAND AND A CITY SHRINE

The town's tourist office is on the northwest side of town, by the side of the peaceful landscaped Nong Prajak Park and adjoining lake. Too hot to explore during the day, the paths around the park come alive in the cool of the evening, when lakeside restaurants open for business. Three main roads—Thanon Wattana Nuwong, Thanon Prajak and Thanon Phosi—run parallel to one another and link the park with Thanon Tikattanon. Adjacent to the tourist office is Lak Meuang, the city's shrine, where daily offerings are made. You are more likely to notice a large and garish Chinese shrine, Pu Ya, with a huge statue of a golden dragon inside.

During the Vietnam War, Udon province was home to a number of US air force camps and the city became a popular rest-and-recreation center for servicemen; the plethora of pubs with bar girls is partly a legacy of this era.

INFORMATION

www.udonthani.com

✚ 310 G5 ✉ 16/5 Thanon Mukmontri ☎ 042 325 406 ⊕ Daily 8.30–4.30 🚌 The central bus station is on Thanon Tikattanon; local buses use another bus station at Talat Rungsina on the north side of town 🚆 Udon Thani Station, with daily trains to/from Bangkok ✈ Daily flights to/from Bangkok with Thai Airways, AirAsia and Nok Air; the airport is 2 miles (3km) outside town and the main hotels meet all incoming flights and shuttle guests to the airport for departing flights ❓ Budget (☎ 042 246 805) car rental at the airport

Above *Flower stall in Udon Thani*

NONG KHAI WALK

This walk takes you through the streets of Nong Khai, where you can visit temples, see examples of how French–Lao styles of building have influenced typical Thai–Chinese architecture, and stroll through a street market. For most of the way you are close to, and walking parallel with, the course of the 4,000km-long (2,485-mile) Mekong River.

THE WALK
Distance: 4 miles (6km)
Allow: 2–3 hours
Start/end at: Pantawee Hotel, Thanon Haisok

HOW TO GET THERE
The Pantawee Hotel is in the heart of town.

★ In the absence of a tourist information office, the tour desk at the Pantawee Hotel is the best place to visit for travel and local information. A free copy of the hotel's Nong Khai guide includes a very useful town map. The nearest TAT office is outside of town on Highway 2 (tel 042 421 326, open Mon–Fri 8.30–4.30).

With your back to the hotel entrance, turn to your right and walk to the first set of crossroads and traffic lights. Turn right here onto Thanon Meechai, staying on the right-hand side of the street. Take note of this intersection, as you will return to this point from the other direction at the end of the walk.

❶ Thanon Meechai is one of the four roads in Nong Khai that runs parallel with the Mekong River in a west–east direction, the one farthest from the river being Route 212. Along Thanon Meechai, on the other side of the street, you will see the Danish Baker cafe with its outdoor tables, good for coffee or breakfast. Past this at 702/3 is the Silver Antiques shop with old coins and banknotes for sale. A little farther along on the right is the post office.

About 330 yards (300m) past the post office, at the corner with signposted Soi Srimuang, cross the road and go down the lane to Wat Si Meuang temple.

❷ Nong Khai has many beautiful temples to visit, but the glittering Wat Si Meuang is one of the most photogenic, and is distinguished by a black Buddha image at the temple entrance.

Stay on the left-hand side of Thanon Meechai and continue walking east for another 110 yards (100m) or so. Stop after the signposted Prab-Ho lane on your left, whe you reach the Sawasdee Guest House.

❸ The Sawasdee Guest House, and some similar buildings along this stretch of road, is a fine surviving example of the town's vernacular architecture, much of which is falling prey to modernization. Enter the Sawasdee's lobby, filled with nostalgic objects, to appreciate its Chinese-style design. Consider resting here and having a cold drink or cup of tea.

As you continue to walk along Thanon Meechai, you will see old Chinese–Thai wooden houses with French touches like slatted shutters and small porticoes—a reminder of when Nong Khai was more influenced by colonial Laos than faraway Bangkok.

Continue along Thanon Meechai for 0.5 miles (1km). When you pass a sign pointing right for Luang Pho Phra Sai, cross to the other side of Thanon Meechai and turn right down Phochai Road to Wat Pho Chai, at the bottom on your right.

❹ Wat Pho Chai, perhaps a little too glossy and theatrical for its own aesthetic good, receives more devotees than any other shrine in Nong Khai because it houses the revered Luang Pho Phra Sai, a Buddha image that was brought from Laos to Thailand in 1850 under perilous circumstances. The head of the sitting Buddha image is made of pure gold, and the body is bronze. Murals tell the story of the image's journey from Laos, including the capsizing of the raft that was carrying it across the Mekong River and its miraculous recovery.

Return to Thanon Meechai, cross the road and walk down toward the river, turning left at the river.

❺ Walking along this quiet riverside setting you will pass a large golden Buddha staring across to Laos. Monks from the temple often stroll along this promenade, shaded from the heat of the sun by their umbrellas. The bridge you can see farther up the Mekong is the 0.75-miles (about 1.2km) long Friendship Bridge, completed in 1994 with the help of funds from Australia. Visas for Laos can be obtained on the other side of the bridge and Vientiane, the capital, is a half-hour taxi ride away.

At the end of the promenade, if the entrance to the main market is closed, turn left and walk through a small covered market that leads to Thanon Prab-Ho and back onto Thanon Meechai. Turn right here, back past the lane that led to Wat Si Meuang, and turn right at the next turning down Soi Srisaget to get back to the riverside. If the entrance to the main market is open, however, walk straight through the market and avoid the detour.

❻ The market is an interesting one, full of clothes and arts and crafts from Thailand. There are also goods smuggled via Laos from former Soviet states in Asia. The market is spread out along Thanon Rimkong as far as Tha Sadet, a pier where only Thais and Laotians can cross the Mekong River.

Continue walking westward past Tha Sadet, with the Me Kong Guest House on your right and Nobbi's restaurant on your left. Turn left at the end of Thanon Rimkong, which will bring you to the west end of Thanon Meechai. Turn left here to return to the crossroads where a right turn will take you back to the Pantawee Hotel. If you're feeling hungry stop here. Alternatively, continue along Thanon Meechai, where you'll find the Danish Baker cafe on the left.

WHERE TO EAT/STAY
DANISH BAKER

This is an excellent café for breakfast or a meal. The atmosphere is affable and the large menu includes Thai and Western dishes. There are a couple of tables outside.

✉ Thanon Meechai, Nong Khai
🕐 Daily 9–9 🍴 L B100, D B200

SAWASDEE GUEST HOUSE

Rest and enjoy the nostalgic atmosphere with a cold drink.

✉ 403 Thanon Meechai, Nong Khai
☎ 042 412 502

Opposite *Nong Khai has abundant charm*
Below *An elaborate shrine in Nong Khai*

LOEI TO NONG KHAI

This drive begins inland at the town of Loei and heads north toward the Mekong River, 31 miles (50km) away. On reaching the river that divides Thailand from Laos, the drive follows its course for 125 miles (200km) to Nong Khai. Vehicular traffic is very light—only the occasional truck or bus is to be seen—and the Mekong is often in view as this scenic route takes you through a very rural region of the northeast.

THE DRIVE

Distance: 137 miles (220km)
Allow: 4–6 hours
Start at: Loei
End at: Nong Khai

★ The market town of Loei (▷ 123), 31 miles (50km) south of the Mekong River, is a provincial capital and benefits from a university on its northern outskirts. You pass the university on your left as you head out of town.

Leave Loei, heading north on Route 201, signposted to Chiang Khan. You will soon leave the town behind and the traffic will thin out.

❶ The forest-clad hills of Phu Rua National Park (▷ 123) form the scenic background to your left, while nearer to the roadside you will

see farmers at work in their paddy fields. Loei is one of Thailand's least spoiled provinces, and the mountain scenery and absence of industry is evident as you head north toward the border.

After 31 miles (50km), turn right at the T-junction (intersection) to drive into the small town of Chiang Khan. You are still on Route 201, which now becomes the main road through the town, but look for the numbered *sois* (small side roads) leading off to your left. Turn down Soi 8, and at the bottom turn right at the T-junction (intersection). Park along this road, Thanon Chai Khong, close to the river.

❷ Chiang Khan (▷ 119), on the banks of the Mekong, has a dry and dusty atmosphere that blends

in well with the old wooden shophouses that line Thanon Chai Khong. It is worth calling in at the Rimkong Guesthouse for a cold drink or coffee. Its rooms overlook the Mekong and they are fitted with mosquito nets. You will see yellow warning flags along the street alerting people to the problem of malaria-carrying mosquitoes.

Either leave the car and walk eastward for around 1km (just under a mile) or drive in that direction, parking just after Soi 20 by Wat Thakhok.

❸ There are fine views of the river from this point, and Wat Thakhok, with balustrades and painted shutters, is a good example of the way Thai architecture in the Mekong region reveals a French–Laotian

Opposite *Sun sinking below the Northern Mountains near Loei*

accent. The first European to explore the Mekong was a Frenchman, Francis Garnier, whose expedition in the 1860s led to the discovery of Angkor Wat.

Drive up Soi 21 to join Route 211 and turn left to continue driving eastward toward Pak Chom, 23 miles (37km) away.

❹ The road to Pak Chom is a slow and windy one, passing forested hillside and with the Mekong usually in view as it drifts by on its long journey from Tibet to the south of Vietnam. Pak Chom itself is a one-street town which was the site of a refugee camp for 15,000 Hmong people, displaced here after the victory of the Communist Pathet Lao in Laos in 1975. The refugees have been resettled around the world, and Pak Chom has returned to its quiet, sleepy state.

Drive through Pak Chom continuing on Route 211 and, after 31 miles (50km) and between kilometer stones 97 and 98, look for a sign pointing to Than Thip Falls. Route 211 continues via the large village of Sang Khom.

❺ After Pak Chom, the road improves and stays closer to the river. Water buffalo and big-eared humped cattle lounge by the wayside, banana plants grow on both sides of the road, and the only passing vehicle will be an occasional pickup truck. After 16 miles (26km) you pass a small village where the school has a sign up by the side of the road—"Please Visit Us"—inviting visitors to drop in and give pupils a chance to practice some English.

The sign for the Than Thip Falls takes you off the road for five minutes to the first of two waterfalls surrounded by forest. It is possible to swim here.

Return to Route 211 and after 12.5 miles (20km) on the road past Sang Khom, look for a sign pointing left to Wat Hin Mak Peng. Drive through the temple's entrance—separated by a long, low white wall—and park your vehicle in the compound.

❻ Wat Hin Mak Peng (▷ 129) has a landscaped garden with giant bamboo and remarkably lifelike wax effigies of the monk who founded the monastery. Built close to the river, you can walk down the steps to the riverbank.

Continue driving on Route 211, heading toward the village of Si Chiang Mai.

❼ Around Si Chiang Mai, look out for the racks of spring roll wrappers drying in the sun (▷ 129).

Keep going along Route 211 for the final 36 miles (57km) to reach Nong Khai. There will be more traffic along this stretch of road, and you will lose sight of the river at times. When you are 7 miles (11km) from Nong Khai, the road joins the three-lane Route 2 for the final drive to your destination.

WHERE TO EAT
BUOY GUEST HOUSE

If Buoy Guest House is without guests, food may not be available, in which case continue along Route 211 for a further 440 yards (400m) and eat at the unassuming bamboo shack on the left, opposite the police station. There is no menu and little choice, but you can be assured that the food is freshly cooked and plentiful.
✉ Located on the left-hand side of the road, signposted on Route 211 in the middle of Sang Khom ☎ 042 441 065
🕐 Daily 8–8 ⬥ B200 per person, per night

TOURIST INFORMATION
LOEI TOURIST OFFICE
✉ Thanon Charoenrat, Loei
☎ 042 812 812

CHIANG KHAN

CHIANG KHAN GUEST HOUSE

Chiang Khan Guest House is not only a good place to stay (▷ 146), but it also can arrange various excellent tour activities, either guided or independent. Boat tours along the Mekong are charged by the boat, not, as more usual, the number of passengers.

✉ 282 Chiang Khan Road, Chiang Khan ☎ 042 821 691 ✋ Boat trips: 2 hours B1,000; motorcycle rental: B200 per day; mountain bike rental: B100 per day

KHON KAEN

9TH AVENUE PUB

A popular disco and nightclub that benefits from a sophisticated lighting system and a revolving bandstand. The club opens at 9pm, but not much happens until after 11pm, two hours before it closes. There are DJs every night.

✉ Sofitel Raja Orchid Hotel, 9/9 Thanon Prachasumran, Khon Kaen ☎ 043 322 155 🕐 Daily 9pm–2am ✋ Free admission

CHONNABOT SILK VILLAGE

Chonnabot (▷ 121) is the best-known silk village close to Khon Kaen and you will easily spot the women working away on their looms outside their homes in the shade. Visitors are welcome to linger and observe the fascinating process, and vendors sell the women's work on the streets.

✉ Chonnabot village 🕐 Daily 9–5

CHOPHAKA

Beautiful silk and fabrics, jackets, tops, scarves, ties—more clothes for women than men—and gorgeous axe pillows sold unpadded so that taking a couple home is quite feasible. Silk is sold by the meter, starting at around B1,000 for about 4 yards (3.6m). Expect to be given a 15 percent discount off the marked prices. Chophaka is a friendly shop and English is spoken.

✉ 3/12 Thanon Prachasumran, Khon Kaen ☎ 043 228 359 🕐 Daily 8–8

DARHA SPA

Decorated in classic Thai-Bali style and set in relaxing grounds, this spa offers a wide range of health and beauty treatments, from basic massages and reflexology to the Vichy shower, where water is heated to body temperature and sprinklers are then used to stimulate circulation and aid detoxification. There is also a private steam room, a hydro room and a styling salon.

✉ 45/25 Soi Ummart 4, Thanon Pimpisoot, Khon Kaen ☎ 043 237 554 🕐 Daily 10–10 ✋ B300–B500

KING COBRA VILLAGE

A visit to the King Cobra Village (▷ 118), located 31 miles (50km) northeast of Khon Kaen, is more a form of light entertainment than a way of finding out about cobras. There is a "boxing" ring with audience seating, and the warm-up show is performed by young children handling non-poisonous snakes, followed by the main individual bouts between village snake handlers and their cobras. Pose for a photograph afterward, if you wish, with your favorite snake from the show languidly wrapped around your neck.

✉ Ban Khok Sa-Nga, northeast of Khon Kaen ☎ 081 974 9499 🕐 Daily 7–5 ✋ To look around the village and see the snakes B10; admission for a performance depends on the number of visitors

Opposite Shelves full of brightly colored silks in Rin Thai Silk shop in Khon Kaen

PRATHAMAKANT LOCAL GOODS CENTER

A virtual supermarket of regional arts and crafts, this vast store is a blessing if you want to do a lot of shopping under one roof, and with fixed prices and no hassle from sales staff. There is a wide choice of cotton and silk clothes for men . and women, as well as silverware, jewelry and craft goods like carved wooden elephants. If buying silk by the meter, this store offers a wide range of colors to choose from. Prices are reasonable too, at B290 a meter for two-ply silk, and from B1,450 for *mutmee*—"tied strings"—which gets its name from the method of using dye-resistant string to create unusual patterns in the cotton thread before weaving.

✉ 79/2–3 Thanon Ruen Rom, Khon Kaen ☎ 043 224 080 🕐 Daily 9–8

RIN THAI SILK

A selection of silk clothes, mostly for women but with some shirts and ties. A meter/yard of plain silk costs from B300. Prices are more or less fixed, and not much English is spoken. Thanon Namuang is one of Khon Kaen's main streets, and Prathamakant Local Goods Center (▷ above), where silk prices can be compared, is a short walk away.

✉ 412 Thanon Namuang, Khon Kaen ☎ 043 220 705 🕐 Daily 8–6.30

SILK VENDORS

As well as the retail shops in Khon Kaen, individual vendors also congregate on the sidewalk opposite the Sofitel Raja Orchid Hotel and display their produce for sale. The quality varies, but if you are not seeking top-quality silk then these vendors offer good prices for different-size lengths of material. There are no marked prices and you are expected to bargain, but this is not Bangkok and opening prices are not ludicrously high.

✉ Thanon Prachasamran, Khon Kaen 🕐 Daily 9–7

ZOLID DISCO

This large disco hall offers loud music and flashing lights. Plenty of friendly locals on weekends help fill the place up, creating a lively atmosphere. There's not a lot of variety in drink choices, but the local beers and whiskeys are good value for the money if you're not too picky.

✉ Charoen Thani Princess Hotel, Thanon Si Chan, Khon Kaen ☎ 043 220 400 🕐 6pm–midnight ✋ Free admission

MUKDAHAN
INDOCHINA MARKET

This is one of those markets where making a purchase is less important than just being in the place, and, given that Mukdahan is way off the regular visitor's trail, you can hardly expect to find what you are looking for. Lao–Thai trade is the genesis of the market, and inexpensive goods are brought over the Mekong River from Vietnam and Laos. Thai cotton and silk make it back across the river to Laos and such fabrics are your most likely buy.

✉ The Promenade, Mukdahan 🕐 Daily 7–5

NAKHON RATCHASIMA (KORAT)
JIRANAI

Jiranai is one of the best shops in Korat for quality silk. Prices start at around B750 for a meter/yard of *mutmee* silk, half that for a plain pattern, rising to over B1,500 for more intricate patterns. Silk shirts and blouses are also available, though there is not a wide range. To find the shop, walk along Thanon Phokang from the Thao Suranari shrine in the middle of town; it is on the corner at the end of the first block, on your right.

✉ 140/2 Thanon Phokang, Nakhon Ratchasima (Korat) ☎ 044 243 819 🕐 Mon–Sat 9–6

KORAT NIGHT BAZAR

Korat is not well known for its nightlife, but the city's bustling night bazaar is a good place to come to experience a slice of northeastern culture up close. The centrally located market has been established as an outlet for locally produced crafts and souvenirs, and there are plenty of places dotted about to eat and drink—local style!

✉ Thanon Manat, Nakhon Ratchasima (Korat) 🕐 Daily 6pm–10 pm

THE MALL

www.themalldepartmentstore.com
The Mall is the largest shopping complex in Nakhon Ratchasima (Korat), and aside from offering a cool and convenient place to do any necessary shopping, there is also a wide range of entertainment facilities on offer, including a cinema, a fun park, bowling and a swimming pool. The usual fast-food restaurants are here, as well as a food court and a number of western-style coffee shops. The Mall is popular with the locals, drawing large crowds on weekends and holidays.

✉ 1242/2 Mitrapap Highway, Nakhon Ratchasima (Korat) ☎ 044 231 000 🕐 Mon–Fri 10.30am–9.30pm, Sat–Sun 10–9.30

NAKHON RATCHASIMA ZOO

This family-friendly attraction is the only public zoo in the northeastern region and is home to more than 700 species of land animals, birds, reptiles and aquatic creatures. You can make your way around the zoo on an open bus, golf-cart or even a bicycle. There's a public park, children's play area, dinosaur park, restaurant, souvenir shop and an exhibition hall.

✉ Thanon Chalermprakiet Ram 9 Nakhom Ratchasima (Korat) ☎ 044 934 531/3 🕐 Daily 8–7 ✋ Adult B100, child B50

NONG KHAI
MEKONG BOAT TRIP

The boat will not depart for just a couple of passengers, but most evenings it attracts enough people to justify taking off up the Mekong River. Food is served on board if you order it before departure time, but the standard rice dishes are disappointing and it may be more fun to just sit back and relax with something from the reasonably priced drinks list. The boat heads up toward the Friendship Bridge before turning to return along the Laos side, passing fish farms and people washing clothes in the river. You will feel a long way from home as you see the real Thailand.

✉ Thanon Kaeworawut, Nong Khai (just beyond the Mut Mee Guest House) ☎ 042 412 211 🕐 Daily at 5.30pm 🖐 B150

NOBBI'S

Open as a restaurant from 8am, Nobbi's brightens up with fairy lights at night and is popular with assorted northern Europeans needing a fix on meatballs, home-made sausages, sauerkraut, chicken goulash and smoked ham. With 140 types of beer, especially German imports, and Italian wine starting at B395 a bottle, the restaurant becomes a busy late-night pub.

✉ 997 Thanon Rimkong, Nong Khai ☎ 042 460 583 🕐 Daily 8am–11pm

PANTAWEE HERBAL SPA

Massages at Pantawee come in different forms and strengths, from vigorous Thai ones by graduates of the Wat Po medical school in Bangkok to a less robust massage with herbal oils. There are other health and beauty treatments available, and these include an all-over body scrub, leg waxing and a herbal bath. There is also a hair salon.

✉ Pantawee Hotel, 1049 Thanon Haisoke, Nong Khai ☎ 042 411 568 🕐 Daily, 24 hours 🖐 Facial B900; body scrub B500

STREET MARKET

This traditional market, encountered on a walking tour around the town (▷ 136–137), occupies the east end of Thanon Rimkong and it starts at Tha Sadet, the small tower-shape building marking the official crossing point on the river for Thais and Laotians. Spreading eastward from here, the covered market has a multitude of small and large stands selling a good selection of clothes, arts and crafts, binoculars,

toys, household goods and miscellaneous goods from Laos.

✉ Thanon Rimkong, Nong Khai 🕐 Daily 9–6

VILLAGE WEAVER HANDICRAFTS

This is a good place to purchase *mutmee*. About 3.3-yard (3m) long lengths of *mutmee* vary in price from B1,600 to B4,500. Silk and cotton shirts, including free-size silk skirts, tops and skirts are also available. Smaller craft items on offer include woven pencil cases, slippers and purses. Everything has a marked price, but you can expect a 10 percent discount off that. The handicrafts shop was set up in 1982 as a self-help project for local villagers to help them supplement their meager incomes.

✉ 1151 Chitapanya Lane, Thanon Prachak, Nong Khai ☎ 042 411 236 🕐 Daily 8–7

VILLAGE WEAVER HANDICRAFTS WORKSHOP

This is a branch of the main Village Weaver Handicrafts shop (▷ above), but it is a little nearer to the middle of town, at the corner of Thanon Haisoke and just a little way down from the Pantawee Hotel.

✉ 1020 Thanon Prachak, Nong Khai ☎ 042 422 652 🕐 Daily 8–7

PHIMAI

PHIMAI'S BANYAN TREE

The Khmer temple at Phimai (▷ 127) may not excite children as much as adults but Sai Ngam, nearby, will appeal. The single banyan tree is like a small forest, and you can buy small turtles to release into the nearby pond for good luck. Small birds can also be purchased and released.

ROI ET

ARTS AND CRAFTS

There is no English sign for this shop, but it is easy to find by following the shophouse numbers; look for the display of traditional musical instruments in the window. Goods include axe pillows, fabrics, tops, baskets and boxes and a small amount of jewelry. Prices

are marked, but bargain hard to secure a reasonable price.

✉ 383–385 Thanon Phadung, Roi Et 🕐 Daily 9–6

SURIN

NIGHT BAZAAR

The night bazaar is fun to wander around for its variety of food—grilled locusts are a local delicacy—clothes for the fashion-conscious and general bric-a-brac. Surin is the center of a local silk-weaving industry and during the day there are usually women displaying silk for sale on the street, where the night bazaar meets Thanon Tannasarn. There are also a number of small shops around town selling silk, mostly to the north of the night bazaar in the vicinity of the roundabout on Thanon Tannasarn.

✉ Thanon Krungsrinai, Surin 🕐 Bazaar daily 6pm–9pm; street vendors daily 9–5

THAT PHANOM

RENU NAKHON SILK VILLAGE

Renu Nakhon is a weaving village that is best visited on a Wednesday, when the weekly fair comes alive and there are countless stands displaying cotton and silk for sale. Prices are reasonable.

✉ Renu Nakhon, That Phanom 🕐 Daily 8–8 🚌 Take the inland turning on Route 212, 4 miles (6km) north of That Phanom

UBON RATCHATHANI

ART HOME

Next to the Laithong Hotel, this modest shop has an interesting selection of skirts, dresses, silk, handbags and axe pillows. The prices are very reasonable—lower than at other shops of this kind in town. Be sure to check out the bargain-price clothes hanging outside on rails.

✉ 52 Thanon Pichitrangsan, Ubon Ratchathani ☎ 045 254 335 🕐 Daily 8am–7pm

MAYBE

A small collection of authentic local cotton woven using traditional designs. Prices are reasonable, less than half what you would pay for quality cotton fabrics in Bangkok or Chiang Mai. To find Maybe, head up past Punchard on Thanon Ratchabut, take the first right along Thanon Srinarong then continue for 0.3 miles (0.5km); the shop is on the right.

✉ 124 Thanon Srinarong, Ubon Ratchathani ☎ 045 254 452 🕓 Daily 8–7

PUNCHARD
www.punchard.net
Punchard, between the museum and the tourist office, is the most upmarket arts and crafts store in Ubon and has some great gift items. There is also a branch on Thanon Padang (156 Th Pha Daeng, tel 045 265 751). To find the main shop, turn right with your back to the tourist office and take a right turn at the first corner; Punchard is on your right.

✉ 158 Thanon Ratchabut, Ubon Ratchathani ☎ 045 243 433 🕓 Daily 9.30–8.30

RAN SIRIPA
Ran Siripa sells beautiful handmade handicrafts, including silk and cotton textiles, clothing, bags, baskets and small gift items. There is very little English spoken, but with sign language and a notepad to scribble prices on you can always get by. Prices are very reasonable.

✉ 388 Thanon Upalisaan, Amphor Muang, Ubon Ratchathani ☎ 045 241 569 🕓 Daily 7.30–6

U-BAR AND E-BAR
These two competing discos are located on the same street and are the hottest hangouts for college kids and twenty-somethings, where visiting DJs and bands from Bangkok often perform. E-Bar is the newer of the two and is quickly overtaking U-Bar in popularity, but both are full on weekends and holidays.

✉ Thanon Phichit Rangsan, Ubon Ratchathani ☎ 045 265 141 🕓 Daily 7pm–1am

UDON THANI
CHAROENSRI COMPLEX
The anchor tenant, Robinson's Department Store, adds some

FESTIVALS AND EVENTS

MID-FEBRUARY TO EARLY MARCH
THAT PHANOM FESTIVAL
Phra That Phanom is commemorated and celebrated in a week long event in the small town of That Phanom (▷ 132).

APRIL
PHANON RUNG FESTIVAL
This festival in the town of Phanom Rung (▷ 126) commemorates the Khmer ruins of the town. It begins with a procession through town to the temple and climaxes with a superb sound-and-light show in the evening.

MAY/JUNE
ROCKET FESTIVAL
Across the northeast but especially in Yasothon and Nong Khai, the Rocket Festival has to be seen to be believed. Home-made

substance to Udon Thani's most modern shopping mall. The smaller outlets sell clothes, shoes and accessories, but the department store generally offers better quality goods. There is a food center on the third level and a movie theater on the top level that shows English-language blockbuster movies.

✉ Thanon Prachak, Udon Thani ☎ 042 242 777 🕓 Daily 10–8

CHAROENSRI HEALTH AND SPA
A full menu of health and beauty massages is on offer; choose from a traditional Thai one to a 45-minute anti-cellulite session. Facial treatments range from a half-hour facial brightening to longer detoxifying sessions. There are also Jacuzzi bathtubs, herbal saunas, hot compresses and mineral baths for relaxation.

✉ Charoensri Grand Royal Hotel, 271 Thanon Prachak, Udon Thani ☎ 042 343 555 🕓 Daily 10–10 ✋ Facial B400–2,000

bamboo rockets of great size and power are hauled up the launching pad and fired into space to the accompaniment of merrymaking.
🕓 Mid-May to mid-Jun

PHI TA KHON FESTIVAL
This distinctive festival takes place in the town of Dan Sai, 50 miles (80km) southwest of Loei, and its animist elements suggest origins predating Buddhism. Celebrants dress up in wild and ghoulish costumes, don garish masks and generally have a good time.

JULY
CANDLE FESTIVAL
Ubon Ratchathani is the best place to enjoy this annual carnival, although you will see other similar events. Parades of huge carved candles take over the streets.
🕓 Mid- to late July

IRISH CLOCK
This cosy Irish tavern serves great food and has some good accommodation available upstairs. Enjoy Thai, Irish and popular Western fare with free WiFi and imported beer on tap. It is furnished in dark wood with the latest soccer matches shown on the widescreen TV.

✉ 19/5 Thanon Sampanthamit, Udon Thani ☎ 042 247 450 🕓 Daily 7am–midnight

YASOTHON
AXE PILLOW VILLAGE
Ban Sri Than is an attractive village, located 12 miles (20km) east of Yasothon, dedicated to the production of beautiful axe pillows. You can watch them being made by the villagers, underneath their houses, and they can be purchased here.

✉ Ban Sri Than, Yasothon 🕓 Daily 10–8
🚗 Take Route 202 out of Yasothon, and just after kilometer stone 18 turn right for the remaining 2 miles (3km)

PRICES AND SYMBOLS

The prices given are the average for a two-course lunch (L) and a three-course dinner (D) for one person, without drinks or wine.

For a key to the symbols, ▷ 2.

KHON KAEN

KAEN INN RESTAURANT

This is a comfortable and popular hotel restaurant. The Thai food is best enjoyed during the evening, when live entertainment enlivens the atmosphere.
✉ Kaen Inn Hotel, 56 Thanon Klangmuang, Khon Kaen ☎ 043 245 420 ③ Daily 7am–2pm 🖐 L B200, D B400

LOONG YUEN

Two or more people can enjoy a feast of Cantonese dishes, including roast duck, deep-fried prawns, chicken with a lemon sauce, and hot-and-sour soup, but there are also hotter Sichuan offerings.
✉ Sofitel Raja Orchid Hotel, 9/9 Thanon Prachasumran, Khon Kaen ☎ 043 322 155 ③ Daily 11.30–2.30, 6–10 🖐 L B400, D B450

NAMNUNGRAPLA

There are plenty of dishes to choose from at this air-conditioned Vietnamese-Thai restaurant. Starters include shrimp and sugarcane rolls or papaya salad, and main dishes like chicken cooked with herbs and pork grilled with spices.
✉ 61 Thanon Klang Muang, Khon Kaen ☎ 043 236 296 ③ Daily 9–9.30 🖐 L B230, D B275

SAIGON

The setting is a little public, located on the second floor of the grand Pullman Khon Kaen Raja Orchid hotel (▷ 146), but there are indoor and outdoor tables to choose from, and this is one of the best places to enjoy authentic Vietnamese cuisine in Thailand; the chef is from Hanoi.
✉ Pullman Khon Kaen Raja Orchid Hotel, 9/9 Thanon Prachasumran, Khon Kaen ☎ 043 322 155 ③ Daily 6pm–10pm 🖐 D B500

LOEI

BOTUN RESTAURANT

The most comfortable place to enjoy local food in Loei, and there is an excellent choice of seafood on the menu. Prices are good value when compared with hotel restaurants of this kind. The *tom yam* soup with Mekong fish is suitably fiery and the sun-dried fish and mango salad is justifiably popular. This is *the* place to drink Thailand's best attempt at wine-making, Chateau de Loei.
✉ Loei Palace Hotel, 167/4 Thanon Charoenrat, Loei ☎ 042 815 668 ③ Daily 6am–midnight 🖐 L B220, D B350

RABBIENG NAAM

This delightful little restaurant has a lovely view of the mountains, making it a charming place to sit outside and enjoy your meal. Many of the traditional Thai dishes are served here, but the specialty is fresh fish from the restaurant's own nearby pond.
✉ Mariwon Road, Loei ☎ 042 811 332 ③ 10am–11pm 🖐 L B150, D B300

NAKHON RATCHASIMA (KORAT)

PRINCESS CAFÉ

Close to the heart of the city, the Princess Café serves a buffet lunch and a selection of reasonably priced Thai, Chinese and international dishes from its all-day menu. A house band performs nightly from 7.30pm. If you prefer truly Chinese cuisine, try the Empress Restaurant on the same floor.
✉ Royal Princess Hotel, 1137 Thanon Suranaree, Nakhon Ratchasima (Korat) ☎ 044 256 629 ③ 6am–10pm 🖐 L B180, D B230

WAN VARN

A short walk from the Thao Suranari shrine in the middle of the city, the

Opposite Menu written in Thai and English

dark wood interior offers a calm escape from the sun. There's an odd style to the place—antique clocks, pictures, posters, tennis rackets, a saxophone and other assorted objects fill the walls. The menu of Thai dishes includes a variety of noodles, salads, stir-fries and seafood, as well as spring rolls and grilled spare ribs.

✉ 101–103 Thanon Mahadthai, Nakhon Ratchasima (Korat) ☎ 044 244 509 🕐 Daily 10–10 ✋ L B140, D B250

NONG KHAI
DAENG NAEM–NUANG

The place to enjoy Vietnamese food, even if the choices are limited, in the comfort of a bright and cheerful, air-conditioned restaurant. The specialty is *naem nuang*, which comes to you in the form of barbecued pork, vegetables and a peanut sauce and a set of thin rice sheets with which to roll up the mixture.

✉ 526–527 Thanon Rimkong, Nong Khai ☎ 042 411 961 🕐 Daily 6am–8pm ✋ L B200, D B250

MUT MEE

Tables under a bamboo-thatch shade on the banks of the languid Mekong River provide an atmospheric scene for this popular restaurant attached to the guesthouse of the same name. A curry is made fresh each day, and vegetarians have the option of a tofu version. House specials include *gai rat sors som* (chicken in orange), and wine is available by the glass. Breakfast is served, and for a light lunch there are half-baguettes.

✉ 1111 Thanon Kaeworawrut, Nong Khai ☎ 042 460 717 🕐 Daily 7.30am–9.30pm ✋ L B120, D B170

PHIMAI
BANYAN TREE RESTAURANT

Facing the banyan tree, 1.2 miles (2km) from the Khmer temple, this restaurant looks like a food center, but there is just one kitchen. The menu is not in English and little English is spoken so you must look around and point at some dishes that look interesting. Inexpensive but tasty food.

✉ Sai Ngam, Phimai 🕐 Daily 11–11 ✋ L B100, D B140

ROI ET
ONE-OH-ONE RAAN BURNG KONG

This quiet place, frequented by the locals, serves a range of popular Thai dishes. The *tom yung goong* is well recommended. The staff are friendly and helpful, but be prepared to take out your phrase book as little English is spoken here. Wine is not served here.

✉ 326 Ronnachaichanyut Road, Roi Et ☎ 043 512 477 🕐 Daily 10–10 ✋ L B150, D B300

SURIN
WAI WAN RESTAURANT

A congenial restaurant that is conveniently located in the heart of Surin; from the train station walk straight down Thanon Tannasarn, the main street heading into town, and Thanon Sanitnikhomrat is the second turning on the left (if you reach the traffic circle (roundabout) you have gone too far). The food is a mix of Thai and Western favorites, including steak and chips.

✉ 44–46 Thanon Sanitnikhomrat, Surin ☎ 044 515 140 🕐 Daily 8am–9pm ✋ L B150, D B350

UBON RATCHATHANI
BAN KHUN PU

The chef of this self-styled American-Thai restaurant gained 30 years of experience in Illinois restaurants, which provides you with a satisfying meal, whether you order a Thai dish, or one of the variations of steak, soup or pasta combinations. The atmosphere is warm, and prices are reasonable, although there is no wine list.

✉ Thanon Charoenrat, Ubon Ratchathani ☎ 045 240 910 🕐 9.30am–10pm ✋ L B150, D B350

SAKORN

There is an English menu here, though very little English is spoken. Persevere, as the food is inexpensive but exceptional. The dining room facing the street has fans but there is also a room indoors with air-conditioning. Try the fried chicken with ginger and onions, or a green curry.

✉ 64–70 Thanon Pha Daeng, Ubon Ratchathani ☎ 045 241 101 🕐 Daily 10–10 ✋ L B90, D B160

SINCERE

A charming and intimate restaurant with a tiny bar, soft music and an appealing menu that includes lobster bisque, appetizers of salmon, snails and clams, a choice of steaks or a fish dish like baked sea bass, and desserts like crêpe Suzette.

✉ 126 Thanon Saphasit, Ubon Ratchathani ☎ 045 245 061 🕐 Mon–Sat 11–11 ✋ L B300, D B600

UDON THANI
BELLA ITALIA

A traditional wood-fired oven delivers fresh and piping hot pizzas from mid-morning onward. The pizzas and fresh bread are the best reasons for coming here, but there are also pasta dishes and steaks. There's also a children's menu.

✉ 1st Level, Charoensri Complex, Thanon Prachak, Udon Thani ☎ 042 343 134 🕐 Daily 11am–1am ✋ L B220, D B350

KRUA TONG SRI MUANG LUNCH BUFFET

Come here early, for the lunch buffet, which is the best-value food spread in the city—sushi, sashimi, Japanese chicken burgers, fried catfish and chili *tom yam* soup, beef in paprika sauce, fried squid, sea bass and Chinese plum, fish steaks, beef, chicken and pork. Live music in the evening and a menu of Thai food and some grills in the way of steak, spare ribs and pork chops. The fish deserves a recommendation—either the Mekong fish with a spicy sauce or the snake-head fish. Be sure to make reservations at weekends.

✉ Charoensri Grand Royal Hotel, 277/1 Thanon Prachak, Udon Thani ☎ 042 343 555 🕐 Daily 11–2, 6–11 ✋ L B200, D B300

PRICES AND SYMBOLS

Prices are the lowest and highest for a double room for one night. Breakfast is included unless noted otherwise. All the hotels listed accept credit cards unless otherwise stated. Note that rates vary widely throughout the year.

For a key to the symbols, ▷ 2.

CHIANG KHAN

CHIANG KHAN GUEST HOUSE

This home-away-from-home wooden guesthouse has plenty to offer guests, with great views of the river provides neat rooms, good food, useful local information and a range of tour packages.

✉ 282 Chiang Khan Road, Chiang Khan ☎ 042 821 691 💷 B150–B300 🛈 14

CHIANG KHAN HILL RESORT

www.chiangkhanhill.com

This is the only resort in the area and it's made up of beautiful Thai-style buildings set among grass lawns with flowering trees and shrubs, and right on the river's edge. Rooms include furnished bungalows, suites and single rooms. The restaurant serves Thai and international dishes and a range of drinks.

✉ 28/2 Thanon Ruam Chai Narumit, Chiang Khan ☎ 042 821 285 💷 B800–B4000 🛈 50 🌊 Outdoor

KHAO YAI

GREEN LEAF GUEST HOUSE

It's budget accommodation, but if you are planning to spend as much time as possible in the park then Green Leaf is perfect. The restaurant is inexpensive tours into the park are conducted by an expert.

✉ Thanon Thanarat, kilometer stone 7.5, Pak Chong ☎ 044 365 073 💷 B200–B300 🛈 12

KHON KAEN

KAEN INN HOTEL

This is a gregarious hotel in the heart of town. It's good value for money, with well-kept rooms that come with TV and a fridge. There's a snooker room, barber shop, massage parlor, 24-hour coffee shop, and a restaurant with evening entertainment (▷ 144).

✉ 56 Thanon Klangmuang, Khon Kaen ☎ 043 245 420/30 💷 B750–B1,600 🛈 160 🌊

PULLMAN KHON KAEN RAJA ORCHID

www.accorhotels.com

This is a superb hotel in many respects, with local artwork dotted around the lobby and restaurants. The graceful style extends to the bedrooms, where Isan woodcarvings and handwoven silks are to be found. There are Italian, Vietnamese and Chinese restaurants, a microbrewery on the premises, and a basement complex—The Underground—for evening entertainment. A shuttle bus serves the airport for all flights.

✉ 9/9 Thanon Prachasumran, Khon Kaen ☎ 043 322 155 💷 B2,600–B3,500 🌊 🍸 Outdoor

SAWASDEE HOTEL

In the middle of the city, close to shops and places to eat, Sawasdee Hotel is a good-value place in Khon Kaen. The standard rooms have the benefit of good-size bathrooms; better rooms face away from the main road and come with tea- and coffee-making facilities. Other facilities include a laundry room with a washing machine.

✉ 177–179 Thanon Namuang, Khon Kaen ☎ 043 221 600 💷 B400–B900 excluding breakfast 🛈 72 🌊

KO PHET

LAMAI HOMESTAY/GUEST HOUSE

www.thailandhomestay.com

The Lamai offers amazingly good accommodation in a quiet rice village where you will experience rural Thailand up close. Rates include transfer from Korat bus station or

Opposite *One of the many resort hotels*

Bua Yai railway station and breakfast in the garden. Lots of activities and excursions are available.

✉ Kok Phet, Bua Yai, near Nakhon Ratchasima (Korat) ☎ 062 585 894 💷 B500; 3- or 5-night all-inclusive packages from B6,000 ⓘ 4 ⚑ Some

LOEI
LOEI PALACE HOTEL
www.amari.com

Loei does not look the kind of town that would have a comfortable and classy hotel like this one on its doorstep. Bedrooms are spacious and smart, and there's a good restaurant with Thai–Chinese and international food (Botun ▷ 144) and a pub and restaurant with karaoke.

✉ 167/4 Thanon Charoenrat, Loei ☎ 042 815 668 💷 B1,900–B4,600 ⓘ 156 ⚑ ⛱ Outdoor 🏳

NAKHON RATCHASIMA (KORAT)
DUSIT PRINCESS
www.dusit.com

This is the best hotel in the city in terms of facilities, with a good pool, a traditional Chinese restaurant and the more modern Princess Café (6am–10pm), with a Thai-European buffet every night and a Japanese corner. The location is not perfect, north of the North Gate, and too far to walk into town, though *songthaews* run into town along Thanon Suranarai.

✉ 1137 Thanon Suranarai, Korat ☎ 044 256 629 💷 B1,200–B1,765 ⓘ 186 ⚑ ⛱ 🏳

SRIPATANA HOTEL
www.sripatana.com

This is a good-value hotel, located less than 0.6 miles (1km) from the railway station, with a coffee shop, 24-hour room service, a fair-size pool and large bedrooms with bath and shower. If you are staying in Korat for only a night, Sripatana Hotel is well worth considering.

✉ 346 Thanon Suranarai, Korat ☎ 044 251 652 💷 B730–B1,280 ⓘ 180 ⚑ ⛱ Outdoor

TOKYO HOTEL

Not as good value as the Sripatana but the next best place—the rooms with a fan are especially cheap but they have no hot water; the air-conditioned rooms are the same size, and cost almost twice as much. The hotel is conveniently located in the middle of town.

✉ 256–258 Thanon Suranarai, Korat ☎ 044 242 788 💷 B260–B450 excluding breakfast ⓘ 35 ⚑ Some

NONG KHAI
MUT MEE
www.mutmee.com

On the bank of the Mekong River, inexpensive accommodation and a good restaurant are two reasons for staying here. The place is clean and there is a relaxed feel. Popular with travelers, it has a small art gallery next door, yoga, reiki and astrology courses, and meditation classes.

✉ 111/4 Thanon Kaeworawut, Nong Khai ☎ 042 460 717 💷 B730–B1,280 excluding breakfast ⓘ 29 ⚑

PANTAWEE HOTEL
www.pantawee.com

The Pantawee is the best place to stay in Nong Khai. The location is convenient and there is a choice of rooms, a 24-hour restaurant and bar, internet access any time and friendly staff. Many of the bedrooms have a computer with free internet use. There is also a useful travel desk and information on local tours and bus connections, and a large open-air tub for cooling down in.

✉ 1049 Thanon Haisoke, Nong Khai ☎ 042 411 568 💷 B600–B2,600 ⓘ 105 ⚑

SI SAKET
KESSIRI HOTEL

The Kessiri is definitely the best place for a good night's sleep in Si Saket. It is in the middle of town, and easily reached by *tuk-tuk*. The rooms are comfortable and there is a restaurant downstairs. Discounts are often available if demand is slack.

✉ 1102–1105 Thanon Kukhan, Si Saket ☎ 045 614 007 💷 B850–B1,600 ⓘ 93 ⚑

UBON RATCHATHANI
LAITHONG HOTEL
www.laithonghotel.net

This is the plushest hotel in Ubon Ratchathani. The restaurant is a mixture of Thai, Chinese and international food, the lobby serves cocktails and there is live music some evenings. There's free transport to and from the airport.

✉ 50 Thanon Pichitrangsan, Ubon Ratchathani ☎ 045 264 271 💷 B1,300–B3,000 ⓘ 124 ⚑ ⛱ Outdoor

TOKYO HOTEL

This is the best-value hotel in Ubon Ratchathani and very adequately equipped. The beds in the clean rooms with cable TV are new and firm, plus there is a little breakfast corner in the lobby and a secure parking area. From the museum, walk north up Thanon Chayangkun and you will see the sign on the left side of the street.

✉ 360 Thanon Opparat, Ubon Ratchathani ☎ 045 241 739 💷 B220–B600 excluding breakfast ⓘ 110 ⚑ Some rooms

UDON THANI
CHAROEN HOTEL

Showing its age a little, this is still a decent place to stay. The rooms are fine—all have a fridge and cable TV. Breakfast (B165) is not included in the room rate but is available at the restaurant, which also does a lunchtime buffet. There is internet access available in the hotel and a choice of single or double beds.

✉ 549 Thanon Phosri, Udon Thani ☎ 042 248 155 💷 B800–B900 excluding breakfast ⓘ 250 ⚑ ⛱ Outdoor

CHAROENSRI PALACE HOTEL

Well, maybe not a palace but very good value for a one-night stay in Udon and just a short *tuk-tuk* ride (B30 to B40) away from the bus or train station. The bedrooms are large and well kept, with cable TV and fridge, plus there's an attractive little Italian restaurant (Vittorio Piccola Roma) just up the road.

✉ 60 Thanon Phosri, Udon Thani ☎ 042 242 611 💷 From B380 excluding breakfast ⓘ 70 ⚑

THE NORTH

Thailand's highest mountains mark the boundaries of the country's northernmost region and ring its ancient moated capital, Chiang Mai. Once the heart of the old Lanna kingdom; a recent revival of Lanna architecture is infusing the city once again with a sense of elegance. The city is one of the largest in Thailand, yet the old quarter retains small-town charm with its central brick roads and renowned Sunday night markets. Today, Chiang Mai is a major hub for commerce, tourism, education and politics.

Northern Thailand was intersected by the Silk Road, an ancient commerce route linking neighboring China, Burma (Myanmar) and Laos. The trail was a conduit for silk, tea, spice, timber, medicine, opium and other valuable goods. The ancient caravans are lost to romantic history, and thankfully, too, the trade in opium has been greatly curtailed by programs initiated by the current king. The area was once the center of the infamous "Golden Triangle" (which includes Myanmar, Laos and Northern Vietnam) and, until recently, the name referred to the illicit trade in heroin here. The term has since been appropriated by the tourism industry and infused with a connotation of exotic adventure.

The northern mountains are the birthplace of Thai culture and now home to numerous hill tribes. Nomadic Hmong with intricate embroidery, Karen women wearing V-neck tunics, baggy-panted Lahu men, Lisu crowned with tasseled turbans, Akha women with indigo shirts and ornate headdresses, Mien silversmiths, and the infamous long-necked Padaung all call this region home, and the many handicraft villages are among the region's top attractions.

National Parks, such as Doi Inthanon and Doi Pui, offer boundless outdoor activities. The jungle-covered heights are challenging terrain for hikers, while the deep valleys are cut by fast-flowing rivers, perfect for kayaking. Upland trails lead to remote hill-tribe villages where visitors receive a warm welcome.

BO SANG

Umbrellas are the specialty of this village, 5 miles (8km) northeast of Chiang Mai. The story goes that some 100 years ago a local monk was traveling in Myanmar and asked a craftsman there to mend his umbrella. The monk, Phra In Tha, was surprised to see him use *sa* paper, made from mulberry tree bark. Phra In Tha took the technique home to Borsang and showed Thai villagers how to make *sa*-paper umbrellas. The largest workshop, the Borsang Umbrella Centre (tel 053 338 466; daily 8–5) is in the center of the village. For a fee of B100 upward you can have your own design painted on an umbrella.

✚ 306 C3 ℹ TAT Northern Office, Region 1, 105/1 Chiang Mai–Lamphun road, Amphoe Muang, Chiang Mai 50000 ☎ 053 248 604/7 ◷ Daily 8.30–4.30

CHIANG DAO
▷ 152.

CHIANG KHONG
▷ 153.

CHIANG MAI
▷ 154–159.

CHIANG RAI
▷ 160.

CHIANG SAEN
▷ 161.

DOI ANGKHANG

Tucked away in the northwestern corner of Thailand, Doi Angkhang is a remote upland range, reminiscent of the former colonial hill stations of Asia. Most of the jungle-clad range is a royal agricultural station, worked by the inhabitants of nearby hill-tribe villages. These villages are largely unspoiled and include a community of Chinese descendants of Kuomintang nationalist Chinese soldiers who fled the advancing forces of Mao Tse Tung. More than 1,000 bird species populate the area, which is criss-crossed by trails

Opposite *Entrance to the Chiang Dao caves*

that visitors can travel on a hired mule. Bungalows can be rented at the Royal Agricultural Station and there's a luxury hotel, the Angkhang Nature Resort (▷ 193).

✚ 306 C1 ℹ The Royal Agricultural Station, Tambon Mae Ngon, Amphoe Fang ☎ 053 450 107/9

DOI INTHANON NATIONAL PARK
▷ 162–163.

DOI MAE SALONG

Drive to this remote mountain community in the far north of Thailand and you'd be forgiven for believing you'd arrived at a Chinese border town. It was settled some 50 years ago by a Nationalist Army regiment fleeing from Mao Tse Tung's Communist forces in China's civil war. Thailand's government allowed the refugees to stay provided they helped in its own efforts to suppress Thai communists. The Chinese integrated well into the local community and became farmers and opened small businesses. Their descendants keep alive many Chinese traditions, however, and the town has a distinctly Chinese character, with its own Buddhist temple, cemetery and specialty shops. It sits atop a 5,577ft (1,700m) mountain range, with magnificent views.

✚ 307 C1 ℹ TAT Northern Office, Region 2, 448/16 Thanon Singhaklai, Amphoe Muang, Chiang Rai 57000 ☎ 053 717 433, 053 744 674/5 ◷ Daily 8.30–4.30 🚌 Regular bus services from Chiang Mai and Chiang Rai

DOI PHU KHA NATIONAL PARK

Northern Thailand's largest national park is also the most remote, covering 658sq miles (1,704sq km) of mountainous terrain bordering Laos. From the 6,140ft (1,872m) summit of Doi Phu Kha, there are breathtaking views deep into Laos, although it's a long trek there from the park headquarters. The rocky outcrops of the mountain are home to the rare "ancient palm," while oaks and other deciduous trees grow at this altitude. Caves

riddle the limestone uplands, and a mountain river flows directly through one, Tham Lot. The waterfalls are spectacular, and one of the pleasures of a stay at the park is a day's trek to either Phufah or Fah Shee Nok cascades for a cooling swim and a picnic in the shade of the jungle. Rooms or chalets can be rented at the park headquarters for B800 to B3,200 per night. The headquarters is reached on the Nan–Pau road. A signpost 37 miles (60km) from Nan indicates the 15-mile (25km) side road to the park.

✚ 307 E2 ✉ Tambol Phu Kha, Amphoe Pua, Nan Province 55120 ☎ 054 70 10 00 🖐 B200 ℹ Tourist Information Service, 46 Thanon Suriyapong, Amphoe Muang, Nan 55000 ☎ 054 710 216 ◷ Mon–Fri 8.30–4.30

DOI SUTHEP/DOI PUI NATIONAL PARK
▷ 164.

DOI TUNG

The Doi Tung mountain southwest of Chiang Rai is the site of a unique royal project to wean hill-tribe farmers away from opium cultivation by encouraging them to engage in profitable handicrafts. The project was begun by the king's mother, the revered "Princess Mother," and is now run successfully by the nonprofit Mae Fah Luang Foundation. The Princess Mother's royal villa (daily 9–5) sits near the summit, overlooking coffee plantations, nurseries and workshops that make up a humming center of commercial activity. The workshops—the "Cottage Industry Center"—turn out textiles, carpets, ceramics and mulberry-paper products, as well as packing coffee that grows on the mountain. Just below the villa is a lodge with 46 rooms (B3,000 to B3,500). Reservations are essential.

✚ 307 D1 ✉ Doi Tung Development Project, Mae Fah Luang, Chiang Rai 57240 ☎ 053 767 015/7 ◷ Daily 7–6 🖐 Royal villa: B70; gardens: B80; Princess Mother Commemoration Hall: B30; ticket for all 3 attractions: adult B150, child half price

INFORMATION

www.chiangdao.com

✚ 306 C2 ℹ TAT Northern Office,
Region 1, 105/1 Chiang Mai–Lamphun
road, Amphoe Muang, Chiang Mai 50000
☎ 053 248 604/7 🕐 Daily 8.30–4.30
🕐 Caves: daily 8.30–4.30 ✋ Park
entrance fee B400

CHIANG DAO

The small market town of Chiang Dao, 46 miles (75km) north of Chiang Mai, is famous for its caves, among the most spectacular in Thailand, which wind deep into the interior of the jungle-clad mountain that broods over the area. The caves penetrate up to 9 miles (15km) into the remarkable mountain, Doi Luang, that leaps straight up out of the rice paddies surrounding the town. Doi Luang stands at 7,300ft (2,225m) and is Thailand's third-highest mountain and perhaps its most spectacular. Its steep, jungle-covered sides are a challenge for the hardiest hiker, but the rewards of a two-day slog up the narrow access path to the summit and back down again are immeasurable, including views to die for. Several species of wildlife, including deer and wild boar, have their home in the impenetrable, forested slopes

A SPECTACULAR DRIVE

The drive to the caves from the main Chiang Mai–Chiang Dao road is spectacular, about 1 mile long (1.5km) avenue lined by high yang trees and fronted by the sheer face of the mountain. Like all caves in Thailand, these come with their own mythology, based on the fable of a local hermit who is said to have lived and meditated in them for 1,000 years. The gods rewarded him by constructing within the caverns a collection of fantastic images, presumably the stalactites, stalagmites and crystallized calcium deposits you'll find within them to this day.

The first two caverns—Tham Phra Nawn (Cave of the Sleeping Buddha) and Tham Phra Seua Dao (Leopard Cave)—are lit, but you'll need to hire a guide with a lantern (B200 per group of eight) to explore farther.

ELEPHANT RIDING

There's much else to keep the visitor in Chiang Dao for a day or two, including an elephant training center (daily 8–5) in the nearby village of Mae Tang. The elephants demonstrate their logging skills and play football (shows daily at 10 and 11), and give rides through the jungle and across a river, where raft trips (B1,000) are also offered.

Above *Romantic view of Doi Chiang Dao Mountain cloaked in mist*

CHIANG KHONG

Sitting on a broad sweep of the Mekong River, Chiang Khong is the major border crossing between northern Thailand and Laos and is a favorite staging post for visitors traveling through Southeast Asia. It's hard for the first-time visitor to believe that this rather rundown riverside town, consisting of little more than one main street, was once the capital of a realm that stretched across northern Laos and into China. It was founded at the start of the eighth century and grew into a powerful city state and important trading post between the east and west.

There's little evidence of the town's grand past now though, apart from one 13th-century *chedi* (monument housing a Buddhist relic) at the riverside Wat Luang. There are ambitious plans to restore the town to its earlier economic importance; eventually it will become a vital element of the great Asian Highway project, linking East and Southeast Asia with a bridge currently being constructed across the Mekong. Large flatbed ferries now carry traffic across the river from a jetty on the edge of Chiang Khong to the small Laotian port town of Ban Xouay. Visitors cross on perilously narrow motor-driven canoes, but you'll need a visa to enter Laos on the other side.

STAGING POST

Chiang Khong is jammed for most of the year with backpackers from all over the world on their way to or from Laos, Vietnam or China. They give the place a cosmopolitan air quite out of proportion to its size, and the modest guest houses that cater to them party deep into the night. The town's markets, strung out along its dusty main street, are awash with goods from Laos and China, mostly textiles and cheap electronic gadgetry, but hill-tribe handicrafts can also be found and are a much better buy.

A LAST RESTING PLACE

On a hill overlooking the river is a reminder of Chiang Khong's more recent history—a cemetery containing the graves of more than 200 Nationalist Chinese soldiers who ended up here after fleeing from Mao Tse Tung's victorious communist army in 1949. Their graves face in the direction of China.

INFORMATION

🗺 307 D1 ℹ️ TAT Northern Office, Region 2, 448/16 Thanon Singhaklai, Amphoe Muang, Chiang Rai 57000 ☎ 053 744 674/5 🕐 Daily 8.30–4.30

TIPS

➤➤ If your guesthouse gets too crowded and noisy with the backpackers who throng high-season Chiang Khong, take an evening stroll along the riverbank path and watch the locals cast their lines into the dark waters of the Mekong in the hopes of hooking something for the family pot (the catfish in these parts are the world's largest).

➤➤ Even if you don't intend to visit Laos, take a ferry ride across the Mekong and at least step on Laotian soil before heading back. Boatmen at the ferry crossing will take you over and back for B50 or so. A longer trip on the Mekong by longtail boat costs between B800 and B1,000.

Below *The peaceful view from Wat Phra That Pha Nago*

INFORMATION

www.chiangmai.online.com

✚ 306 C3   ℹ TAT Northern Office, Region 1, 105/1 Chiang Mai–Lamphun road, Amphoe Muang, Chiang Mai 50000 ☎ 053 248 604/7 🕐 Daily 8.30–4.30

TIPS

➤➤ Touts and scam artists are much less of a problem in sleepy Chiang Mai, than cities to the south, but it is wise to observe all the same precautions here.
➤➤ Have lunch at Ruen Tamarind Restaurant (▷ 189) or Rachamankha (▷ 189) to soak up the "Lanna revival" architecture and peaceful ambience.

Above *The ancient temple complex of Wat Chiang Man, built in the 13th century*
Opposite *The bright fairy lights at Chiang Mai's celebrated Night Bazaar*

INTRODUCTION

Northern Thailand's regional capital is dubbed the "Rose of the North" because of its natural beauty and the profusion of flowers that drape its ancient walls and line its moat and river bridges. Founded in the 13th century by the Lanna King Mengrai, who at first built his citadel slightly south of the present city, it was later forced to move to higher ground by persistent flooding. His new city (Chiang Mai means "new city") grew within a wide moat and defensive walls and bastions. The moat still exists, and many of the ancient fortifications have been reconstructed, giving Chiang Mai much of its charm. Despite its stout defences, Chiang Mai was overrun in the 16th century by Burmese invaders, who sacked the city and carried most of its people off to slavery. Lanna became a Burmese vassal state for nearly 200 years, before the Burmese were driven out in 1774. The Lanna kingdom retained its independence for nearly another century before being absorbed into the Siam state ruling from Bangkok.

WHAT TO SEE
THE OLD CITY

Chiang Mai's old city is a maze of narrow streets and brick-paved lanes leading to ancient *wats* (temples), quiet monastery gardens, hidden bars, restaurants and boutiques. Although the old city is ringed by an efficient one-way traffic system, the roads in the surrounding new city are often as clogged as Bangkok's, and the pollution is only slightly less heavy. Only the most daring visitors rent a car for city sightseeing, so stick to *tuk-tuks* and red-covered *songthaews*. They are responsible for much of the pollution but are still the best way to get around. Taxis are available but still difficult to find. *Samlaws* (tricycle "taxis") are ecologically friendly but slow. Bicycles and motorcycles are easily and cheaply rented, but by far the best way of exploring the old city is still on foot. The old city is about 1sq mile (2.5sq km), and most of the major attractions are to be found within its walls and moat.

WAT CHIANG MAN

Chiang Mai's oldest temple is also its most interesting. Built in 1297–98 by the first Lanna king, Mengrai, on the site of his Chiang Mai palace, Wat Chiang

Man was restored to its present state by the 18th-century monarch, Gawila. The main *viharn* (assembly hall), its beamed ceiling supported by 10 massive teak pillars, is an absolute masterpiece of gold and crimson decoration, but a neighboring, smaller and more modern hall contains the temple's true treasures: the Phra Sila, a carved stone Buddha figure that is said to have originated in India, and the Phra Setangamani, a crystal Buddha reputed to be 1,800 years old. They were placed here by King Mengrai himself and are now contained within a gold and crimson cage, behind three sets of iron bars. At the rear of the main *viharn* is a square, Sukhothai-style *chedi* (monument housing a buddhist relic) supported by 17 elephants, which was constructed here in Mengrai's time and is said to contain a lock of the Buddha's hair.
🕂 157 D2 ✉ Thanon Ratchaphanikai ☎ 053 375 368 🕐 Daily 6am–9pm 💵 Donation box

WAT CHEDI LUANG

Towering above the park-like monastery grounds of Wat Chedi Luang are the bulky remains of an enormous stupa which 15th-century King Saen Muang Ma ordered to be built in the exact center of the old city to safeguard a relic of the Buddha. The king died before it was completed, which was just as well, because an earthquake later destroyed the top of the 282ft (86m) monument—a very bad omen, indeed. Only one of the carved elephants on the stupa's massive base (the most weather-beaten one) dates from those times. Newly added sinuous *nagas*, or mythical serpents, border the remains of steep flights of steps that lead up to golden images of the Buddha sitting in three loges of the stupa. The fourth, east-facing loge, has a replica of the Phra Keo Emerald Buddha that was once safeguarded here before its long journey to Bangkok. Monks once climbed the steps of the stupa to anoint its Buddha images in holy water. Now they employ an ingenious pulley system that carries the water up to the top of the stupa and then tips it over the structure. You're

TIPS

➤➤ Chiang Mai's top tourist draw is its celebrated Night Bazaar (🕂 157 D3), which lines central Thanon Chang Klan for around 1 mile (1.6km) every night from 7pm. There's been a bazaar here for centuries, and although souvenirs now dominate the wares on offer, some of the goods haven't changed a great deal: silks, textiles and hill-tribe handicrafts. The bazaar is held in all winds and weathers, although there's also a permanent building, the Night Market, on this section of Thanon Chang Klan. Some of the stalls and shops here sell genuine antiques. You're expected to bargain—offer half the demanded price and then work toward an acceptable compromise. If you find the Night Bazaar and the Night Market a touch too commercial and if you're in town on a Sunday, make for Thanon Rachadamnoen, which is closed to traffic for the day and turned over to street traders, musicians, artists and craftspeople. In the evening, it becomes a "magical mile," drawing Thais from their homes for a Mediterranean-style "corso" (promenade).

REGIONS • THE NORTH • CITY MAP

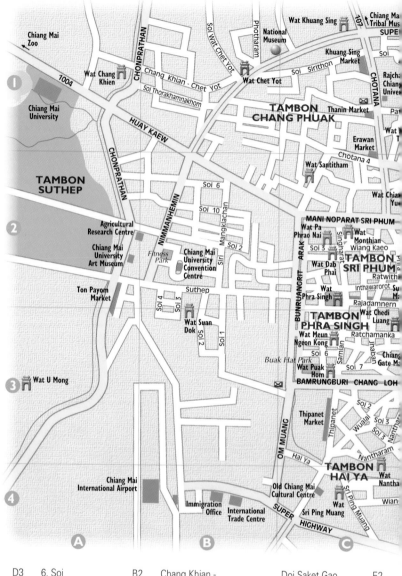

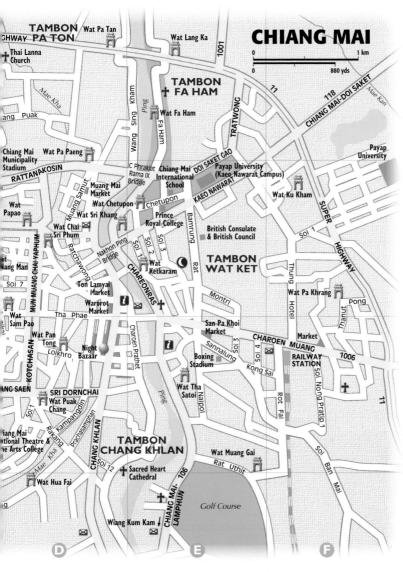

CHIANG MAI

0   1 km
0   880 yds

>> The English-speaking monks of two Chiang Mai *wats* are happy to meet visitors and discuss their cloistered lives, Buddhism and Thai culture. You can find the monks sitting beneath the trees in the compound of Wat Chedi Luang, Thanon Prapokkloa, every afternoon, or on the campus of Mahachulalongkorn Buddhist University, behind Wat Suandok, Thanon Stuep, on Monday, Wednesday and Friday afternoons.

>> Chiang Mai can get quite hot, particularly in March and April. Try to plan your outdoor activities to begin as early in the day as possible, or in the evenings when things have cooled down again. In between, take advantage of air-conditioned shopping plazas, including Gad Suan Gaew, on Huay Gaew Road, and the Airport Plaza.

>> Chiang Mai can get oppressively hot, particularly in March and April.

encouraged to do the same—it's a way of earning merit, avoiding bad luck and easing your journey through the hereafter. The leafy temple grounds contain a 35ft-long (10.5m) reclining 15th-century Buddha, his face contemplating the *chedi*, and a handsome 19th-century *viharn*. Among the neat little chapels that dot the grounds of the temple is one containing the 13th-century city pillar and another housing a jolly 15th-century golden Buddha, his hands clasping his ample belly and an expression of sheer bliss on his broad face. If you visit at 6pm you'll see and hear the monks at evening prayer and, on fine evenings, witness the sun set brilliantly beyond the *viharn's* mountain backdrop—a truly unforgettable sight.

➕ 156 C3 ✉ Corner of Prapokkloa and Rachadamnoen roads ☎ 053 278 595 🕐 Daily 6am–9pm 🖐 Donation box

WAT PHRA SINGH

Chiang Mai's principal temple ensemble dominates the western side of the old city, and its high white walls embrace a collection of centuries-old buildings and *chedis* within tree-shaded park-like grounds. Its oldest structure is a *chedi* built in 1345 to contain the remains of the Lanna ruler Pha Yoo. A modern *viharn*—an airy synthesis of white, red and gold—houses a magnificent gilded Buddha, while the temple's true treasure—a 14th-century Buddha said to have originated in Sukhothai—sits in an older, more modest but exquisitely decorated chapel at the rear.

➕ 156 C2 ✉ Thanon Singharat ☎ 053 814 164 🕐 Daily 7am–9pm 🖐 Donation box

CHIANG MAI TRIBAL MUSEUM

The history, culture and way of life of the hill tribes that inhabit the mountains of northern Thailand are explained and illustrated in this comprehensive museum, located on the outskirts of Chiang Mai. Since many of the villages closest to the city have become little more than small theme parks, crowded with tourist groups and tour buses, a visit to the museum is perhaps the best way to get to know these fascinating but marginalized and often ill-treated

Below left The moat surrounding Chiang Mai's old city

Below right Founded in 1345 to house the ashes of King Kham Fu, the old temple of Wat Phra Singh, in Chiang Mai

people. The handicrafts on show demonstrate their aestheticism, imagination and skill with textiles, basketwork, bamboo, rattan and tropical woods.

✛ Off map at 156 C1 ✉ Ratchamangkla Park, Thanon Chotana (the Mae Rim road) ☎ 053 210 872 🕓 Mon–Fri 9–4 ✋ Donation box

NATIONAL MUSEUM

www.thailandmuseum.com

The history of the Lanna kingdom and its culture are well documented and displayed in Chiang Mai's premier museum, a large Lanna-style building on the edge of the city. Among the exhibits, distributed in six sections over two floors, is a fine collection of local San Kamphaeng porcelain dating from the 14th century.

✛ 156 B1 ✉ Chiang Mai–Lampang road ☎ 053 221 308 🕓 Wed–Sun 9–4 ✋ B100

MORE TO SEE

WAT CHET YOT

One of Chiang Mai's most attractive temple compounds sits on the busy "superhighway" that rings the city. In the center of lawns and paved walkways is the seven-spired *chedi* (Chet Yot) after which the temple is named. It was built in 1455 as a local memorial to the temple in Bodhgaya, India, the village where the Buddha was said to have gained enlightenment.

✛ 156 B1 ✉ Chiang Mai–Lampang road ☎ 053 221 947 🕓 Daily, no fixed hours

WIANG KUM KAM

Only in 1984 did archeologists discover that King Mengrai's first Chiang Mai capital was downriver from the present city. He first chose a site on a bend in the Ping River, but discovered the folly of his choice in the first rainy season, around 1293, when floods inundated the new settlement. Nevertheless, at least six temples were built there, and their ruins have now been laid bare. You can tour them in a horse and carriage (B200) or by tram (B250).

✛ Off map at 157 E4 ✉ 3 miles (5km) south of Chiang Mai on the Chiang Mai–Lamphun road ☎ 053 277 322 🕓 Daily 8–5

Above *One of the bastions of the old city walls in Chiang Mai*

INFORMATION

www.chiangraiprovince.com
307 D1 TAT Northern Office, Region 2, 448/16 Thanon Singhaklai, Amphoe Muang, Chiang Rai 57000
☎ 053 717 433, 053 744 674/5 Daily 8.30–4.30

TIPS

>> Chiang Rai's night market rivals Chiang Mai's for size and variety. It's open every evening from 6–11.
>> Don't miss Khun Kon Forest Park (daily 9–6), 18 miles (29km) south of Chiang Rai, which has the highest waterfall in Chiang Rai province. The park also has some picturesque hill-tribe villages.

Above *Serpents guard the temple of Wat Phra Kaew*
Below *Buddha statues at Wat Phra Singh*

CHIANG RAI

Chiang Rai possesses three of the region's most historic temples. Thailand's northernmost city is also an ideal center from which to tour the Golden Triangle and the mountains that border Myanmar (Burma) and Laos. Chiang Rai is older than Chiang Mai, founded in 1256 by King Mengrai, who moved his capital progressively southward from its original site on the Mekong River. King Mengrai later founded Chiang Mai and moved the capital there, after which the Burmese conquered Chiang Rai and maintained control for several centuries. It later became a vassal of Chiang Mai in 1786.

HISTORIC TEMPLES

One of its temples, Wat Phra Kaew (daily 6am–8pm), sheltered the fabled Emerald Buddha on its long journey to Bangkok. A modern copy, donated in the late 1990s by a Chinese millionaire, now sits in the main *viharn* of the temple. Chiang Rai's oldest temple, Wat Doi Tong (daily 6am–8pm), built before the arrival of King Mengrai, commands a hilltop site above Wat Phra Kaew. The climb there, through shady woodland, is well worth the effort for the view of Chiang Rai and the Kok River that embraces the city. It's said that King Mengrai also made the climb and planned the layout of his future capital from this superb vantage point.

Chiang Rai's third temple of note, Wat Phra Singh (daily 6am–8pm), dates from the 14th century and has a handsome Lanna-style *viharn* with some very fine wood carving, bronze Buddha images and murals. It once boasted one of northern Thailand's most beautiful Buddha statues, the Phra Buddha Singh, which was carried off to Chiang Mai by King Mengrai. It's now the finest feature of Chiang Mai's Wat Phra Singh, and the one you see in Chiang Rai's temple of the same name is a later copy.

SHOPPING BARGAINS

Chiang Rai has an excellent night bazaar to rival Chiang Mai's. It's also well stocked with hill-tribe handicrafts, brought down from the nearby mountains every evening by women of the six hill tribes of the region: the Akha, Yao, Meo, Lisu, Lahu and Karen.

The bazaar, just off Thanon Phaholyothin, is the place to eat authentic northern Thai food, from any of the stalls that line the road. Due to the outstanding natural scenery, Chiang Rai is a prime launching point for trekking to hill-tribe villages, where additional craft shopping opportunities abound.

CHIANG SAEN

Neglected for many years, this fascinating Mekong River town is being restored to the important status it once held in Thai history and is destined to become one of the major ports of the Mekong River once again. Visit Chiang Saen and you'll find a town humming with activity as construction workers expand its harbor facilities and modernize the installations to create a 21st-century port that will be able to handle freighters and barges from Myanmar (Burma), China and Laos.

Between the harbor and the town center, archeologists are excavating the ancient citadel of Chiang Saen and the town's 800-year-old foundations. The original settlers here were thought to be Tai migrants from Yunnan, China, arriving in the middle of the sixth century. The historical city was later founded in the 13th century by Mengrai, who used it as a stepping stone to creating the Lanna kingdom, setting up his royal residences first here, then in Chiang Rai and finally in Chiang Mai. At its peak, the city had more than 75 temples within the city wall, and more than 60 outlying temples.

ANCIENT CHIANG SAEN

Invading Burmese forces laid waste to ancient Chiang Saen in 1588, and a disastrous fire two centuries later gutted the rebuilt city. Modern construction and looting have also taken more recent tolls on the ruins and antiquities. But the foundations and walls of the old city are now being laid bare, and many finds from Chiang Saen's early history are in the local museum (702 Thanon Phaholyothin, tel 053 777 102; Wed–Sun 8.30–4.30; adult B100, child under 14 free). Established nearly 50 years ago, the museum is one of the most important in northern Thailand, tracing not only the origins of the Lanna kingdom but the prehistory of this region of the Mekong valley. Among the museum's treasures is a very beautiful 16th-century bronze depicting the emblematic Lanna flame, found in the Mekong. A graceful 19th-century Burmese receptacle attests to the influence Burma once wielded.

WAT PA SAK

Dating from Mengrai's time is Wat Pa Sak and its stepped *chedi*, said to contain holy relics brought here from across the Mekong when the city was founded. The temple's name, Pa Sak, means "teak forest," referring to the hundreds of teak trees planted to provide wood for construction. Nearby is an octagonal temple, Wat Phra That Luang, dating from the 14th century.

INFORMATION

✚ 307 D1 ℹ TAT Northern Office, Region 2, 448/16 Thanon Singhaklai, Amphoe Muang, Chiang Rai 57000 ☎ 053 744 674/5 🕐 Daily 8.30–4.30

TIP

➤➤ Don't miss the longtail boats berthed below the customs post on the main riverside boulevard, which take visitors across the Mekong to an island that is Laotian territory, although you don't need a passport. The boatmen charge B500 to B600 for the trip.

Above *Monks in saffron robes beside the Mekong River at Chiang Saen*

INFORMATION

www.thaiparks.com
✛ 306 B3 ☎ 053 268 550 🕙 Daily
6–6 ℹ TAT Northern Office, Region
1, 105/1 Chiang Mai–Lamphun Road,
Amphoe Muang, Chiang Mai 50000
☎ 053 248 604/7 🕙 Daily 8.30–4.30
✋ Adult B200, child B100, vehicles B30

TIP

» For the best views of Doi Inthanon
avoid the most direct route (Route 108
until Chom Tong, then the country road to
the summit)—drive farther on Route 108
until Hot, then take the country road to
Mae Chaem and from there to the summit
of the mountain. From the valley floor, the
Doi Inthanon massif is displayed in all
its majesty.

Above *Waterfall at the Doi Inthanon
National Park*

INTRODUCTION

Doi Inthanon is Thailand's highest mountain, named after Chiang Mai's last
ruler, Inthawuchayanon, and it dominates a national park where tigers still
roam. The nature-loving ruler Inthawuchayanon was so enchanted by this wild
mountainous region, just 50 miles (80km) from his Chiang Mai palace, that
he ordained his ashes to be buried on its 7,645ft (2,330m) summit. A modest
white *chedi* in a forest clearing contains his remains at a spot called "the
roof of Thailand." The serpentine route to the top winds through two distinct
climatic zones, from tropical jungle to deciduous oaks and evergreen firs. In
just 18 miles (30km) the average nighttime temperature drops in winter from a
pleasant 70°F (21°C) to near freezing, with a record of 17.5°F (-8°C).

Spectacular waterfalls—including Thailand's highest—are easily accessible,
either on foot or by vehicle, and hill-tribe villages welcome overnight visitors.
Just below the summit and Inthawuchayanon's grave are two other, larger
chedis erected in honor of the present king and queen.

WHAT TO SEE
MOUNTAIN VIEWS

The direct route up Doi Inthanon winds gradually through thick forest that
obscures any view of the summit. For an impression of the height and sheer
magnitude of the Doi Inthanon massif turn left just before the summit onto
Route 1192, which leads to the isolated weaving village of Mae Chaem. From
the valley floor you have a breathtaking view of this grand mountain.

PLANT LIFE

Giant rhododendrons and delicate varieties of roses grow in profusion on
the park's upper slopes, and wild orchids cling to the massive trees of the
impenetrable jungle. Thick rain forests and towering stands of bamboo clothe
the mountain's tropical zone, while teak and pine grow under close Forestry
Department supervision and are hence untouched by illegal loggers.

ANIMAL LIFE

Tigers have been spotted on Doi Inthanon, but they're a very rare sight. You're much more likely to see deer, gibbons, wild boar and Siamese hares. The national park is home to more than 300 bird species (birdwatchers can hire knowledgeable guides at the park headquarters).

WATERFALLS

Doi Inthanon National Park has some of the highest and most beautiful waterfalls in Thailand. They are all well signposted and relatively easy to reach. The highest of them is also the most remote: the 820ft (250m) Mae Ya waterfall, in the southern section of the park. It's a 3-mile (5km) hike but well worth the effort to see this mass of water, higher than Niagara Falls, plunge over a series of steps.

The easiest to reach are the Watchiratan Falls, 13 miles (22km) from the national park turn-off on Route 108, and the Mae Klang Falls, 5 miles (8km) on the same road. Mae Klang, a favorite picnic spot for Chiang Mai families, has a small market and food stands.

Among the most beautiful of the park's falls is the Namtok Siripum. It plunges more than 330ft (100m) over a high cliff towering above a valley where the royal family support an agricultural project, 7 miles (11km) from the edge of the park.

THE ROYAL PROJECT

The Siripum Falls feed trout-breeding tanks, which are one of the most successful enterprises of the national park's royal project. The trout raised here find their way onto the menus of Thailand's leading hotels and, of course, the royal palace. You can enjoy a grilled trout at the simple restaurant that welcomes visitors to the royal project. The trout dishes come in six varieties, including incongruously hot and spicy sauces. The horticultural gardens and greenhouses that make up most of the royal project are a gardener's dream.
🕐 Daily 6–6 ♿ Free

A GOOD HIKE

Doi Inthanon National Park is true hiker's territory, and the area is criss-crossed by wonderful trails connecting the many hill-tribe villages. Walkers can stay in the villages for a modest fee (negotiable with the village elders); the easiest route to the summit of Doi Inthanon involves three overnight stays with Karen communities en route. The route to the summit starts at the Mae Klang Falls and takes you through three conveniently located villages: Mae Aeb, Pa Mon and Pang Somdet.

Above *Queen Sirikit's* chedi *at Doi Ithanon*
Below *Mesmerizing view from the summit of Doi Inthanon at dusk*

INFORMATION

308 B3   TAT Northern Office, Region 1, 105/1 Chiang Mai–Lamphun road, Amphoe Muang, Chiang Mai 50000   053 248 604/7   Daily 8.30–4.30

Wat Phra That Doi Suthep

Doi Suthep   Daily 8–6   Adult B50, child (under 12) free

Phuping Palace

Doi Suthep   Daily 8.30–3.30, except when the royal family is in residence, usually from mid-Jan to early Feb   Palace grounds B50

DOI SUTHEP/DOI PUI NATIONAL PARK

Chiang Mai's "guardian" mountains, 5,065ft (1,544m) Doi Suthep and Doi Pui, rise steeply to the west. Their forested slopes, waterfalls, ponds and lake form the Doi Pui National Park. Doi Suthep's mountaintop temple is one of northern Thailand's most revered places of pilgrimage. It's said that an elephant carrying a Buddha relic was led up the mountain, and on the ridge where it first stopped a *chedi* was built to contain the sacred object. A community of monks later built a temple there.

Until 1935 the only way to reach the temple was along a steep jungle path. Today it's a 10-minute journey on a well-paved road to the entrance of the park. A pleasant, shady path leads from the national park entrance on Thanon Huay Kaew about 3 miles (5km) up the mountain, emerging on the main road, where you can flag down one of the many red *songthaews* that cruise the route.

WAT PHRA THAT DOI SUTHEP

The broad, leafy terrace of the temple complex sits like a shelf below the summit of Doi Suthep, at 3,543ft (1,080m), and commands a spectacular view of Chiang Mai below. The extensive temple ensemble of chapels (*bot*), assembly halls (*viharn*), chedis (the main one covered in gold leaf), Buddha images and frescoed cloisters took shape over the past seven centuries. Don't leave without striking one of the sonorous bells that border the terrace. *Songthaews* (B50) set out on the steep mountain road from parking areas on Thanon Huay Kaew, Thanon Sri Poom and outside the Wat Prasingh on Thanon Samlan. From the Doi Suthep parking area it's a long but pleasant climb up a broad flight of steps to the temple, but if that seems too daunting then an ugly funicular also makes the journey.

PHUPING PALACE

The king's summer residence near the summit of Doi Suthep is more like an alpine lodge than a palace. The house itself is closed to the public, but the grounds are worth visiting for the rose garden alone.

DOI PUI MEO

From the parking area below Phuping Palace a road leads 2.5 miles (4km) to a Meo hill-tribe village. The main street is lined by makeshift shops and workrooms where Hmong women create handicrafts.

Below Looking towards Chiang Mai's guardian mountains

FANG

www.dnp.go.th

Fang, founded in the 13th century by the Lanna king Mengrai, is the gateway to one of Thailand's newest national parks, Mae Fang. It's a beautiful region of mountains, valleys, waterfalls, hot springs and a rich variety of flora and fauna, including deer, sloth, wild boar—and even bears. About 43 miles (70km) of the park borders Myanmar, and it's a remote highland region rising to Thailand's second-highest mountain, Doi Phahompok (7,497ft/ 2,285m). The 4-mile (7km) hike to the summit of the mountain is rewarded by a breathtaking view of the border region between Thailand and Myanmar. A circular route takes you past caves and two waterfalls. Next to the park entrance and headquarters is a natural hot spring with 131ft-high (40m) geysers. Entrance to the park costs B200 (B50 for a vehicle), and bungalows can be rented (B2,000 per night). ✚ 306 C1 ℹ Mae Fang National Park, P.O. 39, Fang District, Chiang Mai 50110 ☎ 086 430 9748 ⏰ Daily 8.30–4.30

HANG CHAT

www.lampang.go.th

In a forest, just off the Lampang–Chiang Mai highway and 10 miles (16km) north of Hang Chat, is Thailand's National Elephant Institute and Conservation Center. This is where the king stables his white elephants, although you'll have to sign up for an elephant-training course to view them. More than 30 other elephants populate the center, giving demonstations and taking visitors for rides. One group paints pictures, which have fetched big prices at auctions in London and New York. Another group plays instruments and has cut two CDs. Performances take place daily at 10, 11 and 1.30; adult B70 child (under 14) B30. Visitors can see the elephants bathing at 9.45 and 1.45. Rides are B400 for 30 minutes.

The center rescues neglected and sick elephants, which are treated in its hospital. Among the patients are elephants who suffered hideous wounds when stepping on landmines in Myanmar.

Just 6 miles (10km) north of the center is Hang Chat's renowned farmers' market, Kad Tung Khwian. When local villagers established the market 20 years ago it won notoriety for offering live snakes and exotic animals. Nowadays, it's a much tamer but there are still plenty of stalls to browse, and everything from Lampang pottery to hand-forged swords are available here. ✚ 306 C3 ℹ Tourist Information Lampang, Tessaban Lampang ☎ 054 219 300 ⏰ Mon–Fri 8.30–4.30

LAMPANG

▷ 166–167.

LAMPHUN

▷ 168–169.

MAE HONG SON

▷ 170.

MAE SAI

This dusty frontier town is the northernmost point of Thailand, connected by a short river bridge with neighboring Myanmar (Burma). Its chief attraction is its easy access to Myanmar. Until Thailand recently changed its visa policy, the border town was a popular place for expatriates to leave the country and re-enter Thailand with a new visa. You can join them by walking across the bridge over the narrow Mae Sai River and paying US$5 for a day's Burmese visa. That allows you to wander around Myanmar's frontier town, run-down Tachilek, and shop for gems and Burmese souvenirs in the riverside market, as well as stock up on cheap liquor and cigarettes in the town's duty-free shop.

Mae Sai has a famous temple, Wat Phra That Doi Wao. It's known as the scorpion temple because of a large sculpture of the poisonous creature common in these parts. If the climb is too formidable then a motorcycle taxi will take you there for B10. Either way, the trip is worth it for the view from the terrace.

Above *Hill-tribe children from Doi Mae Salong*

✚ 307 D1 ℹ TAT Northern Office Region 2, 448/16 Thanon Singhaklai, Amphoe Muang, Chiang Rai 57000 ☎ 053 717 433 ⏰ Daily 8.30–4.30 🚌 Regular bus services from Chiang Mai and Chiang Rai

MAE SARIANG

Mae Sariang is a convenient overnight stop on the Chiang Mai–Mae Hong Son loop, but also an ideal center from which to explore the Thai–Myanmar (Burmese) border region. It's a pretty town, with a large population of ethnic Karen from neighboring Myanmar. One of its most notable temples, Wat Mandalay, is Burmese in origin, with Buddhist sculptures by Burmese craftspeople, including a Buddha image brought to the town in the late 19th century by a servant of Mandalay's King Thibaw. The servant fled to Mae Sariang when the British conquered Mandalay, and in 1909 oversaw the construction of Wat Mandalay, which provided a safe haven for his cherished Buddha. The monastery has another claim to fame—a banyan tree reputed to be a scion of the bodhi tree in India, under which Siddhartha Gautama, the Buddha, attained enlightenment. ✚ 306 A4 ℹ Tourist Information Centre, Old District Office, Thanon Khunlumphrapas, Amphoe Muang, Mae Hong Son 58000 ☎ 053 612 982/3 ⏰ Mon–Fri 8.30–4.30 🚌 Regular bus services from Chiang Mai and Chiang Rai

INFORMATION

www.lampang.go.th

✚ 307 C3 ❶ Tourist Information, Tessaban Lampang (Lampang Municipality) ☎ 054 219 300

🕐 Mon–Fri 8.30–4.30

INTRODUCTION

Northern Thailand's second-largest city struggles to maintain its historic role as a major commercial and cultural center and tends to be bypassed by tourists on their way to Chiang Mai. It has much to offer, however, including a relaxed riverside lifestyle and one of Thailand's most magnificent temples.

Lampang was once a major teakwood-trading center, surrounded by thick forest and sitting on a navigable river, the Wang. Although later development did little to beautify the city, some handsome timber-built mansions still stand on its uncongested streets and quiet lanes. In its heyday, the elephants employed by timber companies nearly outnumbered the population. The city's importance as a timber-trading center brought the railway in the early 20th century, and several trains a day connect it with Bangkok to the south and Chiang Mai to the north. Long-distance buses between Bangkok and the north stop at Lampang's large bus station, which also serves outlying towns. There's also an airport, but the flight schedule is erratic. The compact city center is easy to cover on foot, although you'll need to take a taxi or *songthaew* to visit its top attraction, the Wat Phra That Lampang Luang, 11 miles (18km) to the south.

WHAT TO SEE

COCKERELS AND HORSES

The city's mascot is a cockerel, and early in its history it was known as the City of White Roosters (Kukkudnakorn). A rooster decorates the ceramics for which Lampang is famous.

The city is also famous for its horse-drawn carriages, the only place in Thailand where this romantic and ecologically friendly mode of transportation is used. You'll pay more for the privilege than the locals, but the fare (B150 to B300 depending on the tour length) is worth it and it's a great way to see the city. Lampang's horse-drawn carriages can't be flagged down like normal taxis. There are special carriage stands on several street corners.

WAT SRICHUM

The Burmese ruled Lampang for two centuries and built several beautiful temples during their time. This is the biggest—and the biggest of all 31 Burmese temples in Thailand. The half-brick and half-timber *viharn*, or assembly hall, has a Burmese-style Buddha image and murals giving a Burmese perspective of the lives of the Buddha.

✉ Thanon Sichum ⊕ Daily 6am–8pm 🖐 Free

WAT CHEDI SAO

"Chedi Sao" means "20 *chedis*," and local lore has it that if you can count all of them, then you are in for good luck. The white *chedis*, of different sizes and topped with gold, pose a tantalizing mystery. It's not clear exactly what purpose they served or how old they are. The unearthing on the site of amulets from the Haripunchai period indicates that some are more than 1,000 years old.

✉ Tambon Tonthongchai, off Thanon Chae Hom ☎ 054 320 233 ⊕ Daily 6am–8pm 🖐 Free

CHINESE QUARTER

Chinese traders set up businesses in Lampang as it grew in economic importance, and their 19th-century shophouses and homes line Thanon Talad Gae (Old Market). The intricately carved balustrades are fine examples of Chinese craftsmanship.

✉ Southwest bank of the Wang River

BAN SAO NAK

This city mansion is Lampang's finest teak house, built in 1895 in a mixture of Burmese and Lanna styles. Its walls contain an intriguing display of Burmese and Thai antiques.

✉ 6 Thanon Ratpattana ☎ 054 227 653 ⊕ Daily 9–5 🖐 Adult B50, child (under 14) B25

MORE TO SEE

WAT PHRA THAT LAMPANG LUANG

It is well worth the 11-mile (18km) drive from Lampang to view this large temple complex, one of Thailand's most beautiful *wats*. It stands so far outside the present city because the Haripunchai Queen Chamtewi established her royal residence for a while here in the eighth century, when Lampang itself was an insignificant settlement. The temple compound was built as a fortress, on a mound and surrounded by stout laterite walls. Despite these formidable defenses, it was overrun by the Burmese in one of their forays into northern Thailand. But a local prince drove them out, and the bullet hole marking the spot in a *chedi* (monument housing a Buddhist relic) fence where he shot dead the Burmese commander is a revered memento of those times.

The temple museum also has a small Buddha image, said to have been carved from the same stone that produced the revered Emerald Buddha in Bangkok.

The most curious feature of the temple, however, is a tiny chapel that serves as a camera obscura—a hole in its gnarled door throws a reverse picture of the outside *chedi* onto a screen. Only men may view it, though. Women are denied entry to the chapel, which stands above a hallowed imprint of what's said to be the Buddha's foot.

✉ On highway 1034, 2 miles (3km) west of Ko Kha ⊕ Daily 6am–8pm 🖐 Free

Below *Gilt painting of* Thevada (angels) *at Wat Phra That Lampang Luang*

INFORMATION

http://thailand.sawdee.com/lamphun
✚ 306 C3 ℹ Lamphun Information Office, opposite Wat Haripunchai main entrance ☎ 053 561 430 🕐 Mon–Fri 8.30–4.30

TIP

➤➤ Visit Wat Haripunchai at sunset and marvel at the glow acquired by the temple's golden *chedi*, and the mystery as night falls on the monastery grounds, illuminated by fairy lights.

INTRODUCTION

Most visitors to northern Thailand head straight for Chiang Mai, bypassing its neglected neighbor, the pretty town of Lamphun that is only a half-hour drive to the south and notable for two temples that are among Thailand's finest. Lamphun was founded in AD680, making it possibly Thailand's oldest city, nearly six centuries older than Chiang Mai. For most of its early years it was ruled by the powerful Chamthewi dynasty, which gave Thailand's history one of its most glamorous monarchs—Queen Chamthewi, who ruled in the eighth century. From the 13th century onward it lost its influence to Chiang Mai.

Today, Lamphun is a quiet backwater, a pretty town and northern Thailand's smallest provincial capital, with a lazy river, flower-bordered moats and some well-restored remains of the original city walls. There are only a couple of comfortable hotels and few good restaurants, so the town and its outstanding temples are best visited on a day trip from Chiang Mai, 18 miles (29km) away.

WHAT TO SEE

WAT CHAMTHEWI

The temple that carries the name of the first ruler of early Lamphun, the legendary eighth-century Queen Chamthewi, was built under her instructions and became her home after she abdicated at the age of 60. She spent most of her remaining years meditating within its walls, until her death at the age of 92. She was cremated within the temple compound and her ashes were sealed in a *chedi*, a five-tiered sandstone structure with 60 Buddha figures standing in curved niches. The *chedi* is in good repair, although the original golden top disappeared long ago, giving the temple its alternative name—Wat Kukkut ("broken-top pagoda"). The temple's other monument of note, the Rattana Chedi, is almost as old as Chamthewi's, built by the 12th-century King Phaya Sapphasit. It's also decorated with Buddha images standing on ascending platforms. The modern *viharn* is a riot of color, its teak-planked ceiling supported by 10 high columns covered in glass mosaics. In much more restrained taste is a neat little cruciform-shape chapel, with elaborate Lanna-style roof decoration and lifelike bronze statues of revered abbots. The grounds of the chapel, complete with palm garden, offer a peaceful retreat.

✉ Thanon Lamphun–Rimping 🕐 Daily 6am–7pm ✋ Free

WAT HARIPUNCHAI

The center of Lamphun is dominated by this large and immensely interesting temple ensemble, where fact and fable are woven in a fascinating account of the entwined origins of the city and its most famous *wat* (temple). The Buddha is said to have visited the area in one of his incarnations and to have been fed myrobalan fruit by two hermits.

Tradition has it that he was so touched by their hospitality that he ordained a city to be built on the site. Its name was to be Haripunchainakorn—the "city where myrobalan was eaten." The name Haripunchai derives from two ancient words meaning a kind of tropical fruit and the verb "to eat." As a memento of his visit, the Buddha is said to have given the two hermits a lock of his hair, which they placed in a glass urn and buried at the site. Two centuries later, the Haripunchainakorn ruler Artitayaraj transferred the relic to a large golden urn and placed that within a golden *chedi*.

The *chedi* still stands, despite the ravages of centuries, which reduced much of the monastery to rubble. The 121ft-high (37m) stupa is the tallest *chedi* in northern Thailand and towers over the monastery compound and its ensemble of 17 temples, chapels and pagodas. Apart from the *chedi*, there's much else of compelling interest to see: the modern *viharn* has a collection of Buddha images, all watched over by towering bronze and gilt statues; the monastery library is a bijou building of stucco and teak with an intricately carved roof; and the belfry contains, allegedly, the world's largest gong— 10ft (3m) in diameter, more than 100 years old and still splendidly sonorous.

✉ Thanon Chaimongkol 🕐 Daily 6am–7pm ✋ B40

Below left *The shrine to Queen Chamthewi's great war elelphant*
Below right *Golden dragons on the roof of one of the buildings at Wat Haripunchai*

INFORMATION

www.travelmaehongson.org

⊞ 306 A2 ℹ Tourist Information Centre, Old District Office, Thanon Khunlumphraphat, Amphoe Muang, Mae Hong Son 58000 ☎ 053 612 982/3 🕓 Mon–Fri 8.30–4.30

TIPS

» Virtually every hotel, guesthouse and tour operator in Mae Hong Son offers an outing to a village inhabited by the so-called Long-neck Women. It should also be noted that these Burmese refugees have no rights as citizens and are confined to living in these villages, which some have labeled human zoos. Admission is collected at the entrance of many villages by Thai staff, and it is questionable whether these refugees receive any financial benefit.

Below *Peaceful Chom Kham Lake with Mae Hong Son behind*

MAE HONG SON

Undiscovered by outsiders until about 20 years ago, this remote, mountain-ringed town still has a pioneer feel to it. Half the inhabitants of Mae Hong Son and the surrounding countryside are ethnic Shan, who have their roots in neighboring Myanmar (Burma). They trade not only at the town's markets but across the nearby border, and not all the goods are legal. Some of the region's most hardened drugs traffickers are based in Shan State, which borders Mae Hong Son province. Thai and international anti-drugs squads work secretly in Mae Hong Son, and although they keep a very low profile, there's a tangible atmosphere of intrigue in the rarified mountain air.

For a fine view of Mae Hong Son, nestled around the small lake in the town center, climb Doi Kong Mu, a hill at the southwestern edge of town. At the top is a 19th-century Shan temple, Wat Phra That Doi Kong Moo, with a fine *chedi* containing the ashes of Shan monks.

CHOM KHAM

The town's picturesque lake, Chom Kham, is bordered by a pleasant park and two very pretty Burmese-style temple ensembles—Wat Chom Kham and Wat Jong Klang. Wat Chom Kham was built in 1827 by Shan benefactors, who kept the temple simple, while positioning two Shan maidens as welcoming statues at its white stucco entrance. Neighboring Wat Jong Klang, built about 50 years later, has an excellent museum (daily 8–6, donation required) containing a remarkable collection of carved figures depicting scenes from the Jataka legend. The figures, carved in Myanmar, are wonderfully lively representations of local characters.

On the northern edge of town, Wat Hua Wiang has a Burmese-style Buddha that draws pilgrims from throughout northern Thailand.

THAM PLA

Among the many caves in the mountains around Mae Hong Son, the most curious is the Fish Cave, a grotto in a cliff above the main Pai road, Route 1095, some 10 miles (16km) outside the town. A small cistern-like pool just inside the grotto is crammed with mountain carp, while others fight to join them from a river outside. The attraction the dark, dank pool holds for the fish is a mystery that has never been explained. Thais hold the pool in mystical reverence and it's a favorite local excursion destination. The cave (free) is on the edge of the Tham Pla Pha Sua National Park and is reached by a riverside path from the park headquarters.

Above *Painting is just one of the skills performed by elephants at the Mae Sa Elephant Camp*

MAE SA VALLEY

The Mae Sa Valley loop skirts the Doi Suthep and Doi Pui mountain range outside Chiang Mai, winding for a circular 62 miles (100km) through jungle and farms worked by hill-tribe communities. It is lined for much of its length by resorts, wayside restaurants, orchid farms and tourist attractions. Traveling the route from central Chiang Mai (via Mae Rim) you first of all reach, after 12 miles (20km), the Mae Sa Elephant Camp (Mae Rim–Samoeng road; tel 053 206 247, www.maesaelephantcamp. com; daily 7–2.30, with elephant shows at 8, 9.40 and 1.30; adult B120, child B80), where three times a day elephants present a show of their skills, from rolling logs to playing football. They can paint pictures, too, and their works of art are on show in Gallery Maesa.

Farther on lies the Queen Sirikit Botanic Garden (Mae Rim–Samoeng road; www.qsbg.org; daily 8.30–5; adult B40, child B10, vehicles B100), a 2,470-acre (1,000ha) stretch of mountain forest and parkland opened in 1993 and now under royal patronage. A 3.5-mile (6km) road through the park passes through a stunning variety of natural flora, from thick stands of bamboo to carpets of delicate lilies. A three-floor-high hothouse contains a miniature rain forest, while nearby greenhouses nurture more varieties than are listed in the average gardener's manual. Around 350 species of orchid thrive in the park's nursery, which has an excellent English-language explanation of the idiosyncracies of this exotic plant. Several orchid gardens are also to be found along the Mae Sa route.

Build time into your itinerary for at least a half-day drive along the spectacular Mae Sa route, beginning at the signposted turn-off just beyond Mae Rim (the Chiang Dao road) and ending your tour with lunch or an early evening meal at the lovely Lanna Resort just before the "loop" ends at the Chiang Mai–Hang Dong road. A rented car and chauffeur costs from B1,500 to B2,000 plus petrol for the day.

✚ 306 B3 🛈 TAT Northern Office, Region 1, 105/1 Chiang Mai–Lamphun road, Amphoe Muang, Chiang Mai 50000 ☎ 053 248 604/7 ⊘ Daily 8.30–4.30

MAE SOT

The small market town of Mae Sot is an important border crossing to Myanmar (Burma) and a haven for refugees from Burmese oppression in the Karen frontier region. Karen refugees and migrant workers give the town a distinctly Burmese character. There are two main refugee camps—Mae La and Mawker—a number of "safe houses" and a famous clinic devoted to treating needy Karen, all of which welcome visitors and material assistance. The town market is full of Burmese goods, particularly gemstones (but caution is advised when buying these). The border is west of the town, where the Thai–Myanmar Friendship Bridge crosses the narrow Moei River. There's a lively market here, too, but be careful when offered obvious contraband, particularly cigarettes.

From the hilltop temple Wat Phra That Doi Din Kiu (daily 7–7; free) you have views of the Moei River and Myanmar. Mae Sot is also the start point of one of Thailand's most spectacular mountain routes, the "Sky Highway" to Um Phang, a village so remote it's known as "the end of the world." The 74-mile (120km) highway, Route 1090, winds through and across mountain ranges, past waterfalls, hill-tribe villages and two national parks; the scenery is stunning. At journey's end, the mountain-village of Um Phang, there's a wildlife sanctuary.

✚ 308 B6 🛈 TAT Northern Office, Region 3, 193 Thanon Taksin, Tambol, Nong Luang, Amphoe Muang, Tak 63000 ☎ 055 514 3413 ⊘ Daily 8.30–4.30

NAN

Founded in the 13th century, Nan was once a powerful principality but now slumbers in its isolated corner of northern Thailand, near the Laos border. There are only two roads in and out of the town, and although it has an airport, the flight schedule is haphazard. Nevertheless, it's well worth visiting, if only for the spectacular drive there and to visit one of Thailand's most stunning temples, Wat Pumin. The 186-mile (300km) drive from Chiang Mai, on almost deserted modern highways, sweeps and winds through verdant mountain valleys, teak and bamboo forests, rice paddies and past mountainside hill-tribe homesteads. Nan itself has a quiet charm, and if you're seeking peace and quiet, away from the tourist hustle and bustle, then this is the place to be. Even 16th-century Wat Pumin (daily 9–6) is usually deserted, despite its fame. The interest of its 19th-century frescoes lies in their unconventional beauty and historical context. Unlike most other temple murals, these record scenes of contemporary everyday life, populated by caricatures of local characters. They are also a unique historical record, picturing the arrival of French colonial soldiers and Dutch traders in fully rigged sailing ships and an early steamer.

The home of the last ruling prince of Nan, a national mansion, is now also the town museum (Thanon Suriapong, 054 772 777; daily 9–4; B100), famous for its 3ft-long (1m) black elephant tusk, which is revered by local people for its supposed auspicious properties.

✚ 307 E3 ℹ Tourist Information Office, 46 Thanon Suriyapong, Amphoe Muang, Nan 55000 ☎ 054 710 216 ◷ Mon–Fri 8.30–4.30 🚌 Regular bus services from Chiang Mai

PAI

Pai is a convenient halfway stop on the mountainous road between Chiang Mai and Mae Hong Son, but it's also a pretty spot to spend a day or two. Well-heeled Bangkok businesspeople first discovered Pai, then the once-quiet market town became popular with backpackers seeking an alternative scene. These days, other tourists are making a reappearance in Pai, spurred on by resort development and daily flights from Chiang Mai. A quiet backwater Pai is not, but thankfully there are nearly equal numbers of foreign and Thai tourists.

In high season—November to March—you can escape the crowds by heading off into the nearby hills, either alone or as part of an organized trekking group. Tours into the countryside and to nearby Shan, Lisu and Lahu hill-tribe villages are organized by most of Pai's several resorts, one of which, the Belle Villa, is among the region's best addresses (▷ 193).

The Mo Paeng waterfall, 5 miles (8km) from town, is a delightful picnic spot and has cool pools for swimming. The town has little of interest, apart from a couple of small temples—Wat Phra That Mae Yen is worth visiting at sunset for its misty views over the town and the mountains beyond. Most Pai restaurants, bars and cafes line the main street, Chai Songkram, or border the sleepy river, the Pai—crossed by a bridge "stolen" from Chiang Mai by Japanese forces in World War II and reerected here to

facilitate their advance into Myanmar (Burma). Tha Pai Hot Springs, 14 miles (7km) from town, is a pleasant place to visit in the afternoon.

✚ 306 B2 ℹ Tourist Information District Office, Amphoe Muang, Pai 58000 ☎ 053 612 982 ◷ Mon–Fri 8.30–4.30 🚌 Regular bus services from Chiang Mai

PHAYAO

Like so many other small northern Thai towns, Phayao was once a powerful regional center, ruled by a 13th-century monarch so influential that he played a key role in founding the city of Chiang Mai. King Ngum Muang entered into a blood-sealed pact of friendship with Chiang Mai's first ruler, Mengrai, guaranteeing the new city's security, and is honored for his services with statues in central Chiang Mai and on the peaceful shores of Phayao's lake, Kwan Phayao.

Today's Phayao has little to offer the visitor except its picturesque landscape and tranquil lake, northern Thailand's largest stretch of fresh water, whose hyacinth-covered surface is bordered by far-off mountains. It's an angler's paradise and boats can be rented at the waterfront for around B300 to B400 per day. The day's catch lands on the menus of the restaurants that line the lake's promenade, a pleasant spot to take a stroll as the sun sets into the water's western edge.

A temple, Wat Sri Khom Kham (daily 6am–8pm) sits on the edge of the lake, a short walk from the promenade. Next door is the Phayao Cultural Exhibition Hall (tel 054 410 058; Mon–Sat 8.30–5; B40), a museum of local history and culture. The main *viharn* houses Thailand's largest Lanna-style Buddha, 65ft (20m) high and 56ft (17m) broad, so massive that it took Phayao craftspeople 33 years to construct.

✚ 307 D2 ℹ Provincial Public Relations Office, Salaklang Jungwat Phayao, Amphoe Muang, Phayao 56000 ☎ 054 481 704 ◷ Mon–Fri 8.30–4.30 🚌 Regular bus services from Chiang Mai

Above *The fertile landscape around Nan*

PHRAE

This provincial market town was once an important center of Thailand's teak trade, and its former prosperity is evident in many of the late 19th-century timber-built mansions within the remains of its ancient walls. The finest of them lies 1 mile (about 1.5km) outside the city, though, in the village of Ban Pa Maet. The astonishing building, Ban Prathap Chai (daily 9–5; B20), is an ensemble of antique homes reconstructed on foundations of 130 massive teak columns. It's still a private home, but visitors are invited to wander through its teak-floored rooms, lined with cabinets full of family photographs and mementoes. The ground floor is taken up by a collection of stands selling local handicrafts, most of them (of course) made from teak.

Phrae has several superb historic temples to visit, the oldest of which, Wat Luang, has a 13th-century, stepped *chedi* (monument housing a Buddhist relic) guarded by well-weathered elephants.

🛑 307 D4 ℹ️ Provincial Public Relations Office, Salaklang Jungwat Phrae, Thanon Chaiyaboon, Amphoe Muang, Phrae 54000 ☎ 054 511 566 🕐 Mon–Fri 8.30–4.30

SOP RUAK AND SAM LIAM THONG KHAM

An undistinguished frontier town on the banks of the Mekong River, Sop Ruak claims to be the gateway to Thailand's fabled Golden Triangle and has two museums devoted to the cause of its fame: opium.

Sam Liam Thong Kham (the Golden Triangle) has no defined borders and can refer to a large region covering border areas of Thailand, Myanmar (Burma) and Laos or to the point where the frontiers actually meet, at the confluence of the Mekong and Ruak rivers. About 1 mile (1.5km) downstream lies the small, one-street town of Sop Ruak, once a stronghold of the renegade Burmese drug baron Khun Sa. Although he and his Mong Tai Army controlled the opium trade, Thailand has effectively put an end to his operations on Thai territory, and Khun Sa is now semiretired.

A magnificent narcotics museum now stands where opium poppies once grew. The House of Opium (tel 053 784 060; www.houseofopium.com; B50) in the south of Sop Ruak can be visited; look for the green tin-roofed pagoda just above the entrance gate. On the riverbank

where smugglers once plied their trade, a large, gilded Buddha statue stands watch.

Two of the region's finest hotels overlook the Golden Triangle: the Imperial Golden Triangle Reort (▷ 192) and the Anantara. From the terraces of each hotel there are views of the Mekong and the uplands of Laos and Myanmar.

Across the road from the Anantara is the Hall of Opium (tel 053 784 444/5/6; www.goldentrianglepark.com; Tue–Sun 10–3.30; adult B300, child under 12 free), a spectacular edifice dominating a small valley above the Mekong. You enter through a tunnel where weird music and the simulated smell of opium fill the air and phantasmagoric bas reliefs adorn the walls. The tunnel ends in a lobby filled with blinding light, where the story of opium is related on illuminated panels. Subsequent rooms explain the history of other drugs—even the history of tea.

🛑 307 D1 ℹ️ TAT Northern Office, Region 2, 448/16 Thanon Singhaklai, Amphoe Muang, Chiang Rai 57000 ☎ 053 717 433 🕐 Daily 8.30–4.30

Below left *The peaceful scene where the Mekong and Ruak rivers join*
Below right *Abundant lotus flowers near Pai*

SOPPONG

www.soppong.com

When Pai gets too crowded, nature-lovers make for the village of Soppong, 28 miles (45km) farther along Route 1095 to Mae Hong Son. Soppong, also known as Pang Ma Pha, is a hill-tribe settlement straddling the main road and a center for trekkers heading out into the surrounding mountains. It has about half a dozen guesthouses and simple restaurants with names like Jungle Guest House and Little Eden. Two local caves are of interest: Tham Lot, which has a weird collection of stalactite and stalagmite formations, and Coffin Cave, named for a number of prehistoric wooden coffins found in its labyrinths.
✚ 306 B2 ℹ Soppong River Inn, Soppong 58150 ☎ 053 617 107 ✋ B300–B1,200 per night

TAK AND THE BHUMIPHOL DAM

▷ 175.

THA TON

Sitting prettily on a bend of the Kok River, almost next to the Burmese border, Tha Ton is one of the most appealing little towns in this remote northwestern corner of Thailand.

Below *Bridge over the Kak River at Tha Ton*

Its hilltop temple, dominated by a revered "white Buddha," is a place of pilgrimage and draws people of all nationalities for its meditation sessions. The courses in vipassana meditation, as well as accommodations and food, are free, although a donation is expected. Even if you're not participating in the courses, it's well worth the effort to climb to the terraced temple for a fine view of the mountains of neighboring Myanmar (Burma) beyond.

Boats set out here for the four-hour river trip to Chiang Rai, where you can catch a bus back to Tha Ton. A longtail boat leaves daily at 12.30 (B350) or a boat, accommodating six people, can be chartered for B2,200. A covered raft takes two days to make the trip, stopping for the night at a riverside guesthouse en route. The trip, including accommodations and all meals, costs B2,700. A new raft is built for every trip, so reserving one week in advance is required (tel 053 459 427, fax 053 373 224). Boats and rafts leave from the TAT pier in the center of town.
✚ 306 C1 ℹ TAT Northern Office, Region 2, 448/16 Thanon Singhaklai, Amphoe Muang, Chiang Rai 57000 ☎ 053 717 433 ⏰ Daily 8.30–4.30

UTTARADIT AND THE SIRIKIT DAM

Uttaradit played a central role in finally ridding northern Thailand of Burmese domination, and its most famous hero, Phraya Pichai, who fought alongside Taksin the Great in the late 18th century, is commemorated with a statue in front of the Provincial Hall. Phraya Pichai, who also played a role in ushering in the Chakri dynasty that followed Taksin's overthrow, is portrayed in full battle dress and brandishing a sword in each hand. One of his ceremonial swords, other weapons and objects from this period, as well as from Uttaradit's earlier history, are exhibited in the Uttaradit Cultural Center (Thanon Paetwa; Wed–Sun 8–5).

Uttaradit is also the gateway to the Sirikit Dam and the Phu Soi Dao National Park, two areas of outstanding beauty. The Sirikit Dam wall, 371ft (113m) high and 2,657ft (810m) long, is the highest in Thailand and blocks the Nan River, forming a large picturesque lake dotted with islands that were once mountaintops.
✚ 307 D4 ℹ TAT, 193 Thanon Taksin, Amphoe Muang, Tak 63000 ☎ 055 514 341/2/3 ⏰ Daily 8.30–4.30

TAK AND THE BHUMIPHOL DAM

Birthplace of King Taksin the Great, who took his name from his hometown, Tak is not only one of northern Thailand's most historic areas but also the gateway to a very scenic region and the country's largest dam. Tak today has little to remind the visitor of its former glory, except a shrine containing a statue of its most famous son. His portrait hangs on the walls of many homes, shops and restaurants, and a national park on the road to Mae Sot bears his name: the Taksin Maharaj National Park.

WALLED CITY

The original walled city of Tak lies 15 miles (25km) from today's bustling market town on the Ping River, although little remains apart from a 13th-century hilltop *chedi* (monument housing a Buddhist relic) said to have been built by King Ramkhamhaeng of Sukhothai.

WAT MANI BANPHOT

This ancient temple on Thanon Phaholyohtin houses a 13th-century Buddha image fashioned in the Chiang Saen style of the early Lanna kingdom.

TAKSIN MAHARAJ NATIONAL PARK

This small national park (tel 055 511 429; B200) halfway between Tak and the Thai–Myanmar (Burmese) border town Mae Sot was originally named after the krabak yai tree, Thailand's largest, which grows in profusion in the area. The park is one of northern Thailand's most beautiful nature reserves, surrounded by forested mountains. Hiking trails criss-cross its 37,000 acres (14,980ha).

BHUMIPHOL DAM

Thailand's largest dam, named after the current king, stretches from just north of Tak into neighboring Chiang Mai province. Houseboats make the 87-mile (140km) overnight trip across the dam and then up the Ping River to a jetty where travelers can catch a bus to nearby Chiang Mai; for reservations tel 055 549 509. Longtail boats make shorter pleasure trips that include lunch at a floating restaurant and stops for swimming or fishing. A small resort below the dam wall has comfortable accommodations in bungalows (tel 055 599 093).

✠ 308 B5

INFORMATION

✠ 308 C5, B5 ℹ TAT, 193 Thanon Taksin, Amphoe Muang, Tak 63000
☎ 055 514 341/2/3 🕐 Daily 8.30–4.30

Above *Standing on the Bhumiphol Dam*

DRIVE

THE MAE HONG SON LOOP

Chiang Mai is the charming capital of northern Thailand and the starting point for many scenic drives through the surrounding mountains. The Mae Hong Son Loop is one of the most spectacular, named after the remote town that marks the drive's halfway point. The road to Mae Hong Son from Chiang Mai has endless hairpin bends, but the drive is punctuated by so many spectacular mountain vistas that it's worth it.

THE DRIVE
Distance: 310 miles (500km)
Allow: 2–3 days
Start/end at: Chiang Mai

With its rich history, Chiang Mai demands a stay of at least three or four days in order to get to know its old town, a warren of lanes enclosed by walls and a wide moat.

★ Leave Chiang Mai on Route 107, through the one-street suburb of Mae Rim, and after 25 miles (40km), take a left turn at the market town of Mae Malai onto Route 1095, signposted to Pai and Mae Hong Son. The road winds through paddy fields, orchards and hill-tribe villages, gradually climbing to the foothills of the Doi Ang Ket mountain range. The province of Chiang Mai ends in a valley 31 miles (50km) from Mae Malai, and the point where Mae Hong Son province begins is also the site of one of the few large villages en route, Mae Sae.

❶ Mae Sae has a predominantly Muslim population, and simple restaurants on either side of the road serve *khao soy* (Burmese-style noodles in a rich meat broth). It's an ideal spot for lunch.

Continuing on Route 1095, watch out for the viewpoint on the right, 6 miles (10km) from Mae Sae.

❷ The view from the mountainside terrace is breathtaking, and on a clear day you can see Thailand's third-highest mountain, Chiang Dao's Doi Luang, 31 miles (50km) away.

The road descends now into the valley of the Pai River, and as you approach the popular little resort town of Pai, watch out for a disused multispan bridge on your right.

❸ The bridge was erected by Japanese forces as they headed for Myanmar (Burma) at the height of World War II.

Pai straddles the river of the same name 3 miles (5km) farther on, 80 miles (130km) and a three-hour drive from Chiang Mai.

❹ If you arrive in Pai during the low season you may be tempted to stay overnight, enticed by its laid-back atmosphere, its restaurants, bars and comfortable guesthouses. In high season the small town can be impossibly crowded, and the pull of Mae Hong Son, a farther 75 miles (120km), may be stronger.

The Mae Hong Son road (still Route 1095) winds its way through the hill-tribe village of Soppong, past tracks leading to waterfalls and caves.

❺ The most accessible and one of the most mysterious caves is Tham Pla (Fish Cave; ▷ 170), 5 miles (8km) north of Mae Hong Son. The cave is part of the Tham Pla Pha Sua National Park, and the 20-minute walk to the grotto, with its dark pool packed with fish, is a pleasant riverside stroll. Tham Lot (6 miles/10km north of Soppong) is another cave, but the road there is rough in the rainy season.

Return to Route 1095 and continue onto Mae Hong Son.

Opposite *Patchwork of rice paddies near Mae Hong Son*

❻ Mae Hong Son nestles around a small lake surrounded by mountains. There's enough here—including a cluster of Burmese-style temples—to keep the visitor occupied for several days. If you've driven the six-hour journey from Chiang Mai, then at least an overnight stay is recommended. Walk in the late afternoon up to the hilltop temple Wat Phra That Doi Kong Moo and bask in the sun as it sets over the Burmese mountains to the west of the town.

From Mae Hong Son, Route 108 continues directly south, through forests of teak and conifers. Just beyond the village of Huai Pong, 25 miles (40km) south of Mae Hong Son on the right-hand side of the road, you'll find a cemetery.

❼ This is one of more than 30 wartime cemeteries containing the remains of Japanese soldiers who died in the area during their retreat from Myanmar (Burma) in August, 1945. The next town, Khun Yuam, 18 miles (30km) farther south, has a fascinating little museum with a dust-gathering collection of weapons, uniforms, helmets, personal possessions and photographs left behind in the town by the retreating Japanese. There's also a small Japanese cemetery and shrine in the Shan temple compound opposite.

From Khun Yuam, Route 108 runs across a highland ridge, through forests and plantations of teak and conifers, to the market town of Mae Sariang, 43 miles (70km) south.

❽ Mae Sariang (▷ 165) is close to the Burmese border and has a large population of Karen refugees and migrants. Some of the local shops and restaurants serve as art galleries if you want to purchase work by Karen artists. Mae Sariang also has two very comfortable

hotels if you choose to break your journey here. Make sure that you carry your passport for police checkpoints.

From Mae Sariang, Route 108 does an abrupt left turn toward Chiang Mai, an easy 118-mile (190km) run, descending from the border highlands to the Mae Ping River valley. The road swings past the heavily forested Ob Luang National Park and through Hot, a rebuilt version of an old town submerged by the waters of the great Bhumiphol dam. At the village of San Pa Tong, 41 miles (66km) north of Hot, turn right on Route 1013 to Lamphun, then left on Route 106, back to Chiang Mai through an avenue of towering *yang* trees.

WHERE TO EAT/STAY
BELLE VILLA
(▷ 193).
✉ 113 Moo 6, Huay Poo-Wiang Nua Road, Pai ☎ 053 698 226/7 ⓘ Restaurant daily 6am–10pm

RIVERSIDE HOTEL AND RESORT
(▷ 193).

✉ 6/1 Moo 2 Langpanich Road, Mae Sariang ☎ 053 683 066 ⓘ Restaurant daily 11–11

ROOKS HOLIDAY HOTEL AND RESORT
✉ 114/5–7 Thanon Khunlumprapas, Mae Hong Son ☎ 053 612 324/9 ⓘ Restaurant daily 11–11

PLACES TO VISIT
THAM LOT
ⓘ Daily 9–5 🖐 Free

THAM PLA
ⓘ Daily 9–5 🖐 Free

WORLD WAR II MUSEUM
✉ Mae Hong Son road, Khun Yuam (Thai-Japan Friendship Memorial Hall)
ⓘ Daily 8–4 🖐 Adult B50, child free

TOURIST INFORMATION
MAE HONG SON TOURIST OFFICE
www.travelmaehongson.org
✉ Old District Office, Thanon Khunlumprapas, Amphoe Muang, Mae Hong Son 58000 ☎ 053 612 982/3

PAI TOURIST OFFICE
✉ District Office, Amphoe Muang, Pai 58000 ☎ 053 612 982

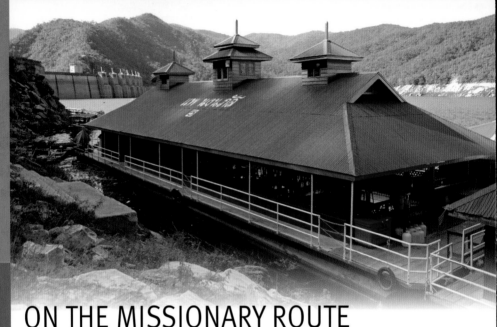

ON THE MISSIONARY ROUTE

As late as a century ago, missionaries and traders found the easiest and fastest route from Bangkok to the northern outpost of Chiang Mai was by boat, following the network of rivers that lead into the Ping River. You can cover a 87-mile (140km) stretch of this route on board a motorized houseboat, an adventurous way to see one of northern Thailand's wildest regions.

THE RIVER TOUR
Distance: 87 miles (140km)
Allow: 2 days
Start at: Bhumiphol Dam wall
End at: Ban Doi Tao

HOW TO GET THERE
The Bhumiphol Dam is 37 miles (60km) north of Tak, a half-hour journey by rented car or *songthaew* pickup taxi (there's a taxi stand at Tak's bus station). If your boat is leaving early in the morning you might want to stay the first night in one of the comfortable bungalows at the base of the dam—it's a very beautiful area in which to spend a day and an evening. The bungalow resort is operated by Thailand's Electricity Generating Authority, and accommodations can be booked by phoning 055 599 093.

★ The Bhumiphol Dam, named after Thailand's present king, is the country's biggest and one of the world's top 10 largest dams. It supplies most of Thailand's hydroelectric power.

The houseboat jetties are close to the vast concrete wall of the dam, and the adventure begins as you board one, tottering along a narrow gangplank. Your "boat" is a plank-floored platform on cylindrical floats (often just empty oil barrels), beneath a thatched roof. There are a few tables and plastic chairs, a rudimentary kitchen and arguably the most important item of all: a karaoke stage, complete with large-screen TV and mega-speakers. You're traveling with Thais as company, and karaoke is an essential item on almost every

Thai's holiday itinerary. If the music gets too loud, you can usually escape to a sun-deck.

❶ The first stop is a floating restaurant at the head of the main dam. The menu is understandably dominated by fish fresh from the dam. The *tabtim* from Bhumiphol Dam are locally famous, and if you can persuade the cook to fry them in garlic you're in for a treat.

❷ If the skipper feels there's time he'll make a stop at one of the dam's few islands, Valentine, where you can take a swim or just catnap on its sandy beach.

The dam narrows now as its waters wind through a gorge that leads into the Ping River. The northern side of the dam is bordered by the Mae Ping National Park, a wild and beautiful mountainous region traversed by just one narrow road. Thick jungle clothes the rocky sides of the narrowing dam, which takes a sharp right turn before yielding to the Ping river. The river, as narrow as 66ft (20m) in places, snakes between the dense jungle-covered uplands of the Mae Ping National Park and the heights of Doi Mon Chong (3,737ft/1,139m) and Doi Lang Muang (5,078ft/1,548m), mountains that dominate one of the wildest and remote regions of northern Thailand.

❸ An overnight stop is made at the tiny river settlement of Kaeng Ko, at the western entrance to the Mae Ping National Park. Supper is served on board, and your bed is on board, too—or, strictly speaking, on boards. You sleep on deck, on thin mattresses. But a glass or two of Thai whisky and an evening of karaoke should guarantee a good night's sleep.

As dawn creeps up the mist-shrouded river, the crew cast off and serve the passengers a Thai breakfast of rice soup. It's now only a 25-mile (40km) chug up river to Doi Tao lake and the journey's end. Through a break in the mountains on the western bank the Mae Lai River

joins the Ping and together, when in full flood, they create a lake 12.5 miles (20km) long.

❹ Ban Doi Tao lies halfway up the eastern side of the lake. It's a simple village, with a few noodle shops for lunch and an incongruous modern shopping plaza with souvenir stores.

Pickup taxis operate a service from Ban Doi Tao to Hot, 28 miles (46km)

north, from where you can catch a bus to Chiang Mai, a farther 59 miles (95km) north. Nineteenth-century missionaries and traders completed the entire distance on the Ping River, but of course such modern temptations as buses didn't exist in those days.

WHEN TO GO

The best time to make the trip is at the end of the rainy season, in September or October. In the dry season (Nov–end Feb), the Doi Tao lake at the northern end of the route is liable to dry out so that only the Bhumiphol Dam can be navigated, but even a one-day excursion on its mountain-ringed waters is a memorable experience.

TOURIST INFORMATION
TAK TOURIST OFFICE
✉ TAT, 193 Thanon Taksin, Amphoe Muang, Tak 63000 ☎ 055 514 341/2/3
🕓 Daily 8.30–4.30

Opposite *The floating restaurant next to the Bhumiphol Dam*
Left *The best way to explore the dam is by boat*

WALK

CHIANG MAI'S GUARDIAN MOUNTAIN

The vast majority of visitors to Chiang Mai's mountainside temple, Wat Phra That Doi Suthep, travel there by red *songthaew* pickup taxi. However, by doing so they miss out on the spectacular scenery enjoyed by hikers who make the journey on foot.

THE WALK
Distance: 5 miles (8km)
Allow: 4 hours
Start at: Thanon Huay Kaew, Chiang Mai
End at: Wat Phra That Doi Suthep temple

★ Start at the entrance to the Namtok Monthatarn waterfall, at "KM 7" on Route 1004 between Chiang Mai Zoo and Wat Phra That Doi Suthep.

The well-signposted and paved minor road to the falls enters the Doi Suthep and Doi Pui National Park, and you'll have to pay B200 admission at the entrance kiosk (this is the fee for entering any Thai national park). The 2-mile (3km) walk to the falls, where the strenuous hike up the mountain truly begins, snakes its way through thick forest. Note the way the planners divided

the road around one particularly revered tree, a centuries-old *yang* tree that towers majestically over its deciduous companions which stand on either side.

❶ A resort-like settlement of national park buildings and a camping ground lies at the foot of the main falls, which plunge 200ft (60m) over granite rocks into deep pools that then feed a narrow mountain river. The *montha* tree is abundant in these parts, and in the winter months it bears beautiful red-and-white flowers. Cool off in the falls or take a break at the refreshment pavilion (daily 9–5).

Venture upward into the dark green forest, which hangs above the mountain valley like a theater backdrop. The path follows the falls

as they plunge over eight separate cascades, each as dramatic as the next. The enclosing forest contains ever more numerous upland evergreens, towering pines and other firs. Young teak fight for space on the mountain with hardy deciduous trees, undergrowth and stands of bamboo and upland palms. Large orchids cling to ancient wood (don't pick any–it's illegal). In the occasional clearing, clouds of butterflies can burst into view–the mountain has dozens of varieties.

❷ Keep an eye open for monkeys, wild boar and small "barking" deer. And keep a very wary eye open for snakes; at least two highly venomous species of pit viper have made their home on the mountain. Pythons also lurk in the thick brush. If you encounter a "crocodile salamander," however, don't be alarmed—they're harmless. Doi Suthep is one of only four locations in Thailand where they are found. The forest teems with birdlife; among the 300 varieties found on Doi Suthep and Doi Pui mountain are pheasants, jungle fowl and parrots. If you're very lucky you might catch a glimpse of an eagle soaring above the mountainside.

About 1.2 miles (2km) from Namtok, Monthatarn another superb waterfall, Namthok Sai Yai, comes into view.

❸ Namthok Sai Yai is another of the mountain's many beautiful waterfalls, and offers an opportunity to cool off before tackling the steepest part of the hike.

A few hundred meters beyond the falls, the trail meets a dirt road skirting the mountaintop. Turn left and follow it for 330 yards (300m) before rejoining the signposted path to the Doi Suthep and Doi Pui National Park headquarters. Shortly after reentering the forest, watch out for a small white *chedi* (pagoda) on your left. It's one of the mountain's mysteries—no one knows how old

it is or who placed it here. Another few hundred meters farther on stands a venerable old fig tree, perhaps the only one this deep in the forest.

❹ The fig tree signals the approach of the National Park headquarters, where a welcome rest and refreshment await you at a simple outdoor restaurant (daily 9–5).

The trail has skirted the hike's goal, Wat Phra That Doi Suthep, which lies through the forest to the left of the National Park headquarters. Head for the park exit, turn left on the paved road and follow it for 0.6 miles (1km).

❺ The fairground-like bustle around the entrance to the temple is a stark contrast to the peace you've experienced on the mountain hike here, but there's no alternative to plunging into the crowds thronging the temple grounds.

There is, however, an alternative to the final stage of the hike, the broad flight of 300 steps that leads up to the main temple compound. A funicular railway now makes that part of the journey easy, and visitors

who have braved the 5-mile (8km) hike to get to the temple can be excused for giving in and buying a B30 ticket to ride it.

❻ Red *songthaews* wait at the bottom of the funicular to take visitors the 7.5 miles (12km) back down the mountain to Chiang Mai.

WHEN TO GO
The best time to tackle this hike is very early in the morning, to avoid walking in the midday sun. But even if the journey does get hot, there are waterfalls and wayside pools in which to cool off.

PLACE TO VISIT
WAT PHRA THAT DOI SUTHEP
🕐 Daily 8–6 ✋ Adult B50, child (under 12) free

TOURIST INFORMATION
CHIANG MAI TOURIST OFFICE
✉ TAT Northern Office, Region 1, 105/1 Chiang Mai–Lamphun Road, Amphoe Muang, Chiang Mai 50000 ☎ 053 248 604, 053 248 607 🕐 Daily 8.30–4.30

Opposite *The rooftops of the Wat Phra That Doi Suthep complex*
Below right *The enormous bronze bell at Wat Phra That Doi Suthep*
Below left *The Naga staircase at the temple*

WHAT TO DO

Above *Spend the day, relaxing at one of the superb spas at Chiang Mai*

CHIANG DAO
BUA TONG WATERFALL
Just off the road between Chiang Mai and Chiang Dao is one of the region's most unusual waterfalls, Namtok Bua Tong. The water flows over the rocks in seven distinct colors, picked up from the calcium carbonate content of the spring water. It's a beautiful picnic spot on the road north.

🚌 The falls are on the road east from Mae Taeng, 29 miles (47km) north of Chiang Mai, to Mae Khachan

CHIANG MAI
ACTIVE THAILAND
www.activethailand.com
For the full range of guided adventure tours, this is a good one-stop place to shop. Options include trekking, cycling, rafting and kayaking tours, from one-day outings to five-day trips into the mountains featuring a close-up view of hill-tribe culture and lifestyles.

✉ 420/3 Thanon Chang Klan, Chiang Mai 🕿 053 204 664 🕐 Office hours 8–5 💷 B2,200–B12,000

BAAN TAWAI
Antiques and reproductions provide the sole livelihood of this one-street village, 5 miles (8km) south of Chiang Mai (take the Hang Dong road, Route 108). Whatever you're looking for, you should find it here, from small carved objects to Chinese medicine chests and ancient armoires. An interesting morning can be spent prowling around the shops and warehouses.

✉ Hang Dong, Chiang Mai 🕐 Daily 9–6

BRASSERIE
Locally famed guitarist Tuk performs most nights at this riverside venue. He plays everything from rhythm and blues to reggae, fronting a band that draws a big crowd nightly until late. Combine a visit with a dinner date on the romantic, lantern-hung terrace overlooking the Ping River.

✉ 37 Charoenrat Road, Chiang Mai 🕿 053 241 665 🕐 Daily 11pm–1am 💷 B50–B250, Wine B900

CHIANG MAI LAND
Chiang Mai Land is a vibrant 0.5 miles (0.8km) of bars, restaurants, karaoke joints and

two of Chiang Mai's best discos. The action starts at 9pm and continues until after midnight.

CHIANG MAI NIGHT SAFARI PARK
www.chiangmainightsafari.com
Very few tigers now roam Thailand's forests, but you can see them in something like their natural habitat at Chiang Mai's Night Safari Park. They're among more than 100 species of wildlife in the 100-acre (40ha) reserve at the foot of the Doi Suthep mountain range, 6 miles (10km) from Chiang Mai. Other big cats you might be fortunate enough to spot in your rented car headlights, include leopards, jaguars and civets. There's a restaurant onsite.

✉ Kilometer stone 10, Chiang Mai–Hod road 🕿 053 999 050 🕐 Mon–Fri 1pm–midnight, Sat–Sun 10am–midnight 💷 Adult B100, child B50

CHIANG MAI RACE TRACK
A day at the races in Chiang Mai is a great opportunity to see Thais lose their cool and their shirts. The track is run by the military authorities with great professionalism. There's a tote, an English-style paddock and the Doi Suthep mountain as a backdrop.

✉ Chiang Mai–Mae Rim road, kilometer stone 5 🕓 Sat 2–6 💰 B20 (B100 for the VIP grandstand)

CHIANG MAI ZOO

Chiang Mai's zoo, on the slopes of Doi Suthep, has the only two giant pandas in captivity in Southeast Asia, on loan from China. It's otherwise not a very spectacular zoo by international standards, but the forest setting of the cages and enclosures has pleasant, shady walks. If you get tired, an electric trolley bus tours the grounds.
✉ Doi Suthep Road ☎ 063 608 661 🕓 Daily 8.30–5 ✋ Adult B100, child (under 14) B50; to view the pandas; adult B100, child (under 14) B50

CHIENGMAI GYMKHANA CLUB

www.chiengmaigymkhana.com
Chiang Mai is ringed by championship golf courses (the Lanna Golf Club, tel 053 211 556, and the Green Valley Country Club, tel 053 298 249–51, are among the best), but if you only have time for a leisurely nine holes then the century-old Chiengmai Gymkhana Club is a tantalizing 10-minute tuk-tuk ride from the middle of the city. The club itself is worth visiting for its colonial atmosphere and the beauty of the grounds. Clubs and shoes can be rented. There is a restaurant and bar.
✉ Chiang Mai–Lamphun road, Chiang Mai ☎ 053 241 035 🕓 Golf course daily 6–5.30 ✋ B300 for 9 holes, caddy B100

EXTREME SPORTS CENTRE

www.chiangmai-xcentre.com
Set in the Mae Sa Valley alongside other tourist attractions like elephant camps, snake farms and orchid farms, the Extreme Sports Centre offers something totally different from the rest. The North's only bungy jump is 164ft (50m) high over a lagoon. Other options for adrenaline junkies include racing through the jungle in an off-road buggy, go-karting around a dirt track, or if you arrive with a group there is paintball, with full safety equipment and the latest in paintball weaponry provided. Once you've worn yourself

out, there is a bar and restaurant where you can discuss the day's events. Transportation is available from Chiang Mai.
✉ 263 Moo 1, Mae Rim–Samoeng road, Mae Rim ☎ 053 297 700 🕓 Daily 9–6 ✋ Bungy jump B1,500; off-road buggy B2,000 per hour; go-kart B600 per 10 minutes; paintball B600 per 50 pellets

GEMS GALLERY

Claiming to have the world's largest jewelry showroom, the Gems Gallery is certainly impressive. In addition to browsing the beautiful items for sale, you can also watch jewelry makers busy at their craft in the workshops, which are attached to the showroom.
✉ 80/1 Moo 3, Chiang Mai–San Kampaeng road ☎ 053 339 307–10 🕓 Daily 8.30–5.30

HUEN SOONTAREE VECHANONT

A famous Thai mother-and-daughter combination can frequently be heard singing at this very ethnic riverside Thai restaurant. Soontaree runs the establishment, while her daughter is often on tour or recording. Other resident singers and instrumentalists also appear nightly on the canopied stage. The northern Thai food served here is also excellent.
✉ 208 Thanon Patun, Chiang Mai ☎ 053 872 707 🕓 Daily 4pm–midnight ✋ Dinner B300, Wine B750

MAE RIM SHOOTING RANGE

Try your hand and your aim with a rifle or a revolver at northern Thailand's best-equipped shooting range. Beginners and experts are welcomed, and the selection of arms ranges from simple air guns to sophisticated rifles.
✉ Kilometer stone 2, Mae Rim–Samoeng road ☎ 053 112 383, 081 595 7113 🕓 Daily 9–6 ✋ B1,700

NORTHERN PARK EMPORIUM

www.otop-online.com
If your flight's delayed at Chiang Mai airport then fill in the time by visiting the nearby Northern Park Emporium, a government-supported trade center packed with fine local

arts and crafts. The imaginatively designed items of furniture may be too bulky to bring home, but the center's showroom and galleries have plenty of fascinating small items of Lanna workmanship.
✉ Mahidol Road (the airport turn-off), Chiang Mai ☎ 081 672 0987 🕓 Daily 9–5

NORTHERN VILLAGE

Two floors of this vast shopping mall are devoted to Lanna-style and northern Thai contemporary arts and crafts. The display is arranged like a village crafts center, with individual stands selling anything from handwoven textiles to ceramics and decorative carved items.
✉ Central Airport Plaza, Airport Road, Chiang Mai ☎ 053 999 199 🕓 Mon–Fri 10.30–9, Sat–Sun 10–9

OASIS SPA

There are so many spas in and around Chiang Mai that you could spend two weeks just being pampered. Among the longest established is the Oasis Spa, whose treatments range from a B2,700 "pampering" (aromatherapy, body scrub, massage and facial) to a four-hour complete program costing B5,700. There are two branches on opposite sides of the city.
✉ 102 Thanon Sirimuangkarajan and 4 Thanon Samlan, Tambol Pra Singh, Chiang Mai ☎ 053 815 000 🕓 Daily 10–10

OLD CHIANGMAI CULTURAL CENTER

A visit to Chiang Mai is incomplete without a trip to a kantoke dinner and show. "Kantoke" is the word for the trays in which northern Thai food is served. Performances of traditional music and dance are presented on a stage on one side of the restaurant.
✉ 185/3 Thanon Wualai ☎ 053 274 540, 053 202 993–5 🕓 Daily 7–9.30 ✋ Kantoke dinner B350

THE OLD MEDICINE HOSPITAL MASSAGE SCHOOL

www.thaimassageschool.ac.th
This is reputedly the best Thai massage school in the north.

The 10-day courses, costing B5,000, include instruction in herbal medicine, and an official government-approved certificate is given to successful students. The school also offers weekend courses in reflexology (B2,500).

✉ Thanon Wualai (opposite Old Chiang Mai Cultural Center), Chiang Mai ☎ 053 201 663, 053 275 085 ⏰ Daily 9–4

THE OTOP SHOP

www.pcinter.com

The OTOP (One Tambol, One Product, ▷ 21) shop concept was established under the umbrella of the Department of Export Promotion, to provide a platform whereby a *tambol* (a community group) specializing in the production of a particular product could market their wares both domestically and in the international markets. Standards are high, prices are very reasonable, and the range is large: Ceramics, wooden dolls, hand-woven silks and cane-ware are just some of the items you will find here.

✉ 29/19 Thanon Singharat, Chiang Mai ☎ 053 482 591 ⏰ Mon–Fri 8–5.30, Sat 9–6

THE PEAK

www.thepeakadventure.com

Embark on outdoor adventures, such as rock climbing, abseiling, off-roading and trekking with the area's leading experts.

✉ 28/2 Thanon Chang Klan (behind the Night Bazaar), Chiang Mai ☎ 053 800 567/8 ⏰ Daily 6–10 🍴 Trips start from B1,500

THE PUB

Despite a complete overhaul of the interior after many decades of business, all the character of a typical countryside English tavern still remains. Guinness and John Smith beers are on tap at reasonable prices, soccer is shown on television, and aside from their regular menu of Thai and Western food, English-roast lunches are served every Sunday. The garden bar is a welcome retreat in the cooler

months, and comfortable rooms are also available for those who want to stay the night.

✉ 198 Huay Kaew, Chiang Mai ☎ 053 211 500 ⏰ 12–12 🍴 Imported draught B200; Sunday roast B250

RIVERSIDE BAR AND RESTAURANT

Chiang Mai's "tuppies" (Thai yuppies) pack this sprawling riverside bar and restaurant every night. They love its mix of Thai and Western music, played by live bands. If the bar area gets too noisy you can escape the decibels at an outside table on the riverbank. The food is so-so, but it's the music that draws the crowds.

✉ 9–11 Thanon Charoenrat, Chiang Mai ☎ 053 243 239 ⏰ Daily 10am–1am 🍴 Lunch B150, dinner B200. Wine B600, other drinks B60–B160

ROYAL ORCHID COLLECTION

www.siamroyal.com

Rose blossoms and orchid blooms are set in glass and gilt to form original table decorations by the Siam Royal Orchid company. They are available at the company's retail outlet on the second floor of the Northern Village shopping precinct at the Central Airport Plaza.

✉ 94–120 Charoenmuang Road, Chiang Mai ☎ 053 245 598 ⏰ Mon–Sat 8–5

SHINAWATRA THAI SILK

www.shinawatrathaisilk.co.th

The Shinawatra company is Thailand's oldest industrial silk manufacturer, founded in 1929. Its products range from silk household items and fashion accessories to bespoke silk clothing, even shoes.

✉ 145/1–2 Chiang Mai–San Kamphaeng Road ☎ 053 221 076 ⏰ Daily 8.30–5.30 🍴 Free

SPICY

Chiang Mai bars close at 1am, but for some obscure reason this one stays open until 4am, sometimes later. The "action" is limited to karaoke TV screens, over-amplified music and, for men, the attentions of off-duty servers.

✉ Thanon Chayaphum 20, Chiang Mai ☎ 053 246 488 ⏰ Daily 9pm–4am 🍴 Drinks B60–B120

SUAN RACHAPRUEK

Originally established to commemorate the 60th anniversary of the King's ascension to the throne (▷ 19), these botanic gardens have been scaled down somewhat from their former glory, when countries from all over the world were invited to establish floral exhibits in honor of the king. Even so, the present exhibition is still quite spectacular, especially the central palace pavilion and the manicured gardens that surround it. Research and education centers dot the grounds, and there is a shuttle bus (B20) to take you around. As the park is quite a way out of town, you might consider planning your visit here in conjunction with a trip to the nearby Night Safari Park (▷ 182), with its resident tigers and other big cats.

✉ Next to the Night Safari Park, Chiang Mai–Hod road ☎ 053 114 110 ⏰ Daily 9.30am–6pm 🍴 B50

TA-WAN DECOR

A small area of fantastic upmarket boutiques has arisen in the lane adjoining the Amari Rincome Hotel on Thanon Nimmanheimin. Ta-Wan Decor is on the corner and is probably the best of them, selling an attractive selection of handicrafts and furniture, ranging from chairs to exquisitely carved items that you'll want to take home with you.

✉ 1 Thanon Nimmanheimin, Soi 1, Chiang Mai ☎ 053 894 941 ⏰ Mon–Sat 10–6

TEA HOUSE SIAM CELADON

More than a dozen varieties of tea and delicious homemade pastries are served in the colonial setting of a century-old restored timber-built mansion on Chiang Mai's busiest shopping street. Celadon and textiles are on sale in the front showrooms.

✉ 158 Thanon Tha Pae, Chiang Mai ☎ 053 234 518 ⏰ Daily 9.30–6

Left *Boats on the Kuang River, Lamphun*
Below *Old Chiangmai Cultural Center*

U.N. IRISH PUB
Test your general knowledge of all things meaningful and trivial on busy Thursday nights at 8.30. Snacks are provided, and there are prizes for the biggest know-all, though the relaxed atmosphere means fun for all.

✉ 24 Thanon Ratchawithi, Amphoe Muang, Chiang Mai ☎ 053 214 554 🕐 Thu 8.30pm

CHIANG RAI
BAN LORCHA
Chiang Rai's Tourism Development Project is working to prevent hill-tribe villages in northern Thailand from becoming commercial "theme parks," and has started a pilot program at the Akha village of Lorcha, near Thaton. It charges admission, but the money is divided into a village fund for orphans, widows and the elderly. The Hilltribe Tourism Development Foundation aims to expand the scheme to other communities. The small entrance charge covers a tour of the village and a demonstration of traditional handicraft skills.

✉ Thaton–Mae Chan road, Chiang Rai 🕐 Daily 8–5 ✋ B20

CHARIN GARDEN RESORT
Northern Thailand residents traveling between Chiang Mai and Chiang Rai make a point of stopping at this unusual roadside cafe to stock up on its celebrated range of homemade cakes and pies. The array of delicious fancy cream cakes, cheesecakes and fruit tarts and pies is astonishing.

✉ 83 Moo 1, Tambol Mae Suay, Chiang Rai ☎ 053 717 272 🕐 Daily 7–7

CHIANG RAI WINERY
World leaders, including US President George W. Bush, have drunk the fruit wine of Thailand's leading winery. The wine is made from a wide variety of tropical and semitropical fruits and herbs. You can buy a bottle or two at the winery retail outlet.

✉ 160 Moo 7, Baan Tung, Yaow Sri, Chiang Rai 🕐 Mon–Sat 9–5 ✋ Wine B200–B400

HILLTRIBE HANDICRAFT MUSEUM/SHOP
www.pda.or.th/chiangrai
Embroidery and woven fabrics made in hill-tribe villages near Chiang Rai are sold in a shop adjoining Chiang Rai's Hilltribe Museum. The handiwork is of a very high quality and remarkable value. Profits from the enterprise go to community development projects.

✉ 620/1 Thanon Tanalai, Chiang Rai ☎ 053 740 088 🕐 Mon–Fri 9–6, Sat–Sun 10–6

THAM PLA
If you're driving from Chiang Rai to Mae Sai on Highway 1, watch out for the sign to Tham Pla, about 7 miles (12km) north of Mae Chan. Although it translates as Fish Cave, Tham Pla is the home of hordes of monkeys.

✉ Ban Khunnaam Nangnom, Mae Chan 🕐 Daily, 24 hours ✋ Free

WATERFORD VALLEY GOLF COURSE
Globetrotting golfers say this magnificent championship course located outside Chiang Rai is among Southeast Asia's finest. It's laid out on a plateau, ensuring cooler temperatures and more breezes than many other northern Thailand courses, making play more enjoyable. Lakes and creeks provide plenty of water, while tropical vegetation adds to the hazards of the course and the magnificent mountains furnish an impressive backdrop.

✉ 33 Moo 5, Tambol Wiang Chiang Rung, Chiang Rai ☎ 053 953 425–8 🕐 Daily 8–4 ✋ Mon–Fri B1,100, Sat–Sun B1,650

LAMPANG
SRISAWAT CERAMICS
Lampang has Thailand's richest source of white clay, and its beautiful ceramic products are highly prized. Much of it bears the city's famous insignia (a cockerel). In December a ceramics festival is held throughout Lampang city.

✉ 316 Phaholyotin Road, Lampang ☎ 054 225 931 🕐 Mon–Sat 9–5

LAMPHUN

LAMPHUN'S OLD BRIDGE

Lamphun is proud of its wooden, covered bridge spanning the Kuang River, which is like a local version of Venice's Rialto Bridge. The bridge is lined with stands selling excellent local products.

✉ Just below the tourist office, Lamphun ⏰ Daily 8–6

SERAPEE WINERY AND RESTAURANT

Northern Thailand's only vineyard, in a quiet village between Lamphun and Chiang Mai, produces two varieties of white wine, which the German owner serves in his adjacent restaurant. The wines are from hardy European stock and are entirely chemical free. They're light and crisp.

✉ Serapee ☎ 084 803 1977 ⏰ Fri 6–10, Sat–Sun 11.30–10

MAE HONG SON

WORLD WAR II MEMORIAL MUSEUM

Roughly midway between Mae Sariang and Mae Hong Son, the World War II Memorial Museum commemorates the hundreds of Japanese soldiers who died here on their retreat from Allied armies in Myanmar (Burma). Local people took the Japanese in, nursing many back to health and burying those who died. A local historian later gathered the belongings they left behind.

✉ Khun Yuam, kilometer stone 98, Route 108 ⏰ Thu–Tue 9–5 💲 B10

MAE SA

JUNGLE BUNGY JUMP

If bungee jumping is your thing, this is the only outfit in northern Thailand. If it doesn't appeal, you can watch the enthusiasts fling themselves into the air.

✉ 229 Moo 1, Tambol Mae Rim, Amphoe Mae Rim, Chiang Mai ☎ 053 297 700, 081 885 1912 ⏰ Daily 9–6 💲 B2,000

MAE SA BUTTERFLY AND ORCHID FARM

You can walk through clouds of tropical butterflies at this attractive roadside halt on the way to the Mae Sa valley. The butterflies live in a netting enclosure, along with a mass of colorful orchids. A shop sells packed kits for visitors to take home and grow their own orchids. There's also an airy terrace restaurant.

✉ Mae Rim–Mae Sa road, kilometer stone 10 ☎ 053 297 152 ⏰ Daily 9–5 💲 Adult B40, child (under 14) B20

MAE SA SNAKE FARM

Snake handlers play with deadly poisonous cobras and vipers in the arena of the Mae Sa Snake Farm. Snakes are also "milked" for their venom in demonstrations.

✉ Mae Rim–Samoeng road, kilometer stone 3 ☎ 053 860 719 ⏰ Daily 8–4 💲 Adult B200, child (under 14) B100

MAE SA WATERFALL

Mae Sa's spectacular waterfall was attracting visitors from Chiang Mai and beyond before any of the other attractions on this mountain route were opened. It descends a mountain slope in eight stages and during the rainy season is a breathtaking sight. The waterfall is in a national park, so you'll be charged to see it.

✉ Mae Rim–Samoeng road, kilometer stone 4 ⏰ Daily 8–5 💲 B200

PAI

B-BOP BAR

This is a legendary jazz club, reputedly better than even Bangkok's best. The brick and timber walls and teak rafters ring nightly to every kind of beat, from blues to reggae music.

✉ Highway 1095, opposite the tourist police station ☎ 095 608 561 ⏰ Nightly 9–1 💲 Free admission

SIPSONGPANNA ART GALLERY

Attached to the charming Sipsongpanna Bungalow is an attractive art gallery showing the work of the many talented artists who have made their home in Pai. Prices are very reasonable and the work on show is impressive.

✉ 60 Moo 5 Viang Neua, Pai ☎ 053 698 259, 017 351 786 ⏰ Daily 8–6

THAI ADVENTURE RAFTING

www.thairafting.com

This Chiang Mai tour company organizes two-day whitewater-rafting trips on the wild Pai River. The expedition leaders are fully qualified and know the region and its rivers, so you're in good hands.

✉ 16 Moo 4 Thanon Rangsiyanon, Pai ☎ 053 699 111 ⏰ Daily 9–5 💲 B2,500 (2-day trip)

PHAYAO

BAN SAN PA MUANG

This small village, 10 miles (16km) from Phayao, is famous for the handicrafts made from the fibers of the water hyacinths that grow in the Kwan Phayao Lake. Many locals specialize in the craft.

✉ LTAT Northern Office, Region 2, 448/16 Singhaklai Road, Chiang Rai ☎ 053 717 433

SAN KAMPHAENG

HOT SPRINGS

Follow the signs from San Kamphaeng or take a *songthaew* to these sulphur springs, set in a valley of flower gardens and woods. Two geysers also feed a swimming pool and baths. Bungalows with private hot tub can be hired for B150 for two hours or rented overnight for B800.

✉ San Kamphaeng ⏰ Daily 7–6 💲 B30 (B50 for use of the pool)

TAK

BHUMIPHOL DAM GOLF CLUB

The golf club, nestled in a mountain valley below Thailand's largest lake, claims to be "one of the finest in Asia." It's certainly one of the least expensive—green fees for a day's play on the 18-hole course are B400, and a caddy costs B180. The course is beautifully landscaped in a river valley just below the dam.

✉ Bhumiphol Dam, Tak ☎ 055 599 093 ⏰ Daily 8–5 💲 Green fees B400, caddy B180

HILL-TRIBE MARKET

Silverware and textiles made by the Lahu, Lisu and Hmong are sold at this country market on the road between Tak and Mae Sot. Locally

grown fruit and vegetables are also piled high on the market stands.
✉ Tak–Mae Sot highway 105, kilometer stone 29 🕐 Daily 6–6

MYSTERY HILL

If you're traveling by car from Tak to the border town of Mae Sot you can experience a rare phenomenon at a section of the road called "mystery hill." Stop your vehicle at the foot of the hill, switch off the engine and sit back in amazement as the car appears to roll up the hill, albeit a natural optical illusion. This strange phenomenon attracts travelers from all over Thailand.
✉ Tak–Mae Sot highway 105, kilometer stone 68

UTTARADIT
KESANI RAFT TOUR

Houseboat rafts ply the still waters of the vast Sirikit Dam, and a cruise on one of them is a great away-from-it-all experience. The rafts can be rented for the day or for an overnight trip. Meals and bedding are included in the cost.
✉ Sirikit Dam, Ban Tha Rua ☎ 081 605 6211 🕐 Daily 8–10 💷 B2,500–B3,500

LAB LAE

Lab Lae got its peculiar name (meaning "Invisible Town") because, for many people in earlier times, it was a forest-hidden refuge from wars in the region. Today, it's a lively handicrafts center and a producer of langsad fruit.
✉ 5 miles (8km) east of Uttaradit on Route 1045

SAK YAI WILDLIFE RESERVE

"Sak Yai" means "large teak tree," and that's the chief attraction of this reserve. The tree is said to be about 1,500 years old and the largest in Thailand. Wildlife in the park includes civets and 40 rare bird species, so binoculars are recommmended.
✉ 42 miles (70km) east of Uttaradit (Route 1047) ☎ 055 258 028 🕐 Daily 8–6 ✋ Entrance fee B200

FESTIVALS AND EVENTS

FEBRUARY
CHIANG MAI FLOWER FESTIVAL

February is the month when Chiang Mai bursts into bloom, and the first weekend is devoted to a riotous floral display along two sides of the old city moat.
ℹ TAT Northern Office, Region 1, 105/1 Chiang Mai–Lamphun road, Amphoe Muang, Chiang Mai ☎ 053 248 604 🕐 First weekend in February

STRAWBERRY FESTIVAL SAMOENG

Chiang Mai's best strawberries come from this nearby mountain community. Punnets of freshly picked strawberries, wine, jam, jellies, desserts and bonbons are for sale at village stands.
ℹ TAT Northern Office, Region 1, 105/1 Chiang Mai–Lamphun road, Amphoe Muang, Chiang Mai ☎ 053 248 604 🕐 Second weekend in February

APRIL
SONGKRAN (WATER FESTIVAL) CHIANG MAI

Songkran is celebrated in even the smallest village in Thailand, but nowhere as colorfully as in Chiang Mai. The moat surrounding the old city provides unlimited water for festivities in which everyone gets drenched.

ℹ TAT Northern Office, Region 1, 105/1 Chiang Mai–Lamphun road, Amphoe to Muang, Chiang Mai ☎ 053 248 604 🕐 April 13–15

MEKONG BOAT RACES CHIANG SAEN

Boat races on the Mekong River, featuring crews from Thailand, Laos, China and Myanmar (Burma), are a highlight of the *Songkran* Festival in Chiang Saen. The climax, though, is the crowning of the Queen of the Golden Triangle.
ℹ TAT Northern Office, Region 2, 448/16 Thanon Singhaklai, Chiang Rai ☎ 053 717 433 🕐 Middle of April

NOVEMBER/DECEMBER
SUNFLOWER FESTIVAL MAE HONG SON

www.travelmaehongson.org
The six-week season when the famous sunflowers bloom on the mountains surrounding Mae Hong Son is celebrated with a seemingly endless program of cultural and popular events, ranging from performances of traditional music and dance to a Miss Sunflower contest.
ℹ Tourist Information Centre, Old District Office, Thanon Khunlumphraphat, Amphoe Muang, Mae Hong Son ☎ 053 612 982/3 🕐 Nov to mid-Dec Mon–Fri 8.30–4.30

Right *The tricky process of extracting venom from a king cobra*

THE NORTH • WHAT TO DO

REGIONS

Above *Enjoy elegant dining in beautiful surroundings in Chiang Mai*

PRICES AND SYMBOLS
The prices given are the average for a two-course lunch (L) and a three-course dinner (D) for one person, without drinks or wine.

For a key to the symbols, ▷ 2.

BAN SOP RUAK
BORDER VIEW
On the edge of Ban Sop Ruak is the luxury Imperial Golden Triangle (▷ 192) with this first-class restaurant. Its name is very apt, because from its broad terrace diners have a fine view of the Mekong and the mountains. The Thai cuisine is excellent, and the fish comes from the Mekong.
✉ Imperial Golden Triangle Resort, 222 Ban Sop Ruak (Ban Sop Ruak–Mai Sai road), Chiang Saen ☎ 053 784 001 ⓒ Daily 6am–11.30pm 🖐 L B180, D B300

CHIANG DAO
CHIANG DAO NEST MINI-RESORT
www.nest.chiangdao.com
This restaurant has achieved national fame because of the extraordinary

culinary skills of resident chef Wicha. Her menus feature such dishes as local buffalo steak in red wine sauce followed by hot chocolate soufflé. She makes her own bread and pasta and uses only locally grown vegetables. Many of her best customers drive from Chiang Mai, 40 miles (65km) away to sample her exquisite cuisine.
✉ 144/4 Moo 5, Chiang Dao ☎ 053 456 242, 086 017 1985 ⓒ Daily 8am–9pm 🖐 L B180, D B400

CHIANG MAI
THE ANTIQUE HOUSE
The suitably named Antique House, built in 1870, is one of Chiang Mai's few buildings under an official protection order. The beautiful timber-built house is rather cramped and the main dining area is in a relatively modern extension, but the setting is authentic Lanna. Classical string music is played in the evenings, which adds to the amotsphere. The menu is also genuine northern Thailand—the pork and ginger curry (*hang led*) is especially recommended.

✉ 71 Thanon Charoen Prathet, Chiang Mai ☎ 053 276 810 ⓒ Daily 11am–midnight 🖐 L B300, D B500

THE EMPRESS RESTAURANT
www.empresshotels.com
This restaurant has a relaxed yet smart setting. The buffet lunch is very popular among Thais and foreigners alike, with a wide variety of Thai and international dishes laid out from which diners choose. All the food is superbly cooked and presented of roast meats, *dim sum*, croquet potatoes, noodle dishes, fresh sushi and Royal Thai cuisine make up just a part of the spread. A good selection of cakes and sweets is available to finish off your meal. The evening set menu is well worth trying, and varies slightly each night. A good selection of drinks is also available.
✉ The Empress Hotel, 199 Chang Klan Road, Chiang Mai ☎ 053 270 240 ⓒ Daily 11.30–2, 6–11 🖐 L B250, D B450

HUEN PHEN
Phen's house (*huen* in northern Thai) is two restaurants in one, catering to two distinct classes of clientele.

By day, the open-sided streetfront dining area caters to a busy Thai lunchtime crowd and offers a simple, cheap menu. In the evening, the ancient, cluttered Lanna house at the rear opens up to offer diners a more stylish dining experience. The menu then is studded with northern Thai specialties such as delicious *sai uwa* sausage, *nam prik* sauce and mouthwatering *hang led* pork and ginger curry.

✉ 112 Thanon Rachamanka, Chiang Mai ☎ 053 277 103 ⓒ Daily 8.30–3, 5–10; closed last Mon in month ✋ L B90, D B220

KHAOMAO-KHAOFANG RESTAURANT
www.khaomaokhaofang.com

This restaurant is well located for people visiting Suan Rachapruek, the Night Safari or heading south toward Hang Dong. Two great domes above a lotus pond, waterfalls and rich greenery create a semitropical jungle setting in which to enjoy the great range of mostly Thai and northern Thai dishes. The fish dishes are especially recommended and come in a variety of styles. Western dishes are also available.

✉ 181 Mu 7 Rachapruek Road, Nongkwai, Chiang Mai ☎ 053 838 444 ⓒ Daily 11–10 ✋ L B250, D B350

RACHAMANKHA
www.rachamankha.com

Tucked just behind Wat Phra Singh, next-door to the hotel, Rachamankha has a beautiful temple-like setting in the courtyard of a "Lanna Revival" style mansion, filled with antiques from Laos, China, Myanmar, and Thailand. In addition to the beautiful interior and peaceful atmosphere, the great food and being serenaded by live dulcimer music makes for a magical evening. The cuisine focuses on Thai Mayanmar and Tai Yai (a local hill tribe), with salads and European options. Try the Ravioli Napolitano or the Prawn Myanmar Masala Curry. There's a good choice of wines, too.

✉ 6 Rachamankha 9, Phra Singh, Chiang Mai ☎ 053 904 111 ⓒ Daily 7am–10pm ✋ L B500, D B850

THE RIVERSIDE
www.theriversidechiangmai.com

The popular Riverside, on the Ping River, opened in the early 1980s and has now grown into a popular sprawling place where you can dine on Thai or international food. Alternatively, find a table for drinks near one of two stages where live bands play every night. For something entirely different you could take a river cruise and have dinner served aboard, then cram yourself into one of the bars for drinks and music on your return.

✉ 9–11 Charoenrat Road, Chiang Mai ☎ 053 243 239 ⓒ Daily 10am–1am ✋ L B250, D B350

RUEN TAMARIND RESTAURANT
www.tamarindvillage.com

The Thai dishes here are outstanding, but it is its "Lanna Revival" architectural setting that makes this fine dining hideaway exceptional. Owned by the folks at Rayavadee Resort in Railay, and designed by the owner of the Rachamankha, the restaurant–hotel's lineage promises a special evening. The alternate restaurant entrance is just around the corner on Pha Pokklao Street.

✉ 50/1 Thanon Ratchadamnoen, Tamarind Village, Chiang Mai ☎ 053 418 896 ⓒ Daily 7am–11pm ✋ L B200, D B400

SLEE BANYAN
www.centarahotelsresorts.com

About 15 minutes drive southeast of the city, Siripanna's boutique resort-restaurant is the perfect stop for outings into the countryside. The indoor-outdoor setting is surrounded by architecture that is reminiscent of a "Lanna Revival" city with raised moatlike swimming pools, towers, and encampments. Choose from international, Thai, and Asian dishes, with plenty of options for the whole family. Despite being a boutique resort, the restaurant can accommodate large groups.

✉ Siripanna Villa Resort, Chiang Mai, 36 Rat Uthit Road, Wat Ket, Chiang Mai ☎ 053 371 999 ⓒ Daily 6am–10.30pm ✋ L B500, D B850

SUNFLOWER CHINESE RESTAURANT
www.centarahotelsresorts.com

Set on the top floor of Centara's Duangtawan tower near the night market, the Sunflower offers the most spectacular aerial view of Chiang Mai. This Cantonese restaurant offers delicious *dim sum* while you enjoy the view. Come back another night for to enjoy delicious pasta at Marco Polo on the 1st floor.

✉ Centara Duangtawan Hotel Chiang Mai, 132 Loykroh Road, Chang Klan, Muang, Chiang Mai ☎ 053 905 000 ⓒ Daily 11–2.30, 6–10.30 ✋ L B300, D B400

CHIANG RAI
CABBAGES & CONDOMS

This rural version of Bangkok's famous Cabbages & Condoms restaurant is just as quirky—an entrance sign welcomes visitors with the words "You have arrived at the rubber triangle," and free condoms are handed out with the after-dinner peppermints. The underlying purpose, however, is serious, and the restaurants' founder is a respected Thai anti-AIDS campaigner. Oh, and the food is very good here, too.

✉ 153 Moo 6, Tambon Pangiew, Amphoe Wiangpapao, Chiang Rai ☎ 053 952 312/3 ⓒ Daily 7am–10pm ✋ L B120, D B250

CHAM CHA

Chiang Rai's tourist office is next door to this busy restaurant, and its staff are among its best clients, along with officials from the nearby city hall. Their patronage is a guarantee of the excellence of the Thai food, particularly the kitchen's *pad thai*, a hearty helping of noodles laced with meat or fish. The downstairs dining area gets very crowded, but there are usually spare tables upstairs.

✉ Thanon Singhaklai, Chiang Rai ☎ 053 744 191 ⓒ Mon–Sat 7–4 ✋ L B100

HAWNARIGA

A cool stream, stocked with fish, runs through this thatch-roof, open-sided restaurant. Order steamed tabtim with garlic and herbs and it will be served straight from the water. Other northern Thai specialties on the menu include *sai uwa* sausage with a spicy dip. The restaurant is easy to find—it's next to the city clock tower, from which it gets its Thai name.

✉ 402/1–2 Thanon Banpapragarn, Amphoe Muang, Chiang Rai ☎ 053 711 062 🕐 Daily 9am–10pm 🖐 L B100, D B140

SALUNGKHAM

Northern Thai dishes such as *yang ruam* (grilled beef and local sausage) and *khai tun* (steamed whipped eggs) are the specialties of this popular ethnic restaurant. From the upstairs teak-floored terrace you can watch your meal being prepared in the open kitchen below. Non-smokers have their own area on the ground floor.

✉ 834/3 Thanon Phaholyothin, Amphoe Muang, Chiang Rai ☎ 053 717 192 🕐 Daily 10.30–10.30 🖐 L B150, D B200

KHUN YUAM
BAN FARANG

The only restaurant of any standard on the "loop" route between Mae Hong Son and Mae Sariang is roughly halfway, in the village of Khun Yuam. The open-sided, orchid-hung terrace dining area is part of a guesthouse catering to visitors to the nearby World War II Museum, and it has an international menu. The pork or chicken steaks with a herb sauce are very tasty, while the pancakes are a popular local specialty.

✉ 499 Moo 1, Khun Yuam, Mae Hong Son ☎ 053 622 086 🕐 Daily 6am–10pm 🖐 L B150, D B200

LAMPANG
BAAN FAI LAMPANG

This is a popular restaurant specializing in northern Thai food. The *nam prik noom* (a dish consisting mostly of mashed green chili peppers that is surprisingly mild-tasting) is popular among the locals. There are also many traditional Thai dishes from other parts of the kingdom on the menu if you find the

northern food just a little too unusual for your palate. The restaurant is next to a lovely teak house that adds to the traditional setting and laid-back atmosphere.

✉ Baan Fai Lampang, Pahonyothin Road, Lampang ☎ 054 335 238 🕐 Daily 10am–9.30pm 🖐 L B150, D B250

THE RIVERSIDE BAR & RESTAURANT

From the teak-floored terrace of the Riverside you have fine views of the Wang River and a temple's golden spires breaking through nearby woods. The rambling old building has a collection of dining areas, inside and outdoors, linked by a bandstand where live music is played most nights. Good Thai and Western dishes are served—the snow peas and calf's liver are particularly recommended. So are the excellent pizzas that come from a genuine brick oven.

✉ 328 Thanon Tipchang, Lampang ☎ 054 221 861 🕐 Daily 11–midnight 🖐 L B150, D B200

LAMPHUN
TONFAI

Mind your head as you enter this ancient teak-built home on the riverside road a few paces from Lamphun's tourist office. It must have been built for very short people. The upstairs dining room (remove your shoes first) has greater clearance, with high wooden rafters supporting uncovered roof tiles. Unglazed windows look out over the river and are shuttered when the weather gets cool. The northern Thai menu has exotic dishes like curried frog and chicken's innards; the fried rice variations are hearty and tasty.

✉ Thanon Chaimongkol 1, Lamphun 🕐 Sun–Sat 11–11 🖐 L B120, D B150

MAE HONG SON
BAI FERN

The "Fern Leaf" is one of Mae Hong Son's oldest established and most popular restaurants, well patronized by Thai businesspeople and their families. A live band plays most nights in the larger of the two dining

rooms, so if you're looking for peace and quiet take a table in the smaller, cozier bar area. The menu is full of imaginative variations of northern Thai specialties—the pork ribs and pineapple are especially good.

✉ 87 Thanon Khunlumprapas, Mae Hong Son ☎ 053 611 374 🕐 Daily 10–10 🖐 L B250, D B350

GOLDEN TEAK

Mae Hong Son's most prestigious restaurant is in the Imperial Tara Hotel, its large picture windows looking out over lush tropical gardens. Oriental rugs are spread between the wickerwork tables and chairs. The menu is a mix of Thai, Chinese and international dishes, and the vast breakfast buffet is a good start to the day touring.

✉ Imperial Tara Hotel, 149 Moo 8, Tambol Pang Moo, Mae Hong Son ☎ 053 684 444 🕐 Daily 6am–midnight 🖐 L B350, D B550

MAE SAI
SAISHOL

This is the northernmost restaurant in Thailand, and from its first-floor dining room you can look over the small border river below and directly into Myanmar. The inexpensive menu has some very tasty northern Thai dishes—try the *khai yat sai* (meat-filled omelet), and if the weather's hot order a refreshing Thai-style sweet iced tea to accompany your meal.

✉ 86/2 Thanon Chonlapatan, Mae Sai 🕐 Daily 7am–9pm 🖐 L B100, D B120

MAE SARIANG
RIVERSIDE

The stunning view from the wooden deck of this attractive guesthouse restaurant makes up for the simplicity of its menu. Tables look out over a bend of the Yuam River, flanked by rice paddies and sugarcane fields and backed by the far-off mountains. The menu has mostly Thai rice and noodle dishes, although an "American breakfast" is served until noon.

✉ 85 Thanon Langpanich, Mae Sariang ☎ 053 682 592 🕐 Daily 8am–10pm 🖐 L B80, D B120

NAN

CHUMPOO-THIP
www.thecityparkhotel.com
The stylish City Park Hotel's
Chumpoo-Thip restaurant serves
fresh produce from its own kitchen
garden, which diners are invited to
stroll around while waiting for their
orders. The fish with Thai pepper
sauce and the restaurant's own
version of the Isan dish *lab* are
highly recommended.

✉ The City Park Hotel, 99 Thanon
Yantarakitkosol, Nan ☎ 054 741 343
🕐 Daily 7am–midnight 🖐 L B180,
D B200

RUEN KAEW
The Nan River meanders past the
outside terrace of this flower-
smothered rustic restaurant on the
edge of Nan. Locals pack the place
at weekends to listen to its Thai
bands and singers, who perform
nightly. The excellent northern Thai
food is also a big draw—try the
honey-baked chicken.

✉ 1/1 Thanon Sumondhevaraj, Nan
☎ 054 710 631 🕐 Daily 10am–11pm
🖐 L B150, D B200

SURIYA GARDEN
Chinese specialties such as Canton-
style pig's trotters feature on the
extensive menu of this large, airy
restaurant overlooking the Nan River.
On warm evenings, take a table on
the wood-floored waterfront deck.
A Thai band and vocalists perform
nightly.

✉ 9 Thanon Sumondhevaraj, Nan
☎ 054 710 687 🕐 Daily 10am–midnight
🖐 L B150, D B200

PAI

BAAN PAI
The Baan Pai ("Pai Home") is a
favorite with locals and visitors alike,
serving Thai and Western dishes in
the relaxed surroundings of an old
timber-built house on one of Pai's
two main streets. The Thai menu
includes the usual range of rice and
noodle dishes, while the Western
fare encompasses everything from
hamburgers to pizzas. The mashed
potato is the best in town.

✉ 7 Moo 3, Thanon Rangsiyanont, Pai
☎ 053 699 912 🕐 Daily 8am–midnight
🖐 L B120, D B200

BURGER HOUSE PAI
In the middle of town, this
restaurant has 36 seats and is run
by a friendly American. There are
12 different hearty burgers and
plenty of baguettes to choose from
(including some vegetarian fillings),
with breakfast items on the menu to
help start the day.

✉ 14 Moo 4, Rangsiyanont Road, Pai
☎ 053 399 093 🕐 Daily 9–9 🖐 L B150,
D B200

NONG BEER
From the open-sided main dining
room at this popular restaurant you
have a fine view of paddy fields and
the mountains beyond. The Thai
menu includes such favorites as
spicy *Pad Thai* noodles and green
and red curries.

✉ Thanon Rangsiyanont, Pai ☎ 053 699
103 🕐 Daily 10–10 🖐 L B100, D B140

PHAYAO

SANG CHAN
The fishing nets draped across
the glass facade of this lakeside
restaurant signal that this is *the*
place to find the best of the day's
catch and is highly recommended.
Tilapia is its specialty, grilled
with garlic or chili. The beamed
and pillared restaurant has the
friendly feel of an Italian lakeside
trattoria and it's a favorite weekend
destination of local Thai families.
There's an attractive, flower-bordered
front garden for alfresco dining.

✉ 17/4 Chai Kwan Road, Phayao ☎ 054
431 971 🕐 Daily 9am–10pm 🖐 L B150,
D B200

PHRAE

MAEYOM PALACE HOTEL
(RUAN TOMYOM)
The outdoor restaurant, open only
in the evening, has a lovely relaxed
feel to it. The staff are very friendly
and helpful, and while the menu
features a range of both international
and Thai cuisine, the fish dishes are
the specialty here. The steamed

Above *Traditional Thai cuisine is colorful,
and created using a wide range of fresh
produce and spices*

fish with Thai herbs is especially
recommended. No wine is served.

✉ Maeyom Palace hotel (Ruan Tonyom),
181/6 Yantarakijkosol Road, Phrae ☎ 054
521 028/35 🕐 Daily 5–11pm 🖐 L B120,
D B150

NAKHON PHRAE TOWER HOTEL
The Nakhon Phrae Tower Hotel's
restaurant is Phrae's top dining
establishment and popular with
the locals. It is very good value and
serves a large variety of excellent
Thai and Chinese dishes—try the *lab
muang kwa* or *pla kang phad cha*.

✉ 3 Thanon Muanghit, Phrae ☎ 054 521
321 🕐 Daily 7am–1am 🖐 L B120, D B250

THA TON

CHANKASAM
Just 22 yards (20m) from Tha
Ton's boat pier, this open-air Thai
restaurant is recommended for
a good lunch to prepare for the
four-hour river trip to Chiang Rai.
Fish from the Kok River lands on
the restaurant menu and gets into
the excellent *tom yam pla maenam*
(spicy river fish soup). The traditional
Thai breakfast (*kao tom* rice soup) is
also served from 7am.

✉ 209 Moo 3, Tambon Tha Ton, Amphoe
Thaton ☎ 053 459 313 🕐 Daily
7am–10pm 🖐 L B80, D B120

Above *The region has many fine hotels.*

PRICES AND SYMBOLS

Prices are the lowest and highest for a double room for one night. Breakfast is included unless noted otherwise. All the hotels listed accept credit cards unless otherwise stated. Note that rates vary widely throughout the year.

For a key to the symbols, ▷ 2.

BAN SOP RUAK

IMPERIAL GOLDEN TRIANGLE RESORT

www.imperialhotels.com

Set high above the Mekong River, all rooms have terraces overlooking the river and the mountains. The terrace of the restaurant (▷ 188) is a perfect spot to relax and watch the setting sun.

✉ 222 Ban Sop Ruak (Ban Sop Ruak–Mai Sai road), Chiang Saen 57150 ☎ 053 784 001 ✋ B4,120–B19,420 🛏 73 (20 non-smoking) 🏊

CHIANG DAO

RIM DOI RESORT

www.rimdoiresort.com

This pretty resort is located on the edge of the mountains. Guests stay in simply furnished bungalows, chalets or in more stylish, teak-

walled and furnished lakeside rooms. An attractive restaurant and karaoke bar also overlook the water.

✉ 46 Moo 4, Muang Ngay, Chiang Dao ☎ 053 375 028/9, 017 066 876 ✋ B200–B700 excluding breakfast 🛏 60

CHIANG MAI

CENTARA DUANGTAWAN HOTEL

www.centarahotelsresorts.com

This high-rise, luxury hotel with parking is conveniently located beside the Saturday Walking Market and the Chiang Mai Night Market. Dine in the Chinese restaurant on the top floor for great views, relax in the outdoor pool, or indulge in a spa treatment at the Cenvaree.

✉ 132 Loykroh Road, Chang Klan, Muang, Chiang Mai ☎ 053 905 000 ✋ B1,200–B1,600 🛏 48 🏊 🏖 🎾

RACHAMANKHA

www.rachamankha.com

Designed by the same architect of the Tamarind Village, this boutique hotel has a peaceful temple-like atmosphere. The spacious rooms are beautifully furnished with Lanna, Burmese or Chinese antiques, and open out onto either the lush tropical gardens or a secluded courtyard swimming pool. Parking and free WiFi is also available.

✉ Thanon Rachamankha, Soi 9, Chiang Mai ☎ 053 904 111 ✋ From B8,300 🛏 25 rooms, 2 suites (all non-smoking) 🏊 🏖 Outdoor

TAMARIND VILLAGE

www.tamarindvillage.com

One of the best Lanna-style boutique hotels in Chiang Mai. Rooms look over gardens dominated by tamarind trees, while cloisters surround a swimming pool with an open-sided restaurant. Non-smoking rooms and parking are available.

✉ 50/1 Thanon Ratchadamnoen, Chiang Mai 50200 ☎ 053 418 889 ✋ B4,950–B13,600 🛏 45 🏊 🏖 Outdoor

CHIANG RAI

THE LEGEND RESORT AND SPA

www.thelegend-chiangrai.com

This hotel is built in Lanna style on an island in the Kok River, just a short walk from the city center. Rooms are furnished with antiques and reproductions, while public areas are a mixture of whitewashed walls and teak. The restaurant and pool are on the river bank, with mountain views. Parking is available.

✉ 124/15 Moo 12 Thanon Kohloy, Amphoe Muang, Chiang Rai 57000 ☎ 053 910 400 ✋ B3,300–B7,500 🛏 78 (all non-smoking) 🏖 Outdoor

THE WHITE HOUSE
www.chiangraiprovince.com
The White House is a charming villa-style guesthouse with simple but clean, comfortable rooms. Many rooms lead onto a terrace overlooking the pool.
✉ 789 Thanon Phaholyothin, Chiang Rai ☎ 053 713 427 ✋ B350–B1,200 excluding breakfast ⓘ 30 ☷ Outdoor

CHIANG SAEN
GIN'S GUESTHOUSE
The Mekong River practically flows at the end of the garden of this friendly Thai home. Ask for a room on the upstairs floor of the main house, where you'll share a large, lounge with other guests. Gin, the man of the house, will arrange tours.
✉ Rim Kong Road, Chiang Saen ☎ 053 650 847 ✋ B200–B700 excluding breakfast ⓘ 12

DOI ANGKHANG
ANGKHANG NATURE RESORT
www.amari.com
The mountains and forests of Doi Angkhang embrace this haven of luxury. The large and airy rooms are furnished in teak and local fabrics. In its fine restaurant, the menu features only organic products from the nearby royal agricultural project.
✉ 1/1 Moo 5, Baan Koom, Tambon Mae Ngon, Amphoe Fang, Chiang Mai 50320 ☎ 053 450 110 ✋ B3,800–B8,000 ⓘ 72 rooms (23 non-smoking), 2 suites ☷ Outdoor ⏀

LAMPANG
PIN HOTEL
The modern, neat and clean Pin is tucked away on a quiet lane linking two of Lampang's busiest streets (parking available). Rooms are decorated in pastel shades and light woods. A spacious lounge adjoins the breakfast room and restaurant.
✉ 8 Suandok Road, Lampang ☎ 054 322 283/4, 054 221 509 ✋ B500–B1,100 excluding breakfast ⓘ 59 🛇

LAMPHUN
HOTEL SUPAMIT
The functional rooms hardly match the palatial promise of the vast lobby, with its grand, Siamese-style porticoed entrance, but most of them have fine views. There's ample parking and a noisy karaoke lounge.
✉ 204/10 Thanon Jamma Dhavi, Lamphun ☎ 053 534 865 ✋ B250–B600 ⓘ 78 (some non-smoking)

MAE HONG SON
ROOKS HOLIDAY HOTEL AND RESORT
Mae Hong Son's largest hotel, Rooks has a tour desk where guests can reserve excursions. The comfortable rooms overlook tropical gardens or the mountains. Parking is available.
✉ 114/5–7 Thanon Khunlumprapas, Mae Hong Son 58000 ☎ 053 612 324/9 ✋ B2,200–B2,820 ⓘ 114 (some non-smoking) 🛇 ☷ Outdoor ⏀

MAE SAI
PU TAWAN RESORT
On a hillside above Mae Sai, this romantic resort is a peaceful retreat from the bustle below. Eighteen air-conditioned bungalows are set in lush gardens, half with Bali-style bathrooms open to the sky.
✉ 414 Moo 10, Tambol Weangpangkham, Mae Sai ☎ 053 640 727, 086 913 9502 ✋ B500–B800 excluding breakfast ⓘ 36 🛇

MAE SALONG
MAESALONG FLOWER HILLS RESORT
The tea plantations of the Queen Mother's Mae Fah Luang project clothe the mountainsides below this restful resort. The bungalow rooms are simple but comfortable; the most expensive have views of the mountains and gardens.
✉ 779 Moo 1, Maesalong-Nok, Mae Fah Luang, Chiang Rai ☎ 053 765 496/7 ✋ B1,000–B2,700 excluding breakfast ⓘ 40 🛇 Some

MAE SARIANG
RIVERSIDE HOTEL AND RESORT
www.riverhousehotels.com
From these sister properties you have a fine view of the Yuam River and the mountains. The rooms are made of wood, so smoking is discouraged. Parking is available.
✉ 6/1 Moo 2 Langpanich Road, Mae Sariang ☎ 053 683 066 ✋ Hotel B850–B1,250; resort B1,400–B2,800 ⓘ Hotel 12, resort 42

MAE SOT
CENTARA MAE SOT HILL RESORT
www.centarahotelsresorts.com
The sleek exterior of the hotel towers over Mae Sot. The carpeted, bamboo- and rattan-furnished rooms are a comfortable retreat.
✉ 100 Asia Road, Mae Sot ☎ 055 532 601/8 ✋ B2,800–B3,200 ⓘ 113 (33 non-smoking) 🛇 ☷ Outdoor ⏀

NAN
DHEVARAJ HOTEL
Nan's top hotel is a high-rise with rooms clustered around a central courtyard, where bands often perform. Parking is available.
✉ 466 Sumondhevaraj Road, Nan 55000 ☎ 054 751 577 ✋ B500–B3,500 ⓘ 152 🛇 ☷ Outdoor ⏀

PAI
BELLE VILLA
www.bellevillaresort.com
The teak bungalows are equipped as well as a five-star hotel's suites. The restaurant overlooks a pool, rice paddies and distant mountains.
✉ 113 Moo 6, Huay Poo–Wiang Nua road ☎ 053 698 226/7 ✋ B2,850–B3,850 ⓘ 40 🛇 ☷ Outdoor

PHAYAO
GATEWAY HOTEL
The Gateway's pink exterior makes it hard to miss. It's a modern hotel with rooms of international standard. There is a gym and pool offer welcome relaxation. Parking is available.
✉ 7/36 Pratuklong 2 Road, Phayao 56000 ☎ 054 411 333-5 ✋ B1,000–B1,100 ⓘ 108 🛇 ☷ Outdoor ⏀

PHRAE
MAE YOM PALACE THANI
This central hotel is a good base for exploring. Rooms are small but have a TV. Parking is available.
✉ Thanon Yontra Kritgoson 181/6, Phrae ☎ 054 521 028 ✋ B1,200–B3,500 ⓘ 104 🛇 ☷ Outdoor

CENTRAL THAILAND

Thailand's most populous region has many unspoiled villages and towns that figured in the country's history but now sit neglected among the rice paddies and orchards that are important in supporting the local economy. The central plains of Thailand are aptly referred to as the country's rice bowl, providing food for much of the country. With Thailand's northeast, the center is the least visited region of the country and retains a quaint, laid-back charm.

Directly north of Bangkok lie ancient ruined cities, preserving the secrets of Thailand's imperial past. Ayutthaya, now World Heritage Site of Ayutthaya, was the Siamese capital of Thailand for four centuries prior to the foundation of Bangkok in 1782. Although usually crowded with visitors, Ayutthaya still retains a peaceful atmosphere and quiet charm. Further north, Lop Buri dates to the 12th century. Its ancient temple architecture, built by the Hindu Khmers, is occupied by an army of spoiled monkeys who are honored with a yearly festival. Sukhothai is the birthplace and original capital of the Thai kingdom. Dating from the 13th century, traditional Thai art and architecture evolved from the examples that flourished here.

Lying northeast of Bangkok, is Kanchanaburi, capital of one of the country's most beautiful provinces in Thailand, and more than just the site of the bridge over the River Kwai. The surrounding province, by the same name, is considered one of the most beautiful in the country. Further north, the last stretch of the infamous Death Railway draws visitors seeking relics of Japanese occupation during World War II. Between Kanchanaburi and the Three Pagoda Pass, the Erawan Falls on the Kwai Yai River is the crown jewel of Erawan National Park and one of the most photographed nature scenes in Thailand.

In contrast to the peace and quiet of the national park, is the best and biggest floating market at Damnoen Saduak, near Ratchaburi, about 62 miles (100km) west of the capital. Boats have been plying their wares here on the Khlong River and its canals for centuries, and visitors can try their hand at bargaining for souvenirs while afloat.

INTRODUCTION

Thailand's capital for more than four centuries (when the country was known as Siam), Ayutthaya is still a vibrant living city and a World Heritage Site. You'll find a glorious history within its weathered ruins.

Ayutthaya was founded in 1350 by the U thong ruler King Ramathibodi I, who recognized the strategic advantages of the site, which was enclosed by three rivers, giving the city a natural defensive "wall" and providing an abundant supply of water for a rapidly growing population. Over the following 417 years, Ayutthaya extended its realm over much of present-day Thailand and into Cambodia. It swallowed up Sukhothai and even the Khmer capital, Angkor. Magnificent royal palaces and more than 400 Buddhist monasteries were built, and visiting emissaries from the West compared Ayutthaya at the height of its power in the 17th century to Paris, London and Venice. But the seeds of Ayutthaya's destruction had already been sown; successive rulers were unable to contain the constant threat of invasion from neighboring Myanmar (Burma), and in April 1767 the city succumbed to a 15-month siege and was destroyed by the victorious Burmese.

WHAT TO SEE

THE OLD CITY

Although the old city of Ayutthaya is fairly compact, you'll need to choose some kind of transportation to visit all the important sights. *Tuk-tuks* charge about B200 an hour, but drivers will settle for less for a half-day or all-day rental. Bicycles are the cheapest option (under B50 a day) and can be rented at the rail station or the Chao Phrom Market at the end of Thanon Horattanachai.

WAT PHRA MAHATHAT

After collecting your bicycle at the rail station or Chao Phrom Market head down Thanon Horattanachai to the Phra Ram pond. At the edge of the water stands ancient Wat Phra Mahathat. This served for centuries as the royal temple, where rulers worshiped and participated in Buddhist rites. Its Khmer-style stupa towered over the city, but collapsed in the 17th century, leaving only the monumental base to hint at its original size. The stupa was rebuilt but collapsed again in 1911, and archeologists discovered a hoard of golden objects in the ruined base.

The temple grounds are studded with other *chedis* (monuments housing a Buddhist relic) from various periods and contain the massive head of a Buddha image, entwined in the roots of ancient fig tree.

➕ 199 B1 🕐 Daily 8–4 ✋ B50

WAT RATBURANA

Across the road from Wat Phra Mahathat stands another of Ayutthaya's most interesting temples, built on the site where the 15th-century King Intharachathirat and two of his sons were cremated. The two sons died in a duel fought to decide the succession to King Intharachathirat's throne, and two *chedis* were built on the site where they were killed to contain their ashes. The temple's main stupa, Ayutthaya's best-preserved one, was found recently to contain not only the usual Buddha relics but also priceless collection of royal golden objects, including 500-year-old votive tablets and containers, now in Ayutthaya's Chao Sam Phraya National Museum. Stairs lead down to the vault, where the relics and the gold were kept, within walls covered with beautiful antique frescoes.

➕ 199 B1 🕐 Daily–4 ✋ B50

INFORMATION

http://thailand.sawadee.com/ayutthaya

➕ 314 D9 ℹ️ TAT Central Region 6, 108/22 Moo 4, Amphoe Phra Nakhon Si Ayutthaya ☎ 035 246 076/7 🕐 Daily 8.30–4.30

Opposite *Built in 1384, the tall Khmer-style towers of Wat Phra Mahathat in the ancient capital of Ayutthaya*

TIPS

>> Try to avoid the midday sun when touring Ayutthaya's historical sites. Early morning and late afternoon are the best times, particularly for photos.

>> The evening hours at Wat Chai Wattanaram are magical, when the setting sun burnishes the ancient temple walls .

>> An easy way to see the riverside temples is to rent a boat. There are several operators in front of the Hua Ro Market on the Lop Buri River (around B200 per hour for a tour of the old city).

>> Free, detailed maps of Ayutthaya's sights and of the Bang-Pa-In Palace are available from Ayutthaya's TAT office.

Below *A Buddha image among the roots of a banyan tree, Wat Phra Mahathat*

THE GRAND PALACE AND WAT PHRA SRI SANPHET

Turn right outside the main entrance to Wat Ratburana and follow the northern edge of Phra Ram pond to the ruins of the former Grand Palace and the royal temple, Wat Phra Sri Sanphet. The palace, described by early Western emissaries as the finest in all Asia, was destroyed by the Burmese in 1767, but the ruins of its six royal halls give an idea of its size and beauty.

The royal temple, Wat Phra Sri Sanphet, was built in 1448, incorporating two large *chedis* for the remains of two early kings. The main *viharn*, Viharn Phra Mongkhon Bophit, built in 1500, contained an astonishing Buddha image, 52ft (16m) high and covered in 374lb (170kg) of pure gold. But the Burmese stripped it of its gold when they sacked Ayutthaya, and the core of the Buddha was later taken to Bangkok and put in a memorial *chedi* there. An immense bronze Buddha image, one of the largest in Thailand, now sits in the *viharn*.
➕ 199 B1 🕐 Daily 7–6 ✋ B50

WAT LOKAYA SUTHA

Head across the narrow canal behind the Grand Palace ensemble to find Wat Lokaya Sutha. This temple compound is worth visiting for its huge reclining Buddha, 122ft (37m) long, the head resting on a lotus. It was built of stucco-covered brick in the Middle Ayutthaya period.
➕ 199 A1 🕐 Daily 7–6 ✋ Free

AYUTTHAYA HISTORICAL STUDY CENTER

Before setting out on a tour of Ayutthaya, a visit to this very instructive information center is advised. Multimedia technology re-creates the magnificence of ancient Ayutthaya and immerses you in its history, giving you all the background information you need to understand the architecture and history of the temple complex.
➕ 199 B2 ✉ Thanon Rotchana ☎ 035 245 124 🕐 Wed–Fri 9–4.30, Sat, Sun 9–5 ✋ B40

CHAN KASEM PALACE

The original palace that stood here was destroyed by the Burmese in 1767, but rebuilt by King Mongkut in the 19th century as a private residence during his visits to Ayutthaya. Today it serves as a history and natural history museum.
➕ 199 B1 ✉ Hua Ro Market ☎ 035 251 586 🕐 Wed–Sun 9–4 ✋ B30

CHAO SAM PHRAYA NATIONAL MUSEUM

Golden objects and a jewel-encrusted sword recovered from the *chedis* of Ayutthaya's royal temples are the highlight of this very interesting museum. Although the collection is impressive, it's still only a portion of what the *chedis* once held—much of the gold placed there by Ayutthaya's rulers as tokens of merit was carried off by looters.
➕ 199 B2 ✉ Corner of Thanon Rotchana and Thanon Khlong Tho ☎ 035 241 587 🕐 Wed–Sun 9–4 ✋ B150

MUSEUM OF THAI VESSELS

Models of more than 200 traditional Ayutthaya and old Siamese vessels were built by a local historian and craftsman, Phaithun Khaomala, who gives private tours of the museum on request.
➕ 199 B1 ✉ Thanon Bang Lan ☎ 035 241 195 🕐 Daily 9–3

ROYAL ELEPHANT PALACE (ELEPHANT KRAAL)

www.elephantstay.com

A palisade of massive teak logs encircles the grounds where wild elephants were trained for warfare in Ayutthaya's heyday. The last round-up was in May 1903 in a presentation for King Chulalongkorn, who took his place in a royal pavilion where early rulers would personally select their war elephants. The

pavilion still stands, together with a Buddhist sanctuary for elephant *mahouts*. Tame elephants now take visitors for rides (B500 per half-hour).
✚ 199 B1 ✉ Thanon Khumkunphan Paton, Phranakhon Si Ayutthaya ☎ 08 0668 7727 🕐 Daily 9–5

WAT PHANAN CHOENG

This temple complex predates the founding of Ayutthaya, and the large gilded Buddha image, the Phra Buddha Trittana Nayok, that sits in its *viharn* was cast 20 years before King Ramathibodi set up his residence there. A popular myth says tears flowed from the eyes of the Buddha when the Burmese sacked Ayutthaya. The 63ft (19m) Buddha statue is so high and the *viharn* so small that no photographer has yet succeeded in capturing the entire figure.
✚ 199 C2 🕐 Daily 7–6 👆 Free

WAT YAI CHAI MONGKHON

This massive structure, with its distinctive octagonal-base, bell-shape stupa, was built by King Naresuan the Great to celebrate his victory in 1592 over Burma's crown prince in an elephant-back duel. It's a suitably proud and flamboyant construction, ringed by seated Buddhas in poses of contemplation. Nearby is a sublime sleeping Buddha.
✚ 199 C2 🕐 Daily 8–4 👆 B20

WAT CHAI WATTANARAM

Dominating the banks of the Chao Phraya River opposite the southwestern corner of the old city, this very beautiful temple ensemble was built in 1630 by King Prasatthong in memory of his mother. The main stupa, 115ft (35m) high, and the cluster of smaller ones around it are all built in the Khmer *prang* style, indicating to historians that they might have been constructed to celebrate the King's victory over the Khmer empire.
✚ 199 A2 🕐 Daily 9–6 👆 B50

TIP

❯❯ Several monasteries of outstanding interest lie outside the old city, in the southeast corner of town, adjacent to the main highways 3477 and 3059. These include Wat Phanan Choeng and Wat Yai Chai Mongkhon (▷ left).

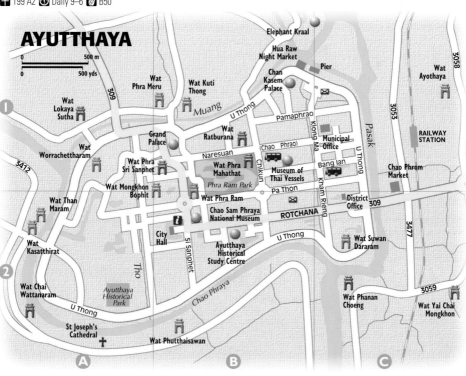

INFORMATION

314 D9 Daily 8–4 B100

TAT Central Region 6, 108/22 Moo 4, Amphoe Phra Nakhon Si Ayutthaya

035 246 076/7 Daily 8.30–4.30

BANG-PA-IN

The small village of Bang-Pa-In, 11 miles (18km) south of Ayutthaya, is famous for its hauntingly beautiful royal palace ensemble, a slightly surreal blend of architectural styles, built on and around three river islands.

The original palace, built in the 16th century by Ayutthaya King Prasat Thong, was destroyed in the Burmese invasion that wiped out the Siamese capital in 1767. It was then rebuilt by Rama IV as a retreat from the new court in Bangkok and became a favorite country residence of his successor Rama V, King Chulalongkorn. On one of his outings to the palace, the boat carrying his wife capsized and she drowned. The devastated king built a white cenotaph in her memory.

ARCHITECTURAL STYLES

Mongkut and his successor, Chulalongkorn, were influenced by Western styles of architecture, and the structures they built are an eclectic but aesthetically successful mixture. The one truly Thai building, the Isawan Thippa-At Pavilion, a fragile concoction with four porches rising to a delicate spire, appears to float in the middle of one of the lakes.

On the riverbank opposite is another ethereal structure, the Krachom Trae Pavilion, an octagonal bandstand-like affair with a domed roof supported by slender pillars. Completing the ensemble in this part of the grounds are three structures that illustrate the regard that Mongkut and Chulalongkorn had for European classical architecture: a graceful bridge with elegant statues of Greek gods and goddesses on its parapets; the Warophat Phiman Throne Hall, an elegant mansion with a classical portico of Corinthian pillars; and the royal temple, Wat Niwet Thammaprawat, with a Gothic interior complete with stained-glass windows. The Rama throne still stands in the Throne Hall, and Thailand's royal family often spends short breaks in the residential section.

Behind the Throne Hall is a curious European-style house, the Uttayan Phumisathian Royal Mansion, filled with beautiful French furniture from the reign of Napoleon III. Yet another royal mansion, Wehat Chamrun, was built in Chinese style with donations raised by Chinese merchants. Completing the ensemble is a curious observatory, the Withunthatsana Tower, a Legoland-like structure dominating the smallest island.

Below *The pavilions of Bang-Pa-In Palace*

CHANTHABURI

Chanthaburi is the center of Thailand's gems trade. Its "gem road"—Thanon Sri Chan and Trok Krachang—is transformed on weekends into the country's liveliest gemstone market. Dealers come from as far away as Myanmar (Burma), Malaysia and Cambodia to haggle, and it's been estimated that as much as 10 million baht changes hands on a busy weekend.

The town was an outpost of the Ayutthaya realm in the reign of King Taksin the Great, and remains of his fort can be seen on Thanon Tha Chalaep. Taksin is still highly revered in Chanthaburi, and a blue-domed circular shrine stands in front of one of the restored walls of the fort, with a statue of the king inside. Sturdy cannons from the 19th-century reign of Rama III also front the wall. Taksin was a superstitious warrior, and Wat Phlub, a temple built in his honor, has a rectangular stupa where potions were concocted to help in his military campaigns.

Just outside the town is a small national park, Nam Tok Pliew, named after its chief attraction, a waterfall that descends over several steps into a clear pool stocked with fish. Overnight accommodations (tel 025 620 760) are available in the park.
➕ 315 F11 ℹ️ TAT Central Region Office Region 4, 153/4 Thanon Sukhumvit, Amphoe Muang, Rayong 21000 ☎ 038 664 585 🕐 Daily 8.30–4.30

DAMNOEN SADUAK FLOATING MARKET
▷ 202.

ERAWAN NATIONAL PARK AND SAI YOK YAI NATIONAL PARK

These small national parks, lying on either side of the 323 highway between Kanchanaburi and the Three Pagodas Pass, have two of Thailand's most beautiful waterfalls. The Erawan Falls, on the Kwai Yai River (the "big" River Kwai), are probably the most photographed scene in Thailand. The much smaller Sai Yok Yai Falls, on the Kwai Noi River (the "small" River

Kwai), however, are every bit as picturesque. Longtail boats ferry visitors from the Sai Yok Yai National Park headquarters (tel 025 620 760) to the foot of the falls (B400). Houseboats can also be rented for the day (B1,000) or for an overnight trip on the river (B2,000). To rent one, tel 081 856 8754.
➕ 314 C8, B9 🕐 Daily 8.30–4.30
🎫 B400, child (under 14) B200 ℹ️ TAT Central Region Office Region 1, Thanon Saeng Chuto, Amphoe Muang, Kanchanaburi 71000 ☎ 038 511 200, 034 512 500 🕐 Daily 8.30–4.30

KAMPHAENG PHET

An important garrison citadel in both the Sukhothai and Ayutthaya eras, Kamphaeng Phet is today a busy market town. Sections of the old city walls, dating from the 15th century, have been restored and incorporated in the modern urban sprawl, while the most important ruins now form the Kamphaeng Phet Historical Park (tel 055 711 921; daily 8–5; adult B150, child B100), 1 mile (1.6km) from the city center. Three reconstructed statues from the early Ayutthaya period include a gracefully recumbent Buddha. The surviving chedis also show Ayutthaya influence. During excavations, many important objects were uncovered, and most of them are on display in the Kamphaeng Phet National Museum (Thanon Pin Damri, Nai Muang, tel 055 711 570; Wed–Sun 9–4; B100).
➕ 308 C6 ℹ️ TAT Northern Office Region 3, 193 Thanon Taksin, Tambol Nong Luang, Amphoe Muang, Tak 63000 ☎ 055 514 341/3 🕐 Mon–Sat 8.30–4

KANCHANABURI
▷ 203–204.

KO SI CHANG

www.ko-sichang.com
Ko Si Chang is an unlikely tourist destination due to its small size, inherent lack of commercialism and near absence of beach life. For some, however, this makes the quaint little island all the more appealing. The only decent, albeit

Above *The Catholic cathedral in Chanthaburi*

small, sandy beach is located at Hat Tham Pang (meaning collapsed beach). Pebbles, rocks and steep ledges ring most of the island, making for some dramatic scenery and perfect photo opportunities. The area is also perfect for kayaking and snorkeling among coral reefs.

The main attraction here is the palace grounds of Rama V. Built as a convalescent home for ailing royalty, King Rama V eventually lost interest in its construction and moved the teak palace to the site in Bangkok known as Vimanmek Palace (▷ 72–73). The grounds have been restored and beautified, however, making it a lovely place for a walk under the frangipani trees, followed by a picnic.

The other point of interest here is Saan Chao Paw Khao Yai, an impressive Chinese temple, which predates the palace by several centuries. The temple was founded when seafarers from Ming China reported a light shining from a cave in the darkness. Around the New Year, the site draws thousands of Chinese visitors.
➕ 314 E10 ℹ️ Ko Si Chang Pier 🚢 Boats from Ko Si Chang to Si Racha run hourly from 6am to 6pm for B60. Boats going the opposite direction run hourly from 7am–8pm

➕ 314 D10 🚌 Buses to Damnoen Saduak leave every 20 mins from 6am to 9pm from Bangkok's Southern Bus Terminal; 2-hour journey, B80 🚗 Follow highway 4 west from Bangkok and turn left at kilometer stone 80 onto the Bang Phae–Damnoen Saduak road

DAMNOEN SADUAK FLOATING MARKET

The floating market at Damnoen Saduak is one of Thailand's top visitor attractions but has still managed to retain much of its historic character. It is a survivor from the days when floating markets were the commercial hub of Bangkok, when the city's roads were its waterways—the Chao Phraya River and the canals that feed off it. Early travelers called Bangkok the "Venice of the East." The romantic image has long since faded, but floating markets do exist, although those within Bangkok are disappointingly small and stocked mostly with cheap tourist curios.

The best and biggest floating market in the Bangkok region is at Damnoen Saduak, near Ratchaburi, about 62 miles (100km) west of the capital. Boats have been plying their wares here on the Khlong River and its canals for centuries, and although the market is now geared more toward visitors, locals do still shop there.

SHOPPING AFLOAT

On a busy market day, hundreds of flat-bottomed punts jam the waterways, paddled by female market traders wearing the deep-blue jackets and straw hats traditionally favoured by Thai farmers. Their boats are piled high with everything you can think of, from fruit and vegetables and household supplies to handicrafts and, increasingly, souvenirs. There are even floating kitchens, on some of the boats, serving noodles and fried rice, although ordering food from them and keeping your balance on a choppy canal can be a hazardous business. The only way to experience the market firsthand is to rent a boat (B300 per hour) and join the throng. The market women can be importunate, so stay firm but polite—a few words in Thai can help here.

Like all Thai markets, Damnoen Saduak's version is best visited in the morning—the earlier the better. After about midday, the market tends to wind down, and there may be disappointing number of boats still pying their trade.

Below *Market sellers still wear traditional wide-brimmed hats*

INTRODUCTION

Site of the bridge immortalized by the film *The Bridge on the River Kwai* (1957), Kanchanaburi is also the capital of one of Thailand's most beautiful provinces. Kanchanaburi's official position as capital of the western province of the same name, one of Thailand's most beautiful regions, is overshadowed by its fame as the site of the World War II bridge built by the Japanese, using Allied prisoners as forced labor. The remains of the bridge and a second, more modern construction stand in the center of Kanchanaburi, where an open, riverside plaza is packed with visitors most of the year. The war cemetery containing the remains of prisoners who died building the bridge is 0.3 miles (0.5km) away, bordered by an information center explaining the project's dark history. A section of the original line runs from Kanchanaburi to a remote station, Nam Tok, on the edge of the Erawan National Park.

WHAT TO SEE

THE BRIDGE

Virtually every visitor to Kanchanaburi travels there to view the remains of the bridge made famous by the film *The Bridge on the River Kwai*. For many it's also a pilgrimage to the sites where more than 12,000 Allied prisoners of war died between 1943 and 1945 while building the "Death Railway" with which Japan hoped to win the war in Southeast Asia.

The wooden bridge depicted in the film spans a non-existant gorge, but the bridge is actually no more than a few wooden stumps across a flat area. A more stable one, built with metal support spans imported from Sumatra, has been reconstructed and carries trains running along the original "Death Railway" route. It is 902ft (275m) from one side of the bridge to the other bank of the Kwai River.

INFORMATION

www.kanchanaburi-info.com

314 C9 TAT Central Region Office Region 1, Thanon Saeng Chuto, Amphoe Muang, Kanchanaburi 71000 034 511 200, 038 512 500 Mon–Sat 8.30–4.30 and TAT and Kanchanaburi Tourist Police, Kanchanaburi Railway Station, 1 Thanon River Kwai, Kanchanaburi 71000 034 512 795 Daily 24 hours Regular bus service from Bangkok

Above *Waterside buildings at Kanchanaburi*

TIPS

›› The city of Kanchanaburi is the capital of one of Thailand's most beautiful mountain regions, which is well worth exploring. Take Route 323 into the mountains as far as the Three Pagodas Pass on the Thai-Burmese border.

›› Rather than staying in a hotel near the river, you could go one step further and choose one that is literally on the river. There are a number of floating hotels in and around Kanchanaburi, ranging from very basic bamboo house-rafts to fully furnished "floatels."

DEATH RAILWAY

A train service (twice daily; single ticket B100) runs from Bangkok's Thonburi railway station to the end of the line, at Nam Tok, on the edge of the Erawan National Park some 37 miles (60km) northwest of Kanchanaburi. Beyond Kanchanaburi, the line runs through virgin jungle and inches its way along a long trestle bridge clinging to the side of a river gorge—the journey is not for the faint-hearted.

The railway line's Kanchanaburi station is part of a large plaza adjoining the bridge and lined with souvenir stands and shops. A short walk away is the World War II Museum, containing an eclectic display of dusty mementoes. The museum (tel 034 512 596; daily 8–6.30; B40) is housed in a riverside temple complex which also describes the history of Thailand using larger-than-life statues of historical figures. The history of the "Death Railway" is told with a fragmentary collection of exhibits and explanatory labels, with their interpretation of Japan's wartime policies and conduct.

Another worthwhile stop is the nearby Death Railway Museum (www.tbrconline.com; daily 9–5; adult B150, child B50), which is officially known as the Thailand–Burma Railway Centre. The museum gives a comprehensive and informative history of the whole railway.

WAR CEMETERY

The hideous toll of Japan's conduct during World War II, in this remote corner of Asia, is evident at the war cemetery, where the remains of nearly 7,000 former Allied prisoners of war lie buried beneath simple bronze plaques. This serene, park-like patch of beautifully maintained land was given in perpetuity to Britain, Australia and the Netherlands by Thailand. The cemetery is located on a busy two-lane highway, Thanon Saengchuto, about 0.6 miles (1km) from the centre of Kanchanaburi.

HELLFIRE PASS

About 400 of those who lie in Kanchanaburi War Cemetery died on one stretch of the "Death Railway", a series of cuttings known as "Hellfire Pass," 50 miles (80km) northwest of Kanchanaburi, on highway 323. They were literally worked to death, hacking a way for the railway through a rocky mountainside. Under pressure to complete the cuttings in four months of 1943, the Japanese put their slave force of Allied prisoners of war and Asian conscripts to work on shifts of up to 18 hours. The work went on through the night, to the light of lanterns, flares and bonfires—giving the scene an inferno-like look and giving the pass its name: "Hellfire." Remains of wooden railway sleepers mark the route through the cuttings, between rocks where broken implements still lie embedded. A museum (daily 9–5; free) at the site tells the story of the construction of the Death Railway and Hellfire Pass in a series of vivid photographs and contemporary documents.

Below *The graves of Allied prisoners of war, most of whom died while working on the "Death Railway"*

MUANG SING HISTORICAL PARK

The Kanchanaburi area was the westernmost outpost of the Angkor-based Khmer empire in the 13th to 14th centuries, and one of the strongest citadels of King Jayavoraman VII was Muang Sing—"Lion City." Much of it was built in the style of the Khmer Bayon temple complex at Angkor. Siam's first Chakri king, Rama I (1782–1809), discovered the existence of the old city, and his archeologists uncovered traces of a large and productive community within its earth and brick ramparts. At the center of the site is a tall Khmer *prang*, or tower, in very good condition. A nearby museum has copies of a fine series of Bodhisattva images. Bodhisattva was a four-armed god worshiped by the Khmer—a very benign being judging by the blissful smiles on the handsome faces of the images.

✚ 314 C9　✉ On highway 3085, 12 miles (20km) west of Kanchanaburi　🕓 Daily 8–4　🎫 B30

LOP BURI

Lop Buri's resident tribe of monkeys have made this ancient city world famous, but the city has plenty of history and interesting sites to offer visitors. The origins of Lop Buri are lost in the mists of prehistory, but by the sixth century it was an important bulwark of the expanding Dvaravati empire. The Khmer took it over in the 10th century and held it until the powerful kingdom of Sukhothai overran it. Ayutthaya succeeded Sukhothai as masters of Lop Buri, and King Narai made it his second capital. Narai welcomed Westerners to his court, and Lop Buri today is an eclectic mixture of Khmer and Ayutthaya ruins and colonial-style buildings.

THE DVARAVATI AND KHMER ERAS

Lop Buri's most famous landmark, the Phra Prang Sam Yot, probably dates from Dvaravati times and was later enlarged by the Khmers, who built its three distinctive *prangs*, or towers, representing the Hindu trinity of Brahma, Vishnu and Siva. The oldest Khmer tower, Prang Khaek, adjoining the market on Thanon Vichayen, is also a Hindu shrine of great beauty. Khmer towers also dot the extensive grounds of Wat Phra Si Maha That.

THE FRENCH INFLUENCE

King Narai constructed an impressive palace ensemble in a mixture of Siamese and French styles. He clearly intended the Phra Narai Ratchaniwat Palace (built 1665–77) to impress visiting Western dignitaries, including the French nobleman Chevalier de Chaumont, King Louis XVI's ambassador to Siam. Three handsome mansions were built, in one of which, the Suttha Sawan Pavilion, King Narai died in 1688. One of his successors, the fourth Chakri monarch, King Rama IV, built his own residence here, the Phiman Mongkut Pavilion. The restored palace now houses government offices and the Somdet Phra Narai National Museum.

MONKEY BUSINESS

A famous tribe of monkeys has made its home in the temple compound at Wat Phra Gan. You'll see them perched on buildings around the city and ganging up on fruit-stall owners to steal their favorite treats. The locals not only leave them alone but revere them as a source of good luck and income for the community; once a year a local hotelier treats the monkeys to a party at which they're fed delicacies at trestle tables set up in the temple grounds. They're a favorite visitor sight, but don't go too near—these spoiled little monkeys bite.

INFORMATION

✚ 309 E8 ⓘ TAT Central Region Office 7, Thanon Rop Wat Phrathat, Amphoe Muang, Lop Buri 15000 ☎ 036 422 768/9 🕐 Daily 8.30–4.30 🚉 Lop Buri

Somdet Phra Narai National Museum
www.thailandmuseum.com
☎ 036 41 14 58 🕐 Wed–Sun 8.30–4
✋ B30

Below *The spoiled resident monkeys at Lop Buri are revered by the locals*

NAKHON PATHOM

Site of the world's largest stupa, Nakhon Pathom also claims to be Thailand's oldest city, with some of the country's most ancient Khmer ruins. The marvelous golden stupa, Phra Pathom Chedi (B40), 767ft (234m) high and taller even than Rangoon's celebrated Shwe Dagon, was built in 1853 over the remains of a pagoda constructed more than 2,000 years ago to enshrine Buddha relics.

Within the monastery compound surrounding the *chedi* (monument housing a buddhist relic) are four *viharn*, each facing a different cardinal point of the compass, and containing a variety of Buddha images. The statues on the *chedi* terrace include an unusual representation of Buddha seated in a chair. Nearby are the ruins of the temple Wat Phra Man, believed to have been built in the same period as the *chedi*. Just outside the town is a former royal palace ensemble, Sanam Chandra, built by King Rama VI in a variety of styles (including English Tudor) as a country retreat and with a shady park reminiscent of European country estates. Within Nakhon Pathom are European-style buildings that served as backdrops in *The Killing Fields* (1984).

➕ 314 D9 ℹ️ TAT Central Region Office Region 1, Thanon Saeng Chuto, Amphoe Muang, Kanchanaburi 71000 ☎ 034 511 200, 038 512 500 🕐 Mon–Sat 8.30–4.30

PATTAYA AND THE EAST COAST
▷ 208–209.

PHITSANULOK

Birthplace of Ayutthaya's 16th-century King Naresuan the Great, Phitsanulok served as the capital of Siam from 1448 to 1488. A shrine in the compound of the local Phittayakom school stands on the site of the palace where Naresuan was born. The city is today a busy industrial and commercial center, and a good base from which to tour this region of central Thailand. Pilgrims stream to the city throughout the year to pay homage at what is thought to be the country's finest Buddha image, the Phra Buddha Chinnarat, which sits in a *viharn* of Wat Phrasri Rattana Mahathat (daily 7.30am–6pm; B40). The official town history records that the Sukhothai-style gilded figure was cast in 1357, although some scholars place its true origins as far back as the 11th century.

An irresistible, nationally famous attraction in Phitsanulok is the eccentric, eclectic Sergeant Major Thawee Folk Museum (26/148 Thanon Wisutkasat; Tue–Sun 8.30–4.30; B50). The museum is a jumble of arts, crafts and curiosities.

➕ 309 D5 ℹ️ TAT Northern Office Region 3, Surasi Trade Centre, 209/7–8 Thanon Borommtrailokanat, Amphoe Muang, Phitsanulok 65000 ☎ 055 252 742/3 🕐 Daily 8.30–4.30 🚂 Phitsanulok

PRACHINBURI

The town of Prachinburi is a low-key destination, most notable for its unique hospital touting traditional herbal remedies. The Chaophraya Abhaibhubejhr Hospital shop (32/7 Moo 12, Thanon Prachin-Ahuson, tel: 037 213 610) is open from 8am to 8pm.

Ancient Khmer temple ruins dot the countryside of surrounding Prachinburi Province. Sa Morakot is located southeast of town in the village of Ban Sa Khoi. The Sa Morakot Archeological Site is a large complex of Buddhist monuments dating from the ninth to 13th centuries. The temples were constructed of laterite and brick, though only the bases remain. The reservoir here was constructed during the reign of Jayavarman VII. Its waters are considered sacred and used for coronation ceremonies. Si Mahosot Ancient Town dates back to the Dvaravati period. More than 100 monuments have been uncovered, though most are mere foundations and irrigation systems. Many of the Hindu relics, as well as Buddhist relics from Sa Morakot, are housed in the Prachinburi National Museum.

➕ 315 E9 ℹ️ TAT (182/88 Thanon Suwannason, Prachinburi ☎ 037 312

284 🚂 From Hualamphon train sation in Bangkok (B45 to B120), 2.5hrs 🚌 From Mo Chit bus station in Bangkok (B95 to B120)

SANGKHLA BURI AND PHRA CHEDI SAM ONG

Although this southernmost border crossing between Thailand and Myanmar (Burma) played a vital role in the history of relations between the two countries, most visitors now make the 124-mile (200km) journey to Phra Chedi Sam Ong (the Three Pagodas Pass) from Kanchanaburi (▷ 203–204) to see where the "Death Railway" of World War II passed. Thailand ripped up its part of the ill-renowned railway after the war, but a rusting section of it can be seen on the Burmese side of the border. On the Thai side, a short, symbolic section of the original track was laid out in front of a "Border Peace Temple." The temple was erected opposite the three pagodas by Japan and Thailand in 2002.

Seven years previously, a group of former Allied prisoners of war who had worked on the railway placed a "time capsule" at the three pagodas site. The capsule—to be opened on April 25 (Anzac Day), 2045—has a large bronze plaque relating the history of the "Death

Railway" and plotting its route. It passed just 151ft (46m) from the three pagodas, which in turn marked the route successive Burmese armies took to invade Siam in the 16th to 18th centuries. The pagodas, white *chedis* (monuments housing a buddhist relic) only 20ft (6m) high, are a disappointing sight, standing forlornly in a patch of ragged ground bordered by a market selling cheap Burmese and Chinese goods.

The nearest Thai town to the Three Pagodas Pass is Sangkhla Buri, 6 miles (10km) south, at the head of the vast Wachiralongkon Dam. The outskirts of the town, including a temple, were submerged to create the dam, and a popular outing for Thais is to rent a boat to view the underwater ruins. A new, pyramid-style temple was built high above the dam, and a fine view can be enjoyed from its terrace.

🚏 308 B7 ℹ️ TAT Central Region Office Region 1, Thanon Saeng Chuto, Amphoe Muang, Kanchanaburi 71000 ☎ 034 511 200, 038 512 500 🕐 Mon–Sat 8.30–4.30

SAWANKHALOK

A dusty little town with just one main street, Sawankhalok was once the center of a thriving ceramics industry whose products were prized by palaces and wealthy households far beyond the boundaries of ancient Siam.

The special qualities of the soil in the alluvial plain surrounding Sawankhalok were recognized as long as 1,200 years ago. The rulers of nearby Sukhothai and Si Satchanalai prized the locally produced celadon and other ceramics particularly highly and made a royal tradition of presenting beautiful tableware and decorative pieces to the imperial courts of China, from where it found its way to Japan. Many fine examples are on display at the Sawankhalok Museum, about 0.6 miles (1km) outside the town on the Phitsanulok road. You can purchase a combined ticket for Sukhothai Historical Park, Ramkhamhaeng Museum, Si Satchanalai Historical Park and

Sawankhalok kilns: adult B150, child (under 14) B100.

Celadon Kiln Site Study and Conservation Center is a huge area of centuries-old kilns being excavated at the village of Ban Ko Noi, 2.4 miles (4km) north of Si Satchanalai (daily 9–12, 1–4.30; adult B20, child (under 14) B10). More than 500 kilns have so far been discovered, although only two are open to the public. A small museum displays some of the wares recovered during the excavations, including celadon pieces in remarkably good condition.

🚏 308 D5 ℹ️ TAT Northern Office Region 3, Surasi Trade Centre, 209/7–8 Thanon Boromtrailokanat, Amphoe Muang, Phitsanulok 65000 ☎ 055 252 742/3 🕐 Mon–Sat 8.30–4.30

SI RACHA

Sitting between the Provincial capital of Chonburi and Pattaya, the once-quiet fishing port of Si Racha is growing. Korean and Japanese migrant workers have helped to spur development, by bringing large shopping centers, upscale housing,

and plenty of great restaurants. The old wooden piers and colorful fishing fleet, however, retain much of their charm. What the town does lack are lots of tourists—for the moment. Si Racha's biggest claim to fame is the internationally famous Siracha Chili Sauce, which is great paired with the local seafood. Animal lovers will enjoy the modern Khao Kheow Open Zoo, or the Si Racha Tiger Zoo, with more than 200 large cats. Not far off the coast, Ko Si Chang offers a quiet island escape with a cliff-side Chinese Temple, though Ko Samet is also available for those who prefer their exotic islands with a few more entertainment options.

🚏 314 E10 🚌 B40 for 3 hours 🚆 Departs from Bangkok's Hua Lamphong Station at 6:55am. Departs from Si Racha at 2:50pm. From Mo Chit and Ekamai stations in Bangkok between 5am and 9pm 🚢 Depart hourly from Si Racha to Ko Si Chang between 7am and 8pm for B60. From Ko Si Chang, boats depart hourly between 6am and 6pm

SI SATCHANALAI

▷ 210–211.

Opposite *Golden Buddha at Phra Pathom Chedi, Nakhon Pathom*
Above *The Sawankhalok Museum contains many beautiful ceramics*

INFORMATION

www.whitesandsthailand.com
www.pattayacity.com/pattaya
✚ 314 E10 ℹ TAT Central Office,
609 Moo 10, Pra Tumnak, Tambon Nong
Preu, Pattaya City ☎ 038 42 76 67
🕐 Mon–Fri 8.30–4.30

Above Bang Bao traditional fishing
village in Ko Chang

INTRODUCTION

First-time visitors to Pattaya either hate the resort or love it. It's Thailand's premier playground, unashamedly brash, with an urban beachside setting, but also within a short distance of a marine national park and two quiet islands, which are perfect for diving and snorkeling.

Fifty years ago, Pattaya was a quiet fishing village, embraced by long expanses of deserted beaches. Thailand's early boom years attracted the country's newly rich, who built holiday homes on its pristine coast. Then came the Vietnam War and the first aircraft carrying American servicemen for "rest and recreation." The sex industry flourished and has continued to be a hallmark of the city. Now there's much more recreation than rest, with entire streets of restaurants and go-go bars doing brisk trade, and maintaining the town's raunchy reputation as a tourist playground. It is possible, however, to enjoy a few days in Pattaya and have little or no contact with the seedier side of the town, provided certain areas are avoided. And although much of the town and its surroundings are decidedly downmarket, there is a smart, ritzy side to Pattaya, which boasts luxury hotels, exclusive golf courses and a pony polo club.

WHAT TO SEE
THE BEACHFRONT

Likewise, Pattaya has become a popular family holiday destination, with plenty of water sports and beachfront diversions. The urban beach where the city spills right out onto the sand means that the beach is easily accessible and some of the most spectacular views of the bay are to be had from the top of the city's high-rise malls and hotels. There are also major shopping centers, such as the Central Festival, cinemas and bountiful restaurants to keep the family busy and entertained without ever going near the beach.

KO SAMET

Ko Samet is named after the samet or cajeput tree, which flourishes here and is prized for its essential oil and lumber used in boat building. This small island off the Rayong coast is a marine national park (B200 entry fee), and is a paradise for scuba-divers and snorkelers. Although, there is so much development here that its hard to believe that conservation is a major focus. Nonetheless, most of the 14 beaches are sandy and less crowded than on the mainland. The more isolated beaches are found on the north and west coasts of Ao Hin

Those wanting to enjoy some nightlife should head to Hat Sai Kaew (Diamond Beach) on the island's northeastern side. The beaches are good here, too, with brilliant white sand, and there are excellent opportunities around the island for diving and snorkeling. The best diving, however, is at Hin Pholeung, where manta rays and whale sharks can be seen swimming in the vicinity of two tall underwater ledges. Ferries run to the island from the small town of Ban Phe, 10 miles (16km) east of Ranong.

✚ 315 F11

KO CHANG

Thailand's second-largest island (after Phuket) is also a marine park, offering some of the region's best diving. Over the last decade massive tourist growth has placed pressure on the island's infrastructure, and while much of Ko Chang's natural beauty remains, it is not the quiet and pristine getaway it used to be. Half a dozen waterfalls are within hiking distance of the coast. The best include Nam Tok Thuan Mayon, Nam Tok Khlong Plu and Nam Tok Khiri Phet.

Most of the best beaches are on the west side of the island, which—like Ko Samet—has its Hat Sai Kaew (Diamond Beach), a 3-mile (5km) stretch of glistening white sand fringed with beautiful palms and backed by thickly forested hills. Currents here are strong—obey warnings posted at beaches—and can be dangerous. Elephant trekking opportunities are available and popular on the island.

ELEPHANT CAMP

Ban Kwan Chang Elephant Camp is one of the best, including feeding and bathing the elephant. A 1-hour "ride" costs B900. Other popular island activities are kayaking, mountain biking and bird watching. Ferries run to the island from Laem Ngop, near Trat.

✚ 315 G11

TIP

➤➤ City transportation is by *songthaew*. Just flag one down and name your destination–a city journey usually costs B18–B40.

Below *Spirit house on the beach at Ko Samet*

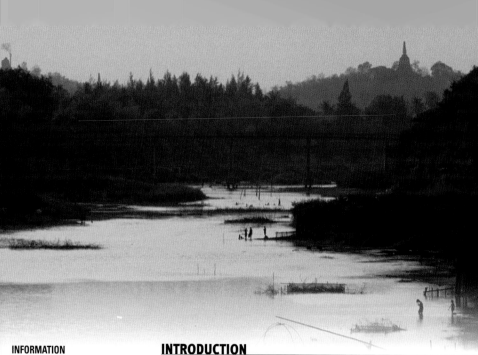

INFORMATION

✚ 307 C4 🕐 Daily 8–4 💵 B100–B220, vehicle B50 ℹ Historical Park Information Centre ☎ 055 679 211

TIPS

❯❯ Two other temple ruins that are worth visiting are Wat Khao Phanom Phloeng (next to Wat Khao Suwan Khiri) and Wat Nang Phaya (at the park entrance), where well-preserved bas-reliefs of flowers on the stone balustrades are reminders of how artistry and aesthetic imagination flourished in the Sukhothai period.

❯❯ Although it's a World Heritage Site, the Si Satchanalai Historical Park is difficult to find and badly signposted. The best way to visit is to book an organized tour at your hotel in Sukhothai or rent a car and driver. The more adventurous take a bus from Sukhothai to Si Satchanalai and persuade a *songthaew* driver there to take them to the historical park (about B100).

Above *The peaceful Yom River at dusk*

INTRODUCTION

Si Satchanalai was traditionally ruled by the crown prince of Sukhothai, 50 miles (80km) to the north and several days' journey by elephant in those times. The greatest of the Sukhothai monarchs, King Ramkhamhaeng, is believed to have built one of the most beautiful of the 134 temples and monuments that make up the Si Satchanalai Historical Park. The park is now (like Sukhothai) a UNESCO World Heritage Site.

Si Satchanalai found itself at the center of a historic confrontation in the mid-14th century, when Siam split into northern and southern realms, placing Sukhothai and its satellite city in a kind of buffer zone. In the century-long struggle that followed, several monarchs tried unsuccessfully to bolster the historic eminence of Sukhothai and Si Satchanalai. In 1438, Sukhothai was annexed by the mightier, southern Siam kingdom of Ayutthaya, and Si Satchanalai faced no choice but to be also absorbed. Its fate was sealed by the renown of its ceramics: they were highly prized by the rulers of Ayutthaya, who grew rich on exporting the ware as far as Japan and the Philippines. The rise of Ayutthaya, and subsequently Bangkok, eclipsed both Sukhothai and Si Satchanalai, which faded over the centuries into provincial towns with little political or cultural influence.

WHAT TO SEE
CITY RUINS

An undistinguished, unassuming town, Si Satchanalai is famous for the nearby ruins of a 700-year-old city that was rivaled in northern Siam only by mighty Sukhothai. The once magnificent city of Si Satchanalai is now a disorderly collection of mostly ruined brick and laterite reminders of its past glory. The riverside site ranges over 2.7sq miles (7sq km), the heart of the original city surrounded by a 39ft-wide (12m) moat. It's a placid, almost neglected place, lacking the infrastructure of the Sukhothai Historical Park and consequently not overrun by overseas tourists.

WAT KHAO SUWAN KHIRI

For an overview of the site, make your way to the northwestern corner and climb the small hill to this 14th-century temple, believed to have been built by Sukhothai's King Ramkhamhaeng. From the tiered base of its huge *chedi* (monument housing a Buddhist relic) you have a fine view of the park and surrounding countryside.

WAT CHANG LOM

Immediately to the south of Wat Khao Suwan Khiri is the park's most impressive temple complex, Wat Chang Lom, with another large, bell-shaped *chedi* supported by 39 elephants *(chang)* and with a staircase lined by Buddha figures. Four of the elephants face the cardinal points of the compass, an important architectural feature in the Sukhothai period.

WAT CHEDI JET THAEW

The most beautiful ensemble, however, is Wat Chedi Jet Thaew, just south of Wat Chang Lom. It's named after the seven *(jet) chedis* in various states of repair that stand in well-ordered rows before the ruins of the *viharn* where centuries ago monks gathered to pray. The *chedis* contain the ashes of members of Si Satchanalai's ruling families.

CHALIANG

About 0.6 miles (1km) to the south is the ancient city of Chaliang. The two temple sites here, Wat Chao Chan and Wat Phra Si Rattana Mahathat, were most probably built in the 12th and 15th centuries, respectively. The laterite temple site of Wat Phra Si Ratana displays a large sitting Sukhothai Buddha, and a smaller standing statue. Less than a 0.6 miles (1km) to the west, Wat Chao Chan contains a Khmer tower built during the reign of King Jayavarman VII (1181–1217) of Angkor. The two temples receive relatively few visitors.

Below *The impressive ruins of Wat Chang Lom with its* chedi *supported by elephants*

TIPS

›› In front of Wat Chang Lom, renowned for its carved elephants, is a real elephant, which the owner rents out for rides (B100 for 15 mins) around the historical park. A trolley train also tours the park (B20).

›› Every year, on April 7–8, newly ordained monks are carried through the village of Ban Hat Sieo, near Si Satchanalai, on elephant back. It's a vibrant procession of up to 30 elephants, decorated with traditional trappings and textiles woven in the village.

›› Si Satchanalai Historical Park is in one of central Thailand's most remote regions, a rugged, mountainous stretch of virgin forest and tropical jungle. Waterfalls, caves and hot springs are all accessible from the park's headquarters, where timber-built chalets can be rented.

INFORMATION

www.wayfarersthailand.com/sukothai.htm

✚ 308 D5 ℹ Historical Park Information Office ☎ 055 69 75 27, 055 69 73 10 🕓 Daily 8.30–4.30

TIPS

➤➤ There are a few refreshment stands en route in the park, but it's best to carry a bottle or two of water, particularly in the hot season (February–end June).

➤➤ The park is vast (27sq miles/70sq km), so rent a bike (B30), either at the entrance or from one of the shops opposite.

Above *The remains of Wat Mahathat Sukhothai*

INTRODUCTION

The mystical sound of the name alone and its epiphanic meaning—"Dawn of Happiness"—sum up the irresistible attraction of this great historic city, now a World Heritage Site. Stand today amid the ruined temples and *chedis* of the Sukhothai Historical Park and it's hard to imagine that eight centuries ago this small patch of Siam ruled an empire from Laos in the north to the Malay peninsula in the south.

In the 13th century Sukhothai became the heart of a widespread uprising against rule by the Khmer, who had penetrated much of the region from their base in Angkor, in today's Cambodia. Sukhothai was the scene of the decisive victory over the Khmer, when a Siamese prince, Phor Khun Bang Klang Thao, defeated the city's Khmer commander in an elephant duel. The victorious prince, renamed Sri Indraditya, founded a dynasty that ruled the Sukhothai empire for nearly 150 years.

Sukhothai reached the height of its power and influence under the rule of the great Ramkhamhaeng, who was only 19 when he ascended the throne in 1279. During the 20 years of his rule, Sukhothai flourished as no other Southeast Asian city. Inscriptions found in its ruins tell us that the city was a citadel of freedom and tolerance. Free trade was allowed, taxes were minimal, slavery prohibited—King Ramkhamhaeng even installed a bell that any citizen with a grievance could ring and summon the monarch to sit in judgment. It couldn't last—Sukhothai declined with the rise in power of Ayutthaya in the south and the Lanna kingdom in the north. It was finally annexed by Ayutthaya in 1438, and faded rapidly in importance.

WHAT TO SEE
GETTING TO THE SIGHTS

The Sukhothai Historical Park is 7.2 miles (12km) from "new" Sukhothai, a busy but uninteresting market town on the Yom River. There are guesthouses and simple restaurants near the park, but for an extra few hundred baht, greater comfort and convenience can be found in new Sukhothai. Red *songthaew* pickup taxis run between the new city and the park (B20). The entrance fee includes a map. A new information center opposite the park houses fine reproductions of the treasures that were excavated at Sukhothai and taken to the National Museum in Bangkok.

SUKHOTHAI HISTORICAL PARK AND RAMKHAMHAENG MUSEUM

King Ramkhamhaeng introduced Theravada Buddhism to the region he ruled. The original Khmer and Hindu influences persisted, however, and their imagery is found at many of the 21 sites that make up the historical park. Nearly 200 temples, *chedis* (monuments housing a Buddhist relic) and monuments are scattered over the verdant area of lawns, trees and ponds—fortunately, only about 10 are really worth study. They are all well marked on the map provided at the entrance booth. Most of the finds from the Sukhothai ruins are in the National Museum in Bangkok, but enough were kept in Sukhothai to make a visit to the Ramkhamhaeng Museum interesting. It contains many examples of temple art from his era, including some fine Buddha statues. The museum is to the left of the Historical Park.

🕐 Park: daily 6–6; museum: daily 9–4 ✋ Park: B100; museum: B150; combined ticket for Sukhothai Historical Park, Ramkhamhaeng Museum, Si Satchanalai Historical Park and Sawankhalok kilns: B350

WAT MAHATHAT

Located in the heart of the wall-enclosed center of the old city, this temple compound is the largest and most interesting Sukhothai site. Although probably built at the start of the Sukhothai era, it was enlarged and renovated by King Ramkhamhaeng's son, Loe Thai, whose religious devotion was blamed for the temporal decline of the Sukhothai empire. Although Loe Thai is accused of neglecting matters of state, his artistic and religious energies bequeathed a magnificent ensemble to Sukhothai. He built the Sri Lankan-style lotus-bud *chedi* that still stands as a symbol of Sukhothai. The *chedi* was constructed to contain two Buddha relics brought back from Sri Lanka by a Sukhothai monk. The *chedi* stands at the head of a collection of 200 smaller ones, ranked like assembled soldiers and each containing the ashes of leading monks and citizens of ancient Sukhothai.

WAT SRA SRI

Here you'll find the famous "walking Buddha," an original Sukhothai creation and—like the lotus-bud *chedi* of Wat Mahathat—a timeless symbol of the city at the height of its creativity and power. The Buddha strides elegantly past the temple's main *chedi*, also in the Sri Lankan style. The temple compound takes up two islands surrounded by a lake swimming with lotuses.

WAT SRI CHUM

An enormous Buddha statue, 49ft (15m) high and 36ft (11m) wide, dominates the superb temple compound of Wat Sri Chum, one of the 116 that have been found outside the old city walls. The statue is in remarkably good condition, as is a series of frescoes of about the same age that decorates a passageway between the *wat's* outer walls.

WAT SRI SAWAI

Evidence that the Sukhothai rulers absorbed Hindu and Khmer influences into the architecture of their capital is to be found everywhere in this temple. Even its name derives from the original Thai word for the Hindu god Shiva. Two Khmer-style *chedis* still contain some original Buddha figures and Hindu deities, exemplifying the strange amalgam of cultural influences that left their mark on ancient Sukhothai.

WAT TRAPHANG NGOEN

Named "The Temple of the Silver Pond," this ruined ensemble also stands on an island in one of the many lakes and reservoirs that must have added greatly to the beauty of the ancient city. Its 13th-century *chedi* is capped with the typical Sukhothai lotus bud and has niches that once held Buddha images.

TIPS

➤➤ Avoid touring the Sukhothai Historical Park at midday, when the sun can be very hot. Early morning and late afternoon are the best times to visit, particularly for photographers.

➤➤ Although the historical park is 7.2 miles (12km) from present-day Sukhothai, consider staying in the new town, where the choice of accommodations is larger and eating possibilities more plentiful.

Below *Giant Buddha at Wat Sri Chum*

INFORMATION

www.dnp.go.th

🕂 308 B8 ℹ️ Thong Pha Phum National Park ✉️ P.O.Box 18, Amphur Thong Pha Phum, Kanchanaburi 71180 ☎️ 013 820 359, 081 382 0359 or 025 620 760 🕐 8.30–4.30 (visitor center 💰 B200

INTRODUCTION

Tall limestone peaks shrouded in mist and dense rain forest are fashioned by gushing waterfalls sustaining a diverse ecosystem. With few tourists, Thong Pha Phum National Park is an optimum place to spot wildlife, including wild elephants, tigers, sun and moon bears, muntjacs, civets, mountain goats, buffalos, toucans and hornbills.

The park is located 40 miles (65km) from the town of the same name. To reach the park from town, head to the Amphur Sangkhlaburi intersection on Highway 323 and turn left, heading for 25 miles (40km). At the park headquarters take the winding Route 3272, through jungles and mountainous countryside into the heart of the park.

Thong Pha Phum covers 432sq miles (1,120sq km) and is part of a vast corridor of interconnected national parks, including Kaeng Krachan, Khao Laem, Sai Yok, the Thung Yai Naresuan Wildlife Sanctuary, and adjacent forests of Myanmar. The park has three distinct seasons, with a summer from February to May, winter from November to January, and a rainy season in between. Accommodations within the park are available in the form of imaginative tree houses for B1,200 per night. Tents are also available for B150. A restaurant is located on site, though menu choices are modest.

WHAT TO SEE

WATERFALLS AND VIEWS

The crown jewel of the park is the 98ft-high (30m) Jok Ka Din Waterfall, 2.5 miles (4km) from the park entrance and 0.6 mile (1km) from the Burmese village of Ee Tong. Bi Teng Waterfall is active year-round, though difficult to reach. Ranger-led hikes pass through dense forests full of wildlife. Other falls include the three-tiered Khao Yai Waterfall, Dip Yai Waterfall, which is part of the same stream system, and Huay Muang Waterfall and cave.

Glorious views abound in Thong Pha Phum. The most scenic and accessible are the viewpoint on the summit of Khao Khad, near Jok Ka Din Waterfall and the highest elevation point in the park, Nern Sao Thong Mountain or "Flagstaff Mountain" (a permanent military base along the border, though visitors are

Above *Forested hills in Thong Pha Phum National Park*

permitted to visit and take in views of Thailand, Myanmar and the Andaman Sea), and the Km 15 Viewpoint—offering great views of Vajiralong Reservoir. The underlying karst mountains are pock-marked with caves. Khao Noi is a popular cave attraction located in Taling Daeng Village, with lovely stalactite and stalagmite formations and a Buddha image displayed inside.

THONG PHA PHUM TOWN
The quaint little town of Thong Pha Phum is nestled between misty mountains and lush rain forests. The town has only one main road, with a large market full of Burmese imports at the center. A lovely Mon-style hilltop temple overlooks the town, reached by taking the riverfront road and a walk across the small footbridge. Thong Pha Phum is a bit of a one-horse town so visitors should stock up on any unusual items before they arrive.

SURROUNDING LAKES, HOT SPRINGS AND WATERFALLS
Water is the main theme of the attractions within the park. Hin Dat Hot Springs (open daily 6am–10pm, B10) consists of two 108°F (40°C), spring-fed geothermal pools, a cold natural stream and a massage pavilion. The springs are just 9 miles (15km) south of Thong Pha Phum town, reachable via the Sangkhlaburi-Kanchanaburi bus on Highway 323.

Along the same road, Nam Tok Pha That (B200) is a lovely multi-tiered waterfall with few visitors and great swimming opportunities. Pha Tat waterfall is 18 miles (30km) south of town, or another 9 miles (15km) from Hin Dat.

VAJIRALONG RESERVOIR
About 7.5 miles (12km) west of Thong Pha Phum is the scenic Vajiralong Reservoir (formerly known as Khao Lam). The 45-mile (73km) long lake has several satisfactory accommodation options. Local hotels can arrange hiking and boat trips on the lake.

INFORMATION
Buses between Kanchanaburi and Sangkhlaburi stop in Thong Pha Phum. The air-conditioned bus journey can take from 1.5 to 2.5 hours. Buses run from Thong Pha Phum to Bangkok's Northern Terminal every 90 mins and cost B200.

TIP
❯❯ As with any national park in Thailand, be sure to bring mosquito repellent, sun screen, long pants (trousers), a hat and suitable walking shoes. Particularly during rainy season, leeches can be pests in the forests. Leeches are not poisonous and are not known to pass on blood parasites but secondary infections are possible if their bites are not kept clean.

Below The precarious bridge at Thong Pha Phum National Park

THE SLOW BOAT TO AYUTTHAYA

Thailand's former capital and now a World Heritage Site, Ayutthaya is less than one hour's drive from Bangkok on motorway number 1, but travelers with the time (and money) can make the journey the way the Siamese did centuries ago, by riverboat.

THE CRUISE

Distance: 87 miles (140km)
Allow: 3 days
Start/end at: Bangkok

Day trips are offered by a number of Bangkok tour operators, but the most unforgettable journey to and from Ayutthaya is a trip on one of the two luxuriously converted rice barges of Manohra Cruises (www.manohracruises.com). These 100-year-old barges are built of solid teak—from the fat, squat hull to the polished decks and paneling in mahogany and padua wood. The barges are the last word in luxury. Admission to attractions en route is included in the barge fare (approx. US$2,000 (B66,000) per night).

DAY ONE

★ The voyage begins at the Manohra Cruises Chao Phraya river pier, in front of the riverside Marriott Resort and Spa. A steward welcomes you aboard with a cool fruit cocktail and then shows you to your stateroom, a snug but roomy, and luxuriously appointed, teak-walled and floored cabin with private bathroom and, of course, superb river view.

❶ En route to Ayutthaya the barge glides past some of Bangkok's leading riverside sights, including the Grand Palace ensemble (▷ 87–90) and Wat Arun (the Temple of Dawn; ▷ 84). A stop is also made at the Royal Barges Museum (▷ 80), where the King's own barge is kept.

The barge cruises its way gently past lines of rice barges battling upriver at walking pace behind tiny tugs. Longtail skiffs and outboard dinghies skip from side to side of the busy river. Lunch is served on the open-sided dining deck as the barge heads into the hinterland of Nonthaburi province, past simple timber-built riverside homesteads and farms, each with their own pier and moored flat-bottomed boat.

❷ At the first bend in the river, the barge passes the island of Kret, which is home to a community of ethnic Mon people famous for their pottery kilns.

At 4pm, traditional tea is served on the rear deck: dainty sandwiches, scones and patisserie, accompanied by a choice of teas, some of them from Thai estates.

After tea, a stop is made at Wat Pathum Khon Ka so you can feed the fish there. This is a traditional merit-making act that is meant to assure travelers of a trouble-free journey, not just to Ayutthaya but throughout life.

❸ The barge ties up for the night a few miles north at Wat Bang Na. This 18th-century temple is famous for its mummified body of an abbot who died in 1988. His perfectly preserved body rests in a glass coffin.

Later, sundowner cocktails are served on the barge, and dinner is served against the beautiful backdrop of the illuminated temple.

DAY TWO
The barge moors so that passengers can make a pre-breakfast visit to Wat Bang Na.

❹ At the temple, passengers fill the eating bowls of the monks as they set out on their alms rounds—another merit-making act that helps Thais on their way to nirvana.

As the barge heads nearer Ayutthaya, an Italian lunch is served as a reminder, perhaps, that the Siamese capital was open to all aspects of Western culture, from food to architecture.

❺ The first Ayutthaya stop is Wat Phanan Choeng (▷ 199), a 14th-century temple that stood here before the capital was founded. The Buddha in the temple's *viharn* is one of Thailand's oldest.

An elegant stretch limousine picks passengers up for the drive into Ayutthaya and a tour of its ancient monuments and temples. Part of the tour can be made riding on an elephant, if you choose. After the tour, the limousine carries passengers back to the barge,

which is now moored at another temple, Wat Niwet Thamaprawat.

❻ Wat Niwet Thamaprawat is part of the Bang-Pa-In palace ensemble, 11 miles (18km) south of Ayutthaya. The temple was built by King Rama V in European neo-Gothic style, complete with stained-glass windows.

Dinner, served on the barge, features a menu of traditional "royal Ayutthaya" dishes.

DAY THREE
After a full English breakfast, passengers tour Bang-Pa-In.

❼ Bang-Pa-In is an eclectic ensemble of imposing buildings, built on a river island as a summer retreat by Ayutthaya's King Prasat Thong (ruled 1630–55). When the Burmese sacked Ayutthaya in the late 18th century, Bang-Pa-In fell into neglect and disuse, but King Rama IV restored much of it 80 years later. His successors Rama V and Rama VI carried on his work, adding a collection of royal mansions and pavilions unmatched in Thailand.

The barge now heads back to Bangkok, riding on the swift downriver current, calling at

the Royal Folk Arts and Crafts Centre at Bang Sai, an hour or so downstream (▷ 220).

❽ The center was established as a royal project to encourage farmers and their families to take up ancient crafts, such as basketry, silk weaving and dyeing, wood carving and carpentry. Products can be bought at the center's shop.

Lunch is served as the barge winds through the rice paddies north of Bangkok, and tea is taken as the skyscrapers of the capital come into view. At 6.30pm, the barge ties up at the Manohra Cruises Chao Phraya river pier.

WHEN TO GO
The sunsets on the Chao Phraya river are one of the main attractions of the cruise, and the best time of year to enjoy them is the dry season, from December to the end of February.

TOURIST INFORMATION
AYUTTHAYA TOURIST OFFICE
✉ TAT Central Region 6, 108/22 Moo 4, Amphoe Phra Nakhon Si, Ayutthaya
☎ 035 246 076/7 ⏰ Daily 8.30–4.30

Opposite and above Traveling and dining in style on a Manohra rice barge

WALK

KANCHANABURI WALKING TOUR

This walking tour takes you to the various fascinating and thought-provoking WWII sites around Kanchanaburi, mixed with some local culture at the market. The route follows the riverfront for much of the way and features several museums and some excellent places to stop for drinks or meals.

THE WALK
Distance: 2 miles (3km)
Allow: 1hr plus time for visits
Start/End at: TAT Kanchanaburi

The Tourism Authority of Thailand office (tel 034 511 200, open 8.30–4.30) is on the southeast side of town on Saeng Chuto Street (across from the bus station) and provides free city and provincial maps. They can also answer any questions about the sights to be visited on the walk.

★ From the local Tourism Authority of Thailand office, head southwest on Wisuttharangsi Street for about 440 yards (400m), toward the riverfront and on to the JEATH (Japan, England, America/Australia, Thailand, and Holland) War Museum.

❶ The JEATH War Museum is run by monks at Wat Chaichumphon and displays the horror and hardship that the Allied prisoners endured under

Japanese occupation. The museum is housed inside bamboo huts, much like the ones that the prisoners were forced to live in.

Walk north on Pak Phraek Street for 330 yards (300m) to the City Gate. Just on the right is Lak Meuang (the city pillar) on the street by the same name, in front of City Hall.

❷ Lak Meuang is a sort of spiritual foundation for Kanchanaburi, built to placate local spirits. Such pillars were constructed in historical cities throughout the country. Nearby is a renovated section of the old city wall, with three original cannons.

Back on Pak Phraek Street, head north along the riverfront for about 220 yards (200m) to reach the central market on the right. The market is a great place to pick up local souvenirs, cheap drinks, fresh fruit and snacks. Head north for

another 330 yards (300m) to pass Wat Neua, a Chinese temple, named Wat Thavorn Wararam on the left, and then a Chinese cemetery on the right. The Allied War Cemetery is straight ahead on Chaokunen Street.

❸ Of the 100,000 people who died here under the Japanese, 6,982 are thought to be buried in the Dok Rak Kanchanaburi War Cemetery (Allied War Cemetery). Nearly half of them were British, and the remainder mainly from the Netherlands and Australia. More than 90,000 others who died (buried elsewhere) were mostly Asian prisoners from Thailand and surrounding countries. For every 0.6 miles (1km) of track laid in the "Death Railway," 38 men died—most of them under the age of 25. An annual memorial service is held both here and at "Hellfire Pass" (▷ 204) on Anzac Day (April 25).

④ Directly across the street from the Allied War Cemetery is the Thailand-Burma Railway Center, now known as the Death Railway Museum. The museum's nine galleries portray the history of the "Death Railway" and the horrific treatment of the Allied and Asian prisoners of war under the Japanese construction project. The collection is perhaps the most comprehensive portrayal of the period found at any of the local attractions, told through scale models, artifacts and an extensive selection of photos. A video produced by the survivors is particularly vivid and enlightening.

The food vendors at Prasopsuk market, across the street on Saeng Chuto, provides another great stopping point for snacks and refreshments. Heading northwest for 0.6 miles (1km), Mae Nam Khwae Street leads back toward the River Kwai, passing a long stretch of bars, restaurants and guesthouses and eventually leading to the Death Railway Bridge. After visiting the bridge, return here for lunch or an afternoon cocktail—a fitting way to end the walk. Check out The Floating Restaurant or Keeree Tara. Both are beautiful riverside restaurants serving fresh fish, which is caught in the River Kwai each morning.

⑤ The War Museum is a strange and surprising collection of random relics from the war and ancient Thai artifacts. Housed in two buildings, the heavy reliance on rather camp wax dummies makes it hard to take the displays seriously.

Next door to the War Museum is the infamous Bridge over the River Kwai (Death Railway Bridge). The original wooden bridge was constructed in 1943, but was later replaced by a steel bridge. Only the outer spans on the present bridge

are original, as the center planks and braces were destroyed by an Allied bombing raid in 1945. The bridge is, of course, the focus of the whole town, and so draws tourists and touts in large numbers. Linger at the entrance too long and you'll find yourself swamped by street hawkers and con artists. The crowds of visitors reach their apex in late November and early December when there is a two-week reenactment of the Allied bombing raid on the Death Railway.

After your walk there are plenty of *songthaews* and taxis waiting to take you from the bridge back to your hotel.

WHERE TO EAT
THE FLOATING RESTAURANT
▷ 227.
✉ 415 Moo 1, Thanon River Kwai Kanchanaburi ☎ 034 625 053 ⏰ Daily 8.30am–11pm

KEEREE TARA RESTAURANT
▷ 227.

✉ 431/1 Mae Naam Kwai Road, Tarmakaam, Kanchanaburi ☎ 034 624 093 ⏰ Daily 11am-midnight

PLACES TO VISIT
THE DOK RAK KANCHANABURI WAR CEMETERY (ALLIED WAR CEMETERY)
✉ Thanon Saeng Chuto ⏰ Daily 8–6

JEATH WAR MUSEUM
✉ Thanon Wisuttharangsi C034 511 263 ⏰ Daily 8.30–6 ✋ B30

WAR MUSEUM
✉ Wat Chaichumphon, Ban Tai River Kwai Kanchanaburi ☎ 034 515 203 ⏰ Daily 8–6.30 ✋ B40

THAI-BURMA RAILWAY CENTER (DEATH RAILWAY MUSEUM)
www.tbronline.com
✉ 73 Thanon Chaokunen ☎ 034 510 067 ⏰ Daily 9–5 ✋ Adult B150, child B50

TOURIST INFORMATION
KANCHANABURI TOURIST OFFICE
✉ TAT Central Region Office Region 1,Thanon Saeng Chuto, Amphoe Muang Kanchanaburi 71000 ☎ 034 511 200/034 512 500 ⏰ Mon–Sat 8.30–4.30

Opposite *Exterior of the JEATH Museum, made to look like a POW hut*
Right *Walking across the the River Kwai*

WHAT TO DO

AYUTTHAYA

BAN BANG SADET
Women of this small village, located 7.5 miles (12km) north of Ayutthaya (Highway 309), make so-called "court dolls," encouraged by a project launched by Thailand's queen. The finely crafted clay figures depict villagers in poses of everyday life, as well as characters from folk plays. They are on sale at the village temple and make great souvenirs to take home.
⊠ A. Pa Mok, Ayutthaya ⊙ Daily 8–6

BAN RATSADON BUMRUNG
The residents of this small village, 22 miles (35km) northeast of Ayutthaya (routes 329 and 340), make fine handicrafts from the water hyacinths that grow in the area. The pliable roots of the plants are made into wickerwork trays, baskets, bags and even hats.
⊠ A. Don Chedi, Ayutthaya

BOAT TOURS
Several companies operate one-day boat trips from Bangkok to Ayutthaya. They include: Chao Phraya River Express Boat (☎ 022 225 330) and River Sun Cruises (☎ 022 669 125).

BUFFALO VILLAGE
A herd of more than 50 buffalo works the fields and rice paddies of this farm museum near the town of Suphan Buri, 25 miles (40km) west of Ayutthaya, demonstrating a way of rural life that is being eroded by the advance of mechanization. Rice-harvesting and threshing methods are demonstrated in the working environment of a traditional village.
⊠ Tambol Si Prachan, Amphoe Si Prachan, Suphan Buri ☎ 035 582 591 ⊙ Daily 9–6 ✋ Adult B300, child (under 14) B210

ROYAL FOLK ARTS AND CRAFTS CENTER
Local farmers and their families are trained at this royal project to learn new skills in handicrafts and folk art. On a 14-acre (5.5ha) site, they produce basketwork, hand-woven silk and cotton, wood carvings, traditional dolls, artificial flowers and furniture. The products are sold at the center's own shop.
⊠ Tambol Chiang Yai, Amphoe Bang Sai ☎ 035 366 252–3 ⊙ Daily 9–5 ✋ Adult B100, child B50

THA SADET BIRD SANCTUARY
Open-billed storks, painted storks, herons, cormorants, night herons and white ibises have made their home in this watery spot just 9 miles (15km) west of Suphan Buri. Bring your binoculars and visit at sunset to see them return to their nests.
⊠ Suphan Buri–Don Chedi road (Highway 322), Suphan Buri 🛈 TAT Central Region Office, Region 6, 108/22 Moo 4, Tambol Pratu Chai, Ayutthaya ☎ 035 246 076/7 ⊙ Daily 8–4 ✋ Free

WAT SA KAEO
This 300-year-old temple between Ayutthaya and Ang Thon (Highway 309) cares for needy and orphaned children and has a handicrafts center producing traditional hand-woven textiles, tablecloths and bed linen.
⊠ Ban Pa Mok, A. Ang Thong ⊙ Daily 7–6

BANG-PA-IN

BANG-PA-IN PALACE
Boat tours (▷ 216–217) run from Bangkok to Bang-Pa-In Palace, set upon islands along the banks of the Chao Phraya River. The magnificent summer palace of the kings of Thailand dates back to the 17th century. After falling into disuse it was revived by King Mongkut (Rama IV) in the 19th century. Visitors are

Opposite Topiary in the Summer Palace of King Chulalongkorn at Bang-Pa-In

allowed to view the outer palace compound, with its blend of Thai and European design styles.
☎ 035 261 044 🕐 Daily 8–3.30 💷 B50

CHANTHABURI
LAEM SINGH BEACH
Chanthaburi is only about 16 miles (25km) from the coast, and its most popular beach is in the Pak Nam district, near the mouth of the Chanthaburi River. Pine trees shade the beach from the afternoon sun, and there are many bars, restaurants and food stands along its length.

OASIS SEA WORLD
Dolphins are the attraction at this marine park on the coast south of Chanthaburi. The park is a conservation and breeding center, but the dolphins also present shows for the public, jumping through hoops and playing football (daily at 9, 11, 1.15, 3 and 5, weekends at 7am also). The park gardens are alive with butterflies, and the nearby Laem Sing River has picnic rafts.
✉ Tambol Pak Nam, Chanthaburi ☎ 039 399 015, 039 363 238–9 🕐 Mon–Fri 9–6, Sat–Sun 6.45–6 💷 B180, swim with dolphins B400 per hour

KANCHANABURI
THUNG YAI–HUAI KHA KHAENG WILDLIFE SANCTUARY
Described in the 1980s as Thailand's "largest remaining wilderness," this region, bordering Myanmar (Burma) northwest of Kanchanaburi, is a beautiful stretch of unspoiled forested mountains, inhabited by 28 endangered species of wildlife, including tigers. It is the only national park in Thailand that is also a World Heritage Site. It is easily accessible on Route 323 between Kanchanaburi and the Three Pagodas Pass, and a visit to the sanctuary is an unforgettable experience.
✉ Tambol Labam, Amphoe Lan Sak, Uthaithani 61160 ☎ 087 840 0316 🕐 Daily 8–6.30 💷 Adult B200, child B100

KO CHANG
BB DIVERS
www.bbdivers.com
BB Divers offers a range of PADI courses and dive trips to suit all levels. The beginners course (B3,500) takes you through all the necessary stages to get you exploring the bountiful marine life around Ko Chang.
✉ Bang Bao Pier 16/2, Ko Chang ☎ 039 558 040/086 129 2305 💷 1-day tour B2,000–2,400; dive master certification B25,000

CANOE AND KAYAK RENTAL
For a relaxing trip along the coastline and inner islands, try paddling a canoe or kayak. Operators can be found on most beaches, either as independent operations or in conjunction with a resort. "Triyaks" (three-person kayaks) at Kai Bae Hut Shop are well maintained and come with life jackets.
✉ Kai Bae Hut Shop, Kai Bae Beach, Ko Chang 🕐 Daily 9–6 💷 Triyaks B150 per hour; tandems B100 per hour per person

THIDA YACHTING CO LTD
www.sailing-in-thailand.com
Thida Yachting offers two skippered fiberglass boats, which depart from the Salak Phet seafood restaurant and resort in Salak Phet bay on the southeast corner of Ko Chang to sail you around the archipelago. The best time of year is November to March, when steady winds and a not-too-hot climate ensure a pleasant voyage. All food and accommodations are provided on board the boat.
✉ (Office) 3601/257-258 Soi Chalaem Nimit, New Road, Bangkhlo, Bangkok ☎ 022 919 124, 081 933 3691 💷 2-day trips available from BB9,000; 3-day trips from B13,300; charter B37,800 per day

LOP BURI
BAN THA–KRAYANG BRASS ARTISANS CLUB
The little village of Ban Tha–Krayang has been a center of brass casting for generations and the leading craftspeople have formed themselves into a "club." They turn out works of great skill and beauty, from replicas of famous sculptures to completely original creations.
✉ 168 Moo 1, Tambol Thalay Chup Son, Amphoe Muang, Lop Buri ☎ 036 421 469 🕐 Daily 8–6

BEE FARM
This country bee farm is a hive of information on Thailand's thriving apiary business. The owners readily show visitors how the hives work and how honey is extracted. The bees feed on nearby sunflowers and produce sweet nectar, which makes beautiful honey, which is sold in the farm's own shop and throughout the region.
✉ Soi 24 Sai Tri, Moo 9, Tambol Pattana Nikom, Lop Buri ☎ 036 639 292 🕐 Daily 8–6 💷 Free

BOAT MUSEUM
The timber-built sermon hall at this restored temple, 5.5 miles (9km) south of Lop Buri, has been converted into a fascinating museum of boats. Among the array of historic local craft is a single-seat barge typical of those used to navigate the canals in past centuries.
✉ Wat Yang Na Rangsi, Tambol Talung, Lop Buri ☎ 036 656 402 🕐 Daily 7–6 💷 Free

KHAO PHRA NGAM DIAMONDS
The Lop Buri area is famous for its sparkling gems, misleadingly called diamonds by the locals. They are in reality highly polished and skilfully cut quartz stones, most of them made at a production center in the Lop Buri district of Tambol Khao Phra Ngam.
✉ Tambol Khao Phra Ngam, Lop Buri 🕐 Mon–Sat 9–5

PA SAK CHONLASIT DAM
Catch a northbound local train (run daily) at Saraburi and ride the single-track line across the 3-mile (5km) wall of the Pa Sak Chonlasit Dam, central Thailand's largest. The railway line runs alongside the Pa Sak River and next to much of the 22-mile (35km) length of the dam, at

221

the northern end of which is a very beautiful waterfall, Namtok Wang Kan Loeng. A special train runs from Bangkok to the dam on weekends and public holidays.

✉ Lop Buri train station ☎ 036 411 022
✋ B200 return

PRACHA SUK SAN ARTS AND CRAFTS CENTRE

Ban Kluai is one of three villages near Lop Buri producing Thailand's coveted *mutmee* silk. You can watch it being woven at the village's arts and crafts center, which also has a sales outlet.

✉ 84 Moo 4, Tambol Ban Kluai, Amphoe Ban Mi ☎ 036 471 847 🕐 Daily 7–5

SUNFLOWER FIELDS

In November and December, thousands of visitors flock to the sunflower fields of Patthana Nikhom, 28 miles (45km) east of Lop Buri, when Thailand's largest area of sunflowers bursts into bloom.

✉ Tambol Patthana Nikom, Lop Buri
🕐 Nov, Dec

Opposite and below *The vibrant Don Wai market (near Wat Rai Khing)*

THAM KHANG KHAO

Every evening millions of bats turn the sky black above Wat Khao Wongkot, near Lop Buri, as they stream out of the bat cave to feed. The phenomenon lasts at an hour.

✉ Wat Khao Wongkot, Khao Sanam Chaeng, Amphoe Ban Mee, Lop Buri
🕐 Daily at around 6pm

NAKHON PATHOM
AIR ORCHIDS & LAB

Billed as Thailand's only "orchid supermarket," this vast emporium sells more than 40 species. It's an orchid-lover's paradise and a treat for any gardener—and there's no sales pressure. Visitors are given a free cup of coffee or tea and left to wander the paths and shelves that take up nearly half an acre.

✉ Thambon Salaya, Nakhon Pathom
☎ 089 494 9900 🕐 Daily 7–5 ✋ B50

DON WAI MARKET

The riverside community of Nakhon Chaisi plies its wares as it has for centuries in Nakhon Pathom's

most vibrant market. Goods of every description are on offer, and traditional food is served at innumerable stands. Get there early to see the market at its busiest.

✉ Tambol Nakhon Chaisi, Nakhon Pathom
🕐 Daily 6–6

NATURE TREK

Cruise the quiet waters of the Nakhon Chaisi River on a tastefully converted 50ft (15m) rice barge. Many interesting temples and wooden homes are on the riverbanks. The barge takes 50 passengers on day trips and 12 on overnight cruises.

✉ Lamphraya Market, Bang Len, Nakhon Pathom ☎ 025 561 225 🕐 Times vary
✋ B1,600–B2,100

SAMPHRAN GARDEN

Thailand's most spectacular garden grew from a small patch of land developed by a Bangkok mayor as a country retreat. His hobby was rose-growing, and roses are still the prime attraction of the extremely beautiful estate that grew from the mayor's relatively modest garden. A peaceful nature path through the 70-acre (28ha) estate winds past banks of damask roses, orchid galleries, ponds of lotus and water lilies, a banana grove and topiary and ixora gardens.

✉ Thanon Pet Kasem, Tambol Samphran, Nakhon Pathom ☎ 034 322 5893 🕐 Daily 8–5 ✋ Entry B40, show B450

SAMPHRAN RIVER CRUISES

Longtail boats leave at 9am every morning from the Samphran District Office pier for two- to three-hour cruises on the Nakhon Chaisi River and its canals. The itinerary includes stops at fruit orchards, orchid farms and a house where traditional sweets are made.

✉ Samphran District Office landing stage, Tambol Samphran, Nakhon Pathom
🕐 Daily 9am–11am ✋ B300

THAI HUMAN IMAGERY MUSEUM

Uncannily lifelike sculptures of Thai historical figures and ordinary people

are exhibited in this version of a Western waxworks. All the kings of the Chakri dynasty are brought to life in a truly artistic royal pantheon.
✉ Kilometer stone 31, Thanon Boromarajajonani, Nakhon Pathom ☎ 034 332 607, 034 332 109 🕐 Mon–Fri 9–5.30, Sat–Sun and public holidays 8.30–6 ✋ Adult B200, child (under 14) B100

PATTAYA

ALANGKARN CULTURAL SHOW
www.alangkarnthailand.com
Reputedly Thailand's biggest entertainment complex, the Alangkarn has an auditorium with a 230ft-long (70m) stage and seating for 2,000, where elaborate performances of traditional music and dance and historical tableaux are presented. The complex also includes cinema screens, a shopping mall and restaurant.
✉ 2/7 Moo 2, Jomtien, Pattaya ☎ 022 161 869 🕐 Thu–Tue 5pm–10pm ✋ B1,200–B1,400, including dinner

BLUES FACTORY
www.thebluesfactorypattaya.com
Hammond organ enthusiasts crowd the Blues Factory, which has Thailand's only fully functional instrument. The "Factory" also has some of Pattaya's best showbands, and a happy hour that starts at 9pm.
✉ Soi Lucky Star, Walking Street, Pattaya 🕐 Daily 8.30 till late ✋ Cocktails from B100

CENTRAL FESTIVAL
www.centralfestival.co.th
Pattaya's grandest shopping center is part of a large empire of luxury shopping malls, resorts and spa that are found in all the major tourist and commercial centers in Thailand. This high-rise monument to commerce can easily be seen from the beach and the main road, and is the best place to find international brands of electronics, clothing, cosmetics and just about anything else. There is a cinema on the top floor and plenty of entertainments to keep the whole family happy for a few hours.
✉ Pattaya 2 Road, Pattaya ☎ 026 351 111 🕐 10am–11pm

MINI-GOLF
This 18-hole mini-golf course is the only one of its kind in Pattaya, and with its ample natural shade it is quite pleasant to play your way through even on hot days. Good lighting means night games can also be enjoyed, concluding at the 19th Hole bar and restaurant, where there is a large-screen TV for major sporting events.
✉ The Mini-Golf Pub (The MG Pub), 191/1 Mu 10 Thappraya Road South, Pattaya ☎ 038 250 318 🕐 Daily 10am–11pm ✋ Adult B120, child B60

MINI SIAM
A rather unusual collection of more than 80 exquisitely crafted miniature replicas of famous structures around the world. The Bridge Over the River Kwai features in the collection, together with the Eiffel Tower, Statue of Liberty, Sydney Opera House and Bangkok's Grand palace.
✉ 387 Moo 6, Thanon Sukhumvit, Pattaya ☎ 038 717 333, 038 727 666 🕐 Daily 7am–10pm ✋ Adult B250, child (under 14) B120

NONG NOOCH TROPICAL BOTANICAL GARDEN
www.nongnoochtropicalgarden.com
The 600-acre (240ha) garden was originally destined to be an orchard. After an overseas trip the owner was inspired to make something more of it, and today the botanical garden is only one part of a range of displays on offer. There is also a zoo and Thai Cultural Center showcasing Thai drama, martial arts and sports. There are restaurants in the gardens.
✉ Kilometer stone 163, Thanon Sukhumvit (Highway 3), Pattaya ☎ 038 429 321 🕐 Daily 8–6 ✋ Adult B400, child B200

RIPLEY'S BELIEVE IT OR NOT MUSEUM
www.ripleysthailand.com
You can't miss Pattaya's Ripley's—the fuselage of a Vietnam-era DC3 projects from the building. The museum incorporates a cinema with "dynamic motion seating."
✉ Royal Garden Shopping Plaza, 218 Moo 10, Thanon Chai Hat, Pattaya ☎ 038 710 294/8 🕐 Daily 11–11 ✋ Adult B380, child (under 14) B280

ROYAL GARDEN SHOPPING PLAZA

This large shopping mall has several floors of shops, selling everything from beautiful Thai textiles and handicrafts to brand-name fashions and accessories. There are several restaurants and cafes for refreshments and, on the top floor, Pattaya's famous Ripley's Believe It or Not Museum (▷ 223).
✉ 219 Moo 10, Thanon Chai Hat, Pattaya ⏰ Daily 11–11

TIFFANY'S

Tiffany's is famous for presenting the first transvestite extravaganza in Asia. Copied now throughout Thailand, it has a stunning cast of transvestites and transgenders, gorgeously costumed and ingeniously choreographed. This is a fantastic show and it's all tastefully done—you can take the whole family.
✉ 464 Moo 9, Second Street, Pattaya ☎ 038 421 700 ⏰ Three shows nightly at 6, 7.30 and 9 💰 B500–B800

TOM'S GEMS

Tom's Gems has been in business since 1975 and has built up a sound reputation for providing quality, reliability and service. It also prides itself on fashioning jewelry to order from customers' own designs.
✉ 239/2 Moo 10, South Pattaya, Pattaya ☎ 038 422 811, 038 429 811 ⏰ Daily 11–11

UNDERWATER WORLD

A 330ft-long (100m) tunnel allows visitors to walk through schools of sharks and giant rays at this fascinating attraction.
✉ 22/22 Moo 11, Thanon Sukhumvit, Pattaya ☎ 038 756 879 ⏰ Daily 9–6 💰 Adult B400, child (under 14) B200

VIMARN TAI TALAY (THE YELLOW SUBMARINE)

The Yellow Submarine is a purpose-built, 48-seat, tourist submarine made in Belgium, and offers a novel way to comfortably view the spectacular underwater world of fish and coral. Passengers are taken by ferry to Lan island, where they are transferred to the submarine for a 45-minute dive, reaching depths of up to 98ft (30m).
✉ 311/7 Moo 10, South Pattaya ☎ 038 415 234 ⏰ Daily 10, 11.20, 1 💰 Adult B2,000, child B740

WORLD GEMS COLLECTION

www.worldgems.co.th
The latest jewelry technology is on display at this immense gems store, where visitors are invited to take part in instruction on the complicated business of gemology. Instruction personnel and sales staff are all highly qualified, and all gems are sold with guaranteed documentation.
✉ 98 Moo 6, Thanon Pattaya Nua, Pattaya ☎ 038 412 333 ⏰ Daily 8.30–6.30

PHITSANULOK
BUDDHA CASTING FACTORY

Buddha images of all sizes are made at this long-established factory, which still uses the age-old method of casting from wax molds. Most of the Buddhas are in bronze, and you can follow the entire manufacturing process.
✉ Thanon Wisutkasat (opposite the Folklore Museum), Phitsanulok ☎ 055 301 668 ⏰ Daily 8–5.30 💰 Free

THE GREEN ROUTE

Phitsanulok is the starting point of a "Green Route," which follows Highway 12 eastward for 80 miles (130km) through some of the region's most beautiful countryside. It ends at the junction of Highway 21, which leads to Phetchabun and Bangkok. There are plenty of rest stops en route, and Phetchabun has a wide range of hotels and guesthouses to choose from.
✉ Phitsanulok–Nam Nao National Park

LADY JANE'S PUB

Lady Jane is in reality a Thai woman from Chiang Mai who is one of Phitsanulok's most popular landladies, running an English-style pub with uncanny knowledge of how the British like their beer served.
✉ 2/1 Thanon Baromatrailokanart, Phitsanulok ☎ 055 225 280, 081 688 4275 ⏰ Daily 6pm–midnight

PHITSANULOK PLAZA

Phitsanulok Plaza is a pleasure palace of bars, pubs and clubs, offering a wide range of venues and entertainment.
🕐 Daily 9am–midnight

PHU HIN RONG KLA NATIONAL PARK

www.dnp.go.th
This remote national park, 56 miles (90km) east of Phitsanulok (Route 12), was a stronghold of Thailand's banned Communist Party from 1968 to 1972 and the scene of heavy fighting between die-hards and government forces. A 2-mile (3km) trail from the park headquarters leads to the old Communist headquarters (now a museum), a small cafe and a shop. The park is now a peaceful, wild region with a weird feature: a huge field of stones, broken by deep fissures.
✉ PO Box 3, A. Nakhon Thai, Phitsanulok ☎ 055 233 527

SI SATCHANALAI
LUMTAD ANCIENT SILVER

Superbly crafted gold and silver jewelry was made in Si Satchanalai and Sawankhalok, as well as ceramics, for the rulers of Sukhothai, and you can buy fine reproductions of ancient designs at this wonderful litttle workshop in the traditional village of Tachai.
✉ 13 Moo 3, Amphoe Si Satchanalai, Tachai ☎ 055 631 589, 055 679 068
🕐 Daily 8–5

SATHORN CRAFT CENTRE

Locally produced textiles and fine jewelry are sold at a rustic crafts center at the northern end of Si Satchanalai's one main road. There is a small museum at the center, which also includes a coffee shop.
✉ Uttaradit Road, Si Satchanalai
🕐 Daily 9–6

Opposite *The imaginative facade of Ripley's Believe it or Not Museum in Pattaya*
Right *Performance of the traditional Bamboo Dance*

FESTIVALS AND EVENTS

FEBRUARY
KING NARAI THE GREAT FESTIVAL

Lop Buri's principal festival honors the Ayutthaya king with sound-and-light shows, theater performances, music and stands selling everything from food to handicrafts.
🛈 TAT Central Region Office 7, Thanon Rop Wat Phrathat, Amphoe Muang, Lop Buri ☎ 036 422 768/9

MARCH
PATTAYA MUSIC FESTIVAL

Pattaya's international music festival takes over the town center for three days, with an emphasis on multicultural and folk music.
🛈 TAT Central Region Office 3, 609 Moo 10, Thanon/Phratamnak, Amphoe Banglamung, Chonburi 20260 ☎ 038 427 667 🕐 Mid-March

APRIL
LOY KRATONG FESTIVAL

Thailand's *Loy Kratong* celebrations are beautiful, and nowhere more impressive than in Sukhothai, where candlelit floats are launched on the lakes and ponds of the ancient city. Hot-air balloons are also sent off into the night sky above the ruins.

✉ Sukhothai Historical Park 🛈 Sukhothai Provincial Office ☎ 055 614 531, 055 611 619

NOVEMBER
MONKEY BANQUET

Monkeys are a major tourist draw in Lop Buri and are rewarded on the last Sunday of November with a "banquet" at the Wat Phra Gan shrine (▷ 205) and Phra Prang Sam Yot temple. Bananas and other popular fruit, sweetmeats of every kind and even bottles of soft drinks are laid out on decorated tables for the partying monkeys.
🛈 TAT Central Region Office 7, Thanon Rop Wat Phrathat, Amphoe Muang, Lop Buri ☎ 036 422 768/9

DECEMBER
RIVER KWAI FESTIVAL

The bridge over the River Kwai and the wooden remains of the original structure are the centerpiece of this week-long festival. The river is the setting for a spectacular sound-and-light show, and its banks are lined with food and craft stands, as well as music arenas.
🛈 TAT Central Region Office, Region 1, Thanon Saeng Chuto, Amphoe Muang, Kanchanaburi ☎ 034 511 200 🕐 Early Dec

Above *Relaxing at a popular open-air tourist restaurant in Sukhothai*

PRICES AND SYMBOLS
The prices given are the average for a two-course lunch (L) and a three-course dinner (D) for one person, without drinks and wine.

For a key to the symbols, ▷ 2.

AYUTTHAYA
CHAINAM
Riverside Chainam is popular with visitors for its full Western breakfasts, accompanied by fresh Thai coffee. The main menu is a mix of Western and Thai dishes, but traditional fried rice and noodles dominate the menu.
✉ Thanon U-Thong (opposite Chan Kasem Palace), Amphoe Muang, Ayutthaya ☎ 035 252 013 🕐 Daily 8am–9pm ✋ L B150, D B200

CHAO PHRAYA HUT
Named after and set beside the Chao Phraya River, this restaurant serves freshly prepared Thai food.

Specialties include delicious fried yellow curried crab and steamed mixed seafood cake. Although you'll need to travel a few miles (kilometers) outside Ayutthaya to reach it, the journey is definitely well worth your while when you see the setting and taste the food. There is no wine served here.
✉ 45/1 Moo 8 Baanmai, Pranakhonsri, Ayutthaya ☎ 035 398 200 🕐 Daily 10–10 ✋ L B150, D B250

IRASHAIMASE RESTAURANT
This is one of several restaurants in the U-Thong Inn Hotel and it serves a lovely selection of Japanese dishes. You can watch the sushi chef prepare your selection. The friendly staff are dressed in traditional Japanese style. There is no wine served here, but the California Maki is highly recommended.
✉ U-Thong Inn Hotel and Conference Center, 210 Rojana Road, Ayutthaya ☎ 035 212 531 🕐 Daily 11–2, 5–12 ✋ L B300, D B450

PASAK RIVER QUEEN
The big attraction of this waterside restaurant is its riverboat, the *Pasak River Queen*, which makes a nightly cruise (at 6.30pm) around Ayutthaya, with an on-deck à la carte dinner service. Dinner on land, on the restaurant's riverbank terrace, comes cheaper, but is probably not as fun. Fish is, of course, the thing to order; the *tom yam pla mae nam* (spicy fish soup) is delicious.
✉ 116 Moo 2, Borpong Nakornluang, Ayutthaya ☎ 035 724 520, 035 724 504, 035 724 519 🕐 Daily 10–10 ✋ L B160, D B200 (boarding fare B139)

SIAM
Freshwater lobster is the Siam's house specialty. It's expensive (B300) but well worth the outlay. Other traditional Thai dishes are cheaper, and the restaurant also serves a number of Vietnamese specialties. It's right opposite the entrance to Wat Mahathat, ideally located for refreshment after touring the temple compound.

✉ 11/3 Moo 1, Thanon Maharach, Tambol Pratuchai Pranakronsri, Ayutthaya ☎ 035 211 070 🕐 Daily 9–9 🖐 L B150, D B200

CHANTHABURI

CHOMLOM CHOMCHAN

On hot evenings, this open-air riverside restaurant is a delightful place to eat. The food is truly Thai, with an emphasis on fish dishes. The sea bass fishcakes *(tod man pla)* and the spicy seafood soup *(tom yam talay)* are especially recommended.
✉ Tambol Tarat, Chanthaburi ☎ 039 332 532 🕐 Daily 11–11 🖐 L B150, D B200

KAMPHAENG PHET

THREE J GUEST HOUSE

The friendly "Three J" has a rustic terrace restaurant serving Thai dishes of high quality at very reasonable prices. The *pad thai* are particularly good. The guesthouse is also a good base for touring the area, offering tourist information and a ticket service.
✉ 79 Thanon Rachavitee, Tambol Naimuang, Kamphaeng Phet ☎ 055 713 129, 055 720 384 🕐 Daily 8am–9pm 🖐 L B100, D B150

KANCHANABURI

FELIX RIVER KWAI RESORT

www.felixriverkwai.co.th
The finest accommodation in the area also hosts one of the best places to dine. The Palm Garden Brasserie serves Thai and international cuisine while The Good Earth serves Cantonese and dim sum. The Rantee Lounge is a pleasant place to relax after dinner, with a live band from the Philippines. There are other cafes and bars scattered around the complex with varying hours.
✉ 9/1 Moo 3, Thamakham, Amphoe Muang, Kanchanaburi ☎ 034 551 000 🕐 Daily 7am till late 🖐 L B200, D B350

FINE THANKS

Here you'll find a large restaurant and bar with plenty of seating inside and out. Fine Thanks is a popular place with Thais and foreigners alike, and the food caters to all tastes, with a mixture of Western and Thai

dishes. The atmosphere gets louder as the night goes on, especially if soccer is showing on one of the restaurant's big screens.
✉ 2/8 Songkwai Road Baannua, Kanchanaburi ☎ 034 621 152 🕐 Daily 6pm–2am 🖐 D B250

THE FLOATING RESTAURANT

This is the best of the pontoon restaurants that cluster around the River Kwai Bridge. In fact, it's one of the best dining-out venues of the entire region, with a great atmospherere and an outstanding 40-page menu encompassing the pick of traditional Thai fare. Six varieties of fish are on offer, besides a range of delicacies such as soft-shell crab and large farmed prawns. Draft Thai and Japanese beer is served.
✉ 415 Moo 1, Thanon River Kwai, Kanchanaburi ☎ 034 625 053 🕐 Daily 8.30am–11pm 🖐 L B150, D B250

KEEREE TARA RESTAURANT

Set beside the River Kwai, the Keeree Tara Restaurant is beautifully located, with the dining tables on terraces leading down to the river's edge, and is highly recommended. The specialties here include dried green curry and salted river fish, all delightfully presented. It's a bit more pricey than other restaurants around, but the quality of the food and location definitely justify the extra expense.
✉ 431/1 Mae Naam Kwai Road, Tarmakaam, Kanchanaburi ☎ 034 624 093 🕐 Daily 11am–midnight 🖐 L B300, D B450

KO SAMET

PANORAMA RESTAURANT

www.moobantalay.com
Enjoy a refreshing sea breeze as you dine at this restaurant, which is in a delightful open structure on the beach. There are two menus in the evening: the à la carte, and the set menu, which varies each night. There is plenty of superbly cooked fresh fish, as you would expect from a beautiful beachside restaurant.

✉ Moobantalay, Noina Bay, Ko Samet ☎ 081 838 8682, 038 644 251 🕐 Daily 7am–10pm 🖐 À la carte B400; set menu B900 for 2 people

SEA VIEW RESTAURANT

Dine here in the shade of casuarina trees, at the edge of a quiet beach. The seafood couldn't be fresher, and the prawns couldn't be larger. Western dishes predominate but there's also a Thai menu. Cocktails are served in an atmospheric bar beneath high wooden rafters.
✉ Ao Prao Resort, 60 Moo 4, Tambol Phe, Ko Samet ☎ 038 644 100–2 🕐 Daily 7am–10pm 🖐 L B150, D B250

LOP BURI

BUALUANG

Members of the Thai royal family eat at this charming garden restaurant when visiting Lop Buri so you'll be in good company here. You can choose from favourite "royal dishes," such as *yam kan ka-na goong krab* (spicy Chinese broccoli with shrimp) or deliciously succulent *phoo-nim tod kratiem prik thai* (soft crab fried with garlic and pepper).

Below *Seafood restaurant in Pattaya*

✉ 46/1 Thanon Paholyothin, Tambol Thasala, Amphoe Muang, Lop Buri ☎ 036 614 227–30, 036 422 669 🕓 Daily 11–11 ✋ L B200, D B250

LOP BURI STEAKHOUSE

Lop Buri Steakhouse serves excellent beef steaks. The salads are crisp and fresh, and there's an extensive Thai menu.
✉ Thanon Phahon Yothin, Amphoe Muang, Lop Buri ☎ 036 615 880 🕓 Daily 10–10 ✋ L B200, D B250

SANGSAWANG

This no-nonsense Thai restaurant, opposite the main entrance to Lop Buri zoo, serves local fare at very reasonable prices. Try the *yam mamuang* (spicy mango salad), followed by *pla samlee tod krab* (a grilled river fish).
✉ 11–16 Amphoe Muang, Lop Buri ☎ 036 411 632, 036 613 685 🕓 Daily 10–10 ✋ L B100, D B150

NAKHON PATHOM
INN-CHAN

The Rose Garden Resort's stylish Thai restaurant uses herbs gathered from the resort's kitchen garden. Enjoy traditional dishes such as *tom yam* soups and the sauces that accompany the fresh river fish. The cool, airy restaurant is an ideal place to end the day in the Rose Garden.
✉ The Rose Garden Resort, Thanon Pet Kasem, Tambol Yaicha, Nakhon Pathom ☎ 034 322 589 🕓 Daily 11–2.30 ✋ L B300

PATTAYA
ART CAFÉ

www.artcafe-thailand.com
Rabbit, lamb and ostrich are some of the more exotic items on the imaginative menu of this Mediterranean-style eatery. The steaks are enormous, but vegetarians are also provided for, with dishes such as lentil salad with eggplant (aubergine) mousse. Local artists display their works here.
✉ 285/3 Moo 5, Naklua Soi 16, Pattaya ☎ 038 367 652 🕓 Daily 11–11 ✋ L B250, D B400

CENTRAL FESTIVAL

www.centralfestival.co.th
For Western fast-food, ice cream, donuts and coffee, there is no better place to head than Pattaya's largest shopping mall. Some excellent restaurants are also resident here, including The Orangery by the Sea, which serves a broad selection of Asian, Russian and French cuisine, or Khao Suay, serving all the usual Thai favorites.
🕓 Daily 10am–11pm

PARADISE

You dine in style here beneath a high ceiling that's supported by arched walls covered with hand-painted rain forest murals. Tables are laid with crisp white linen and vases containing fresh flowers. The menu matches the exotic decor, with such specialties as crocodile and lobster. The Thai menu has all the usual favorites, such as spicy shrimp soup and sweet-and-sour pork or chicken, all priced at under B100.
✉ 215/62–63 Second Road, Pattaya, Chonburi ☎ 038 723 177 🕓 Daily 8am–10pm ✋ L B250, D B300

PIC KITCHEN AND JAZZ PIT

This elegant Thai-style restaurant and pub is an old Pattaya favorite, close to the Beach Road and the sea. There are four pavilion dining areas, in two of which diners sit on the polished teak floor, Thai-style. The food isn't cheap, but many of

Below *Floating restaurant in Phitsanulok*
Opposite *The cozy Dream Café in Sukhothai*

the dishes—the *nam prik khai poo*, for instance—are memorably good so are the wines. The Jazz Pit Pub serves up some great music.

✉ 255 Soi 5, Pattaya 2 Road, Pattaya ☎ 038 428 374 ⏰ Daily 8am–midnight 🖐 L B400, D B600

–5° SUPPERCLUB & –5° ICEBAR

www.minus5pattaya.com

This is one of the chicest spots in Pattaya for dinner, with an all-white interior and light-blue lighting. While the Supperclub may look like an icebox, the Icebar actually is, with entry limited to 20 minutes per ticket and freeflow vodka shots (B500 per ticket or B300 between 6–8pm). Warm up at the restaurant by choosing from the extensive menu, which includes Thai, Asian-fusion and pasta dishes, with 3- and 4-course set menus priced around B1,110 and B1,350 respectively.

✉ Amari Nova Suites, 254 M.9, Soi Petchtrakool, Pattaya ☎ 038 426 768 ⏰ Reservations from 11am, or 6pm till late 🖐 L B600, D B1,110

THAI HOUSE

The Thai House is a Thai-style pavilion with sweeping eaves and able to seat 800 diners. Performances of traditional music and dancing are given every evening. The menu is international, with some original dishes such as *goong pad* "baby corn" (sautéed shrimp with young maize corn).

✉ 171/1 Moo 6, Naklua, Bang Lamuang, North Pattaya, Chonburi ☎ 038 370 579–81 ⏰ Daily 10am–11pm 🖐 L B200, D B250

PHITSANULOK
NA NAM

From the terrace of this large, open-air restaurant you have a great view of the river, making it a romantic place for an evening out. The Thai menu has such exotic specialties as "flying salty chicken" (*gai khua kem*). The fish dishes are particularly tasty—try *pla neung sea we* (steamed river fish in soy sauce).

✉ Thanon 89/4 Wangchan, Amphoe Muang, Phitsanulok ☎ 055 216 404, 055 230 444 ⏰ Daily 11–11 🖐 L B200, D B250

PHAE FAH THAI

Phitsanulok is renowned for its "floating restaurants" which sit directly on the river, their large, airy teak-floored terraces like an ocean liner's promenade deck. The Phae Fah Thai is among the best.

✉ 100/49 Thanon Bhuddabucha, Amphoe Muang, Phitsanulok ☎ 055 242 743 ⏰ Daily 11–11 🖐 L B200, D B250

PHAE SONG KWAE

This floating restaurant takes diners out onto the river on dinner cruises, leaving at 6 and 8 every evening. A band plays on board and also on shore in the large dining terrace. Fish dishes dominate the menu, and

this is *the* place to try barbecued prawns (*goong phao*).

✉ 21 Thanon Wangchan, Amphoe Muang, Phitsanulok ☎ 055 242 167 ⏰ Daily 11–11 🖐 L B150, D B250

RAYONG
COTE JARDIN

The Novotel's elegant Cote Jardin restaurant is among Rayong's best, serving a select menu of international and Thai dishes in the dining room or on the outside terrace. It's widely known for the quality of its seafood—the *gaeng pet talay*, a seafood curry, is one of its outstanding specialties.

✉ Novotel Coralia Rim Pae, 45/Moo 3, Thanon Pae Klaeng Kram, Rayong ☎ 038 648 008 ⏰ Daily 6am–midnight 🖐 L B500, D B700

SANGKHLA BURI (THREE PAGODAS PASS)
SONGKALIA RIVER HUT AND RESORT

From a table at this lakeside resort's open-sided restaurant you can watch fishermen at work on the vast Khao Laem reservoir, hauling in the catch that lands on the day's menu. The specialty of the lake and the restaurant is *pla red*, delicious in garlic or sweet-and-sour sauce. Traditional Mon dishes from Myanmar (Burma) are also on the menu—the pork or chicken *hang led* curry is spicy but is excellent.

✉ Sangkhla Buri lake road ⏰ Daily 11–10 🖐 L B120, D B150

SUKHOTHAI
THE DREAM CAFÉ

This attractive little restaurant, with wood-paneled walls and polished teak and tile floors, is divided up into cozy dining areas and nooks and crannies. Every corner and wall space is filled with bric-a-brac, small antiques and old clocks. The menu is an imaginative mixture of Thai and Western food. There's a guesthouse extension, the Cocoon.

✉ 86/1 Thanon Singhawat, Amphoe Muang, Sukhothai ☎ 055 612 081 ⏰ Daily 10am–11pm 🖐 L B200, D B250

PRICES AND SYMBOLS

Prices are the lowest and highest for a double room for one night. Breakfast is included unless noted otherwise. All the hotels listed accept credit cards unless otherwise stated. Note that rates vary widely throughout the year.

For a key to the symbols, ▷ 2.

AYUTTHAYA
AYUTTHAYA GRAND HOTEL

The white facade of the Grand dominates the market area. Rooms range from simply furnished to spacious suites. Parking is available. ✉ 55/29 Moo 1, Tambol Tanu, U-Thai, Ayutthaya ☎ 035 335 483/91 ✋ B500–B1,800 🚪 122 🆑 🏊 Outdoor 🍽

AYUTTHAYA RIVERSIDE

This modern hotel with parking has rooms furnished in local textiles. One of the two restaurants is on the river, and dinner cruises embark every evening. ✉ 91/1 Moo 10, Tambol Kamang, Amphoe Pranakorn, Ayutthaya 13000 ☎ 035 234 873/7 ✋ B1,200–B1,800 🚪 102 🆑

KRUNGSRI RIVER HOTEL

www.krungsririver.com
Rooms are furnished with fine fabrics and drapes. Guests can dine in the restaurant or on the hotel's riverboat. Parking is available. ✉ 27/2 Moo 11, Thanon Rajchana, Tambol Kamang, Ayutthaya 13000 ☎ 035 244 333 ✋ From B1,800–B4,000 🚪 212 (60 non-smoking) 🆑 🏊 Outdoor 🍽

CHANTHABURI
MANEECHAN RESORT AND SPORT CLUB

www.maneechan.com
This top-quality resort with parking has excellent sports and spa facilities. The modern, comfortabe rooms have twin queen-size beds. ✉ 110 Moo 11, Thanon Sukhumvit, Tambol Plub Pla, Chanthaburi 22000 ☎ 039 343 777/8 ✋ B1,500–B2,800 🚪 72 (all non-smoking) 🆑 🏊 Outdoor 🍽

SUANRIMTHARN RESORT

This is neat little resort is set in beautiful rolling countryside with a mountain backdrop. Accommodations are in charming Swiss-style chalets, with balconies overlooking gardens, a pool and a fish pond. The restaurant serves Vietnamese, Thai and Western dishes. Parking is available. ✉ 139 Moo 1, Tambol Khaowongkot, Amphoe Khanghang Maew, Chanthaburi 22160 ☎ 019 236 332 ✋ B1,590–B4,000 🚪 16 (2 non-smoking) 🆑 🏊 Outdoor

KANCHANABURI
RIVER KWAI CABIN

From the gardens of this jungle resort you have a fine view of the most spectacular stretch of the "Death Railway." Accommodations are in simple bivouac-style cottages or riverbank cabins. ✉ 28/234 Moo 7, Kanchanaburi ☎ 029 678 181/4 ✋ 2-night package B4,580, includes 5 meals and activities 🚪 20 🆑

RIVER KWAI VILLAGE HOTEL

www.riverkwaivillagehotel.com
The River Kwai Village Hotel sits within a tropical forest bordered by the Kwai Noi River. You can stay in one of the hotel's moored "raftels," (houseboats). The "village" has a full entertainment program, including a jungle bar with live bands and buggies for exploring the forest. Parking is available. ✉ 74/12 Moo 4, Tha Sao, Kanchanaburi ☎ 083 242 1120, 022 517 828 ✋ B2,400–B4,200 🚪 140 🆑 🏊 Outdoor

KAMPHAENG PHET
PHET HOTEL

www.phethotel.com
This hotel is convenient for shopping and seeing the sites. The rooms are compact and simply furnished

Opposite *Royal Cliff Beach Hotel, Pattaya*

(suites available). There is a restaurant serving international and local food, a lounge and a pub.
✉ 189 Bumrungraj Road, Kamphaeng Phet ☎ 055 712 810 ✋ B700–B900 🛏 215 💳 ❄ Outdoor

KO SAMET
AO PRAO
www.sametresorts.com
In the quiet season, this resort has bargain special offers. Rooms are rustic but luxurious; the more expensive front the sea, but they are all only a short walk from the beach.
✉ 60 Moo 4, Tambon Phe, Rayong ☎ 038 644 100/3 ✋ B6,000–B16,500 🛏 52 💳

SAMET VILLE RESORT
www.sametvilleresort.com
This huge resort takes up an entire section of coast. Accommodations are in comfortable wooden bungalows, many on the beach.
✉ 88/1 4 Tambon Phe, Rayong 21160 ☎ 038 651 681/2 ✋ B900–B1,500 🛏 60 (all non-smoking) 💳 Some

LOP BURI
LOPBURI INN
Lop Buri's biggest hotel occupies a city corner block. Its six floors have 130 attractively furnished rooms. Thai, Chinese and Western cuisine is served in its Lopburi Cafe. ✉ 28–29 Thanon Narai Maharach, Amphoe Muang, Lop Buri 15000 ☎ 036 412 300, 036 412 609, 036 412 802 ✋ B600–B1,200 🛏 130 💳

LOPBURI INN RESORT
Each of the 100 rooms at this resort hotel is named after a Thai province and furnished in provincial style. The restaurant is one of Lop Buri's best.
✉ 144 Thanon Paholyothin, Amphoe Muang, Lop Buri ☎ 036 420 777, 036 421 453 ✋ B1,400–B1,750 🛏 100 💳 ❄ Outdoor 🍴

PATTAYA
CHANAGAN GUEST HOUSE
This cheerful little guesthouse is set at the back of a small street in Pattaya's quiet, family-friendly Jom

Tien Beach. Rooms are spacious, with English-speaking cable channels. The friendly owner speaks fluent English.
✉ 75/244 Moo 12 Soi 6, Jom Tien Beach Road, Pattaya ☎ 089 938 4196 ✋ B500–B700 🛏 52 (all non-smoking) 💳

GRAND JOMTIEN PALACE HOTEL
www.hotelsjomtien.com
Ask for a west-facing room to enjoy the sunset over the Gulf of Thailand. All rooms have balconies; those facing inland are cheaper. Other rooms overlook the gardens, with their three pools. Parking is available.
✉ 356 Thanon Jomtien Beach, Pattaya, Chonburi 20260 ☎ 038 231 405 ✋ From B1,250–B1,850 🛏 52 (all non-smoking) 💳 ❄ Outdoor 🍴

GREEN PARK RESORT
www.greenparkpattaya.com
All rooms at this resort overlook its huge, landscaped pool. There are also 16 bungalows set among tropical gardens. The resort's Park Restaurant serves Thai and international dishes.
✉ 240/5 Moo 5, Soi Pingpa, North Pattaya, Chonburi 20150 ☎ 038 426 356–8 ✋ B2,825–B8,000 excluding breakfast 🛏 193 💳 ❄ Outdoor

ROYAL CLIFF BEACH HOTEL
www.royalcliff.com
This vast resort is set in 64 acres (26ha) of clifftop parkland with its own beach. There are five swimming pools, ten restaurants and four bars. It has five-star accommodations, with a presidential suite.
✉ Royal Cliff Bay, Pattaya, Chonburi 20150 ☎ 038 250 421 ✋ B6,400–7,770 excluding breakfast 🛏 1,122 (400 non-smoking) 💳 ❄ Outdoor 🍴

PHITSANULOK
PHITSANULOK THANI HOTEL
Phitsanulok's top hotel is a high-rise, close to the river. Rooms are large and airy. The restaurant serves Thai and Western cuisine.
✉ 39 Thanon Sanambin, Amphoe Muang, Phitsanulok 65000 ☎ 019 495 394 ✋ B1,000–B4,000 🛏 110 rooms (22 non-smoking), 4 suites 💳

RAYONG
BAAN PAE CABANA
If you're catching the boat to Ko Samet island it's worth adding a night or two at this mainland resort, which offers free transfers to the ferry station. Many of the 35 thatched and timber-built bungalows overlook the sea. The resort has a wide range of water sports.
✉ 206/1–2, Moo 3, Tambol Klaeng 21160 Rayong ☎ 038 648 489 ✋ B2,825–B6,350 🛏 35 💳 ❄ Outdoor

SI SATCHANALAI
WANG YOM RESORT
The Si Satchanalai Historical Park is just a short walk from this charming resort hotel. Accommodations are in comfortably furnished bungalows. The main building has an excellent restaurant, too.
✉ 78/2 Moo 6, Si Satchanalai ☎ 055 631 380 ✋ B800 🛏 4 (all non-smoking) 💳

SUKHOTHAI
ANANDA MUSEUM GALLERY HOTEL
This hotel has luxurious rooms with fine reproductions and local textiles. Original Sukhothai dishes are served in its Celadon garden restaurant.
✉ 10 Moo 4, Banlum, Muang Sukhothai ☎ 055 622 428/30 ✋ B2,500–B3,100 🛏 32 💳

LOTUS VILLAGE
www.lotus-village.com
This resort-style hotel is tucked away between Sukhothai's new market and the Yom River, with cozy timber-built bungalows. Credit cards are not accepted. Parking is available.
✉ 170 Thanon Ratchathanee, Sukhothai ☎ 055 621 484 ✋ B1,000–B1,700 🛏 20 rooms, 2 villas (all non-smoking) 💳 Some

RAJTHANEE HOTEL
A business hotel, the Rajthanee offers comfort and good facilities. Rooms are comfortable with full-size tubs. The airy terrace restaurant serves Thai and Western food.
✉ 229 Thanon Charodvitheetong, Sukhothai ☎ 055 611 031, 055 611 308, 055 612 877 ✋ B500–B700 🛏 83 💳 ❄ Outdoor

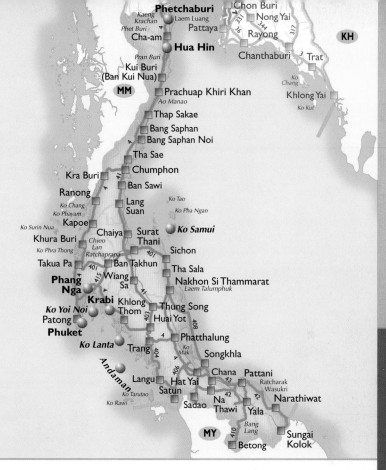

THE SOUTH

You are never far from crystal-clear water in southern Thailand and, together with luxury hotels, fantastic shopping, wildlife-rich national parks and some of the world's most beautiful beaches, it is not surprising that it is one of the world's favorite playgrounds. The tropical beach resorts and exotic islands here receive millions of visitors each year, which has inspired rapid development of the coastline in many resorts with world-class accommodations, dining and plenty of opportunities for water-based activities, such as snorkeling, diving and canoeing.

Southern Thailand is characterized by its tall limestone cliffs, offshore islands and palm-lined beaches, making a picturesque setting for luxury vacations and Hollywood films alike. Most tourists pass through the upper panhandle on a night train or bus from Bangkok to reach beaches further south, missing many beautiful old temples, sleepy coastal fishing villages and karst landscapes that lie between the high-density resorts.

Travelers tend to spend most of their time on the islands of the western Andaman Coast, particularly Phuket, which attracts beach-lovers in their thousands. There are, however, quieter alternatives such as of Krabi, which has a lesser sense of that rampant, visitor-fueled mania for building Ko Bubu, a Robinson Crusoe-style island with limited accomodations; or Ko Phayam, where there are no cars and a local population of around 400 people.

Once a haven for budget-conscious backpackers, prices in southern Thailand are still surprisingly reasonable and the area has plenty to offer all types of travelers. You can experience glorious seascapes and sandy beaches, stay in a bamboo hut or five-star resort. During the day there's diving and snorkeling in Ko Tao and Ko Phi Phi, rock climbing in Ao Nang and Railay, and birdwatching in the rain forests of Khao Sam Roi and Khao Sok national parks. For those looking to pamper themselves, Phuket and Ko Samui islands offer endless spa choices, cocktails on the beach and fresh seafood. For all-night, full-moon parties and beach bars, the youthful and young-at-heart head to Ko Pha Ngan.

ANDAMAN COAST

Lush vegetation and limestone peaks punctuate the landscape with alarming beauty; equally arresting are the dramatic seascapes of turquoise water and tropical islands famed for their beaches and coral reefs.

Thailand's Andaman coast begins at Ranong, close to the border with Myanmar (Burma), and stretches south for 342 miles (550km) until it reaches the border with Malaysia. Geographically and culturally constant, it is distinguished by stunning scenery and a human landscape populated by a mix of ethnic Chinese in urban areas and Thai Muslims in the countryside. Fields of rice are less common than plantations of rubber, palm oil and coconut trees. The Andaman coast bore Thailand's brunt of the 2004 tsunami, but recovery programs were speedily implemented.

WHEN TO VISIT

Weather conditions, due to the impact of the southwest monsoon, need to be borne in mind. When the rain comes in, starting in May and lasting until mid-October, it hits the Andaman coast more persistently than other regions of Thailand, and passenger services to outlying islands are suspended or reduced depending on local conditions. The rainy season, though, is not a barrier to enjoying a successful holiday along the Andaman coast—accommodations are discounted and less advance planning is required.

PLACES TO VISIT

The most visited destination on the Andaman coast is Phuket (▷ 250–252). The beaches are superb and the overall level of services, accommodations and activities are second to none, but the island can feel busy. Krabi (▷ 246–247) to the east, with its own nearby beaches and easygoing character, is an ideal alternative in this respect. So are the excellent white-sand beaches of Ko Lanta (▷ 240), easily reached from Krabi. From Ko Lanta it is easy to island-hop to tiny Ko Jum (Ko Pu; ▷ 239) and Ko Bubu (▷ 239) or the better-known Ko Phi Phi (▷ 241). Diving and snorkeling are always a possibility along the coast, with the outstanding opportunities available around Ko Similan (▷ 241) and Ko Surin Nua (▷ 241) especially popular.

GETTING AROUND

Excellent transportation links make traveling to and along the Andaman coast easy. Other than on Phuket, roads are rarely busy and car rental is easily arranged in the main towns. Boat services to offshore islands are frequent and usually well organized.

INFORMATION

http://andamanthailand.com

✚ 316 A15–318 C18 ☷ 75 Thanon Phuket ☎ 076 212 213 🕐 Daily 8.30–4.30 🚂 To Trang, then a bus 🚌 From Bangkok ✈ From Phuket, Krabi and Ranong 🚗 Highway 4 from Bangkok

TIP

» Find time to watch the sun set over the Andaman Sea, preferably from a beach.

Opposite *Coconut palms and jungle by the beach at Ko Tarutao*
Below *A longboat sitting off Ao Nang in Krabi*

ANG THONG NATIONAL MARINE PARK

The national park consists of more than 40 small islands. The islands' wildlife is protected, and long-tailed macaques, wild pigs, monitor lizards and langurs have the run of the place, and are not too difficult to spot. There is also a rich birdlife, but you will need binoculars to make the best of this. The park's headquarters are located on the largest island, Koh Wua Talab (island of the sleeping cow). The island has five bungalows to rent but facilities are basic with no hot water or electricity at night. Camping is also permitted on the island via organized tour companies in Ko Samui.

Access to the marine park is controlled, but there are several boat rental and kayak operators in Ko Samui, some 19 miles (30km) to the east, including Ko Pha Ngan, who organize kayaking and camping trips in the park. One of the most popular day trips from Ko Samui includes a visit to Ko Wua Talab where you can, footwear and energy permitting, climb up a 1,400ft (430m) hill to the highest point of the park for panoramic views over the entire archipelago and the mainland.

Caves on many of the islands have intriguing rock formations, and a popular sight is Tham Bua Bok, which has unusual shaped stalactites and stalagmites, which resemble lotuses. Many of the park's hundreds of beaches are remote, surrounded by coral reefs, and offer superb swimming and snorkeling opportunities.

🚩 316 C15 ☎ 077 286 025 💷 Park entrance adult B400, child (under 14) B200; day trips from Ko Samui B1,000–1,600 🚤 From travel shops on Ko Samui daily; less frequently from Ko Pha Ngan

BAN KRUD

The charming fishing town of Ban Krud sits on the edge of an expansive stretch of white sand and crystal waters backed by luscious palm and casuarinas trees. Ban Krud occupies 3 miles (5km) of beach at the northern end of Thong Lang Bay.

The beach changes names to Don Samran and Thong Lang as it extends southward. Ban Krud is the perfect place to relax. In fact there's not much else to do other than eating, drinking and swimming. The only tourist attraction here, other than the beach itself, is the 49ft-high (15m) Buddha and Wat Phra, with its colorful stained-glass windows, on the northern cape of Khao Thangchai. The Buddha was built by a joint US-Thai company to sweeten local attitudes toward their proposed coal-fueled power stations. The token was not fruitful, however, as the power stations were not permitted to be built, and locals shunned the temple site.

🚩 316 C12 🚌 Buses stop at Highway 4, where songthaews and motorbike taxis pick up passengers for delivery to the beach 5 miles (8km) away 🚆 Ban Krud train station with service to Bangkok and Phunphin (near Surat Thani)

CHA-AM

Between Hua Hin (▷ 238) and Phetchaburi (▷ 249), Cha-am is busy on weekends, when families from Bangkok and elsewhere arrive. At other times it lapses into a sleepy beach-based destination. Amenities are condensed into a 2-mile (3km) stretch facing the sea. The classy resorts, though, are spread out to the north and south, with beach areas more or less exclusively their own, and a stay here is made easier with your own transportation. The beach in the heart of Cha-am is not perfect but is safe for swimming. It also has a choice of places to eat and mid-range accommodations.

🚩 314 D11 🛈 Highway 4, a 15-min walk south of the main hub ☎ 032 471 005 🕐 Daily 8.30–4.30 🚌 Buses from Bangkok (southern bus station) every hour (☎ 032 425 307)

CHUMPHON

The main highway from Bangkok splits into two at Chumphon: one branch accessing the Andaman coast to the west and the other heading due south for the Gulf coast in the east. The town's bus terminal, with regular connections to and from Bangkok and destinations along the east and west coasts, makes Chumphon a busy place. The town is fully geared up for folk with plans to move on elsewhere. There are plenty of knowledgeable travel agents who can provide information as well as transportation and day trips, including the popular route to Ko Tao (▷ 244). Numerous places offer internet access, as well as car and motorbike rental.

The most appealing beach is 7.5 miles (12km) north of town, known variously as Tha Wua Lan and Thung Wua Laem, and is served by regular songthaews. It has a good sandy stretch of beach, as well as canoes for rent, a dive center at the large Chumphon Cabana hotel, a choice of accommodations and some excellent seafood restaurants. Snorkeling trips to offshore islands can be arranged through the dive center, from the beach-sited hotels or from travel shops in town. In Chumphon town, day trips to Pha To, 62 miles (100km) inland to the southwest, are organized for water rafting on the Lang Suan River.

There are plenty of places to stay that offer simple accommodations for a few nights. The food scene is more encouraging, with lively food stands set up at night along the main street near the train station, and plenty of restaurants and bars.

🚩 316 C13 🛈 Thanon Paramin Manka, ☎ 077 511 024 🕐 Mon–Fri 8.30–4.30 🚌 Main terminal on Thanon Tao Tapao (☎ 077 507 209) 🚆 Daily express trains from Thonburi (077 511 103) ✈ The airport (☎ 077 591 263/72) is 22 miles (35km) north of town 🚗 Contact Infinity Travel for diving trips (Thanon Thatapao ☎ 077 501 937 for guided tours; www.cabana.co.th)

HAT YAI

In the deep south, 580 miles (933km) from Bangkok, Hat Yai is a major-league southern Thailand transportation hub. The city bustles relentlessly with commercial life, day and night, and seems more Chinese and Malay in character than Thai. Three long streets, numbered Niphat

Uthit 1, 2 and 3, run north–south through the town and parallel to the road with the train station. On and around these streets are hotels, guesthouses, places to eat, travel agents and the tourist office.

Just 3.75 miles (6km) outside the city is the flower-filled Hat Yai Municipal Park. There are several interesting statues, a Brahman shrine and a pavilion in the middle of the pond, as well as a number of food stalls. A little further afield, but a relatively easy day trip from Hat Yai, is the beautiful Ton Nga Chang Waterfall in the Ton Nga Chang Wildlife Sanctuary.

Note that recent unrest in the Pattani area (▷ 244) has at times spread as far as Hat Yai.

🚉 319 D18 🔢 1/1 Soi 2, Thanon Niphat Uthit 3 ☎ 074 243 747 🕐 Daily 8.30–4.30 🚆 Daily trains from Bangkok (074 261 290, 074 243 705) 🚌 Buses and minivans use various points around town; Cathay Tour (Thanon Niphat Uthit 2 ☎ 074 354 104) reserves tickets and runs its own minivan services ✈ Daily flights to/from Bangkok from the airport 7.5 miles (12km) southwest of the town with Thai Airways, Orient Thai, Nok Air and One-Two-Go

HUA HIN
▷ 238.

KHAO LAK
The beaches at Khao Lak, looking out to the Andaman Sea just off Highway 4 and an hour by road from Phuket Airport, were the heart of a thriving and cosmopolitan holiday scene until the tsunami in December 2004. Destruction was widespread, especially to the main hub at Nang Thong, though most of the area has been rebuilt and little visible evidence of the tsunami remains other than poignant memorials.

Khao Lak is a base for trips to offshore islands and the hub for dive operators specializing in Ko Similan (▷ 241) and Ko Surin Nua (▷ 241). Travel shops in Khao Lak will all reserve you trips to Khao Sok National Park (▷ right) and day trips into nearby Mynamar (Burma), too.

🚉 316 B16 🚌 Buses and minivans from Phuket, Ranong, Surat Thani, Krabi and Phang Nga

KHAO SAM ROI YOT NATIONAL PARK
www.dnp.go.th/National_park.asp
The 38sq miles (98sq km) Khao Sam Roi National Park derives its name, "300 Mountain Peaks" from the 1,968ft-high (600m) limestone cliffs towering above pristine beaches and coastal wetlands. Thailand's largest freshwater marsh is found here, intermingling with mangrove forests and mud flats, forming a vast habitat for endemic and migratory birds. One of the few places in the country where the purple heron breeds, the park is also home to painted storks, grey herons, spotted eagles and black-headed ibises. Mammals found in the park include muntjac, lorises, pangolins, crab-eating macaques, serows and fishing cats. Khao Sam Roi boasts two sandy beaches, but the three main caves are more notable. Tham Phraya Nakhon is the most popular, containing a pavilion built for King Rama V in 1890. Earlier in 1868, King Rama IV came to the park to observe a total solar eclipse that he predicted himself. He contracted malaria from the insufferable mosquitoes here and later died.

For transport to and within the park, try Hua Hin Adventure Tour (www.huahinadventuretour.com, 032 530 314).

🚉 314 D11 ✉ Hat Laem Sala ☎ 089 533 8664 🚆 Arrive in Pranburi then take a songthaew (B300) to the park 🚌 To reach the park from Hua Hin, take Highway 4 to Pranburi and turn left at the main intersection. Turn right at the police station and travel a further 12.5 miles (20km) to the park entrance. The park's headquarters are 9 miles (15km) farther on at Hat Laem Sala

KHAO SOK NATIONAL PARK
www.khaosok.com
Accessible from either of southern Thailand's two coasts, Khao Sok National Park is dense in rain forest, rich in wildlife, including gibbons, leopards and deer, and distinguished

Above *Stalls in a Muslim market in Hat Yai*

by limestone peaks that dominate the scenery. With more than 180 species of birds, a pair of binoculars is useful. Walking trails lead from the park headquarters into the dense interior, and a day's walking would cover the trek to and from the Ton Gloy waterfall, with time for swimming. There are plenty of accommodations; visitor amenities are spread out along the access road (from the main road to the visitor center) and many of the guesthouses also function as restaurants. Elephant trekking, canoeing and jeep safaris can be arranged, and guides can be hired in the park for trips to caves and a lake, with camping or accommodations in simple raft houses on the lake.

🚉 316 B15 ✉ Highway 401, east of Takua Pa ⛔ Park entrance adult B400, child B200; guided day trip around B1200, overnight trip B1,800–B2,900, night safari B500 🔢 Park Visitor Center ☎ 077 395 025 🕐 Daily 8–6 🚌 Buses from Takua Pa (1 hour); from Bangkok or Hua Hin take a bus for Surat Thanis but get dropped off 12.5 miles (20km) before at the junction for buses to Takua Pa, which pass the park entrance; from Phuket or Khao Lak take a bus for Surat Thani and get dropped off at the park entrance; minivans also run from Krabi and Ko Samui 🚌 On Highway 401, coming from Takua Pa or Surat Thani, the park entrance is at kilometer stone 109 📖 *Waterfalls and Gibbon Calls*, Thom Henley (available in the park)

INFORMATION

www.hua-hin.com

314 D11   Corner of Thanon Damnernkasem and Thanon Phetkasem, ☎ 032 532 433   Mon–Fri 8.30–4.30, Sat, Sun 9–5   Daily trains from Bangkok ☎ 032 511 073   Buses for towns to the north and south, including Phuket and Krabi, depart/arrive at various spots around town. Minibuses to Victory Monument in Bangkok depart from opposite the Esso/Tesco garage on Thanon Damnernkasem   Daily flights to/from Bangkok from airport (☎ 032 520 343) 3.7 miles (6km) north of town

TIP

❯❯ The finest stretch of sandy beach, safe for swimming, is between Sofitel Centara Grand Resort and Hua Hin Marriott.

Above *The gardens at the Sofitel Centara Grand Resort, formerly the Railway Hotel, Hua Hin*

HUA HIN

Visited by royalty for more than a century and with a good beach and a wide range of amenities for tourists, Hua Hin is increasingly popular with visitors from around the world. King Rama VI commissioned the building of a palace in Hua Hin for his family in the 1920s, then Rama VII built another one, and in the same decade the Thailand–Malaysia railway line began running down this side of the coast. Soon after a train station was opened, the grand Railway Hotel followed and guidebooks of that era began referring to the new sedate bathing destination as Hua Hin-on-Sea. It retained a genteel image until the 1980s—and even today it is a far cry from Pattaya (▷ 208–209)—but high-rise hotels, golf courses, a burgeoning array of bars, nightlife entertainment, fresh seafood restaurants and a jazz festival every June have transformed Hua Hin into a lively beach resort.

Trains to and from Bangkok take more than 5 hours at the best of times and trains back to the capital depart at unhelpful hours, but the teakwood train station itself, a five-minute walk from the middle of town, retains an old-fashioned charm.

ROYAL BEACH RESORT

The three armed vessels out at sea, rendered innocuous-looking at night when lit up by fairy lights, reflect the fact that Thai royalty still stay in their palace with a private stretch of beach. This leaves 3 miles (5km) of beach for everyone else, and some restaurants have extensions built on stilts over the sand. There are plenty of shops for visitors—souvenir stalls, tailors, artists' studios and a modest department store—as well as travel agents offering various excursions and spas to suit most budgets.

THE RAILWAY HOTEL

A member of the royal family with interests in the State Railway of Thailand commissioned an Italian architect to design the Railway Hotel, built in 1923. Its splendid style appealed to the makers of the film *The Killing Fields* (1984), who used it as a set, but a renovation project in the 1980s transformed it into the Sofitel Central—it is now part of the Sofitel Centara Grand Resort and Villa Hua Hin (▷ 270). It is worth visiting for its topiary gardens, open-air lobby and Museum Café. The current king reportedly spends time here to escape from Bangkok's polluted air.

KO BUBU

This Robinson Crusoe island is so small that there is only the one place to stay, and with just 30 rooms the island cannot get too crowded. It is the ultimate place to chill out, relax on the 220-yard (200m) long beach, read a novel or two and take frequent plunges into the warm sea—between May and the end of October, at least, when boats run and accommodations are open (Bubu Island Resort; 075 618 066; Nov–Apr; B400–B1,000 per night). ✚ 320 18 C17 🚢 From Ban Ko Lanta on the east coast of Ko Lanta, and Krabi travel agents reserve tickets for through transportation from Krabi

KO CHANG

Not to be confused with the larger island with the same name on Thailand's east coast, Ko Chang is a small, tree-clad island 4 miles (7km) off the coast in the Andaman Sea, with a scheduled boat service to and from Ranong (▷ 253). The rainy season sees nearly all the island's guesthouses closing down and boat journeys become unpredictable. Ko Chang, inhabited by fishing families and farmers of cashew nuts and rubber trees, has a lovely relaxed pace of life where very little happens—this is what is likely to attract you. Accommodations are all fairly simple, and the best bedrooms have their own bathrooms, fans and mosquito nets; air-conditioning is not available because mains electricity has not yet reached the island. Nearly all the guesthouses serve meals. The best beaches are on the west coast, the one at Ao Yai being especially suited to a couple of days spent lazing about and watching the sun set over Myanmar (Burma). It takes half an hour to walk across to the mangrove-fringed east coast. ✚ 316 B14 🚢 Boats depart Nov–end May from Saphan Pla (3 miles/5km outside of Ranong and reached by *songthaew*) to Ao Yai (1hr) usually twice a day in the morning ❓ Only a few necessities are available at small shops on the island so you should bring items like sunscreen and insect repellent with you

KO JUM (KO PU)

The island (also known as Ko Pu) is located halfway between Ko Lanta and Krabi, and the passenger boats that ply their way regularly between these places are met by longboats that set out from Ko Jum's west coast to pick up visitors. Mangrove trees cling to the east coast, but the west coast has sandy beaches and a modest selection of inexpensive and mid-range bungalow operations that use generators in the absence of mains electricity. As with Ko Bubu, most accommodations are closed between June and the end of October; at other times there is not a lot to do and nightlife is a rather low-key affair. To some, Ko Jum is a true retreat from urban blues; to others, it borders on the comatose. ✚ 318 B17 🚢 From Ko Lanta (45 min) or Krabi (1.5hrs), and from Laem Kruat (30 min) on the mainland southwest of Krabi

KO LANTA

▷ 240.

KO PHA NGAN

www.kohphangan.com; www.watkowtahm.org

A 45-minute boat trip away from Ko Samui, the island of Ko Pha Ngan possesses many qualities that will endear it to those who find the island of Ko Samui just a tad too developed for its own good. There are superb beaches on the east coast, though they remain remote because there is no surfaced road on this side of the island. Many boats dock at Thong Sala on the west coast, and from here a good road heads north and south to reach most of the accommodations and restaurants. Activities on the island include horseback riding on the beach, meditation courses at Wat Khao Tham and famous full-moon parties on the southernmost promontory of Hat Rin. A plethora of shops and services have turned parts of Hat Rin into a mess, and finding a quiet place to stay is becoming more and more difficult. From here, though, a longtail boat runs a taxi service up the east coast for those wanting more relaxing places to stay. The west coast north of Thong Sala has a good mix of accommodations, neither as remote as the east coast nor as noisy as Hat Rin. ✚ 317 D14 🚢 From Surat Thani and from Na Thon on Ko Samui to Thong Sala; speedboats from the north coast of Ko Samui to Ko Tao stop at Thong Sala, plus there are services to Hat Rin; daily services between Ko Tao and Ko Pha Ngan

Above *Wooden bungalows on Sunrise Beach, Ko Pha Ngan*

INFORMATION

☩ 318 C17 ℹ No official tourist office but information and useful free maps readily available from travel agents on the island 🚢 From Phuket, Krabi, Ao Nang and Ko Phi Phi outside of the rainy season 🚌 Year-round from Krabi and involving two short ferry crossings

KO LANTA

Visit Ko Lanta and you can enjoy superb beaches and a fast-developing infrastructure that caters to visitors with varying budgets. Not surprisingly, Ko Lanta continues to increase this island's popularity so you won't have the place to yourself. It is best visited between November and April.

Only a few years ago, Ko Lanta was the destination of choice for discerning backpackers. Though readily accessible outside of the rainy season, the island remained relatively undeveloped and there were only a few, fan-cooled bamboo-and-thatch bungalows strung out along the west-coast beaches catering to island-hoppers. Budget accommodations are still available, but so too is an increasing range of middle- and high-priced options. What has not yet changed is the relaxed pace of life, with beach bars and restaurants lighting up along the west coast and beckoning to visitors as night approaches.

EXPLORING THE ISLAND

Shops and amenities, including ATMs, are spread across the west coast, especially, around Ban Sala Dan, where boats arrive and depart, and along the nearby beach of Hat Khlong Dao. The entire west coast, served by a good road that skirts the beaches, is continuing to develop with new resorts, restaurants and bars. The east coast has a different character because there are no beaches, but this is where many of the 20,000 or so islanders live and work their farms. Motorcycles and jeeps are easily rented either in Ban Sala Dan or from your accommodations, and a trip down the east coast to the old town of Ko Lanta offers an alternative to beach life. Snorkeling, diving and kayaking are equally easy to arrange. Elephant rides are popular but may also involve trekking, so bring suitable footwear.

BEACHES

Hat Khlong Dao beach is within easy walking distance of the pier, and its long and broad expanse of beautiful golden sand ensures its popularity without ever making it seem busy or crowded. The next beach, Ao Phra-Ae, is equally appealing and it is only with Hat Khlong Khong, 1.2 miles (2km) to the south and midway down the coast, that rocks begin to pepper the sand at low tide. Unbroken sand continues at the next two beaches and, as you continue south, the coves become more secluded until the road ends near the Pimalai Resort & Spa (▷ 270).

Below *The beautiful tree-backed beach on Ko Lanta*

KO PHAYAM

This trim little island, about 6 miles (10km) long by 4 miles (7km) wide, is reached by boat in two hours from Ranong. The island has no cars, just beautiful sandy beaches, hornbills flying overhead, a laid-back feel and inexpensive accommodations. It is the perfect place to relax, snorkel and enjoy the beautiful coastline. Numerous shady paths leading to its remote bays make for good walking.

Only a few hundred people live here, making their living from fishing, farming, rubber plantations and the small-scale visitor scene. Between June and the end of October, when the boat service from the mainland becomes unpredictable and many of the bungalows close for the rainy season, the residents mostly have the island to themselves. There is one village, on the northeast coast, with the island's main pier, plus a few shops, restaurants, a solitary bar and narrow roads that lead to the island's two bays. Motorcycle taxis wait at the pier to take visitors to their beachside accommodations. The most attractive, and longest, beach is Ao Yai, 3 miles (5km) away in the southwest of the island. Most of the places to stay are close to this beach, and some rent out snorkeling gear and boogie boards.

The other bay is at Ao Kao Fai, in the north of the island; parts of it are not ideal for swimming but accommodations are available here. Motorcycles can be rented, but for the short hops between the village and the two bays it is easier to take a motorcycle taxi. All the bungalow operations have restaurants and many of those at Ao Yai set up little beach bars in the high season; there is also Oscar's Bar in the village. Some of the bungalows run trips to Ko Similan and Ko Surin Nua (▷ both right) as well as local snorkeling excursions. Travel shops in Ranong (▷ 253) will reserve your choice of accommodations on Ko Phayam and transportation to the boat pier from town.

🚏 316 B14 🚤 Boats depart at 9am and 2pm from Saphan Pla (3 miles/ 5km outside of Ranong and reached by *songthaew*); during high season (Dec–end Feb) 🖐 B150 for a 2hr trip

KO PHI PHI

Ko Phi Phi consists of two islands but only the larger Ko Phi Phi Don is inhabited, with the smaller island, Ko Phi Phi Le, only visitable on day trips. The tsunami disaster of 2004 wreaked havoc on Ko Phi Phi, hitting the densely packed area of Ao Tan Sai, causing the buildings to collapse and killing hundreds of people. The northern shoreline of the island, where there are some high-quality resort hotels, was unaffected, and this is where people come for a relaxing few days to enjoy the beautiful beaches and crystal clear waters. The quality of the diving and snorkeling around the island is first rate.

🚏 318 B17 🚤 Boats depart from Krabi; boats also run to/from Ao Nang and Laem Phra Nang Nov–end May; also from Phuket

KO SAMUI

▷ 242–243.

KO SIMILAN

www.thaiforestbooking.com
www.dnp.go.th

Ko Similan, 40 miles (64km) off shore, is the largest of the nine islands that make up the magnificent Mu Ko Similan National Park, generally agreed to be one of the most thrilling spots in Thailand for diving and snorkeling. The water is clear to a depth of 98ft (30m), but rough sea conditions close the park in the rainy season. The most convenient way to experience the mesmerizing underwater life is to join one of the many tours available from travel agents in Phuket or reserve a trip with one of the dive operators, mostly based in Khao Lak (▷ 237). A day trip is feasible, especially for snorkeling, but note the travel time from Phuket is three hours one way; two- to four-day packages are more feasible but are also more expensive because of the additional cost of staying on board

a boat or using the park bungalows on Ko Miang, the second-largest island and the park's administration headquarters.

🚏 318 A16 🕐 Mid-Nov to mid-May 🖐 Entrance adult B400, child B200; day trips from Phuket or Krabi B2,900; 2-day/1-night B3,900; 3-day/2-night B4,900 ℹ️ National Park Office, Thap Lamu pier, 4 miles/7km south of Khao Lak ☎ 076 411 913; guided tours, see www.similanthailand.com; www.phuketdivers.com; www.seadragondivecenter.com

KO SURIN NUA

www.thaiforestbooking.com
www.dnp.go.th

Mu Ko Surin Marine National Park is made up of five small islands—Ko Surin Nua, Ko Surin Tai, Ko Ree, Ko Glang and Ko Khai (or Ko Torinla)—37 miles (60km) off shore; Ko Surin Nua (north) is where the park headquarters is stationed and where accommodations are available. The shallow reefs surrounding 3-mile (5km) wide Ko Surin, where the water is clear to a depth of well over 98ft (30m), are justly praised for the exceptional quality of marine life and coral gardens on view to divers and snorkelers. Dive operators in Phuket (▷ 250–252), Khao Lak (▷ 237), Ranong (▷ 253) and Ko Chang (▷ 239) run live-aboard trips, and from Ko Phayam (▷ left) snorkeling day trips are available. Independent travel is also possible, but advance reservation of accommodations through the park office is advisable.

The Songkhran New Year in April is celebrated on Ko Surin Tai (south) with a large gathering of *chao ley*, the so-called sea travelers who have lived in this region, ignoring the marine borders between Malaysia, Thailand and Myanmar (Burma), for centuries. During the festivities, longtail boats take visitors on Ko Surin Nua across the narrow channel that separates the two islands.

🚏 316 A15 🕐 Mid-Nov to mid-May 🖐 Entrance adult B400, child B200; day trips from the pier at Kura Buri B1,700 ℹ️ National Park Office, Tab Lamu pier, 4 miles (7km) south of Khao Lak ☎ 076 491 378

INFORMATION

www.planet-scuba.net
www.samui.org
www.kohsamui-info.com
✚ 317 D15 🈁 Na Thon ☎ 077 420
504 🕐 Daily 8.30–4.30 🚢 Boats
depart from Pak Nam Tapi pier (☎ 077
426 092) east of Surat Thani, and from
Don Sak pier (☎ 077 426 000) on the
coast 43.5 miles (70km) east of Surat
Thani; an all-night boat departs from Ban
Don pier in Surat Thani; vehicle ferries,
which also carry foot passengers, run
from Don Sak pier ✈ Bangkok Airways
flies to/from Bangkok, Phuket, Krabi,
U-Tapao (close to Pattaya) and Singapore
🚆 Train–bus–boat combined tickets
to/from Bangkok reservable in advance
at Bangkok's Hua Lamphong station
🚌 Bus–boat combined tickets to/from
Bangkok reservable at the Southern Bus
Terminal in Bangkok; travel shops in
Bangkok, Hat Yai, Krabi and Phuket all
reserve bus and boat tickets to Ko Samui
and usually include transportation to/
from the piers

Above *Looking along the beautiful Lamai Beach on Ko Samui*

INTRODUCTION

Fishing families were the earliest inhabitants here; a trade in coconuts came later. The island's interior is still home to forests of coconut and durian trees shrouding numerous waterfalls. Well known only among backpackers until the 1980s, hoteliers and entrepreneurs gradually began moving in, a regular ferry service was established and an airport was up and running before the end of that decade. The high season now sees more than 20 flights a day landing from Bangkok and the numerous ferries from the mainland are packed full.

People are drawn to Thailand's third-largest island for its outstanding, palm-fringed beaches. Massages on the beach and visits to spas can be complemented by a more active excursion to the Ang Thong National Marine Park or a wide choice of water sports. Ko Samui is 15 miles (25km) wide and 13 miles (21km) long, and renting a 4WD vehicle or a motorcycle for a day or two opens up the island using the main 4169 road and the smaller roads signposted off it. During the day *songthaews* run at fixed rates to all the beaches. At night, they operate more like taxis and fares are negotiable; regular, unmetered taxis also run.

Ko Samui can be enjoyed any time of the year, but the weeks between October and mid-April are the busiest in terms of visitors to the island; accommodations need to be reserved well in advance for this period. Rainy spells are more common from late May to the end of September but rarely last long enough to spoil a visit. It's usually not long before the sun is shining again.

STAYING IN KO SAMUI

Chaweng has generally expensive accommodations, but this is the place to stay if you want an active time. The beach at Lamai is a delight and quieter than Chaweng, but some find the area's nightlife a little too lively, seeming in places to attract more single men than families or couples. Maenam, popular with backpackers, has budget accommodations, a so-so beach but a laid-back atmosphere and calm nightlife. Choeng Mon, in the island's northeast corner, has a happy balance: a white-sand beach with slingchairs laid out at night around modest bonfires, unhurried restaurants, suitable for families and couples but with buzzing Chaweng not far away. Bophut is tranquil as well, with a modicum of shops, water-sports facilities and places to stay and eat.

WHAT TO SEE

ANG THONG NATIONAL MARINE PARK
This park consists of many of the 80 islands in the Samui archipelago, and is easily visited in a day from Ko Samui, and is a great place to see wildlife.
➕ 318 C15 ✋ Park entrance B400; day trips from Ko Samui B600 📧 From travel shops on Ko Samui daily; less frequently from Ko Pha Ngan

CHAWENG
Possessing the longest and loveliest of Ko Samui's beaches, Chaweng on the east coast is the social heart of the island. The 4-mile (7km) stretch of beach, which slopes gently into the sea, can seem busy, but there is space for everyone even with the multitude of available water sports: sailing, windsurfing, parasailing, snorkeling, water-skiing and kayaking. Behind the palm trees, the scene is less idyllic as visitor-oriented developments continue to mushroom; after dark the area's main street becomes a crowded and busy night bazaar with restaurants, bars and discos jostling for your attention. Here too you will find clinics, a hospital (tel 077 230 781; www.sih.co.th), pharmacies, travel agents, internet facilities and a sprawling colony of resorts, hotels, bungalows, spas and massage parlors. Restaurants serve a variety of food, including refined cuisines, but for atmosphere consider leaving the main drag and pick a bungalow-operated place on the beach where you can hear the rhythm of the waves in the background. Chaweng has the best concentration of shops on the island, and as well as the usual stands retailing DVDs and light clothing there are also fashion boutiques and arts and crafts stores.
➕ 317 D15 (inset) 🚌 The 4169 ring road has a turnoff for Chaweng that becomes its main street and also accesses the airport

BIG BUDDHA BEACH
The beach gets its name from the 39ft-high (12m) seated Buddha that gazes down on the hedonistic scene below. The Buddha figure, erected in 1972, and temple are reached via a short causeway and, while not especially remarkable, they have become a popular, "been-there-seen-that" kind of place and can be fun to visit. Souvenir stands are abundant along the way to the ornate, dragon-decorated steps of the temple, and coin-operated machines dispense ready-made amounts of rice as nominal alms for the monks. From the top of the temple steps there are panoramic views of the north coast. The beach itself is not the best that Ko Samui has to offer, but there are places to stay for those seeking a resort-like retreat away from the main action.
➕ 317 D15 (inset) 🚗 Signposted off the 4169 road in the northeast of the island

NA MUANG WATERFALLS
With a rented vehicle, the south coast is worth exploring. The Na Muang Waterfalls, a few kilometers inland, are a pleasant destination along the way, but avoid weekends, when visitor overload is a problem. There are two falls, and the first one, close to the road, has a large pool suitable for swimming. The second waterfall is more spectacular, and is about 1 mile (1.5km) away on foot along a signposted trail. You have the option of taking an elephant ride there from below the first fall, but you will regret the journey if you don't pack a supply of drinking water. If time is limited, see the first waterfall, and skip several others that are nearby also. From the higher waterfall there are views that stretch away beyond the southern shoreline. The 4170 road, completing a loop that hugs the southern shoreline closer than the 4169, accesses Laem Hin Khom; from here a small road leads to an attractive bay from where there are fine views out to sea. Dotted around the southern coastline are one-off places to stay that provide a sense of privacy and exclusiveness.
➕ 317 D15 (inset) 🚌 Signposted off the 4169 road on its inland stretch in the south of the island

TIPS
➤➤ Spend the day relaxing and being pampered at the Tamarind Springs spa in Ko Samui (▷ 261).
➤➤ On a rented motorcycle take extra care navigating the twisting roads and unforeseen hazards and always wear a helmet and suitable clothing; the slightest fall can result in nasty injuries.

Below *Pamper yourself at the Tamarind Springs spa*

KO TAO

www.on-koh-tao.com

This is a tiny island compared with Ko Samui and Ko Pha Ngan, a short way to the south, and attracts scuba-divers thanks to the exceptional clarity of the water. There are beaches, though, where non-divers or snorkelers can enjoy themselves, and for such a small island there are a surprisingly large number of places to stay. The south and west sides are where most of the bungalows and resorts are to be found, close to Mae Hat, where boats arrive and depart from, and these can all be full between December and the end of March. Many close down from early June to early September, when sea conditions can be unpredictable. Mae Hat has a healthy cluster of restaurants, bars, dive operators and amenities like ATM machines and internet access, and it serves as the terminus for *songthaews* and motorcycle taxis to the more scattered and remote resorts on the east coast. The best beach for swimming and snorkeling, Ao Leuk, is at the bottom of the east coast, and there is a walkable track connecting it with Mae Hat.

⊞ 317 D14 🚢 Various companies depart from Chumphon; there are also boats from Ko Pha Ngan, some of which start in Ko Samui 🔗 For guided tours, see www. bigbluediving.com; www.planet-scuba.net

KO TARUTAO

www.johngray-seacanoe.com
www.thaiforestbooking.com

The single best reason for heading into the deep south on the Andaman coast is to visit Ko Tarutao, the largest of the 50 or so islands that make up the Ko Tarutao National Marine Park and the site of the park headquarters. The only accommodations are in rented tents or park bungalows, which, though fairly basic and lacking hot water, can still fill up around Christmas and Thai holiday periods; try to reserve in advance. Activities you can sign up for include boat trips through the mangrove swamps, hill-climbing

to watch the sunset, walks to a waterfall and to sandy beaches where turtles come ashore to lay their eggs, and spotting whales and dolphins off the coast.

⊞ 318 C18 🛈 Park visitor center on Ko Tarutao ☎ 074 729 002; park visitor center at Pak Bara ☎ 074 783 485 🚢 Boats depart from Pak Bara (2 daily; 1.5 hours) and from Thammalang pier south of Satun town

KO YAO NOI ISLANDS

▷ 245.

KRABI

▷ 246–247.

NAKHON SI THAMMARAT

This large town is not a major transportation hub or jumping-off point for one of the offshore islands. One long road, Thanon Ratchadamnoen, bisects the town on a north–south axis and *songthaews* run all the way up and down it throughout the day and evening. But, at the southern end of Thanon Ratchadamnoen is Wat Mahathat, a stupendous temple that dates back to the 13th century and is the most striking in appearance of any temple outside of Bangkok. A short walk farther south brings you to the National Museum (Wed–Sun 9–4; B30; www.thailandmuseum. com) and its specialist collection of art and craft items from southern Thailand. Nielloware (*kruang tom*)—a hard-to-find decorative craft that involves rubbing a compound of metals into etched silverware—is a local specialty, and a range of small household items of nielloware can be purchased from any of the handicraft shops on Thanon Thachang, which is close to the tourist office. Thai shadow theater is also kept alive in the town and there's a workshop (south of Wat Mahathat, Soi 3, Thanon Si Thammasok, tel 075 346 394; daily 8–5), where the art is demonstrated and puppets are for sale.

⊞ 318 D16 🛈 TAT office in Sanam Na Muang, in the heart of town ☎ 075 346 515 🕔 Daily 8.30–4.30 🚌 Buses from Bangkok (12 hours), Hat Yai (3 hours), Krabi

(3 hours), Phuket (5–7 hours) ✈ Flights from Bangkok with Nok Air, AirAsia, One-Two-Go 🚆 Trains from Bangkok

PAK NAM PRAN

Between the towns of Hua Hin and Chumphon, the quaint fishing town of Pak Nam has a lengthy, white-sandy beach catering mainly to wealthy Bangkok residents with second homes, and expats with inside knowledge on the local boutique hotels. Pak Nam is another beach where there's not much to do but soak up the sun, swim and snorkel or watch dolphins from the beach. It does, however, serve as a convenient base to explore nearby Khao Sam Roi Yot National Park. There are several local restaurants and small shops here, but there isn't much to speak of in terms of nightlife. The beach, which is named Hat Naresuan, is pleasant however, and visitors are likely to have long stretches to themselves. The colorful shrimp and crab boats are the subject of many photos.

⊞ 314 D11 🚗 From nearby Pranburi town, turn east off of Highway 4 onto Road 3168 🚆 Nearest station for the Southern Rail Line is located 15.5 miles (25km) south of Hua Hin 🚌 Available from Bangkok to Hua Hin and Pranburi, with *songthaews* available for the remainder

PATTANI

Pattani and the other southern provinces of Narathiwat and Yala are more ethnic Malay Muslim than Thai Buddhist. Currently, however, this region is best avoided except for essential travel, as there has been violence and insurgency (reaching as far as Hat Yai, ▷ 236–237). There is strong support in this area of southern Thailand for regional autonomy from the Thai government and a separatist movement has made itself heard in recent years. If you are heading overland to Malaysia, the town of Sadao (Songkhla province) is the recommended alternative.

⊞ 319 E18 🚌 From Hat Yai and Yala 🚆 From Bangkok to Yala, an hour away by bus

KO YAO NOI ISLANDS

The beautiful islands of Ko Yao represent a frontier in Thailand's rapid coastal tourism development. The name Ko Yao means "Long Island," and Ko Yao Noi and Ko Yao Yai mean Little Long Island and Big Long Island respectively. The setting on both islands with the many surrounding islets and karsts is beautiful—no matter which beachside hotel visitors choose, there will always be a great view. While Yao Yai is the larger of the two by far, Ko Yao Noi is much more popular.

WILDLIFE AND BEACHLIFE

There are numerous beaches on Ko Yao Noi, and while swimming is excellent at high tide, many become mud flats at low tide. The island has numerous options for outdoor activities, including rock climbing, kayaking, snorkeling, birdwatching and walking through the densely rainforested interior. Frequently sighted animals include cobras, eagles, macaques, gibbons and monitor lizards.

The 4,000 residents on the island are overwhelmingly Muslim Thais, therefore it is best to dress conservatively to avoid offense. Likewise, alcohol is only sparsely available. The central "metropolis" of Ko Yao Noi is Ban Tha Kai, a quaint little town with the main post office, central market, ATM and a number of shops and food stalls.

Accommodations are spread around both islands and far from the piers, so it's a good idea to arrange free pickup to guesthouses in advance. The islands are fairly rustic—most stretches of road are unpaved, and there are few western-style restaurants.

KO YAO NOI'S BEACHES

Hat Klong Jaak was one of the first beaches to receive tourist accommodations and has the best nightlife on the island. Nearby Hat Pasai is a lovely beach easily accessed from Klong Jaak. A few miles to the north, Hat Tha Khao is the backpacker beach with the cheapest accommodations. The village of Ban Tha Khao, located here, hosts a busy pier with boats to Krabi. Nearby Hat Sai Taew, or Temple Beach, is the nicest on the island. The name derives from a Buddhist sect that owns the land adjacent to the beach.

INFORMATION

318 B16, B17 Most boats arrive from Phuket and Krabi, with service also available from Ao Nang and Phang Nga. Taxis meet arriving boats and deliver passengers to island guesthouses for around B100. Boats from Phuket leave at the Bang Rong pier, departing hourly during daylight for B120 (approximately 1hr 20 mins). Boats arrive at Tha Suka and Tha Manok piers on Ko Yao Noi. Boats from Krabi leave at the Ao Thalen pier, 22 miles (35km) north of town, several times daily between 10am and 4pm, for B210 (approximately 1hr). Boats arrive at Tha Kao pier on Ko Yao Noi. Boats between Yao Noi and Yao Yai can easily be arranged at any time during daylight hours at the adjacent piers.

Above *Traditional longtail boat waiting at Ko Yao Noi*

INFORMATION

www.yourkrabi.com
www.johngray-seacanoe.com

➕ 318 B17 ℹ Thanon Utrakit, north of town on the road to the bus terminal ☎ 075 622 163 🕐 Daily 8.30–4.30 🚌 To/from Bangkok's Southern Terminal (12hrs), Hat Yai (4–5hrs), Ko Samui (bus/boat, 7 hours), Phang Nga (2hrs), Phuket (3–4hrs), Ranong (5 hours), Surat Thani (2.5hrs); the bus station (☎ 075 611 804) is north of town, too far to walk, but *songthaews* run regularly into town 🚆 From Bangkok overnight to Surat Thani, then a bus (16hrs) ✈ From Bangkok with Thai Airways, Bangkok Airways and Phuket Air; the airport (☎ 075 636 541) is 11 miles (18km) east of town 🚢 Boats to Ko Lanta and Ko Jum mid-Oct to mid-Apr (2hrs); to Ko Phi Phi all year (1.5hrs); tickets usually include transfer to the pier 📖 *Krabi: Caught in the Spell—A Guide to Thailand's Enchanted Province*, Thom Henley ✋ One-day snorkeling trips B1,000; kayaking trips B1,000–B2,000

INTRODUCTION

Krabi achieves a rewarding balance between visitor-related facilities, excellent transportation links to offshore islands and local beaches, good accommodations and an intrinsically appealing Thai flavor, and is a less-touristy alternative to Phuket. The denizens of Krabi (pronounced *gra-bee*) province's eponymous capital are well used to people staying around for a day or two before moving on.

This small fishing town is a principal hub for onward travel to some of the region's most popular islands, including Ko Phi Phi (▷ 241), with its diving and snorkeling opportunities, and Ko Lanta (▷ 240), with its superb beaches. As townsfolk go about their business, there is a pleasant air of nonchalance toward visitors. Evenings can be pleasant around town, especially on Thanon Kongka and its walkway by the side of the Krabi River. At around 5.30pm mobile food and drink stands are wheeled into place here, powered up from gas canisters; the seafood is unpacked from ice boxes and customers start drifting by as tables and chairs are laid out.

There are no "must-see" attractions in Krabi town, but the numerous travel shops located around town will book you on a one-day trip to nearby islands that includes snorkeling gear, a packed lunch and transfers to and from your accommodations.

WHAT TO SEE

BEACHES, CORAL REEFS AND MANGROVE SWAMPS

A popular excursion is paddling in a kayak through the slightly creepy world of mangrove swamps or trips to the *hongs* farther up the coast from Krabi. The most visited local beach is Ao Nang, a resort area in its own right with plenty of amenities, and easily reached in half an hour by *songthaew* from Thanon Maharat, Krabi's busy main street. Just southeast of Ao Nang is a small, lush-green peninsula, Laem Phra Nang (Railay), where limestone cliffs hover precipitously over the clear emerald water and white sandy beaches.

Rock-climbing is a big draw here, as are snorkeling and diving, and bungalow accommodations can be reserved in Krabi or Ao Nang when you arrive. Transportation from Krabi to Railay is easy—by boat in less than an hour from the riverfront pier or just a few minutes from Ao Nang—but, as with Ao Nang, it is feasible to base yourself in Krabi and then make day trips.

AO NANG

The charming beach town of Ao Nang serves as a sort of back-door entrance to nearby Railay Beach (Laem Phra Nang), Phuket, and the beautiful islands of the Andaman coast. Ao Nang is smaller than neighboring Krabi, the provincial capital and consequently many buses bypass it, requiring travelers to catch a *songthaew* from Krabi to complete their journey.

Most travelers only spend a night or two here before using the well-organized boat services to visit nearby islands. Facilities are much more substantial here than the outlying islands or Railay, so it's a good idea to stock up on any necessary items before heading out.

Snorkeling, sunbathing and beachcombing are the only real daytime activities, with bar hopping and shopping the main pastimes in the evening. The most dramatic scenery is at Ao Phai Plong, a private beach occupied by the Centara Grand Hotel.

✚ 318 B17 🚤 To Ko Phi Phi and Ko Lanta for about B500 at 2.5hrs each. To Railay from B80–B120 throughout the day. Frequent boats to Phuket and other islands 🚌 Generally *songthaew* between Krabi and nearby towns

KLONG MUANG

www.klongmuang.com

Just around the corner from Ao Nang, Klong Muang is a quiet, relatively undeveloped beach just off the tourist map. A few luxury hotels have popped up recently however, such as the Sheraton Krabi Beach Resort, Sofitel Krabi Phokeethra Golf & Spa Resort and Phulay Beach Resort, suggesting Klong Muang may soon become one of the many vacation satellites of Krabi. For now there's not much to do here but soak up the sun, swim in the crystal seas and enjoy the ambience of the tropical Andaman coast.

There's no nightlife here to speak of—for that, head to nearby Ao Nang—but there's plenty of great seafood, caught in the bay each morning and delivered to the restaurants along the beach.

🚌 Just a few kilometers west of Ao Nang

LAEM PHRA NANG

www.railay.com

The beautiful peninsula of Laem Phra Nang sits between Ao Nang and Krabi, bounded by dramatic rainforest-crowned karsts. The peninsula is inaccessible by road, only reachable by boat via the surrounding towns. Before boutique resort hotels and guesthouses arrived, the dominant residents were macaques and gibbons who still occupy the limestone peaks, coming down to beg and steal food from tourists. The landscape is dramatic too, with karsts punctured by countless caves—there is even a hanging lagoon called Sa Phra Nang, which is only reachable via a dangerous climb.

Known by the tourism industry as Railay, there are four superb beaches in the area, including Hat Ton Sai (a popular backpacker's beach with plenty of good-value accommodations), Hat Rai Leh West (the landing beach for Ao Nang and outlying islands), Hat Rai Leh East (more of a mud flat and landing for Krabi), and Hat Tham Phra Nang (occupied exclusively by the luxurious Rayavadee resort, though graciously open to the public).

🚤 Longtail boats from Ao Nang to Hat Rai Leh West and Hat Ton Sai are B80–120, leaving throughout the day. Longtail boats from Hat Rai Leh East to Khong Ka (Krabi) leave several times a day or when full, and cost B200.

Opposite *Longtail ferry boats moored along the shore at Ao Nang*
Below *Saffron-robed monks at Wat Tham Seua Temple*

INFORMATION

www.johngray-seacanoe.com
www.seacanoe.net
www.sayantour.com
http://phangnga.sawdee.com
🚑 318 B16 👋 Park entrance B200;
Elephant Belly Cave tours B500; tours
of Phang Nga Bay from B500/B800 for a
half/full day, plus B250 for overnight stay
on Ko Panyi; *hong* tours B2,000–B2,800,
overnight *hong* tours B9,000 🚌 From
Phuket, Krabi and Surat Thani; the bus
station (☎ 076 412 014) is in the heart
of town 🚤 Tours of Phang Nga Bay
depart from Tha Don pier, 5.5 miles (9km)
south of town (reached by *songthaew*)

TIP

>> Establish exactly what is covered by
a Phang Nga Bay tour before committing
yourself.

Below *The towering limestone rocks in
Phang Nga Bay*

PHANG NGA

The town of Phang Nga is the starting point for trips into the Phang Nga
National Marine Park and its breathtaking vista of limestone formations.
Highway 4 passes right through Phang Nga and, though the town itself is less
than absorbing, everything you might need is usefully gathered around the
middle of town and its bus station: hotels, restaurants, banks, ATMs, post
office and numerous travel shops. From any of these travel shops it's easy to
arrange tours in the bay, as well as a local two-hour trip to Elephant Belly
Cave. The cave is a natural tunnel through the cliff that stretches for 0.6 miles (just
over 1km) and involves some canoeing and sometimes wading as well.

THE BAY EXPERIENCE

Vessels motor their way into Phang Nga Bay and head for the limestone rocks
that tower out of the water up to a height of 328ft (100m). You will undoubtedly
be taken to the cleft Khao Ping Gan (Leaning Rock), also known as James
Bond Island because it provided the set for Scaramanga's headquarters in *The
Man With the Golden Gun*. It has inevitably suffered from the hype, and the
beach and cave area has a surplus of souvenir vendors and overpriced seafood
restaurants.

The standard tour also takes in the picturesque Muslim village of Ko Panyi,
built on stilts over the water around a mosque-bearing rock. Overnight bay trips
involve staying in the village and, like the early-morning trips from town, they
improve the quality of the experience by avoiding the crowds of visitors that
build up from mid-morning onward.

THE HONGS

Thai for "room," a *hong* is a tidal lagoon entered by sea canoe through narrow
openings in rock. Once inside, you are surrounded by water, dwarfed by
vegetation-covered rocks and aware of an eerie silence. The *hongs* of Phang
Nga Bay are the focus of day-long trips that are mostly organized from Phuket
and Krabi by reputable companies. The tours include lunch and hot drinks and
provide time for swimming and sunbathing on a beach. They can be fun as well
as educational if you have your own canoe to paddle and if the tour leader is
knowledgeable about the *hong's* ecosystem. Best of all are the two-day/one-
night trips.

PHETCHABURI

Within day-trip distance of Bangkok or Hua Hin, the ancient *wats* of Phetchaburi are a big draw, and the best of them can be appreciated on a walking tour of the town. There is no tourist office or obvious town center, but the backpacker's hotel, Rabieng Rim Nam Guest House, is a useful source of information and a central base. It is located at Chomrut Bridge at the junction of Thanon Chisa-in and Thanon Damnoen Kasem. *Samlors* from the train or bus station will bring you here, and the walking tour below begins from here.

A WALKING TOUR

Cross Chomrut Bridge and turn right onto Thanon Phongsuriya, passing the Chom Klao Hotel. Wat Yai Suwannaram is on the right-hand side of the road after 38 yards (350m). Notice the 18th-century murals decorating the *bot* (main sanctuary) with images of Indra, Brahma and other divinities. There are two other *wats* farther down the street on the other side, but limited time is better spent ignoring these and turning right instead into Thanon Phokarong. After an eight-minute walk down this street, turn right into Thanon Phrasong, where Wat Kamphaeng comes into view on your right. Built to worship Hindu gods in the 12th century, nose your way around the *wat* to appreciate its ancient lineage. Leaving here, continue along Thanon Phrasong and pass two undistinguished *wats* on either side of the street.

WAT MAHATHAT

Cross the river by the main junction, and ahead of you looms the stately Wat Mahathat. This is the town's most visited and most photogenic *wat*, and there is plenty of fine artwork and decorative detail to examine. From Wat Mahathat walk up Thanon Damnoen Kasem to return to Chomrut Bridge and your starting point. The Rabieng Rim Nam Guest House has a good restaurant and makes a suitable place to rest and recuperate.

KHAO WANG

From Thanon Phongsuriya at Chomrut Bridge, a short *samlor* taxi ride will bring you to this hill. It is an exhausting walk to the summit, where the former king's (Rama IV) summer house is now a museum (daily 9–4; adult B70, child B30); there is a cable car (daily 8.30–5.30; B64).

INFORMATION

✚ 314 D10 🛈 Tourist information from Rabieng Rim Nam Guest House ☎ 032 401 983 🚌 Bangkok (2.5hrs), Hua Hin (1.5hrs), Cha-am (45 min) 🚆 Bangkok (up to 8 daily; 3hrs), Hua Hin (1hr); Cha-am (35 min)

TIP

»» The graceful old library in the middle of the pond in Wat Yai Suwannaram is worth seeking out.

Above *Rama IV's summer house at Khao Wang is covered in intricate carvings*

INTRODUCTION

Thailand's premier resort, Phuket (pronounced poo-ket) has enough diversity to accommodate most tastes. Patong is hedonistic, Phuket town is historical; beaches in the west are long and sandy and those in the northwest are quiet. Each beach area has its own character, which affects to some extent the kind of holiday you will experience. Phuket town, on the east coast and without a beach, deserves a visit and is worth considering as an accommodations base. It has its own identity and appeal, best appreciated on foot (▷ 254–255), and there are regular *songthaews* throughout the day between the town and the west-coast beaches. After about 5.30pm the *songthaews* stop running, but *tuk-tuks* are readily available. Transportation between the beaches is by way of *tuk-tuks* (B300–B400) and taxis and it is easy to rent motorcycles or jeeps (but take care: Motorcycle accidents on Phuket are alarmingly frequent).

Merchants from India and Arab lands were stopping off in Phuket at least as early as the ninth century, but it was another 700 years before the first European traders arrived. Pearls and tin were the valuable commodities, Chinese immigration followed and the English introduced modern methods of tin-mining in the early 20th century. The wealth generated by the tin trade turned Phuket town into the prosperous island capital that is revealed in the lobby museum of the Thavorn Hotel.

Tin remains important, as does rubber, coconut and fishing, but in recent years tourism has become the main source of revenue. The 2004 tsunami brought financial hardship, as hotel occupancy rates and visitor numbers plummeted. Patong beach, though, looked more enticing than it had for decades: The quality of the sea water improved and only 13 percent of Phuket's dive sites were found to have suffered damage. Since the rebuild, Phuket has flourished and become busier than ever.

WHAT TO SEE

WEST COAST BEACHES

Ao Patong has a terrific beach and is dense with hotels and amenities—this is the place to arrange water sports—but while it has an energetic nightlife it has a noticeably seedy side as well and some find the whole place vulgar. Family-friendly Ao Karon offers a better balance of activities and relaxation, though the beach lacks shade, and it's just a short hop north to experience

INFORMATION

www.phuket.com
www.phuket.net
www.phuketmagazine.com
www.phuket.com/coralisland
www.santanaphuket.com
www.johngray-seacanoe.com
www.seacavecanoe.com
www.andamanseakayak.com

➕ 318 B17 ℹ️ 191 Thanon Talang, ☎ 076 212 213 🕐 Daily 8.30–4.30 ✈️ Phuket International Airport (☎ 076 327 230) is in the northwest of the island, 20 miles (32km) from Phuket town. Airport buses will take you to your hotel, but only taxis are available for the return journey (B400 upward, but metered taxis charge B50 for 0–1.25 miles (0–2km) and B7 for every subsequent 0.6 mile (1km) ☎ 076 232 192). Airlines flying to Phuket include Thai Airways, Bangkok Airways, Phuket Air, Orient Thai, Nok Air, One-Two-Go and AirAsia 🚌 Regular routes to/from Krabi (3–4 hours) via Phang Nga (2.5hrs), and Chumphon (6.5hrs), Nakhon Si Thammarat (7hrs), Hat Yai (6–8hrs) and Ranong (5–6hrs); bus journeys to/from Bangkok are usually overnight and take 12–15hrs. Phuket town bus station (☎ 076 211 977) is at the eastern end of Thanon Phang Nga; *songthaews* to the west coast

Opposite *The spectacular Ton Sai waterfall at Khao Pra Thaeo*
Above *Laem Phromthep on Phuket island*

beaches line up along Thanon Ranong in Phuket town 🚉 To Surat Thani, then a bus to Phuket (6hrs)

TIPS

➤➤ Observe the beach warning flags as riptides and strong currents can occur, especially between May and the end of October.

➤➤ The tourist office issues a leaflet setting out the *tuk-tuk* fares between the beaches and the *songthaew* fares from Phuket town.

➤➤ As always in Thailand, ignore anyone, including foreigners, who approaches you on the street here and tries to initiate a conversation or offer helpful advice. It is always a scam.

Below *The clocktower roundabout in Phuket town*

frenetic Patong in small doses. Farther south, the beaches of Kata Yai and Kata Noi benefit from an equally genial air and are home to some good hotels and restaurants. North of Patong, the first beach is the relatively low-key Kamala, which has most amenities close at hand. Once you move farther north, to Bang Tao, you are entering luxury-hotel territory, where visitors tend to confine themselves to their resort facilities. The next beach up, Nai Thon, has a sense of privacy due to the lack of hotel developments and public transportation (a taxi from Bang Tao is necessary). Just to the north is Nai Yang, a sedate and shaded beach with accommodations and agreeable restaurants looking out to sea. The last beach on the west coast, just north of the airport, is at Mai Khao; it stretches for a glorious 11 miles (17km), with the J W Marriott hotel the only sizeable development.

KHAO PHRA THAEO WILDLIFE PARK

The tourist office in Phuket town dispenses a useful small guide to the park that describes the Ton Sai Waterfall Nature Trail, which draws your attention to rain forest characteristics like the huge buttresses of the Dipterocarpus species of trees and a particular species of palm (*kerriodoxa elegans* Dransfield) that is found only in Phuket. The waterfall itself is eye-catching only during the rainy months—between June and the end of October, when there is enough water to produce a good flow. It is possible to walk along a trail from the waterfall to the Gibbon Rehabilitation Center (tel 076 260 492; www.gibbonproject.org; daily 9–4; donation required), but with your own transportation the center is more directly reached using the directions given in the driving tour (▷ 254–255).

✚ 318 B17 ✉ Amphoe Thalang ☎ 076 311 998 🚌 *Songthaew* to Thalang, turn right and walk the 2 miles (3km) to the entrance or take a motorcycle taxi 🚗 Turn right at Thalang on the 402 road, 13 miles (21km) from Phuket town

TRIPS AND TOUTS

Phuket has hundreds of small businesses catering to visitors, with water sports and sea-canoeing trips into Phang Nga Bay (▷ 248) being the most popular. Diving and snorkeling trips are highly rated due to the close proximity of spectacular reefs, and packages for novices as well as those with experience are available. Half-day and full-day snorkeling trips to Coral Island (Ko Hai) off the southeast coast are readily arranged in any travel shop. Water sports, such as jet-skiing, are also popular, but ask your hotel to recommend a reputatable hire firm. Some jet-ski renters, have been known to claim that customers have "damaged" machines in order to extort ten of thousands of baht from them. Thai cookery classes are also popular and good Thai cuisine is served at a number of restaurants.

Part of the Phuket experience is lying on one of the more popular beaches and being offered a massage, cold drinks and sliced fruits, a sarong or trinkets of some kind. Vendors outside tailor shops will suggest you buy a suit or two, and at night the beach roads are awash with stalls selling clothing, DVDs and other items. There are no hard sells, and lots of smiles, but be prepared to bargain. Some of the best shopping on the island is in Phuket town, with specialist arts and crafts shops as well as department stores and street stalls.

MORE TO SEE

VEGETARIAN FESTIVAL

Every year for nine days between late September and November (the dates are determined by the start of the lunar month), a major Vegetarian Festival takes place. The festival is not just about avoiding meat products and visitors are treated to dramatic and noisy processions in Phuket town, which involve entranced devotees skewering themselves with sharp objects and walking over red-hot coals.

RANONG

Only a narrow estuary separates Ranong from Mynamar (Burma) and this gives the town an engaging border atmosphere, where Thais and Burmese mix freely with Malays and Chinese. Day trips into Myanmar are easy to arrange with any of the travel shops around town and Ranong is also the base for trips to Ko Chang (▷ 239) and Ko Phayam (▷ 241). Thanon Ruangrat is Ranong's main street and here you will find shops, hotels, restaurants and internet access.

➕ 316 B14 ℹ Tourist and tour information from Pon's Place, Thanon Ruangrat
☎ 077 823 344 ✈ AirAsia flies from Bangkok 5 days a week; the airport is 15 miles (20km) south of town 🚌 Buses serve Bangkok (10hrs), Chumphon (3hrs), Phuket (5–6hrs), Krabi (6hrs), Surat Thani (3–5hrs), Phang Nga (5hrs) and Hat Yai (5hrs); the bus station is south of town on Highway 4 but many buses will also stop in the middle of town and there are also private bus companies 🚢 Boats to Ko Chang and Ko Phayam depart from the pier at Saphan Pla, 3 miles (5km) out of town and served by *songthaews*

SONGKHLA

The most pleasant town on the Gulf Coast south of Hua Hin, Songkhla has charm and character. Bus stops, amenities and places to visit are clustered in a small area around Thanon Jana, the main street that runs from the fishing port on the west side of town. The National Museum (Thanon Jana, tel 074 311 728; www.thailandmuseum.com; Wed–Sun 9–12, 1–4; B40) is housed in an elegant century-old building and displays a collection of local art and objects. Songkhla is a walkable town and to the north of Thanon Jana there is a forested hill, Khao Tung Kuan, from the top of which the geography becomes clearer, with the Gulf of Thailand to the north and Thale Sap lagoon to the west. Just north of the hill is Hat Samila, an 5-mile (8km) stretch of shaded beach. South of Thanon Jana lies the eye-catching Wat Matchimarat on Thanon Saiburi.

➕ 319 E18 🚌 Regular services to/from Hat Yai (▷ 236–237), 15 miles (25km) away, from where there are good road and air links

SURAT THANI

A less-than-arresting town, traffic-choked Surat Thani is where you are likely to find yourself in the course of reaching or departing from Ko Samui or Ko Pha Ngan. Touts congregate around the bus and train stations and you should be circumspect regarding their deals, especially any that involve private buses and accommodations. If you get stuck waiting for a train, the Queens Hotel (tel 077 311 003) has a few good bedrooms. A million miles away from Surat Thani in some respects, but only 37 miles (60km) by road, is the unruffled town of Chaiya, with its ancient *wats* and 10-day meditation programs at the International Dharma Heritage (tel 077 431 661; www.suanmokkh. org). Local buses from Surat Thani travel to Chaiya and buses between Chumphon and Surat Thani will drop you off at the turnoff for Chaiya. One event not to miss in September/October is the start of the 11th lunar month and the Buddhist Chak Phra Festival in Surat Thani. It is celebrated with processions on the town's river and on the streets.

➕ 316 C15 ℹ 5 Thanon Talatmai
☎ 077 288 817 🕐 Daily 8.30–4.30
🚌 Buses serve Bangkok (10 hours), Hat Yai (4 hours), Krabi (2–3 hours), Nakhon Si Thammarat (2 hours), Phang Nga (3hrs), Phuket (5hrs) and Ranong (4hrs) 🚆 To/from Bangkok (12hrs), including overnight services; the train station at Phum Phin is 8 miles (13km) west of town, from where buses and shared taxis travel into town
❓ Train, bus, plane and boat tickets can be reserved at Phantip Travel (293/6–8 Thanon Talatmai ☎ 077 272 230) 🚢 To Ko Samui (▷ 242–243) or Ko Pha Ngan (▷ 239); www.seatranferry.com ✈ Thai Airways flies daily to Bangkok; the airport is 17 miles (27km) north of town, by minibus from Phantip Travel

Right *A painted fishing boat, decorated in the colorful Kor Lae style*

TRANG

www.trangonline.com
www.trangislands.com
There are no "must-see" sights in Trang but the town has good transportation links, a fair choice of easy-to-find hotels and places to eat and a helpful tourist office—all of which increase the appeal of coming here for the superb island beaches that lie some 25 miles (40km) to the west. If you have been to Phuket and found it too commericalized then the islands near Trang will come as a very pleasant surprise.

All the travel agent shops in the heart of town offer various packages to one or more islands that are easy to arrange. Staying on the mainland, there are opportunities for canoeing, trekking trips and excursions to scenic waterfalls, and the travel shops in town have all the details (from B750 for a day trip to nearly B2,000 for a three-day trek).

➕ 318 C17 ℹ Thanon Ruenrom near the night market ☎ 075 215 867 🕐 Daily 8.30–4.30 🚆 Two overnight trains daily between Bangkok and Trang 🚌 Daily to and from Bangkok (13hrs), Hat Yai (3hrs), Krabi (2hrs), Nakhon Si Thammarat (3hrs), Phuket (4.5 hours) ✈ Daily to and from Bangkok Thai and AirAsia, tel 075 219 923

PHUKET TOWN TO KRABI

While Phuket island can sometimes seem too busy, the town of Krabi is characterized by an easygoing pace. A drive between the two takes in this change of tempo. The drive crosses three of Thailand's provinces, accesses the region's photogenic scenery and also takes you through a rural landscape of rubber and palm oil plantations where Thai Muslims live and work.

THE DRIVE

Distance: 102 miles (165km)
Allow: 1 day
Start at: Phuket town
End at: Krabi

Phuket town (▷ 251–252), on the east side of Phuket island, is a workaday community quite different in character from the lighthearted, beach-based life of the island's west coast.

★ Follow signs out of Phuket town for Route 402, the main highway, also signposted to the airport. Go ahead at the traffic lights where the road to the left is signposted for Patong beach. Stay on Route 402, which leads to the large Heroines Monument traffic circle (roundabout), 6 miles (10 km) north of Phuket town.

① The Heroines Monument in the middle of the traffic circle commemorates the defeat of an invading army from Myanmar (Burma) in 1785 and the defiant leadership offered by two women who organized a female army and expelled the enemy.

Turn off to the right onto the signposted Route 4027 for the Gibbon Rehabilitation Center in Khao Phra Thaeo Wildlife Park (▷ 252).

② The Gibbon Rehabilitation Center is 1.2 miles (2km) down a signposted turning to the left off Route 4027. Visitors are introduced to the work of the volunteer-run center, helping gibbons rescued from captivity to return to forest life. Gibbons used to freely roam the forests of Phuket and were routinely kept as

pets; although this is now illegal, the animals remain endangered. A 15-minute walk along a riverside track from the center leads to the scenic Bang Pae Falls.

Continue on Route 4027, which rejoins Route 402 near the turnoff for the airport. Do not take the airport road but continue northward on the 402, crossing the Sarasin Bridge and the empty beach on your left. After a few miles (kilometers), bear right on the 402, signposted for Phang Nga, along a two-lane highway. Be careful here—slow down for the bends in the road. You are now in the province of Phang Nga.

③ The province of Phang Nga, separating the provinces of Ranong and Phuket, is noted for its landscape of limestone mountains. Each rock formation rises up in dramatic isolation, though before you see these mountains a more characteristic sight is row upon row of rubber trees laid out in straight lines with cups attached ready to collect the sap.

After passing through the attractive small village of Takua Thung, 6 miles (10km) before Phang Nga, look for a sign on the left pointing to Wat Tham Suwankhuha.

❹ Two caverns make up the fascinating temple cave of Wat Tham Suwankhuha, replete with Buddhist images and dominated by a large, awkwardly proportioned reclining Buddha.

Back on the main road, surrounded by an array of limestone peaks, note the right turn at the traffic lights, signposted for Krabi. For a lunch break, though, carry on straight at the traffic lights to enter the main street of Phang Nga town (▷ 248). After lunch, turn around and head back to the traffic lights to take the road to Krabi.

❺ The road to Krabi crosses a small bridge, with views of homes built on wooden platforms in the river, and five minutes later on your left you pass a golden Buddha figure sitting splendidly beneath a towering limestone peak.

When you see a signpost saying 3 miles (5km) to Thap Put, take the next right turn onto a small road that runs through a palm oil plantation. This detour will take you through a seemingly endless vista of palm oil trees, a valuable cash crop in this part of the country. This road does eventually rejoin the main Krabi road, or you can return to Route 415 and continue via Thap Put.

At Thap Put turn right to join Route 4, which leads to Krabi through a Muslim neighborhood and into the province of Krabi.

❻ The mosque on the right-hand side of the road is evidence of the fact that many of the people living in this area are Muslims, but you will also see *wats* (temples). The province of Krabi, like Phang Nga, is characterized by a karst landscape, and it provides an engaging backdrop for the final leg of this journey to the town of Krabi.

WHERE TO EAT
PHANG-NGA INN
Phong Nga's smartest hotel, signposted in the middle of town, has a restaurant on the ground floor. ✉ 2/2 Soi Lohakit, Phang Nga ☎ 076 411 963 🕐 Restaurant daily 7am–9pm

PLACE TO VISIT
GIBBON REHABILITATION CENTER
www.gibbonproject.org
✉ Bang Pae Wa, Phuket ☎ 076 260 492 🕐 Daily 9–4 ♿ Entrance to the national park B200

TOURIST INFORMATION
PHUKET TOWN TOURIST OFFICE
✉ 191 Thanon Talang Phuket ☎ 076 212 213

KRABI TOURIST OFFICE
✉ Thanon Utrakit ☎ 075 622 163 🕐 Daily 8.30–4.30

Opposite *Local boats in the shallow waters just offshore from Tham Phra Nang Beach*
Above *White-handed gibbon, one of the many residents of the Gibbon Rehabilitation Center in Phuket*

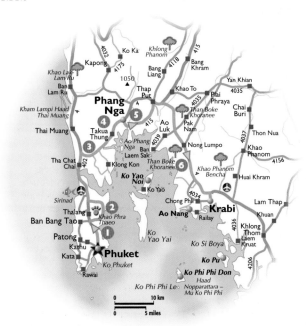

PHUKET TOWN

This walk introduces you to the provincial capital of Phuket, its vernacular architecture, a small local museum and the everyday life of the townspeople. It also takes in a wide range of shops where you may be tempted to make a purchase. If it's a hot day, but comfort yourself with knowing that the walk ends at an ice-cream parlor in an air-conditioned building.

THE WALK

Distance: 1 mile (1.5km)
Allow: Half an hour, plus time for visits
Start/end at: The fountain traffic circle (roundabout) where Thanon Ranong and Thanon Rasada meet

HOW TO GET THERE

From the east coast beaches, take a taxi or one of the *songthaews* that run regularly into town.

★ The fountain traffic circle can be considered the heart of the old town. Look for street names in English on a blue background. Thanon Rasada is where the *songthaews* to the beaches depart, but find the signposted Thanon Yaowarat that heads north.

Walk a short way up Thanon Yaowarat and take the first right turn, with an old-fashioned Chinese pharmacy on the corner, into Thanon Phang-Nga. Pass the On Hotel on your left and, before reaching a set of traffic lights, gaze upward to observe the traditional shophouses along this street.

❶ Some of the shophouses are rather dilapidated and showing their age; they were built a century ago for Chinese shopkeepers in the economic heyday created by tin-mining on the island. A well-preserved example on this street, at No. 90—now the Le Dix clothes shop—is best seen from the left-hand side of the street.

At the traffic lights, turn left into Thanon Phuket and cross to the other side of the street to appreciate the architecture of Siam City Bank.

❷ The Siam City Bank is a grander example of the kind of buildings constructed in the second half of the 19th century, when the island's capital was rebuilt here to replace the old capital of Thalang, destroyed by the Burmese in 1800.

Walk along to the first crossroads and turn left, at the Honda store, into Thanon Thalang for a street full of fine examples of wooden shophouses built in the Sino-Portuguese style.

❸ The Sino-Portuguese style was brought to Phuket by Portuguese traders and Chinese merchants who were familiar with this architecture from the ex-Portuguese port of Melaka to the south of Thailand. The building style is characterized by shutters, louver windows and decorative carvings on the exterior in stucco and wood. Look for the engraved dragons that reveal the Chinese influence. Number 37, on the right-hand side, is now the Talang Guest House (▷ 272), a good example of how these buildings can be preserved into the 21st century without losing their character. Before reaching the guesthouse, a modern art gallery on the other side of the street is open for business, but Thanon Thalang is full of more traditional shops selling everyday goods and fabrics.

At the crossroads, where Thanon Thalang meets Thanon Yaowarat, turn left to return to the walk's start point, but consider a spot of shopping before stopping for lunch.

❹ The Wood and Stone shop at No.55 Thanon Yaowarat, on the right-hand side of the street, is worth a browse for gifts. A few doors down at Rinda Magical Art (No. 27), you may catch the resident artist at work. Close to the fountain traffic circle, at 10 Thanon Rasada, Pui Fai has a large selection of affordable

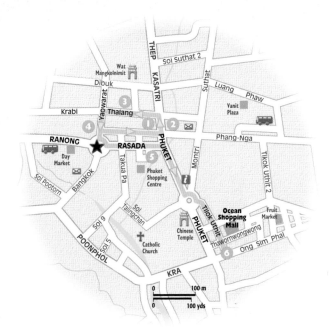

arts and crafts. Here, too, you will find a lunch spot suitably named The Circle.

After lunch, continue to walk down Thanon Rasada for an art shop and a small museum.

❺ The Soul of Asia shop is on the left, and farther down on the right is the Thavorn Hotel and its lobby museum, with old photographs and memorabilia of the town's history.

Continue walking down the street to a traffic circle and then turn right onto Thanon Phuket, passing the tourist office on your left. At the clock traffic circle, head down the street signposted Thanon Tikok Uthit to the end where there is a Boots pharmacy on the right. Walk straight across the crossroads here and head toward the green-and-white building of Robinson's department store.

Opposite *An elegant Portuguese-style house in Thanon Thalong*
Left *Corner of the Siam City Bank building in the town centre*

❻ You will be surrounded by shops, with clothes stands spilling onto the pavement and the Robinson Ocean Plaza, with Robinson's department store and a cinema. Inside Robinson's, on the ground floor, you can rest from the heat in the air-conditioned ice cream parlor or Mr Donut.

From here, you can either retrace your steps to the start point or take one of the many taxis or *tuk-tuks* waiting outside the shops back to your hotel.

WHERE TO EAT
THE CIRCLE
✉ On the fountain traffic circle
☎ 081 091 2187 ⏰ Daily 9–6

PLACE TO VISIT
THAVORN HOTEL LOBBY MUSEUM
✉ 74 Thanon Rasada ☎ 076 211 333
⏰ Daily 8–5 ♿ B30

TOURIST INFORMATION
PHUKET TOWN TOURIST OFFICE
www.phuket.com
✉ 191 Thanon Talang Phuket
☎ 076 212 213 ⏰ 8.30–4.30

Above *Learn to cook Thai food at Time for Lime cookery school in Ko Lanta*

HAT YAI

DIANA COMPLEX SHOPPING CENTER

While Hat Yai tends to lack the activities and facilities appealing to many visitors and, in particular families, the Diana Shopping Center provides a modern shopping and entertainment environment to keep everyone happy. Aside from western franchise restaurants like KFC, Pizza Hut and Swensens, there is also a bowling alley and a five-screen cinema complex. Many of the Western movies shown here are dubbed in Thai, so be sure to check before you purchase your ticket—ask for a movie "with soundtrack".
✉ 55/3 Thanon Sripoowanart, Hat Yai ☎ 074 272 222 🕒 Mon–Fri 10.30–9, Sat–Sun 10–9

HUA HIN

BUCHABUN THAI COOKING COURSE

A 9am start, with a pickup from your hotel, and a trip to the local market to shop for the ingredients. The cooking school is a short distance away, and you will learn how to make Thai curry paste, *tom yam* soup, *hor mok* (steamed seafood with fish curry) and Thai desserts. The course finishes at 3pm. Reserve by phone or at the school itself.
✉ 22 Thanon Dechanuchit, Hua Hin ☎ 032 531 220, 081 572 3805 🖐 B1,500

HUA HIN BREWING COMPANY

Decked out in the style of a Thai fishing village, with a 5,000L (1,100-gallon) wooden beer barrel, this gregarious pub attracts a good cross section of Hua Hin visitors of all ages. Food is available, as are some interesting house specials:

Elephant Tusk, a dark ale; Sabai Sabai, a wheat beer; and Dancing Monkey, a lager. A Thai band provides live entertainment from 9pm onward, and after around 11.30pm a lively atmosphere kicks in.
✉ Hilton Resort and Spa, 33 Thanon Naresdamri, Hua Hin ☎ 032 512 888 🕒 Daily 6pm–2am

ROYAL HUA HIN GOLF CLUB

Located just five minutes from the middle of Hua Hin, this golf club—the first course in Thailand and designed by a Scottish railway engineer—was opened in 1924. The superb 18-hole, par-72 course length is 6,700 yards (6,126m), and you can rent clubs from B500. Costs are higher on weekends and public holidays.
✉ Hua Hin Prachuabkirikhan ☎ 032 512 475 🕒 Daily 6–6 🖐 Green fees, including caddy and hotel transfers B2,000

SASI GARDEN THEATRE

A set Thai meal precedes the show of classical Thai dance, a display of Thai martial arts and a rousing drum dance called *theod theung*. Two episodes from the *Ramayana* are also presented in the form of a masque. After the show, live Thai traditional music continues to be played if you want to linger. Seats can be booked through any travel agent in Hua Hin.

✉ 83/159 Nhongkae, Hua Hin ☎ 032 512 488, 081 880 4004 🕐 Daily 7pm–9pm ✋ Adult B750 (excluding drinks), child (5–10) B600

WORLD NEWS COFFEE

On the same street as the Hilton (and under the same management), this is a pleasant and airy cafe where you can connect to the internet and while away some time reading the international newspapers and magazines—hence the name of the place, presumably—over a coffee and some cake. There are tables outside as well.

✉ 33 Thanon Naresdamri, Hua Hin ☎ 032 512 888 🕐 Daily 8am–11pm ✋ B50–B110

KO LANTA
SAME SAME BUT DIFFERENT

A short distance past the Pimalai Resort in the far south of the island, Ba Kan Tiang Beach is a contender for the ultimate chill-out beach in southern Thailand. Come here to while away an evening and feel a million miles away from home. You'll find wooden tables, lantern lights, cool music in the background and a simple menu of various deep-fried starters and curries. Bring a torch to find your way back to the road in the darkness.

✉ Ba Kan Tiang Beach, Ko Lanta ☎ 081 787 8670 🕐 Daily 10am–midnight ✋ L B150, D B200

SUMATE KOH LANTA YAI SAFARI

www.sumatekohlantasafari.com

You can reserve elephant treks direct with this company, through your accommodations or any of the agents in Sala Dan, and there are other companies offering fairly identical trips. An elephant trek can be a little more strenuous than you might think, so check the itinerary to see how much walking is involved and wear something sturdier than sandals on your feet.

✉ 284 Moo 2 Pra-ae Saladan, Ko Lanta ☎ 075 684 845

TIME FOR LIME

www.timeforlime.net

Time for Lime is a well-established cookery school on Ko Lanta with a weekly "menu" of classes. A typical day covers the preparation of curry paste, *satay* with chicken, spicy prawn soup, seafood with chili paste and barracuda in red curry. A typical evening class covers fresh spring rolls with dips, green curry with chicken and fried rice with vegetables. The course fee includes a Thai meal—not the one you prepare! Vegetarian courses can be arranged, as can babysitting and taxis.

✉ Klong Dao Beach, Ko Lanta ☎ 075 684 590, 099 675 017 🕐 Daily 4–9pm ✋ Day classes: B1,800

KO PHI PHI
HIPPIES

On the beach, just east of the pier and before the PP Villa Resort, Hippies is fairly typical of Ko Phi Phi's nightlife. The food is not the best reason for coming here, but as darkness descends and the fairy lights dimly illuminate the bamboo seats and tables, the laid-back atmosphere can prove enticing. The pace quickens as the night lengthens and soft 1960s music gives way to brasher and more insistent beats.

✉ Ton Sai, Ko Phi Phi ☎ 081 970 5483 🕐 Daily 7pm–2am

KO SAMUI
ARK BAR

www.ark-bar.com

The Ark caters to a younger crowd, with its vibrant staff, chillout funk music played throughout the day, and dance music until all hours of the night. The beachside location

makes it ideal for a daytime drink, also. Accommodations are available at the attached bungalows, though it is not recommended for those who like to go to sleep early.

✉ Beach Road, central Chaweng ☎ 077 422 047 🕐 Daily 8am–2am

BELLINI

An Italian restaurant with a neat bar where a good wine list competes for attention with some crafty cocktails from well-stocked shelves. The atmosphere is very relaxed for this part of Ko Samui, and Soi Colibri has so far managed to keep a low profile.

✉ 46/26 Soi Colibri (Chaweng Boulevard), Chaweng ☎ 077 413 831 🕐 Daily 6pm–11.30pm

BLACK JACK

An English-owned, English pub that has been around for 10 years. All the premier league soccer and other major sporting events are shown here. There is a pool table and a nice upstairs terrace. There are snacks and plenty of draught beer.

✉ Chaweng Beach Road, Chaweng, Ko Samui ☎ 077 413 214 🕐 Daily 5pm–2am

BLUE STARS

www.bluestars.info

Blue Stars offers well-organized adventure trips to Ang Thong National Park, overnight kayaking, and snorkeling among the tidal lagoons of the park.

✉ 169/1 Moo 2, Tambol Bophut, Chaweng Beach Road ☎ 077 413 231 🕐 Daily 9am–midnight ✋ Day trips: adult B2,200, child B1,400

CENTARA SPA

www.centaraspa.com

Massages, aromatherapy and body wraps make up the treatment packages that come with tempting names, such a Earthly Pleasures, Seize the Day and Essential Male. Half and full-day programs.

✉ Centara Grand Beach Resort Samui, Chaweng Beach, and Centara Villas Samui, Natien Beach, Ko Samui ☎ 077 230 500 (Chaweng), 077 424 020 (Natien) 🕐 Daily 8.30–8

COCO BLUES BAR

Open for breakfast and lunch, this family-friendly bar and restaurant comes alive each evening with a band playing blues-style, funky music. The energetic atmosphere makes for a great evening. The full schedule and live broadcasts are listed on the website. You'll find Cajun and creole food—gumbo and blackened chicken are popular—a balcony bar and a good drinks list that includes some Blues Specials. ✉ 161/9 Moo 2, Chaweng Beach Road, Chaweng, Ko Samui ☎ 077 414 354 🕓 Daily 9am–2am

DISCOVERY

www.discoverydivers.com

Discovery offers what is probably the least exacting introduction to scuba-diving, with the entire learning facilities available on site. You begin learning to dive in the training pool, attend lessons in air-conditioned classrooms and finish by using one of the company's on-dive boats. There are one- and four-day courses, as well as advanced courses up to PADI Divemaster status. ✉ Amari Palm Reef Resort, Chaweng Beach ☎ 077 413 196 🕓 Daily 10–6 ✋ PADI course B10,000, scuba trips from B3,999

EASY DIVERS

www.easydivers-thailand.com

Easy Divers is one of the leading dive centers on the island, and it has offices on all the main beaches. The European-managed company has been around for over 10 years, and its PADI dive courses are well established. ✉ Opposite Sand Sea Resort, Lamai Beach ☎ 077 413 373 ✋ Courses from B1,700 (child over 8 B1,000), 4-day PADI courses B14,750

FROG AND GECKO

Away from the hustle and bustle of Chaweng, there are two places for a good evening of entertainment at the Bophut waterfront called Fisherman's Village. One is an Australian sports bar, the Billabong, and the other is the English-style Frog and Gecko. The busiest night of the week is Wednesday —arrive earlier to get a seat—when a pub quiz gets under way at 8pm. Indian food is served, and there's a large television screen for satellite-beamed soccer. ✉ Fisherman's Village, Bophut, Ko Samui ☎ 077 425 248 🕓 Wed–Mon noon–2am

HEALTH OASIS RESORT

www.healthoasisresort.com
"Relax, cleanse, rejuvenate" is the motto of the Health Oasis Resort, which offers a range of fasting, colonic cleansing and pampering programs. Accommodations are also available, from simple rooms with fans to air-conditioned bungalows. Plus there's a vegetarian restaurant, and a rather special service that claims to establish your vortex location. Full details of all the treatments are on the website.

✉ 26/4 Moo 6, Maenam, Ko Samui ☎ 077 236 255 ⏰ Daily 8–8

PEACE TROPICAL SPA

www.peacetropicalspa.com
Facial therapies, massage, reflexology and body treatments are on the menu here, as well as packages like a two-hour session that includes a steam room visit before a massage, or a combined body scrub and body wrap. The Happy Hour package includes an oil massage and facial treatments.

✉ 17 Moo 1, Bophut ☎ 077 430 199 ⏰ Daily 10–10 🖐 Massages B1,500, body treatments B1,000–B2,600, facials B1,600–B2,000, packages B2,000–B5,500

SAMUI INSTITUTE OF THAI CULINARY ARTS

www.sitca.net
Daily cooking classes and food-carving courses from a professional institution, SITCA, are on offer at the Samui Institute of Thai Culinary Arts. A culinary shop (and an online mail-order service) is also run by SITCA, where you can purchase ingredients and equipment. The morning cooking class starts at 11.30, and three dishes are taught by 1; the afternoon class starts at 4 and lasts two hours. You eat together with the other participants and can bring along a friend for free.

✉ Central Samui Beach Resort, South Chaweng Beach Road ☎ 077 413 172 ⏰ Mon–Sat 11.30–1, 4–6.30 🖐 B1,950

Opposite *Enjoy a beauty treatment in a room built into the rocks at the Tamarind Springs spa in Ko Samui*

SAMUI MONKEY THEATER

Coconut harvesting is a major industry on Ko Samui, and macaque monkeys make up a large part of the industry's workforce. These small, clever monkeys are trained to climb the trees to select the ripe coconuts. During the thrice-daily, one-hour shows, you'll get to see how they work and how they play too.

✉ Kao Phra Village, Boh Pud, Ko Samui ☎ 077 960 128, 089 118 9688 ⏰ Shows daily 10.30, 2, 4 🖐 B300

SAMUI OCEAN SPORTS AND YACHT CHARTER

www.sailing-in-samui.com
Samui Ocean Sports provides sailing courses for beginners, and Lasers and Hobie cats are available for off-the-beach rental. If you want to get even further from the beach, monohulls and catamarans can be arranged for both skippered or chartered cruises around the Samui archipelago. Flotilla cruises can also be arranged: led by an experienced skipper, you can still be captain of your own boat and enjoy the company of other sailing enthusiasts out on the water.

✉ Chaweng Regent Beach Resort, 155/4 Moo 2, Tambon Bophut, Ko Samui ☎ 081 940 1999 🖐 Lasers and Hobie cats start from B600 per hour; half-day private skippered charter cruise starts from B4,500

SANTIBURI SAMUI COUNTRY CLUB

www.santiburi.com/HomeGolf.asp
Surrounded by a dense palm-tree jungle, the 18-hole golf course here gives stunning views of the ocean and out toward Phangan island. All but very experienced golfers will find the undulating gradients and winding fairways a challenge. Relax after your game in the comfortable clubhouse or enjoy a meal and the views in the restaurant. A driving range is also available. For non-golfers there is a spa here, too.

✉ Santiburi Resort, 12/12 Moo 1, Maenam, Ko Samui ☎ 077 421 700 ⏰ Daily 6–6 🖐 Green fees B3,500 for 18 holes (includes golf cart and caddy); golf club rental B700–B2,000

SPA RESORT MEDITATION

www.spasamui.com
You do not need to be staying at the resort to join its meditation or yoga classes. Every morning at 7.30 free meditation classes are held on the beach by the resort. They are followed by yoga and *chi-gung*. Every month there are also five-day retreats. The website has full details.

✉ Spa Resort, Lamai Beach, Ko Samui ☎ 077 230 855 ⏰ Daily 9–7 🖐 Yoga B250

TAMARIND SPRINGS

www.tamarindretreat.com
On the main road between Chaweng and Lamai, with a peaceful hillside setting, Tamarind Springs is one of the island's most sophisticated massage centers. As well as the standard two-hour Thai massage, there is also an oil massage that takes half an hour less, plus separate face, foot and head massages. There are also a number of packages that cater to couples and which begin with a session in the aromatic herbal steam room. Towels and garments are provided.

✉ 205/3 Thong Takian, Tambon Maret ☎ 077 424 221 ⏰ Daily 10–8 🖐 Packages B4,500–B7,500

THE THREE MONKEES

www.3-monkeys.com
A pub and restaurant, between the Beachcomber Hotel and the Silver Sand Resort, with a sociable atmosphere and a sense of fun. There's a pool table, papers to read, food throughout the day (with a free glass of wine), movies and sporting events shown on TV, and a corner with free internet access.

✉ Chaweng Beach Road, Chaweng, Ko Samui ☎ 081 821 9388 ⏰ Daily 10am–1am

KRABI (AO NANG)
THE IRISH ROVER

The Irish Rover is a cozy pub, open for breakfast, lunch and dinner and serving draught Guinness and a range of imported beers. It's a good place to read the English newspapers, or watch sport. You'll find it just off the main beach road, opposite the police station.

✉ 249/8 Thanon Ao Nang, Ao Nang
☎ 075 637 607 🕐 Daily 7am–1am

KING CLIMBERS
King Climbers have a good reputation for safety and high teaching standards. A range of climbing courses are offered, from absolute beginner courses to advanced climbing and rescue techniques. All the guides have a minimum of five years of climbing experience and ACGA accreditation, and all their equipment is imported from Europe and America.

✉ 249/11 Thanon Ao Nang, Ao Nang
☎ 075 637 125 🕐 Daily 9–5 ✋ Half-day course B1,000; 1-day course B1,800; 3-day course B6,000

TROPICAL HERBAL SPA AND RESORT
www.tropicalherbalresort.com
This spa offers massages in an exclusive and relaxing environment, though with prices to match. A variety of treatments and therapies are available, including traditional Thai massage, royal Thai massage and massages with oils and herbal scrubs imported from around Asia and the West, all designed to leave you feeling relaxed and rejuvenated. A full range of facial and body treatments is also available.

✉ 20/1 Moo 2, Ao Nang ☎ 075 637 940
🕐 Daily 10–7 ✋ B750 for 1 hour; B1,200 for 2 hours

PHUKET
ANCHAN RESORT AND SPA
www.anchanresort.com
Traditional Thai massage along with other massages and body treatments. This is one of the most glamorous spas on the island, offering luxurious, personalized service within intimate and private surroundings, and conveniently located near beautiful Bang Tao Beach. Top-class accommodations and dining are also available.

✉ 325 Moo 2, Thanon Srisoonton, Tambon Cherngtalay, Phuket ☎ 076 271 250

🕐 Daily 9–6 ✋ Thai Massage B850 for 90 mins; body wraps from B2,400

ANGUS O'TOOL'S
www.otools-phuket.com
This well-stocked pub, just 330 yards (300m) from Karon beach, provides a cool place and a wide range of stouts and ciders. It opens from 10am, when it serves breakfasts, and it has two big screens playing major sporting events from around the world. Things tend to get very merry before closing time at 2am. Air-conditioned rooms upstairs are also available.

✉ 516/20 Phatak Road, Karon Beach, Phuket ☎ 076 398 262 🕐 Daily 10am–2am

BODY AND MIND DAY SPA
www.body-mindspa.com
Hydrotherapy, body wraps and facials are on offer, as well as massages, aromatherapy and sport. Various packages are available, such as a body scrub and aromatherapy massage (two hours; B2,400). The setting is stylish and suitably serene for treatments that leave you calm and revitalized. You'll find it at the end of Karon Beach, before the Central Karon Village resort.

✉ 558/7–12 Thanon Patak, Karon Beach
☎ 076 398 274 🕐 Daily 11–10
✋ B600–B4,200

BLUE NOTE BAR
In the middle of Soi Easy, a bar and complex on Thanon Bangla, Blue Note is one version of Patong nightlife. A DJ plays mainstream rock and pop, regulars play darts, and major sports events on TV take precedence. Cocktails and beers are both available.

✉ Soi Easy, Thanon Bangla, Patong
☎ 076 344 146 🕐 Daily 2pm–3am

CENTRAL FESTIVAL PHUKET
www.centralfestival.co.th
Central Festival Phuket is an ultra-modern shopping and entertainment complex providing fashion and beauty products from around the world, giftware, sporting equipment, electronics, hardware and virtually

Above *Eat dinner and catch dinner a Vegas-style show at the Phuket Fantasea*

every other household item you could think of. Try out the Food Terrace for well-cooked local and Asian dishes, or take in one of the latest movies showing at the SFX Coliseum Cinema Centre on the third floor.

✉ 74–75 Wichitsongkran Road, Phuket town ☎ 076 291 111 🕐 Daily 10–10

CHAN'S ANTIQUES
www.chans-antique.com
Proclaiming to be the largest antiques and art dealer on the island, and with over 20 years' experience, Mr Chan Sae Sim, the owner and founder of Chan's Antiques, has developed a steadfast reputation for quality of goods and service. If you are looking to invest in Asian art, seeking a lasting memento of your trip to Thailand, or wish to pick up a gift that is a little more classy than the tacky items found along the beachfront then this is the place to come. Prices start at around B500 for small carved wooden ornaments.

✉ 99/42 Thanon Chalermprakiat, Phuket town ☎ 076 261 416 🕐 Daily 8.30am–6pm

Above *Gain a PADI qualification during your stay on Ko Samui with one of the diving schools*

CLUB MED DINNER AND DISCO

The Half Day Pass provides time for an activity or two as well as a shower before the buffet dinner, which includes beer and wine, followed by after-dinner live entertainment, either a band indoors or a flying trapeze show outside, and later a disco on a dance floor of sand.
✉ Club Med, Thanon Kata, Karon ☎ 076 330 456 🕑 Half-day pass valid 7.15pm–1am 👆 Half-day pass adult B2,800, child (age 4–11) B1,400

CLUB MED MINI CLUB

A Day Pass at the luxurious Club Med resort includes lunch and activities, and you don't need to be staying at the resort. Some activities, like the bungee bounce and flying trapeze, are only for children aged over 13. There is an afternoon package that covers just the activities.

✉ Club Med, Thanon Kata, Karon ☎ 076 330 456 🕑 Daily 10–6 👆 Day Pass child (age 4–10) B1,040, child (over 11) B2,080; activities only package child (4–10) B400, child (over 11) B800

CORAL GRAND

www.coralgranddivers.com
This diving company covers Ko Samui, Ko Tao and the Similan Islands, as well as Phuket. Snorkeling trips to Ang Thong National Park are popular, and their standard scuba-diving Open Water Course takes three and a half days. More advanced courses available.
✉ Similian, Chalong, Phuket 83100 ☎ 076 383 699 🕑 Daily 9–5 👆 Dive trips start from B19,000

CORAL SEEKERS

www.coralseekers.com
Coral Seekers has speedboats for snorkeling trips around the island, with package deals that include transport to and from your hotel and snorkeling gear. Half- and full-day trips are organized regularly and water skiing is also an option.

✉ 16 Soi Teuson, Samkong, Phuket town ☎ 076 354 074 🕑 Daily 8–5 👆 B3,500–B37,500

DIVE ASIA

www.diveasia.com
Dive Asia has been in Phuket for over 25 years and has a good reputation as *the* place to go to learn diving, from Discover Scuba Diving to NITROX courses and IDC/CDC programs for those with previous diving experience. One-day dive trips feature alongside cruises that take you to prime locations off the Similan and Surin islands.
✉ 24 Karon Road, Karon Beach, Phuket ☎ 076 330 598, 076 284 117 🕑 Daily 11–9 👆 From B2,990

HIDEAWAY DAY SPAS

www.phuket-hideaway.com
A wonderful spa with plunge pools and traditional Thai aromatherapy, hand massages, hair and skin treatments, rejuvenating body wraps and salt scrubs.
✉ 157 Thanon Nanai, Patong, Phuket ☎ 076 340 591 🕑 Daily 10.30–8

LAGUNA PHUKET GOLF CLUB

www.lagunaphuketgolf.com
Located just 20 minutes from
Phuket International Airport and
25 minutes from Phuket town is
this superb par-71 resort course,
designed by Max Wexler and David
Abell. The Andaman Sea is in view
for much of the game as you play
your way through coconut groves
and tropical lagoons and over the
undulating fairways that make this a
challenge for players of all abilities.
Other features include a driving
range, putting greens, practice
bunkers and chipping areas.
✉ 34 Moo 4, Srisoonthorn Road,
Cherngtalay, Phuket ☎ 076 270 991
🕐 Daily 6.30–5 💰 Green fee:
B1,970–B4,200, caddy fee: B250, club rental:
B900–B2,200

MOLLY MALONE'S

Unexciting meals are always
available here, but at night a band
enlivens the place considerably and

there is a sociable atmosphere. For
more of the same, turn right outside
and walk around the corner to
Scruffy Murphy's.
✉ Thanon Thawiwong (Beach Road),
Patong ☎ 076 292 771 🕐 Daily
10am–2am, live music: 9.45

MOM TRI'S THAI COOKING CLASSES

www.boathousephuket.com
Every weekend Chef Tamanoon of
the Boathouse hotel and restaurant
conducts Thai cooking classes. In
the high season you need to reserve
a place in advance as these classes
are popular. Recipes and apron are
yours to keep.
✉ Kata Beach, Phuket ☎ 076 330 015
🕐 Sat–Sun 10–2 💰 2-day course B4,095;
1-day course B2,574

P&P GREAT OPTICAL

Most kinds of lenses and frames
are available here. Bring your own
prescription or have your eyes

assessed here. A similar place,
Washington Optic, is in Phuket town
at 52 Thanon Rasada. Both places
should have prices less than those in
Europe or North America.
✉ 6 Thanon Bangla, Patong ☎ 076 340
227 🕐 Daily 10am–11pm 💰 From B3,800

PATONG PARK

Bungy-jumping from 60m (200ft)
above a pool, the tallest jump in
southern Thailand, with professional
jumpmasters on hand.
✉ Soi Kebsap 2, Thanon Sainamyen,
Patong ☎ 076 345 185 🕐 Daily 10–7
💰 B1,650

PERFECTION SPA AND BEAUTY SALON

This salon is on Chao Fa Road, just
under halfway between Phuket town
and Chalong, and offers a range of
treatments, from a haircut, manicure
or pedicure to a full makeover. There
is a mixed spa for men and women
and a separate women-only spa
room. The gallery attached to the
spa displays and sells the work of
local artists.
✉ 1/10 Moo 1, Soi Songkhun, Chao Fa
Road ☎ 076 264 295 🕐 Tue–Sun 10–8

PHUKET FANTASEA

www.phuket-fantasea.com
A nightly dinner buffet followed by
a show that defies easy labeling,
this claims to be a window into
Thai culture via the style of Las
Vegas. There is certainly something
spectacular about the show. It
tells the story of Kamala, the prince
of an enchanted kingdom, and it
provides the narrative for a stage
spectacular featuring elephants, a
tiger, water buffalo and acrobats,
plus light and sound effects. Children
will love it; adults need to be in the
mood for an extravaganza of dancing
and set pieces worthy of an epic
film. The buffet food is as good as
can be expected of a place catering
to up to 4,000 diners a night. Tickets
can be reserved at any travel shop in

Left *Phuket Fantasea promises a good
evening's entertainment*

Phuket and transportation there and back for B280 can be arranged.

✉ Kamala Beach ☎ 076 385 111 (reservations), 076 385 000 (information)
🕐 Fri–Wed buffet at 6pm, show at 9pm
🍴 Dinner and show: adult B1,700, child (age 4–12) B1,500; show only: B1,500

PHUKET RIDING CLUB

www.phuketridingclub.com
Take your horse for a stroll on the beach or into the woods or coconut plantations around the club. Instructors are available for beginners and guides are available on request, with tours through a variety of terrain. Children are welcome.

✉ 95 Thanon Vises, Rawai Beach, Phuket
☎ 076 288 213 🕐 Daily 7–7 🍴 B650 per hour

PHUKET THAI COOKERY SCHOOL

Northeast of Phuket town and offering free transportation from Patong, Kata, Karon and Phuket town, this is a popular place where courses begin with a visit to a local market for ingredients. Lunch or dinner is included in the fee. A course in Thai vegetarian cooking is also available.

✉ 39/4 Thanon Thepatan, Rasada ☎ 076 252 354 🕐 Daily 8–5 🍴 Mon–Thu B1,900, Fr–Sat B2,200

ROCK & BOWL

This is the largest bowling alley in Phuket, and it attracts a good crowd of locals, expats and visitors. Food, calling itself American-breakfast, is always available. Children will enjoy Rock & Bowl as well, with disco music and flashing lights around the place.

✉ Patong Park, Soi Kebsap 2, Thanon Sainamyen, Patong ☎ 076 345 898
🕐 Noon–2am 🍴 B90 per game per person, shoes B30

SANTANA DIVING AND CANOEING

www.santanaphuket.com
Another well-established diving operation in Phuket, this first outfit to establish itself at Patong has its own vessel for live-aboard trips to

FESTIVALS AND EVENTS

SEPTEMBER/OCTOBER
VEGETARIAN FESTIVAL

www.phuket.com/festival/vegetarian.htm
This festival of vegetarian delights, more about gruesome acts of self-torture than dietary restrictions, lasts for more than a week, and Phuket is the place to experience the event at its most extreme. Check with

the Similian Islands and reefs off the coast of Mynamar (Burma). One-day trips around Phuket take place daily, and beginners are welcomed as well as experienced divers.

✉ 49 Thanon Thaweewong, Patong Beach ☎ 076 294 220 🕐 Daily 10–9 🍴 From B3,500

SARASIL ART GALLERY

Watercolor and oil paintings range over a wide subject area, from the ordinary and realistic to the highly abstract. Prices are equally varied, from a few thousand baht to B40,000. You will pass this gallery on the Phuket walk (▷ 256–257).

✉ 121 Thanon Phang-Nga, Phuket town
☎ 076 224 532 🕐 Daily 8am–9pm

SAXOPHONE

Saxophone provides a relaxing environment where you can enjoy a meal, a drink and good music. There is seating inside and out, the staff are friendly, and the band plays western and local music, with a skilled saxophone player to keep the bar worthy of its name.

✉ 188/2 Thaweewongse Road, Patong Beach, Phuket ☎ 076 346 167 🕐 Daily 3pm–1am

THE SENSE SPA

This is one of Phuket's more tastefully designed spas to be found outside of a five-star hotel. On offer are Thai and Swedish massages, body scrubs, body wraps, hair waxing, facials and packages that include the Sense of Wellbeing treatment, which

the local tourist office about events happening at different temples around the island. Smaller events take place in Krabi and around Phang Nga.

ℹ Tourist office, 73–75 Thanon Phuket
☎ 076 21 22 13 🕐 Late September to early October

takes over three-and-a-half hours to complete and costs B4,235.

✉ 2/12 Kata Plaza, Thanon Kata, Karon, Phuket ☎ 076 333 014 🕐 Daily 10–10
🍴 B1,650–B6,000

SPHINX

The best food at this restaurant is the Thai dishes, and there is a cocktail list to accompany your food. But the main attraction is upstairs in the theater, where the resident Pharaohs dance troupe performs routines from Broadway musicals like *Cats*, reenactments of scenes from classical Thai myths and some comedy. The atmosphere is gregarious. Reserve for dinner or show, or both.

✉ Thanon Rad Uthit, Patong ☎ 076 341 500 🕐 5pm–midnight; performances Wed–Mon 9pm and 10.30pm 🍴 Dinner B1,200 (child under 12 B900) for Thai menu; B1,400 and B1,050 for European menu

TARN TARA SPA

www.tarntaraspa.com
Conveniently located close to Wat Chalong, off the road between Phuket town and the beaches of Karon and Kata, this is a restful lakeside spa and a restaurant with a health-conscious menu. The basic three-hour Andaman Sunshine package includes an oil massage, facial treatment, shampoo or foot massage and a session in a steam bath or pool. You can reserve treatments online.

✉ 58/11 Moo 6, Thanon Chao Far, Chalong, Phuket ☎ 076 521 746 🕐 Daily 9am–11pm 🍴 B3,000–B5,500

PRICES AND SYMBOLS

The prices given are the average for a two-course lunch (L) and a three-course dinner (D) for one person, without drinks or wine.

For a key to the symbols, ▷ 2.

HUA HIN

CIAO

Facing a superb stretch of Hua Hin's beach, the thatched, open-air Ciao looks its best at night when lit by candles and a cool breeze blows in from the sea. Pizzas and a Caesar salad are always on the menu and expect to find veal, pork or lamb chops and lobster.

✉ Marriott Hotel, Hua Hin ☎ 032 511 881 ◷ Daily 11–11 ✋ L B800, D B1,300

MAHARAJA RESTAURANT

The friendly staff in this well decorated restaurant are only too happy to help you choose from the menu. Some of their most popular dishes are chicken tikka masala and tandoori prawns. There is a decent selection of wine, too.

✉ 25 Naresdamri Road, Hua Hin ☎ 032 531 122 ◷ Daily 11–10 ✋ L B200, D B400

WHITE LOTUS

High up on the 17th level of the Hilton (▷ 270), the White Lotus has tables inside or on the balcony overlooking the town and the beach. There's *dim sum* for lunch and a helpful menu, as well as a wine menu that suggests wines for the Chinese dishes, which include tempting appetizers like Alaskan scallops and asparagus, and dishes like stir-fried prawns with apple in an orange and lemongrass sauce. Intimate at night, the elevation takes you away from the gregarious street activity 17 levels below.

✉ Hua Hin Resort and Spa, 33 Thanon Naresdamri, Hua Hin ☎ 032 512 888 ◷ Mon–Sat 11.30–2.30, 6.30–10.30 ✋ L B250, D B1,100

KO LANTA

BAAN LANTA RESTAURANT

This lovely restaurant is right on the beach looking out to sea. It's a perfect place to enjoy the fresh seafood or the international dishes

on the menu. Recommended is the red snapper with lemon, or the popular *tom yung goong*. Wine is not served.

✉ Baan Lanta Resort and Spa, Kan Tieng Bay, Ko Lanta Yai ☎ 075 665 091 ◷ 7am–10pm ✋ L B250, D B350

MR BEAN'S

English food comes into its own on Wednesdays and Saturdays when the place is booked out for the roast lamb dinners. Indian food is available on Friday nights, but the normal menu is one of cottage pie, chili con carne, fish and chips (french fries), shepherd's pie and huge cholesterol-packed breakfasts.

✉ Klong Dao Beach, Ko Lanta ☎ 015 975 182 ◷ Daily 8am–midnight ✋ L and D B200–B300

SALA THAI RESTAURANT

An evening meal watching the sun go down and the candles light up is a memorable experience. Fresh seafood and dishes in the style of Royal Thai cuisine are beautifully prepared. There are also international dishes and a wide range of drinks available.

📧 Royal Lanta Resort and Spa, Klong Dao beach, Ko Lanta ☎ 075 684 361 🕐 Daily 7am–10pm 🖐 L B500, D B700

SEA SIDE
As Sea Side is next to the pier, with tables over the water, it is convenient if you're caught in Ban Sala Dan waiting for a boat. On the menu are chicken and noodles, curries, sandwiches and salads, plus it's open for breakfast of pancakes, toast and eggs. It also has a good line in shakes.

📧 Ban Sala Dan, Ko Lanta ☎ 015 987 340 🕐 Daily 8–7 🖐 L and D B100

KO SAMUI
CHEF CHOM'S
Thai cuisine at Chef Chom's aspires to the exquisite in the luxury setting of the Tongsai Bay Hotel. It is a place to dress up for and a couple of diners is the minimum needed to do justice to the menu. Arrange for a

taxi to collect you if you do not have your own transportation.

📧 Tongsai Bay Hotel, 84 Moo 5, Bophut, Ko Samui ☎ 077 425 015 🕐 Daily 11–6, 7–10 🖐 L B1,000, D B1,300

THE CLIFF BAR AND GRILL
High on the mountain with great views, this is one place you need to reserve as it is very popular, despite being a relative newcomer. The only other problem you'll find here is what to choose from the extensive Mediterranean menu. Champagne is also available to celebrate a memorable dining experience.

📧 On the cliff between Chaweng and Lamai Beach, Ko Samui ☎ 077 414 266 🕐 12–11 🖐 L B500, D B800

THE ISLANDER
The Islander is a well-managed pub-restaurant with a vacation atmosphere—a place where you can wear shorts. Aside from the Thai and

Western food, there is a sports area that shows soccer games, and a children's menu.

📧 Central Chaweng, Ko Samui ☎ 077 230 836 🕐 Daily 8am–2am 🖐 L B500, D B700

POPPIES
Poppies comes into its own at night when the place is lit up and people are mingling. It's a popular, longstanding restaurant where you would not feel out of place for having dressed up a little. Try to reserve a table by the sea, under swaying pandan trees, for the full romance factor. Seafood, pizza and meat dishes are on offer, and there's occasional live entertainment at weekends. Reservations are essential during the high season.

📧 Central Chaweng, Ko Samui ☎ 077 422 419 🕐 Daily 7am–11pm 🖐 L B500, D B1,200

SPA RESORT RESTAURANT
www.thesparesort.net
The restaurant at the well-known Samui Village Spa Resort (▷ 271) is mostly raw foods or vegetarian, and this is what it does best, but chicken and fish are also an option with many of the dishes. It's open for breakfast and serves all day from a big menu of Western salads, soups, sandwiches, spaghetti and tacos, as well as Thai food like *pla goong* (prawns sautéed with lemongrass, onions and mint leaves).

📧 Lamai Beach, Ko Samui ☎ 077 230 855 🕐 Daily 7am–10pm 🖐 L B150, D B300

ZICO'S BAR & GRILL
www.zicossamui.com
This street-side Brazilian barbecue sits across from the Centara Grand Beach Resort, and is part of their large empire of properties. Samba dancers from São Paolo, dressed in elaborate costumes, dance the Samba and the Axe, adding a touch of Rio carnival to any meal. The

Left *A table with a sea view at Poppies Restaurant in Ko Samui*

menu changes daily, but the main focus is seafood, beef, chicken and pork cooked on the grill.

✉ 38/2 Moo 3, Tambon Bo Phut, Ko Samui ☎ 077 231 560 🕓 Daily 5pm–1am till late 🍽 D B790

KRABI

CARNIVORE

www.carnivore-thailand.com

If you want to get your teeth into a good steak then this is the place to go. Tuck into imported beef and choice sauces, served in generous helpings and with a choice of wines. Reservations are recommended.

✉ 127 Moo 3, Krabi ☎ 075 661 061 🕓 Daily noon–11pm 🍽 L B300, D B500

RUEN MAI

This is one of the best Thai restaurants in the area. The spicy salads and traditional curries are well worth a try, although let the staff know if you want the spiciness toned down. A wide range of vegetarian dishes is also available.

✉ Maharat Road, Krabi town ☎ 075 631 797 🕓 Daily 10.30–10 🍽 L 150, D B200

VIVA

Bread at Viva is made fresh each morning. On the menu are omelets, crêpes, soup, bruschetta, salads, antipasti, more than 30 types of homemade pasta—including unusual dishes like *gamberi piccanti* (spicy garlic prawn)—thin-crust pizzas (you can take away) and imported steaks. It's a friendly restaurant, which opens onto the street without being noisy at night. Wheat beer from Germany and Italian wines are available.

✉ 29 Thanon Pruksa Uhtit, Krabi ☎ 075 630 517 🕓 Daily 10am–11pm 🍽 L B200, D B450

YAYA RESORT

http://yaya-resort.com

One of Railay's last remaining havens for backpackers and budget travelers, Yaya Resort not only has the cheapest accommodations, but also the most reasonably priced food in the area. The menu is typical of a backpacker's diner,

Above *Elegant dining in the open air at Baan Rim Pa Piano Bar & Restaurant in Phuket*

with an international menu of tasty pancakes, pizzas, burgers, pasta, Indian and Thai dishes. Movies are shown at every night 8pm.

✉ Sunrise Beach, Railay, Krabi ☎ 075 819 460 🕓 7am till late 🍽 L B130, DB180

PHUKET

BAAN KLANG JINDA

www.baanklung.com

A 10-minute walk or short ride by *tuk-tuk* from the heart of town to the top of Thanon Yaowarat will bring you to a grand, century-old edifice that was built as the government's revenue-collecting office. It looks best at night when the grounds are lit up and there are outdoor tables on the green. There's live music in the lounge bar Monday to Saturday from 7pm to 8pm before the band shifts to the dining room and then the lounge from 10pm for another two hours.

✉ 158 Thanon Yaowarat, Phuket town ☎ 076 221 777 🕓 Mon–Sat 11–2, 5–midnight 🍽 L B250, D B500

BAAN RIM PA PIANO BAR & RESTAURANT

www.baanrimpa.com

Reservations are essential at Patong's most elegant restaurant, on high ground across from the Novotel Hotel and facing the beach. The food includes *yam hua plee gluay* (banana blossom salad) and chicken in pandanus leaves. There's jazz music nightly except Monday.

✉ 223 Prabaramee Road, Patong, Phuket ☎ 076 340 789 🕓 Daily noon–10.30pm 🍽 L and D B1,000

BAAN YIN DEE RESTAURANT

www.baanyindee.com

In the Baan Yin Dee Resort, this prestigious restaurant overlooking Patong Bay offers a fusion of European and Thai food. After your meal you can sit back and listen to the piano while enjoying some of their fine wines or spirits.

✉ 7/5 Muean Ngen Road, Patong Beach, Phuket ☎ 076 294 104 🕐 Daily 11–5, 6–10.30 🖐 L B800, D B1,000

BEACH HOUSE

The Beach House is at the south end of Patong beach, just before the Seaview Hotel, and is managed by a Swedish-Thai couple. You'll find Thai food alongside hamburgers and the like. It's a quiet retreat from the main action, with sea views.

✉ 6 Thanon Thaweewong, Patong, Phuket ☎ 076 345 639 🕐 Daily 7am–11pm 🖐 L B250, D B300

BOATHOUSE WINE & GRILL

Rebuilt after the tsunami of 2004, the restaurant is as close to the beach as possible and makes for an idyllic scene at night. There are set menus of Thai or French cuisine plus an à la carte menu—the rock lobster with green curry, Armagnac and thermidor sauce is a popular choice, as is the Australian lamb. There is an excellent wine list.

✉ Kata Beach, Phuket ☎ 076 330 015 🕐 Daily 7am–10.30pm 🖐 L B900, D B1,500

THE CLIFF

Try to arrive to watch the sunset over Karon and take your time over the menu of Mediterranean and Asian food, which includes scallop salad, crabs with celery root salad, beef carpaccio, and prawns sautéed in Parma ham. Finish with crème brûlée and chocolate mousse.

✉ Coastal road between Karon and Patong, close to Centara Villas, Phuket ☎ 076 286 300 🕐 Daily 6–11pm 🖐 D B990

CUCINA

www.marriott.com/hktjw

Cucina has an open kitchen with brick-built pizza oven, a carpeted dining area and a terrace for alfresco dining. A popular dish is *zuppa zio pino*, a kind of bouillabaise. A solo guitarist plays nightly and the atmosphere can be romantic in a low-key way; reserve a table facing the sea for the best views.

✉ J W Marriott Phuket Resort & Spa, 231 Moo 3, Mai Khao Talang, Phuket ☎ 076 338 000 🕐 Daily 6pm–11pm 🖐 D B1,500

MANI'S GERMAN BAKERY

Between Kata and Karon, at the east end of Soi Bangla, this is the place for rye, wholemeal, malt and onion bread. Pretzels, too. It's open for breakfast sausages, meatloaf and cold cuts, and a smaller outlet of the bakery can be found near the Chalong Circle.

✉ Soi Bangla, Karon, Phuket ☎ 076 396 882 🕐 Mon–Sat 7am–1pm 🖐 L B150

METROPOLE RESTAURANT

www.metropolephuket.com

On the second level of the Metropole Hotel, the menu here is a mixture of Thai and international dishes: curries, grilled pork chops, fried wild boar, and prawns with asparagus. The desserts are uninspiring, but compensation comes in the form of a live band or singer performing most nights on the restaurant's small stage.

✉ Metropole Hotel, Thanon Montri, Phuket town ☎ 076 214 020/9 🕐 Daily 6pm–10pm 🖐 D B1,200

MOM TRS

Head to this restaurant during the day for dream views looking down on Kata Noi Beach and, at night, the sound of waves dashing on the rocks below. The sophisticated menu changes regularly, but expect dishes like mango gazpacho, stir-fried lobster and *ped palo* (duck with spices, garlic and peppercorn sauce). The serious wine list includes organic bottles, and there's a choice of seven high-quality wines by the glass.

✉ Boathouse Regatta, Royal Phuket Marina, Kata Noi Beach, Phuket ☎ 076 360 855 🕐 Daily 6.30am–11.30pm 🖐 L B720, D B1,150

ORIENTAL SPOON

www.twinpalms-phuket.com

Just north of Kamala beach, this restaurant attracts island residents as well as visitors so the menu changes every so often and various specials are usually available. Expect good and familiar dishes, such as Caesar salad, pork spare ribs and grilled chicken.

✉ Twin Palms Hotel, 106/46 Moo 3, Surin Beach, Phuket ☎ 076 316 500 🕐 Daily 7am–11pm 🖐 L B700, D B950–B1,250

RUAMJAI

A short way past the bus stops for the *songthaews* to the beaches, look for the bright yellow sign displaying Ruamjai's name. Inside is fan cooled, with plenty of tables, a tiled floor and friendly staff, and there's a choice of about a dozen vegetarian dishes at lunchtime. Very clean and very inexpensive.

✉ Thanon Ranong, Phuket town ☎ 076 222 821 🕐 Daily 6.30–4.30 🖐 B130 (all-day menu)

SALVATORE'S

www.salvatorestaurant.com

A bright and cheerful restaurant with artwork on the walls and Latin jazz playing in the background. On the menu here are favorite dishes, such as a shrimp cocktail or Parma ham and salad, pasta dishes, such as fettuccine with crab meat, a range of pizzas, more expensive T-bone steaks and plenty of tempting desserts.

✉ 15 Thanon Rasada, Phuket town ☎ 076 225 958 🕐 Tue–Sat 12–2, 6–11, Sun 6–11 🖐 L B350, D B700

SAWASDEE

Sawasdee is an Arab-Thai-themed restaurant—the shimmering gilded dome as you enter blends aspects of a Thai temple with those of a mosque—but the food is all Thai at night and more European at lunchtime; breakfast is also available. It's easy to find—opposite Sawasdee Village in Kata.

✉ 65 Thanon Katekuan, Kata, Phuket ☎ 076 330 979 🕐 Daily 6–10.30, 11–2, 6–11 🖐 L B400, D B600

Above *Choose from a range of resort-style hotels in Hua Hin*

PRICES AND SYMBOLS

Prices are the lowest and highest for a double room for one night. Breakfast is included unless noted otherwise. All the hotels listed accept credit cards unless otherwise stated. Note that rates vary widely throughout the year.

For a key to the symbols, ▷ 2.

HUA HIN

HILTON HUA HIN RESORT & SPA

www.hilton.com/huahin
Every room has an ocean view from its balcony and all the amenities of a five-star hotel. The three-in-one alfresco restaurant serves Thai, Japanese, Italian and Western food, and there's also a Chinese restaurant. There's a bar with jazz at night, a spa, squash and tennis courts and a children's club.
✉ 33 Thanon Naresdamri, Hua Hin ☎ 032 512 888 🖐 B7,560–B9,360 🛏 296 (87 non-smoking) 🔇 🏊 Outdoor 🍽

PATTANA GUEST HOUSE

huahinpattana@hotmail.com
The Pattana is an oasis of calm with attractive bedrooms, and a good kitchen serving up hearty breakfasts.
✉ 52 Thanon Naresdamri, Hua Hin ☎ 032 513 393 🖐 B325–B550 excluding breakfast 🛏 12

PUANGPEN VILLA HOTEL & P. P. VILLA

ppvillahotel@hotmail.com
If you want an affordable but presentable place to stay close to the beach and all the town's amenities, then this may fit the bill. The rooms have a fridge and safe deposit box, and the beach is five minutes down the road.
✉ 11 Damnernkasem, Hua Hin ☎ 032 533 785 🖐 B1,200–B1,500 excluding breakfast 🛏 40 🔇 🏊 Outdoor

SOFITEL CENTARA GRAND RESORT AND VILLA HUA HIN

www.centarahotelsresorts.com
Almost on the beach with one- and two-bedroom bungalows, some with sea views, this resort also incorporates the former Railway Hotel (▷ 238). The restaurant overlooks the beautiful pool. Tours and car rental can be booked via the hotel.
✉ 1 Thanon Damnernkasem, Hua Hin ☎ 032 512 021 🖐 B5,000–B6,100 🛏 42 bungalows; 207 rooms 🔇 🏊 Outdoor 🍽

KO LANTA

PIMALAI RESORT & SPA

www.pimalai.com
Occupying 40.5ha (100 acres) of land adjoining a 900m (980-yard) sandy beach at the southwest corner of the island, this is the most luxurious hotel on Ko Lanta. Rooms have polished teak floors, bamboo curtains, decorative Thai art, and a balcony with a fan. You'll find all the amenities of a five-star resort, including a spa, restaurants and a dive center with a good reputation.
✉ 99 Moo 5, Ba Kan Tiang Beach, Ko Lanta ☎ 075 607 999 🖐 B8,500–B14,500 excluding breakfast 🛏 79 🔇 🏊 🍽

SALATAN RESORT

www.salatanresort.com
This family-run bungalow resort is on the beachfront at the northern end of Ko Lanta Yai, away from the main town but within walking distance of a small village, restaurants and nightclubs. Bungalows are basic but clean and comfortable, with many of them offering a good view out to sea from the balcony.
✉ 166 Moo 1 Saladan, Ko Lanta, Krabi ☎ 075 684 111 🖐 B950–B2,250 🛏 26 🔇 🏊 Outdoor

WHERE ELSE!

www.lanta-where-else.com
Halfway down the west coast, all the bungalows come with a fan and the better ones have hammocks

on their balconies. All the beds are equipped with mosquito nets, and there are open-air bathroom facilities. The mood is laid-back and there are internet facilities, motorcycles and cars for rent, massage and a pool table.

✉ 149 Moo 2 Klong Khong Beach, Ko Lanta ☎ 075 667 024 ✋ B300–B1,500 ⓘ 20

KO PHI PHI
BAY VIEW RESORT
www.phiphibayview.com
The bungalows are built atop pillars on high ground, and all rooms have a fridge and minibar; the higher-priced ones have tea- and coffee-making facilities. The restaurant is virtually on the beach; the pool is shared with a nearby and pricier resort.

✉ Laem Hin, Ko Phi Phi ☎ 075 621 1223 ✋ B3,400–B10,500 ⓘ 105 🔆 🏊 Outdoor

PHI PHI NATURAL RESORT
www.phiphinatural.com
This resort is in the northeast of the island, a lot quieter than the Tonsai area. The resort is beginning to show its age but it is a well-run and friendly place with spacious bungalows; the standard ones are the least attractive while the seaview deluxe ones with balconies are the most sought after.

✉ Moo 8, Leam Tong Beach, Ko Phi Phi ☎ 075 613 010 ✋ From B3,300–B4,300 ⓘ 70 🔆 🏊 Outdoor

KO SAMUI
AMARI PALM REEF RESORT
www.amari.com/palmreef
All the rooms, set in tropical gardens on the beachfront, have a balcony or terrace. Facilities include two bars (one of which is a swim-up pool bar for cocktails), two restaurants, a spa and an air-conditioned squash court.

✉ Chaweng Beach, Ko Samui ☎ 077 422 015 ✋ B4,900–B6,000 ⓘ 187 🔆 🏊 Outdoor

ANANTARA LAWANA
www.anantara.com
A wooden walkway leads through gardens and arches to the entrance

of this very stylish boutique hotel. There's an Italian restaurant on the pool terrace, a spa with inviting treatments, and the Eclipse Bar, where aquarium fish tirelessly circumnavigate glass vases. The pool is heavenly and there are gardens.

✉ B99/9 Moo 1, Bophut Bay, Ko Samui ☎ 077 428 300 ✋ B6,200–B8,500 ⓘ 106 (32 non-smoking) 🔆 🏊 Outdoor 🍽

CENTARA GRAND BEACH RESORT SAMUI
www.centarahotelsresorts.com
About 15 minutes from the airport and half an hour from the ferry piers, this large four-level hotel is designed so that every bedroom has a view of the sea. There are lots of leisure facilities—sailing, windsurfing, pool games, sauna, tennis courts, bicycles—and a spa. For dining there are Japanese and Thai restaurants; the Palm Grove serves an excellent range of international food.

✉ 38/2 Moo 3 Borpud, Chaweng Beach, Ko Samui ☎ 077 230 500 ✋ B4,200–B8,000 ⓘ 203 🔆 🏊 Outdoor 🍽

CENTARA VILLAS SAMUI
www.centarahotelsresorts.com
You'll find this place tucked away in the southeast of the island on the Natien Beach near Hua Tanon, a fishing village on the coast about 18.5 miles (30km) from the airport. Facilities include a spa, snorkeling day trips, bicycles for guests' use and table tennis. The villas with fridge and satellite TV are just minutes away from the beach. There's good seafood and barbecues, and a shuttle bus to Chaweng and Na Thorn.

✉ 111 Moo 2, Tambon Maret, Natien Beach, Ko Samui ☎ 077 424 020 ✋ B5,885–B7,400 ⓘ 100 🔆 🏊 Outdoor

THE LIBRARY
www.thelibrary.co.th
Located on the popular Chaweng Beach, this is the island's chicest hotel and has some of the best-appointed rooms available. Each room (or page, as they are called)

includes an Apple Mac computer with free internet access, large widescreen television, large bathtub and elegant bath products, and free coffee and tea.

✉ 14/1 Moo 2 Bo Phut, Ko Samui ☎ 077 422 7678 ✋ B16,520–B18,880 🔆 🏊 Outdoor 🍽

SAMUI VILLAGE SPA RESORT
www.thesparesort.net
Bungalows and villas are mostly around the pool; the more expensive ones have a kitchen, lounge and bathroom. The resort runs courses based around cleansing fasts, vegetarian food, yoga and meditation. You can reserve online.

✉ Lamai Beach, Ko Samui ☎ 077 230 855 ✋ B500–B7,700 ⓘ 46 🔆 🏊 Outdoor

SANTIBURI BEACH RESORT GOLF & SPA
www.santiburi.com/
On the northern tip of Samui at Mae Nam Beach, 7.5 miles (12km) from the airport, this resort has a superb location amid gardens that seem to go on forever. The Vimarnmek restaurant caters to international tastes but the seafood is better. A spa and fitness center are on the premises, as is a dive school.

✉ Mae Nam Beach, Ko Samui ☎ 077 425 031 ✋ B13,500–B26,000 ⓘ 71 🔆 🏊 Outdoor 🍽

KRABI (AO NANG)
KRABI LA PLAYA
www.krabilaplaya.com
Set in beautiful gardens and only 165 yards (150m) from the beach, this quiet resort is a great place to relax. There are three choices of rooms—Superior, Deluxe and Poolside Deluxe—each well appointed and decorated in a contemporary Thai style. The pool has several whirlpools and a walk-in bar; next to the pool you can treat yourself to a traditional Thai massage. The restaurant offers Thai, Asian and Western cuisines.

✉ 143 Moo 3, Tambon Ao Nang, Amphoe Muang, Krabi ☎ 075 637 015 ✋ B2,500–B6,200 ⓘ 79 🔆 🏊 Outdoor

SABAI MANSION AND SPA
www.sabaimansion.com
There's a good range of rooms at this hotel, including ones suitable for families, most of which have air-conditioning; the least expensive rooms have fans. It's a short walk to the beach, and there's a fridge and safety box in the rooms.
✉ 249 Moo 2, Ao Nang, Krabi ☎ 075 637 643 💵 B100–B1,050 excluding breakfast 🛏 26 🏊 Some rooms 🏊 Outdoor

KRABI TOWN
KRABI CITY SEAVIEW HOTEL
www.krabicityseaviewhotel.com
Within walking distance of the heart of the town, this hotel has some rooms facing the river and away from the traffic. The most expensive rooms have the most cramped bathrooms, making the mid-priced ones better value. All the bedrooms have showers (no baths), TV and minibar. There's a breakfast room on the top floor, and a garden between the hotel and river.
✉ 77/1 Thanon Kong Kha, Paknum, Krabi ☎ 075 622 885 💵 B600–B1,500 excluding breakfast 🛏 30 🏊

PHETCHABURI
FISHERMAN'S VILLAGE
www.fishermansvillage.net
Less than an hour's drive north along the coast from Hua Hin is Haad Chao Samran, as yet unspoiled by tourist development. Each traditional, air-conditioned villa has all the amenities you would expect from a boutique resort, including indoor and outdoor showers. The resort has lovely sea views over a quiet beach. There is also a spa that offers more than 30 treatments. The friendly staff are happy to advise you on the local activities and the chef gives cooking lessons on request.
✉ 70 Moo 1, Haad Chao Samran, Phetchaburi ☎ 032 441 370 💵 B2,000–B4,800 🛏 32 villas 🏊 Outdoor

PHUKET
CENTARA KARON RESORT
www.centarahotelsresorts.com
One of the best resorts on the island, Centara Karon has a broad range of accommodations available including high-rise hotel rooms with beach views, competively priced family suites, and spacious boutique-style villas with private Jacuzzis. The hotel hosts several restaurants, large conference rooms with views of the beach, a childcare facility, and Centara's signature SPA Cenvaree. Parking is available.
✉ 502/3 Patak Road, Karon Beach, Phuket ☎ 076 396 200 💵 B4,900–B6,000 🏊 Outdoor 3 🍴

CLUB MED
www.clubmed.com
A sprawling place dominating the beach, especially appealing to families with young children. All meals are organized as buffets, mixing Thai, Japanese and Western food, with unlimited beer and wine.
✉ Thanon Kata, Karon, Phuket ☎ 076 330 456 💵 B4,200–B15,500 including all meals and activities 🛏 304 🏊 Outdoor 🍴

FRIENDSHIP BUNGALOW
This place is easy to reach, being directly across from the *songthaews* and taxi station, and good value because the rooms have hot water and a fridge and the beach is nearby.
✉ 177/7 Thanon Koktanod, Karon, Phuket ☎ 076 330 499 💵 B650–B1,800 🛏 22

J W MARRIOTT PHUKET RESORT & SPA
www.marriott.com/hktjw
A resort in the northwest of the island, close to the airport, and a stroll away from a 10.5-mile (17km) beach. The bedrooms are elegant, spacious and have balconies. There's spa, Thai cooking classes and a six-hole pitching and putting green. There is also an ATM machine.
✉ 231 Moo 3, Mai Khao Talang, Phuket ☎ 076 338 000 💵 From B9,000–B12,000 excluding breakfast 🛏 265 (133 non-smoking) 🏊 Outdoor 🍴

KATATHANI
www.katathani.com
Stretching for 930 yards (850m) in front of Kata Noi Beach, the rooms are generous in size and, except for the ground level ones, have balconies for watching the sunsets. Polished wood and stone characterize the style of the resort and there are four restaurants (including a seafood grill on the beach), two tennis courts, cooking classes, five pools and a spa.
✉ 14 Thanon Kata Noi, Kata, Phuket ☎ 076 330 124 💵 B4,000–B7,000 🛏 479 🏊 Outdoor 🍴

MOM TRI'S BOATHOUSE AND VILLA ROYALE
www.boathousephuket.com
The Boathouse—"a hotel for people who prefer not to stay in hotels"—is on three floors overlooking the beach. Villa Royale, 330 yards (300m) away, is even more luxurious, with pavilions, landscaped terraces and Balinese-inspired interior design. Facilities include beach chairs and umbrellas, two great restaurants, a spa and a cookery school.
✉ Kata Beach, Phuket ☎ 076 330 015 💵 From B4,200–B10,000 excluding breakfast 🛏 33 (Boathouse), 3 suites and studios (Villa Royale) 🏊 🍴 Outdoor

PHUKET ISLAND PAVILION
Not within walking distance of the town center but this is a pleasant hotel with a spa, a small pool, an outdoor pub at street level and a lounge bar with music at night. Rooms are functional, with a safe deposit box, minibar and tea- and coffee-making facilities.
✉ 133 Thanon Satoon, Phuket town, Phuket ☎ 076 210 445 💵 B1,320–B2,500 🛏 105 (33 non-smoking) 🏊 Outdoor

TALANG GUEST HOUSE
This clean, three-floor guesthouse has plenty of character and a choice of rooms with or without air-conditioning, and is a good-value place to stay. The best rooms are on the top level—the third floor—spacious and overlooking the street and roof tops. It is considered to have the best budget accommodations in Phuket town.
✉ 37 Thanon Thalang, Phuket town, Phuket ☎ 076 214 225 💵 B350–B450 🛏 13 🏊 Some

PRACTICALITIES

Practicalities gives you all the important practical information you will need during your visit from money matters to emergency phone numbers.

BEFORE YOU GO
CLIMATE

>> Thailand has three seasons, governed by monsoons but subject to regional variations. See www.climate-zone.com/climate/thailand.

>> The cool season is from November to the end of February, and in the north temperatures can drop low enough at night to require a sweater. Daytime temperatures average 79°F (26°C).

>> The hot season lasts from March to the end of May and is felt most in the northeast, where temperatures can reach 104°F (40°C) in the day.

>> The rainy season lasts from June to the end of October and is the most variable of the three seasons. On the Andaman coast, in the southern region, the rain is persistent enough to cause some bungalow operations to close down until late October. The choppy water may also affect boat timetables. On the Gulf Coast rainfall is most likely between October and January. In Bangkok and the central region, September and October see the heaviest rainfall.

WHEN TO GO

>> The cool season is the most pleasant time to visit Thailand and as the demand for hotel rooms and seats on sleeper trains and domestic flights rises there is the most need for planning ahead.

>> The north and northeast are oppressively hot from March to the end of May. The Andaman coast is at its best from November to the end of May.

>> For weather information, see www.tmd.go.th/en/.

INOCULATIONS

Inoculations are not compulsory but it makes sense to consult your doctor about immunizations, especially against typhoid and hepatitis, and to ensure that your 10-year polio and tetanus boosters are up to date. For information on malaria, ▷ 277.

WHAT TO TAKE

>> Bring with you any necessary prescription drugs. Pharmacies, however, have a range of medicines and English-speaking staff to give advice. You are allowed to bring in up to 30 days' worth of medication without a license from the Thai Food and Drug Administration. Narcotics are forbidden, but certain types of psychoactive substances

BANGKOK
TEMPERATURE

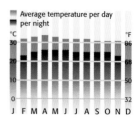

RAINFALL

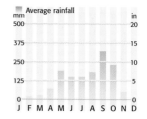

CHANG MAI
TEMPERATURE

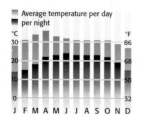

RAINFALL

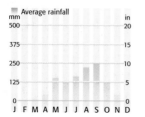

SONGKHLA
TEMPERATURE

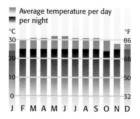

RAINFALL

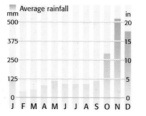

UBON RATCHATHANI
TEMPERATURE

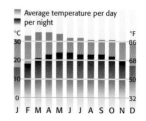

RAINFALL

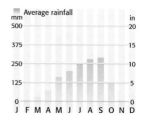

(categories 2, 3 and 4) are permitted with a doctor's certificate. If in doubt, always carry a doctor's note with you.

>> Malaria and other diseases are spread by mosquitoes during the night and day. You should pack mosquito repellent, although it is available in Thailand.

DOCUMENTS
ESSENTIAL ITEMS
>> Passport (with at least six months validity)
>> Visa (if required; ▷ below)
>> Travel tickets and documents
>> Insurance documents
>> Credit/debit cards
>> Prescription medicines
>> Driver's license (if renting a car an International Driving Permit is supposed to be produced, but a national license is usually accepted)
>> First-aid kit

PASSPORTS AND VISAS
>> Your passport must be valid for at least six months from the date of entry into Thailand.
>> Most passport holders from Western Europe, North America, Australia and New Zealand do not require a visa and are allowed to stay for up to 30 days after the date stamped in their passport on arrival. At airports, passport and visa regulations do change so always check before you travel.
>> Visa requirements can be checked at the website for Thailand's Ministry of Foreign Affairs—www.mfa.go.th/web/12.php—or through your travel agent or Thai embassy.
>> Sixty-day tourist visas can be applied for in advance through your country's Thai embassy or consulate, but allow up to two weeks for this. Two photos and a small processing fee may be required. At the time of writing, the visa fee has been waived temporarily.
>> The 30-day tourist visa can be extended by 10 days at immigration offices in Thailand. Visitors can also make a short visit across Thailand's land borders and obtain a new 15-day visa at immigration offices in Thailand. Visas on arrival at the Thai borders now expire after 15 days, but may be extended for an additional seven days.

CUSTOMS
Visitors entering Thailand have a duty-free allowance of 0.22 gallons (1 liter) of spirits or wine and 200 cigarettes. A license is required to export antiques or Buddha images, although it is not usually enforced for the mass-produced Buddha images. Any ancient object, religious or secular, requires a license that reputable antique shops will organize for you.

TRAVEL INSURANCE
>> Take out a comprehensive health and travel insurance policy, which covers medical and personal effects.

TIME ZONES
Thailand is 7 hours ahead of Greenwich Mean Time (GMT), and there is no adjustment for daylight saving.

CITY	TIME DIFFERENCE	TIME AT 12 NOON THAILAND
Amsterdam	−6	6am
Auckland	+3	3pm
Bangkok	0	12 noon
Berlin	−6	6am
Brussels	−6	6am
Chicago	−13	11pm*
Dublin	−7	5am
Johannesburg	−5	7am
London	−7	5am
Madrid	−6	6am
Montréal	−12	12 midnight*
New York	−12	12 midnight*
Paris	−6	6am
Perth, Australia	+1	1pm
Rome	−6	6am
San Francisco	−15	9pm*
Sydney	+3	3pm
Tokyo	+2	2pm

* = the previous day

>> If you rent a car or motorcycle, check what your insurance covers.
>> If you are planning to go diving, or any other adventure activies, check the terms of your policy beforehand.
>> Make sure you know what to do if you need to claim. Keep details of the policy with you.
>> Report stolen goods to the police to obtain a signed, dated and stamped statement for your insurer.

THAI EMBASSIES AND CONSULATES ABROAD

COUNTRY	ADDRESS	WEBSITE
Australia	111 Empire Circuit, Yarralumla, Canberra, ACT	http://Canberra.thaiembassy.org
	Tel (02) 6206 0100	
New Zealand	2 Cook Street, Karori, PO Box 17226, Wellington,	www.thaiembassynz.org.nz
	Tel (644) 476 8616/9	
South Africa	840 Church Street, Eastwood, Arcadia 0083, Pretoria	www.thaiembassy.co.za
	thaipta@lin01.globsl.co.za	
	Tel (27 12) 342 5470	
UK (& Ireland)	29–30 Queen's Gate, London, SW7 5JB	www.thaiembassyuk.org.uk
	Tel 020 7589 2944	
USA	1024 Wisconsin Avenue, Washington DC 20007	www.thaiembdc.org
	Tel (202) 944 3600	
Canada	180 Island Park Drive, Ottawa, Ontario KIY OA2	www.magma.ca/~thaiott/mainpage.htm
	Tel (613) 722 4444	

MONEY

THE BAHT

➤ The Thai currency is the baht (B), which comes in denominations of:

B20	green
B50	blue
B100	red
B500	purple
B1,000	beige

➤ The larger the note, the larger the denomination. All notes carry Western as well as Thai numerals.

➤ Coins come in B10, B5, B2, and B1. There are also 25 and 50 satang/cent coins but these are worth very little and are rare.

➤ Some hotels and diving companies quote their rates in US dollars, a legacy of the baht's dramatic fall in the 1990s.

BEFORE YOU GO

➤ Use a combination of traveler's checks and bank cards rather than only one means for making payments and obtaining cash.

➤ Before you travel, check with your credit and/or debit card company that your card can be used to withdraw cash from ATMs in Thailand. It is also worth checking what fee will be charged for withdrawals and what number you should call if your card is stolen.

TRAVELER'S CHECKS

➤ Traveler's checks are a convenient way to carry money as you can claim a refund if they are stolen or lost.

➤ Traveler's checks get a better rate of exchange than cash. There is a fixed commission rate of B23 per check (some hotels may charge more). Try to avoid carrying too many small denomination checks. Sometimes there is a charge made when you buy the checks, but shop around because this rate varies and sometimes there will be no charge if paying from your bank account.

➤ Traveler's checks in dollars are the most common and familiar in Thailand, but sterling ones and; euro checks are accepted in the more popular destinations. Traveler's checks can be exchanged in banks, exchange booths and many hotels.

ATMS

➤ ATMs are common across Thailand, including airports, and accept Visa and MasterCard, usually with instructions in English. There is usually a charge for each withdrawal.

➤ Not every island will have a bank and/or ATMs but islands like Ko Samui, Ko Chang and Ko Lanta do. For ATM locations visit www.mastercard.com and www.visa.com

BANKS AND EXCHANGE BOOTHS

Banks open Monday to Friday, from 8.30am to 4.30pm, but close on public holidays. In major destinations like Phuket, Ko Samui, Chiang Mai, and areas in Bangkok like Thanon Sukhumvit and Thanon Khao San, exchange booths keep longer hours.

WIRING MONEY

➤ In an emergency, money can be wired from your home country, but the agent handling the transaction will make a charge. Moneygram (www.moneygram.com) and Western Union (www.westernunion.com) are the two major agents.

➤ Money can also be wired from your home bank to a bank in Thailand but it will take at least two days.

CREDIT AND DEBIT CARDS

Credit and debit cards can be used in many hotels and the more expensive restaurants. Department stores and an increasing number of shops will also accept cards, but some shops will expect the customer to pay the percentage charge made by the card company. Cash can often aid bargaining.

LOST/STOLEN CREDIT CARDS

The following numbers can be used in an emergency to report lost or stolen credit cards.

MasterCard	Tel 026 704 088/97
Visa	Tel 001-800-11-535-0660
American Express	Tel 022 730022/44
Diners Club	Tel 022 383 660

TIPPING GUIDE

Restaurants	10%
Hotel porters	B10–B20
Taxis	Rounded up to the nearest 10 baht

TIPPING

Tipping is becoming normal in Thailand, especially in hotels and restaurants that cater to visitors.

TAXES

➤ The value added tax (VAT) of 7 percent that is applied to many goods and services can be reclaimed by visitors to Thailand if the shop operates a VAT refund service. Collect a VAT refund form at the shop at the time of purchase and present it to the airport VAT office before departure with your receipt.

➤ Top-end hotels will usually add a 7 percent hotel tax plus a service charge that averages around 10 percent. These charges are usually indicated by a ++ sign after a quoted room rate.

EXCHANGE RATES

For the latest exchange rates, check online at www.oanda.com or www.xe.net/ucc.

PRICES OF EVERYDAY ITEMS (BANGKOK)

These are average prices. Expect to pay around the same in Phuket but less in other regions of the country.

ITEM	BAHT
Petrol	B30–B35 0.22 gallons (per liter)
Lunch	B50–B350
Skytrain or subway ticket	B10–B40
Cup of coffee	B50–B80
Bottled water	B12–B25
International newspaper	B150–B250
Taxi—short ride	B70–B150
Internet access	B1–B2 per minute
Meal for two in mid-range restaurant	B300–B500

HEALTH

BEFORE YOU GO

>> It is essential to have full health and travel insurance arranged before you arrive in Thailand because in the event of a mishap, all costs are your responsibility. There is no form of public insurance coverage.

>> If you have existing home insurance of the all-risks, comprehensive kind, check to see if it includes the loss of personal possessions while traveling abroad.

>> Similarly, if you have a private medical policy, check to see if it covers you when in Thailand.

>> Before committing yourself to a particular health and travel insurance plan, make sure that you know what it covers in terms of any adventure sports you might be planning, especially diving and trekking, and costs arising from an accident with a rented vehicle. You may have to pay a premium to cover diving or trekking.

IF YOU NEED TREATMENT

>> If you need to seek treatment for a non-emergency ailment, consider in the first instance visiting the nearest pharmacy, where there will be a professional, English-speaking pharmacist on duty who can offer advice on possible medicine and/or the advisability of consulting a doctor.

>> If you need to visit a doctor, check with staff at your hotel for a conveniently located doctor. If you are staying in a four- or five-star hotel there may be a hotel doctor on call.

You will need to pay for a doctor's consultation and for any medication that is prescribed. You'll need a receipt to claim on your insurance.

>> If you need to visit a hospital (▷ 280), check with staff at your hotel for the nearest one and arrange for a taxi to take you there. The general standard of hygiene and healthcare at major Thai hospitals is high and English-speaking doctors will be available. Keep receipts for any payments that need to be made.

>> In an emergency, get to a hospital as soon as possible and get someone to contact your embassy and health insurance company if you have to be transported to a larger hospital, to Bangkok or back to your home country.

WATER

>> It is not advisable to drink water direct from a tap—Thai people do not drink tap water. Bottled water is available everywhere and because of the climate you are likely to find yourself always needing to have a supply ready to hand. In good hotels it is usually safe to use tap water to brush your teeth but if you're in any doubt, use bottled water.

>> In the cheapest restaurants the water that may be brought to your table in a jug will have been previously boiled and cooled. If you are unsure ask for bottled water or use your own.

HEAT

>> It is important to protect yourself from the effects of the sun,

especially if you are fair-skinned. Even if not sunbathing, it is more comfortable during the hot parts of the day to wear sunglasses and/or a hat or peaked cap.

>> If you are going to sunbathe be sure to use a high-protection sun cream and be careful not to spend too long in the sun, especially during your first few days. It is very easy in Thailand to turn yourself lobster red in a very short time; and as well as looking silly, the experience is damaging to your skin and can prove quite painful. Beware of sunburn on your back and neck while snorkeling; consider wearing a T-shirt and using water-resistant sun cream.

>> You will experience dehydration if you do not drink enough water so keep a supply of bottled water always at hand.

>> Heat rash and fungal infections can be a minor problem, but talcum powder is available everywhere.

MALARIA AND DENGUE FEVER

>> Mosquito-borne malaria and dengue fever (known as kai-leuad-awk) are still common in border regions, with fatalities reported every year, particularly among small children. Urban areas like Phuket and Chiang Mai are usually free of both diseases, though outbreaks do occur from time to time.

>> Check whether the area you are intending to travel to is at risk. In areas that are at risk, especially during the rainy season, mosquito repellent containing the DEET compound should be used on the

USEFUL HEALTH WEBSITES

WEBSITE	DESCRIPTION
www.who.int/en	World Health Organization
www.tripprep.com	Travel Health Online
www.state.gov/travel	US State Department Travel Information
www.tmb.ie	Advice and information from the Tropical Medical Board
www.doctorbackhome.com	Doctor Back Home
www.nhsdirect.nhs.uk	Useful guide to illnesses and what to do about them
www.doh.gov.uk; www.fco.gov.uk/travel	Health and travel advice from the British government
www.cdc.gov/travel	Official US site on health information across the globe
www.healthfinder.com	Links to health organizations and medical sites, giving a comprehensive range of health advice from the US Department of Health
www.travelhealth.co.uk	Tips and information

body and clothes after dusk when mosquitoes are about. Screens covering windows are usually fitted in bedrooms and a mosquito net is fitted around beds. Mosquito coils are often lit at night and left burning in the bedroom or outside on a balcony or verandah. They are not a fire risk and the very mild smoke keeps mosquitoes at bay. Mosquito coils and nets are inexpensive and readily available in shops and department stores in Thailand.

›› If you are going to an area at risk, discuss with your doctor the use of anti-malarial drugs. They need to be taken before, during and after your stay in a malaria-risk area.

HEALTH HAZARDS BY THE SEA

›› Bites from jellyfish, torn skin from coral and splinters from standing on a sea urchin are risks while swimming or on the beach. It's therefore a good idea to keep your feet covered at all times with rubber soles. The spikes from sea urchins, which are painful and not dangerous, need to be removed one by one from the skin; try to soften the skin first with ointment. Clean and carefully wash any cuts to the skin and apply an antiseptic.

›› Seek medical advice if you are unlucky enough to be stung by a jellyfish or bitten by a sea snake. Try to keep calm and still, do not apply a tourniquet, and arrange for transportation to the nearest hospital or doctor.

Above *An umbrella is a useful way to shade yourself from the sun*

HEALTHY FLYING

›› Visitors to Thailand may be concerned about the effect of long-haul flights on their health. The most widely publicized concern is Deep Vein Thrombosis, or DVT. Misleadingly called "economy class syndrome," DVT is the forming of a blood clot in the body's deep veins, particularly in the legs. The clot can move around the bloodstream and could be fatal.

›› Those most at risk include the elderly, pregnant women and those using the contraceptive pill, smokers and the overweight. If you are at increased risk of DVT see your doctor before departing. Flying increases the likelihood of DVT because passengers are often seated in a cramped position for long periods of time and may become dehydrated.

To minimize risk:
Drink water (not alcohol)
Don't stay immobile for hours at a time
Stretch and exercise your legs periodically
Do wear elastic flight socks, which support veins and reduce the chances of a clot forming

EXERCISES

1 ankle rotations	**2 calf stretches**	**3 knee lifts**
Lift feet off the floor. Draw a circle with the toes, moving one foot clockwise and the other counterclockwise	Start with heel on the floor and point foot upward as high as you can. Then lift heels high, keeping balls of feet on the floor	Lift leg with knee bent while contracting your thigh muscle. Then straighten leg, pressing foot flat to the floor

Other health hazards for flyers are airborne diseases and bugs spread by the plane's air-conditioning system. These are largely unavoidable but if you have a serious medical condition seek advice from a doctor before flying.

OTHER HEALTH HAZARDS

›› Rabies is prevalent in Thailand, and dogs (or other animals) should not be approached or patted. Worms can be picked up through the feet; wear something on your feet at all times, especially if staying in inexpensive beachside accommodations.

›› The most common health complaint experienced by visitors is a bout of diarrhea brought on by unfamiliar or contaminated food. This is best treated by taking lots of fluids and waiting two or three days for your stomach to settle. Medicines like Imodium, which only treat the symptoms, are useful if you have to travel but they do not speed up recovery time. Medication from a doctor may be necessary if the diarrhea persists and your temperature rises.

SPAS, HEALTH CENTERS, PRIVATE HOSPITALS AND CLINICS

›› Thailand has plenty of excellent spas and health centers offering a variety of courses and treatments promising physical well-being and mental relaxation. Massages of the head, feet or whole body, facial therapies, aromatherapy, hydrotherapy, body detoxification, meditation and yoga are available. Private hospitals and clinics offer dental treatment, health checks, minor surgery and plastic surgery.

›› In every town or city in Thailand you will find small private clinics, often run by just one doctor. Outside of large cities, an appointment is not necessary and it is a matter of showing up and waiting your turn. Such clinics usually dispense any drugs prescribed by the doctor who treats you. Pharmacies are very common, often with an English-speaking member of staff.

›› Private dental clinics can be found in every town, and appointments can often be made at short notice.

›› See Finding Help (▷ 280) for addresses and phone numbers of hospitals in Bangkok, Chiang Mai and Phuket.

BASICS

ELECTRICITY

Voltage in Thailand is 220 volts. The most common socket takes two round pins, although sometimes they take two flat pins and others take both. If you are packing electrical items you may need an adaptor plug. American appliances using 110 to 120 volts will need an adaptor and a transformer. Mid-range and more expensive hotels will have 110-volt shaver outlets.

CHILDREN

>> Nearly all restaurants welcome children, although not many will have high chairs or children's menus. A request to tone down the chili, however, usually works and most large hotels have restaurants serving international food.

>> Accommodations are usually charged by a room rate, not the number of occupants. Extra beds tend only to be available in the top-end hotels but rooms with three beds are not uncommon.

>> Disposable diapers (nappies) are available, but washable ones should be packed as a backup. The restrooms in four- and five-star hotels are a good bet when in need of changing facilities.

>> Buggies can be difficult to handle, because the streets are so bumpy and there are few ramps. Car seats are not available in taxis or rented cars.

TOILETS

>> Public toilets are not common in Thailand, but no one will object to you using the facilities in a hotel or guesthouse. All restaurants will have their own toilets.

>> Modern toilets are found in hotels, restaurants and places that attract visitors from abroad.

>> The alternative to a modern toilet takes the form of a tiled area, level with the floor surface, without a toilet seat and requiring the user to squat. A bucket and scoop will be nearby, with a tap to refill if necessary. Toilet paper is not always provided.

CAR RENTAL

>> Driving is not easy and is best avoided in Bangkok because of the complex road network, the difficulty of reading traffic signs in Thai and the challenge of finding parking.

>> Driving a rented vehicle outside of Bangkok is feasible. (▷ 54–55).

>> Car rental can be arranged in advance through the internet using a reputable company like Budget (www.budget.co.th) or through the many agencies that can arrange car rental. In destinations like Ko Samui, Phuket and Chiang Mai there are numerous places offering car rental, but it is advisable to use a reputable company because the less expensive deals may not always provide proper insurance.

LOCAL WAYS

>> Visitors to a Thai home are expected to leave their footwear outside.

>> Losing your temper in public does not impress Thai people—they will be embarrassed by such behavior.

>> The royal family is protected from criticism by laws making it an offence to utter derogatory remarks or behave improperly in matters affecting them. Thais stand for the playing of the royal anthem in cinemas and at prestigious occasions, and you are expected to show respect by doing the same.

>> Women are not supposed to touch or hand anything directly to a Buddhist monk. Images of the Buddha are treated with respect.

>> Shaking hands is not common among Thais. A familiar form of greeting is the placing of the hands together at chest height with fingertips almost reaching your chin, as if in prayer. The general rule is that the junior person in a relationship or encounter initiates a *wai*.

>> The term *khun* is used as a mark of respect in addressing people, orally or in writing, and comes before the person's first name. Sirinate Meenakul, for example, would be Khun Sirinate.

>> Rules of decorum make it rude to touch another person's head.

Dress Codes

>> Apart from a few restaurants in Bangkok (▷ 106–109), formal dress is not required for dining. Better restaurants expect diners to be smartly attired, but this usually means not shorts.

>> A dress code does apply when visiting the Grand Palace (▷ 87–90) in Bangkok, and for temples visitors are expected to be modestly dressed. Footwear is always removed and left outside a temple.

>> Thai people are modest and dress accordingly and while shorts and short-sleeved tops are fine for beaches and casual situations, dress more smartly when meeting Thais in non-casual social situations.

Scams

Be aware of scams involving overly helpful, smartly dressed people at Bangkok's railway station or airport. They usually work on commission for a travel agent or unlicensed taxi company. Around places such as the Grand Palace or Jim Thompson's House in Bangkok, do not accept tours, as this is often an excuse to take you to overpriced shops.

CONVERSION CHART		
FROM	TO	MULTIPLY
BY		
Inches	Centimeters	2.54
Centimeters	Inches	0.3937
Feet	Meters	0.3048
Meters	Feet	3.2810
Yards	Meters	0.9144
Meters	Yards	1.0940
Miles	Kilometers	1.6090
Kilometers	Miles	0.6214
Acres	Hectares	0.4047
Hectares	Acres	2.4710
Gallons	Liters	4.5460
Liters	Gallons	0.2200
Ounces	Grams	28.35
Grams	Ounces	0.0353
Pounds	Grams	453.6
Grams	Pounds	0.0022
Pounds	Kilograms	0.4536
Kilograms	Pounds	2.205
Tons	Tonnes	1.0160
Tonnes	Tons	0.9842

FINDING HELP

PERSONAL SECURITY

>> Make a list of the numbers of your traveler's checks and keep this with your proof of purchase (necessary for a claim) and the contact number to use in case the checks are lost or stolen. Make sure you keep this information separate from the checks themselves.

>> Keep a photocopy of the main page of your passport showing your photograph and personal details and the page with the stamp of your Thai visa, and keep these separate from your passport. Also consider keeping the number of your passport, or a scanned copy of the relevant pages, in an email which can be retrieved if necessary. The same could be done with the details of your travel and health insurance documents and your air tickets.

>> Don't keep wallets or purses in back pockets or any open pocket that might be a temptation to a professional thief. The general level of street crime and pickpocketing is low in Thailand but in high-profile parts of Bangkok—around the Grand Palace, Wat Traimet and on the Chao Phraya River Express boats—pickpocketing is more common.

HOSPITALS IN BANGKOK

Bangkok General Hospital, 2 Soi Soonvijai 7, Thanon Phetchaburi Mai ☎ 023 103 000; emergency ☎ 023 103 456; 24-hour call center ☎ 023 103 000; www. bangkokhospital.com. This hospital also has a dental surgery.
Bumrungrad Hospital, 33 Sukhumvit Soi 3 ☎ 026 672 000; emergency ☎ 026 672 999; www.bumrungrad.com

Travmin Bangkok Medical Centre, 8th Floor, Alma Link Building, 25 Soi Chitlom, Thanon Ploenchit ☎ 026 551 024

HOSPITALS IN CHIANG MAI

Chiang Mai Ram Hospital, Thanon Boonreuangrit ☎ 053 224 851/8
Lanna Hospital, Thanon Superhighway ☎ 053 999 777
McCormick Hospital, Thanon Kaew Nawarat ☎ 053 921 777

HOSPITALS IN PHUKET

Bangkok Hospital Phuket ,Thanon Yongyok Uthit ☎ 076 254 425; www.phukethospital.com
Phuket International Hospital, Airport Bypass Road ☎ 076 249 400; emergency ☎ 076 210 935; www.phuketinternationalhospital.com

POLICE

>> As well as the regular police you will see in cars and on motorcycles, who you cannot assume will speak English, there are special tourist police whose job is to assist visitors with difficulties. They can be contacted on a special tourist police 24-hour telephone line ☎ 1155. In parts of Bangkok, Chiang Mai and Phuket, and some smaller popular tourist destinations, such as Hua Hin and Pattaya, the tourist police have their own office or sidewalk cubicle, often stationed near the local tourist office.

>> If you have property stolen or lost you will need to report the incident to the police and obtain an official document proving you have lodged a report as this will be needed to make a claim on your insurance. This cannot be done with

the tourist police, but they will advise on where to go.

>> In a non-criminal emergency, the emergency number for the fire services is ☎ 199 and for the police it is ☎ 191. However, the person answering the phone may not speak English, so it is better to use the tourist line number ☎ 1155.

CONSULAR OFFICES IN CHIANG MAI	
COUNTRY	**CONTACT DETAILS**
Australia	Tel 053 492 480
Canada	Tel 053 850 147
Germany	Tel 053 838 735
UK	Tel 053 263 015
US	Tel 053 252 629

EMERGENCY TELEPHONE NUMBERS	
Police	191
Tourist police	1155
Fire service	199

Above A policeman on a street in Thailand

EMBASSIES AND CONSULATES IN BANGKOK		
COUNTRY	**ADDRESS**	**CONTACT DETAILS**
Australia	37 Thanon Sathorn Tai	Tel 023 446 300
Canada	15th Floor, Abdulrahim Place, 990 Thanon Rama IV	Tel 026 360 540
Germany	9 Thanon Sathorn Tai	Tel 022 879 000
Ireland	28th Floor, Q House, Lumphini Building, 1 Thanon Sathorn Tai	Tel 026 777 500
New Zealand	14th Floor, M Thai Tower, All Seasons Place, 87 Thanon Witthayo	Tel 022 542 530
UK	14 Thanon Witthayo	Tel 023 058 333
US	120 Thanon Witthayo	Tel 022 054 000

COMMUNICATION

TELEPHONES

>> The most expensive rates for calling abroad will be from your hotel room, while an internet-phone link from an internet cafe may set you back as little as B30 per hour. For a slightly higher charge, a high-quality connection can be obtained by using Thaicard, a phonecard issued by CAT (Communications Authority of Thailand), or the Pinphone 108 issued by TOT (Telephone Organization of Thailand) and available from post offices and many shops in denominations of B300 or B500. The cards can be used with the international telephones found near or in a post office, and dotted around cities and large towns.

>> In popular destinations and resorts, including airports, there are also Lenso telephone booths where you can make international calls using pre-paid Lenso cards or your credit card. Lenso phone cards are sold in shops near the payphone.

PAYPHONES

>> Payphones will accept either just coins or just phone cards for calls within Thailand. Phone cards in various denominations can be bought from shops, including 7-Eleven, and hotels.

>> Coin phones (blue or silver) are available for local (B1) and inter-provincial calls (B6–B15 per minute). Card phones are usually orange and blue, and are found in shopping malls and tourist areas, as well as at postal and telephone offices.

>> When making a call within Thailand, use the full area code even when you are phoning within the

Above *A sign advertising an internet cafe in Phuket*

area. Seven-digit numbers preceded by 01, 04, 05, 06, 07, 08, and 09 are mobile or satellite phone numbers and will cost more than landline numbers.

MOBILE PHONES

>> If your cell phone doesn't work with Thailand's networks, inexpensive phones can be readily purchased.

INTERNET

>> Most hotels and guesthouses, as well as many cafes have computer terminals available for customers, and charge between B120–B250 per hour. Rates are cheapest in the far north. Old-style internet cafes with numerous computer terminals are less common than they once were, but can still be found in tourist and rural areas. Some also offer other services, such as printing, international calls using the internet, burning photo CDS, and uploading content onto iPods.

>> While Thailand's constitution claims to grant freedom of speech, certain topics are off-limits and there have been cases where foreigners have been imprisoned for criticizing the monarchy. Visitors should take great care when including politics or other sensitive topics in blogs.

>> WiFi is everywhere in Thailand, but it almost never free. Most networks require a pre-paid card or cell SIM card and membership. True WiFi and other providers have

patch service in major cities. Most providers now collect personal information and log all internet transmissions, in accordance with Thai law, so use caution when viewing or sending sensitive information.

CALLING THAILAND FROM ABROAD

The international country code for Thailand is 66, and this is followed by the area code for the region of Thailand with the initial zero missing, then the local number. To call from the US, dial 011+66+area code+number; from the UK, dial 00+66+area code+number.

CALLING ABROAD FROM THAILAND

To call the US, dial 009, 007 or 001 (in order of increasing quality and expense), then 1, then the area code and the local number. To call the UK, dial 001, followed by 44, then the area code with the initial zero missing and then the local number.

MAIL

>> Stamps can be bought in post offices. Hotels and guesthouses also sell stamps.

>> Parcels must be packed and sealed at special counters in post offices. The rate for a non-airmail parcel under 5kg is B1,650 to the UK and B1,110 to the US. Airmail rates are B2,420 and B2,950 respectively.

INTERNATIONAL DIALING CODES	
Australia	61
Ireland	353
New Zealand	64
UK	44
US	1
For international directory enquiries and operator, tel 100.	

OPENING TIMES AND NATIONAL HOLIDAYS

BANKS

›› Monday to Friday from 8.30am to 4.30pm, though some may close at 3.30pm.

›› Exchange booths, easy to find in resort destinations, Bangkok and Chiang Mai, keep longer hours and are often open seven days a week from 9am to as late as 9pm or 10pm.

POST OFFICES

Most post offices open Monday to Friday, 8.30am to 4.30pm, and on Saturday from 9am to noon. Some may close for lunch and stay open an hour or more longer.

MUSEUMS

Many museums in Thailand open daily from 9.30am to 4.30pm or 5pm, but when there are exceptions, as with the National Museum in Bangkok, they usually close on Monday and Tuesday.

SHOPS

Most shops open Monday to Saturday from around 9am to 8pm or 9pm and many keep the same hours on Sunday. Department stores tend to open at 10am. In resort areas and popular destinations, shops catering to visitors will stay open seven days a week.

OFFICES

General office hours are Monday to Friday, 8.30am to 4.30pm or 5pm and on Saturday from 8am to noon.

PHARMACIES

General hours are from 9am to 8pm, including Sunday.

Right *You will find banks and ATMs in all the major towns, cities and resorts*

NATIONAL HOLIDAYS

Banks and offices close on national holidays and many museums close on Thai New Year.
The Chinese New Year is not a national holiday, but many restaurants and businesses close.

January 1	New Year's Day
Late January to early March	Makha Bucha Day
April 6	Chakri Day
April 12–14	Song Khran (Thai New Year)
May 1	National Labor Day
May 5	Coronation Day
One day in the first half of May	Royal Plowing Ceremony
July	Khao Pansa (start of Buddhist Lent)
August 12	Queen's Birthday
October 23	Anniversary of Rama V's death
December 5	King's Birthday
December 10	Constitution Day

TOURIST OFFICES

TOURIST OFFICES

TAT (Tourist Authority of Thailand; www.tourismthailand.org) Open daily 8.30am to 4.30pm, unless otherwise stated
TAT Helpline
Tel freephone 1672 daily 8am to 8pm

Bangkok: Head Office
1600 Thanon Phetchaburi Mai, Makkasan, Ratchathewi, Bangkok 10400
Tel 022 505 500
Email: center@tat.or.th

Bangkok: Local Office
4 Ratchadamnoen Nok Avenue, Banglamphu
Tel 022 831 555

Bangkok: Suvarnabhumi Airport
Main terminal, second floor
(No tel)

Ayutthaya
108/22 Moo 4, Tambon Phratoochai, Ayutthaya
Tel 035 246 076
Email: tatyutya@tat.or.th

Chiang Mai
105/1 Thanon Chiang Mai–Lamphun, Chiang Mai
Tel 053 248 604, 053 248 607
Email: tatchmai@tat.or.th

Kanchanaburi
14 Thanon Saeng Chuto, Kanchanaburi
Tel 034 511 200

Nakhon Ratchasima (Korat)
2102–2104 Thanon Mittaphap, Nakhon Ratchasima (Korat) Tel 044 213 666
Email: tatsima@tat.or.th

Phuket
191 Thanon Talang, Phuket town
Tel 076 212 213
Email: tatphket@tat.or.th

TAT OFFICES ABROAD

London
1st Floor, 17–19 Cockspur Street, Trafalgar Square, London SW1Y 5BL
Tel (020) 7925 2511
Email: info@tourismthailand.co.uk

New York (also covering Canada)
61 Broadway, Suite 2810 New York, NY 10006
Tel (212) 432 0433
Email: info@tatny.com

Los Angeles
611 North Larchmont Boulevard, 1st Floor, Los Angeles, CA 90004
Tel (323) 461 9814
Email: tatla@ix.netcom.com

Sydney (also covering New Zealand)
Level 20, 56 Pitt Street, Sydney NSW 2000
Tel (020) 9247 7549
Email: info@thailand.net.au

USEFUL WEBSITES

www.wunderground.com/global/TH.html
Useful daily weather updates for the whole of Thailand.

www.travelforum.org/thailand/index.html
Information about resorts and sights in throughout Thailand.

www.tourismthailand.org
Thai tourist board official website.

www.sawadee.com
Regional information, maps and online hotel bookings.

www.thaifocus.com
All forms of transportation with links to timetables, car rental etc.

www.khaosanroad.com
Dedicated to Thanon Khao San, the backpackers' area of Thailand.

www.travelfish.org/country/Thailand
Travelfish's online guide to Thailand, which includes a travelers' forum.

www.thaiworldview.com/tv/cinema.htm
Reviews of Thai movies with.

www.siam-info.de/English/poisonous_animals.html
Information on poisonous animals and treatment of bites and stings.

www.martialartsphuket.com
A Thai kickboxing camp in Phuket.

www.thailandlife.com
Features on culture and local crafts.

www.thaipro.com
Thai web directory with links to hundreds of Thai sites.

www.seameo.org/vl/thailifearts/artscrafts.htm
Dedicated to Thai crafts.

www.onebag.com
A useful guide to traveling light.

www.movieseer.com/th
Find cinemas and showtimes across Thailand.

www.embassyworld.com
Database of embassies worldwide.

www.cybercaptive.com
Database of cybercafes worldwide, giving street addresses.

www.thaifocus.com/disabledt.htm
Assistance for disabled travelers.

www.paddleasia.com
Phuket-based company offering kayaking trips and nature holidays.

www.asianbiketour.com
A company based in Chiang Mai that offers motorcycle touring holidays.

www.railay.com/railay/climbing/climbing_intro.shtml
A reputable climbing school in Krabi.

www.thecrag.com
Accounts of rock-climbing spots in Thailand.

http://divehappy.com/category/Thailand
Information on diving in Thailand.

www.activethailand.com/kayaking
Information and links to kayaking organizations, chiefly in the north.

http://johngray-seacanoe.com
Reputable kayaking tour company in Phuket.

www.activethailand.com/rafting
A company based in Pai that organizes whitewater rafting tours.

www.muaythai.com
Lots of information about kickboxing.

www.cyclingthailand.com
Bicycling routes in Thailand.

www.wfb-hq.org
World Federation of Buddhists, with list of meditation centers.

http://across.co.nz/thaichurches.html
Directory of churches in Thailand and Thai churches overseas.

FILMS, BOOKS AND MEDIA
FILMS

>> Thailand has been the location for many movies. It has stood in on many occasions for Vietnam, particularly in the *Deer Hunter* (1978), and has itself been represented in film by other countries, notably the 1999 movie *Anna and the King* based on the novel by Anna Leonowens *(The English Governess and the Siamese Court)*. The movie was filmed in Malaysia, since its production and distribution was banned in Thailand—the film and its previous incarnations suggested a romantic involvement between the king of Thailand and the governess, which was considered insulting to the Thai royalty.

>> Thailand has been presented to the public in several famous movies over the decades. *Brokedown Palace* (1999) tells the relatively true story of two Australian girls committed to 30 years for a drugs offence. In 2000 *The Beach* was both set in and filmed on Ko Phi Phi, which made the islands enormously popular and no longer a well-kept secret. The opening scenes are set in Bangkok and feature Leonardo De Caprio arriving in Thanon Khao San and viewing the Reclining Buddha in Wat Pho.

>> James Bond has, of course, hung out in Thailand a few times. In *The Man with the Golden Gun* (1974) Christopher Lee's secret lair was hidden offshore at Ao Phang Nga, and 1997's *Tomorrow Never Dies* returned to the same spot.

>> Thailand has its own movie industry, turning out thrillers, musical comedies and more. Yongyooth Thongkonthun's *Iron Ladies* (2000), based on the true story of how a team consisting mainly of gay men, transvestites and transsexuals won the Thai national volleyball championships in 1996, received a considerable international viewership. In 2001, Wisit Sasanatieng's *Tears of the Black Tiger* won the Dragons & Tiger Award for best new director at Vancouver and was selected for Cannes. The film tells a traditional story in a very up-to-date way, creating images that resemble hand-colored photographs.

>> In 1989 Jean-Claude Van Damme's movie *The Kickboxer* brought Thai martial arts to a world audience.

BOOKS

>> For the historical background of the country, you can do no better than the single volume *Thailand: A Short History* by David K. Wyatt (Yale University Press, 1982). *Southeast Asia* by Mary Somers Heidhues (Thames and Hudson, 2001) is also a usefully concise history of Thailand and the region. *Lords of the Rim* by Sterling Seagrave (Bantam, 1995) remains a popular, albeit exaggerated, tale of Chinese influence in southeast Asia, including Thailand.

>> There are a number of interesting and useful books that focus on Bangkok. Nancy Chandler's *Map of Bangkok* (Nancy Chandler Graphics, 2005) is currently in its 23rd edition and comes in the form of a fold-out map of the city center with separate maps of key areas like Sukhumvit, Chatuchak and Chinatown. Only information of possible interest to visitors and expatriates is included, and there is a wealth of local detail assiduously collected by residents of the city. The website www.nancychandler.net has details of other, like-minded publications. *The Grand Palace Bangkok*, by Naengnoi Suksri (Thames and Hudson, 1999), is a richly illustrated guide in color—one of those books you may wish you had consulted before visiting the Palace.

>> For those who intend to visit Kanchanaburi *The River Kwai Railway: The Story of the Burma-Siam Railway*, by Clifford Kinvig (Conway Maritime, 2005), tells the harrowing story of the prisoners of war and slave workers who worked and died on the construction of the railway line. Along similar lines but in the form of a novel is

Above *Shopping in Siam Square, Bangkok*

Pierre Boule's *The Bridge on the River Kwai* (Bantam Books, 1990). Best of all on the subject of the Thai–Myanmar railway and its construction is *Railway Man* by Eric Llomax (Jonathon Cape, 1995), who survived the experience and returned to meet the man who brutalized him.

>> *The National Parks and Other Wild Places of Thailand*, by Stephen Elliott (New Holland, 2006), is an up-to-date guide to Thailand's non-urban attractions.

>> Travel literature about the region to look out for includes *Adventurous Women in South East Asia* by John Gullick (OUP), which recounts the adventures of assorted eccentric women travelers of the 19th century. *The Gentleman in the Parlour*, by W. Somerset Maugham (Vintage Classics, 2001), is a classic tale first published in 1935, of an Englishman abroad, on a journey across southeast Asia and Thailand. A more modern and offbeat account of travel in Thailand is *Thailand: The Last Domino* by Richard West (Michael Joseph, 1991), who gives a lively account of his journeys across the country, packed with historical and cultural detail.

>> For those who want to understand the cultural mores of

Thai society there are several books to choose from. *The Arts of Thailand*, by Steve van Beek (Thames and Hudson, 1999), is an excellent, beautifully illustrated account of Thai architecture, sculpture and painting. *Thailand: A Survival Guide to Customs and Etiquette*, by Robert Cooper and Nanthapa Cooper (Graphic Arts Center Publishing, 2005), is a new edition of what used to be the *Culture Shock!* series. It is up to date and full of information, though aimed more at the expatriate than the visitor.

>> *Phra Farang*, by Phra Peter Pannapadipo (Arrow books, 2005), is the story of how a businessman becomes a Buddhist monk in Bangkok. *The Path to Buddha*, by Steve McCurry (Phaidon, 2003), is illustrated with photographs from Tibet, but the explanations and account of Buddhism relate to Thai culture also. *The Essence of Buddha: The Path to Enlightenment*, by Ryuho Okawa (Time Warner, 2003), offers a general introduction to the philosophy of Buddhism while *An End to Suffering: The Buddha in the World*, by Pankaj Mishra (Picador, 2004), manages to do the same but in a more perceptive manner, weaving philosophy, history, biography and politics. One of the best practical manuals for putting the philosophy of Buddhism into practice is *Change Your Mind: A Practical Guide to Buddhist Meditation*, by Paramananda (Windhorse Publications, 1999).

>> A number of books have been written by Westerners who have been imprisoned for serious drug offences in Bangkok's notorious Bang Kwang prison, dubbed the Bangkok Hilton. The title of Warren Fellows' account, *The Damage Done: Twelve Years of Hell in a Bangkok Prison* (Mainstream Publishing, 1999), leaves little to the imagination; nor does another account, by Sandra Gregory and Michael Tierney, entitled *Forget You Had a Daughter: Doing Time in the Bangkok Hilton* (Vision, 2003). Sandra Gregory, who was caught

smuggling heroin at Bangkok airport in 1993, was eventually transferred to a British prison and released in July 2000.

>> Thai cooking has to be one of the most fashionable styles around at the moment, and there are any number of good, simple books on Thai food and its preparation. A great start can be made with *Asian Greens*, by Anita Loh-Yien Lau (Apple Press, 2001), which has clear illustrations of each and every strange vegetable that you see in Thai markets and Asian stores back home and explains what to do with it. Two books by Jackum Brown, *Thai Cooking* and *Vegetarian Thai Cooking* (Hamlyn, 1999), offer good glossaries and simple instructions on many of the regional variations, from jungle curry to steamed pomfret. In a similar vein is *The Book of Thai Cooking* (Salamander, 2001), which also offers pictures of equipment, basic ingredients and illustrated instructions for over 100 recipes. *A Little Taste of Thailand* (Murdoch Books, 2004) is an affordable book of recipes, from street food to curries. The most comprehensive account of Thai cuisine is *Thai Food*, by David Thompson (Pavillion Books, 2002), a doorstop of a book with some 300 recipes, extensive information on ingredients and superb photographs.

>> If you experience a Thai massage and want to learn the technique then the best book on the subject is *Step-by-Step Thai Massage*, by Mann and McKenzie (Asia Books, 2004). It is a highly practical manual, with photographs illustrating each and every stage, and should be available in most Bangkok or Chiang Mai bookshops.

>> Wildlife enthusiasts can look out for *A Photographic Guide to the Birds of Thailand*, by Michael Webster and Chew Yen Fook (New Holland, 2002), or *Field Guide to the Birds of Thailand*, by Craig Robson (New Holland, 2005).

>> There are several good accounts of dive sites in Thailand, including *Diving South East Asia: A Guide to*

the best *Dive Sites in Indonesia, Malaysia, the Philippines and Thailand*, by Kal Muller (Periplus). *Dive Guide Thailand*, by Paul Lees (New Holland, 2005), is now in a new and updated edition with practical information, advice and maps on 140 dive and snorkel sites.

>> *The Magic of Bangkok*, by Sean Sheehan (New Holland, 2003), is an inexpensive book of photographs and text, a reminder of what you saw in the country's capital.

TELEVISION

>> Thailand has a plethora of land-based and satellite TV channels. The only cable TV company, UTV, offers several English-language movie channels (all heavily censored), sports channels, Western and Asian imported sit-coms and TV series, CNN, BBC World TV, the Discovery Channel and more. Satellite channels offer a similar range and include Thai variety shows and movies. Land-based TV stations are mostly government owned and air fairly safe run-of-the-mill dramas, documentaries and news shows.

RADIO

>> Thailand has hundreds of radio stations, owned and run by local government bodies. Bangkok has good Thai music stations, and BBC World Service, Radio Canada, Radio New Zealand, Voice of America and more can be picked up on short wave bands.

NEWSPAPERS

>> There are two English-language daily newspapers available in Thailand: the *Bangkok Post* and *The Nation*. The *Bangkok Post* tends to have rather more international material while *The Nation* focuses on local news. Both are widely available in cities and larger towns. In addition, the Singapore edition of the *International Herald Tribune* is available in Bangkok and the *Asia Wall Street News* can often be found in major bookstores.

SHOPPING

BARGAINING

Bargaining is the order of the day in markets and many shops, and it is generally only in modern shopping malls and department stores that fixed prices apply. Bargaining is not always fun—it can be time-consuming and frustrating—and a shop with fixed prices can sometimes be a welcome relief, especially when you are not sure of a fair price. In Bangkok, when shopping for handicrafts, the government-run Narai Phand is a good place to start because it retails products from all parts of Thailand, and silk can be bought by length. Don't hesitate to bargain in markets or in smaller shops, even if they have price tags. There are no hard and fast rules about how to start negotiating. You'll soon know if you are offering too low a price. Decide what you think the item is worth and start some way below what you are prepared to pay. It helps to check the fixed-price stores first to get an idea of what the shop owner is prepared to accept. Alternatively, bid half the asking price and work up to a price between the two.

In the northeast, asking prices tend to be more reasonable, and a discount of 10 to 15 percent is often the most you should expect. In the night markets of Ko Samui and other beach destinations, initial prices can sometimes be a little outrageous.

FABRICS

Thailand cottons and silks are versatile and are usually of excellent quality so well worth seeking out. Slightly coarser and with a more comfortable feel than Chinese silk, Thai silk can be bright or subtle, with an attractive dull sheen. It is made in small villages, especially in the northeast of the country, by craft workers, and a visit to a silk-weaving village is a memorable experience.

Cottons are also handwoven in the northeast of the country and shopping can be a rewarding experience. Cotton fabrics can be bought as lengths of cloth or as brightly patterned sarongs, several of which will easily convert to curtains or bedspreads. Look out too for handwoven scarves in rough cotton thread. Another great purchase in Thailand is the wonderfully simple axe pillow, a bright triangular cushion, which is surprisingly sturdy. Bought ready stuffed, they can be unwieldy to get home, but it is possible to find them without the stuffing.

TAILORED CLOTHES

Bangkok tailors usually have a wide range of patterns or they can copy a suit that you have brought or even a photograph. You should make sure you go to a reputable tailor, not one who offers to make up your garment overnight and throw in all kinds of gifts into the bargain. Consider carefully the motives of anyone offering a recommendation for a particular shop because they may be receiving a commission for every potential customer they bring in. Prices will vary depending on the cloth you choose—imported cloth, especially that of Italian origin, is more expensive—and the amount of time you can give the tailor to make up the suit. Be careful about the number of/absence of vents, buttons, whether it should be single- or double-breasted, what the lapels will look like, the style of the pants (trousers) or skirt. Dressmakers can do similar wonders with a picture or a dress you want copied.

OFF THE PEG

There is an excellent choice of garments, in every style, fabric and color, to be bought around Thailand—hippy chic, street-smart urban wear, clothes by Thai designers, imported European fashions. There aren't many bargains in the imported items, but cheap cotton pants (trousers) and T-shirts are a good buy. If you buy fake items, remember that these things are knocked out by the thousand and have a very brief life expectancy—the little crocodiles fall off first, followed by a general unraveling and the occasional dissolution in the washing machine while turning all your clothes green. Be aware that it may also be illegal to import fake goods back to your home country. Locally made shoes and bags are good bargains, and at MBK in Bangkok (▷ 98) you can get a good line in ski wear, but check all the zips work.

ARTS AND CRAFTS

Hill-tribe crafts are available in Chiang Mai and Chiang Rai, and in Bangkok, and there are some very pretty woven shoulder bags, clothes and quality jackets to be had. There is also jewelry and basketware. Each tribe has its own pattern for woven cloth, but lots of it is turned out on a large scale these days. Craft items come in a bewildering multitude of forms, and although you will find carved wooden elephants and Buddhas by the thousand, you will also see exquisitely made lacquer vases, celadon and woven accessories for the most sophisticated of homes.

It is hard to beat Chiang Mai for dedicated arts and crafts shopping—and you may end up having to purchase additional luggage in order to transport all your must-have buys home. Here, you will find a dazzling array and concentration of shops, and it does not take long to get a feel for the value of the goods that you are looking at. Lacquerware items are especially enticing, combining beauty and craft skill. Perfect gifts for the folks at home, they're also suitable for packing away in your luggage. Other products, like paper umbrellas, are equally attractive but a little more difficult to transport home; the beautiful paper stationery on sale is

easier to carry and makes a lovely gift. If your luggage space is limited, stick to smaller items like silver-crafted utensils and jewelry.

ANTIQUES AND COUNTERFEITS

If you decide to buy a genuine Thai antique you will have to obtain a permit to take it out of the country; any reputable dealer can arrange this. Look for the TAT-approval sticker on the door or window. Buddha images are not supposed to be taken out of the country. As in some other Southeast Asian countries, there is a brisk trade in crafted "antiques" that are actually new and made in large numbers.

The faking business extends to designer clothes, watches, DVDs, software and music, and Bangkok's Thanon Khao San and Patpong areas are famous for their stands packed with such items. Panthip, a shopping mall in Bangkok, is notorious for its illegal copying of DVDs and CDs and the Thai authorities largely look the other way.

Clockwise from left *A craftsman making decorative items in Ko Samui; clothing and jewelry stalls in the Indian quarter of Phahurat in Bangkok; hand-crafted baskets and wicker balls, displayed for sale at an open-air market in Nong Khai*

If you are lucky while in Thailand you may come across a performance of *Lakhon*—an ancient dance drama dating back to the 17th century. The dramas use traditional tales and often retell the lives and stories of the Buddha, from the Indian epic story the *Ramayana* and local fables. They are popular both in Bangkok and in the countryside.

Most performers are women who wear beautifully elaborate costumes and masks and who dance using highly stylized and symbolic movement, accompanied by a *phiphat* orchestra.

Another form of dance drama is *Khon*—a more sophisticated version of *Lakhon*. All movement is again stylized—the dancers are silent and accompanied by a chorus that sings and chants the story as it is performed. It can be seen at Bangkok's National Theatre and in cultural shows in restaurants in the main tourist areas. The masks you see in tourist shops are copies of those worn during the *Khon* performances.

Likay is a very entertaining comic form of dance drama. The stories are more contemporary and are often made up by the troupes. The troupes work on makeshift stages, often wear modern dress and involve improvisation, audience participation and general wackiness, all in Thai of course. Performances last around five hours and you can wander in and out of one without offending anyone. If you come across one, it is well worth watching for a while. In the south of the country you may come across shadow puppet theater, more common in Malaysia. Huge puppets play out traditional Thai stories from behind a screen, the audience watching the shadow thrown onto it to the accompaniment of music.

CINEMA
Cinema is very popular in Thailand, far outweighing traditional dance dramas in the public's idea of a good night out. Bangkok has plenty of cinemas, many showing Chinese movies, which depend on car chases, martial arts, romance and comedy, usually all in one film. Anyone who has taken a long bus ride in Thailand will know the quality of these movies, which are probably more interesting for not knowing what the characters are saying—guessing why they're running around is half the fun. Western movies are also very popular and are usually subtitled rather than dubbed, but you should check beforehand. Thailand now has its own film industry and you should look out for subtitled versions of Thai movies. Every performance of a movie involves the playing of the royal anthem, and the audience stands for the duration.

Left to right *A poster advertising a Chinese opera in the Chinatown district of Bangkok; inside Siam Square mall where there are cinemas, shopping, entertainment and restaurants; a bar just off Silom Road in Bangkok; night food market in Sisaket*

BARS AND CLUBS

Theme bars are increasingly popular, ranging from sports bars with large screens to British pubs with beer gardens, and there are also Wild West saloons and antique-filled bars full of red silk and cushions. Many visitors find it more interesting to avoid the dance clubs and enjoy the beach bars that open up at night, after the sunbathers have given up for the day. Candles flutter in the dark of the evening; you can listen to the waves breaking on the shore or the beguiling rhythms of Buddhist music playing in the background.

DRINKS

Beer in Thailand is taxed relatively heavily. Local beers include Singha, a lighter version called Singha Gold, and Kloster, as well as cheaper beers such as Chang, Cheers, Beer Thai and Leo. Heineken and Carlsberg are widely available, and recently Guinness and Kilkenny's have become more widespread, especially in Irish pubs. Wine in Thailand is mostly imported and relatively expensive, although there are a few Thai vineyards; Chateau de Loei is probably the best of these. Thai whisky is popular and inexpensive, and the 35 percent proof Mekong whisky can be mixed to produce a pleasant drink.

OPENING HOURS

Regular bars and clubs generally close at 1am. In some areas this extends later to 2am. Live music venues and dance clubs usually stay open until 2am.

THE GAY SCENE

The gay scene in Thailand, like its straight counterpart, has both a sleaze element and some good places for a night out. In Bangkok, Chiang Mai, Phuket and Pattaya there are many gay bars. Lesbian-oriented venues are far less obvious. There are a few mixed gay bars but in Thailand lesbian women tend to keep a low profile. For information on the gay scene try www.dreadedned.com or www.utopia-asia.com.

NIGHT MARKETS

Talat yen is the name for the night markets that open in most towns at around 6pm and which are dedicated to open-air, inexpensive eating. It's one of the least expensive ways to eat in Thailand and the atmosphere is entertainment in itself. Carts with butane heaters set up, deep-frying, barbecuing, stir-frying, and you wander around choosing a few dishes from different stands and then find a place to sit. The vendor will keep his eye on where you go and bring your food over, and the bill gets sorted out between the various vendors afterwards. This is the place to try out local specialties and to watch Thai families out for a night enjoying themselves.

BANGKOK

Bangkok has the most diverse and organized nightlife scene in Thailand. A free entertainment magazine, *BK Magazine*, which comes out on the first and third Friday of each month, has a useful nightlife section with up-to-date listings of the kind of music on offer at the various bars and clubs around the city. *BK Magazine* can be found in places like Starbucks, Delifrance and Blockbuster, as well as in bookshops, restaurants and cafes. The two English-language newspapers, *Bangkok Post* and *The Nation*, both have useful weekend editions that contain entertainment and nightlife listings.

SPORTS AND ACTIVITIES

BICYCLING

Renting a bicycle is possible even in quite small towns, and you can spend a day at your leisure visiting local sights. Bicycle rental is inexpensive, and local motorists are usually careful to avoid accidents, although bicycling may not be advisable in Bangkok or other big cities. If you intend to make a holiday of it, bringing your own mountain bicycle is an option. Roads for the most part are paved and have soft shoulders if you need to move over for a larger vehicle. Real aficionados can find plenty of mountain tracks to hurtle along. You should, however, bring spare parts, a medical kit, a bicycling helmet and reflective clothing. Also, make sure your insurance covers bicycling accidents. Bicycles can be taken on trains for a small charge, and there is rarely a charge on buses; ▷ 283 for useful websites.

COOKERY CLASSES

It's a long way to travel just to learn to cook, but when you get home your friends will be seriously impressed by the wonderful Thai dishes you can put together. Good places to find courses are Bangkok, Chiang Mai, Kanchanaburi, Hua Hin, Phuket and Ko Samui. The farther afield you choose your course, the more unusual ingredients you will encounter. In the northeast this will run to scorpions and silkworms! Courses usually include trips to the market to collect ingredients.

Local markets are a good place to buy those pesky utensils that you are required for cooking fragrant Thai cuisine, such as bamboo steamers, slotted spoons, and deadly looking cleavers you will have difficulty getting through airport security (and might be illegal to import to your home country). Dried herbs and spices are a good buy in markets.

KAYAKING

Most of the good kayaking centers are on the Andaman coast, where there are lots of interesting inlets, caves and lagoons to explore. Kayaking is especially suitable for cruising some of the shoreline's fascinating mangrove swamps. Phuket has very good centers with courses and accompanied kayaking trips, as well as equipment rental. In the north of Thailand there are river kayaking opportunities; ▷ 283 for useful websites.

MEDITATION

Thailand has meditation centers and an increasing number of them are offering classes for foreign visitors, chiefly in English. In Bangkok there are lots of centers where you can just roll up and sit quietly for an afternoon but if you want to spend a little more time learning meditation techniques there are centers in

more off-the-beaten-track places. These must be reserved in advance.

Longer meditation retreats are not for the faint-hearted. Many segregate the sexes, insist on white clothing, have a vow of silence and ask you not to leave the center while you are learning meditation techniques. Abstinence from food after noon and from drugs, alcohol and sex throughout, plus a 4am wake up call puts many people off. That said, the benefits of a few days spent learning concentration and how to focus your thoughts can be quite life changing. Instruction and accommodations are often free, although the centers usually expect a donation. For useful websites, ▷ 283.

ROCK CLIMBING

Southern Thailand's Andaman coast is home to several climbing spots, especially around Krabi, where rock climbing in the limestone rock formations has become popular. On Laem Phra Naeng there are climbing schools all within short distances of both holiday accommodations and good climbing locations. Courses run from a half-day's instruction to a three-day course, and equipment is available to rent. Rock climbing on the limestone rocks in Railay and Ton Sai in the Krabi area is a popular activity. You are in a harness and roped together. The rope is fixed to metal bolts permanently placed in the rock so if you do slip your fall is safely arrested. Average physical fitness is required, with the mental ability to concentrate more important than muscles. It is a thrilling experience, with every moment focused on the rock and your two hands and legs, and an adrenaline rush is guaranteed. For useful websites for climbing centers in Thailand, ▷ 283.

SCUBA DIVING

Scuba diving is enormously popular in the warm, reef-filled waters of southern Thailand. It is almost impossible to find a beach resort without a diving school or rental shop, and the huge number of offshore islands offer hours of exploration. Complete novices and expert divers are catered to, and the long coastlines mean that diving is possible all year round. The Andaman coast offers the clearest waters and safest conditions between December and April, while the Gulf of Thailand offers favorable weather conditions for diving all year. For your own safety, especially if you are a novice, there are several precautions you should take before choosing a dive course.

It is essential to check on the company's PADI (Professional Association of Divers) certificate and membership of IRRA (International Resorts and Retailers Association). This means checking on their website and asking lots of questions. Don't go for the cheapest course—in order to get customers the school may be cutting corners. Find out what kind of boat is used to take you to the dive sites—you want a nice big one with a radio and a first-aid box and spare equipment.

Check that your travel insurance covers you for accidents while diving and check with the company you book with that insurance is included for the duration of the course.

Look on the Dive Happy website (▷ 283), which has a forum section where people give accounts of their trips. Anyone who has been badly treated generally lets everyone know about it. The site also has information on the hundreds of dive sites and companies running diving courses. While diving, don't break off bits of coral, don't ask your instructor to anchor on a reef and don't buy any coral products.

SNORKELING

Most dive schools and equipment rental places also cater to visitors wanting to snorkel. All beaches have rental equipment and some opportunities for the sport, but it might be a good idea to check the dive centers to see if they will take snorkelers on one of their trips where there will be better

opportunities than along the beach where you are staying. If you buy a snorkeling mask hold it against your eyes without putting on the strap, breathe in and let go. If the mask fits you it will stay in place. If it is the wrong size or shape for your face it will fall off. Bring your own snorkel if you plan to spend some time in southern Thailand.

TAKRAW

A type of cross between volleyball and basketball without the use of hands, *takraw* is a team game played with a hollow rattan ball. There are several versions of it, one played with teams of three on a volleyball pitch and another with larger teams using basketball-type nets. Other versions have the players standing in a circle simply keeping the ball airborne, and judges award points on the beauty or skill of the hit rather than actually getting goals. Since the players can't use their hands and have to keep the ball in the air, it can be a very acrobatic performance.

Opposite *Bicyclists in Tad Ton National Park*
Above *Rock climbing near Krabi*

THAI BOXING

Muay Thai, or Thai boxing, is extremely popular in Thailand and is the equivalent of soccer in Europe or baseball in the US. Events are regularly shown on TV and there are stadiums dedicated to the sport around the country. Bangkok has two stadiums and is probably the best place to take in some professional games. The start of the game is a highly ritualized ceremony accompanied by live music from a *phiphat* orchestra. Each boxer follows a pattern of making obeisance to the four quarters of the compass and to his home province. He then performs a dance. When the actual fighting begins, it is less spiritual and more physical. Those of a delicate nature might not want to watch as the bout gets under way, with frenetic betting going on as the match progresses and the wailing *phiphat* getting faster and louder. Some visitors might want to attend a kickboxing school; ▷ 283 for useful websites.

TREKKING

If you travel to northern Thailand then a trekking trip may well be the highlight of your stay. November to February is the best time. You need to be fit to undertake a trek since it invariably includes quite strenuous uphill walking in hot conditions and some curious meals.

TAT (the Tourism Authority of Thailand) has a list of accredited companies who organize these tours. Do not just go with the people your guesthouse suggests—they get a commission for each person they send. Find out how many people will be on the trek—a large party can make life difficult. A typical trip lasts about four days and includes a trek through the mountains with overnight stays in local villages. When meeting these people, try not to interfere too much with their lifestyle. Do not take valuables with you beyond your camera, unless you are prepared to lose them. Robberies are now rare but still possible.

WHITEWATER RAFTING

Some exciting trips can be had during the rainy season (July to November), when the rivers are full. Most organized and popular are stretches of the Umphang and Mai Khlong rivers. In Pai, in northern Thailand, some excellent trips can be organized—two days along the Pai River through rapids and gorges, camping at night. Less challenging river trips are organized on the Kwai River, near Kanchanaburi; ▷ 283 for useful websites.

WINDSURFING

Thailand is famous for its superb water sports and good windsurfing centers. You'll find plenty of opportunities for windsurfing at Pattaya, Ko Samet and Ko Samui. The best winds in the Gulf of Thailand are from February to April and on the Andaman coast from September to December. Equipment will suit amateurs and beginners, and the temperate water means that wetsuits are not necessary.

HEALTH AND BEAUTY

SPAS

Most spas include the usual range of facials, aromatherapy, body wraps, baths in exotic substances and general pampering. Many resorts will have at least one spa connected to a five-star hotel, and you do not need to be a guest to book a session.

At some spas you remain fully clothed while others provide disposable underwear or a hospital-type garment. Some massages use aromatherapy oils on the back and others offer a hot stone massage, based on the idea that stones harvested from volcanic lava are rich in energy and release their therapeutic value when heated and applied to the body in a stroking motion by the masseur. Small heated stones are also placed on key energy points of the body, the heat penetrating the body to relax muscular tension.

THAI MASSAGE

A good massage should make you feel refreshed and energized, as blood circulation is stimulated and tension points relaxed. While most forms of massage that Westerners are familiar with tend to manipulate flesh to relieve tension, Thai massage is based on the idea that most problems with the flesh and the mind are caused by the blocking of energy as it flows through the body. The treatment is aimed at relieving these blockage points in order to restore equilibrium. It is a very strange sensation—a kind of pleasant abuse with the massage therapist using her feet, elbows and knees as well as her hands for the workout. The recipient also finds their limbs being manipulated into strange positions. There is a massage therapist on every beach where there are overseas visitors. A massage should last one or two hours and cost around B200 to B300. In Chiang Mai there are several schools that teach these massage techniques.

Below *Thailand is famous for it health and beauty spas*
Right *Beginning of a Buddhist festival in Bangkok*

FOR CHILDREN

ACCOMMODATIONS
Hotels rarely make an extra charge for children if they sleep in their parents' room.

HYGIENE
The usual rules for sensible hygiene apply doubly to children. Make sure their hands are washed regularly, deal with any cuts and scrapes straightaway, and ensure they don't binge on too many mangoes at once. They should also be told to keep away from stray animals—in addition to their poor cleanliness, rabies is not uncommon.

SNORKELING
In southern Thailand, snorkeling can be an enthralling experience for children who are able to swim, but adult supervision is constantly required because it is such an absorbing activity that snorkelers can easily lose their sense of distance and direction. There is also the danger of sunburn to the back of the neck and back. Snorkeling packages are usually advertised in resort areas. From Krabi, for example, there are popular four-island day trips that provide masks and snorkels (and life jackets), and children will enjoy the journey by speedboat and the fish-feeding sessions. You may want to consider packing your own gear for children since these may be less readily available in Thailand.

FESTIVALS AND EVENTS

The Chinese New Year, which falls sometime between **mid-January and late February**, is the occasion for celebrations by Thai-Chinese, especially in Bangkok and Phuket.

On a full moon in **February**, *Maha Puja* is a Buddhist merit-making occasion with nighttime processions to local temples.

Late February to mid-April sees kite-flying contests—Sanam Luang in Bangkok is a popular venue.

The Phanom Rung Festival in the last week in **March** celebrates the restoration work at Phanom Rung Historical Park with a procession and sound-and-light shows.

Usually around **mid-April**, *Songkhran* is the most exuberant national holiday. For visitors, its most conspicuous feature is the dousing of everyone with large amounts of water—be prepared for a soaking.

The most solemn day of the Buddhist year is *Visakha*, in **May**, when the life, enlightenment and death of Buddha are commemorated.

In **July/August**, a Candle Festival in Ubon Ratchathani brings three days of parades. This marks the Buddha's first sermon and the beginning of the traditional period of retreat for Buddhists.

Around **mid-October to mid-November**, the Kathin Festival marks the time when new monastic garments are offered by the laity to the temples' monks.

The **full-moon week in November** brings *Loy Kratong*, when a multitude of small boats, made of plant leaves, are set afloat to carry blessings of incense, flowers and candles to celebrate the end of the rainy season.

Bangkok and other big cities in Thailand have their share of Western-style restaurants serving international cuisine, fast-food joints and trendy Asian fusion places. Better than this, almost every small town has roadside stands, cafes and restaurants serving freshly made, delicious regional dishes, as well as the old Thai favorites of tom yam, green curry and fried rice.

CURRENT TRENDS

The two eating capitals of Thailand are Bangkok and Chiang Mai, but there are culinary surprises to be savored all over the country. Thai cafés and restaurants abound, but there are also the big chains more familiar in the West, as well as places serving European cuisine and American-style steakhouses. You don't have to try unusual food if you choose, but the range and variety of cuisines is one of the joys of eating in Thailand. South Indian vegetarian venues are dotted around, as are Indian Muslim venues serving *roti* and chicken *biryani*. Chinese food is also well represented and is strongly influenced by Thai elements.

Vietnamese food finds a presence in the northeast. Thai food ranges from noodle-based dishes to curry, fried rice, salads and soup.

PRICING

Canteens charge around B60 for a main course, while slightly more upmarket places charge up to B150 and more. Classy hotel restaurants charge prices equal to those in restaurants in Europe. Service charges of 10 percent plus 7 percent VAT have begun appearing on bills, even in many fast-food restaurants. Street stands are inexpensive and well worth a try for little snacks. Tipping is not necessary where there is already a service charge.

FRESHNESS

Many of the best and cheapest places to eat, where you will sit down in a real Thai atmosphere and be among Thai people, are the market stands and small, primitive-looking cafes. Most Thai dishes are cooked in minutes and use fresh ingredients picked or slaughtered

not too far away from where you are actually eating, so freshness of food is rarely a consideration. Hygiene should never be ignored, though, and you should always check that meat and fish are fully cooked. Also make sure that your own hands are washed carefully before eating, and that your choice of venue is full of happy, healthy-looking customers. If you have a delicate digestive system, work your way up to full-on chili-laden curries and avoid too much exotic fruit at first. Buy unpeeled fruit and peel it yourself. Bottled water is best and avoid salads and homemade ice-cream in places that don't appear to be very clean and well-maintained.

THAI REGIONAL CUISINES

Thai food is a mixture of indigenous cooking fused with some Chinese and Indian styles. It can be chili fueled or quite bland, depending on the origin of the dish and the region of the country. It typically uses ginger, and galangal, two very similar roots which are chopped and used for flavoring. Galangal in particular gives it that special Thai taste. Coconut thickens the sauce and adds its own rich taste to the blend, while lime leaves, fresh cilantro (coriander) leaves, Thai basil and whole fresh peppercorns usually end up in there too. Lemongrass, chopped or ground, is another essential ingredient. Other ingredients include peanuts for thickening, tiny pea-size eggplants, *nam pla* or fish sauce made from anchovies and occasionally tamarind to add a tangy taste, such as that in *tom yam* soup (▷ 296).

Beyond the typical Thai dishes there are plenty of regional variations. Northern Thailand has dishes that are closely akin to those of Myanmar (Burma). Noodles, both fried and boiled, are common, and sticky or glutinous rice is more widely used, primarily because it grows better there. To the south of Thailand, Malay cuisine begins to influence and green curry sauce gives way to Panang curry where cilantro (coriander) root replaces fresh herbs, and peanuts are used to thicken the sauce. Satay—barbecued meats on skewers served with spicy peanut sauce—ubiquitous in Malaysia, is common.

Thai desserts are not desserts as the West have come to know them. Real Thai restaurants tend not to serve them, and the posh ones keep them as a sop to our sugar-fueled palates. Cakes, which can be bought on the street, are often made with sticky rice and coconut cream and bear the colors of pandanus leaves or taro. Pancakes are made from rice flour and coconut milk, rolled up around fresh fruit and sprinkled with palm sugar and dried coconut flakes. Look out for coconut custard, often served with fresh lychees or banana, *met kanun* or "jackfruit seeds" (nothing to do with actual jackfruit)—split yellow lentils made

into donuts and glazed with syrup, or tapioca and coconut, much nicer than the tapioca that older Brits will remember from school dinners. Fried bananas, sticky rice served with mangoes, and roasted jackfruit seeds are all popular.

VEGETARIAN OPTIONS
The more religious Buddhists like to spend at least one day a week being vegetarian and there are dedicated restaurants serving all kinds of vegetarian food. The trouble is spotting them, since they are often run by monks close to a temple and unadvertised. Their name is *raan ahaan jeh*, but this may not help if the words are in Thai. Try asking around. Be aware that regional standards of vegetarian cooking might not be as strict as those found in the West, including dishes that contain fish sauce or meat products.

Tourist areas are aware of the vegetarian market among their *farang* visitors and often have a veggie element to their menus. Most places can take out the meat if you ask them, and since a Thai meal is generally made up of a plate of rice and lots of other side dishes you can easily pick the meat-free ones. Vegetarian fried rice is negotiable in most places, and even vegans can arrive at an arrangement with hand waving, the expression *mai sai* (without) and pointing. The glory of regular Thai cafes and restaurants is that the food is cooked as you order it, so you can choose what goes into it. Cheese and cow's milk are rarely part of Thai cuisine.

EATING ETIQUETTE
Thai food is usually eaten with a spoon and fork, the spoon making the journey to your mouth and the fork used to get the food onto the spoon. Most food is in tiny bite-size pieces so a knife is not necessary. Noodle dishes require chopsticks, and Chinese restaurants always provide them. You can hold your bowl up close to your mouth in your other hand. If you aren't comfortable with chopsticks, no one minds

providing a fork and spoon. If you are eating with a group then each person will get their own bowl of rice, while the shared food is brought out in big dishes.

Take a little from one dish and then refill. Don't stack up a whole meal at once. Sticky rice and Indian food is often served without utensils and eaten with the right hand, never the left. Again, if you're not happy to eat with your fingers, you won't cause offense if you ask for a spoon and fork.

STRANGE FRUIT
Custard apples and soursop are round, greenish scaly-skinned fruit with creamy flesh which tastes a little like spicy pears. Durian *(turian)*, the gigantic hedgehog-like fruit, is a definite acquired taste—a little like garlic-flavored custard. It has a distinctive and pungent smell and is often banned in hotel rooms and on public transport. Thais love it and will spend ages choosing their fruit to get the right degree of softness. Jackfruit *(khanun)* is a bumpy fruit whose flesh is like fruity bubblegum.

Mangosteen *(mang khud)* looks like a cross between an eggplant (aubergine) and an apple, with purple skin which breaks into five sweet segments with a bit of a bite to them. Papaya *(malakho)* is better known in the West. Ripe papaya is soft with orange flesh and makes excellent milkshakes. It mixes well with melon and pineapple in many a Thai breakfast. Pomelo *(som-o)* is like a giant greenish grapefruit with a sharp taste. Its flesh is less juicy than grapefruit.

Rambutan *(ngo)* and lychees *(linchi)* are very similar fruits, rambutan being the hairy version. The flesh around the stone inside is very sweet and juicy. They have a short season and don't keep well. Star fruit *(mafueng)*, shaped like an elongated star, is pale green and tastes very much like a sweeter version of pea pods. Dragon fruit is also popular. This shockingly bright cerise, oval, scaly fruit, is about the size of an elongated ostrich egg.

In popular destinations menus will be in English but it is worth learning a few words in Thai. Spellings vary; curry is spelled *gaeng* or *kaeng*, and *popiah* (spring rolls) sometimes appear as *bapia*, *paw* or *pia*. If you don't eat some items, learn the expression *mai sai*—"without." Boiled or filtered water is *nam piao*. Salt is *kleua* and sugar is *nam tan*.

BASICS
Ahaan ta-lay seafood
Ba-mee (krawp) egg noodles (fried)
Gai chicken
Kai egg
Kao rice
Kao neeyo sticky rice
Kung prawns
Kwey teeyo assorted rice noodles
Muu pork
Neua beef (or generally, meat)
Plaa fish
Puu crab
Tahu tofu

SOUP
Gaeng jeut curry soup with meat, usually pork, and vegetables
Tom kar gai chicken soup with coconut
Tom yam kung hot-and-sour soup with prawns

RICE DISHES
Kao gaeng curry and rice
Kao pat gai/muu/kung fried rice with chicken/pork/prawns
Kao pat sapporot pineapple fried rice
Kao suay steamed rice

NOODLE DISHES
Ba mil haeng egg noodles fried with egg, meat and vegetables
Kow soi Chiang Mai fried noodles
Kway thiaw mil nam rice noodles in a soup of chicken broth
Kway thiaw rat na rice noodles in thick sauce with vegetables
Pat thai flour noodles cooked with assorted meat and vegetables, bean sprouts and occasionally tofu

The previous dishes can be made with either rice noodles (*kway thiaw*) or egg noodles (*ba mil*).

CURRY
Gaeng keeyo waan green curry
Gaeng Mussaman Muslim beef and potato curry
Gaeng pet red (in color but also hot) curry
Gaeng pet gai/neua spicy chicken/beef curry
Gaeng phaneng regular chicken/beef curry

MEAT DISHES
Gai tua chicken in peanut sauce
Gai pat bai kraprao fried chicken with basil leaves
Gai pat naw mai chicken with bamboo shoots
Gai yang garlic chicken
Muu preeyo waan sweet-and-sour pork
Neua pat gratiam prik thai beef with garlic and pepper
Neua pat naam man hoy beef in oyster sauce
Si klok pork and crab sausage

EGG DISHES
Kai yat sai omelet stuffed with pork and/or vegetables

FISH DISHES
Plaa neung pae sa steamed fish with ginger and vegetables
Plaa pao grilled fish
Plaa preeyo waan whole fish fried with lots of ginger
Plaa rat phrik whole fish cooked with chilies
Tord man plaa fishcakes

SALADS
Som tam very spicy salad of green papaya and tomatoes
Yam tang kwa cucumber salad

VEGETABLE DISHES
Pak put ruam mit stir-fried mixed vegetables
Tahu sod sai stuffed soy bean cake

VEGETABLES
Grathiam garlic
Makeua eggplant (aubergine)
Mekeua thet tomato
Mun farang (tord) potatoes (fries)
Naw mai bamboo shoots
Pak vegetables
Pat pak lai yang stir-fried veg
Phrik chili
Phrik yuak peppers
Taeng kwaa cucumber
Tua lentils (or peas or beans)
Tua ngawk bean sprouts

Phom kin ahaan jay I am a vegetarian (man)
Di-chan kin ahaan jay I am a vegetarian (woman)
Mai sai without

FRUIT
▷ 295.

DESSERTS
Gluay buat chee bananas in sweet coconut sauce
Gluay kak banana fritters
Kanom beung pancakes stuffed with coconut cream and egg
Kao neeyo mamuang sticky rice with mango
Met kanun sweet glazed lentil dumplings
Sungkeeya fuk tawng steamed custard in pumpkin shell
Sungkeeya maprow on coconut cream custard

DRINKS
Bia beer
Chaa tea
Chaa rawn hot tea
Chaa yen iced tea
Gluay pun banana shake
Kaafe coffee
Naam kaeng ice
Naam manao lime juice
Naam plao drinking water
Naam som orange juice
Naam yen cold water
Ohliang iced coffee

Opposite *Food stall at Sirikit Reservoir*

Popular destinations offer a range of accommodations, from exclusive and luxuriously appointed five-star hotels to budget places with dorms, guesthouses and camping sites. Rates at all of them vary according to demand and time of year, falling during the rainy season and escalating in the high season, rising even higher if there is a big festival or event in town. Apart from at quality hotels, it is normal practice to be shown your room before you agree to stay. In cheaper places you should check the shower and hot water, and that the door locks, and, if appropriate, the availability of mosquito nets and how well the windows close. Note that non-smoking rooms are not common in Thai hotels, and very rarely found in establishments with fewer than five stars.

UPMARKET HOTELS

All the really big names in luxury hotels feature prominently in the big resorts and in Bangkok. There are some home-grown Thai chains too— Amari and Dusit stand out among them. All of these charge much lower rates than their equivalent in the West and if you have the budget for it this would be your chance to experience luxury hotel living for a while. The really exclusive places are small boutique-style hotels with individually furnished rooms, internet access in each room, DVD players and music systems, room service, the ubiquitous spa, a pool, several exclusive restaurants and sometimes a beer garden and bar.

Many of these luxurious hotels, especially in the off-peak season, will offer huge discounts if you walk in and ask for a room or email at short notice. They also offer equally big discounts if you reserve via the internet either through a reservations agency or on the hotel's own website. There are a number of reservations agencies in Bangkok airport, and Thai Airlines will arrange discounted reservations for their passengers.

RESORT ACCOMMODATIONS

Resort can mean five-star luxury with fitness center, pool, spa, tennis, and golf buggies to drive you around, or just a set of thatched wooden huts on the beach. Most resort destinations in Thailand have their own website with photographs of the various hotels and their facilities so it would be wise to do some research before you make your reservation. If a resort is not on the internet it is probably small with few facilities.

THAI-CHINESE HOTELS

Most small towns have several well-run, clean and efficient Thai-Chinese family-run hotels, which

Opposite and above Expect high levels of service and excellent accommodations in Thailand

offer a range of accommodations with options of fan, air-conditioning, bath and fridge. The cheapest rooms will be fan cooled with a simple shower and double bed. The best rooms will be air-conditioned with a bathroom, including a bath, hot water, fridge, TV and phone in the room. These last few items raise the price considerably. You should ask to be shown the choices of rooms and check that all the facilities are actually working. Ask for a room at the back to avoid the noise of traffic. European-looking visitors may be offered a special high rate so bargain before agreeing to stay. Most of these hotels will be on the main street in town and have a good coffee shop serving Chinese or Thai food.

GUESTHOUSES

Guest houses of one kind or another are manifold all over Thailand and range from budget hotel-type buildings to very simple wooden and thatch buildings with a couple of rooms. They are right at the budget end of Thai accommodations and often run only to a shared bathroom, a fan-cooled room and a double bed.

The advantage of the best of them, besides their cheap rates, is that they are run by people who are used to Western tourists, can organize trips and often have internet access, as well as good notice boards, other visitors to swap stories with and good traveler information. They rarely take advance reservations so you should turn up before noon to reserve your room for the night.

HOSTELS

These are the cheapest form of accommodations in Thailand and are really more like the old European-style youth hostels, fairly primitive facilities with dorm rooms but also some air-conditioned doubles. You need to be a member of Hostelling International to stay at a Thai youth hostel. Membership costs B300 per year or an extra fee of B50 (in addition to the room rate) for one night.

CAMPING

Most of Thailand's campsites are in national parks and facilities are fairly basic. You don't really need a tent as parks have equipment for rent. If you do rent a tent then check that the zips work—you don't want to share your sleeping bag with some of the park's denizens. You will need a flashlight, a lightweight sleeping bag or sheet and a sleeping mat, plus cooking equipment, drinking water, insect repellent and food. Accommodations in Thailand are so cheap that, unless you love the outdoors, bringing all that equipment seems a little unnecessary. Lots of the parks also have inexpensive bungalows and longhouses, which might make a more comfortable alternative, although they tend to be based around groups of six or more people. You should reserve your park accommodations in advance at www.thaiforestbooking.com. Camping is also allowed on islands and beaches, although few people bother with a tent.

Below *Visitors can choose to stay in luxury hotels to quirky boutique hotels, in Thailand*

Thai has its own complex script, which is very different from any European language. Here we provide a simple transliteration using the English alphabet.

Courtesy and respect is very important in Thai society, and people consider hierarchy, status and seniority when addressing one another. The safest option is to refer to yourself ("I") as *phom* (if you are male) and *dichan* (if you are female), and address the other person as *khun* (this can be followed by his/her first name). To be polite, men should add *khrap* to the end of sentences and women should add *kha*. Please choose the appropriate alternative indicated in this guide such as *phom/dichan*, etc.

Thai words in this guide have been transliterated as closely as possible to how they are actually pronounced in Thai. However, there are certain characters which are pronounced differently and should be drawn to your attention. They are:

ua = ou	as in	t**ou**r
bp = p	as in	s**p**are or s**p**ort
dt = t	as in	s**t**op or s**t**ool
uae	as in	**uaggh**

Thai is a tonal language with five different tonal sounds (flat, high, low, rising and falling) denoted by four tonal marks. These tones vary the meaning of a sound. For example, *mai* in a high pitch means "new/again/another," whereas *mai* in a low pitch means "no." The transliteration of Thai tonal sounds has not been attempted in this guide, to keep the notation simple.

Thai verbs do not have tenses. Words or phrases, such as "now," "two days ago," "tomorrow" are used to indicate present, past or future. Articles (a, an and the) do not exist in Thai. Adjectives come after nouns. Thus "a red apple" is "apple red" in Thai.

Learning a few simple words in Thai is quite easy, as many Thai words are monosyllabic. The locals will appreciate it if you can learn to exchange a few words with them in Thai.

NUMBERS

0	**soon**
1	**nung**
2	**song**
3	**saam**
4	**see**
5	**hah**
6	**hok**
7	**jet**
8	**bpaet**
9	**gaow**
10	**sib**
20	**yee-sib**
30	**saam-sib**
40	**see-sib**
50	**hah-sib**
60	**hok-sib**
70	**jet-sib**
80	**bpaet-sib**
90	**gaow-sib**
100	**nung-roi**
1,000	**nung-pan**
million	**lahn**
quarter	**nung nai see**
half	**khrung**

USEFUL WORDS

yes
chai
no
mai
please
garunah
thank you
korb-khun
you're welcome
Mai pen rai khrap/kha
excuse me!
Kor-toht khrap/kha!
where
tee-nai
here
tee-nee
there
tee-nan
when
muae-rai
who
khrai
why
tam-mai/pro arai
may I/can I?
Phom/dichan kor...dai mai?

COLORS

black	**see dam**
pink	**see chom-poo**
red	**see daeng**
purple	**see muang**
orange	**see som**
brown	**see nam-dtaan**
yellow	**see luaeng**
green	**see kiew**
turquoise	**see kiew-om-fah**
white	**see kaow**
gold	**see torng**
silver	**see ngern**
gray	**see tao**
blue	**see nam-ngern**

CONVERSATION

I don't speak Thai
Phom/dichan poot pah-sah Thai mai dai
Do you speak English?
Khun poot pah-sah angkrit dai mai?
I don't understand
Phom/dichan mai khao-jai
My name is...
Phom/dichan chue...
What's your name?
Khun chue arai?
Hello, pleased to meet you
Sawatdee khrap/kha. Yin-dee tee dai roojak khun
This is my wife/husband/daughter/son
Nee panraya/sah-me/loog-saow/loog-chai khong phom/dichan
Where do you live?
Khun yoo tee-nai?
I live in...
Phom/dichan yoo tee...

PRACTICALITIES WORDS AND PHRASES

Good morning
Sawatdee
Good afternoon/evening
Sawatdee
Goodbye
Lah-gone khrap/kha, Sawatdee
How are you?
Sabaai-dee rue khrap/ kha?
Fine, thank you
Sabaai-dee, korb-khun
I'm sorry
Phom/dichan kor-toht

SHOPPING
How much is this?
Tao-rai khrap/kha?
Where can I buy...?
Phom/dichan ja sue ... dai tee-nai?
I'm just looking, thank you
Dern doo tao-nan khrap/kha, korb-khun
I'll take this
Phom/dichan ao an-nee khrap/ kha
Do you accept credit cards?
Chai bat credit dai mai?
Can you measure me please?
Wat dtua hai phom/dichan noi khrap/kha?

MONEY
Is there a bank/currency exchange office nearby?
Taew nee mee ta-nah-kaan/tee laek-plian ngern taang-bpra-tet mai?
I'd like to change sterling/dollars into Thai baht
Phom/dichan dtong-garn laek ngern bporn/dollar bpen ngern baht.
Can I use my credit card to withdraw cash?
Phom/dichan ja chai bat credit torn ngern-sot dai mai?
I'd like to cash this traveler's check
Phom/dichan dtong-garn laek cheque dern-taang bpen ngern-sot

GETTING AROUND
Where is the train/bus station?
Satah-nee rot fai/rot bus yoo

tee-nai?
Does this train/bus/ferry go to...?
Rot fai/rot bus/ruae-kaam-faak nee bpai...rue bplao?
Where can I buy a ticket?
Sue dtua dai tee-nai khrap/kha?
Please can I have a single/return ticket to...
Kor sue dtua tiew-diew/bpai-glap bpai...khrap/kha
Where can I find a taxi (stand)?
Ja hah taxi (queue rot-taxi) dai tee-nai khrap/kha?
How much is the journey?
Khah rot tao-rai?
Please turn on the meter
bpert meter duoy khrap/kha
air-conditioned bus
rot-bus dtid-air
skytrain
rot fai-fah
underground
rot dtai-din
airport
sa-naam bin
(longtail) boat
ruae (haang-yaow)
ferry
ruae kaam-faak
bicycle
rot jak-gra-yarn
motorcycle
rot mor-dter-sai

TOURIST INFORMATION
Where is the tourist information office/tourist information desk, please?
samnak-ngaan kormoon garn-tong-tiew/panaek kormoon garn-tong-tiew yoo tee-nai khrap/kha?
Do you have a city map?
Khun mee paen-tee muaeng rue-plao?
What is the admission price?
Kah kao chom tao-rai khrap/kha?
Are there guided tours?
Mee tour nam-tiew mai khrap/kha?
Can we make reservations here?
Sam-rorng tee tee-nee dai mai khrap/kha?
Do you have a brochure in English?
Khun mee brochure pah-sah angkrit mai khrap/kha?

IN TROUBLE/ILLNESS
Help!
Chuoy duoy!
Stop, thief!
Yut, kamoy!
Call the fire brigade/police/an ambulance
Riak noy-dap-ploeng/dtam-ruat/ rot payah-baan duoy
I have lost my passport/wallet/ purse/handbag
Passport/kra-bpau-ngern/ kra-bpau-sapaai khong phom/ dichan haai
I have had an accident
Phom/dichan dai rap u-bat-dti-het
I need information for my insurance company
Phom/dichan dtong-garn kormoon samrap borisat bpra-gan-pai khong phom/dichan
Excuse me, I think I am lost
Kor-toht khrap/kha. Phom/dichan kit wah phom/dichan long-taang
I need to see a doctor/dentist
Phom/dichan dtong bpai hah mor/mor-fan
Where is the hospital?
Rong-payah-baan yoo tee-nai?
I feel sick
Phom/dichan roo-suk kluen-sai
I am allergic to...
Phom/dichan pae...
Can I have a painkiller?
Kor yah gae-bpuat noi khrap/kha?

RESTAURANTS AND HOTELS
A table for..., please
Kor dto...tee-nang khrap/kha
Do you have the menu in English?
Khun mee menu pah-sah angkrit rue-plao?
Could we sit there?
rau nang tee-nan dai mai?
Could I have bottled still/sparkling water?
Kor naam-kuat tammadah (nam plau)/naam-kuat rot sah duoy khrap/kha?
The food is cold
Ah-haan yen bpai
The meat is overcooked/too rare
Nuae suk gern-bpai/mai suk
Is service included?
Ruam kah borigarn duoy mai

khrap/kha?
waiter/waitress
panak-ngaan-serve
I am a vegetarian
Phom/dichan taan mang-sa-wirat
I have made a reservation for…
nights
Phom/dichan jong hong-pak
wai…kuen
Do you have a room?
Khun mee hong waang mai?
How much per night?
Rah-kah tao-rai dtor kuen?
The room is too hot/too cold/dirty
Hong rorn gern-bpai/naow gern-
bpai/sok-ga-prok gern-bpai
Double/single room
Hong koo/hong diew
With bath/shower
Mee aang aab-naam/naam-fak-
bua
Twin room
Hong dtiang-koo
Please can I pay my bill?
Phom/dichan kor jaai kah bill
duoy khrap/kha?

IN THE TOWN
on/to the right
yoo/bpai taang kwah
on/to the left
yoo/bpai taang saai
opposite
dtrong-kaam
straight on
dtrong bpai
north
nuae
south
dtai
east
dta-wan-ork
west
ta-wan-tok
free
free
donation
bor-ri-jaak
open
bpert
closed
bpit
monastery/temple
wat
monument

anusah-waree
palace
wang/pra-raat-chawang
town
muaeng
street/road
tanon
island
ko
river
mae-naam
bridge
sa-paan
village
moo-baan
mountain
poo-kao
beach
haat/chaai-talay
canal
khlong
alley
dtrorg/soi
embassy
sa-taan-toot
market
dta-laat
police station
sa-tah-nee-dtam-ruat
no entry
haam kao
entrance
taang kao
exit
taang org
men (toilets)
hong-naam chaai
women (toilets)
hong-naam ying

DAYS/TIMES/MONTHS
Monday
wan jan
Tuesday
wan ang-karn
Wednesday
wan put
Thursday
wan pa-ru-hat-sa-bordee
Friday
wan suk
Saturday
wan sau
Sunday

wan ah-tit
night
glang-kuen
day
glang-wan
morning
dtorn-chao
afternoon
dtorn-baai
evening
dtorn-yen
today
wan-nee
yesterday
muae-waan-nee
tomorrow
wan-prung-nee
month
duaen
January
mak-ga-rah-kom
February
gum-pah-pan
March
mee-nah-kom
April
may-sah-yon
May
pruet-sa-pah-kom
June
mi-tu-nah-yon
July
ga-rak-ga-dah-kom
August
sing-hah/kom
September
gan-yah-yon
October
dtu-lah-kom
November
pruet-sa-ji-gah-yon
December
tan-wah-kom

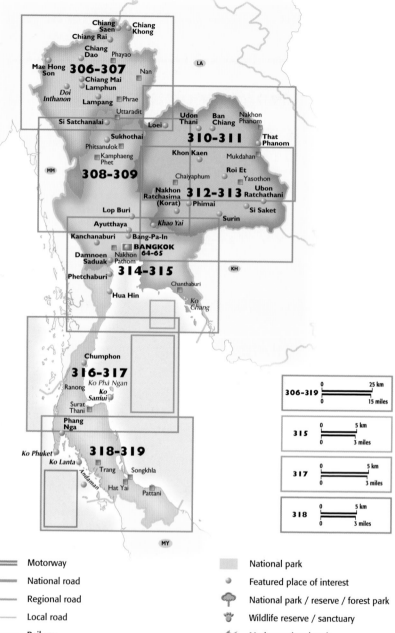

Map index

- Chiang Saen
- Chiang Khong
- Chiang Rai
- Chiang Dao
- Phayao
- Mae Hong Son
- 306-307
- Nan
- Chiang Mai
- Lamphun
- Doi Inthanon
- Lampang
- Phrae
- Uttaradit
- Si Satchanalai
- Loei
- Udon Thani
- Ban Chiang
- Nakhon Phanom
- 310-311
- That Phanom
- Sukhothai
- Phitsanulok
- Kamphaeng Phet
- Khon Kaen
- Mukdahan
- 308-309
- Chaiyaphum
- Roi Et
- Yasothon
- Nakhon Ratchasima (Korat)
- 312-313
- Ubon Ratchathani
- Lop Buri
- Phimai
- Si Saket
- Ayutthaya
- Khao Yai
- Surin
- Kanchanaburi
- Bang-Pa-In
- BANGKOK 64-65
- Damnoen Saduak
- Nakhon Pathom
- Phetchaburi
- 314-315
- Chanthaburi
- Hua Hin
- Ko Chang
- Chumphon
- 316-317
- Ranong
- Ko Pha Ngan
- Ko Samui
- Surat Thani
- Phang Nga
- Ko Phuket
- 318-319
- Ko Lanta
- Trang
- Songkhla
- Andaman
- Hat Yai
- Pattani
- LA
- MM
- KH
- MY

306-319	0		25 km
	0		15 miles
315	0		5 km
	0		3 miles
317	0		5 km
	0		3 miles
318	0		5 km
	0		3 miles

Legend

- ═══ Motorway
- ─── National road
- ─── Regional road
- ─── Local road
- ----- Railway
- International boundary
- – – Administrative region boundary
- ■ City / Town / Village
- Built-up area

- National park
- Featured place of interest
- National park / reserve / forest park
- Wildlife reserve / sanctuary
- Marine national park
- Waterfall
- Airport
- 621 ▲ Height in metres
- Ferry route

MAPS | THAILAND

MAPS

Map references for the sights refer to the atlas pages in this section or to the individual town plans within the regions. For example, Phuket has the reference 318 B17, indicating the page on which the map is found (318) and the grid square in which Phuket sits (B17).

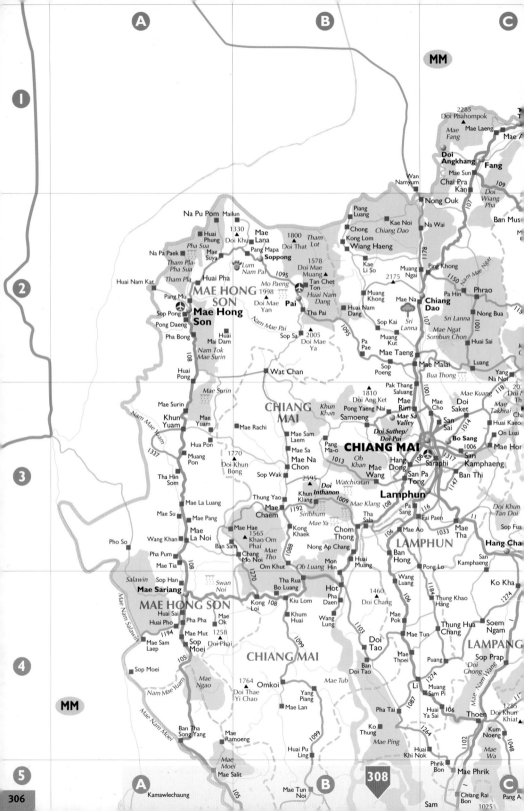